1 & 2 TIMOTHY/
TITUS
A Commentary in the Wesleyan Tradition

ID0879060

*New Beacon Bible Commentary

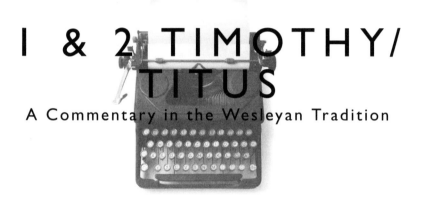

1 & 2 TIMOTHY/ TITUS

A Commentary in the Wesleyan Tradition

David A. Ackerman

BEACON HILL PRESS
OF KANSAS CITY

Copyright 2016 by Beacon Hill Press of Kansas City

Beacon Hill Press of Kansas City
PO Box 419527
Kansas City, MO 64141
www.BeaconHillBooks.com

ISBN 978-0-8341-3559-8

Printed in the United States of America

All rights reserved. No part of this publication may be reproduced, stored in a retrieval system, or transmitted in any form or by any means—for example, electronic, photocopy, recording—without the prior written permission of the publisher. The only exception is brief quotations in printed reviews.

Cover Design: J.R. Caines
Interior Design: Sharon Page

Unless otherwise indicated all Scripture quotations are from the *Holy Bible, New International Version®* (NIV®). Copyright © 1973, 1978, 1984, 2011 by Biblica, Inc.™ Used by permission. All rights reserved worldwide. Emphasis indicated by underlining in boldface quotations and italic in lightface quotations.

The following versions of Scripture are in the public domain:

The King James Version of the Bible (KJV).

The following copyrighted versions of Scripture are used by permission:

The *Common English Bible* (CEB), copyright 2011. All rights reserved.

The *Contemporary English Version* (CEV). Copyright © 1995 by American Bible Society.

The Holy Bible, English Standard Version (ESV), copyright © 2001 by Crossway Bibles, a division of Good News Publishers. All rights reserved.

Good News Translation® (*Today's English Version*, Second Edition) (GNT). Copyright © 1992 American Bible Society. All rights reserved.

The Jerusalem Bible (JB), copyright © 1966 by Darton, Longman & Todd, Ltd., and Doubleday, a division of Bantam Doubleday Dell Publishing Group, Inc.

The *Lexham English Bible* (LEB). Copyright 2012 Logos Bible Software. Lexham is a registered trademark of Logos Bible Software.

The *New American Standard Bible®* (NASB®), © copyright The Lockman Foundation 1960, 1962, 1963, 1968, 1971, 1972, 1973, 1975, 1977, 1995.

The *New English Bible* (NEB), © the Delegates of the Oxford University Press and the Syndics of the Cambridge University Press 1961, 1970.

The *New King James Version* (NKJV). Copyright © 1979, 1980, 1982 Thomas Nelson, Inc.

The *Holy Bible, New Living Translation* (NLT), copyright © 1996, 2004, 2007, 2013 by Tyndale House Foundation. Used by permission of Tyndale House Publishers, Inc., Carol Stream, IL 60188. All rights reserved.

The *New Revised Standard Version* (NRSV) of the Bible, copyright 1989 by the Division of Christian Education of the National Council of the Churches of Christ in the USA. All rights reserved.

The *Revised Standard Version* (RSV) of the Bible, copyright 1946, 1952, 1971 by the Division of Christian Education of the National Council of the Churches of Christ in the USA. All rights reserved.

The Message: The Bible in Contemporary Language (TM), copyright © 1993, 1994, 1995, 1996, 2000, 2001, 2002. Used by permission of NavPress Publishing Group.

The *Holy Bible, Today's New International Version®* (TNIV®). Copyright © 2001, 2005 by Biblica. All rights reserved worldwide.

Library of Congress Cataloging-in-Publication Data
Names: Ackerman, David A. (David Allen), author.
Title: 1 & 2 Timothy-Titus / David A. Ackerman.
Other titles: First & Second Timothy-Titus
Description: Kansas City, Missouri : Beacon Hill Press of Kansas City, 2016.
 | Series: New Beacon Bible commentary | Includes bibliographical
 references.
Identifiers: LCCN 2016003645 | ISBN 9780834135598 (pbk.)
Subjects: LCSH: Bible. Pastoral epistles—Commentaries.
Classification: LCC BS2735.53 .A25 2016 | DDC 227/.8307—dc23 LC record available at http://lccn.loc.gov/2016003645

The Internet addresses, email addresses, and phone numbers in this book are accurate at the time of publication. They are provided as a resource. Beacon Hill Press of Kansas City does not endorse them or vouch for their content or permanence.

10 9 8 7 6 5 4 3 2 1

DEDICATION

To my wife, Rhonda
To my daughter, Shan
To my son, Joel

COMMENTARY EDITORS

General Editors

Alex Varughese
> Ph.D., Drew University
> Professor of Biblical Literature
> Mount Vernon Nazarene University
> Mount Vernon, Ohio

Roger Hahn
> Ph.D., Duke University
> Dean of the Faculty
> Professor of New Testament
> Nazarene Theological Seminary
> Kansas City, Missouri

George Lyons
> Ph.D., Emory University
> Professor of New Testament
> Northwest Nazarene University
> Nampa, Idaho

Section Editors

Robert Branson
> Ph.D., Boston University
> Professor of Biblical Literature
> Emeritus
> Olivet Nazarene University
> Bourbonnais, Illinois

Alex Varughese
> Ph.D., Drew University
> Professor of Biblical Literature
> Mount Vernon Nazarene University
> Mount Vernon, Ohio

Jim Edlin
> Ph.D., Southern Baptist Theological
> Seminary
> Professor of Biblical Literature and
> Languages
> Chair, Division of Religion and
> Philosophy
> MidAmerica Nazarene University
> Olathe, Kansas

Kent Brower
> Ph.D., The University of Manchester
> Vice Principal
> Senior Lecturer in Biblical Studies
> Nazarene Theological College
> Manchester, England

George Lyons
> Ph.D., Emory University
> Professor of New Testament
> Northwest Nazarene University
> Nampa, Idaho

CONTENTS

GENERAL EDITORS' PREFACE

The purpose of the New Beacon Bible Commentary is to make available to pastors and students in the twenty-first century a biblical commentary that reflects the best scholarship in the Wesleyan theological tradition. The commentary project aims to make this scholarship accessible to a wider audience to assist them in their understanding and proclamation of Scripture as God's Word.

Writers of the volumes in this series not only are scholars within the Wesleyan theological tradition and experts in their field but also have special interest in the books assigned to them. Their task is to communicate clearly the critical consensus and the full range of other credible voices who have commented on the Scriptures. Though scholarship and scholarly contribution to the understanding of the Scriptures are key concerns of this series, it is not intended as an academic dialogue within the scholarly community. Commentators of this series constantly aim to demonstrate in their work the significance of the Bible as the church's book and the contemporary relevance and application of the biblical message. The project's overall goal is to make available to the church and for her service the fruits of the labors of scholars who are committed to their Christian faith.

The *New International Version* (NIV) is the reference version of the Bible used in this series; however, the focus of exegetical study and comments is the biblical text in its original language. When the commentary uses the NIV, it is printed in bold. The text printed in bold italics is the translation of the author. Commentators also refer to other translations where the text may be difficult or ambiguous.

The structure and organization of the commentaries in this series seeks to facilitate the study of the biblical text in a systematic and methodical way. Study of each biblical book begins with an **Introduction** section that gives an overview of authorship, date, provenance, audience, occasion, purpose, sociological/cultural issues, textual history, literary features, hermeneutical issues, and theological themes necessary to understand the book. This section also includes a brief outline of the book and a list of general works and standard commentaries.

The commentary section for each biblical book follows the outline of the book presented in the introduction. In some volumes, readers will find section *overviews* of large portions of scripture with general comments on their overall literary structure and other literary features. A consistent feature of the commentary is the paragraph-by-paragraph study of biblical texts. This section has three parts: **Behind the Text**, **In the Text**, and **From the Text**.

The goal of the **Behind the Text** section is to provide the reader with all the relevant information necessary to understand the text. This includes specific historical situations reflected in the text, the literary context of the text, sociological and cultural issues, and literary features of the text.

In the Text explores what the text says, following its verse-by-verse structure. This section includes a discussion of grammatical details, word studies, and the connectedness of the text to other biblical books/passages or other parts of the book being studied (the canonical relationship). This section provides transliterations of key words in Hebrew and Greek and their literal meanings. The goal here is to explain what the author would have meant and/or what the audience would have understood as the meaning of the text. This is the largest section of the commentary.

The **From the Text** section examines the text in relation to the following areas: theological significance, intertextuality, the history of interpretation, use of the Old Testament scriptures in the New Testament, interpretation in later church history, actualization, and application.

The commentary provides **sidebars** on topics of interest that are important but not necessarily part of an explanation of the biblical text. These topics are informational items and may cover archaeological, historical, literary, cultural, and theological matters that have relevance to the biblical text. Occasionally, longer detailed discussions of special topics are included as **excurses.**

We offer this series with our hope and prayer that readers will find it a valuable resource for their understanding of God's Word and an indispensable tool for their critical engagement with the biblical texts.

Roger Hahn, Centennial Initiative General Editor

Alex Varughese, General Editor (Old Testament)

George Lyons, General Editor (New Testament)

AUTHOR'S PREFACE

The Pastoral Epistles were an enigma to me for many years. Classes in my doctoral program on the writings of Paul generally assigned them to pseudonymity. They were treated as addendums to Paul's thought. I first immersed myself in these letters when I taught a graduate course on them in Papua New Guinea over a decade ago. But I had not worked systematically through the murky waters of the scholarly debates until I was asked to write this commentary. As a result, I came to the project with few preconceived ideas.

The journey of discovery has been rewarding. I have been challenged not only intellectually but also personally and spiritually. I believe that whenever we approach Scripture with sincere seeking and humility, we experience transformation. This has been my experience in writing this commentary.

My goal in this project has been to write in such a way that readers will be able to hear the Holy Spirit speak into their own lives and situations. It is my prayer that this commentary will allow these Pauline Letters to speak afresh to a new generation. These letters are much more than ancient correspondence between missionary colleagues. These letters hold power for the present and hope for the future.

The research and writing of this commentary took considerable time, often encroaching on other priorities in my life. Those who have suffered most have been my family. I truly appreciate their patience and endurance with my many hours of preoccupation with my "computer." Many friends and family have asked about my progress and offered encouragement along the way. I appreciate the opportunity given to me by denominational leaders and the editors of this series to write this commentary. Final glory must be given to God who calls, equips, and enables us in Christ Jesus to be his instruments of change and renewal by the power of the Holy Spirit.

David A. Ackerman

ABBREVIATIONS

With a few exceptions, these abbreviations follow those in *The SBL Handbook of Style* (Alexander 1999).

General

→	see the commentary at
‖	parallel(s)
AD	anno Domini (precedes date)
BC	before Christ (follows date)
ca.	*circa*, around
cf.	compare
ch(s)	chapter(s)
d.	died
diss.	dissertation
e.g.	*exempli gratia*, for example
esp.	especially
frag.	fragment
ibid.	*ibidem*, in the same place
lit.	literally
LXX	Septuagint
MS(S)	manuscript(s)
MT	Masoretic Text
n(n).	note(s)
NT	New Testament
OT	Old Testament
Q	Qumran
repr.	reprinted
s.v.	*sub verbo*, under the word
v(v).	verse(s)
vs.	versus

Modern English Versions

ESV	English Standard Version
GNT	Good News Translation (Today's English Version)
JB	Jerusalem Bible
KJV	King James Version
LEB	Lexham English Bible
NASB	New American Standard Bible
NEB	New English Bible
NIV	New International Version (2011)
NIV84	New International Version (1984)
NKJV	New King James Version
NLT	New Living Translation
NRSV	New Revised Standard Version
RSV	Revised Standard Version
TM	The Message
TNIV	Today's New International Version
TNT	*The Translator's New Testament*
UBS[4]	*The Greek New Testament*, United Bible Societies, 4th ed.

Print Conventions for Translations

Bold font	NIV (bold without quotation marks in the text under study; elsewhere in the regular font, with quotation marks and no further identification)
Bold italic font	Author's translation (without quotation marks)

Behind the Text:	Literary or historical background information average readers might not know from reading the biblical text alone
In the Text:	Comments on the biblical text, words, phrases, grammar, and so forth

From the Text: The use of the text by later interpreters, contemporary relevance, theological and ethical implications of the text, with particular emphasis on Wesleyan concerns

Old Testament

Gen	Genesis	Dan	Daniel		
Exod	Exodus	Hos	Hosea		
Lev	Leviticus	Joel	Joel		
Num	Numbers	Amos	Amos		
Deut	Deuteronomy	Obad	Obadiah		
Josh	Joshua	Jonah	Jonah		
Judg	Judges	Mic	Micah		
Ruth	Ruth	Nah	Nahum		
1—2 Sam	1—2 Samuel	Hab	Habakkuk		
1—2 Kgs	1—2 Kings	Zeph	Zephaniah		
1—2 Chr	1—2 Chronicles	Hag	Haggai		
Ezra	Ezra	Zech	Zechariah		
Neh	Nehemiah	Mal	Malachi		

New Testament

Matt	Matthew
Mark	Mark
Luke	Luke
John	John
Acts	Acts
Rom	Romans
1—2 Cor	1—2 Corinthians
Gal	Galatians
Eph	Ephesians
Phil	Philippians
Col	Colossians
1—2 Thess	1—2 Thessalonians
1—2 Tim	1—2 Timothy
Titus	Titus
Phlm	Philemon
Heb	Hebrews
Jas	James
1—2 Pet	1—2 Peter
1—2—3 John	1—2—3 John
Jude	Jude
Rev	Revelation

Old Testament (continued):

Esth	Esther
Job	Job
Ps/Pss	Psalm/Psalms
Prov	Proverbs
Eccl	Ecclesiastes
Song	Song of Songs/ Song of Solomon
Isa	Isaiah
Jer	Jeremiah
Lam	Lamentations
Ezek	Ezekiel

(Note: Chapter and verse numbering in the MT and LXX often differ compared to those in English Bibles. To avoid confusion, all biblical references follow the chapter and verse numbering in English translations, even when the text in the MT and LXX is under discussion.)

Apocrypha

Bar	Baruch
Bel	Bel and the Dragon
1—2 Esd	1—2 Esdras
Ep Jer	Epistle of Jeremiah
Jdt	Judith
1—2 Macc	1—2 Maccabees
3—4 Macc	3—4 Maccabees
Sir	Sirach/Ecclesiasticus
Tob	Tobit
Wis	Wisdom of Solomon

NT Apocrypha and Pseudepigrapha

Acts Paul	*Acts of Paul*
Acts Pet. Paul	*Acts of Peter and Paul*
Acts Pil.	*Acts of Pilate*

OT Pseudepigrapha

3 Bar.	*3 Baruch*
1 En.	*1 Enoch*
Jan. Jam.	*Jannes and Jambres*
Jub.	*Jubilees*
Sib. Or.	*Sibylline Oracles*
T. Dan.	*Testament of Daniel*
T. Jud.	*Testament of Judah*

Dead Sea Scrolls and Related Texts

1Qap Gen	*Genesis Apocryphon*
1QpHab	*Pesher Habakkuk*
1QS	*Rule of the Community*
4Q559	*Biblical Chronology*
CD	*Damascus Document*

Philo

Alleg. Interp.	*Allegorical Interpretation*
Contempl. Life	*On the Contemplative Life*
Creation	*On Creation*
Flacc.	*In Flaccum*
Flight	*On Flight and Finding*
Leg.	*Legum allegoriae*
Legat.	*Legatio ad Gaium*
Moses	*On the Life of Moses*
QG	*Questions and Answers on Genesis*
Spec. Laws	*On the Special Laws*

Josephus

Ant.	*Jewish Antiquities*
J.W.	*Jewish War*
Vita	*Vita*

Rabbinic Literature

'Abot	*'Abot*
B. Bat.	*Baba Batra*
Ber.	*Berakot*
Tg. Jer.	*Targum Jeremiah*
Tg. Ps.-J.	*Targum Pseudo-Jonathan*

Apostolic Fathers

Apos. Con.	*Apostolic Constitutions*
Barn.	*Barnabas*
1 Clem.	*1 Clement*
2 Clem.	*2 Clement*
Did.	*Didache*
Herm. Mand.	*Shepherd of Hermas, Mandate*
Ign. Magn.	Ignatius, *To the Magnesians*
Ign. Pol.	Ignatius, *To Polycarp*
Ign. Smyrn.	Ignatius, *To the Smyrnaeans*
Ign. Trall.	Ignatius, *To the Trallians*
Pol. Phil.	Polycarp, *To the Philippians*

Other Church Fathers

1 Apol.	Justin Martyr, *Apologia i*
Apol.	Tertullian, *Apology*
Apol. sec.	Athanasius, *Defense against the Arians*
Bapt.	Tertullian, *Baptism*
Cels.	Origen, *Against Celsus*
Civ.	Augustine, *The City of God*
Com. 1 Tim.	Theodore of Mopsuestia, *Commentary on 1 Timothy*
Com. Sec. Tim.	Ambrosiaster, *Commentary on Second Letter to Timothy*
Comm. Jo.	Origen, *Commentarii in evangelium Joannis*
Comm. Tit.	Jerome, *Commentariorum in Epistulam ad Titum liber*
Div. Image	John of Damascus, *On Divine Image*
Div. Names	Pseudo-Dionysius, *The Divine Names*
Doctr. chr.	Augustine, *Christian Instruction*
Ep. Adelph.	Athanasius, *Letter to Adelphius*
Epist.	Augustine, *Epistulae*
Epist.	Jerome, *Epistulae*
Haer.	Irenaeus, *Against Heresies*
Hist. eccl.	Eusebius, *Ecclesiastical History*
Hom. 1 Tim.	John Chrysostom, *Homiliae in epistulam i ad Timotheum*
Hom. 2 Tim.	John Chrysostom, *Homiliae in epistulam ii ad Timotheum*
Hom. Lev.	Origen, *Homiliae in Leviticum*
Hom. Tit.	John Chrysostom, *Homiliae in epistulam ad Titum*
Idol.	Tertullian, *Idolatry*
Inst.	Cassian, *Institutes*
Int. First Tim.	Theodoret of Cyr, *Interpretation of the First Letter to Timothy*
Int. Sec. Tim.	Theodoret of Cyr, *Interpretation of the Second Letter to Timothy*

Marc.	Tertullian, *Against Marcion*
Pan.	Epiphanius, *Refutation of All Heresies*
Paul. Com.	Severian of Gabala, *Pauline Commentary from the Greek Church*
Praep. ev.	Eusebius, *Preparation for the Gospel*
Quaest. Hept.	Augustine, *Quaestiones in Heptateuchum*
Rule	Benedict of Nursia, *Rule of St. Benedict*
Sac.	John Chrysostom, *Priesthood*
Sent.	Cyprian, *Sententiae episcoporum de haereticis baptizandis*
Serm.	Augustine, *Sermons*
Serm.	Leo the Great, *Sermons*
Spir.	Ambrose, *The Holy Spirit*
Spir. et litt.	Augustine, *The Spirit and the Letter*
Stat.	John Chrysostom, *Ad populum Antiochenum de statuis*
Strom.	Clement of Alexandria, *Miscellanies*
Tract. ep. Jo.	Augustine, *Tractates on the First Epistle of John*
Trin.	Augustine, *The Trinity*
Virg.	Tertullian, *The Veiling of Virgins*

Other Greek and Latin Works

Ann.	Tacitus, *Annales*
Anth. pal.	*Palatine Anthology*
Apol.	Apuleius, *Apology*
Apol.	Plato, *Apology*
Comp. Dem. Cic.	Plutarch, *Comparatio Demosthenis et Ciceronis*
CS	Seneca, *On the Constancy of the Sage*
Def. orac.	Plutarch, *De defectu oraculorum*
Diatr.	Epictetus, *Diatribai (Dissertationes)*
Eloc.	Demetrius, *Style*
Ep.	Pliny the Younger, *Epistulae*
Ep.	Seneca, *Epistulae morales*
Ep. of Diogenes	*Epistle of Mathetes to Diognetus*
Eth. nic.	Aristotle, *Nicomachean Ethics*
Eum.	Aeschylus, *Eumenides*
Evag.	Isocrates, *Evagoras (Or. 9)*
Gnom.	Epictetus, *Gnomologium*
Hist.	Polybius, *Histories*
Hist.	Tacitus, *Historiae*
Hist. of Rome	Livy, *Roman History*
Hymn. Jov.	Callimachus, *Hymn to Jove or Zeus*
Leg.	Plato, *Laws*
Nat.	Pliny the Elder, *Natural History*
Nero	Suetonius, *Nero*
Od.	Homer, *Odyssey*
Off.	Cicero, *De officiis*
Or.	Aelius Aristides, *Oratio*
Or.	Dio Chrysostom, *Orationes*
Pan.	Pliny the Younger, *Panegyricus*
Philops.	Lucian of Samosata, *The Lover of Lies*
Pol.	Aristotle, *Politics*
Resp.	Cicero, *De republica*
Resp.	Plato, *Republic*
Rhet.	Aristotle, *Rhetoric*
Rom. Hist.	Dio Cassius, *Roman History*
Sat.	Juvenal, *Satirae*
Sat.	Petronius, *Satyricon*
Tim.	Lucian of Samosata, *Timon*
Tu. san.	Plutarch, *De tuenda sanitate praecepta*
Vet. med.	Hippocrates, *Ancient Medicine*

Modern Journals and Reference Works

| *ABD* | *Anchor Bible Dictionary* (see Freedman) |
| *BBR* | *Bulletin for Biblical Research* |

BDAG	*A Greek-English Lexicon of the New Testament and Other Early Christian Literature* (see Bauer)
Bib	*Biblica*
BSac	*Bibliotheca sacra*
CBQ	*Catholic Biblical Quarterly*
DPL	*Dictionary of Paul and His Letters* (see Hawthorne)
EDNT	*Exegetical Dictionary of the New Testament* (see Balz)
EuroJTh	*European Journal of Theology*
EvQ	*Evangelical Quarterly*
ExpTim	*Expository Times*
HBT	*Horizons in Biblical Theology*
Int	*Interpretation*
JAAR	*Journal of the American Academy of Religion*
JBL	*Journal of Biblical Literature*
JRelS	*Journal of Religious Studies*
JTS	*Journal of Theological Studies*
NTS	*New Testament Studies*
RB	*Revue biblique*
ResQ	*Restoration Quarterly*
TDNT	*Theological Dictionary of the New Testament*
Them	*Themelios*
TJ	*Trinity Journal*

Greek Transliteration

Greek	Letter	English
α	*alpha*	*a*
β	*bēta*	*b*
γ	*gamma*	*g*
γ	*gamma nasal*	*n* (before γ, κ, ξ, χ)
δ	*delta*	*d*
ε	*epsilon*	*e*
ζ	*zēta*	*z*
η	*ēta*	*ē*
θ	*thēta*	*th*
ι	*iōta*	*i*
κ	*kappa*	*k*
λ	*lambda*	*l*
μ	*mu*	*m*
ν	*nu*	*n*
ξ	*xi*	*x*
ο	*omicron*	*o*
π	*pi*	*p*
ρ	*rhō*	*r*
ρ	initial *rhō*	*rh*
σ/ς	*sigma*	*s*
τ	*tau*	*t*
υ	*upsilon*	*y*
υ	*upsilon*	*u* (in diphthongs: *au, eu, ēu, ou, ui*)
φ	*phi*	*ph*
χ	*chi*	*ch*
ψ	*psi*	*ps*
ω	*ōmega*	*ō*
ʿ	rough breathing	*h* (before initial vowels or diphthongs)

Hebrew Consonant Transliteration

Hebrew/ Aramaic	Letter	English
א	*alef*	ʾ
ב	*bet*	*b*
ג	*gimel*	*g*
ד	*dalet*	*d*
ה	*he*	*h*
ו	*vav*	*v* or *w*
ז	*zayin*	*z*
ח	*khet*	*ḥ*
ט	*tet*	*ṭ*
י	*yod*	*y*
כ/ך	*kaf*	*k*
ל	*lamed*	*l*
מ/ם	*mem*	*m*
נ/ן	*nun*	*n*
ס	*samek*	*s*
ע	*ayin*	ʿ
פ/ף	*pe*	*p; f* (spirant)
צ/ץ	*tsade*	*ṣ*
ק	*qof*	*q*
ר	*resh*	*r*
שׂ	*sin*	*ś*
שׁ	*shin*	*š*
ת	*tav*	*t; th* (spirant)

BIBLIOGRAPHY

Aasgaard, R. 2004. *"My Beloved Brothers and Sisters!" Christian Siblingship in Paul*. London: T&T Clark.

Ackerman, David A. 2006. *Lo, I Tell You a Mystery: Cross, Resurrection, and Paraenesis in the Rhetoric of 1 Corinthians*. Eugene, OR: Pickwick Publications.

Allan, J. A. 1963. The "In Christ" Formula in the Pastoral Epistles. *NTS* 10:115-21.

Apostolic Constitutions. The Ante-Nicene Fathers, vol. 7. Edinburgh: T&T Clark; Grand Rapids: Eerdmans. Christian Classics Ethereal Library, http://www.ccel.org/ccel/schaff/anf07.titlepage.html.

Arichea, D. C., and H. Hatton. 1995. *A Handbook on Paul's Letters to Timothy and to Titus*. New York: United Bible Societies.

Arminius, James. *Works of James Arminius*. Christian Classics Ethereal Library, http://www.ccel.org/ccel/arminius.

Arnold, C. E. 1993. Magic. Pages 580-83 in *DPL*.

Augustine. *On the Trinity. The Nicene and Post-Nicene Fathers*, vol. 3. Translated by Arthur West Hadden. Edinburgh: T&T Clark. Christian Classics Ethereal Library, http://www.ccel.org/ccel/schaff/npnf103.i.html.

————. *St. Augustin: Anti-Pelagian Writings*. Translated by Peter Holmes and Robert Ernest Wallis. Edinburgh: T&T Clark. Christian Classics Ethereal Library, http://www.ccel.org/ccel/schaff/npnf105.i.html.

Aune, David E. 1983. *Prophecy in Early Christianity and the Ancient Mediterranean World*. Grand Rapids: Eerdmans.

————. 1987. *The New Testament in Its Literary Environment*. Philadelphia: Westminster.

Baldwin, Henry Scott. 2005. An Important Word: *Authenteō* in 1 Timothy 2:12. Pages 39-52 in *Women in the Church: A Fresh Analysis of 1 Timothy 2.9-15*. Edited by Andreas J. Köstenberger and Thomas R. Schreiner. Grand Rapids: Baker Books.

Balz, Horst, and Gerhard Schneider. 1993. *Exegetical Dictionary of the New Testament*. Grand Rapids: Eerdmans.

Banker, John. 1987. *A Semantic and Structural Analysis on Titus*. Dallas: Summer Institute of Linguistics.

Barclay, William. 2003. *The Letters to Timothy, Titus, and Philemon*. The New Daily Study Bible. Louisville, KY: Westminster.

Barrett, C. K. 1963. *The Pastoral Epistles in the New English Bible*. Oxford: Clarendon Press.

Barrett, David B., and Todd M. Johnson, eds. 2001. *Christian Trends A.D. 20-A.D. 2000: Interpreting the Annual Christian Megacensus*. Pasadena, CA: William Carey Library.

Bartchy, S. Scott. 1998. Slavery (Greco-Roman). Pages 65-73 in vol. 6 of *ABD*.

Bassler, Jouette M. 1984. The Widows' Tale: A Fresh Look at 1 Timothy 5:3-16. *JBL* 103:23-41.

————. 1996. *1 Timothy: 2 Timothy: Titus*. Abingdon New Testament Commentaries. Nashville: Abingdon.

Batstone, Patricia. 2004. A Many-faceted Faith: 2 Timothy 1:12b. *ExpTim* 115(12):413-15.

Bauer, Walter, Frederick W. Danker, W. F. Arndt, and F. Wilbur Gingrich. 2000. *A Greek-English Lexicon of the New Testament and Other Early Christian Literature*. 3rd ed. Chicago: University of Chicago Press.

Bauernfeind, Otto. 1967a. *mataios*. Pages 519-24 in vol. 4 of *TDNT*.

————. 1967b. *nēphō*. Pages 936-41 in vol. 4 of *TDNT*.

————. 1972. *tynchanō*. Pages 238-45 in vol. 8 of *TDNT*.

Baugh, S. M. 1995. A Foreign World: Ephesus in the First Century. Pages 13-38 in *Women in the Church: A Fresh Analysis of 1 Timothy 2:9-15*. Edited by Andreas J. Köstenberger and Thomas R. Schreiner. Grand Rapids: Baker Books.

Baur, F. C. 1835. *Die sogenannten Pastoralbriefe des Apostels Paulus.* Tübingen: J. G. Cotta.

Beasley-Murray, George R. 1973. *Baptism in the New Testament.* Grand Rapids: Eerdmans.

Behm, Johannes. 1965a. *kainos.* Pages 447-54 in vol. 3 of *TDNT.*

_____. 1965b. *kardia.* Pages 605-14 in vol. 3 of *TDNT.*

_____. 1967a. *noeō.* Pages 989-1022 in vol. 4 of *TDNT.*

_____. 1967b. *nous.* Pages 948-80 in vol. 4 of *TDNT.*

Beker, J. Christiaan. 1980. *Paul the Apostle: The Triumph of God in Life and Thought.* Philadelphia: Fortress.

_____. 1991. *Heirs of Paul: Paul's Legacy in the New Testament and in the Church Today.* Minneapolis: Fortress.

Bernard, John H. 1899. *The Pastoral Epistles: With Introductions and Notes.* London: Cambridge University Press.

Beyer, Hermann W. 1964. *diakoneō.* Pages 81-93 in vol. 2 of *TDNT.*

Bietenhard, Hans. 1967. *onoma.* Pages 242-83 in vol. 5 of *TDNT.*

Black, Robert, and Ronald McClung. 2004. *1 & 2 Timothy, Titus, Philemon: A Commentary for Bible Students.* Indianapolis: Wesleyan Publishing House.

Bonhoeffer, Dietrich. 1959. *The Cost of Discipleship.* Translated by Reginald H. Fuller. New York: Collier Book, Macmillan Publishing.

Bornkamm, Gunther. 1967. *mystērion.* Pages 802-28 in vol. 4 of *TDNT.*

Braun, Herbert. 1968. *planaō.* Pages 228-53 in vol. 6 of *TDNT.*

Brown, Colin, ed. 1986. *The New International Dictionary of New Testament Theology.* 3 vols. Translated by a team of translators, with additions and revisions, from *Theologisches Begriffslexikon zum Neuen Testament,* edited by Lothar Coenen, Erich Beyreuther, and Hans Bietenhard. Grand Rapids: Zondervan.

Büchsel, Friedrich. 1964a. *elegchō.* Pages 473-76 in vol. 2 of *TDNT.*

_____. 1964b. *gnēsios.* Page 727 in vol. 1 of *TDNT.*

_____. 1965. *thymos.* Pages 167-72 in vol. 3 of *TDNT.*

Bultmann, Rudolf, and Dieter Lührmann. 1974. *phainō.* Pages 1-10 in vol. 9 of *TDNT.*

Cadbury, H. J. 1931. Erastus of Corinth. *JBL* 50:42-58.

Calvin, John. 1830. *The Most Celebrated Sermons of John Calvin.* New York: Forbes.

_____. 1964. *The Second Epistle of Paul the Apostle to the Corinthians and the Epistles to Timothy, Titus and Philemon.* Translated by T. A. Smail. Grand Rapids: Eerdmans.

Campbell, Alastair V. 1992. Do the Work of an Evangelist. *EvQ* 64:117-29.

Campbell, Barth. 1997. Rhetorical Design in 1 Timothy 4. *BSac* 154:189-204.

Chrysostom, John. *Homilies on Galatians, Ephesians, Philippians, Colossians, Thessalonians, Timothy, Titus, and Philemon. The Nicene and Post-Nicene Fathers,* vol. 13. Translated by Philip Schaff. Edinburgh: T&T Clark. Christian Classics Ethereal Library. http://www.ccel.org/ccel/schaff /npnf113.titlepage.html.

Clark, Gordon H. 1983. *The Pastoral Epistles.* Jefferson, MD: Trinity Foundation.

Clarke, Adam. 1831. *The New Testament of Our Lord and Savior Jesus Christ.* New York: Peter C. Smith.

Cohen, Shaye J. D. 1986. Was Timothy Jewish (Acts 16:1-3)? Patristic Exegesis, Rabbinic Law, and Matrilineal Descent. *JBL* 105:251-68.

Collins, Raymond F. 1988. *Letters that Paul Did Not Write: The Epistle to the Hebrews and the Pauline Pseudepigrapha.* Good News Studies 28. Wilmington, DE: Michael Glazier.

_____. 2002. *1 & 2 Timothy and Titus: A Commentary.* New Testament Library. Louisville, KY: Westminster John Knox.

Conybeare, W. J., and J. S. Howson. 1962. *The Life and Epistles of Saint Paul.* Repr., Grand Rapids: Eerdmans.

Countryman, L. William. 1980. *The Rich Christian in the Church of the Early Empire: Contradictions and Accommodations.* New York and Toronto: Edwin Mellen.

Deasley, Alex R. G. 2000. *Marriage and Divorce in the Bible and the Church.* Kansas City: Beacon Hill Press of Kansas City.

Deibler, Ellis W. 1973. *The Translator's New Testament.* London: British and Foreign Bible Society. Abbreviated as TNT throughout.

Deissmann, Adolf. 1927. *Light from the Ancient East: The New Testament Illustrated by Recently Discovered Texts of the Graeco-Roman World.* London: Doran.

Delling, Gerhard. 1964a. *artios.* Page 476 in vol. 1 of *TDNT* 1:476.

_____. 1964b. *archē.* Pages 481-89 in vol. 1 of *TDNT.*

_____. 1972a. *tassō*. Pages 26-48 in vol. 8 of *TDNT*.

_____. 1972b. *telos*. Pages 49-87 in vol. 8 of *TDNT*.

_____. 1974. *chronos*. Pages 581-93 in vol. 9 of *TDNT*.

deSilva, David Arthur. 1999. *The Hope of Glory: Honor Discourse and New Testament Interpretation*. Collegeville, MN: Liturgical Press.

_____. 2000. *Honor, Patronage, Kinship and Purity: Unlocking New Testament Culture*. Downers Grove, IL: InterVarsity.

_____. 2004. *An Introduction to the New Testament: Contexts, Methods & Ministry Formation*. Downers Grove, IL: InterVarsity.

Dibelius, Martin, and Hans Conzelmann. 1972. *The Pastoral Epistles*. Hermeneia. Philadelphia: Fortress.

Donaldson, Amy M., Gerald F. Hawthorne, and Timothy B. Sailors. 2003. *New Testament Greek and Exegesis: Essays in Honor of Gerald F. Hawthorne*. Grand Rapids: Eerdmans.

Donelson, Lewis R. 1986. *Pseudepigraphy and Ethical Argument in the Pastoral Epistles*. Tübingen: Mohr Siebeck.

Dunn, James D. G. 1998. *The Theology of Paul the Apostle*. Grand Rapids: Eerdmans.

_____. 2000. The First and Second Letters to Timothy and the Letter to Titus. Pages 775-880 in vol. 11 of *The New Interpreter's Bible*. L. E. Keck, ed. Nashville: Abingdon.

_____. 2010. *Baptism in the Holy Spirit: A Re-Examination of the New Testament Teaching on the Gift of the Holy Spirit in Relation to Pentecostalism Today*. Norwich, UK: SCM Press.

Easton, Burton S. 1947. *The Pastoral Epistles*. London: SCM Press.

Ehrman, Bart D. 2011. *Forged: Writing in the Name of God—Why the Bible's Authors Are Not Who We Think They Are*. San Francisco: HarperCollins.

Ellicott, Charles J. 1883. *The Pastoral Epistles of St. Paul: With a Critical and Grammatical Commentary, and a Revised Translation*. London: Longmans, Green & Co.

Ellingworth, Paul, and Howard A. Hatton. 1995a. *A Handbook on Paul's First Letter to Timothy*. UBS Translator Handbooks Series. New York: United Bible Societies.

_____. 1995b. *A Handbook on Paul's Second Letter to Timothy*. UBS Translator Handbooks Series. New York: United Bible Societies.

_____. 1995c. *A Handbook on Paul's Letter to Titus*. UBS Translator Handbooks Series. New York: United Bible Societies.

Ellis, E. Earle. 1957. *Paul's Use of the Old Testament*. Grand Rapids: Baker.

_____. 1978. *Prophecy and Hermeneutic in Early Christianity: New Testament Essays*. Tübingen: Mohr.

_____. 1993. The Pastoral Epistles. Pages 658-66 in *DPL*.

Evans, Mary J. 1983. *Woman in the Bible*. Downers Grove, IL: InterVarsity.

Falconer, Robert A. 1937. *The Pastoral Epistles*. Oxford: Clarendon.

Fee, Gordon D. 1984. *1-2 Timothy, Titus*. Good News Commentary. San Francisco: Harper & Row.

_____. 1988. *1 and 2 Timothy, Titus*. New International Biblical Commentary. Peabody, MA: Hendrickson.

_____. 1994. *God's Empowering Presence: The Holy Spirit in the Letters of Paul*. Peabody, MA: Hendrickson.

_____. 2007. *Pauline Christology: An Exegetical-Theological Study*. Peabody, MA: Hendrickson.

Fee, Gordon D., and Douglas Stuart. 2003. *How to Read the Bible for All Its Worth*. Grand Rapids: Zondervan.

Ferguson, Everett. 1991. *Topō* in 1 Timothy 2:8. *ResQ* 33:65-73.

_____. 1993. *Backgrounds of Early Christianity*. Grand Rapids: Eerdmans.

Fiore, Benjamin. 1986. *The Function of Personal Example in the Socratic and Pastoral Epistles*. Rome: Biblical Institute Press.

_____. 2007. *The Pastoral Epistles: First Timothy, Second Timothy, and Titus*. Sacra Pagina. Collegeville, MN: Liturgical Press.

Fitzer, G. 1971. *sphragis*. Pages 939-53 in vol. 7 of *TDNT*.

Fitzgerald, J. T. 1992. Virtue / Vice Lists. Pages 858-59 in vol. 6 of *ABD*.

Foerster, Werner. 1964a. *bdelyssomai*. Pages 598-600 in vol. 1 of *TDNT*.

_____. 1964b. *eirēnē*. Pages 400-20 in vol. 2 of *TDNT*.

_____. 1965. *kyrios*. Pages 1039-58 in vol. 3 of *TDNT*.

_____. 1971. *sebomai*. Pages 168-96 in vol. 7 of *TDNT*.

Francis, Fred O., and J. Paul Sampley. 1984. *Pauline Parallels*. Minneapolis: Fortress.

Freedman, David Noel, ed. 1992. *The Anchor Bible Dictionary*. 6 vols. New York: Doubleday.

Funk, Robert. 1967. The Apostolic *Parousia*: Form and Significance. Pages 249-68 in *Christian History and Interpretation*. Edited by W. R. Farmer, C. F. D. Moule, and R. R. Niebuhr. Cambridge: Cambridge University Press.

Furnish, Victor Paul. 1968. *Theology and Ethics in Paul*. Nashville: Abingdon.

———. 1973. *The Love Command in the New Testament*. London: SCM Press.

Goppelt, Leonhard. 1972. *typos*. Pages 246-59 in vol. 8 of *TDNT*.

Gorday, Peter. 2000. *New Testament Vol. IX: Colossians, 1-2 Thessalonians, 1-2 Timothy, Titus, Philemon*. Ancient Christian Commentary on Scripture. Downers Grove, IL: InterVarsity.

Gould, J. Glenn. 1965. The Pastoral Epistles. Pages 541-698 in vol. 9 of *Beacon Bible Commentary*. Kansas City: Beacon Hill Press of Kansas City.

Greenlee, J. Harold. 1989. *An Exegetical Summary of Titus and Philemon*. Dallas: Summer Institute of Linguistics.

Greeven, Heinrich. 1964. *deēsis*. Pages 40-41 in vol. 2 of *TDNT*.

Gritz, S. H. 1991. *Paul, Women Teachers, and the Mother Goddess at Ephesus: A Study of 1 Timothy 2:9-15 in Light of the Religious and Cultural Milieu of the First Century*. Lanham, MD: University Press of America.

Grundmann, Walter. 1964a. *dechomai*. Pages 50-59 in vol. 2 of *TDNT*.

———. 1964b. *dokimos*. Pages 255-60 in vol. 2 of *TDNT*.

———. 1965. *kakos*. Pages 486-87 in vol. 3 of *TDNT*.

Gutbrod, W. 1967. *nomos*. Pages 1022-69 in vol. 4 of *TDNT*.

Guthrie, Donald. 1983. *The Pastoral Epistles*. Tyndale New Testament Commentaries. Downers Grove, IL: InterVarsity.

———. 1990. *The Pastoral Epistles*, 2nd ed. Tyndale New Testament Commentaries. Downers Grove, IL: InterVarsity.

Hanson, Anthony Tyrrell. 1966. *The Pastoral Letters: Commentary on the First and Second Letters to Timothy and the Letter to Titus*. Cambridge: Cambridge University Press.

———. 1982. *The Pastoral Epistles*. New Century Bible Commentary. Grand Rapids: Eerdmans.

Harder, Günther. 1974. *phtheirō*. Pages 93-106 in vol. 9 of *TDNT*.

Harding, Mark. 1993. *Tradition and Rhetoric in the Pastoral Epistles*. PhD diss., Princeton Theological Seminary.

———. 2001. *What Are They Saying about the Pastoral Epistles?* Mahwah, NJ: Paulist Press.

Harding, Mark, and Alanna Nobbs, eds. 2013. *All Things to All People*. Grand Rapids: Eerdmans.

Harrill, J. Albert. 2000. The Use of the New Testament in the American Slave Controversy: A Case History in the Hermeneutical Tension between Biblical Criticism and Christian Moral Debate. *Religion and American Culture* 10.2:149-86.

———. 2006. *Slaves in the New Testament: Literary, Social, and Moral Dimensions*. Minneapolis: Fortress.

Harris, M. J. 1980. Titus 2:13 and the Deity of Christ. Pages 262-77 in *Pauline Studies: Essays in Honor of F. F. Bruce on His 70th Birthday*. Edited by D. A. Hagner and J. J. Harris. Grand Rapids: Eerdmans.

Harrison, P. N. 1921. *The Problem of the Pastoral Epistles*. London: Oxford University Press.

Hauck, Friedrich. 1964a. *hagnos*. Pages 122-24 in vol. 1 of *TDNT*.

———. 1964b. *bebēlos*. Pages 604-5 in vol. 1 of *TDNT*.

———. 1965. *katharos*. Pages 413-17 in vol. 3 of *TDNT*.

———. 1967. *miainō*. Pages 644-47 in vol. 4 of *TDNT*.

Hawthorne, Gerald F., Ralph P. Martin, and Daniel G. Reid. 1993. *Dictionary of Paul and His Letters*. Downers Grove, IL: InterVarsity.

Hays, Richard B. 1989. *Echoes of Scripture in the Letters of Paul*. New Haven & London: Yale University Press.

Heckert, J. 1996. *Discourse Function of Conjoiners in the Pastoral Epistles*. Dallas: Summer Institute of Linguistics.

Heidland, H. W. 1967. *logizomai*. Pages 284-92 in vol. 4 of *TDNT*.

Hendriksen, William. 1957. *New Testament Commentary*. Grand Rapids: Baker.

Hengel, Martin. 1977. *Crucifixion in the Ancient World and the Folly of the Message of the Cross*. Translated by John Bowden. Philadelphia: Fortress.

Hill, David. 1979. *New Testament Prophecy*. Atlanta: John Knox.

Hock, Ronald F. 1978. Paul's Tentmaking and the Problem of His Social Class. *JBL* 97:555-65.

———. 1980. *The Social Context of Paul's Ministry: Tentmaking and Apostleship*. Philadelphia: Fortress.

Hodge, Caroline Johnson. 2007. *If Sons, Then Heirs: A Study of Kingship and Ethnicity in the Letters of Paul*. Oxford: Oxford University Press.

Holmes, J. M. 2000. *Text in a Whirlwind: A Critique of Four Exegetical Devices at 1 Timothy 2.9-15*. Sheffield: Sheffield Academic Press.

Holtzmann, H. J. 1880. *Die Pastoralbriefe, Kritisch und Exegetisch Behandelt*. Leipzig: Engelmann.

Hort, F. J. A. 1980. *Judaistic Christianity*. Grand Rapids: Baker.

Houlden, J. L. 1989. *The Pastoral Epistles: I and II Timothy, Titus*. Philadelphia: Trinity Press International.

Hutson, C. R. 1997. Was Timothy Timid? On the Rhetoric of Fearlessness (1 Corinthians 16:10-11) and Cowardice (2 Timothy 1:7). *Journal of the Chicago Society of Biblical Research* 42:58-73.

Irenaeus. *Ante-Nicene Fathers*, vol. 1. Edited by Alexander Roberts and James Donaldson. http://www.ccel.org/ccel/schaff/anf01.i.html.

Jewett, Robert. 1971. *Paul's Anthropological Terms: A Study of Their Use in Conflict Settings*. Leiden: Brill.

Johnson, Luke Timothy. 1978. II Timothy and the Polemic against False Teachers: A Re-examination. *JRelS* 6-7: 1-26.

_____. 1987. *1 Timothy, 2 Timothy, Titus*. Knox Preaching Guides. Atlanta: John Knox Press.

_____. 1996. *Letters to Paul's Delegates*. The New Testament in Context. Valley Forge, PA: Trinity Press.

_____. 1999. *The Writings of the New Testament*. Minneapolis: Fortress.

_____. 2001. *The First and Second Letters to Timothy*. Anchor Bible. New York: Doubleday.

Judge, Edwin Arthur. 1960. *Social Pattern of the Christian Groups in the First Century: New Testament Ideas of Social Obligation*. London: Tyndale.

Karris, R. J. 1973. The Background and Significance of the Polemic of the Pastoral Epistles. *JBL* 91: 549-64.

Kasch, Wilhelm. 1968. *rhyomai*. Page 1002 in vol. 6 of *TDNT*.

Käsemann, Ernst. 1969. *New Testament Questions of Today*. Philadelphia: Fortress.

Keck, Leander E. 1974. On the Ethos of the Early Christians. *JAAR* 42:435-52.

Kee, Howard Clark. 1980. *Christian Origins in Sociological Perspective: Methods and Resources*. Philadelphia: Westminster Press.

Keegan, T. J. 2006. *First and Second Timothy, Titus, Philemon*. New Collegeville Bible Commentary. Collegeville, MN: Liturgical Press.

Kelly, J. N. D. 1963. *A Commentary on the Pastoral Epistles*. Black New Testament Commentary. London: A & C Black.

Kenny, Anthony J. P. 1986. *A Stylometric Study of the New Testament*. Oxford: Clarendon Press.

Kidd, Reggie M. 1990. *Wealth and Beneficence in the Pastoral Epistles*. SBL Dissertation Series 122. Atlanta: Scholars Press.

Kittel, Gerhard. 1964. *akoloutheō*. Pages 210-16 in vol. 1 of *TDNT*.

Kittel, Gerhard, and Gerhard Friedrich. 1964-76. *Theological Dictionary of the New Testament*. 10 vols. Translated and edited by Geoffrey William Bromiley. Grand Rapids: Eerdmans.

Knight, George W. 1979. *The Faithful Sayings in the Pastoral Letters*. Grand Rapids: Baker.

_____. 1992. *The Pastoral Epistles*. The New International Greek Testament Commentary. Grand Rapids: Eerdmans.

Koester, Helmut. 2000. *Introduction to the New Testament, Vol. 2: History and Literature of Early Christianity*. Berlin: de Gruyter.

Köstenberger, Andreas, and Terry L. Wilder, eds. 2010. *Entrusted with the Gospel: Paul's Theology in the Pastoral Epistles*. Nashville: B&H Publishing.

Köstenberger, Andreas, and Thomas R. Schreiner, eds. 1995. *Women in the Church: A Fresh Analysis of 1 Timothy 2:9-15*. Grand Rapids: Baker.

Kroeger, Catherine Clark. 1986. 1 Timothy 2:12—A Classicist's View. Pages 225-44 in *Women, Authority & the Bible*. Edited by Alvera Mickelsen. Downers Grove, IL: InterVarsity.

Küchler, M. 1986. *Schweigen, Schmuck and Schlier: Drei neutestamentliche Vorschriften zur Verdrängung der Frauen auf dem Hintergrund einer frauenfeindlichen Exegese des Alten Testaments im antiken Judentum*. Freiburg: Universitätsverlag.

Kümmel, Werner Georg, and Howard Clark Kee. 1975. *Introduction to the New Testament*. Nashville: Abingdon.

Ladd, George Eldon. 1993. *A Theology of the New Testament*. Grand Rapids: Eerdmans.

Lane, William L. 1965. 1 Timothy 4:1-3: An Early Instance of Over-realized Eschatology? *NTS* 11.2:164-67.

Lang, Friedrich. 1971. *sōreuō*. Pages 1094-96 in vol. 7 of *TDNT*.

Lea, Thomas D., and Hayne P. Griffin. 1992. *1, 2 Timothy, Titus*. The New American Commentary 34. Nashville: Broadman Press.

Lee, John A. L. 2003. *A History of New Testament Lexicography*. New York: Peter Lang.

Liefeld, Walter L. 1999. *1 & 2 Timothy, Titus*. NIV Application Commentary. Grand Rapids: Zondervan.

Lightfoot, J. B. 1885a. *The Apostolic Fathers, Part I: Clement* (2 Vols.). London: MacMillan & Co.

_____. 1885b. *The Apostolic Fathers, Part II: S. Ignatius, S. Polycarp* (3 vols.). London: MacMillan & Co.

Lilema, Chinyama Joe, and Rodney L. Reed. 2011. An Evaluation of Polygamy Policy in the Church of the Nazarene in Africa: Africa Central Field Case Study, Africa Nazarene University. *Didache: Faithful Teaching*. 10:2. http://didache.nazarene.org/index.php?option=com_docman&task=doc_view&gid=824&Itemid=51.

Lillie, William. 1975. Pauline House-Tables. *ExpTim* 86.6:179-83.

Louw, J. P., and E. A. Nida. 1996. *Greek-English Lexicon of the New Testament: Based on Semantic Domains*. New York: United Bible Societies.

Luck, Ulrich. 1974. *philanthrōpia*. Pages 107-12 in vol. 9 of *TDNT*.

MacDonald, Margaret Y. 2010. Kinship and Family in the New Testament World. Pages 29-43 in *Understanding the Social World of the New Testament*. Edited by Dietmar Neufeld and Richard E. DeMaris. London and New York: Routledge.

Maddox, Randy. 1994. *Responsible Grace: John Wesley's Practical Theology*. Nashville: Kingswood Books.

Malherbe, Abraham J. 1977a. Ancient Epistolary Theorists. *Ohio Journal of Religious Studies*. 5:3-77.

_____. 1977b. *Social Aspects of Early Christianity*. Baton Rouge and London: Louisiana State University Press.

_____. 1980. Medical Imagery in the Pastoral Epistles. Pages 19-35 in *Texts and Testaments: Critical Essays on the Bible and Early Church Fathers*. Edited by W. E. March. San Antonio: Trinity University Press.

_____. 1984. "In Season and Out of Season": 2 Timothy 4:2. *JBL* 103:235-43.

_____. 1986. *Moral Exhortation: A Greco-Roman Sourcebook*. Philadelphia: Westminster John Knox Press.

_____. 1988. *Ancient Epistolary Theorists*. Atlanta: Scholars Press.

_____. 1989. *Paul and the Popular Philosophers*. Minneapolis: Fortress.

Malina, Bruce J. 2001. *The World of the New Testament*. Louisville, KY: Westminster John Knox.

Malina, Bruce J., and Jerome H. Neyrey. 1991. *The Social World of Luke-Acts: Models for Interpretation*. Edited by Jerome H. Neyrey. Peabody, MA: Hendrickson.

Marshall, I. Howard. 1976. Orthodoxy and Heresy in Earlier Christianity. *Them* 2:5-14.

_____. 1999. *A Critical and Exegetical Commentary on the Pastoral Epistles*. International Critical Commentary. Edinburgh: T&T Clark.

Maurer, Christian. 1971. *synoida*. Pages 898-919 in vol. 7 of *TDNT*.

Maxwell, John C. 1999. *The 21 Indispensable Qualities of a Leader: Becoming the Person Others Will Want to Follow*. Nashville: Thomas Nelson.

McDonald, Lee M. 1995. *The Formation of the Christian Biblical Canon*. Peabody, MA: Hendrickson.

McEleney, N. J. 1974. The Vice Lists of the Pastoral Epistles. *CBQ* 36:203-19.

McRay, John. 2007. *Paul: His Life and Teaching*. Grand Rapids: Baker.

Meeks, Wayne A. 2003: *The First Urban Christians: The Social World of the Apostle Paul*. New Haven, CT: Yale University Press.

Meier, John P. 1973. *Presbyteros* in the Pastoral Epistles. *CBQ* 35:323-45.

Methodist Church. 1936. *The Book of Offices: Being the Orders of Service Authorized for Use in the Methodist Church*. London: Methodist Publishing House.

Metzger, Bruce. 1994. *A Textual Commentary on the Greek New Testament*, 2nd ed. New York: United Bible Societies.

Meyer, Marvin, ed. 2007. *The Nag Hammadi Scriptures*. New York: Harper Collins.

Michaelis, W. 1967. *leōn*. Pages 251-53 in vol. 4 of *TDNT*.

Michel, Otto. 1967a. *oikos*. Pages 119-59 in vol. 5 of *TDNT*.

_____. 1967b. *homlogeō*. Pages 199-220 in vol. 5 of *TDNT*.

Miller, James D. 1997. *The Pastoral Letters as Composite Documents*. Cambridge: Cambridge University Press.

Minor, Eugene E. 1992. *An Exegetical Summary of 2 Timothy*. Dallas: Summer Institute of Linguistics.

Montague, George T. 2008. *First and Second Timothy, Titus.* Grand Rapids: Baker.

Moo, Douglas J. 1980. I Timothy 2:11-15: Meaning and Significance. *TJ* 1.1:62-83.

———. 1981. The Interpretation of 1 Timothy 2:11-15: A Rejoinder. *TJ* 2.2:198-222.

Moore, Arthur Lewis. 1966. *The Parousia in the New Testament.* Leiden: Brill.

Mott, Stephen C. 1978. Greek Ethics and Christian Conversion: The Philonic Background of Titus 2.10-14 and 3.3-7. *NovT* 20:22-48.

Moule, C. F. D. 1965. The Problem of the Pastoral Epistles: A Reappraisal. *Bulletin of John Rylands Library* 47:430-52.

Mounce, William D. 2000. *Pastoral Epistles.* Word Biblical Commentary. Nashville: Thomas Nelson.

Moxnes, H., ed. 1997. *Constructing Early Christian Families: Family as Social Reality and Metaphor.* London: Routledge.

Moyise, Steve. 2010. *Paul and Scripture: Studying the New Testament Use of the Old Testament.* London: SPCK.

Murphy-O'Connor, Jerome. 1991. 2 Timothy Contrasted with 1 Timothy and Titus. *RB* 98:403-18.

———. 1995. *Paul the Letter-Writer: His World, His Options, His Skills.* Collegeville, MN: Liturgical Press.

Neumann, Kenneth J. 1990. *The Authenticity of the Pauline Epistles in the Light of Stylostatistical Analysis.* Atlanta: Scholars Press.

Neyrey, Jerome H. 2005. "First," "Only," "One of a Few," and "No One Else": The Rhetoric of Uniqueness and the Doxologies in 1 Timothy. *Bib* 86:59-87.

Ngewa, Samuel M. 2009. *1 & 2 Timothy and Titus.* African Bible Commentary Series. Grand Rapids: Zondervan.

Oakes, Peter. 2010. Urban Structure and Patronage: Christ Followers in Corinth. Pages 178-93 in *Understanding the Social World of the New Testament.* Edited by Dietmar Neufeld and Richard E. DeMaris. London and New York: Routledge.

O'Brien, P. T. 1977. *Introductory Thanksgivings in the Letters of Paul.* NovTSup 49. Leiden: Brill.

Oden, Thomas C. 1989. *First and Second Timothy and Titus.* Louisville, KY: John Knox Press.

Oepke, Albrecht. 1964a. *apataō.* Pages 384-85 in vol. 1 of *TDNT.*

———. 1964b. *aspilos.* Page 502 in vol. 1 of *TDNT.*

———. 1967a. *mesitēs.* Pages 598-624 in vol. 4 of *TDNT.*

———. 1967b. *nosos.* Pages 1091-98 in vol. 4 of *TDNT.*

Osborne, Grant R. 2000. Resurrection. Pages 931-36 in *Dictionary of New Testament Background.* Edited by Craig A. Evans and Stanley E. Porter. Downers Grove, IL: InterVarsity.

Osiek, Carolyn, and David L. Balch. 1997. *Families in the New Testament World: Households and House Churches.* Louisville, KY: Westminster John Knox.

Padgett, Alan. 1987. Wealthy Women at Ephesus: 1 Timothy 2:8-15 in Social Context. *Int* 41.1:19-31.

The Papal Basilica St. Paul Outside-the-Walls. www.vatican.va/various/basiliche/san_paolo/index _en.html.

Parkin, Robert. 1997. *Kinship: An Introduction to the Basic Concept.* Oxford: Blackwell.

Payne, Philip B. 1981. Libertarian Women in Ephesus: A Response to Douglas J. Moo's Article, "1 Timothy 2.11-15: Meaning and Significance." *TJ* 2.2:169-97.

Pfitzner, Victor C. 1967. *Paul and the Agon Motif: Traditional Athletic Imagery in the Pauline Literature.* Leiden: Brill.

Philo. 1993. *The Works of Philo.* Translated by C. D. Yonge. Peabody, MA: Hendrickson.

Pietersen, Lloyd K. 2004. *The Polemic of the Pastorals: A Sociological Examination of the Development of Pauline Christianity.* London: T&T Clark.

Porter, Stanley E. 1996. Pauline Authorship and the Pastorals: Implications for Canon. *BBR* 6:105-23.

———. 2005. *The Pauline Canon.* Leiden: Brill.

Poythress, Vern Sheridan. 2002. The Meaning of *Malista* in 2 Timothy 4:13 and Related Verses. *JTS* 53.2:523-32.

Preisker, Hebert. 1967. *orthos.* Pages 449-51 in vol. 5 of *TDNT.*

———. 1968. *periousios.* Pages 57-58 in vol. 6 of *TDNT.*

Quell, Gottfried. 1965. *kyrios.* Pages 1058-59 in vol. 3 of *TDNT.*

Quinn, Jerome D. 1990. *The Letter to Titus: A New Translation with Notes and Commentary and an Introduction to Titus, I and II Timothy, The Pastoral Epistles.* Anchor Bible 35. Garden City, NY: Doubleday.

Quinn, Jerome D., and William Wacker. 2000. *The First and Second Letters to Timothy.* Eerdmans Critical Commentary. Grand Rapids: Eerdmans.

Richards, E. Randolph. 2004. *Paul and First-Century Letter Writing: Secretaries, Composition, and Collection*. Downers Grove, IL: InterVarsity.

Richards, William A. 2002. *Difference and Distance in Post-Pauline Christianity*. New York: Peter Lang.

Ridderbos, Herman. 1975. *Paul: An Outline of His Theology*. Translated by John Richard De Witt. Grand Rapids: Eerdmans.

Robbins, Vernon K. 1996. *The Tapestry of Early Christian Discourse: Rhetoric, Society, and Ideology*. London: Routledge.

Robertson, Archibald Thomas. 1931. *Word Pictures in the New Testament*, Vol. 4. Nashville: Broadman Press.

Rohrbaugh, Richard L. 2010. Honor: Core Value in the Biblical World. Pages 109-25 in *Understanding the Social World of the New Testament*. Edited by Dietmar Neufeld and Richard E. DeMaris. London and New York: Routledge.

Roloff, Jürgen. 1988. *Difference and Distance in Post-Pauline Christianity*. Zürich: Benziger Verlag.

Rudolph, Kurt. 1984. *Gnosis: The Nature & History of Gnosticism*. Translated by Robert McLachlan Wilson. San Francisco: HarperCollins.

Saarinen, Risto. 2008. *The Pastoral Epistles with Philemon and Jude*. Grand Rapids: Brazos Press.

Schlier, H. 1964a. *anechō*. Pages 359-60 in vol. 1 of *TDNT*.

_____. 1964b. *aphisthēmi*. Pages 512-13 in vol. 1 of *TDNT*.

_____. 1964c. *arneomai*. Pages 469-71 in vol. 1 of *TDNT*.

Schliermacher, Friedrich. 1807. *Über den sogenannten Ersten Brief des Paulus an den Timotheus: Ein Kritisches Sendschreiben an J. C. Gass*. Berlin: Realbuchhandlung.

Schmitz, Otto. 1967a. *parangellō*. Pages 761-65 in vol. 5 of *TDNT*.

_____. 1967b. *parakaleō*. Pages 793-99 in vol. 5 of *TDNT*.

Schneider, B. 1967. *Kata pneuma hagiosynes* (Romans 1:4). *Bib* 48:367-85.

Schneider, J. 1972. *Timē*. Pages 169-80 in vol. 8 of *TDNT*.

Scholer, David M. 1986. 1 Timothy 2:9-15 and the Place of Women in the Church's Ministry. Pages 192-219 in *Women, Authority & the Bible*. Edited by Alvera Mickelsen. Downers Grove, IL: InterVarsity.

Schreiner, Thomas R. 2005. An Interpretation of 1 Timothy 2:9-15: A Dialogue with Scholarship. Pages 85-120 in *Women in the Church: A Fresh Analysis of 1 Timothy 2.9-15*. Edited by Andreas J. Köstenberger and Thomas R. Schreiner. Grand Rapids: Baker Books.

Schrenk, Gottlob. 1964a. *graphō*. Pages 742-73 in vol. 1 of *TDNT*.

_____. 1964b. *dikē*. Pages 174-224 in vol. 2 of *TDNT*.

_____. 1965. *heiros*. Pages 221-83 in vol. 3 of *TDNT*.

Scott, E. F. 1936. *The Pastoral Epistles*. Moffat New Testament Commentary. London: Hodder and Stoughton.

Seebass, Horst. 1976. *Hosios*. Pages 236-38 in vol. 2 of *NIDNT*.

Skeat, T. C. 1979. Especially the Parchments: A Note on 2 Timothy 4:13. *JTS* 30:173-77.

Smith, Craig A. 2006. *Timothy's Task, Paul's Prospect: A New Reading of 2 Timothy*. Phoenix: Sheffield Phoenix Press Ltd.

Smith, R. E., and John Beekman. 1981. *A Literary-Semantic Analysis of 2 Timothy*. Dallas: Summer Institute of Linguistics.

Southern, Pat. 2006. *The Roman Army: A Social and Institutional History*. Oxford: Oxford University Press.

Spicq, C. 1969. *Les Épîtres Pastorales*. Études Bibliques. Paris: J. Gabalda.

Stählin, Gustav. 1964. *aiteo*. Pages 191-95 in vol. 1 of *TDNT*.

_____. 1967a. *mythos*. Pages 762-95 in vol. 4 of *TDNT*.

_____. 1967b. *xenos*. Pages 1-36 in vol. 5 of *TDNT*.

_____. 1968. *prokopē*. Pages 703-19 in vol. 6 of *TDNT*.

_____. 1974. *chēra*. Pages 440-65 in vol. 9 of *TDNT*.

Stewart, Eric C. 2010. Social Stratification and Patronage in Ancient Mediterranean Societies. Pages 156-66 in *Understanding the Social World of the New Testament*. Edited by Dietmar Neufeld and Richard E. DeMaris. London and New York: Routledge.

Stott, John R. W. 1973. *The Message of 2 Timothy*. Downers Grove, IL: InterVarsity.

_____. 1996. *The Message of 1 Timothy and Titus*. Leicester / Downers Grove, IL: InterVarsity.

Stowers, Stanley. 1984. Social Status, Public Speaking and Private Teaching: The Circumstances of Paul's Preaching Activity. *NovT* 26:59-81.

_____. 1986. *Letter Writing in Greco-Roman Antiquity*. Philadelphia: Westminster.

Strathmann, H. 1967. *latreuō*. Pages 59-63 in vol. 4 of *TDNT*.

Sturm, Richard E. 1989. Defining the Word "Apocalyptic": A Problem in Biblical Criticism. Pages 17-48 in *Apocalyptic and the New Testament, Essays in Honor of J. L. Martyn*. Edited by Joel Marcus and Marion Soards. Sheffield: JSOT Press.

Sumney, J. 1999. "God Our Savior": The Fundamental Operational Theological Assertion of 1 Timothy. *HBT* 21:105-23.

Theissen, Gerd. 1982. *The Social Setting of Pauline Christianity: Essays on Corinth*. Translated by John H. Schütz. Philadelphia: Fortress.

Thiselton, Anthony C. 1978. Realized Eschatology at Corinth. *NTS* 24:510-26.

Thurston, B. B. 1989. *The Widows: A Women's Ministry in the Early Church*. Minneapolis: Fortress.

Towner, Philip H. 1989. *The Goal of Our Instruction: The Structure of Theology and Ethics in the Pastoral Epistles*. Sheffield: JSOT Press.

_____. 1994. *1-2 Timothy and Titus*. The IVP New Testament Commentary Series. Downers Grove, IL: InterVarsity Press.

_____. 2006. *The Letters to Timothy and Titus*. New International Commentary on the New Testament. Grand Rapids: Eerdmans.

Trebilco, P. R. 2004. *The Early Christians in Ephesus*. Wissenschaftliche Untersuchungen Zum Neuen Testament 166. Tübingen: Mohr Siebeck.

Twomey, Jay. 2009. *The Pastoral Epistles Through the Centuries*. Blackwell Bible Commentaries. Chichester, UK: Wiley-Blackwell.

Van Neste, Ray. 2004. *Cohesion and Structure in the Pastoral Epistles*. London: T&T Clark.

Verner, David C. 1983. *The Household of God: Social World of the Pastoral Epistles*. SBL Dissertation Series 71. Chico, CA: Scholars Press.

Von Rad, Gerhard. 1964. *doxa*. Pages 238-42 in vol. 2 of *TDNT*.

Walker, Peter. 2012a. Revisiting the Pastoral Epistles—Part I. *EuroJTh* 21.1:4-16.

_____. 2012b. Revisiting the Pastoral Epistles—Part II. *EuroJTh* 21.2:120-32.

Wall, Robert W., with Richard B. Steele. 2012. *1 and 2 Timothy and Titus*. Two Horizons New Testament Commentary. Grand Rapids: Eerdmans.

Wallace, Daniel B. 1996. *Greek Grammar Beyond the Basics*. Grand Rapids: Zondervan.

Ward, Ronald A. 1974. *Commentary on I and II Timothy and Titus*. Waco, TX: Word Books.

Waters, Kenneth L. 2004. Saved through Childbearing: Virtues as Children in 1 Timothy 2:11-15. *JBL* 123.4:703-35.

Watson, D. A. 2000. Education: Jewish and Greco-Roman. Pages 308-13 in *Dictionary of New Testament Background*. Edited by Craig A. Evans and Stanley E. Porter. Downers Grove, IL: InterVarsity.

Wesley, John. 1813. *Explanatory Notes upon the New Testament*, vol. 2. London: Thomas Cordeux.

_____. 1986. *The Works of John Wesley*, 14 vols. Edited by Thomas Jackson. Reprint of 1872. London: Wesleyan Conference Office. Kansas City: Beacon Hill Press of Kansas City.

Wilckens, Ulrich. 1971. *sophia*. Pages 465-528 in vol. 7 of *TDNT*.

Williams, David J. 1999. *Paul's Metaphors: Their Context and Character*. Peabody, MA: Hendrickson.

Williams, P. J., Andrew D. Clarke, Peter M. Head, and David Instone-Brewer. 2004. *The New Testament in Its First Century Setting*. Grand Rapids: Eerdmans.

Wilson, Stephen G. 1979. *Luke and the Pastoral Epistles*. London: SPCK.

Winter, Bruce W. 2003. *Roman Wives, Roman Widows: The Appearance of New Women and the Pauline Communities*. Grand Rapids: Eerdmans.

Witherington, Ben. 1988. *Women in the Earliest Churches*. Cambridge: Cambridge University Press.

_____. 2006. *Letters and Homilies for Hellenized Christians, Volume 1: A Socio-Rhetorical Commentary on Titus, 1-2 Timothy and 1-3 John*. Downers Grove, IL: InterVarsity.

Wright, N. T. 1997. *What Saint Paul Really Said*. Grand Rapids: Eerdmans.

_____. 2005. *Paul in Fresh Perspective*. Minneapolis: Fortress.

Young, Frances. 1994. *The Theology of the Pastoral Letters*. New Testament Theology. Cambridge: Cambridge University Press.

TABLE OF SIDEBARS

INTRODUCTION

First and Second Timothy and Titus appear toward the end of the collection of letters in the NT attributed to Paul the apostle. These three letters have been collectively labeled "Pastoral Epistles" for three centuries. They have prompted many historical challenges and debates among interpreters from the earliest days of the church until the present. Scholars disagree widely about their meaning, authorship, and canonical status.

It is seldom necessary to resolve such debated historical issues to find spiritual application in Scripture. However, awareness of these issues may shed light on some of their more difficult passages. Many aspects of these are interrelated. Here, we can offer only a brief overview of the main issues to set the stage for the commentary.

A. The Pastorals as a Literary Unit

The Pastoral Epistles follow the nine community letters and precede Philemon in the Pauline collection. They have been organized not chronologically but stichometrically—from the longest to the shortest—since the late second century (as attested in the Muratorian Canon; Quinn 1990, 3).

They stand out from the other Pauline letters because of their unique style, content, and personal nature. They allege to have been written to individuals rather than to churches. This distinguishes them from the rest of the NT (except 3 John). Although Philemon bears the name of an individual, other names are listed in its salutation, including "the church that meets in your home" (Phlm 2).

Titus was first labeled a "Pastoral Epistle" by D. N. Berdot in 1703. Paul Anton gave 1 and 2 Timothy this designation later in 1726. Long before that, Thomas Aquinas in the thirteenth century described 1 Timothy as "virtually a pastoral rule." "Pastor" is the NT word for the "shepherd" leader of the flock of God's people (Acts 20:28; Eph 4:11; 1 Pet 5:2). This designation for these letters continues to be used because the letters were written to persons with pastoral responsibility. They are the only NT letters written to such persons. Although they are grouped together in the canon and share many similar themes, there are no internal indicators that the letters were meant to be grouped as such or were written to be studied together. But the texts themselves suggest that they were written by the same person and about similar issues.

Taking the claims within the letters at face value, it appears that Paul gave Timothy and Titus administrative tasks under his authority. The letters offer his directions for stabilizing churches that were being infiltrated by false teachers and doctrines. First Timothy and Titus particularly address leadership issues in the churches. But the letters are much broader in their scope. They incorporate a number of themes beyond simply the mechanics of pastoral service. Paul recognized leadership abilities in Timothy and Titus and advised them as to how to connect these in difficult situations that required careful guidance.

Recent scholars—notably Philip H. Towner (2006, 88-89) and Luke Timothy Johnson (2001, 63-99)—have challenged the widely held assumption that these letters should be interpreted as one literary unit. They insist that each letter should be interpreted first on its own, although insight can still be gained by comparing them to one another. Treated on its own, it appears that "each letter is addressed to a situation that close analysis shows to be at once internally consistent and completely inconsistent with the situation addressed by the other two letters" (Johnson 2001, 89).

Paul did not write the Pastoral Epistles as manuals for pastoral ministry. Admittedly, there is important information in them about church leadership and development. Rather, these letters offer the practical wisdom of a seasoned missionary and church planter for situations requiring extreme care and serious correction. They offer guidance intended to enhance the strong leadership of Timothy and Titus and emerging leaders in the Christian communities they led.

B. Authorship

Scholars have debated the authorship of these three letters more than any other Pauline letter in modern times. All three claim Paul the apostle as their author (1 Tim 1:1; 2 Tim 1:1; Titus 1:1). One's decision on this one issue impacts the way we interpret the letters and reconstruct early church history. There are two major and divergent streams of scholarly opinion about the authorship of the Pastorals: they are authentically Pauline or they are pseudonymous. The latter view typically assumes that they were written a generation or two after Paul's death, offering what the authors believed the apostle would have said had he still been alive. These two opposing positions may be further distinguished as representing four perspectives (the names enclosed in parentheses identify scholars who have championed each):

1. The traditional view is that Paul was the author (Kelly, Guthrie, Simpson, Spicq, Michaelis, Towner, Johnson).
2. The secretary view is that Paul used an amanuensis (Mounce). He expressed the apostle's ideas in his words (Jeremias). Some identify Luke as this unstated co-author (Moule, Quinn and Wacker, Witherington, Wilson).
3. The fragmentary view is that a second-century author composed the letters, using genuine Pauline material (Harrison, Scott, Easton, Falconer).
4. The pseudonymous perspective is that someone else—a disciple of Paul—wrote in Paul's name (Dibelius and Conzelmann, Kümmel, Barrett).

1. Paul as the Assumed Author

Most of the historical information we have about Paul comes from either Acts or Paul's own writings. Neither of these gives a complete picture of his life and ministry. The Pastorals provide information not found in Acts or the undisputed epistles. This fact prompts questions about their authorship, date, and historical reliability.

Scholars appeal to two different approaches to establish whether Paul wrote these letters: (1) internal claims within the letters themselves and (2) external, early church witnesses.

a. Internal Claims

Until the nineteenth century, there was almost a unanimous consensus that Paul wrote these letters, since the letters themselves claim Pauline authorship. The letters mention twenty-five contemporaries of Paul—coworkers, friends, and enemies, twelve of whom appear in other Pauline letters. Autobiographical statements like 1 Tim 1:12-14 cohere with the presentation of Paul in Acts. The two central figures of the letters, Timothy and Titus, appear as companions of Paul in the undisputed Pauline letters and Acts. Many personal details in the letters indicate intimate knowledge of the Pauline mission: For example, the names of the false teachers Hymenaeus and Alexander (1 Tim 1:20), Onesiphorus (2 Tim 1:16-18), the church workers Artemas and Tychicus (Titus 3:12) who were to replace Titus in Nicopolis, and others. Timothy's mother and grandmother are named in 2 Tim 1:5.

b. External Claims

Pauline authorship of the Pastorals was almost universally accepted in the early church. Questions remain as to how early they were recognized. The earliest possible allusion appears toward the end of the first century—in Clement of Rome's letter to the Corinthians (ca. 95) and Ignatius of Antioch's letter to the Ephesians (ca. 110). In his letter to the Philippians (4:1 and 9:2), Polycarp of Smyrna (ca. 117) may allude to 1 Tim 6:7, 10 and 2 Tim 4:10. But the clearest early external testimony dates from the end of the second century. Irenaeus (ca. 180) seems to quote from these letters in his *Against Heresies* (2.14.7—1 Tim 6:20; 3.14.1—2 Tim 4:10-11; 1.16.3—Titus 3:10). The Muratorian Canon lists all three books as by Paul. But its date is contested—ca. 170-300. Tertullian (ca. 160-225) wrote that Marcion (ca. 84-160) knew and rejected the Pastorals, requiring a date before Marcion (*Marc.* 5.21).

There is no evidence that anyone in the early church rejected these letters, except the heretic Marcion (Marshall 1999, 8). He rejected them on theological grounds—their emphasis on God's desire to save everyone, the goodness of the created order, and positive view of marriage (Johnson 1996, 3).

The Pastoral letters were not included in the early third-century manuscript of the Pauline Letters p[46] or in the important fourth-century Codex Vaticanus. The earliest fragmentary manuscript to include them is a single page of the second-century p[32]. This fragment contains Titus 1:11-15 on one side and 2:3-8 on the other. The earliest complete manuscript evidence comes from Codex Sinaiticus (ca. 350).

2. Challenges to Pauline Authorship

a. The History of the Debate

The basic argument against Paul as author focuses on style, vocabulary, themes, and church structure. Those who challenge strict Pauline authorship claim that these better fit the second than the first century. They conclude that an unknown person in the second century wrote in Paul's name.

J. E. C. Schmidt's 1804 examination of the vocabulary of the letters led many scholars to doubt their authenticity. In 1807, Friedrich Schleiermacher questioned the plausibility of biographical data in the letters, which seemed inconsistent with Paul's other letters. A consensus emerged in critical German scholarship, centered in Tübingen, that questioned Pauline authorship. F. C. Baur (1835) argued that the Pastorals had a different style and vocabulary than Paul's other letters, the biographical data did not match, and the letters do not logically develop theology in the same way as Paul's other letters.

This position has been refined and defended by numerous so-called liberal interpreters over the past two centuries. Many British and American scholars have consistently offered a dissenting, conservative voice. Toward the end of the twentieth century, the liberal position claimed to represent the consensus of NT scholarship, but this claim is overstated.

Conservative scholars claim that there is no evidence that the early church accepted forgeries. All documents known to be pseudepigraphical and written in the name of an apostle, they allege, were rejected by the early church (Mounce 2000, cxxiv). Liberals, of course, disagree (see, e.g., Ehrman 2011).

There has been a noticeable shift in the past fifty years. Recent commentaries in respected series and critical NT introductions have increasingly accepted these letters as genuinely Pauline (see Witherington 2006, 51).

b. Internal Issues

(1) Vocabulary and Style

One of the most significant challenges to Pauline authorship of the Pastorals is their distinctive language, vocabulary, and style of writing. There are a total of 902 different Greek words in the Pastoral Epistles. Of these, nearly 20 percent (176) occur only here in the NT; 14 percent of the total (130) appear in other parts of the NT but not in Paul's generally accepted letters. Thus, more than one-third of the vocabulary in the Pastorals appears nowhere else in Paul's writings.

The unique subjects addressed in these letters may account for about one-third (over one hundred) of these distinctive terms. The Pastorals include fifty-five words found only in Paul's writings in the NT. But they lack a number of particles (small Greek words often used for transitions and left untranslated in English) that appear in the undisputed letters. Some word groups, frequent in Paul's other letters, are entirely missing in the Pastorals.

Scholars offer a variety of explanations for these differences. Harrison argued on linguistic grounds that many of the distinctive words and phrases in the Pastorals appear more frequently in the second-century Apostolic Fathers than in Paul elsewhere (1921, 70, 165).

Spicq (1969, 1.199), however, has shown that many of these words also occur earlier in the writings of the Jewish philosopher Philo (d. ca. AD 40) and in the Septuagint. This Greek translation of the OT Paul used dates from the second century BC.

Spicq also claims that the Hellenistic flavor of the exhortations in the Pastorals reflects Paul's ability to adapt to his increasingly Gentile churches (Spicq 1969, 1.175, 294). DeSilva asks, If "Paul could use 2,177 different words in the other ten letters, why should he not add another 306 in the Pastorals?" (2004, 737).

The personal nature of the letters may explain some of the stylistic features of the Pastoral letters. Wilson (1979), following Moule (1965, 434), notes that there are significant similarities between the Pastorals and Luke-Acts. He conjectures that Luke (see 2 Tim 4:11) served as Paul's amanuensis for these letters. Witherington similarly opines that the message is Paul's but the words are Luke's (2006, 60). Colossians 4:14 and Phlm 24 and longstanding tradition indicate that Luke was a sometime traveling companion of Paul. The evidence of Lukan vocabulary in the Pastorals has led some scholars to argue that they are a composite of authentic Pauline material and others—disciples of Paul who combined his teachings with their own in order to train pastors for a new generation (Miller 1997).

More recent analyses of the linguistic data have proven ambiguous and inconclusive. Kenny (1986) concludes that all the traditional letters of Paul, except Titus, show the same author. Neumann (1990), however, using different criteria, finds significant differences between the Pastorals and the other Pauline letters.

We must acknowledge that the evidence is inconclusive. Accordingly, Johnson's approach seems the most reasonable, based on the available evidence. He argues that these letters are too short to allow for reliable statistical analysis. Different subject matters and purposes significantly influence style and vocabulary. The vocabulary of the Pastorals differs most where they deal with subjects unique to these letters (1996, 12, 21).

(2) Themes

Another argument against strict Pauline authorship has been that the Pastorals are missing themes common in other Pauline letters. Often noted are justification by faith, the cross of Christ, the church as the "body of Christ," and communion "in Christ." The urgency of the Christ's second coming (in Rom 13:11-14; 1 Cor 7:29; 15:51; and 1 Thess 4:17) is notably diminished in these letters (Beker 1991, 36-47). As we note in the commentary proper, many of these themes are nonetheless implicit, if not explicit, at strategic spots in the Pastorals.

We must also emphasize that none of the supposedly standard Pauline themes appear in all the generally accepted letters. For example, justification language is entirely missing in 1 and 2 Thessalonians. There is no language of holiness in Galatians. These letters never refer to the church using body imagery.

(3) Social Location

At the sociological level, some interpreters argue that the Pastoral letters deal primarily with ethical issues of the urban middle to upper class. Some of Paul's other letters obviously addressed largely poor and powerless believers (see, e.g., 1 Cor 1:26-31). Increasingly upwardly mobile Christians became more prevalent during the second century (Koester 2000, 2:305; Malherbe 1977b, 30-31; Kee 1980, 119). Their social location made them more comfortable with the status quo and less interested in a kingdom that would turn everything topsy-turvy.

As a result, Dibelius called the Pastorals *bourgeois* ("good citizenship"; Dibelius and Conzelmann 1972, 39-41). Kidd (1990, 25) summarizes Dibelius' characterization of early Christianity:

- *a.* Socially Ascendant: Christianity emerged among the lowest class and eventually rose to higher ones.
- *b.* Culturally Accommodative: Christianity adopted Greek and Roman culture over time.
- *c.* Unheroically Conservative: Social ethics became more conservative over time as the urgency of Christ's second coming diminished and matched the various class rankings and power holders within the church.

Spicq (1969; see Kidd 1990, 27) demonstrates that this reconstruction of early Christianity, which argues for a late date for the Pastorals, is overstated. Social concern and social stratification are evident in Paul's other letters. The Pastorals show how Christians expressed their faith in new ways and situations. First Timothy especially (2:10; 6:5-10, 17-19) shows how the pursuit of riches was a problem in Ephesus, one of the wealthiest cities of Asia. But this was not only a second-century problem; it existed in Paul's own lifetime (see, e.g., Phil 3:17-21).

c. Opponents

All three letters address problems related to the influence of teachers of false doctrines. This appears to be the major threat that prompted Paul to write them. There is no consensus as to the identity of these people, what they taught, or the impact the heresy they advocated had on Christians in Ephesus and Crete. Paul wrote these letters to respond to this serious threat. Pietersen (2004, 4) summarizes the evidence found within the letters about these opponents:

1. They came from within the Christian community (1 Tim 1:19; 4:1-4; 5:19-20; 6:21; 2 Tim 2:18; 3:1-7; Titus 1:10-11).

2. There was a clear Jewish element in their error (1 Tim 1:3-4, 6; Titus 1:10, 14; 3:9).

3. Their ethic had an ascetic element, which included forbidding marriage and abstinence from certain foods (1 Tim 4:1-3).

4. The opponents' teaching involved myths (1 Tim 1:4; 4:7; 2 Tim 4:4; Titus 1:14), genealogies (1 Tim 1:4; Titus 3:9), speculations (1 Tim 1:4; 6:4; 2 Tim 2:23; Titus 3:9), disputes about words (1 Tim 6:4; 2 Tim 2:14), profane chatter (1 Tim 6:20; 2 Tim 2:16), concern for knowledge (1 Tim 6:20), a spiritualized view of the resurrection (2 Tim 2:18), rejection of conscience (1 Tim 1:19), and was motivated by financial gain (1 Tim 6:5; Titus 1:11).

Many have attempted to identify the opponents with known heretical movements. It is impossible to identify any one group behind the church problems that occasioned the Pastorals. Differing views on the authorship and dating of the letters inevitably impact every attempt to do so.

- If these letters were written in the second century and are pseudonymous, the opponents could have been gnostics, Cerinthians, or Marcionites.

- If they are authentic, these people shared characteristics with Pauline opponents in such places as Galatia, Corinth, and Colosse.

Thus, it is impossible to use the opponents to date these letters. Gnosticism in the second century was more developed than what is evident in the Pastorals. Many NT writings seem to address what might be called proto-Gnosticism. This developed from the syncretism of Hellenistic Judaism with Christianity and various pagan religions (Fee 1988, 9).

The heretical teachings confronted in the Pastoral letters could have arisen in Paul's lifetime (Kümmel and Kee 1975, 267; Johnson 1996, 13). Misunderstandings of and animosity toward Paul's preaching and mission work arose in many places (2 Cor 11:1-14). All the essential ingredients for later heresies are present in the problems he (and other early Christian leaders) faced during the mid-first century.

The Jewish influence upon the opponents appears in their preoccupation with speculations, genealogies, myths, and circumcision (1 Tim 1:4, 7; 6:20; Titus 1:10, 14; 3:9). This might lead us to expect a more legalistic bent than the Pastorals seem to indicate. Instead, the opponents appear to have been obsessed with "knowledge" (*gnosis* [1 Tim 6:20]). This led to a more libertine (anything goes) ethic. Perhaps, the asceticism the Pastorals oppose was influenced by Platonic dualism, filtered through Hellenistic Judaism (1 Tim 5:11-15; 2 Tim 3:1-

7). Paul's anti-docetic emphases challenge such thinking. He affirms Christ's incarnation and bodily resurrection (1 Tim 3:16; 2 Tim 2:8, 18).

True to his Jewish heritage, Paul, as a strict monotheist, declares that there is one God and one Mediator (1 Tim 2:5). Some Christian converts in Ephesus probably came from the Artemis cult. This may explain some of the immoral behavior Paul was obliged to challenge (2 Tim 3:6). The Ephesian context may also account for their apparent interest in magic (2 Tim 3:13) and asceticism (1 Tim 4:3), especially among the women. Some of the new converts undoubtedly had emotional attachments to their past (Gritz 1991, 116). The Christian converts in Crete may have faced similar issues because of their pagan past.

Paul wrote the Pastoral letters to combat and correct these problems. They had the potential of leading people astray and destroying the church. According to Acts 20:30, he had predicted that such people would attempt to lead believers astray. He used polemic to isolate the opponents because they had rejected or distorted the apostolic gospel (Towner 1989, 24-25).

d. Church Organization

Those who claim the Pastorals are pseudonymous argue that the church structure presumed in them did not emerge until the second century. They evidence an emerging "early Catholicism." In the other letters of Paul, leadership and church structure are based on charismatic gifts. That is, leaders emerged based on their spiritual gifts (Rom 12:6; 1 Cor 12:4-11). The church in the Pastorals seems more developed, more institutionalized. It had grown enough to value organization over spontaneity. Leadership was hierarchically organized with officially ordained bishops, presbyters, and deacons.

To the extent that this characterization is correct, it does not require a late dating. The descriptions of leaders mentioned in the Pastorals were already in use in the earliest church (Eph 4:11-12; Phil 1:1; see Acts 6:1-3; 14:23). First Timothy addresses issues of organization more than do the other Pastorals. Titus treats some of these issues, but not 2 Timothy.

The emphasis on leadership in all three letters is not on specific job descriptions but on the character of leaders. Paul's goal was to develop ethically and theologically sound leaders in the Ephesian and Cretan house churches. The evidence of the letters indicates that this was far more urgent than creating broad ecclesiastic structures.

3. Concluding Thoughts on Authorship

Paul's letters and their historical contexts are complex and many questions remain. However, this should not discourage interpreters from studying them for their theology, spiritual edification, and historical insights.

For many twenty-first-century conservative Christians, the pseudonymous position raises serious questions about the authority of these letters for the church. But in antiquity, disciples of prominent leaders considered it dishonest to present the ideas of their mentors as theirs. So the problem may be partly a matter of cultural differences.

The danger, of course, is that if the Pastoral Epistles are viewed as forgeries, they may be neglected or relegated to a secondary position in comparison to the authentic Pauline Epistles. This effectively silences their witness to the church. Porter (1996) goes as far as to suggest that because the letters are forgeries, they should not be included in the canon.

This raises the issue: Is the Bible as canonized by the church reliable for theology, ecclesiology, and ethics? The early church recognized the authority of these texts in dealing with the gnostic heresies of the second century and for the development of its understanding of church leadership. Other documents were rejected because they failed the test of usefulness and orthodoxy (McDonald 1995, 248). The Holy Spirit worked through those who wrote, received, and canonized the NT.

That Paul stands behind the letters, even if they were composed by another, such as Luke, helps preserve their authority. Witherington argues that it is more important that the letters contain Paul's thoughts than that their grammar, syntax, and vocabulary reflect his style. The Pastorals are Pauline, whether dictated word-for-word by Paul or composed by another attempting to capture his thoughts (2006, 26).

The real issue is not the authority of the purported author of the Pastorals or any other NT book. It is whether or not we will accept the canonical decisions of the church. The authority of the Pastoral Epistles does not depend on anything so fragile as historical arguments for or against Pauline authorship. It rests firmly on their canonical status, which remains unaffected by scholarly debates. This was settled more than a millennium and a half ago. Ordinary believers over a wide geographical area and over several centuries found in these letters evidence that the same Spirit who inspired them continued to inspire those who heard them read in church.

It is entirely possible that the words themselves, not only the ideas, in the Pastorals are Paul's. Style and vocabulary are weak indicators of authorship, because they are influenced by context and purpose of writing (see Mounce 2000, xcix-xcviii). The unique features of these letters can be accounted for because of the different situations confronting both Paul and his addressees. As the churches faced increasing external threats from heretical teachers, Paul adapted his message to deal with these issues. I am of the opinion that the historical and literary evidence supports the traditional view of Pauline authorship more than it does arguments for pseudonymity.

Historical-critical questions address issues of background and composition and neglect the more crucial questions of meaning and significance. Historical questions only take us so far, and answer only certain questions. The Pastoral letters, as part of the biblical canon, bear witness to the thought of the earliest church. These ancient words still speak to contemporary needs.

C. The Pastorals within Paul's Life and Ministry

Considering the letters to be authentic allows us to explore their possible historical background with more precision. Peter Walker (2012a, 2012b) offers a creative and credible overview of the issues related to the dating of these letters, which I summarize below. Those who accept Pauline authorship have taken one of two approaches:

(1) This approach is popular among conservative scholars. It argues that the letters were written after the Acts narrative concludes. They do so because what is found in the letters does not correspond with any events in Acts:

First Timothy and Titus assume that Paul is free and 2 Timothy assumes Paul is in prison awaiting imminent execution. Acts 28 ends with Paul still in Rome, under house arrest, enjoying relative freedom to have visitors.

The traditional conservative theory is that Paul was acquitted after this first imprisonment and then continued his ministry for some time until he was arrested again. First Timothy and Titus were written after this release, and 2 Timothy was written during Paul's second and final imprisonment in Rome.

The significant problem with this theory is that there is no evidence Paul was released from Roman imprisonment. Nero was notoriously cruel and became increasingly paranoid as time passed. It is unlikely Paul received a quick hearing and release. In AD 64, Emperor Nero made Christians scapegoats for a major fire in Rome. This launched a period of intense and official persecution of the church. It was during this time that tradition says both Paul and Peter were martyred.

Conservative interpreters often appeal to *1 Clem.* 5.1—6.1 (AD 96) to support the position that Paul was freed from prison and took the gospel to Spain, as he had planned (Rom 15:24, 28). The Muratorian Canon may have interpreted Clement in this way. Eusebius' mention of this tradition (*Hist. eccl.* 2.22) codified it in church history. But Clement may claim no more than that Paul made it to Rome, where he bore witness to the gospel before the emperor.

(2) The other approach, adopted by Walker, is that the events in 1 Timothy and Titus fit into a window of time during Paul's third missionary journey, mentioned only briefly in Acts 20:1-3:

Paul evangelized in Ephesus and stayed there about two years (Acts 19:10; 20:31). After this, he left Ephesus, probably in the fall of AD 55, for Macedonia (Acts 19:22). While there, he met Timothy in Macedonia and sent him to Ephesus (1 Tim 1:3). He wrote 1 Timothy on his way to Greece, possibly around January AD 56, just a few months after dispatching Timothy. This period may have lasted from fifteen to eighteen months (Acts 20:1-5).

There is a gap at this point in our knowledge of what Paul did. He left Ephesus in the fall of AD 55 and did not arrive in Corinth until December AD 56 or January AD 57. After spending three months there, he set sail for Jerusalem. Paul wrote Titus during this time, possibly from western Macedonia or Illyricum (see Rom 15:19). He wanted to meet Titus in Nicopolis (Titus 3:12), where he planned to spend the winter. Nicopolis was on one plausible route around Greece to Corinth.

Walker's early dating of 1 Timothy fits well with Paul's admonition to Timothy (in 4:12) not to let anyone look down on him because of his youth. Timothy would have been in his mid-twenties. His mission to Ephesus would have been his first major assignment. This explains why Paul went into more detail about his delegate's task in 1 Timothy than in Titus.

If this reconstruction is correct, Titus should be dated earlier than it typically is. Crete was an important island on the major sea routes across the Mediterranean. It was strategic to plant the church there.

We can only guess when the church began there. It is possible that Paul visited the island during his long stay in Ephesus. Acts 19 tells us almost nothing about his activities during this two-year sojourn. We propose that he wrote

44

the letter to Titus sometime after leaving Ephesus, during his long trip around Macedonia.

According to 2 Cor 7:6-16, Paul met Titus (coming from Corinth) in Macedonia in the fall of AD 55. Upon receiving news of problems in Crete, he commissioned Titus to resolve them (→ Titus 1:5). Paul told the Corinthians Titus would be coming soon, perhaps with the letter we call 2 Corinthians (see 2 Cor 8:16-19). After visiting Corinth, Titus could set sail for Crete.

After wintering in Macedonia, Paul commissioned Titus during the spring or summer of AD 56. Soon after, he wrote a letter with further direction for Titus to stay longer and to work to select and solidify new leaders in Crete. The letter we call Titus was sent with either Artemas or Tychicus, whom Paul sent to replace Titus. Titus was then to meet Paul in Nicopolis, where they would spend the winter (→ Titus 3:12). This reconstruction presumes a date for Titus soon after 1 Timothy. This explains why the letters share many similarities.

Clues from Acts and Paul's letters also allow a plausible reconstruction of the occasion for 2 Timothy. Soon after Paul's arrival in Jerusalem with the collection for the poor saints there, Paul was arrested in the temple precincts. He was then moved to Caesarea, where he remained imprisoned for two years. Finally, after a formal appeal, he was shipped to Rome for a trial before the Emperor Nero (Acts 21—28).

Paul likely arrived in Rome in the spring of AD 60. During those first few months, he appeared before some legal officials to explain the nature of his case. This is what he called his "first defense" (2 Tim 4:16), which evidently did not go as planned. He feared that his next and decisive trial would not go well. But he hints that this could be delayed for some time. So he continues to make plans for the mission.

None of Paul's distant colleagues knew where he was during the early days of his Roman imprisonment. Just a few local believers greeted him when he arrived (Acts 28:15). Only Luke was with him at this early point (2 Tim 4:11), which coheres with a widely held reading of "we" sections in Acts 28. Onesiphorus had a hard time locating Paul, because Paul had just arrived in Rome (2 Tim 1:15-18). By the time Paul wrote Colossians from Rome, two of his friends had arrived, John Mark (Col 4:10) and Timothy (Col 1:1).

Second Timothy had invited Timothy and Mark to Rome (2 Tim 4:11). Timothy was present with Paul in Rome when they co-authored Colossians, Philemon, and Philippians. Walker suggests that Paul's last letter was Philippians, which is full of confidence in Christ and hope of future life with him.

If Walker's reconstruction is correct, Timothy arrived in Rome during the fall of AD 60. The letter of Second Timothy was Paul's first chance to contact Timothy and request his help in Rome. Timothy could retrieve the precious belongings Paul left in Troas on his way to Jerusalem with the offering for the saints (4:13; see Acts 20:6-12; Rom 15:17-22).

A strong case can be made, therefore, for Paul having written 2 Timothy at the start of his two-year imprisonment in Rome during his first summer, around early or midsummer of the year AD 60. This early dating for 2 Timothy goes against the prevailing perspective that it was Paul's last letter. It must be acknowledged that this historical reconstruction is tentative but can be supported from the evidence within the Pastorals and the NT.

D. Purpose

There is no universal agreement among scholars on the purpose of the Pastoral letters, but three ideas are usually proposed.

1. The Challenge of Opponents

They are polemical defenses against various false teachers. Their heretical teachings were leading churches astray. Fully one-third of 1 Timothy deals with problems related to the false teachers (1 Tim 1:3). This problem persisted into the writing of 2 Timothy (2 Tim 2:16-17, 23-26; 3:6-9). Titus likewise deals with the threat of false teachers who shared some similarities with Judaizers who were infiltrating other early churches in Paul's mission (Titus 1:10-16). If these situations were not corrected, the influence of false teaching would seriously hamper the mission and lead to misunderstandings of the gospel.

2. Qualified Leaders

In response to the problem of false teachers, Paul gave directions on finding qualified local leadership (1 Tim 3:14-15; Titus 1:5-9). What he wrote in these letters about church leadership is often used to make a case for a late dating. However, a close reading simply shows that he was in the process of helping established churches become more structured in order to confront the onslaught of false teachings and to resolve growing internal issues especially caused by these teachings. Strong local leadership would be the primary way to preserve orthodoxy (Marshall 1976, 8).

3. Personal Concerns

Paul gave instruction to Timothy and Titus about a number of personal concerns. One aim was to encourage both of them to be strong in their ministry and to hold firmly to the truth of the gospel. They had to watch their personal lives and maintain a firm commitment to God's calling. Another area of concern had to do with some of Paul's personal concerns, the need for assistance from trusted colleagues, some personal items, and the continued effectiveness of the Pauline mission.

E. Recipients

The stated recipients of the Pastoral Epistles are Timothy and Titus (1 Tim 1:2; 2 Tim 1:2; Titus 1:4). But the implied recipients include the members of the churches in Ephesus and Crete. The final greeting of each letter shifts from the singular to the plural, indicating that these letters were intended for the churches where Timothy and Titus served (1 Tim 6:21; 2 Tim 4:22; Titus 3:15). Paul had a special bond of friendship, mentoring, and mission with both Timothy and Titus.

I. Timothy

Timothy was a close friend and traveling companion of Paul. He was from Lystra, a Lycaonian town in the Roman province of Galatia, in south central Asia Minor. It is possible that Paul met him and his family on his first missionary trip through the area (Acts 13:49—14:25), ca. AD 46-48. But the first mention of Timothy in Acts (16:1-2) is on his second missionary trip. Acts calls him a "disciple," implying that he was already a believer. His mother Eunice and grandmother Lois were both believers as well (2 Tim 1:5). They had trained him in the Jewish Scriptures (2 Tim 3:14-15). His father was a Greek (*hellēnos*; Acts 16:1). There is no hint in Acts or the letters that he ever became a believer. Acquaintance with both the Jewish and Gentile context would serve Timothy well in his ministry.

By the time of Paul's second visit to the area, Timothy had developed a good reputation among the believers in Lystra and Iconium. This prompted Paul to recruit him for his ongoing mission (Acts 16:2). From that point on, Paul and Timothy had a lifelong relationship. Paul called Timothy his spiritual son (1 Cor 4:17; 1 Tim 1:2; 2 Tim 1:2). Paul and Silas took young Timothy to Troas (Acts 16:8-10), from where they went to Philippi, Thessalonica, and Berea. Timothy and Silas remained in Berea to help the new church there gain strength (Acts 17:14). Later he rejoined Paul and Silas in Corinth (Acts 18:5; 2 Cor 1:19). Timothy and Silas were cosenders with Paul of 1 and 2 Thessalonians. They may have been instrumental in planting the church there (1 Thess 3:1-3). By that point, Timothy had proven his worth as an emissary for Paul.

Timothy was with Paul in Ephesus and Asia on his third missionary tour. So he was involved in the crucial early years in the Ephesian church (Acts 19:22). This relationship would make it easier for him to guide the church later through the troubled waters of false teachers (1 Timothy).

While Paul ministered in Ephesus, he sent Timothy to Macedonia (Acts 18:5), and perhaps on to Achaia, to deliver the letter we call 1 Corinthians. In it he told the church in Corinth that he had sent Timothy to remind them of Paul's way of life (1 Cor 4:17; 16:10-11). By this point in the mission, Timothy already grasped Paul's way of thinking.

Corinth was a difficult church, but Timothy did well in helping them come to unity. He joined Paul about a year later and was with Paul when he wrote 2 Corinthians (1:1). He was with Paul in Corinth when Paul wrote Romans (Rom 16:21). He was again with Paul in Troas at the end of the third missionary journey (Acts 20:4).

Timothy was with the imprisoned Paul in Rome when he wrote Philippians (Phil 2:19-22), Colossians (1:1), and Philemon (1). There was probably no one else in the early church who knew Paul and his thoughts better than Timothy. According to Heb 13:23, at some point Timothy "our brother" was himself imprisoned and expected to be released soon after Hebrews was written. According to tradition, Timothy became the bishop of Ephesus, where he was eventually martyred (Eusebius, *Hist. eccl.* 3.4.6).

2. Titus

Titus was another key missionary colleague of Paul. He is mentioned twelve times in Paul's letters but never in Acts. Paul never indicates how, when, or where Titus became a believer. Like Timothy, Paul calls him his "true son in our common faith" (Titus 1:4). So it is possible that he was converted under Paul's ministry. Titus was a Greek believer who remained uncircumcised (Gal 2:3).

Titus worked with Paul in Corinth and was instrumental in the logistics required to carry out Paul's ambitious collection for the poor in Jerusalem (2 Cor 8:6, 23). He helped deal with the difficult relationship between Paul and the Corinthians (7:6-7, 13-15; 12:18).

At some unknown point, he may have accompanied Paul to Crete. We can be certain only that Paul commissioned him to strengthen the ministry in Crete (→ Titus 1:5). Paul planned to meet Titus in Nicopolis for the winter (Titus 3:12).

Titus' final appearance in the NT canon finds him in Dalmatia as Paul wrote 2 Tim 4:10. According to church tradition, preserved by Eusebius, Titus returned to Crete, where he served as a bishop until his old age (*Hist. eccl.* 3.4.6).

F. Literary Genre and Rhetorical Features

Letter writing was common in the first century. People of all social levels wrote letters—kings, government officials, even common people. Artemon, who collected Aristotle's letters, described a letter as "half a conversation" (Demetrius, *Eloc.* 223). Paul's letters served as substitutes for his personal presence and authority, and extensions of his relationship with the churches. His letters brought unity to the churches under the umbrella of a common theology and ethic.

Handbooks on letter writing were a part of secondary education in the first century (Malherbe 1977a). *Epistolary Styles*, attributed to Demetrius of Phaleron (second to first century BC), described twenty-one letter types used for a variety of reasons and situations. The Pastoral Epistles share features of several of these.

1. Advisory Letters

In advisory letters (*symbouleutikoi*), writers offer judgments on particular matters through exhortation. Or they may show the proper course of action by way of examples. By following these examples, readers will develop a good reputation before others.

The Pastorals use the rhetorical style of paraenesis to exhort and advise readers to pursue or avoid certain behaviors by reminding them of their ethical foundations. Paul reinforces his advice with positive and negative examples. He offers himself as a positive example, urging both Timothy and Titus likewise to be role models to their churches.

Various proofs are used throughout the letters to show the paths to follow and avoid. Paul uses a form of argumentation called polemic (Johnson 1978, 12-14). Polemic is a kind of exhortation in which an author points out the opposite view or behavior in order to highlight the better approach. Paul speaks against opponents only as they relate to Timothy and Titus. He does so to motivate Timothy and Titus with an example of what *not* to do. "The characteristics of the false teachers function simply as contrast to the image of the ideal Christian teacher" (ibid., 11).

Paul's authority is important in the Pastorals because the growing heretical teaching in Ephesus and Crete required strong and decisive action. Timothy and Titus stood in a line of authority that begins with God, was embodied in Christ Jesus, preached by the apostles, and passed on to the leaders of each church. Paul, as a model of a faithful leader, appeals to his trustworthy ethos (credible lifestyle) to add authority to his words. This was part of his strategy for developing the ethos of Timothy and Titus. By connecting them to his message and mission, Paul shows the Ephesians and Cretans that Timothy and Titus have authority to deal with the false teachers.

2. Philophronetic Letters

The Pastoral Epistles also fit the genre of a friendly letter (*philikos*) written by a superior to an inferior to remind this person of a charge or duty. Stowers (1986, 103-4) compares 1 and 2 Timothy to Pliny the Younger's philophronetic letter to Maximus (*Ep.* viii.24). In this letter, Pliny encourages Maximus, his junior, as he is about to assume the post of imperial legate in Achaea. He uses exhortation to remind Maximus of what he already knows and helps him see how to put it into practice.

Paul commissioned both Titus and Timothy to carry on his legacy in his absence. He uses deliberative rhetoric, appealing to the past in order to influence the present. This can be especially seen with his appeal to tradition, confessional language, and "trustworthy saying[s]" (→ 1 Tim 1:15). Second Timothy is the most personal of the three letters. First Timothy focuses on information intended for the Ephesian church. Titus is a mixture of both (Dibelius and Conzelmann 1972, 1).

Harding identifies features of moral exhortation that fit well what Paul does in these letters (1993, 122-43):

a. These letters are written by a superior to inferiors in social or moral rank. Timothy and Titus were Paul's colleagues, but Paul as the apostle and their spiritual father held a position of authority over them.

b. The letters are based on an existing relationship of friendship. There is an intimacy assumed within these letters as Paul appeals to brothers, who had shared ministry challenges with him.

c. The exhortations in the Pastorals are reminders. Paul reminds Titus and Timothy of the tasks to which they knew well God had called them (1 Tim 1:3-4; 2 Tim 1:6, 18; Titus 1:5). They should continue in what they already know.

d. Both positive and negative examples are provided. The author often makes himself an example. Paul provides a number of negative examples of the type of behavior to avoid: Hymenaeus and Alexander (1 Tim 1:20), Jannes and Jambres (2 Tim 3:8), Phygelus and Hermogenes (2 Tim 1:15), and Demas (2 Tim 4:10). Paul serves as an important positive example for imitation.

G. Major Theological Themes in the Pastorals

The theology of the early church developed, in part, in response to pressing social issues (Keck 1974, 435-52). As a church planter and leader in the early mission, Paul functioned as a "pastoral theologian." He was gifted with the ability to contextualize his message to meet the needs of diverse communities. His theology stands behind many of the contextual issues of the Pastorals. Several major themes are interwoven throughout the letters.

1. God as Savior

Paul calls both God and Jesus Christ "Savior" at important points in the letters. God is the initiator and author of salvation. God's desire is that all people be saved (1 Tim 2:3-4). God revealed his plan of salvation in the Mediator, Christ Jesus (1 Tim 2:5). God offers salvation through his grace (Titus 2:11), which appeared in Christ (1 Tim 3:16; Titus 2:13; 3:4). Salvation is a present experience with eternal consequences, which will be completed when Christ returns (1 Tim 1:15-16; 2:3-6; 4:1; 6:14, 19; 2 Tim 1:9-10, 12, 18; 2:8-

13; 3:1; 4:1, 8; Titus 2:11-14; 3:4-7). The Pastorals reflect a high Christology and proclaim the full deity of Christ. Christ entered human experience as the embodiment of God's salvation.

2. Sound Doctrine

The Christology of these letters is defined, in part, against the heretical teachings present in Ephesus and Crete. Paul corrects the false teachings by appeal to "trustworthy saying[s]." These reflect on the core message of the gospel (1 Tim 1:15; 3:1; 4:9; 2 Tim 2:11; Titus 3:8). It was crucial that Timothy and Titus know the gospel well and be effective in communicating it to the Ephesians and Cretans. Their teaching should be "sound" and "healthy." That required it to be accurate and faithful to the apostolic message Paul preached (1 Tim 1:10; 6:3; 2 Tim 1:13; 4:3; Titus 1:9; 2:1, 8). They were to recruit and train leaders of outstanding character (1 Tim 6:11-21; 2 Tim 2:1-26; Titus 1:5-9). These leaders were in turn to preach and teach the gospel in the churches. The health of the church depends on the faithfulness of its leaders.

3. The Ethic of Godliness

The Pastorals show a conservative ethic and emphasize having high moral character. Crucial here is the merging of right belief (orthodoxy) and right living (orthopraxy). Paul does not advocate that converts abandon their places in life. He challenges people of all social levels to live as outstanding models of the best morality within their contexts and to redefine these by their growing relationship with Christ.

The ultimate authority is God, who has allowed and appointed others to lead political, social, and ecclesiological structures. Regardless of their assignment in life, everyone answers to God. The church must model transformed living as "God's household" (1 Tim 3:15). Believers collectively and individually bear witness to the world of God's transforming grace in Christ (vv 14-16). The quality of Christian character bears witness to the power of the gospel (v 7; 5:14; 6:1; Titus 2:5, 9; 3:2, 8). Christians should live in such a way that unbelievers cannot speak ill of them, the church, the gospel, Christ, or God. This is what Paul means by godliness.

COMMENTARY

I TIMOTHY

I. EPISTOLARY PRESCRIPT AND SALUTATION: I TIMOTHY 1:1-2

BEHIND THE TEXT

Paul wrote letters because he could not personally be with the individuals or churches to which he wrote. His letters were written to address specific situations and concerns (Beker 1991, 20). Although he often planned to visit the churches at a later point, his letters express what he would have said if he could have been there in person. His letters were substitutes for his personal presence (Aune 1987, 158-82).

This letter begins with the typical greeting, identification of the sender, recipient, and a salutation. Paul included these elements in his letters but often expanded them, filling each with theological meaning. Some openings are relatively short (1 Thess 1:1), while others are more expansive (Rom 1:1-7; Titus 1:1-4). The salutation of 1 Timothy, like other letters (Rom 1:1-7; Gal 1:1-6; 1 Cor 1:1-3), offers clues about the problems in the churches and their solutions: Some in Ephesus had rejected Paul's authority and interpretation of the gospel. Listening to Timothy, Paul's legitimate spiritual son, offered the solution (Mounce 2000, 4).

The City of Ephesus

Ephesus was one of the major cities of the Roman Empire during the first century. Josephus (AD 37-95), a contemporary of Paul, called it the "metropolis of Asia" (*Ant.* 14.10.11). It was located on the east coast of what is now modern Turkey.

The history of Ephesus stretched back to at least before 1000 BC, when Ionian colonists founded it. Over the next millennia, the city was ruled by Lydians, Persians, Greeks, Seleucids, Ptolemies, and Pergamum. The Romans conquered Ephesus in 41 BC and made it the capital of the Roman province of Asia. By Paul's time, its population was about 100,000, making it the third largest city after Rome and Alexandria.

Ephesus's large harbor, near the mouth of the Cayster River, made it the trading hub of western Asia. Its location, on the major route between Rome and the East, aided in its commerce and strong economy. It also made Ephesus a melting pot of religions and philosophies. The constant traffic between Ephesus and Corinth may explain why Paul addressed similar issues in 1 Corinthians, Ephesians, and 1 Timothy. Ephesus had a mixed population of Greeks, Romans, Jews, and other ethnic groups.

At the center of the religious scene in Ephesus was the cult of Artemis (Roman Diana), the Greek goddess of women, fertility, childbirth, and hunting. The god Apollo was her twin. Artemis worship was widespread throughout Greece and Asia Minor. The Temple to Artemis in Ephesus, the Artemision, built in the sixth century BC, was destroyed around 350 BC and then rebuilt. The largest building in the Greek world at 220 by 425 feet (67 by 130 meters), it stood over 60 feet (18 meters) high and with 127 columns.

The Artemision was one of the seven wonders of the ancient world. It stood at the center of the city, visible from every direction. Artemis worship involved mystery rites and magic (see Acts 19:19). Silversmiths in Ephesus made and sold silver figurines of the goddess. They provoked a riot when Paul's preaching led people to stop buying their idols. The mob cried out, "Great is Artemis of the Ephesians!" (Acts 19:28).

Other religions existed in Ephesus, including the Imperial cult, other mystery religions, and the worship of various Greek and Roman gods and goddesses. There was also a Jewish synagogue in Ephesus where Paul preached for three months (Acts 19:8).

IN THE TEXT

■ 1 Paul begins the letter in the typical style of the time, giving first his name as the author. This style was highly adaptable in the ancient world. Paul's theological creativity can be seen in the opening. He consistently began his letters with the name **Paul**, the only name he ever used for himself in his letters. He first appears in Acts 7:58 under his Hebrew name, Saul. He probably had both names at birth and used them in different situations (McRay 2007, 25-28). He began to go by Paul after Acts 13:9 when he appeared before Cyprus's Roman proconsul Sergius Paulus (Acts 13:7). He continued to use this name throughout his journeys and ministry among the Gentiles.

In a number of letters, Paul mentioned other co-senders (Sosthenes in 1 Corinthians; Timothy in 2 Corinthians, Philippians, Colossians, and Philemon; "all the brothers" in Galatians; Silas and Timothy in 1 and 2 Thessalonians). We cannot say how much these were involved in the writing process. Within these letters it is clear that Paul spoke as their primary authority. He is the only author of this letter.

Paul adds his office to his name with his favorite self-designation—**an apostle**. The Greek *apostolos* is used in two primary ways in the NT. The basic definition is one who has been sent out as an official representative or authorized agent of another (2 Cor 8:23; Phil 2:25). The term is used more specifically for those who had seen the risen Jesus and been commissioned specifically by him to preach the gospel. Jesus had many disciples, but among these, he designated twelve apostles as leaders (Luke 6:13). Paul counted himself part of this select group because of his encounter with Jesus in a vision on the road to Damascus (Acts 9:5, 15; 22:14-15; 26:16-18; 1 Cor 15:8-9; Gal 1:15-16). In the Pastorals the term "apostle" connotes one with authority in the church. In 1 Tim 2:7, Paul restates his calling as an apostle specifically to the Gentiles.

In most of his letters (all except 1 and 2 Thessalonians, Philippians, and Philemon), Paul calls himself **an apostle of Christ Jesus**. In Romans and Philippians he calls himself a "servant"; in Philemon, a "prisoner." This designation is significant because it (1) indicates the source of Paul's apostleship, (2) shows the authority behind his ministry, and (3) identifies his thought with that of Christ.

As with other letters, Paul establishes his ethos at the beginning in order to set a firm foundation for later exhortations. Ethos is the moral character or credibility of an author, the trust in the author the audience has or develops (Aristotle, *Rhet.* 1.2). Although this is a personal letter, it possesses a degree of an official mandate (→ 1 Tim 1:3) from an apostle to his young protégé. It authorizes Timothy to deal with the issues in Ephesus.

The prepositional phrase **of Christ Jesus** translates the Greek genitive case. Here Paul implies that "Christ Jesus" is the *source* of his apostleship. In v 2 Paul will add the descriptive "Lord" to Christ Jesus, suggesting also a master/slave relationship of ownership (see Rom 1:1).

The Pastorals respond to challenges to Paul's authority and interpretation of the gospel (Mounce 2000, 5). Teachers of false doctrines, myths, and genealogies were infiltrating the church (1 Tim 1:3-4), pulling believers away from the truth of the gospel. The problems addressed in 1 Timothy were not new (see Acts 19:8-9). As elsewhere, opponents questioned both Paul's authority and his message (Gal 1:6-9). By mentioning his apostleship and its source at the beginning of the letter, Paul's authority serves as a persuasive force in all that follows.

This letter lends credibility to Timothy's assignment in Ephesus. Authority assumes accountability. There is a direct chain of command, from Christ to Paul to Timothy and finally to the Ephesians. Paul wants both Timothy and the Ephesians to realize this.

Paul's apostleship came **by the command of God our Savior and of Christ Jesus our hope**. This intensifies his apostolic authority. The preposition *kata* has an instrumental force (**by**) with a causal nuance: That is, Paul was an apostle *because of* God's command.

Command (*epitagē*) is a strong word used for both divine and kingly decrees (Delling 1972b, 36-37). In 2 Tim 1:1, Paul uses "will of God" instead of "command of God" to express "the active outworking or expression of the divine will" (Towner 2006, 96). Paul conveys the force of God's call in 1 Cor 9:16: "I am compelled to preach. Woe to me if I do not preach the gospel!"

The command Paul received had two sources: (1) **God** and (2) **Christ Jesus**. Both are genitive nouns modifying the word **command**. Christ called Paul to be an apostle while he was traveling on the road to Damascus (Acts 26:12-19). This experience impacted the rest of his life (→ 1 Tim 1:12-17). When the truth of the gospel was threatened, he appealed to the divine origins of his call and message. In Titus 1:1, he likewise appeals to the command of God to deal with the heretical problems in Crete.

Paul next describes God as **Savior** (*sōtēros*; → 1 Tim 2:3; 4:10; Titus 1:3; 2:10; 3:4). The OT frequently refers to God as the Savior of his people, especially in connection with the exodus from Egypt (Deut 32:15; 2 Sam 22:3, 47; 1 Chr 16:35; Pss 24:5; 25:5; 27:1, 9; 62:2, 6; 65:5; 79:9; 95:1; Prov 29:25; Isa 12:2; 17:10; 25:9; 62:11; Mic 7:7; Hab 3:18). This provided early Christians a solid foundation for their interpretation of Jesus as the one who brought the salvation offered by God (John 3:16; 1 Tim 1:15; 2 Tim 1:10; Titus 1:4; 2:13; 3:6). In the Pastorals, Paul refers to both God and Christ as Savior (2 Tim 1:10; Titus 1:4; 2:13; 3:6). The Father is the architect and initiator of the plan of salvation implemented through the Son (Towner 2006, 97).

It is not accidental that this letter begins by reflecting on God as Savior. The relative concentration of the word *sōtēr* in the Pastorals (ten times) may suggest that Paul had to combat the claims of competing salvation cults of Ephesus and a misunderstanding of salvation by the false teachers (Knight 1992, 61-62). By the first century, the word "savior" was used for various heroes, deities, as well as Roman emperors who earned this title by delivering the people from wars and providing peace.

The other source of Paul's apostleship was **Christ Jesus our hope. Hope** (*elpis*) is a significant part of the Christian message because it anticipates the salvation promised by God. Christ is "the hope of glory" (Eph 1:12, 18; Col 1:27) and the only sure source of this salvation (John 14:6; Acts 4:12; Rom 5:2, 5; 8:24-25; 15:4, 13). John Wesley identified Christ as "the author, object, and ground, of all our hope" (1813, 220). Without Christ, there is no hope (Eph 2:12; 1 Thess 4:13). This hope will be fully experienced by those who believe (1 Tim 4:10) when Christ comes again (1 Cor 15:19-20, 57; Titus 2:13).

Jesus is the personal name; **Christ** is the title. The title consistently comes first in the Pastorals, except in 1 Tim 6:3 and 14, where the phrase is "Lord Jesus Christ." The Greek *Christos* is a translation of the Hebrew *māšîaḥ*, "anointed." Paul identifies Jesus as *the* Messiah, the promised anointed one of God. This became a vital part of his message, especially to the Jews (see Acts 9:20, 22; 17:2-3).

■ **2** This verse identifies the primary recipient of the letter. Although Paul addresses **Timothy**, the target audience includes the church in Ephesus. It will be Timothy's responsibility to pass along and implement Paul's directions.

Paul calls Timothy **my true son in the faith** to express their close bond and special relationship. The adjective **true** (*gnēsios*) designates a legitimate child born in wedlock. In a figurative sense, it can denote a genuine and sincere relationship (Büchsel 1964b, 727). In this verse, it shows the intimacy between Paul and Timothy. Paul boosts Timothy's authority by connecting Timothy to himself. The false teachers who were preoccupied with Jewish myths may have looked down upon things non-Jewish (→ 1 Tim 1:3). So Paul counters that by showing Timothy's legitimacy through this relationship.

Son (*teknon*) literally refers to a *child*. This should not be taken as an indicator of Timothy's age but as an emotive term of fictive kinship (Gal 4:19; Phlm 10; 1 John 2:1, 18; 3:7; 4:4; 5:21; compare 1 Tim 1:18; 2 Tim 1:2; 2:1; and Titus 1:4). The student-teacher relationship was often described as father-son in the ancient world (Mounce 2000, 8).

The prepositional phrase **in . . . faith** (*en pistei*) can be interpreted in two ways: Timothy became Paul's son by being faithful to the calling of God (instrumental) or because their common faith united them (locative). Faith for Paul is the proper response to God's grace (Rom 3:28; Eph 2:8-9). Timothy responded to grace and became Paul's Christian brother. Paul may have had some part in Timothy's conversion (1 Cor 4:15) during Paul's first missionary journey through Lystra, Timothy's hometown (Acts 13:49—14:25). Paul certainly became Timothy's adopted spiritual father and mentor (see Phil 2:22). Their relationship was bonded first and foremost by their common faith in Christ. This description of Timothy would give him additional authority to deal with the problems in Ephesus.

The greeting is given in the form of a prayer: **Grace, mercy and peace from God the Father and Christ Jesus our Lord**. Paul begins all of his letters with similar greetings (see 2 Tim 1:2). He prays for three things for Timothy, each with theological significance.

The first, **grace** (*charis*), resembles the typical Greek greeting "rejoice" (*chairein*). **Grace** is one of the central topics of Paul's letters and is mentioned thirteen times in the Pastorals. *Charis* grants favor or is something attractive. In the LXX, it translates the Hebrew *hên*, "show favor" (see Exod 33:13). Grace is the undeserved experience of God's love in Christ that allows rebellious humanity to experience a right relationship with God. God shows grace by taking the first step in reconciliation—by sending his Son to die in our behalf (Rom 5:1-8). Grace confirms our hope in Christ and sustains us while we wait for his coming again. Grace continues its transformation, leading to holy living (2 Cor 9:8; Titus 2:11-12). Paul closes all of his letters with a benediction of grace (→ 1 Tim 6:21). These references form literary bookends, identifying grace as a succinct summary of his thought.

The second, **mercy** (*eleos*), is compassion to the needy. It is primarily a relational term experienced in covenant. It is the translation for the important Hebrew word *hesed* (**covenantal faithfulness, committed love**) in the LXX. God's unconditional love is evident in his forgiveness and acceptance of sinners. Mercy is God's response to the "dire plight of sinners and their need for divine favor" (Knight 1992, 66).

Grace and mercy are found together in Eph 2:4 and Titus 3:5 (see Heb 4:16). The verbal form, **receiving compassion**, in 1 Tim 1:13, 16, describes the salvation and forgiveness Paul received because of God's grace in Christ. Paul includes grace and peace in all of his greetings, but he adds mercy only in 1 and 2 Timothy, possibly in reflection of salvation (1 Tim 1:14-16; 2 Tim 1:9-10). This greeting reveals Paul's prayer-wish that Timothy might experience the salvation and hope provided by God in Christ (1 Tim 1:1).

The third, the result of grace and mercy, is **peace** (*eirēnē*). Paul uses the typical Hebrew greeting "peace" (*šālôm*) again with theological nuance. Peace is the result of justification and reconciliation with God (Rom 5:1). God is the source of peace (Rom 15:33; 16:20; Phil 4:9; 1 Thess 5:23; 2 Thess 3:16). The world cannot give peace, only Jesus can (John 14:27). Peace with God unites believers (Rom 14:19; 2 Cor 13:11; Gal 5:22; Eph 2:14-18; 4:3; Col 3:15; 2 Tim 2:22) and brings peace with everyone (Rom 12:18). Peace is God's blessing that brings joy to life as God intended. In Heb 12:14, the pursuit of peace is joined with holiness, implying that it is an inner experience that affects how we live outwardly. Peace was something Timothy was to pursue (2 Tim 2:22).

Knight sums up well the relationship of the three terms: "*charis*—God's ongoing forgiveness and enabling, *eleos*—God's sympathy and concern, *eirēnē*—God's tranquility and stability within and among them as individuals and as a Christian community" (1992, 67). These are experienced in new covenant relationship and cannot be counterfeited by the world.

Like Paul's apostleship, there are two sources for these blessings, sharing the same preposition **from** (*apo*): **God the Father and Christ Jesus our Lord**. This implies, first, that with God as **Father**, believers are part of God's family. Through the Holy Spirit, they become God's children, incorporated into God's household (3:15). This enables them to address God as "Abba! Father!" (Rom 8:14-17; Gal 3:26—4:7; Matt 6:9; John 3:5-8).

Second, Jesus' resurrection proved that he is **Lord** (Phil 2:10-11). *Kyrios* has a wide range of meanings in the Bible, from a polite "sir" to a reference to God. It represents someone with power and authority (Foerster 1965, 1041). Jesus was exalted to the supreme position as Lord because of his obedient suffering and death (Phil 2:10-11; Heb 2:6-10). Christians confess that "Jesus is Lord" (Rom 10:9-13). The Holy Spirit empowers us to call God "Father" and Jesus "Lord" (1 Cor 2:7-10; 12:3).

FROM THE TEXT

Christology. Paul was a monotheistic Jew but made room in his thinking for Jesus as Lord (1 Cor 8:4-6). Verse 1 could be translated as **God our Savior, even Christ Jesus our Hope**, taking the Greek word *kai* as "even" instead of "and" (Barrett 1963, 38). Father and Son are so united in Paul's thought that they are one in their actions. Salvation comes from both (→ Titus 2:13). Both Father and Son called Paul to be an apostle and both provide grace, mercy, and peace. In six of Paul's letters, both Father and Son are listed as the source of blessings (Rom 1:7; 1 Cor 1:3; 2 Cor 1:2; Eph 1:2; Phil 1:2; 2 Thess 1:2). There is no evidence that Paul had a fully developed doctrine of the Trinity, something later generations of Christians struggled to articulate. But it is clear that he considered Christ divine.

Hope. There is an innate drive within the human soul that spurs us onward into the unknown, to discover, analyze, and contemplate what is beyond ourselves. Hope addresses a deeper human need for purpose and belonging. Paul found his purpose in belonging to Christ as his "servant" (Rom 1:1). This relationship with Christ the "Master" can be experienced in this life (Col 1:27) through the Holy Spirit (Rom 5:5; 15:13). Fellowship now with Christ provides the hope for future salvation (Gal 5:5). Hope "points to the eschatological dimension of salvation" (Collins 2002, 22). Our present hope rests in the promise of the coming Jesus (Titus 2:13) when "we shall be like him" (1 John 3:2). This hope inspires endurance through the challenges of life (Rom 5:4; 8:25-28).

Authority. Paul had a sense of mission that he passed on to Timothy. Timothy and his mission were part of a greater movement of God. This involved passing on Paul's commands (1 Tim 1:3, 18; 4:6, 11, 13; 5:1, 7; 6:17; 2 Tim 2:2; 4:2; Titus 2:15). Authority is often delegated by those *above* and must be received by those *below.* Timothy was to realize that "he who gives commands is himself under command" (Fee 1984, 35). In addition, the letter provides the necessary status for Timothy's leadership to be recognized within the church. Authority coupled with mission leads to effective leadership in troubled situations.

II. PAUL'S CHARGE TO TIMOTHY ABOUT THE FALSE TEACHERS IN EPHESUS: I TIMOTHY 1:3-20

BEHIND THE TEXT

Paul opens the body of the letter by getting to the heart of the issue in Ephesus: the growing threat of heretical teaching. Missing is his typical thanksgiving section, although vv 12-17 can serve as both a testimony and a variation of a thanksgiving. The absence of a formal thanksgiving creates a greater sense of urgency, similar to Galatians, in which Paul also saw the gospel under attack (Mounce 2000, 15-16). This section ends with the excommunication of two problem people, Hymenaeus and Alexander. Paul gives Timothy the theological context for responding to these problems.

The rhetoric of the letter opening is marked by the hortatory technique of antithesis, in which positive and negative examples are set against each other in order to show the better path to follow (Fiore 1986, 22). This can be seen in the structure:

> Negative: a charge against the opponents (vv 3-4)
>
> Positive: the path to follow (v 5)
>
> Negative: example of lawbreakers (vv 6-11)
>
> Positive: Paul's example of Christ's mercy (vv 12-17)
>
> Positive: Prescription for Timothy to follow (vv 18-19*b*)
>
> Negative: Two examples to reject (vv 19*b*-20)

This use of antithesis denounces the wrong and dangerous approach of the opponents and highlights the positive course for Timothy and the Ephesians. Paul exhorts Timothy to deal strongly with the false teachers, who are examples of "persistent and faithless impiety" (Fiore 2007, 22).

Paul uses the form of indirect command to instruct Timothy how to deal with these teachers. He provides the "data" and assumes Timothy will act on this information. At critical points in the letter, he reminds Timothy of his message and method in order to motivate and instruct Timothy for dealing with the challenges in Ephesus. The opening hints at the *topos* of the letter, the major topics to be covered or frequently mentioned.

A. The Problem of False Teachers and False Doctrine (1:3-7)

IN THE TEXT

■ **3** Paul begins with **as** (*kathōs*) followed by a verb of instruction, **I urged you** (*parekalesa*). Grammatically, this is a dependent clause without a main verb. Translations like the NIV attempt to fix this by treating the infinitive "to stay" as if it were an imperative verb (NASB and ESV "remain"; the NRSV drops "as" and makes "urge" the main verb). This anacoluthon (broken grammatical syntax) creates a sense of urgency that reverberates throughout the letter.

This verse introduces the problem of the teachers who infiltrated the Ephesian church with false doctrine. Paul refers to some previous, unknown command given to Timothy in an earlier conversation. The content of this command is suggested in the second part of this verse.

Acts 19:21-22 mentions that Paul sent Timothy and Erastus to Macedonia before he left Ephesus. At some point, when Paul was going **into Macedonia** (*poreuomenos*, a participle simultaneous with the verb *parekalesa*, **I urged**), he directed Timothy to return to Ephesus to provide strategic leadership to the church. He wrote 1 Timothy soon after sending Timothy on the trip, providing further information and direction. At some point, Paul again met Timothy in Macedonia and then journeyed with others toward Jerusalem.

Timothy is not mentioned again after Acts 20:4, probably because he remained in Ephesus while Paul traveled on to Jerusalem. Paul had planned to visit Ephesus again (1 Tim 3:14-15). According to Acts 20:17-35, Paul met with some Ephesian elders in Miletus, south of Ephesus, on his way to Jerusalem. In vv 29-30 he warned, "I know that after I leave, savage wolves will come in among you and will not spare the flock. Even from your own number men will arise and distort the truth in order to draw away disciples after them." Paul also predicted he would never see them again (v 38).

Perhaps this speech follows up on the problems behind 1 Timothy. It responds to the growing problems of heresy springing up in churches like Ephesus and Crete. In 2 Timothy, written several years later, Paul urged Timothy to leave Ephesus and come to Rome because of his imprisonment there.

The word for **urged** (*parakalesa*) is common in exhortations. This verb is warmer and more personal than **command** (*parangeilēis*) later in the verse (Liefeld 1999, 52). The verb *parakaleō* means to call alongside, or to comfort and encourage, with a sense of personal concern. Paul had shown this concern to Timothy, who was then to respond to the false teachers in a stronger way. The word appears again in 1 Tim 2:1 as Paul begins to deal with specific issues in the Ephesian church.

The purpose (*hina*) of Timothy's stay in Ephesus was *in order to charge certain people not to teach different doctrine*. Command (*parangeilēs*) is sometimes used for military commands or official summons to court (Schmitz 1967a, 762). Followed by the negative *mē* and an infinitive, as here, it means "forbid to do (something)" (Knight 1992, 72). It is used for "didactive and corrective activities associated with the apostolic mission and teaching within the church" (Towner 2006, 108).

Timothy was to carry out Paul's command with a sense of strong authority like a commander or judge (→ 1:18; 2:1; 6:13). "There is a difference between how Timothy and Titus should deal with the opponents and how they should deal with others in the church. In dealing with the opposition they are to command, to speak with the authority given by God through Paul (1 Tim 1:1). But with the others they are to be gentle, urging and encouraging proper belief and conduct" (Mounce 2000, 18).

Paul does not say who **certain people** are at this point, but we can assume that Timothy would know. There was a segment of the church that was adversely influencing the whole group. Paul will name two of these people in v 20.

The problem is that these people were teaching false doctrines. The infinitive **to teach false doctrines** is a compound word with two parts: *hetero*, "of another kind," and *didaskalein*, "teaching." This is the first time in Christian literature that this word occurs, and Paul likely coined it for this situation (see Ign. *Pol.* 3.1). The context of v 3 indicates that this teaching was not simply different; it was false. It is contrasted in 6:3 with "the sound instruction of our Lord Jesus Christ and to godly teaching." Paul's strong words in Gal 1:6-10 imply that any departure from the true gospel he preached was worthy of condemnation. The present tense of the infinitive further suggests that the false teaching was an ongoing activity when Paul wrote this letter and not simply a potential danger.

Paul mentions false teachers throughout the letter (1 Tim 1:18-20; 4:1-8; 6:2-10; also 2 Tim 2:16-18; 3:1-9; 4:3-4, 14-15). Just before the final greetings of the letter, he warns Timothy one last time about this teaching (1 Tim 6:20-21).

The situation in the Ephesian church is ironic: Those who were teaching this false doctrine claimed to be teachers of the law (*nomodidaskaloi* [v 7]). But they did not know what they were saying. The frequency and intensity with which Paul addressed this issue shows the seriousness with which he took this threat. This was more than a personal attack upon him. It threatened the foundations of his message about the one Mediator, Christ Jesus.

■ **4** Paul offers more information about the challenges Timothy faced in Ephesus and the nature of the heresy infiltrating the church. He continues his charge to Timothy to admonish "certain people" of v 3 to avoid two activities (expressed with two infinitives): ***not to be teaching false doctrine*** and ***not to be devoted*** to speculative thought.

Though these are separate activities grammatically, they are closely associated in practice. The false teaching may have involved the two objects of the second infinitive: **myths and endless genealogies**. The word *prosechein* in 3:8 is translated "indulging in" (NIV) and can be more actively understood as "addicted to" (ESV). In 4:13 it is used positively for the devotion Timothy is to have for "the public reading of Scripture, . . . preaching and . . . teaching." It describes the purpose and direction of one's life. Here, the false teachers had become preoccupied with activities that led only to tearing down the church.

The Greek *mythois* refers to fables and imaginary stories, often involving deities. It has the negative connotation of falsehood (→ 4:7; 2 Tim 4:4; Titus 1:14; Stählin 1967a, 762-95). Plato used it in an even more negative sense to refer to deceptive stories that could lead to immorality (Plato, *Leg.* 636C-D, *Resp.* 376E-383C; Towner 2006, 110).

Such myths were a staple in the Ephesian religious context. Some Jews had developed elaborate allegories about creation and patriarchal genealogies that fostered further speculation among the rabbis (→ Titus 1:14). All the ingredients for speculative religion were present in Ephesus when Paul wrote this letter. Early forms of Gnosticism were beginning to cause the church problems. This "proto-Gnosticism" was an amalgamation of Jewish teachings like those seen in Ephesus, merging Platonic dualism with elements of Christianity. These teachings would continue to evolve and became a major problem for the second-century church.

Genealogies were lists of ancestors used to trace one's family tree in order to establish one's bloodline. The problem, however, was that they led to speculation, especially among Jews who had a special interest in tracing their heritage (see, e.g., haggadic literature, *Jubilees*, Philo's QG, 1QapGen, and 4Q559). The word here is modified by the adjective **endless** (*aperantois*), only here in the NT (only in Job 36:26 in the LXX). In other contexts, it refers to something pointless, inconclusive, or unrestrained.

Paul did not object to tracing one's family heritage. Even he did this in an abbreviated way in Phil 3:4-6, and the Gospel writers did this for Jesus (Matt 1:1-17; Luke 3:23-38). But obsessive preoccupation with genealogies led to speculation, which had no value in furthering God's kingdom. Evidently, the false teachers in Ephesus were so absorbed that they misled the church into doctrines that had become counterproductive to the message of salvation.

The Origins of Gnosticism

Gnosticism, as its name implies (from Greek: *gnosis*), was a religion focused upon secret or esoteric "knowledge." Gnosticism taught that there was a vast separation between the transcendent God and sinful world, which had been created by an inferior deity, the "Demiurge." The goal of gnostics was to become free from the body and return to God. Christ, who only "appeared" to be human (there was a strong Docetism among the gnostics), bridged this gap by providing salvation in the form of secret knowledge.

When Gnosticism originated is debated, though clear evidence for it appears in the middle to late second century. Its seeds can be seen in some of the challenges faced by NT writers, such as Paul (→ I Tim 6:20; 2 Tim 2:18) and John (especially I John). A number of texts written by gnostics after the second century were discovered in 1945 in Nag Hammadi, Egypt. The church fathers diligently fought Gnosticism and refer to it throughout their writings (notably Irenaeus, *Haer.*).

Paul ends this verse with the result of these false teachings: **controversial speculations**. The pronoun *haitines*, translated **these**, refers specifically to "genealogies" but is inclusive of "myths." This verse contrasts two different approaches based upon two different understandings of how God works. The first refers to the humanistic pursuit of knowledge about things that do not promote the gospel. The word for "controversy" (*ekzēteseis*), only here in the NT, can also be translated as "speculations" (NRSV).

Paul uses this polemical term to show the dangers of the doctrines of the false teachers. Theirs was not a passive or accidental teaching done out of ignorance. Rather, it is an intentionally promoted (*parechousin*) and persistent perversion by the opponents. The present tense of the verb **promote** ("show," "cause") here suggests an ongoing habit. The ethical consequences of such speculation will lead to the breakdown of community rather than building it up in the faith (see 1 Cor 14:12, 26; Eph 4:29). Paul is establishing early in this letter the parameters for orthodoxy, although at this point, these are given in contrastive terms.

The other approach, which Paul urges Timothy to take throughout this letter, is **God's work** (*oikonomian*). *Oikonomian* refers to the work of a steward who manages a household (*oikos*; Luke 16:2-4; Michel 1967a, 152). Paul uses this term in other letters for the working out of God's plan or the carrying out of God's will as a faithful steward (1 Cor 4:1; 9:17; Eph 1:10; 3:2; Col 1:25). Later in 1 Tim 3:15, Paul describes the church as God's house, which needs to be managed by faithful overseers (3:5). His answer to the problems in Ephesus is to live according to God's principles. He will expound this thought throughout the letter as he deals with men, women, overseers, deacons, and other groups. Proper teaching will lead to an ordered life of ministry for God.

Such service is shown in cooperation through faith with what God is doing. The last phrase of the verse, **which is by faith**, grammatically modifies **work** (*oikonomian*). It gives an important qualification for the stewardship of divine matters. The Greek preposition *en* could be taken instrumentally (**by faith**)—this stewardship is sourced through faith, or locative ("in faith" [KJV])—in "the way God has organized life . . . in the sphere of authentic faith" [Towner 2006, 114]). This is not faith as merely intellectual belief, but faith consistent with the message Paul preached. Timothy is to make sure this message is present in Ephesus. Faith is a significant theme in this letter and is mentioned in 1:2, 4, 5, 14, 19; 2:7, 15; 3:9, 13; 4:1, 6, 12; 6:10-21. Faith is "the trust relationship that is the seedbed in which God works and produces growth" (Knight 1992, 76).

Paul contrasts human folly and divine enablement. The human response to God's work should be faith in cooperation with God's will, not speculation. Paul, the practical theologian, was interested in ministry that makes a difference. He wanted to focus his life on those activities that furthered the cause of Christ (Phil 1:21; 3:13-14). The controversies in Ephesus resulted from human effort. Faith relies on God's enabling strength. God's work will prosper when the focus is the gospel.

■ **5** Paul lays out clearly his solution for the problems in Ephesus. He does not want Timothy to respond to the false teachers through argument, which only leads to more speculation. The essential ingredient Timothy must infuse into the situation is love.

This verse begins a new sentence, which continues until the end of v 7. It begins in Greek with the adversative use of the conjunction *de* ("but," untranslated in the NIV). What Paul lays out in this verse stands in stark contrast to the speculations of the false teachers.

Paul uses the same Greek root for **command** in this verse (the noun form *parangelias*) as he did for Timothy's assignment in Ephesus: to command (*parangelēs*) the false teachers to cease and desist (v 3). He describes here how Timothy is to go about the difficult task of correcting the misguided leaders in Ephesus.

Paul uses the word *telos* to express this motive. *Telos* has many translations, including "perfect," "complete," "mature," and "end" (Delling 1972b, 49-87). But in the present context, it refers to the intended outcome or purpose of **love**.

This is the first of the positive statements that oppose the wrong teachings of the opponents. **Love** is the behavior that should characterize God's household (*oikonomia* [see v 4]). This paragraph is tightly structured around the idea of teaching. Van Neste points out the chiastic structure of this paragraph (vv 3-7), with this verse at the center (2004, 20):

A Improper teaching through false doctrines
> B Negative result of improper teaching—meaningless specula-
> tion
>> C Positive result of proper teaching—love
> B' Negative results of improper teaching—meaningless talk
A' Improper teaching about the Law

The structure highlights the care Timothy is to show in his ministry, both to the larger community of faith and to the errant teachers. If the latter do not change their course, Timothy may need to show tough love, as Paul did with Hymenaeus and Alexander (v 20).

Paul's motive is simply stated in the word **love** (*agapē*), which is best defined by its use. The Christian understanding of love begins with what God has done in Christ. God is the source of love (John 3:16; Rom 5:8; Eph 5:25) and defines love (1 John 4:7-10). Love is the very essence of the Christian faith and should be the characteristic of followers of Christ (John 13:34-35). Love summarizes all the commands of God (Matt 22:37-40; Rom 13:8-10; Gal 5:14). Many NT passages command believers to love one another (Rom 12:10; 1 Pet 1:22; 1 John 3:23).

How is this love possible? It takes both divine assistance and human co-operation. Love is a gift of God that comes in Christ through the Holy Spirit (1 Cor 13; Gal 5:22; 1 Tim 1:14; 2 Tim 1:7). It is both a gift of the Spirit (1 Cor 12:31; 13:13) and something to strive after (1 Cor 14:1). It is often joined with faith in Paul's letters (Gal 5:6; 1 Thess 1:3; 3:6; → 1 Tim 4:12; 6:11; 2 Tim 2:22; 3:10; and Titus 2:2). Love in action ought to mark the people of God. Love was Paul's primary motivation (2 Cor 5:14), and love is the type of response Timothy ought to show his opponents.

Love is resourced by three inner qualities. The first is a **pure heart**. **Heart** (*kardia*) is modified by the adjective **pure** (*katharas*). The vital inner organ took on a more figurative meaning in both Greek and Hebrew. The Hebrew word for **heart** (*lēb*) refers to the depth of a person's being (Pss 17:3; 19:14; 26:2; 44:21; 51:10, 17; 73:1; 139:23; Jer 11:20; 17:10; 20:12). The heart was the seat of emotions, desires, and passions, and the innermost aspect of personhood that responds to God (Behm 1965b, 605-14). Paul knew of the problem of a heart controlled by the power of sin (Rom 1:24). A person's inner disposition will affect how that person lives.

The heart is metaphorically stained with sin in rebellion against God. Thus, it needs to be cleansed (Deut 30:6; Ps 51:10). *Katharas* describes the condition of the heart after the removing of dirt, defilement, or sin. In Israel's cultic system, defilement of various types kept a person from God's presence and had to be removed through washing or sacrifice. A pure heart is the essential quality to see God (Matt 5:8). A purified heart has been transformed through "the light of the knowledge of God's glory displayed in the face of Christ" (2 Cor 4:6; see Eph 1:18). This is accomplished through the power of the Holy Spirit (Rom 5:5; 2 Cor 3:18) in response to faith (Acts 15:8-9).

Katharas occurs eight times in the Pastorals and describes both the heart (1 Tim 1:5; 2 Tim 2:22) and the conscience (1 Tim 3:9; 2 Tim 1:3). Purification comes through the sacrifice Christ made on the cross in our behalf (Titus 2:14). The type of love Timothy must show in Ephesus, and indeed all believers must evidence, can come only from a heart purified from sin and in complete devotion to God.

The second source for love is a **good conscience** (*syneidēseōs agathēs*). *Syneidēsis* occurs six times in the Pastoral Epistles (1 Tim 1:5, 19; 3:9; 4:2; 2 Tim 1:3; Titus 1:15). Both the Greek original and Latin cognate emphasize knowing something in agreement with another. It involves self-awareness that prompts a person to act in a certain way (Maurer 1971, 914).

The conscience develops as people become aware of themselves and their context. Community and culture significantly influence this. The conscience serves as a guide in moral conduct, a moral compass for one's life (Rom 2:15). One motivation for a good conscience in the ancient world was to secure honor and avoid shame. But it is not simply about the opinions of others. The conscience must rely upon some external norm as its basis for judgment. For believers, it is God's law, natural law and revealed (Rom 2:14), and love (1 Cor 8:1-2). The conscience can either accuse or defend us, depending on our compliance with "the law written on [our] hearts" (Rom 2:15).

Two positive adjectives describe "conscience" in the Pastorals: "good" (1 Tim 1:5, 19) and "clear" (1 Tim 3:9; 2 Tim 1:3). Both words refer to a conscience free from condemnation, one that adheres to the truth of the gospel as its norm (1 Tim 1:19). It has not wandered away (1:6), become corrupted or seared by breaking God's laws (1:9-10), rejected the faith (1:19), or been deceived (4:2) like the "seared" consciences of the opponents.

Paul uses two descriptions for the effects of sin upon the conscience. In 1 Tim 4:2, he accuses the false teachers of having consciences "that have been *seared* as with a hot iron," because they have "abandon[ed] the faith" (4:1). Those who reject a good conscience run the risk of a shipwrecked faith (1:19). In Titus 1:15, *corrupted* consciences likewise result from disobedience and unbelief.

The final source for love is **sincere faith** (*pisteōs anhypokritou*). The adjective *anhypokritou* is the opposite of its root *hypokrisis*, "hypocrisy." Thus, it describes something that is genuine, authentic, without pretense, and with integrity. This type of faith has complete trust in God. It has responded to God's grace with complete surrender. One result of this type of faith is a clear conscience before God.

Faith opens the door for love to work. For our love to model God's love in Christ (Rom 5:8), it must be expressed in trust and obedience. Faith and love often appear together in the Pastorals as "the truly Christian virtues" (see 1 Tim 1:14; 2:15; 4:12; 6:11; 2 Tim 1:13; 2:22; 3:10; Titus 2:2; Fee 1988, 42-43). Timothy will need to deal with the problems in Ephesus with such love. Any other approach may lead to division or rejection. The opponents lacked this type of faith because of their hypocrisy (1 Tim 6:5, 10).

■ **6** After the high point of 1:5, Paul turns again to denounce the false teachers in Ephesus. This verse sets up a significant contrast between the ideal of v 5 and the present deviation by the false teachers. The Greek verse begins with **from these** (*hōn*), referring back to the qualities of v 5. The generic indefinite pronoun **some** refers back to the "certain people" of v 3.

There is one verb in this sentence: **have departed**. The participle *astochēsantes* (***missing the target***) precedes the verb and explains why some wander. Because they miss the core qualities of v 5, they wander away into speculation. The verb *exetrapēsan* appears again in 1 Tim 6:21 and 2 Tim 2:18 identifying false teachers (→ 1 Tim 5:15). They had been on the right path, but at some point (aorist) turned off it.

This was not accidental but intentional deviation. Swerving away from the qualities of 1:5 led them to miss the most important goal. "The opponents did not choose to follow the heresy because it was intellectually more acceptable; they chose to abandon love" (Mounce 2000, 26). They had missed the most important and exchanged it for what seemed more interesting. These speculations did not positively transform their character, as the truth of the gospel did. "It was because the triad of graces was neglected that many had turned away from their proper course" (Oden 1989, 57).

Their wandering led them **to meaningless talk** (*mataiologian*—only here in the Bible, but a cognate appears in Titus 1:10—*mataiologoi*). The compound noun refers to worthless discussions that come from not cooperating with God (→ 1 Tim 6:20; 2 Tim 2:16; Bauernfeind 1967a, 519). The teachers offered only empty promises with no positive outcome.

■ **7** Paul claims that the goal of the opponents, **to be teachers of the law**, ironically could not be accomplished. What law were they trying to teach? *Nomodidaskaloi* elsewhere refers only to Jewish teachers (Luke 5:17; Acts 5:34). Were the false teachers promoting a distorted understanding of the Mosaic law (so Mounce 2000, 27)?

Grammatically, this verse depends on the main verb *exetrapēsan* in 1 Tim 1:6. It answers the question: How did they turn aside? This is shown by two dependent participles of cognition, the first leading to the second: they did this **by wanting** (*thelontes*) to be teachers **without understanding** (*mē noountes*).

Two things the false teachers did not know appear in the following relative clauses: **what they are talking about** and **what they so confidently affirm**. The word translated **what** (*ha*) in both phrases is plural, intensifying their misunderstanding of the law. The last word in the sentence, *diabebaiountai*, is an intensified compound of *bebaioun*, **to guarantee**. This supports the NIV paraphrase: **so confidently affirm**. Their total confidence only intensified their complete ignorance.

These "wannabe" teachers desired leadership without the essential qualifications. Their problem was ignorance, but they were not innocently ignorant. They deliberately ignored the truth they should have known (**by swerving**; → v 6). Their ignorance led them only to distort the Law (→ 6:4).

FROM THE TEXT

Challenges to authority. Paul attempts to equip Timothy for the challenges he faced in Ephesus—especially the ignorance of the false teachers. It is extremely difficult for leaders to deal with people who think they know what they are doing but actually have missed the most important point. They are convinced of their perspective and may even be emotionally involved in sharing it with others. The most effective way to deal with such people is to stand on unshakable truth.

As Paul's ambassador, Timothy followed a line of authority originating from "the command of God our Savior and of Christ Jesus our hope" (1:1). It would have been easier to go where the "grass was greener" and the situation not so intense. But Paul wants Timothy to stick it out in Ephesus. It is still tempting to take the easy way out, the path of least resistance, "to drift with the current" rather than to confront such problems head-on (Gould 1965, 556).

Dealing with heresy. It is always difficult to deal with false doctrine, especially when those who teach it are fervent. The best defense against any heresy is to know true doctrine. Throughout the letter, Paul calls Timothy to the essentials of the Christian faith. The firm foundation is the clear message about God as Savior and Jesus as hope. Paul later reminds Timothy that Scripture is the vital source of doctrine (2 Tim 3:16). Misusing or misunderstanding Scripture, as the teachers did, leads only to a shaky foundation (see Matt 7:24-27).

History has a way of repeating itself. There are no new heresies, just old ones in new clothing. What makes a heresy so dangerous is that it distorts the truth. Heresies usually begin within the church but soon take on a life of their own. Those without clear vision and understanding of the gospel might be deceived. Heresy threatens the internal integrity of the church and its external witness to the world (Towner 1994, 43). Strong leadership and knowledge of the truth can guide the church through these murky waters.

The deceit of knowledge. Irenaeus used this passage to warn his readers about gnostics, people who pretended to have knowledge greater than God has revealed and who used clever language to lead people astray. The simpleminded cannot distinguish lie from truth (*Haer.* 1.1).

There are many questions the Bible does not answer. Speculation brings only temporary answers to unanswered questions. Paul turns the focus back to what really matters: the gospel of love.

The core values of orthodoxy. Paul urges Timothy to move the church away from the "interesting" to the "important." Right doctrine is defined, in part, in v 5. What the false teachers taught went against God's way—living by love. They lacked the inner resources of a pure heart, good conscience, and sincere faith. These core values define orthodoxy and bring believers together in unity. One of the dangers of speculation and a weakness of postmodernism is relativism. In this worldview, individuals or social contexts define truth. Indisputable truth draws people together and gives them a basis for community life. John Chrysostom wrote, "For where faith exists there is no need of suspicion. Where there is no room for curiosity, questions are superfluous" (*Hom. 1 Tim.*, quoted by Gorday 2000, 132).

The sources for love. The greatest need in any situation is Christian love. Timothy needed to show tough love toward the Ephesian heretics. Love must be properly sourced. Two approaches are described in this passage: either the empty teaching of the opponents that accomplished nothing but speculation, or love that springs from and leads to transformation. "Knowledge puffs up" but "love builds up" (1 Cor 8:1).

The only way we can love is when our hearts have been purified from sin. There is a vital relationship between the call to love and cleansing from sin. The heart stained with sin (Isa 1:18) and focused upon self-love can be transformed through the Holy Spirit (2 Cor 3:18) to love like Christ (Eph 4:22-24; 5:1-2). Augustine wrote that "the end of all divine Scriptures" is love for God (*Doctr. chr.* 1.35.39, quoted by Gorday 2000, 133).

Although the truths of 1 Tim 1:5 apply to all ministry contexts, they were especially important for Timothy in Ephesus. Love is the primary measure of effectiveness in ministry. The leadership qualities Paul will encourage later in the letter will be unattainable without the core value of love from a pure heart verified by a clean conscience and supported by a sincere faith.

B. The Purpose of the Law (1:8-11)

BEHIND THE TEXT

This section digresses from the problems in Ephesus. However, it is still an integral part to Paul's argument and gives a clue to the purpose of the letter. Paul further defines the error of the false teachers as a misappropriation and misinterpretation of the Law (Sumney 1999, 32). Paul becomes sarcastic toward the opponents. As so-called experts in the Law, they missed the primary purpose of the Law in all their speculations, myth making, and genealogical analysis. Paul also takes a significant step in further defining orthodox teaching. Both of these themes have the effect of sidelining both the teachers and their doctrines.

This section reflects back on v 7 and the focus the false teachers had on the Law. Evidently, they based their speculations on the OT law, since vv 9-10 have obvious parallels to the Ten Commandments. They made two key errors: misusing the Law and misunderstanding the role of God's grace and mercy in salvation (Mounce 2000, 30).

Verses 8-11 form one thematic unit comprising one long complex sentence. This paragraph illustrates the polemical pattern of the whole chapter: It compares two different responses to the Law and to Paul's gospel. The theological theme behind this sentence is the required response of obedience to the call of God heard in part through the Law and experienced fully in the gospel. From this theme comes the ethical question, how ought believers to live?

IN THE TEXT

■ **8** This new paragraph begins with a contrastive *but* (*de*, untranslated in the NIV; "now" [ESV, NRSV]). It refers back to the idea of "teachers of the law" of v 7. There is also a shift from the third person "certain people" to the first person **we know**. Paul often uses **we know** to introduce general Christian truths (Rom 2:2; 3:19; 8:28; 1 Cor 8:1, 4; 2 Cor 5:1). It is unclear who **we** includes, at least Paul and those who agree with him; it excludes the false teachers.

Likewise, the extent of **the law** is unclear. The root for **law** (*nom-*) appears four times in two verses. Because Paul lists vices that reflect the Ten Commandments in 1 Tim 1:9-10, it can be assumed he is speaking about the Jewish law represented in the OT. Usually the word *nomos* in Paul refers to the law given by Moses (Gutbrod 1967, 1069). He deals with similar issues in Titus 1:10 and 14, where the context is explicitly Jewish.

Paul states that the Law **is good.** In a different context and with a different purpose, he writes in Romans that the Law "is holy, and the commandment is holy, righteous and good" (7:12), "spiritual" (7:14), and "good" (7:16). Behind these statements is the conviction that the Law reflects the divine will. The Law reveals what holiness looks like and why holiness is important for relationship with the Holy God.

In this context, the goodness of the Law depends on its use. This is expressed in a conditional clause: **if one uses it properly.** This is a play on words in the Greek and literally means *if someone uses it [the law] lawfully* (*nomimōs*). The Greek word is from the same root as **law** and means agreeable to the Law. In 2 Tim 2:5 it describes an athlete who plays "according to the rules." The Greek subjunctive mood (*chrētai*) here implies a future possibility with some uncertainty of fulfillment. Thus, the Law has the potential of being abused, if it is not allowed to do as it was intended. This is a general, theoretical statement with an indefinite **someone** (*tis*) as the subject.

Since the opponents were misusing the Law, Paul clears up that point before delving into community issues (ch 2 onward). The goal of the Law is to produce love. The way the opponents used the Law would lead to empty speculation, not love.

Law in Paul's Letters

Paul's view of the Law (*nomos*) is complex and debated. He used *nomos* 119 times in his writings, 107 of these in Romans and Galatians. The word originally meant "what is proper" in reference to any norm, custom, usage, or tradition in the political, cosmic, natural, or moral realm. In the religious realm, it referred to the will of a deity (Gutbrod 1967, 1023-24). For the Jews, the Law (Hebrew *torah*) reveals God's will and is a gift from God as a guide to holy living (Rom 7:10, 12), but sin hinders human obedience (7:14, 25).

The Law has two potential effects, depending on one's disposition toward Christ. The Law condemns sin by both defining it and keeping it in check (Rom 5:13, 20; 7:7). Christians may embrace the Law and fulfill it in love (Gal 5:14; 6:2). Sinners reject the Law and live in rebellion against Christ.

■ **9-10** Paul's vice list defines the purpose of the Law in order to show Timothy how the teachers were misguided in their myths and speculations. Verse 9 begins with a participle (*eidōs*), translated as a finite verb in the NIV. It depends on the "we know" of v 8 and carries this idea on to the list of wicked people in vv 9-10. It has a causal sense: **we know** [v 8] . . . *since we know this* [v 9].

There are two major categories in this list: the righteous and everyone else. An imbalance shows Paul's emphasis. First, he expresses that **the law is made not for the righteous** (*didaioō*). Righteousness has a moral quality to it marked by obedience to God's commands. "It is forensic in that the righteous person is declared not guilty and eschatological in that the person will ultimately be declared righteous at the final judgment. It is not only a gift appropriated by faith but also a virtue to be sought" (Mounce 2000, 35-36).

The primary reason the righteous do not need the Law is because they already obey it by nature. They have been made right with God in their response of faith to God's free offer of justification through Christ (Rom 5:17, 21), and they continue to walk in the obedience that faith produces (Rom 1:5; 16:26). Outward obedience to the Law becomes second nature to believers because of the transforming work of the Spirit within them (Rom 8:4; Gal 5:5, 25). The Law has been planted in their hearts through the Holy Spirit (Jer 31:31-34; Ezek 36:27) who fills them with love. They no longer need the Law to correct them (Rom 13:9-10; Gal 5:14, 22).

The disobedient are the ones who need the restraint of the Law (Rom 3:19). Since one of the purposes of the Law is to reveal sin and to bring conviction to the sinner (Rom 7:7, 13), it sets the standard for expected behavior. Because it reveals the will of God, it exposes everything contrary to this will. The Ephesian opponents missed this essential point. Paul artfully summarizes the Decalogue in single words and, at the same time and by polemic, isolates further the false teachers.

Paul lists fourteen types of people, naming "not the sins forbidden by the law but the ones who do what is forbidden" (Knight 1992, 87). The vice list has two major sections: sins against God and sins against humanity. These roughly correspond to the two tablets of the Law—the first four and the last six commandments of the Decalogue (Exod 20:1-17; Deut 5:6-21).

The first group is arranged in assonant pairs—the first five words all begin with *alpha*. This arrangement adds to the rhetorical force of the vices (Collins 2002, 31). No specific commandment stands behind these words. But the general thrust is a rejection of the sovereignty of God, which the first four commandments seek to establish.

Lawbreakers (*anomois*) summarize all the words that follow and imply the most obvious problem: disobedience. **Rebels** (*anypotaktois*) is almost synonymous but has a stronger sense of willful rejection (Rom 8:7; 10:3; Titus 1:6, 10).

Ungodly (*asebesi*) shares the same root as the more positive *eusebeia* ("godliness" or "reverence"), an important virtue in the Pastorals (→ 1 Tim 2:2). The *alpha* privative (*a-*) negates the root *seb-*, "worship." A lack of worship lies at the root of sin. *Asebesi* is often paired, as here, with **sinful** (*hamartōlous*), which describes those who break the Law (Gal 2:15; 1 Tim 1:15; 1 Pet 4:18 [Prov 11:31 LXX]; Jude 15). The first could refer to inner irreverence and the latter to outward disobedience (Fee 1988, 45).

The **unholy** (*anosiois*) are those things that are profane and unfit for worship of God. Paul uses it in 2 Tim 3:2 in a list describing people in the "last days." The root *hosios* is a relational word that denotes that which is worthy to come into the presence of God (Seebass 1976, 2:237; → 1 Tim 2:8; Titus 1:8). This word is partnered with a synonym, **irreligious** (*bebēlois*), which designates something profane or with no sense of God's holy presence (Hauck 1964b, 604). In 1 Tim 4:7, 6:20, and 2 Tim 2:16, it alludes to the activities of the false teachers.

Those who kill their fathers [*patrolōais*] **or mothers** (*mētrolōais*) is an extreme violation of the fifth commandment: "honor your father and your mother" (Exod 20:12; Deut 5:16). These two Greek words only occur here in the Bible and combine "father" and "mother" with *aloaō*, which means to strike fatally or to destroy (see Exod 21:15). Hence, the strong translation **kill**. The worst way to dishonor parents is to beat them or worse, to kill them. Striking a parent was so dishonorable that it was worthy of stoning (Deut 21:18-21). These words are paired with **murderers** (*androphonos*), a rare word that occurs only here in the NT. It corresponds to the sixth command: "you shall not murder" (Exod 20:13; Deut 5:17).

The next two vices refer to sexual sins rejecting the seventh command: "you shall not commit adultery" (Exod 20:14; Deut 5:18). **The sexually immoral** (*porneia*) are those involved in sexual sins of various kinds (Acts 15:20; 1 Cor 6:18; 2 Cor 12:21; Gal 5:19; Eph 5:5; Rev 2:14, 20-21; 9:21).

The next vice (*aresenkoites*) refers to a male engaged in homosexual activity with another man in a consensual arrangement (Lev 18:22; 20:13). In Rom 1:27, this term is used to describe those who reject God and turn to self-gratification (see also Rom 1:24, 26-28). Involvement in this leads to exclusion from God's kingdom (1 Cor 6:9). Homosexuality is clearly condemned in the OT, which may have been the basis for Paul's thought here (Lev 18:22; 20:13). Christ can bring deliverance from such sexual sins (1 Cor 6:11).

Slave traders (*andrapodistais*, only here in the Bible) refers to kidnapping people and selling them into slavery. As a form of stealing, this violates the eighth commandment: "you shall not steal" (Exod 20:15; Deut 5:19). In the OT, the punishment for kidnapping was death (Exod 21:16; Deut 24:7).

Paul does not specifically condemn slavery in his letters. But he does significantly qualify it by elevating slaves within the Christian community to the status of brothers or sisters in Christ, alongside their masters (→ 1 Tim 6:1-2; Phlm 16).

Liars (*pseustais*) refers to speaking a falsehood in order to deceive (Rom 3:4; Titus 1:12). **Perjurers** (*epiorkois*) also lie by breaking an oath. Both of these are violations of the ninth commandment: "you shall not give false testimony" (Exod 20:16; Deut 5:20; see Lev 19:11-12). Paul expands this commandment beyond courtroom perjury (Mounce 2000, 40). The transformed life ought to evidence speaking truthfully to one's neighbor (Eph 4:22-25).

Curiously, there is no reference to the tenth commandment about not coveting (so central in Paul's analysis of sin in Rom 7:7). Why did Paul list these specific sins that reflect so closely many of the Ten Commandments? One possible reason is that these commandments stand at the heart of the Mosaic law, which may have been one of the topics of speculation of the false teachers. Paul is pointing out that the Law was not intended for meaningless discussions that have no eternal value, but for a strong warning to those who would break it. It helps develop a "good conscience" (1 Tim 1:5) in order that a person may be a good steward of "sound doctrine" (v 10). Paul chooses words that specifically fit the context of ch 1 and address social sins that affect the community (Witherington 2006, 197). He may have picked the worst kinds of sins to show the seriousness of the false teachings (Kelly 1963, 49).

Paul gives one last, catchall phrase, **whatever . . . is contrary to . . . sound doctrine**. **Whatever** (*ei ti heteron*) is indefinite and inclusive of sins similar to those already listed. Like Gal 5:21, this list is not complete but only representative. The list has served its purpose, and Paul has no need to continue. The verb **is contrary** (*antikeitai*) reflects back on "is made" (*keitai*) of 1 Tim 1:9. It is found also in 5:14 and shows strong opposition, such as what the "adversary," Satan, gives to widows, and what Paul faced in Corinth (1 Cor 6:9) and Philippi (Phil 1:28).

Sound (*hygiainousē*; source of the English hygiene) is a medical term for whatever produces good health. In the NT, it appears only in the Pastoral Epistles. Greek moral philosophers and Cynics often used medical imagery against opposing ideas they considered "sick" (Malherbe 1980, 121-36). Those Ephesians who had been involved in Artemis worship and its concern for good health may have recognized this word.

The word is an adjectival participle modifying **doctrine** (*didaskalia*). Such *teaching*, when done out of love (1 Tim 1:5), produces a healthy spiritual life. The source of this life-giving teaching is the authority of God (v 1). Healthy teaching, a significant theme in the Pastorals (fifteen times), ought to be the basis for ethical and theological instruction in the church. It should be based on Scripture (1 Tim 4:13; 2 Tim 3:16) and be used for discipleship within the church (Titus 2:2, 8). It was expressed in Paul's preaching passed on to Timothy and Titus (2 Tim 1:13; Titus 2:1). Church leaders must base their lives on such teaching (1 Tim 4:16; 5:17). It is the primary basis for refuting false teachings (Titus 1:9, 13). Sound teaching and the Law serve the same purpose—exposing sin.

Paul uses this imagery as a polemic to define "correct" teaching over against the heretical threat in Ephesus and Crete. False teaching is based only on human curiosity, things that "tickle the ear" (see 2 Tim 4:3). It leads only to the breakdown of community (1 Tim 6:3-5). This teaching must be stopped because it is unhealthy (1 Tim 6:4) and spreads like gangrene (2 Tim 2:17). The false teachings of the opponents would lead only to spiritual sickness within the church. "Healthy teaching leads to proper Christian behavior, love and good works; the diseased teaching of the heretics leads to controversies, arrogance, abusiveness, and strife (6:4)" (Fee 1988, 46).

Vice Lists in Antiquity

Paul's letters offer many "vice lists" (Rom 1:29-31; 13:13; I Cor 5:10-11; 6:9-10; 2 Cor 12:20-21; Gal 5:19-21; Eph 4:31; 5:3-5; Col 3:5-8; I Tim 6:4-5; 2 Tim 3:2-5; Titus 1:7; 3:3). These served the rhetorical purpose of urging readers to avoid particular evil acts. No two lists are identical; each is ad hoc and given for a specific context.

Well before Paul's time, Greeks, Romans, and Jews had developed various vice and virtue lists. These functioned as guides to lifestyles consistent with the values of their authors. Often vices came first, setting in contrast the better way to embrace through the virtues that followed (Malherbe 1986, 138-41; see McEleney's [1974, 218] survey of possible influences upon the vice lists in the Pastoral Epistles).

Paul's vice lists often show behaviors caused by the power of sin in a person's life. Such behaviors result from a rejection of God's grace in Christ or the work of the Holy Spirit upon the conscience. Both of these issues may stand behind the vice list in I Tim 1:9-10.

■ **11** Paul concludes the sentence and paragraph and prepares for his testimony in the following verses. The Greek is literally *according to the gospel*, specifically reflecting back on the "sound doctrine" of v 10. The preposition *kata* designates the norm or standard by which the teaching ought to be evaluated (BDAG 2000, 511). This verse summarizes the whole paragraph (vv 8-11) by shifting the focus from a misuse of the Law to the vital importance of the gospel.

In the NT, **gospel** (*euangelion*) designates the announcement of "good news" of what God has done in Christ in behalf of the human race. Paul reflects in vv 12-17 on how he had experienced the goodness of God's mercy in his own life. The early Christian use of the term may have begun with Jesus' quotation of Isa 61:1-2 (see also 40:9; 52:7; Luke 4:18). Jesus came preaching the "good news of the kingdom" (Luke 4:43). The term was also used in the Imperial cult to describe the military and political success of the emperor (Towner 2006, 131). The emperor Augustus brought sweeping peace to the Roman Empire and was hailed as a savior. The freedom and justice that came with the Pax Romana were viewed as "good news." By the time the Pastorals were written, this news had become old and had been replaced with uncertainty and confusion. Paul's gospel brought good news to this void (see Wright 1997, 41-44; 2005, 59-79).

Paul uses a series of descriptive genitives: **the gospel of the glory of the blessed God**. It is difficult to determine the relation of these words. Does **the glory of** go with **gospel** or with **God**? Does Paul mean the "glorious gospel" (KJV, NRSV) or the gospel that is about the glory of God (NIV, ESV, NEB)? The latter interpretation encompasses the first: **the gospel that tells about the glory of the blessed God.**

What sets the gospel apart from any other type of message is **glory** (*doxēs*). This important biblical word describes the presence, power, and majesty of God. It translates the Hebrew *kabōd*, which means heavy or important (von Rad 1964, 238-42). Moses asked to see God's glory in Exod 33:18. God's glory, his very presence, was so overwhelming that Moses had to hide behind a rock and saw only the fading glory (the "back") of God (33:21-23). No human words can capture the glory of God; only God incarnate could reveal this glory to people (John 1:14; 2 Cor 4:6). The gospel is all about the glory of God, which is best seen in the cross of Christ (1 Cor 1:18). Sin cuts people off from experiencing this glory (Rom 3:23). The goal of Christians is to become participants in God's glory by being transformed into the likeness of Jesus Christ by the Holy Spirit (2 Cor 3:18; 2 Thess 2:14; Titus 2:13).

God is the source of all blessings and happiness. The adjective *makariou* is used with "God" only here and in 1 Tim 6:15. More often, God is described with the similar word *eulogētos* (Rom 1:25; 9:5; 2 Cor 1:3; 11:31; Eph 1:3; 1 Pet 1:3). *Makarios* is found in the many beatitudes in Scripture (e.g., Matt 5:4-11). The gospel is the only source of happiness because it allows us to participate in the divine presence (2 Pet 1:3-4).

God **entrusted** (*episteuthēn*) this message to Paul (1 Cor 9:17; Gal 2:7; Eph 3:2; 1 Thess 2:4; 1 Tim 2:7; 2 Tim 1:11; Titus 1:3). This verb is passive with God as the assumed actor. Paul understood his primary mission to be to preach the gospel (Rom 15:16; 1 Cor 9:14; Gal 1:15-16), and so his letters are devoted to helping the churches understand both the theological foundations and ethical implications of the gospel. God entrusted Paul with the authority and responsibility to carry out this mission (1 Cor 4:1).

This last phrase further establishes Paul's authority while preparing readers for his testimony in the next section. He has introduced several key theological ideas about the gospel while at the same time using polemical language against the opponents. Next, he defines the gospel further in terms of his own experience in order to inspire Timothy to be faithful in his vital mission in Ephesus.

FROM THE TEXT

Correct theology should lead to strong ethics (Furnish 1968). Belief in "God our Savior" and "Christ Jesus our hope" (1 Tim 1:1) ought to determine how we live. If anyone or anything other than these is the foundation, we may be easily deceived and our behavior corrupted. Paul again calls readers to the importance of a transformed heart (v 5) evident in righteous living (v 9).

The Law is a gift of grace that reveals the deepest needs of our hearts. The false teachers misunderstood the basis of the hope of salvation and turned to useless speculations about the Law. The Law was to be a moral guide, to reveal sin so lawbreakers could know the error of their ways. Studying the Law is important because it helps overcome the ignorance of unbelief (Eph 4:17-19).

Nevertheless, the Law serves only a "temporary" role until Christ reigns supreme and the Holy Spirit is allowed to take the lead (Gal 5:25). The church fathers understood this well (see comments of Theodore of Mopsuestia, Theodoret of Cyr, Augustine, and John of Damascus, quoted by Gorday 2000, 140).

Keeping the Law conforms us to the message of the gospel. The goal of the Law is to guide us into loving relationships with God and others (1 Tim 1:5; Rom 13:8-10; see Gorday 2000, 139). Purity of heart leads to social justice. The Holy Spirit will convict lawbreakers and lead the willing to righteous living (John 16:8-11). Verse 10 of 1 Tim 1 significantly influenced the abolition of American slavery in the nineteenth century (Harrill 2000). Experiencing the glory of God through Jesus Christ changes the way we view those around us.

C. Paul's Positive Example of the Truth of the Gospel (1:12-17)

BEHIND THE TEXT

This section continues the theological comparison between Paul's approach and the opponents'. At issue is the authority behind each, with direct implications on the message each proclaimed. The false teachers were self-appointed, whereas Paul was appointed by God. Paul's life illustrates the power of the gospel and serves as a paradigm for transformation. The change in his life adds authority to his words and serves as a test by which to measure the claims of the false teachers. By giving himself as an example, he encourages Timothy to consider the mercy of God for the problems in Ephesus.

At first glance, this section may appear to be a digression from the topic of false doctrine. To the contrary, it is integral to Paul's overall purpose by providing an illustration of "the glorious gospel" of v 11 (KJV). Although the typical thanksgiving section is lacking immediately after the prescript, this section can function as one.

The passage has the following thematic structure:

A Paul's reflections on the change from his former life (vv 12-14)

   B The core truth of the gospel (v 15)

A' Paul's life as a prime example of the power of the gospel (v 16)

   B' A concluding praise to the God who makes it all possible (v 17)

This structure also highlights the key themes: (1) it authenticates Paul's position of authority and places his teaching within orthodoxy; (2) his experience proves the power of the gospel; and (3) his experience shows the priority of faith in salvation (Towner 2006, 135). The climax of the passage comes in v 15 and the "trustworthy saying," a summary of "the gospel concerning the glory of the blessed God" (v 11).

There are several noteworthy literary features here. Noticeably, there is a shift in focus with eight references to the first person ("I," "me"). Several words are repeated. The *pistis* ("faith") word group is used seven times (*episteuthēn* [v 11], *piston* [v 12], *apistia* [v 13], *pisteōs* [v 14], *pistos* [v 15], *pisteuein* [v 16]). The idea of "mercy" (*eleos*) is given in vv 13 and 16. The word *charis* ("grace") can be found in vv 12 and 14. The christological emphasis is evident in the repetition of "Christ Jesus" in vv 12, 14, 15, and 16. Several triads appear: Paul as a blasphemer, persecutor, and insolent person (v 13), which is met by Christ's grace, faith, and love (v 14). The passage culminates with God as incorruptible, invisible, and the only God (v 17).

This passage also offers us a glimpse into Paul's inner life and autobiography (compare Rom 1:1-7; 1 Cor 15:8-11; 2 Cor 11:22-23; Gal 1:13-15; Phil 3:4-11).

IN THE TEXT

■ **12** Paul shifts back to the first person (1 Tim 1:3), used eight times in this paragraph. Although he reflects on his own life, Christ is the focus. Paul serves as an example to Timothy and the Ephesian church of the transforming power of the gospel.

Paul expresses his gratitude using the present tense of the verb **I have** (*echo*) followed by **thanks** (*charis*). The tense suggests that he gave thanks continually or repeatedly (1 Thess 5:18). The Greek word behind **thank** here is translated "grace" in other contexts. Here it refers to favor granted an object of affection (BDAG 2000, 1079; → 2 Tim 1:3). This phrase is basically synonymous with the more typical *eucharisteō* in Paul's other letters (Rom 1:8; 1 Cor 1:4; Eph 1:16; Phil 1:3; Col 1:3; 1 Thess 1:2; 2 Thess 1:3; Phlm 4). Paul thanks, recognizes, and praises God for his sovereign protection and plan of salvation in Christ.

Paul identifies the recipient of his thanks with three substantives in the dative case. The first, *endynamōsanti me*, **to the one who has empowered me**, is a compound verb not found in secular Greek before the NT. In the NT, it refers to religious and moral strengthening (Knight 1992, 93). Its aorist tense suggests that Paul thinks specifically of his conversion experience (Acts 9:5; Mounce 2000, 50).

The second dative stands in apposition to the participle, clarifying the source of Paul's strength as **Christ Jesus** (repeated in 1 Tim 1:12, 14, 15, 16; see 2 Tim 2:1; 4:17; Eph 6:10; in 2 Tim 1:7 the Holy Spirit is the empowering agent).

The third dative, **our Lord**, occurs twice (1 Tim 1:12, 14). Paul leaves no doubt for Timothy or the Ephesians about the solution to their current problems: "This lordship and strengthening is available for all who believe in Christ" (Knight 1992, 93). If Christ can change and use Paul, the possibilities in Ephesus are limitless.

God is usually the receiver of thanks in Paul's letters. Christ may be the recipient here because he is the subject of all the divine activity in this paragraph. Not only did Christ come into the world to die for sinners like Paul, but he is also the exalted Lord, worthy of worship (Fee 2007, 424-25). The second half of the verse expresses two reasons for Paul's thanksgiving (**that** or "because" [*hoti*; ESV, NRSV]).

First, Christ **considered** (*hēgēsato*) Paul to be *faithful* (*pistos*). This aorist tense may refer to Paul's conversion call. *Pistos* usually means "faithful" or **trustworthy** in the Pastorals (Knight 1992, 94). Christ saw potential in Paul and entrusted him with a unique mission. The emphasis is on Christ's calling, not Paul's record of faithfulness. Paul's effective ministry to the Gentiles confirmed Christ's choice (Towner 2006, 138).

Second, Christ appointed (*themenos*) Paul for a special ministry. **Appointing** is an aorist adverbial participle, either instrumental, "by appointing," or telic, "for the purpose of appointing." The aorist tense again indicates that Paul's calling accompanied his conversion (see Acts 9).

One last significant word is **service** or *ministry* (*diakonian*). This word is used in the NT both in a general sense of service to others (John 2:5, 9) and for special responsibility within the church (Acts 1:17, 25; 6:4; 20:24; 21:19; Rom 11:13; 1 Cor 16:15; 2 Cor 3:8, 9; 4:1; 5:18; 6:3; Col 4:17; 2 Tim 4:5). Paul served the one who commanded him to be an apostle (1 Tim 1:1) and had qualified him for this ministry through grace.

To his service uses the preposition *eis* with the accusative case to show the purpose of Paul's calling. Paul believed God had a plan for him even before he was born (Gal 1:15), though only later did he come to realize what this plan was. He brought with him his training in the Scriptures as a Pharisee, his linguistic skills, and his zeal. The same passion he had for persecuting the church was transformed through grace into a passion to preach the gospel. He did not delay fulfilling this call, but immediately "began to preach in the synagogues that Jesus is the Son of God" (Acts 9:20).

■ **13** The sentence begun in 1 Tim 1:12 continues as Paul reflects on his calling and how his life changed when he met Christ. The hinge point between the two parts of his life is his experience of the mercy of Christ (v 16).

Paul introduces his former life with a concessive present participle (*onta*): **Even though I was**. The adverb **once** (*proteron*) places the time period described by the participle as before that of the main verb, **I was shown mercy**. The present tense indicates that Paul was actively blaspheming, persecuting, and acting in violence when Christ showed mercy to him.

Paul describes his former life negatively in three ways: He was **a blasphemer and a persecutor and a violent man**. He may not have intended any kind of sequence with these words, but they match the account of Acts 7:58—8:3.

Blasphemy (*blasphēmos*) is a form of rebellious slander that rejects God (Acts 6:11; 26:9-11). This word occurs seven times in the Pastorals (1 Tim 1:20; 6:1, 4; 2 Tim 3:2; Titus 2:5; 3:2).

Persecutor (*diōktēs*) as a noun occurs only here in the NT. The verb (*diōkō*) is more common. The cognate *diōgmos* means "affliction" (Lam 3:19 LXX). Before his conversion, Paul attempted to "destroy the church" (Acts 8:3; see 1 Cor 15:9; Gal 1:13, 23; Phil 3:6).

Violent (*hybristēn*) describes one so insolent he disregards the rights of others in insulting ways (BDAG 2000, 1022). In Rom 1:30 it refers to those who have proudly turned their backs on God, to their own destruction. Such violent pride ruins relationships and devastates lives. Paul, in his zeal for his Jewish traditions (Gal 1:14), despised the church and its Lord.

In spite of Paul rejecting Christ in these ways, Christ showed him mercy. The stark change made in his life can be seen in the strong adversative *alla* (**but**, untranslated in the NIV, but in the ESV and NRSV). The "once but now" change represents the power of God's grace to transform sinners into saints (see Gal 1:23). Paul's life illustrates what happens when the old way of life is crucified (Rom 6:4; Eph 4:22-24) and "in Christ" a person becomes a "new creation" (2 Cor 5:17).

I was shown mercy (*eleēthēn*) is an aorist passive with Christ (1 Tim 1:2) as the implicit source of this mercy. Paul reflects back on the time when Christ "captured" him (see Phil 3:12) on the road to Damascus. This verse provides a good definition for **mercy**: In spite of Paul's sin, Christ out of sheer, compassionate love called him to a new way of life. Christ did what Paul could not do himself. Behind this verse lies a sense of "awe that even a sinner such as himself was shown mercy" (Mounce 2000, 51).

Paul explains why he was shown mercy in the last part of the verse: **because I acted in ignorance and unbelief**. First, he did not know (*agnoēn*) whom he was persecuting. This was evident when he asked the voice on the Damascus road, "Who are you, Lord?" By persecuting the church, he was actually persecuting Christ (Acts 9:5; 22:8; 26:15). His zeal had blinded him to the mercies of God and the newness of Christ. When he wrote to the Corinthians about the foolishness of the gospel (1 Cor 1:18), he knew from personal experience the power of spiritual blindness (1 Cor 2:8-16).

Was Paul still culpable for this ignorance? The OT law makes a distinction between intentional and unintentional sins (Lev 4:1-35; 22:14; Num 15:22-31; see also Josephus, *Ant.* 3.9.3.230-32). Unintentional sins could be atoned for, but highhanded sins led one to be cut off from the community and from God. Paul did not shake his fist at God in rebellion. He honestly thought Jesus and his followers were heretics. His zeal *against* Christ (Gal 1—2) was transformed and intensified into zeal *for* Christ.

Paul's ignorance was a consequence of his unbelief (*apistia*; Chrysostom, *Hom. 1 Tim.* 3). Although his zeal was driven by ignorance, he still needed to be forgiven. **Because** (*hoti*) requires careful consideration in this regard. Mounce suggests that the word be translated as "since" because "it is giving not the reason for God's mercy but a consideration leading to God's mercy" (2000, 53).

Paul's salvation did not come from any innate qualities within himself or any efforts he had made to be righteous by the Law (Phil 3:4-7). It came through God's mercy. Sin does not elicit God's grace (Rom 6:1); it is the reason divine forgiveness is an act of mercy toward us. Although Paul had been forgiven, the memory of his early life lingered on to remind him of God's mercy.

■ **14** Paul continues the thought of 1 Tim 1:13 (with *de*, **and**, untranslated in the NIV). Three words describe his new life and answer his sinful activities of v 13: **grace**, **faith**, and **love**. In v 13 he received mercy and in this verse he received **grace** (*charis*). Grace is experienced as mercy when it confronts the problem of sin.

The verb **poured out . . . abundantly** (*hyperepleonasen*) is a compound word found only here in the NT. Paul may have coined it for this occasion. The prefix *hyper-* intensifies the meaning of the root *pleonazō*, "abundance" or "increase" (BDAG 2000, 824). This sets the Lord's grace in even stronger contrast to Paul's sin. As the first word of this clause, the verb is even more emphatic. Paul personalizes Rom 5:20: God's grace in Christ "increased all the more" (*hypereperisseusen*), overpowering *his* sin.

The source of grace is **our Lord**. The precise identity of the **Lord** is ambiguous, since God is mentioned in v 17. But v 12 makes "Christ Jesus our Lord" the more natural reading, since Paul seems to allude to his "conversion call." The phrase "grace of our Lord" often refers to Jesus in the closing of Paul's letters (Rom 16:20, 24; 1 Cor 16:23; 2 Cor 8:9; 13:14; Gal 6:18; Phil 4:23; 1 Thess 5:28; 2 Thess 1:12; 3:18; Phlm 25).

The remainder of this verse—(lit.) *with faith and love which is in Christ Jesus*—offers some interpretive challenges. Whose faith and love is this, Jesus' or Paul's? Are faith and love gifts from the Lord or are they the human response to the Lord's grace?

There are three possible answers: (1) One's faith and love are toward Christ. (2) Faith and love are experienced when one is in Christ. Or (3) the faithfulness and love one receives come from Christ.

When faith and love go together in Paul's letters, they always refer to the believer's faith and love toward Christ (1 Cor 13:13; Eph 1:15; 1 Thess 1:3; 3:6; 2 Thess 1:3; Knight 1992, 98). Yet, faith and love are impossible without grace. Both are the result of the Spirit's work within (1 Cor 13:13). "Faith is a response to grace (Rom 3:23-25; Eph 2:8), and faith acts in love (Gal 5:6; cf. 1:5)" (Fee 1988, 52). Paul could love only because of the change that God's grace had made in his life (compare 1 John 4:19).

The prepositional phrase **in Christ Jesus** (*en Christō Iēsou*) identifies the personal sphere within which faith and love are experienced. It "expresses a dynamic existence that is eschatological, relational, and existential" (Towner 2006, 142). Outside of Christ, faith and love become only human efforts that lead to the futility of legalism. "It is only the person 'in Christ' who is able to receive the gifts that are 'in Christ'" (Mounce 2000, 55). The target of faith is God, and the target of love is others. Sadly, the opponents had departed from these key attributes and were headed for ruin (1 Tim 1:6, 19).

■ **15** Paul gives here the first of several "trustworthy saying[s]" (*pistos ho logos*), a formulaic phrase found only in the Pastorals (3:1; 4:9; 2 Tim 2:11; and Titus 3:8). These sayings resemble statements of faith known among Christian communities. They affirm truths self-evident to mature believers. They are used rhetorically to persuade the audiences of some particularly important and relevant truth.

The saying here appears at the critical center of Paul's testimony and highlights the theological basis for the change in his life. The word *pistos* implies that the saying as "faithful" (KJV) is reliable and agrees with the character of God, who is faithful (1 Cor 1:9; 10:13; 2 Cor 1:18-19; 1 Thess 5:24; 2 Thess 3:3; 2 Tim 2:13; Knight 1992, 100). This phrase functions much like the Jewish "Amen" added to the beginning or ending of statements to stress their importance (Collins 2002, 43-44).

Statements are trustworthy because their source is God; the community accepts them as essential truths; and Paul's own testimony verifies them. Paul adapts each saying to a specific context. He isolates the beliefs of the opponents by highlighting the message the Ephesians should accept (Towner 2006, 144-45).

The way this saying is introduced suggests its importance to Paul: It **deserves full acceptance** (→ 4:9). The adjective **full** (*pasēs*) shows that everyone ought to believe this claim. **Deserves** (*axios*) designates something "worthy of" the description that follows, in this case, **acceptance** (*apodochēs*).

What was the source of this saying? Did Paul quote an early creed, baptismal saying, or early hymn? This exact saying is unique here, because of the context of Paul's testimony. But he appears to build on the tradition he received and passed on to his churches (1 Cor 15:3). It clearly articulates the core of the gospel he spent the last half of his life proclaiming. Early Christians did not invent it; it restates a core teaching of Jesus himself (Matt 9:13; Mark 2:17; Luke 5:32; 19:10).

Came into the world is a recurring Johannine theme (John 1:9; 3:19; 11:27; 12:46; 16:28; 18:37). The **world** is the created order presently dominated by the power of sin and death (Rom 5:12). Although all of creation was impacted by what Christ did on the cross (Rom 8:18-25; 1 Cor 15:20-28; Eph 1:7-10), people were the target of his redeeming work.

The aorist tense of **came** refers to the past historical event of the incarnation. It contracts the whole life of Christ into one grand moment in time (Rom 8:3-4; Gal 4:4). "'Coming into the world' is a Jewish idiom for 'taking on earthly, human existence'" (Towner 1989, 79). The humanity of Christ is emphasized in the letter in four christological statements (in 1 Tim 1:15; 2:4-6; 3:16; and 6:12-13; Fee 2007, 421). This verse assumes the preexistence of Christ: The eternal Son decisively entered human history in order to bring salvation to a broken world (1 Cor 8:6; 2 Cor 8:9; Phil 2:6-7; Col 1:15-20).

This purpose is communicated in the infinitive **to save** (*sōsai*; Matt 9:13; Luke 19:10). Christ came to free us from the power and penalty of sin. Paul uses this verb more than any other NT writer. Salvation for him always focused on God "reconciling the world to himself in Christ" (2 Cor 5:19). Christ came to the world to conquer the power of sin, and he will come a second time to conquer the power of death (1 Cor 15:54-57). This victory is guaranteed by his resurrection from the dead (1 Cor 15:20-22). Salvation for Paul is a past, present, and future experience. His own testimony in this chapter shows freedom from the past (Rom 8:24; Eph 2:8-10). He hopes in Christ's future return and the restoration of all things (Rom 11:26; 1 Cor 5:5; Phil 3:20). The past and future provide victory over sin and temptation in the present (1 Cor 1:18; 2 Cor 6:2).

Sinners (*hamartōlous*) is inclusive of all people, since all "have sinned and fall short of the glory of God" (Rom 3:23). Sin is a spiritual brokenness that becomes evident in disobedience, resulting in missing God's plan and falling short of God's best (Rom 5:19; 6:23). Christ came to change our eternal destiny by offering life to replace the spiral into death.

Paul personalizes this statement by referring to himself as an object of this salvation. The degree of his sin is expressed in the adjective **the worst** or **first** (*prōtos*; also in 1 Tim 1:16). There are two major interpretations of this word: (1) It can be taken temporally: Paul was the first of many to comprehend and take the gospel of grace to the Gentiles (Towner 2006, 148). (2) It could refer to degree: Paul was the foremost sinner (BDAG 2000, 894; so NIV, ESV, NRSV); this speaks of the enormity of Paul's sin against God and the church. Most translators choose the second. This is consistent with Paul's testimony in Gal 1:13 that he "intensely [*hyperbolēn*] . . . persecuted the church of God."

Curiously, Paul uses the present tense **I am** (*eimi egō*). Although he had experienced the mercy of Christ, he continued to live in humble dependence on Christ (1 Cor 15:9; Eph 3:8). Salvation was a present, ongoing experience for him. He had no overwhelming sense of guilt. Nor did he continue to struggle with sin. But he possessed "an abiding sense of being a forgiven sinner" (Mounce 2000, 56). "He recognized himself as always having the status of 'sinner redeemed'" (Fee 1988, 53).

This simple confession reveals that Paul did not take sin lightly. The change in his life proves the truth of this "faithful saying" (KJV). If Christ could save a sinner such as Paul, surely he could save the opponents and even the whole world (→ 1 Tim 2:4). The prerequisite is to go from unbelief (*apistia* [1:13]) to believing in Christ alone for eternal life (v 16).

■ **16** The strong adversative **but** (*alla*) shifts the reader's focus from the solution for the sin problem to Paul the sinner, who needed salvation. It contrasts Paul's sin with Christ's mercy. **For that very reason** (*dia touto*) reflects back on why Christ came, given in v 15, and prepares for the specific application of mercy to Paul's own life here. Paul, who was at the top of the list of sinners, was the reason Christ died. This realization made him deeply humble and urged him on to faithful service.

The verb of v 13 is repeated here: **I was shown mercy** (*eleēthēn*). This emphasizes the point of the paragraph—God's mercy (Mounce 2000, 57). This verb connects Paul's life to the purpose infinitive, "to save," from the "faithful saying" of v 15 (KJV). He experienced salvation rather than judgment by being shown mercy. Christ gave Paul a "second chance," a way out of the path of destruction he was on.

The reason why Paul was shown mercy is expressed in a purpose clause (*hina*): *in order that Christ might show immense patience in me*. Paul must have told this story countless times as part of his evangelistic strategy (Acts 9:5, 6, 17; 22:8, 10; 26:15-18). **Display** (*endeixēta*) refers to showing, demonstrating, or causing to be known. Christ wanted to use Paul as example of how far his mercy could go. Even extreme cases such as Paul's, the chief sinner, are not beyond redemption.

Mercy was demonstrated with **patience** (*makrothymia*) modified by the intensive adjective **immense** (*hapasan*). The superlative adjective *hapasan* ("utmost" [NRSV]; "perfect" [ESV, NASB]) highlights the limitless depth of Christ's grace and patience. Paul's intense rampage against believers was more than met with Christ's perfect patience (Rom 5:20). Christ shows patience by not punishing people as their sins deserve (Ps 103:10), but by extending mercy as a way of escape.

In the OT (Exod 34:6; Num 14:18; Pss 86:15; 103:8; Joel 2:13; Jonah 4:2), patience is a key characteristic of God. God is patient so that sinners will repent and be saved (Rom 2:4; 1 Tim 2:4; 1 Pet 3:20; 2 Pet 3:15). Because Christ is patient with sinners, no one is beyond the reach of his mercy.

The main difference between the opponents and Paul is that, whereas he responded in faith to Christ's mercy, they had rejected the truth of the gospel. Paul again (1 Tim 1:16) identifies himself as the recipient of mercy and calls himself **the worst of sinners** ($\rightarrow$ v 15). The word **sinners** (not in the Greek) is presumed from the previous verse.

Why does Paul repeat **worst** a second time? The first reference in v 15 sets up the contrast between mercy and sin. The second reference in v 16 continues this contrast, but it becomes more of an inclusive invitation to all other "sinners" to experience Christ's mercy and salvation. **In me** (*en emoi*) comes in emphatic position as first in this purpose clause and indicates through whom Christ showed patience so others could experience it as well.

Christ's extension of grace must be appropriated in the sinner's life through faith, and the result will be eternal life. Paul's own experience of salvation serves **as an example** [*pros hypotypōsin*] **for those who would believe**. The preposition *pros* in this construction indicates the goal or purpose ("for a pattern" [KJV]) why Christ showed patience with Paul. It was not simply for Paul's own salvation, but for the salvation of others.

Hypotyposis is found only here and in 2 Tim 1:13. It designates a model or sketch (Goppelt 1972, 248). It is related to the more common *typos* ("type" or "example" [1 Tim 4:12; Titus 2:7]). Paul offers himself as an example of service and lifestyle in other places (Phil 3:17; 1 Thess 1:6-7; 2 Thess 3:9).

The specific example offered here is implied in the substantive participle *the ones who would believe* (*tōn mellontōn pisteuein*). This participle followed by a present infinitive forms a periphrasis for the future tense (Knight 1992, 103). The same mercy Paul experienced is available to others who will respond with faith.

The ultimate goal of Christ's coming and offering mercy to sinners is so they might **receive eternal life.** Not everyone sins as Paul did, but all need the same mercy shown him. The Greek preposition *eis* expresses the goal of Christ's coming—*for eternal life.* **Eternal life** (*zōēn aiōnion*), "life of the age to come," can be experienced now. "Life" in the Pastorals "is much more than simple existence; it is a sharing of the eschatological age here and now in anticipation of life in the eschaton, a totally different kind of life" (Mounce 2000, 59). There is a vital connection between how one lives now in faithfulness and in the hope of receiving the promise of eternal life (→ 1 Tim 4:8; 6:12). "Throughout the Pastorals eternal life is never divisible from the reality of salvation in the present age, which itself originates in the Christ event (1 Tim 4:8; 6:12, 19; 2 Tim 1:10; Titus 1:2; 3:7; cf. 2 Tim 1:1)" (Towner 1989, 81).

Paul uses the style of rabbinic argumentation in this section of the letter called *Qal wahomer*, from the lesser to the greater: If Christ's mercy could extend to Paul, it can reach anyone, even the false teachers and their followers. Paul's testimony is vital to his overall argument, precisely because it is an open invitation to experience "grace, mercy and peace from God the Father and Christ Jesus our Lord" (1:2).

■ **17** Paul's reflections on "the grace of our Lord" (v 14) and the mercy he himself received (v 16) cause him to burst forth in a doxology—a song of praise (compare Rom 9:5; 11:36; 16:27; Gal 1:5; Eph 3:20-21; Phil 4:20). A second doxology appears in 1 Tim 6:15-16. The two form an inclusio (literary bookends) of praise surrounding the paraenetic material of the body. These two doxologies are unique in their emphasis on God's "otherness" and "eternity" (Fee 1988, 54; see Aune [1987, 195] on the typical components of NT doxologies).

Paul may quote a liturgical fragment of unknown source. But it is equally possible that he crafted it. Traditional Jewish thought echoes throughout (esp. the Shema of Deut 6:4; see 1 Cor 8:4, 6). What makes this doxology distinctly Christian is its place within its literary context and the implied connection with Christ's redemption mentioned in the prior verses. Father and Son are so intimately united that Paul attributes salvation, grace, mercy, and peace to both (1 Tim 1:1, 2, 15).

The first description of God is as the **king of the ages** (*tō basilei tōn aiōnōn*). God as king is a common and important theme in the OT (Pss 10:16;

74:12; Isa 6:5; Jer 10:10). God's sovereign right to reign appears in the Gospels in Jesus' preaching about "the kingdom of God" (Matt 5:35; 22:1-14).

Jews believe God is eternal (Gen 21:33; Pss 10:16; 74:12; 90:2; Isa 26:4; Hab 1:12). In Jewish thought, there are two ages: the present and the glorious age to come. Thus, the "ages" represent all time—"forever." Paul adopted this scheme but believed that the future age had already begun for believers. God's unending rule has been revealed in the life, death, and resurrection of Jesus Christ.

God is also **immortal** (*aphtharos*), an idea closely related to God's eternality. The word describes something not subject to decay or death. It is used only here and Rom 1:23 for God. In 1 Cor 15:52 it describes the resurrected body. Different Greek words for "immortal" are used in 1 Tim 6:16 (*athanasian*) and 2 Tim 1:10 (*aphtharsian*), despite their identical translation in the NIV.

God as the holy one does not change. He called time into existence (Ps 102:26-27; Isa 41:4; 48:12; Mal 3:6; Heb 1:11-12; Jas 1:17). Pseudo-Dionysius wrote,

> He [God] was not, nor will he be in a static sense. He did not come to be. He is not in the midst of becoming. He will not come to be. No. It is not that he can be defined by the word *is*, but rather he is the essence of being for the things which have being. (*Div. Names* 5.4, quoted by Gorday 2000, 148)

God is **invisible** (*aoratos*) and "lives in unapproachable light, whom no one has seen or can see" (6:16) because of God's utter holiness. The only person ever to see the Father is the Son (John 1:18; 5:37; 6:46; 12:45; 14:9). The closest any human has ever come was Moses, who saw only the fading glory (the "backside") of Yahweh while hiding behind the cleft of a rock (Exod 33:18-23; Heb 11:27). In Scripture, God is known more by his actions, especially in creating the world (Rom 1:20). God became visible through the incarnation of Christ, who is "the radiance of God's glory and the exact representation of his being" (Heb 1:3; see Col 1:15).

The **King** to whom the doxology is addressed is **the only God**. Monotheism, a core doctrine of both Judaism and Christianity, is grounded in the OT. The Shema of Deut 6:4-9, "Hear, O Israel: The LORD our God, the LORD is one," has been foundational in the daily prayers of Jews since Moses. As Christianity spread into polytheistic Gentile areas, it preserved this core confession. The earliest Christians did not consider themselves a separate religion from Judaism but a fulfillment or extension of it. They claimed that the one God became manifest in the person of Jesus Christ (John 5:44; Rom 3:29; 1 Cor 8:4-5; 1 Tim 2:1-6). As the church wrestled to understand and explain the Trinity, it consistently maintained this monotheistic confession.

After describing the object of praise, the doxology gives the element of praise as **honor and glory.** Honor (*timē*) is the respect and admiration given another. Giving honor to others was part of the social core of the Mediterranean world of the first century, and an important Christian virtue (Rom 12:10; 1 Tim 6:1; 1 Pet 3:7). Giving honor to God is an act of worship. It is the response of recognizing who God is and what God has done, especially through Christ (Rev 4:9-11; 5:12-13; 7:12).

Glory (*doxa*) is often paired with honor (Rom 2:7, 10; Heb 2:7, 9; 2 Pet 1:17; Rev 4:9, 11; 5:12, 13; 7:12). When God reveals his glory, the only proper response one can give is worship (Pss 34:3; 63:3; 69:30; 86:12; Isa 66:5; Dan 4:34). "Used in a doxology it signifies desire either that God's radiance continue to be seen in its splendor and glory or that appropriate praise be given in response to it" (Knight 1992, 106). Giving glory "to God for his indescribable gift" of grace in Christ (2 Cor 9:15) ought to be second nature for those who have been redeemed from lives of sin, as Paul was.

The doxology finally gives the time indicator and closing: **for ever and ever. Amen.** This is a common ending formula in NT doxologies (Rom 16:27; Gal 1:5; Phil 4:20; 1 Tim 1:17; 2 Tim 4:18; Heb 13:21; 1 Pet 4:11; 5:11). Literally, Paul wrote ***unto the ages of ages*** (*eis tous aiōnas tōn aiōnōn*). The double plural expresses something that never ends. This doxology invites readers to join the throng around the throne of God singing unending praises to God and the Lamb (Rev 4:9, 10; 5:13). **Amen** invites a pause and reflection by the congregation to what has been said (Mounce 2000, 62).

FROM THE TEXT

This passage provides a number of powerful messages that have inspired the church throughout the ages. At the top of the list must be *the optimism in God's grace to transform sinners into saints.* Paul viewed himself as the worst of sinners because of his persecution of the church. But a dramatic change occurred when Christ showed him mercy on the road to Damascus. The possibilities of grace are limitless because of the source in the eternal King (1 Tim 1:17). The Christian faith is not about our pursuit of God but God's pursuit of us. Charles Wesley's hymn "Depth of Mercy" reflects on Paul's testimony in this passage.

God extends grace to us, but we must also receive it in faith (Eph 2:8-9). Let the cry of our soul echo Augustine: "If Paul was cured, why should I despair? If such a desperately sick man was cured by such a great physician, who am I, not to fit those hands to my wounds, not to hasten to the care of those hands?" (*Serm.* 175.9, quoted by Gorday 2000, 146).

Responding to God's grace must lead to a change in our lives. God forgives our sins, but we need to learn from our past. By being open about his past sinful life, Paul allowed the grace of the Lord to be more evident. We should not glory in our sin but allow God's loving-kindness to shine through the testimony of our transformed lives.

Paul's life also shows that *success in ministry comes not from personal abilities but from openness to divine resources.* Paul found his source of strength in Christ (2 Cor 11:16—12:10; Phil 3:7-14). He encouraged Timothy to stick with the task by giving attention to "a pure heart and a good conscience and a sincere faith" (1 Tim 1:5), which open the floodgates of grace.

Finally, *the proper response to the mercy of Christ Jesus is a life of worship.* This passage invites us to keep our focus on God. The great hymn by Walter C. Smith, "Immortal, Invisible, God Only Wise," was inspired in part by v 17 ("wise" appears in a number of later manuscripts of this verse). In the context of this chapter, this worship praises God for his transforming mercy in Christ Jesus. The transcendent one has become immanently involved in the lives of sinners, offering them salvation. Christ came for a specific purpose: to save the world (v 15). Paul personalizes this and helps us realize that each person is a target of God's grace in Christ.

D. Paul's Charge to Timothy (1:18-20)

BEHIND THE TEXT

This section concludes ch 1 by reminding Timothy of his calling and urging him to remain faithful, unlike those who wandered away from the faith. The polemic of the chapter becomes personal for Timothy, who must apply in Ephesus what Paul has written. Behind this paragraph lies the problem of false teachings. Paul merges reflections on his own experience of the gospel with the vital ministry confronting Timothy.

Verse 18 begins a new thought unit, shifting to two new subjects: Timothy vs. "some" who have wandered away (v 19). The paragraph has two parts, contrasting Timothy (vv 18-19a) and the opponents (vv 19b-20). The opponents were blaspheming (v 20) as Paul did before his Damascus road experience (→ 1:13).

Several verbal links connect these verses with Paul's earlier argument. Verse 18 resumes the concern about the opponents mentioned in v 7. Paul made two digressions from this topic, both critical to the overall thought of the chapter. First, he defined sound doctrine over against the abuse of the Law by the so-called teachers (vv 8-11). Second, to illustrate what sound doctrine looks like and what affect it has, he provided a personal testimony of the change Christ made in his life, from a blasphemer, persecutor, and violent man, to a sinner saved by grace and filled with love and faith (vv 12-17).

Paul then "commands" (*parangelia*) Timothy, as he did in v 3, to apply this teaching with faithfulness. As a metaphorical soldier in the "battle" for the true gospel (v 18), Timothy's primary weapons will be faith and a good conscience. These are two of the key components of the goal Paul outlined in v 5.

When considered with the earlier context of Christ's mercy toward Paul (vv 12-16), Paul's condemnation of apostates should not be read as a hopeless situation. He implies that they can be salvaged, as he was. It will be Timothy's responsibility to present clearly the message of the gospel so that (1) those in the church can discern truth from falsehood and (2) those who have wandered away can have their own consciences pricked in order to return to the faith.

Thus, Paul's command is again out of love (v 5). Timothy is to carry out the same task Paul had throughout his ministry. Paul joins Timothy to this narrative of redemption by reminding him of God's faithfulness in fulfilling his promises to Timothy spoken through prophecies. Timothy is not alone in what he needs to do because he has the eternal King, the "immortal, invisible," and "only God" with him (v 17).

IN THE TEXT

■ **18** The letter again addresses the recipient by name. Paul's paternalistic vocative allows him to shift to the second-person singular **you** to address Timothy directly. This is the second time (v 2) Paul has called Timothy **son** (lit. *child* [*teknon*]). In both instances, **my**, missing in Greek, is supplied by modern translators to reflect the intimacy assumed in this letter.

Paul speaks in the present tense: **I am giving you this command**. This suggests the urgency of the task at hand. *Paratithemai* refers to entrusting something for safekeeping to give to others (BDAG 2000, 772). Paul had entrusted Timothy with the message of the gospel (2 Tim 1:13; 1 Cor 4:17). As the first generation of leaders passed away, it became vital for the next generation to take up the task of preserving orthodoxy (Mounce 2000, 65).

What **this command** entails is not stated here. But the context suggests that it refers to all the exhortations Paul has given to this point. He is passing on to Timothy the "command" he himself had received from "God our Savior and . . . Christ Jesus our hope" (1:1). This is not a direct command in the Greek imperative mood, but an indirect order based on the persuasive power of his letter, his personal relationship with Timothy, and the urgency of the situation.

Paul offers himself as an example of staying true to one's calling. He urges Timothy to do the same in Ephesus. He invites Timothy to recall **the prophecies once made** about him. He does not say what these prophecies were. But since he referred to his call to ministry, he probably means Timothy's similar call (Acts 16:2-4; → 1 Tim 4:14; 2 Tim 1:6).

Paul writes, not on the basis of his own authority, but based on (1) his own testimony, (2) the truth of the gospel (sound doctrine), and (3) divine prophecies about Timothy. He reminds Timothy that the task before him is not Paul's directive but comes through the Holy Spirit (Fee 1988, 57).

So that (*hina*) introduces a clause that gives the key to Timothy's success in his task in Ephesus. Success comes **by recalling** the prophecies. Obedience to these prophecies is assumed by the indirect exhortation of 1 Tim 1:18-19. Timothy's motive ought to be like a soldier on a mission: **that . . . you may fight the battle well**. Similar military imagery in other Pauline letters encourages believers against struggles with opponents or spiritual forces (→ 6:12; 2 Cor 6:7; 10:3-4; Eph 6:11-17; Phil 2:25).

The adversaries in this fight include Satan, Hymenaeus, and Alexander (1 Tim 1:20). This list might be expanded to include those who teach false doctrine (vv 3-4, 6-7) and those who break the law (vv 9-10). The sole weapon in the battle is the truth of the gospel (vv 5, 15). It may be a difficult struggle, but it is worth the pain and suffering. The NIV treats the adjective *kalēn*, **well** as an adverb modifying the verb **fight**. Other translations understand this adjective to describe the type of fight Timothy is in. In this sense, the "good" fight is one that is a noble and worthy undertaking.

■ **19** This verse continues v 18 with an instrumental participle **holding** (*echōn*), expressing how Timothy can be faithful to his calling: he must continue to embrace (present tense) two essential qualities of the spiritual life.

First, **faith** (*pistis*) appears twice in this verse (and frequently elsewhere in the chapter: vv 2, 4, 5, 14, 19). The first has no article, referring to faith as the act of believing. A key characteristic of the Christian life (→ 4:12; 2 Tim 1:5; 2:22; 3:10), faith is the appropriate human response to divine revelation (Matt 17:20; 21:21; Acts 14:9; Rom 14:23; 1 Cor 13:2). The second occurrence has an article and refers to the faith as the authentic content of the Christian gospel.

In the NT, **faith** has an object; it is not simply intellectual assent. "Generally, *pistis* expresses the proper alignment of the individual with Christ and the message about him" (Towner 1989, 146). What Timothy needs most as he deals with problems in Ephesus is to trust God completely. If his faith were to grow weak because of the opposition he faced, he might be unable to complete his mission.

Second, Timothy needs **a good conscience** to guide him through the murky waters of false doctrines making inroads in the Ephesian church. **A good conscience** is paired with **faith** also in 1 Tim 1:5; 3:9; and 4:6-16. It will confirm that his faith is being lived out. "The 'good conscience' is an ethical description of what the Spirit does within the believer to apprehend God's law" (Towner 2006, 158). Timothy must stay spiritually healthy to deal with the sickness infecting the church.

The main problem in Ephesus is that **some have rejected** faith and conscience. Paul strongly warns Timothy about the dangers of rejecting these assets. The pronoun **which** refers specifically to **conscience**, but the basis for a healthy conscience is a strong and obedient faith. The opposite is also true: Weak faith comes from rejecting one's conscience.

The participle *apōsamenoi*, **have rejected**, is instrumental. It shows how the opponents **suffered shipwreck**. Their disaster was the result of not simply ignorance but active rebellion. The aorist tense implies that their ruin had already occurred. The consequences are becoming evident within the church, which explains why Paul wrote. The opponents had turned from a gospel of mercy and grace to speculation about the Law. They could not discern the Spirit's leading because of their rebellion (→ 4:2). The visible consequences of rejecting sound doctrine led to a trajectory of ungodliness illustrated in 1:9-10.

The result of this rejection is suffering **shipwreck with regard to the faith.** Paul knew firsthand the danger of shipwrecks, having been in several himself (Acts 27:27-44; 2 Cor 11:25). This vivid image ought to create a sense of danger about the potential for destruction that comes to those who abandon orthodoxy. The imagery implies that at one time, the opponents were on the right course. As Wesley notes, "Indeed, none can make shipwreck of faith who never had it" (1813, 222).

The Greek article with the second occurrence of **faith** could be equivalent to a personal pronoun: they have shipwrecked their own faith. Or, it could broadly refer to the Christian faith. By damaging their own faith, they caused harm to the faith of others. Thus, they brought disrepute to the Christian faith (Mounce 2000, 67).

■ **20** Paul concludes this chapter with two examples of people who shipwrecked their faith. They represent the danger to others in the Ephesian church who follow false doctrine. This verse continues the Greek sentence begun with v 18, showing a clear connection between the cause and effect of rejecting orthodoxy. The specific names show that this is not only a theoretical possibility but a present danger. **Among them** (*hōn*) identifies **Hymenaeus and Alexander** as among those who have rejected faith and conscience. Beyond their names, we know nothing further about these two heretics. But Timothy and the Ephesians probably recognized the names (for other NT Alexanders, see Mark 15:21; Acts 4:6; 19:33; 2 Tim 4:14-15). The Hymenaeus mentioned in 2 Tim 2:17 could be the same person as here.

Paul **handed** these two men **over to Satan. Satan** and his forces were the key adversaries of the church in Ephesus (3:7; 4:1; 5:15; 2 Tim 2:26). This closing statement poses several interpretive problems:

First, in what sense can Paul "hand over" (*paredōka* from *paradidōmi*, "deliver" or "give over") these men to Satan? The context of this verse assigns the verb a negative connotation. The loving correction Paul advocates in 1 Tim 1:5 would do no good for these two men, who appear to be set in their deviation from the truth. Neither Paul nor Timothy could do anything more to return them to the faith. Their ships had already crashed on the rocks (→ v 19). Paul could only let them struggle on until they realized the error of their ways. He acted with spiritual authority and discernment in a rather harsh and desperate way to correct the situation.

Second, isn't giving someone over to the enemy a cruel punishment? This could be interpreted negatively—that Paul assigned these men to hell. The final purpose (*hina*) clause, however, implies a positive, redemptive purpose: **to be taught not to blaspheme**. The handing over was intended as restorative discipline. His ultimate goal was to help these men realize the implications of their blasphemy, repent, and learn not to blaspheme anymore (compare 1 Cor 5:5; 2 Cor 2:5-11)

Some early church fathers saw the idea of handing over to Satan as a form of excommunication (Gorday 2000, 150). Excommunication was a strategy Paul reserved for extreme situations. The motive for church discipline ought always to be love. Paul did not wish the damnation of these two men. He expelled them from the community to teach them the error of their ways.

The Greek verb translated **to be taught** (*paideuthōsin*) sometimes occurs in the context of discipline (1 Cor 11:32; 2 Cor 6:9; Heb 12:10; Rev 3:19). This learning could come in several forms. On a more personal level, their consciences might be pricked and the spark of faith reignited. This could be helped along by the void and emptiness that would result when they leave fellowship with God and the church community. Their shame may enliven their consciences and draw them back into the community in repentance (compare 2 Thess 3:14).

Hymenaeus' and Alexander's problem was blaspheming (→ 1 Tim 1:13). **To blaspheme** is to reject the leading of the conscience and faith. These two offenders are examples of people caught up in speculations about controversial subjects (vv 3-4), who replace the truth of the gospel with opinions.

FROM THE TEXT

The situation in Ephesus called for strong measures. By this point in his ministry, Paul had seen enough troubles from false teachings to know that he needed to intervene. He sent Timothy to correct those in Ephesus who had strayed from the truth and were in danger of leading others away with them. Such issues still face churches today.

First, *God will call faithful witnesses to lead in preserving the faith.* Timothy had received a special calling in the form of prophecies. Not all leaders in the church will experience such a calling into ministry. Every situation is unique.

But those who do sense a call to guide the people of God ought to respond in faithfulness. What God calls us to do he will enable us to perform. God will do his part, but we must respond in faithful obedience.

Paul urges Timothy at the close of this chapter to remain faithful to the task before him. He could do this by (1) remembering the calling God placed on his life long ago and (2) remaining steadfast to the faith. This entailed obedience to the leadership of the Spirit upon his conscience. God would give the grace, but Timothy needed to remain faithful.

Second, *true doctrine must be preserved and false teachers warned and rejected.* One of the key themes of this chapter is obedience to orthodoxy. Hymenaeus and Alexander had wandered away from the truth and had blasphemed God by rejecting God's leading on their consciences. As a result, they had wrecked their faith and possibly that of others. Faith and a good conscience go hand in hand. Forsaking one leads to the loss of the other. The danger in Ephesus was that the false teachers could draw others away from the truth. The situation was so urgent that Paul gave them over to Satan so they would see their errors and return to the true faith.

One of the most difficult tasks for anyone in leadership is to balance church discipline and gracious forgiveness (Matt 18:15-17; 1 Cor 5:5; 2 Cor 2:5-11; 2 Thess 3:14-15). Paul could appeal to a social force sadly lacking in some contexts today—shame. He considered shunning one away from fellowship enough to awaken the conscience. But sometimes, a person must hit the darkness of the bottom to realize how precious the light is. The community of believers is vital to preserving the faith, disciplining the wayward, and restoring the repentant.

Third, *no one is too far gone to be beyond the reach of divine mercy.* Even after handing the two flagrant offenders over to Satan, Paul is optimistic that they might see their errors and learn not to blaspheme. His own life as the "chief of sinners" illustrates the power of God's grace to transform the sinner into a saint.

Timothy was to approach the opponents in Ephesus with both compassionate love (1 Tim 1:5) and strong conviction (v 19). There may be desperate times when love needs to be "tough," but the arms of grace ought always to be open. Sometimes the only way to balance the two is with deep conviction that comes through a strong faith and a conscience tuned to the Spirit's guidance.

III. BEHAVIOR AND LEADERSHIP WITHIN GOD'S FAMILY: I TIMOTHY 2:1—3:16

BEHIND THE TEXT

In ch 1, Paul exhorted Timothy to deal with the false teachings infiltrating the church in Ephesus. In ch 2, he begins to give specific directions on how to do this. This chapter poses significant interpretive challenges, but also has important implications for the church today. Many of the issues revolve around the intersection of church and culture and how believers should live out their faith in Christ.

Paul encourages Timothy to begin his intervention by praying for the salvation of all people. Prayer is not the main theme but "the stage upon which Paul bases his teaching on the topic of salvation" (Mounce 2000, 76). The setting of this prayer appears to be public worship, though most of what is said could apply to private devotion. The prayer has the specific goal of supporting "the church's universal mission to the world" (Towner 2006, 163).

99

The issues of ch 2 are no longer focused on Timothy and the opponents. Neither is specifically mentioned. Paul's concerns broaden to include the entire church. Over against the false teachings of the opponents (1:3-4, 6-7), Paul begins to set out correct doctrine with optimism in God's grace to transform any sinner into a saint.

There has been some debate whether the section should end with 2:7 or 2:8. Verse 8 continues the theme of prayer, but it is grammatically linked with v 9, which shifts to issues related to women. Chapter 3 begins a new section dealing with overseers. Behind both chs 2 and 3 stands the major theme of strengthening the church through faithfulness to the gospel. This is done while bearing witness to the gospel in the surrounding culture.

The word "all" is used six times (vv 1 [twice], 2 [twice], 4, 6), stressing the *universal* call to prayer for *all* people to experience salvation in Christ. This section can be divided into four parts (Towner 2006, 164):

1. The command to pray is given (vv 1-2).
2. Prayer for *all* is grounded in God's will to save *all* (vv 3-4).
3. God's will to save *all* is given theological backing (vv 5-6*a*). Transition: witnessed at the proper time (v 6*b*).
4. Paul's mission is linked to God's will to save *all* (v 7).

Verses 5-6 form a brief creedal statement. There has been some discussion, but no consensus, on the structure of the statement or its source: Did Paul create this, or is he quoting an early Christian creed or hymn?

One of the challenging background issues of this passage is the relation of church and state. Paul urges Timothy and the Ephesians to pray "for kings and all those in authority" (v 2). Idol worship and emperor adoration were problems in Ephesus and most other cities of the Roman Empire. As Christianity moved away from the protected umbrella of Judaism, both sanctioned and unofficial persecution increased. The issue became, how should believers live in the face of such animosity? The false teachers may have been preaching an overrealized eschatology that led to asceticism and a separation from the culture around them (→ 1 Tim 4:1-5). Paul urges engagement with culture that begins with prayer.

A. Prayer for the Salvation of All People (2:1-7)

IN THE TEXT

■ **1** The transition **then** (*oun*) suggests that this new section continues to deal with how Timothy is to respond to the heretical teachers mentioned in ch 1. Paul begins to give the practical steps Timothy should take to resolve the problems in Ephesus and to build a strong and effective church. *Oun* is often used with the word **urge** (*parakalō*) in exhortations at key turning points in Paul's letters (Rom 12:1; 1 Cor 4:16; Eph 4:1). Urge recalls 1 Tim 1:3, where the past tense of the same word is used, and resumes the exhortation begun in 1:18, though a different word is used there (*parangelian*).

First of all could be taken as either first in a sequence or in priority of importance. But since this is the first specific exhortation to Timothy after the introductory thoughts of ch 1, it probably stresses prayer as the highest priority. God must be looked to as the author of change in Ephesus. The way to access this change is through prayer, and this prayer has a specific goal: the salvation of all.

The placement of this topic at the beginning indicates its importance in Paul's thinking. He modeled praying for others, often beginning his letters by mentioning his constant prayers for the churches (Rom 1:10; Eph 1:16; Phil 1:4; Col 1:3; 1 Thess 1:2 ; 2 Tim 1:3; Phlm 4). What he urges is given with four words for prayer. The unstated "subject" of the passive infinitive is the church: *I urge you all to make these prayers*.

The rhetorical repetition of almost synonymous words for prayer gives a more comprehensive list of what Timothy ought to do. Such grouping is a Semitic literary device that adds breadth to the idea of prayer (Mounce 2000, 79). Because the terms are closely related, it is difficult to use these verses alone to differentiate types of prayers. Together, they provide an inclusive view of how believers ought to pray for others. Each of the terms is in the plural, implying that this is to be done repeatedly by the congregation.

Petitions (*deēseis*) are intercessory prayers made in behalf of others for specific needs (Greeven 1964, 40-41). This word appears twelve times in Paul's letters (→ 1 Tim 5:5 and 2 Tim 1:3). In Phil 1:4 petitions are to be accompanied with "joy"; in 2 Cor 1:11 and Phil 4:6, with "thanksgiving." Prayer requests ought to be given with an attitude of gratitude because of the one to whom the prayer is addressed (Rom 10:1; 2 Cor 9:14; Eph 6:18; Phil 1:4, 19).

Prayers (*proseuchas*) is the most common term for prayer in the NT (122 times, of these 22 are in Paul's letters) and can include all forms of prayer. It often occurs with *deēsis*, as in 1 Tim 5:5, Eph 6:18, and Phil 4:6. God is always the one addressed in these prayers.

Intercession (*enteuxeis*) occurs only in 1 Timothy (here and 4:5 ["prayer" in the NIV]). In secular literature, it identifies a formal petition or appeal to a higher power (Bauernfeind 1972, 238-45). In the present context, the term implies that believers can come boldly before God to ask for the salvation of all people.

Thanksgiving (*eucharistias*) refers to a prayer of gratitude to God. It appears in Paul's prayer reports that introduce many of his letters (Rom 1:8; 1 Cor 1:4; Phil 1:3; Col 1:3; 1 Thess 1:2; 2 Thess 1:3; Phlm 4). Three time aspects appear in prayers of thanksgiving: remembering past actions of God, expressing confidence in the present situation, and displaying hope in the promises of God. Paul reminds believers that "requests are made always in the context of conscious expressions of thanksgiving" (Knight 1992, 115). Prayer should be saturated with thanksgiving because it strengthens one's faith in God (Col 2:7).

These prayers are to be made **for all people**. *Anthrōpōn* is a more inclusive term used in the NT to designate humanity as a race, versus the more specific gender terms "man" (*andras*) or "woman" (*gynaikas*) found in 1 Tim 2:8-10. The word is repeated in v 5 referring to Jesus' humanity (→ v 5). That these prayers should be made for **all** shows the universal scope of grace. Paul believed people of all walks of life could be included in the church (Rom 15:1; 1 Cor 9:22; 2 Cor 5:19; Gal 3:28; Col 3:11). No one is to be excluded from our prayers, not even those who cause hardship (Matt 5:44; Rom 12:14).

■ **2** Paul now gives an example of the "all" of 1 Tim 2:1 by repeating the preposition **for** (*hyper*), which has two objects: **kings** and **those in authority**.

First, prayers ought to be offered for **kings** (*basileōn*). This plural noun with no article suggests a wider reference than the emperor; there were local rulers in many places, especially in Palestine (such as the Herods in Mark 6:14 and Acts 12:1).

Second, Paul urged prayer for *all who are in authority*. This would include all those in civil authority under kings, such as governors and appointed or elected leaders. In the first century, both such leaders were in the upper strata of society.

Early Christians continued the Jewish practice of regularly praying for secular leaders (Ezra 6:9-10; Bar 1:11; 1 Macc 7:33; Philo, *Flacc.* 524; *Leg.* 157, 317; Josephus, *J.W.* 2.17.1). Israel recognized that God is sovereign and can use even pagan leaders to accomplish his will (Isa 7:18-20; 13:4-5; 45:1; Jer 25:9; Towner 2006, 166). Government is part of God's plan to maintain order in the world. Both Paul and Peter commanded early Christians to submit to governing authorities (Rom 13:1; Titus 3:1; 1 Pet 2:13-17).

One key difference distinguished Jews and Christians from their pagan neighbors: They were to pray *for* the emperor, not *to* him. The latter practice was common in the emperor cults of the time (Collins 2002, 53). Because God is "the King of kings and Lord of lords" (→ 1 Tim 6:15), believers need not fear rulers. Instead, we can pray for their salvation because they govern under God's sovereignty.

The reason Paul specifies this group is given in a purpose clause (*hina*): **that we may live**. The verb *diagōmen* with the noun *bion* here refers to how one spends one's earthly life (BDAG 2000, 227)—one's lifestyle (Mounce 2000, 82). The first-person plural could include both believers, who are urged to live godly lives, and those to whom they witness. Paul assumes that if the government is stable and doing its job of maintaining a peaceful and just social order, Christians will be free to share the gospel (1 Thess 4:11-12; → Titus 3:1-2).

The *life* lived in a stable political situation can be **peaceful** (*ēremon*) and **quiet** (*hēsychion*). *Ēremon* describes situations that are quiet, tranquil, and free from outside trouble. Paul knew firsthand how important a peaceful situation was to the spread of the gospel (Acts 13:50-51; 14:5-20; 16:19-21, 39, 40; 17:8-10, 13-14; 19:23-41; 21:31-32).

Hēsychion and *ēremon* are synonyms. In 1 Pet 3:4 *hēsychion* describes the inner tranquility of Christian wives, who witness through their quiet lives to their unbelieving husbands. In 1 Tim 2:11-12, it describes how women can put themselves in readiness to learn. "A Christian's life is not to be quiet of speech, but it should be quiet in nature, a tranquility stemming from a godly and reverent life" (Mounce 2000, 82-83).

Paul describes how this lifestyle is possible in an adverbial prepositional phrase: **in all godliness and holiness**. Godliness (*eusebeia*) is an important term appearing thirteen times in the Pastoral Epistles, and nine of these are in 1 Timothy (2:2; 3:16; 4:7, 8; 5:4; 6:3, 5, 6, 11). In Hellenistic culture it described an attitude of respect toward elders, the dead, one's homeland, rulers, authorities, and of slaves to masters. In the LXX it translates the Hebrew *yirat* in Isa 11:2, 33:6, and Prov 1:7, expressing the reverential awe due Yahweh. The "fear of the LORD" leads to observable conduct consistent with the holiness of God. In the NT, God is always the focus of this word.

Godliness comes from knowing and obeying God (1 Tim 6:3, 5, 6, 11; Titus 1:1). The death and resurrection of Christ Jesus is the source of godliness by the salvation he provides (1 Tim 3:16). Faith in him, expressed in active obedience, leads to godliness (Phil 2:12-13; 1 Tim 4:7-10; 6:5; 2 Tim 3:5).

Godliness is used by Paul only in the Pastorals. It may have been employed by the false teachers to describe their religious disciplines. Their form of godliness misunderstood its substance (→ 2 Tim 3:5; see Towner 2006, 174). The concept of reverence for deity would have been familiar to most Ephesians. *Eusebeia* was an important aspect of Artemis worship in Ephesus (Trebilco 2004, 19-30). Paul uses the antonym *asebeia* to malign the opponents in 1 Tim 1:9; 2 Tim 2:16; and Titus 2:12.

Holiness (*semnotēti*) refers to respectability, seriousness, appropriateness, reverence, propriety, or dignity. It involves worship and respect for the holy (LXX of Prov 8:6; 15:26). This type of behavior is outward and observable. One's inner relationship with God ought to influence one's outer relations with others. It is a quality of life that is contagious as a witness. The resource for holiness is God's work in Christ (Titus 2:2). The noun appears

2:2

here, in 3:4, and in Titus 2:7; the adjective (*semnos*) appears in 1 Tim 3:8, 11, and Titus 2:2.

Both **godliness** and **holiness** were common terms in pagan ethics. Paul expressed "the theology of a dynamic Christian ethics by means of the language of the day" (Towner 2006, 169). By living godly lives, believers make the gospel more appealing to leaders and the rest of society. Both terms are emphasized by **all** (*pasē*), stressing that these activities should penetrate every aspect of life. Believers should be prepared, however, for animosity as their lifestyle comes in conflict with the world around them (→ 2 Tim 3:11-12).

Christians and Civil Authorities

The first century AD was a time of peace known as the Pax Romana (the "Peace of Rome"). The Emperor Augustus (reigned 27 BC to AD 14) initiated a time of peace in the empire that lasted until AD 180. This time was marked by political unity, rule of law, economic development, prosperity, and ease of travel. Various people groups and provinces experienced opportunity for localized administration. The growth of the early church was assisted by this peace and stability.

How Christians relate to governing authorities has been a matter of discussion and challenge since the early church. Jesus respected Roman authority to tax (Matt 22:21). Paul urged the church in Rome to pay their taxes and respect the governing authorities because God established them to uphold justice (Rom 13:1-7). Political power is a gift of God. Titus 3:1-2 implies that there is a saving purpose in our respect for authorities. Christians ought to be model citizens wherever they live. Heinrich Julius Holtzmann famously described this as a status quo, "bourgeois ethic" (*bürgerliche Ethik*): "The civic life is the sphere in which the inner Christian life is outwardly expressed as Christianity in the world" (1880, 307).

■ **3-4** Here Paul explains the reason why Christians should pray for all people. He offers the theological foundation and core motivation for petitioning God in behalf of others. The pronoun **this** refers back to the prayers offered in vv 1-2. Since God desires everyone to be saved, it is **good** that we pray for all.

Pleases (*apodektos*) appears only here and in 1 Tim 5:4 in the NT. It means something that is welcomed and accepted. *Dektos* in the LXX has a cultic sense—a sacrifice acceptable to God (Lev 1:3-4; 17:4; 20:20-21). In the NT, it refers to "spiritual" sacrifices (Rom 15:16; Phil 4:18; 1 Pet 2:5; Grundmann 1964a, 58-59). The sacrifice God wants is prayer aligned with his will and the reason Christ came into the world: to save all people.

These prayers are to be offered *before God our Savior*. The claim of God as Savior (→ 1:1) directly challenged the Imperial cult. In the context of prayer for civil authorities, Paul reminds Timothy (and the Ephesians) that God is the source of salvation, not the emperor, Artemis, or any other.

God's will expresses God's identity. **Who wants** (*thelei*) begins a relative clause with two infinitives that give a glimpse into the character of God. *Thelei* ("desire," "intend") should be interpreted with the full sense of God's purpose and design (Gal 1:4; Eph 1:5, 9; 2 Tim 1:9; Titus 1:2). Both infinitives share the same subject, **all people** (*pantas*).

First, God wants all people **to be saved** (*sōthēnai*). Paul described salvation in his testimony in 1 Tim 1:12-16. Both God (1 Tim 1:1; 2:3; Titus 1:3; 2:10; 3:4) and Christ (2 Tim 1:10; Titus 1:4; 2:13) are called Savior in the Pastoral Epistles. God acted through the agency of Christ to offer salvation to the lost world (2 Cor 5:19). Salvation begins in this life (1 Tim 6:12-15; 2 Tim 4:6-8; Titus 2:11-14) but will be fully realized only in the future (1 Tim 2:15; 4:16; 2 Tim 3:15). The means of salvation is the ransom paid through Christ's death (→ 1 Tim 2:6).

The **all** should not be taken as universalism (that all will someday be saved) nor as election (that only certain people will be saved). Neither can be supported from this passage. Rather, the emphasis is on the universal access to the salvation offered by God (Towner 1989, 84). God, the source of salvation, requires humans to accept this through faith (1:16; 3:16; 4:10). The aorist tense implies the necessity of this decisive decision.

Paul may be countering Ephesian sectarianism, which may have focused too much on speculation about the Law and possibly was indifferent to the salvation of outsiders. God intended salvation not just for Jews, but for all people (Rom 3:27-31; 11:26-32; Gal 3:28; 2 Pet 3:9). Since Christ died for all, all should be the object of Christian prayer.

Second, God wants all people: **to come to a knowledge of the truth**. The aorist tense of this infinitive (*elthein*) also calls for the same type of decision as the first. Two words here deserve comment:

The word **knowledge** (*epignōsis*) with the verb **to come** (*erchomai*) forms an idiom for acquiring new information (Louw and Nida 1996, 27.4). In the Pastorals, knowledge is always associated with the truth (1 Tim 2:4; 4:3; 2 Tim 2:25; 3:7; Titus 1:1). Knowledge for Paul is experiential (Eph 1:17; 4:13; Phil 1:9; Col 1:9-10; 3:10). One moves from ignorantly embracing falsehood to accepting the truth about God. "Conversion" captures the change implied.

The second important word, **truth** (*alētheias*), is the object of this knowledge (→ 2 Tim 2:25; 3:7; Titus 1:1). **Truth** (fourteen times in the Pastorals) is the content of the gospel (2 Cor 4:2; 6:7; 13:8; Gal 5:7; Eph 1:13; Col 1:5; 2 Thess 2:10-12; → 1 Tim 4:10). Paul uses "truth" as a polemic against what readers ought to recognize as false (Towner 2006, 179). The opponents had distorted the truth and corrupted people's minds (1 Tim 6:5) by teaching myths (2 Tim 4:4; Titus 1:14) and that the resurrection had already happened (2 Tim 2:18).

Coming to know the gospel can lead to faith in Christ. Faith in the wrong message is not saving. Paul does not advocate knowledge as salvation. Instead, he offers the false teachers an opportunity to accept the truth as he preached it and escape the consequences of their current path to destruction.

■ **5-6** These two verses are one sentence in Greek and appear in the form of a simple creed. They are significant in the context of the letter and provide a glimpse into Paul's Christology. Whether these are Paul's own words written for this specific occasion or he is quoting an early hymn or primitive confession of faith is unknown. The words are consistent with Jesus' words in Matt 20:28 (Mark 10:45) and agree with early church tradition (1 Cor 11:23-26; 15:3-5). Each line is important to Paul's larger argument and consistent with his preaching (Rom 3:21-30; Gal 1:4; 2:20; Eph 5:22, 25; Titus 2:14).

The opening **for** (*gar*) links the prayer for all in 1 Tim 2:3-4 with the creed in vv 5-6. Within the creed, there is a move from the source of salvation to its means.

The creed opens with a statement that there is only **one God**, an idea consistent with the core Jewish belief confessed in the Shema of Deut 6:4: "Hear, O Israel: The LORD our God, the LORD is one." First-century Jews, especially those of the Diaspora, lived in the midst of pagan polytheism. The early church developed in this same context and went on to flourish in syncretistic environments like Ephesus.

The logic of this whole section can be briefly summarized: Since there is one God who created all things and wants to save all people, it is appropriate and consistent with God's character to pray for the salvation of all people. "Since there is only one God and not several, there can therefore only be one way of salvation" (Marshall 1999, 429).

The essence of this hope is captured in the next line: There is **one mediator between God and mankind, the man Christ Jesus.** The NT consistently states that salvation comes only through Jesus (John 14:6; Acts 4:12; Rom 3:21-30; Gal 2:15-16; 3:8, 14). He is the **mediator** (*mesitēs*), go-between, or negotiator who brings two alienated parties together in relationship (Oepke 1967a, 599; compare 1 John 2:1—"advocate"). A mediator represents one party to another in a covenant (Heb 8:6; 9:15; 12:24). In order to be a representative of humanity, Christ identified with human weakness while at the same time being victorious over sin through total obedience to the Father. Through the incarnation, he became one with those whom he came to save (→ 1 Tim 3:16). He was the perfect image of God (Col 1:15) and the only adequate and sinless ransom (2 Cor 5:21). No one else has ever met this requirement.

Anthrōpos **(the man)** occurs four times in this section (1 Tim 2:1, 4, 5 [twice]). When it is used for Christ this final time, it has no article, empha-

106

sizing the quality of being human (Wallace 1996, 244). Christ's humanity particularly qualified him to be a mediator (Heb 4:15).

The next line shows that Paul has in mind a particular point of Christ's life—his death on the cross (Rom 8:3; Gal 4:4-5; Phil 2:7-8; 1 Tim 1:15; Heb 2:14). The reciprocal pronoun **himself** (*heauton*) points to his voluntary self-giving.

Christ Jesus gave his life as a **ransom** (*antilytron*), a rare word occurring only here in the NT. The Greek word is a compound of the preposition *anti* ("instead of" or "in the place of") followed by the root *lytron*, which refers to the price paid to free captives or buy freedom. The use of the preposition implies substitution. Christ served as an "exchange price" (Guthrie 1990, 86) by giving himself to free humanity from the power and penalty of sin (Rom 6:6; 8:32; Gal 1:4; 2:20; Eph 5:2). This word is similar to the more frequent *apolytrōsis*, "redemption" (Rom 3:24; 8:23; 1 Cor 1:30; Eph 1:7; Col 1:14). In Matt 20:28 (Mark 10:45), Jesus said that he came to give his life as a "ransom" for many. According to Titus 2:14, he gave himself "to redeem us from all wickedness and to purify for himself a people that are his very own, eager to do what is good."

The ransom Christ paid was **for all people**. The preposition **for** (*hyper*) can mean "on behalf of" (representation) or "in the place of" (substitution). It connects the optimism in praying for all people with the salvation possible because of Christ's mediation through the shedding of his blood. The result of mediation is reconciliation for those who accept his offer of mercy (2 Cor 5:17-21).

The awkward syntax of the final line of the creed makes it appear isolated, an afterthought. But on closer examination, this line functions as a link between Christ's death in the previous line and Paul's ministry described in the next verse. Literally, it reads, *the witness [at the] proper times* (*to martu-rion kairois idios*). Ancient scribes and modern translators insert words to make the statement more understandable.

For example, the NIV gives, **This has now been witnessed to at the proper time**. It is difficult to determine what or who the witness is. It could be that the entire creed bears witness to God's plan of salvation. Or, it could point more specifically to the defining historical event of Jesus' death on the cross. The Greek article (*to*) before **witness** would indicate that *the evidence* of God's plan of salvation was that Jesus gave himself as a redeeming sacrifice.

This "testimony" of love (Eph 5:1) took place **at the proper time** (*kairos*; → 1 Tim 6:15; Titus 1:3). At a certain point in history, God's plan of salvation came to fruition. Since the word **time** is plural, there is some question whether it refers to the singular event of Jesus' first coming or also his second coming

(Knight 1992, 124). The preceding reflection on Christ's sacrifice as a human being makes it likely that Paul has in mind the cross event.

This creedal statement stands in strong contrast to any claims of divinity by the emperor. It counteracts any sectarianism of the opponents. The reason the Ephesians ought to be engaged in prayer is so they can be participants with the work of Christ on the cross, since "not to pray for everyone is to treat the death of Christ with contempt" (Mounce 2000, 89).

■ **7** The verse begins with a neuter pronoun *for which* (*eis ho*), connecting Paul's ministry to Gentiles to the universal claims of the gospel given in the earlier verses. His own life proves the truth of his message. The verb **appointed** is in the passive voice; God or Christ Jesus (1 Tim 2:5) was the implied actor. The passive indicates that this calling was not of Paul's choosing. The aorist tense could point back again to his Damascus road experience (→ 1:12-16; Acts 9:15; 22:15; 26:15-18). He often reflects on his calling when he mentions the work of Christ in his letters (2 Cor 5:18-20; Eph 3:7-8; Col 1:25; 1 Tim 1:11-12). The passage returns to the first person of 2:1, which is intensified by an untranslated *egō* (*I myself*). Three nouns (→ 2 Tim 1:11) describe Paul's appointment to ministry:

First, he was appointed a **herald** (*kēryx*). In the ancient world heralds made official public announcements. The noun form here is infrequent in the NT. But the verb (*kēryssō*) occurs nineteen times. The NT places more emphasis on the message, the *kērygma*, than the messenger. The word connotes Paul's missionary activity of evangelism. The term is closely related in meaning to *euangelizesthai*, "to proclaim good news" (Matt 4:23; 9:35; Rom 10:15; Gal 2:2; 1 Thess 2:9).

Second, Paul calls attention again (→ 1 Tim 1:1) to his role as an **apostle**. He was "sent" to proclaim the message about Jesus Christ. Some in Ephesus may have doubted his apostleship, since he was not one of the Twelve who followed Jesus during his earthly life. Paul faced similar criticism in other places (1 Cor 9:1-2; 2 Cor 11:5; 12:11-12; Gal 1—2). **Apostle** identifies not only his mission but also his authority. He was especially called to preach to **Gentiles** (Rom 11:13; Gal 2:8).

Before the last description, Paul interjects an oath: **I am telling the truth, I am not lying**. The threat of false teachings meant the stakes were high (compare Rom 9:1; 2 Cor 11:31; Gal 1:20). Unlike the opponents who had shipwrecked (or were in danger of doing so) their faith (→ 1 Tim 1:19), he had not rejected his calling but stayed the course and faithfully proclaimed the message God gave him (→ 2 Tim 4:7).

Third, Paul refers to his ministry as a **teacher**. He taught *in faith and truth* (*en pistei kai alētheia*). The NIV interprets *pistei* and *alētheia* as adjectives that describe him as a **true and faithful teacher**. However, these are actually nouns. They describe the contents of his teaching (ESV, NASB, NRSV). Faith leads to salvation (1 Tim 1:4, 14-16). It is built upon the truth of the gospel (2 Thess 2:13; Titus 1:1).

Teaching was apparently a problem in Ephesus (1 Tim 1:3, 7). So Paul contrasts the truth of the gospel he taught and the false doctrines and empty speculations taught by the opponents. He was a teacher of the truth (1 Cor 4:17; 2 Tim 1:11) and wanted Timothy to imitate him (1 Tim 4:11, 13; 6:2) and find others in the church qualified to teach it (2 Tim 2:2). Teaching was a gift of the Spirit and an office in the early church (1 Cor 12:28-29; Eph 4:11). Later in the letter, Paul sets out qualifications for those who would teach in the church (1 Tim 2:12; 3:2; 5:17; 6:3).

The recipients of Paul's teaching were **the Gentiles** (*ethōn*), lit. **nations**, a term used in the NT for non-Jews. He believed God had called him to take the message of Christ to the Gentiles (Rom 11:13; 15:16; Gal 2:7-9; Eph 3:1, 6-7). **Gentiles** here, with no article in the Greek, adds to the inclusivity of this whole section. Teaching **Gentiles** the truth of the gospel was how Paul ministered to "all people."

FROM THE TEXT

The false teachers were focusing on the fringes, which can always be debated. They had missed the heart of the issue, which is nonnegotiable. Paul corrects a narrow view about God's purposes in this world and calls Timothy to the core value of the salvation of all people.

The inclusiveness of prayer. Paul charges Timothy and the Ephesians to pray for the salvation of all people. Prayer is a mystery that connects us with the purposes of God. The very nature of God, described in vv 5-6, invites the type of prayer Paul urges here. Praying for all people changes our hearts and leads us to embrace the *missio dei*, because we align ourselves with the character of God our Savior.

The reach of the atonement. This passage makes a major contribution to our understanding of Jesus Christ and confirms the core conviction that he died for all people. This passage is one reason why Jacob Arminius (*Works* 1.3.18.4) and John Wesley proclaimed the doctrine of "free grace" vs. the Calvinist emphases on predestination and limited atonement. One of the texts Wesley used to support his understanding was 1 Tim 2:1-6 (Sermon 128, "Free Grace"). Wesleyans pray for the salvation of all people because we believe God can change anyone. If God could change Saul the persecutor (1:13-16) to Paul the preacher, apostle, and teacher (2:7), there is hope for everyone.

Becoming mediators within culture. The exclusive claims of the gospel confront a world full of pluralism, syncretism, and secularism. Paul knew firsthand the challenges of sharing the gospel in difficult, multicultural situations. He could fulfill his calling only as he connected with God's purposes in Christ. Jesus Christ became the bridge connecting God and all humanity. Paul became a bridge connecting Christ to the Gentile world (v 7). As we seek to become bridge builders in our contexts, the place to start is with prayer.

B. The Faithful Witness of Men and Women (2:8-15)

BEHIND 𝛂 THE TEXT

Verse 8 continues the general topic of prayer introduced in 2:1-3. But it moves from the topic of the prayers to the attitude people should have as they pray. What holds vv 8-15 together is the focus on public, communal worship. But Paul is obviously also concerned about how the church lives out its faith in Christ within the broader culture.

Women are the focus throughout vv 9-15. Verses 9-10 move beyond prayer, which is no longer mentioned, to emphasize how women ought to dress and their attitudes as good learners (vv 11-15). Verses 11-15 function as a parenthetical subunit emphasizing the submissiveness of women.

The behavior Paul advocates for Christians in this section and throughout the letter closely resembles the expectations of the best morality of the pagan culture of that time. We hear something similar today in the expression "family values."

Most Greco-Roman life in the first century revolved around the household (*oikos*). Ethicists taught that the household was the cornerstone of society and vital to the stability of the city-state. The typical household included a father, mother, children, slaves, various workers, and guests (for the classical view, see Aristotle, *Pol.* 1.1253b-1260b26). Each person had a role to play and a way to behave to insure the stability of the home.

Paul builds upon these concepts in his letters by appealing to familial imagery ("God's household" in 1 Tim 3:15) and expected behaviors within the home (Eph 5:22-33; Col 3:18—4:1; 1 Tim 5:1-2; 6:1-2, 17-19; Titus 2:1-8). Martin Luther referred to the Bible's instructions on family life as *Haustafeln* ("household tables")—codes or lists of rules that guided behavior in the home. *Haustafeln* has become a technical term in biblical studies and the concept widely studied.

Many of the challenging issues of the Pastoral Epistles can find some resolution when viewed against the traditional codes of conduct expected at that time. Paul was attempting to develop a new social order (Johnson 2001, 185-86) based in part on cultural expectations but transformed through the message of the gospel. Much of 1 Tim 2:1—6:2 reflects the intersection of the Greco-Roman culture and emerging early Christianity.

Paul may dwell on issues of the *oikos* because the opponents targeted the household, and in particular vulnerable women, contributing to an unstable social structure (→ 2 Tim 3:5-9; Towner 1989, 26-27). Women and slaves were apparently challenging the status quo and upsetting the social equilibrium. There were opportunities in Paul's day for women to move upward in Greco-Roman society. Upper-class women were especially gaining new freedoms (Meeks 2003, 23-24). Some of these new freedoms were not welcomed in the larger cultural context; they were viewed as threats to important and recognized social structures like the family. Still, there is no evidence in the letter that women were teaching heresy in Ephesus or that the false teachers were enlisting women to do so (Towner 1989, 39).

This is one of the more difficult and controversial passages in the entire NT. The scholarly and popular literature on this passage is immense and growing. And no consensus exists. Major studies reach markedly different conclusions.

In this commentary, I can do little more than survey the debate and critique the various approaches scholars have taken. I examine what the text clearly says and offer the major interpretive options when its meaning is disputed. We do not have enough information to be certain. So we must exercise caution in what we assume and conclude; many unavoidable biases are apt to enter into the interpretive process.

We approach this passage with generally accepted, sound interpretive methods and make explicit our assumptions. We consider the social and cultural background of both Paul as the author and of the Ephesians as the implied recipients. We consider the literary context of this passage within the larger concerns of the entire letter. Only after this careful reading do we go beyond the letter to consider other biblical passages.

Believing that "all Scripture is God-breathed" (2 Tim 3:16), we use the "rule of faith" to interpret this difficult text through clearer ones. Doctrine should never be built on controversial or obscure passages. A universal or timeless truth must be supported by all of Scripture. If it is not, the passage should be considered a timely, localized truth. Timeless truths guide localized applications in this and other passages.

Scripture was written within and to specific cultural settings. But it contains timeless truths that are applicable for all times and cultures. The mission of the church will be effective, in part, by how the church relates to social structures.

IN THE TEXT

■ **8** Most modern translations mark a new section with this verse by beginning a new paragraph. **Therefore** (*oun*) connects this verse to the topic of prayer in 2:1-7, but the theme is not what to pray for, but how to pray.

Both 2:1 and 8 begin with first person verbs expressing Paul's desire for prayer in the church: lit. "therefore I urge" and "therefore I want." There is a grammatical link between vv 8 and 9, with the opening verb **I want** (*boulomia*) serving as the main verb for both. This verb expresses Paul's strong desire and should be read fully aware of his apostolic authority just emphasized in v 7. This verb occurs three times in the Pastorals (here; → 5:14; Titus 3:8), always in the context of authority. Two groups are the targets of the verb: men and women.

Paul wants **men everywhere to pray**. The word for **men** (*tou andras*) is different from the one used in 1 Tim 2:1, 4, and 5 (*anthrōpos*) and specifically for Christ Jesus in v 5. *Andras* is translated "husband" in some contexts, but there is usually an indicator that the marital relationship is meant (Towner 2006, 201). Since this is lacking here and the issues are relevant to singles as well as married men, most interpreters take this as more generally applicable to all males.

Why does Paul direct only men to pray here? First, this verse does not preclude women from praying, since Paul gives directions elsewhere about how women should pray (see 1 Cor 11:5). He focuses instead on the specific problem of the attitudes of men in the church when they pray. Possibly in the background may be the Jewish synagogue practice of allowing only men to pray in public. The use of the plural form of "man" here may imply a public setting in which many people are involved in worship. In support of this, the directions Paul gives later in the letter about leadership roles in the public services address men (1:12; 3:2, 5; 4:11-16; 5:17).

Paul's command goes beyond the church in Ephesus, because it exhorts **men everywhere** (*en panti topōi*), repeating the inclusive theme of 2:1-7 and the optimism of "the universal access to God's grace" (Towner 1989, 205). What precisely Paul meant by **everywhere** is impossible to determine. Early believers publicly met in house churches, so minimally this includes any house church in Ephesus. However, prayer is not confined to a particular "place of prayer" or to only a few people. It is to be done by all believers everywhere. The issue here is neither who or where, but how.

The goal of Paul's instruction becomes clearer with a participle of manner explaining how prayers are to be offered: *by* **lifting up holy hands** (*epairontas*). The normal posture for praying in Scripture is standing with arms outstretched (1 Sam 1:26; 1 Kgs 8:22; Pss 28:2; 63:4; 77:2; 88:9; 134:2; 143:6; Isa 1:15; Lam 2:19). The Jews of Paul's day continued this practice. But the emphasis is not on the raised position of one's hands, but on the **holy** (*osious*) condition of those who pray.

The adjective *osious* is an ethical word that refers to moral righteousness. It describes God in Acts 2:27; 13:35; Heb 7:26; Rev 15:4; and 16:5. Hands symbolize here "the entirety of human life, including particularly the central inner dimensions of heart and mind" (Knight 1992, 129; Jas 4:8). Hands that are open and lifted have nothing to hide from God. Those who pray to a holy God must conduct themselves in a way that is acceptable and appropriate to a holy God (Mounce 2000, 108).

The specific behavior men who pray must avoid is given in a final prepositional phrase: **without anger or disputing. Anger** (*orgē*) is the emotional response of displeasure. It often ruins relationships. **Disputing** (*dialogismos*) can simply refer to reasoned discussion (BDAG 2000, 232). But if there is a strong difference of opinion, and if spurred on by anger, discussions can lead to quarrels. In such cases, there may be some underlying causes for grumbling that spill over into arguments (Phil 2:14). Anger creates barriers between people. Left unchecked, anger can become an obstacle between God and the angry person (Matt 5:23; 6:12, 14-15; Eph 4:26-27). Anger and an argumentative spirit divert us from our central concern—the salvation of all people.

■ **9-10** Most of what is described in these verses fits public prayer but can also be applied to Christian living in general. The **also** (*hōsautōs*, "likewise" [ESV, NASB]; "in the same way" [CEB]) connects these two verses with v 8 and the preceding section. Paul's simple message here seems to be that he wants men to pray (v 8) and women to dress (v 9) in appropriate ways. Although the activities are not the same, the attitudes and outcomes are similar (Knight 1992, 132). Women do not need permission to pray (1 Cor 11:2-16), but they must dress so as not to distract others from praying. Verse 9*a* of 1 Tim 2 provides a positive example of appropriate behavior; v 9*b* gives a negative example of behavior to avoid. Verse 10 offers the underlying principle, explaining why one should choose the positive and not the negative.

One of the interpretive issues of this passage is how to translate *gynē*—as "wives" or **women**. The word is translated both ways elsewhere in the NT, depending on the context. Here, as with "men" in v 8, nothing in vv 9-15 indicates that the appeal applies only to married people. Rather, what Paul urges in these verses can apply to women outside the home as well. The absence of an article preceding *gynē* also suggests a broader application (Fee 1988, 71). Paul is likely differentiating "men" and "women" from the "people" of vv 1-7.

The key behavior Paul wants women to practice is **to dress modestly**. The infinitive **to dress** (*kosmein*) actually comes later in v 9 after two prepositional phrases. The first phrase defines what women are to wear, literally *in modest clothing* (*en katastoleēi kosmiōi*). The noun *katastolē* occurs only here in the NT and refers to outward attire or manner of dress (BDAG 2000, 527). One's clothing represents one's behavior (Louw and Nida 1996, 49.14). We still assume this as applied to work and sports uniforms.

Kosmiō is related to the main infinitive of the verse, *kosmein*. This word group describes something that is neat, well organized, orderly, honorable,

2:9-10

and respected by others (BDAG 2000, 560). It is one of the characteristics expected of elders in 3:2, the only other occurrence of the adjective in the NT. When used of clothing, as here, it refers to clothes generally considered respectable and appropriate within the surrounding culture. Though clothing styles change, the essential quality remains: Christian women ought to wear respectable attire that matches the inner character of those ransomed by Christ (2:6).

This becomes clearer with the second prepositional phrase, which shows how to maintain modesty: **with decency and propriety**. Paul uses two terms those in the wider culture would understand. **Decency** (*aidous*, only here in the NT) refers to reverence and respect for others—refusing to cause them shame. Applied to clothing, it describes modest apparel—"appropriate for a specific person or situation" (Mounce 2000, 113).

Propriety (*sōphrosynēs*) is an important personal quality in the Pastorals and refers to good judgment, moderation, self-control, and the feminine virtue of decency and chastity (BDAG 2000, 987; 2 Tim 1:7; Titus 2:12; → 1 Tim 2:15; see also 1 Tim 3:2; Titus 1:9; 2:2, 5, 6, 9, 15).

In Hellenistic culture, modesty and self-control were among the most important virtues for women. These two terms often appear together in Greek literature. In the context of the ancient home and culture, *sōphrosynē* characterized modest wives who could protect the honor of their husbands by the way they dressed (Winter 2003, 101-2).

Paul's instructions next shift to negative examples (marked by *mē*). Women ought to avoid what goes against the standard just given: **not with elaborate hairstyles or gold or pearls or expensive clothes**. The type of hairstyle (*plegmasin*) meant here included pleating and braiding. Having braided hair itself was not the problem; it was a common practice. Elaborate hairstyles characterized fashionable and wealthy women of the first century who had slaves braid their hair using false hair, trinkets, and jewelry (Kelly 1963, 67). This practice originated in Rome in the imperial household. By the end of the first century, the latest styles involved elaborate curls, braids, high wigs, pins, and hair ornaments. Reigning empresses often appeared on coins in Asian cities like Ephesus and on prominent statues. Women looked to such figures for the latest styles (Baugh 1995, 35).

Gold has always been one of the most precious of metals. **Pearls** were costly and precious at that time (Matt 13:45-46; Rev 17:4). Both were difficult and costly to obtain but beautiful in appearance. Women who wore them drew attention to themselves. Courtesans and highly paid prostitutes used both. Women who wore these did not have the best reputations.

Expensive clothes were luxurious garments the wealthy wore. The philosophical schools of the time exhorted women to dress simply and modestly and to avoid such extravagant appearances (Juvenal, *Sat.* 6.492; Petronius, *Sat.* 67; Winter 2003, 104-8).

The problems of "elaborate hairstyles and the wearing of gold jewelry or fine clothes" also appear in 1 Pet 3:3. Some converts within the early church came from the upper economic levels of society. The mention of wealth in 1 Timothy (3:3, 8; 5:6; 6:9-10) implies that there were wealthy people in the Ephesian church. Evidently, some women could afford such luxury items. Their wealth and the lifestyle that went with it may have created problems within the church and hindered their witness among unbelievers (Knight 1992, 136; see Scholer 1986, 201-2).

Verse 10 shifts back to a positive example that broadens into the basic, underlying principle for how women ought to dress. The verse begins with a conjunction (*all'*) that sets up the major contrast between outward adornment that appeals to the senses and the better alternative of **good deeds**, the evidence of inward character that pleases God.

The syntax of this verse is awkward. The prepositional phrase **with good deeds** (*ergōn agathōn*) comes last in the Greek sentence but is put first in the NIV (and NRSV). The verse begins with a vague relative pronoun (*ho*): **what is fitting for women who profess godliness**. What behavior is fitting? Paul could point back to his emphasis on dressing modestly, leaving the details of dress code open-ended. Or, as the NIV implies, he could appeal to a broader principle of good deeds. So, what kind of behavior is **appropriate** (*prepei*)?

The attributive participle **who profess** (*epangellomenas*) in the middle voice refers to an announcement of a promise about oneself or one's intentions to others. Women make a public comment by the way they dress and act. The word translated **to worship God** (*theosebeia*, only here in the NT) refers to showing reverence for God, piety, or how one lives before God (BDAG 2000, 452).

Rather than having the latest hairstyles or being dressed in extravagant clothes, which only draw attention to themselves, Christian women ought to be known for their **good deeds**. Spiritual strength shown in how the women live is more important than their outward adornment.

The Greek preposition *dia* is used with **good deeds**. When followed by the genitive case, as here, it shows the means by which an action is done. In this case, this last phrase in the Greek sentence refers back to the infinitive **to dress**. Women ought to dress themselves metaphorically with good deeds.

Good deeds (*ergōn agathōn*) are "the visible dimension of authentic faith" (Towner 2006, 210) and the proper response to God's grace in Christ (Eph 2:10). The reason Christ gave himself (1 Tim 2:6) was so that we might be eager to do good works (Titus 2:14). *Agathos* in the Pastorals refers to inner moral goodness that becomes visible in how a person lives. This type of life is anchored and resourced by faith in Christ (Rom 2:7; 6:1-23; 7:4; 2 Cor 9:8;

Eph 2:10; Col 1:10). And it is observable to unbelievers (Rom 12:17; 13:1-7; 1 Thess 4:12). Scripture shows what this type of life is like (2 Tim 3:17).

FROM THE TEXT

Although Paul addresses specific issues women faced in the Ephesian context of his day, the principle that guides his directions begins to shine through. The issue was not the specifics of hair, jewelry, and clothing but the principles that guide how one dresses.

Some Christian women in Ephesus had apparently become preoccupied with external matters, which distracted others. They were neglecting the more important matter of character. They should focus their energy (*ergōn*) upon good deeds, not external matters that create only barriers between others. How these women lived would impact the effectiveness of their witness.

Paul was faithful to his calling (2:7) and urges both men and women to be faithful in their own settings in life. For the men, this involved appropriate conduct in prayer (v 8). For women, this involved how they dressed. There is an implied link between the behavior of believers and the salvation of "all people" (2:3).

The New Roman Woman

Many of the ethical issues addressed in this section were also concerns of certain moral philosophers of Paul's day. This is because women then were experiencing increased liberties and opportunities to participate in public life. This passage speaks to the accepted and expected ethical code of conduct of the typical Greco-Roman household. Each person in the household had a role to play. Women lived under the authority of their fathers and husbands. Men had absolute authority over their wives and children. Maintaining the traditional roles of superior and subordinate allowed the household to function smoothly.

A sexual revolution was sweeping the Roman Empire with the emergence of "the new Roman woman." Before the turn of the era, Roman women were expected to have the cardinal virtue of modesty (*sophrosynē*), which was the most common epitaph on women's tombstones of that time. Around 44 BC some changes were made in Roman law that gave more economic and social freedoms to women. Some women began to stretch the bounds of their freedoms in their dress, involvement in civic affairs, and by sexual promiscuity. The difference between the "new Roman woman" and the traditional housewife was often most visible in how they dressed. These "new women" also became known for being loud in public and for interrupting speeches.

Married women were mostly confined to the home. But they increasingly became involved in public life and could even own businesses and land. Roman women had more freedoms than Greek women. Wealthy women had even more freedoms and could come and go as they pleased, often attending public social events. Women of the lower classes usually had no formal education and their lives revolved around the home. Many were forced into slavery and prostitution (see Winter 2003).

These freedoms enjoyed by "the new Roman woman" and the behaviors that accompanied them could have attracted Christian women. Some of them could have come from impoverished settings; others may have brought their pre-Christian behaviors with them.

IN THE TEXT

■ **11** Paul continues his exhortation as to how women ought to behave in community. But he changes to the topic of how they should learn. Verses 11-15 have posed numerous problems of interpretation and application that cannot be solved here.

Paul shifts back to the singular **woman** (*gynē*) without the article. Like v 8, his instructions are broader than the relationship between husbands and "wives." Marriage is not the issue; it is conduct within the community gathered for worship.

Should learn (*manthanetō*) is the only grammatical imperative in this passage; the other exhortations are indirect (vv 1, 8-9). *Manthanetō* refers to learning that comes through instruction. Learning was a vital part of spiritual growth in the early church. The gospel would have been the primary topic of study, with further instruction given about ethical matters (Rom 16:17; 1 Cor 14:31; Eph 4:20, 22; Phil 4:9; Col 1:7; 2 Tim 3:14; Titus 3:14). Women were vital learners in the NT, and their spiritual growth is given a high priority. Jesus gave importance to teaching women and had many female disciples.

This verse should be viewed first as a positive statement. Paul does not prohibit women from learning (→ 5:9-10; Titus 2:4-5), but he puts qualifications on how they should learn. The verb is in the present tense, suggesting that women were already learning in the Ephesian church.

First, women should continue to learn, but do so **in quietness** (*en hēsychia*). The word *hēsychia* can have a range of meanings from absolute silence to a soft-spoken, gentle, meek, and peaceful spirit (1 Thess 4:11; 2 Thess 3:12; → 2 Tim 2:2—in an atmosphere of peace). To be quiet was to refuse to be a rebel, to be respectful and teachable (1 Pet 3:4)—to be a good listener (see Eccl 9:17; Collins 2002, 68).

Some of the young widows in the church had become busybodies and gossipers (1 Tim 5:13). This could have spilled over into worship assemblies and adversely affected their own spiritual growth and the ability of others to learn.

Second, women should learn in **full submission** (*en pasēi hypotagēi*). **Submission** involves coming under the authority of or being subject to another, involuntarily or voluntarily. In the Hellenistic setting of Ephesus, submission involved accepting one's place in society. Maintaining the status quo would result in social stability, harmony, and order (1 Cor 14:32-40; Collins 2002, 69).

Submission was expected of all Christians. First, they were to submit to God (Heb 12:9; Jas 4:7). All will submit one day to Christ (Eph 2:22; Phil 3:21). In general, Christians were to submit to those in authority (Rom 13:1, 5; 1 Cor 16:16; 1 Tim 3:4; Titus 2:9; 3:1; 1 Pet 5:5). Believers were to "submit to one another out of reverence for Christ" (Eph 5:21).

This verse gives no indication as to whom a woman was to submit. Other NT passages urge wives to submit to their husbands (Eph 5:22; Col 3:18; Titus 2:5). But such a narrow reading is not adequate to the inclusiveness of Paul's command and the context of the gathered community. Submission to spiritual leaders was an expected early Christian practice (Heb 13:17; Jas 4:7; 1 Pet 5:5). The specific group here was likely the overseers, who are the focus of the next chapter. Women were to submit to the church authorities who exercised this authority through their teaching (Schreiner 2005, 99).

The word **full** is added for emphasis to show that Paul expects a high level of submission. There should be no arguments but complete willingness to embrace sound doctrine (1 Tim 1:10; 2 Tim 4:3; Titus 1:9; 2:1). Submission is closely related to the quiet spirit Paul also urges here.

Quietness describes the preparation and attitude women must have to learn. **Submission** shows their willingness to accept what they are taught. Elsewhere, Paul exhorts both women and men to have an attitude consistent with that of Christ (Phil 2:5-7).

Teaching and learning were critical issues in the Ephesian church, with the danger of heresy tempting especially the women (2 Tim 3:5-7). Paul urges women to learn. But he puts some cultural conditions upon this. In Paul's cultural and historical context, women were expected to remain silent in a public teaching settings (see 1 Cor 14:34-35). Paul calls for women in the Ephesian church to follow generally accepted public behavior. Some women may have felt liberated by the overrealized eschatology of the false teachers. As a result they had abandoned their traditional roles (Towner 1989, 214), following the cultural tendencies of the imperial period (→ sidebar: "The New Roman Woman," with From the Text for 2:8-15). Women associated with the Ephesian Artemis cult were known for being boisterous.

■ **12** This verse is thematically and grammatically linked to v 11. The topic of teaching and learning continues. But the role of women changes from learners to teachers. Paul continues to explain how women ought to live in community, but he expresses it as an indirect command: **I do not permit** (*ouk epitrepō*). *Epitrepō* makes this "an authoritative demand bordering on the legal" (Mounce 2000, 121; see 1 Cor 14:34; 16:7).

The verb's present tense has created some discussion. Is Paul offering a timeless truth (gnomic present)—"I never allow women to teach . . ."? Or, is he speaking only about the present situation (descriptive)—"I do not allow the women in Ephesus to teach now . . ."? The word itself offers no answer. So the literary and historical contexts alone must determine which option makes better sense (Schreiner 2005, 99-100).

Does Paul's shift to the first person imply that he is giving his own personal judgment on the current troubles in the Ephesian church (Evans 1983, 102)? Note that there are no qualifiers attached to this verb, such as "in all the congregations" (1 Cor 11:16; 14:33-34) or "everywhere" (1 Tim 2:8). Thus, the initial application (at least) is with the Ephesian women.

The verse begins with *de*, a soft contrast translated as "and" or "but" (missing in the NIV) that links vv 12 and 11. The verses are also linked grammatically through parallelism in the subject and verb:

11 "A woman should learn" [positive]

    "in quietness" [two adverbial prepositional phrases expressing

        how women learn]

    "in . . . full submission"

But

12 ***A woman I do not let*** [negative]

    to teach [three parallel infinitives completing the main verb]

       nor

    to have authority

        over a man [governed by both infinitives]

        but [strong contrast leading to a positive infinitive]

    to be in quietness.

Here, Paul indicates that women were not permitted **to teach** (*didaskein*). Teachers were shown great honor in Judaism, in the Greco-Roman world, and within the church (Rom 12:7; 1 Cor 12:28-29; Eph 4:11; 1 Tim 3:2; 5:17; 2 Tim 2:2, 24). Teaching was done in community gatherings.

It is clear from Paul's other letters that women had important teaching roles in his churches (see Phil 4:2-3). But it is unclear what or who they taught. Any teacher needed to be qualified (1 Tim 5:17). This may have presented a challenge for many women, especially Jewish women. Most of them would have been unqualified to teach, because they were not allowed to study the Torah directly. They learned Scripture only from their husbands, but they could encourage their sons and husbands to study (Collins 2002, 71). Gentile women also had little opportunity for education. Without any formal training, most women in the Ephesian church would have been unqualified to teach the more educated men present.

That **woman** (*gynaiki*) has no article in the Greek implies that Paul offers a general principle (→ 2:9 and 11). Women are not prohibited from teaching altogether, since they can teach their children (2 Tim 1:5; 3:14-15) and other women (Titus 2:3-5). Timothy was taught by women (2 Tim 1:5; 3:15).

The NT mentions numerous examples of women teachers in the early church. Some of them worked alongside Paul and Timothy. For example, Priscilla with her husband, Aquila, taught Apollos, who is described as "a learned man." Note that this instruction occurred in Ephesus at Paul's command (Acts 18:2-3, 18, 24-28). Paul elsewhere commands all believers to teach and admonish one another; this likely included women (Rom 15:14; 1 Cor 1:5; 14:26; Eph 5:19; Col 1:28; 3:16).

Thus, women teachers would have been familiar in the Ephesian church. The problem here must not have been *that* women were teachers but with *how* the teaching was done. Paul is likely putting a specific qualification on women's teaching. He mentions no specific topic of teaching here, but we can assume that Paul refers to Christian doctrine and ethics, the subjects of women's "learning" in 1 Tim 2:11.

The second negative infinitive, **to assume authority** (*authentein*), helps narrow the problem facing the women in Ephesus. The meaning of the verb poses a significant interpretive challenge. This is the only time this word occurs in the NT, and it is rare in other literature. *Exousia* is the word Paul typically uses for the exercise of authority (Rom 13:1; 1 Cor 6:12; 7:4; 8:9; 9:4-6, 12, 15; 11:10; 15:24; 2 Cor 10:8; 13:10). His use of a different word here suggests that he has a specific type of "authority" in mind. This seems to be an unusual word for an unusual situation (Scholer 1986, 205).

Kroeger proposes that this word has been wrongly translated and interpreted. The cognate suggests a person initiating or being responsible for an action, situation, or state. Only by extension does it refer to being in charge or ruling over something. Negatively, it has the sense of being responsible for a terrible crime like murder. It can also mean to take matters into one's own hands or to claim sovereignty or authorship. She paraphrases this verse: "I do not allow a woman to teach nor to represent herself as the originator or source of man." She speculates that women may have been teaching a gnostic mythology in which Eve came first and created Adam. This would have appealed to the women of Ephesus who were heavily influenced by the cult of the goddess Artemis (1986, 232).

After extensive review of every known occurrence of the term, Baldwin delineated four primary meanings of the verb: (1) to rule or reign sovereignly; (2) to control, dominate, compel, or influence others; (3) to act independently by assuming authority over or flouting authority; and (4) to be primarily responsible for instigating something. Of these, the second and third options best fit this context (2005, 45, 51).

Some women may have overstepped accepted cultural norms and assumed authority within the church that was not theirs but belonged to leaders (→ ch 3). The reasons for this are unknown. It is possible that the false teachers were leading women to act independently of the authority structures within the church. As the general culture grew more open to liberated women, this mind-set may have found acceptance among some women within the church. We cannot determine whether or not this was some form of proto-Gnosticism or overrealized eschatology.

The use of the negative conjunction *oude* (**nor**) links this infinitive in series with the first. This raises the question of the relation of the two infinitives. Is Paul prohibiting two separate or related activities? Is teaching part of the problem of "usurping" (see KJV) authority? Included with this question is how the phrase **over a man** (lit. *of a man* [*andros*]) fits into the syntax of the sentence. Though this word follows the second infinitive, the structure of the verse suggests that this is the direct object of both infinitives. Thus, the meaning is that a woman is not to teach **a man** or to usurp authority from **a man** within the church.

Apparently, some women tried to lead without the necessary qualifications. They were disrupting the worship and preventing others from learning and coming to salvation, one of Paul's major concerns in this chapter (2:4). *Women* teaching was not the problem; the *manner* in which they did so was. Paul does *not* prohibit women from teaching or leading. Early Christian women taught and had authority over men. They were not, however, to usurp the rightful authority of existing leaders in the church (Evans 1983, 103; Scholer 1986, 205).

Paul's concern is pastoral. He asserts his apostolic authority (v 7) to provide structure in a church that was being adversely affected by teachers of false doctrines (1:7). The **man** in this verse is ambiguous and most likely refers to those in leadership positions in the church. The next chapter mentions two such groups, the overseers and deacons. First Timothy 2:9-15 is closely linked with 3:1-7, and one of the qualifications of an overseer is teaching (3:2). If unqualified women preempted the overseers, doctrinal ambiguity might result. Paul attempts to restore doctrinal purity within the Ephesian church by controlling who teaches. By submissiveness and quietness, women prepare themselves to be taught true doctrine. Thus, learning, they may become qualified to lead.

The final infinitive shifts to the positive: **she must be quiet**. This infinitive stands in sharp contrast (shown by the untranslated *but* [*all'*]) to the previous two infinitives. The word for **quiet** (*hēsychia*) is the same as in v 11. By keeping quiet, women will more easily learn the truth of the gospel. With this approach, they could learn in an orderly way from leaders qualified and gifted to teach. Loud women, who claimed more authority than was theirs, only created barriers for themselves and others in learning sound doctrine.

Education in the Ancient World

Few people in antiquity were formally educated. Most teaching was practical and done in the home. Jewish women were often secluded to home life with little opportunity for formal education. Education was stratified according to one's social position. Wealthy women could receive formal education through private tutors and lectures in the home (→ 2 Tim 3:6). There may well have been some women of wealth and position in the Ephesian church (1 Tim 2:9; 6:17-18). Even average women of first-century Ephesus enjoyed freedoms none before them had. There is not much information available about how women were educated, so caution should be used in making any conclusions.

■ **13-14** Paul next appeals to the Genesis account of creation (v 13) and fall (v 14). What is the relationship of these verses to vv 11-12? Do they provide a theological rationale, or is this merely an illustration? The word **for** (*gar*) can show logical reasoning or introduce an explanation (Towner 2006, 225). Here it probably shows the reason for the injunctions of vv 11-12 (Mounce 2000, 131-32). The experience of Adam and Eve supports Paul's directive.

Verse 13 recalls the order of creation found in Gen 2:7-8, 21-22. **Adam was formed first.** The verb **formed** (*eplasthē*) is also used in the LXX of Gen 2:7, 8, 15, and 19. It describes the process by which God created one thing from another. Adam came **first** in the sequence, then Eve came from the flesh of Adam (2:22). Rabbis used the Genesis passage to support the superiority of Adam—and of males compared to females (Küchler 1986, 17-32). But this logic obviously breaks down because the animals were created before Adam. Are they even more superior? The account of the creation of humanity seems to support equality (see 1:27) and mutuality (2:23-24). Men and women are depicted not "as competitive but as complementary" (Guthrie 1990, 91).

Verse 14 of 1 Tim 2 shifts from Adam as first created to Eve as first to sin. The verse simply states that Adam was not **deceived** (*ēpatēthē*) but Eve (*exapatētheisa*). This deception made her **a sinner.** The verb *apataō* recalls that the serpent "deceived" (*ēpatēsen*) Eve (in Gen 3:13). That is, she was enticed to sin through trickery (Oepke 1964a, 384-85; Eph 5:6; Jas 1:26). The second use of the root here referring to Eve is an intensified form found also in Rom 7:11, 16, 18; 2 Cor 11:3; 2 Thess 2:3. The compound form is stylistic, probably "serving to set the woman and the man apart in the fall and to stress the priority of the woman's deception" (Towner 2006, 229).

Jewish interpretations of the fall blame Eve, as in Sir 25:24, "From a woman sin had its beginning, and because of her we all die" (NRSV). A comparison of Paul's teaching in Rom 5 and 1 Tim 2 suggests that Eve is *not* to blame for sin; she was deceived (2 Cor 11:3). Adam, however, was fully aware of his choice, since he was present at the deception (Gen 3:5 uses plural "you"). Eve was deceived; Adam sinned fully aware. Sin entered the world through disobedience, not deception.

There is a noticeable shift from **Eve** in 1 Tim 2:13 to **the woman** in v 14. There are several possible reasons for this: **The woman** is the word used in Gen 3:13 (*hē gynē*). Paul is broadening his application to women in 1 Tim 2:9-10.

The consequence of Eve's deception is that the woman **became a sinner** (*gegonen parabasei*). *Parabasis* is a "transgression" (Rom 4:15) against God's laws. Adam became a transgressor when he ate the forbidden fruit (Rom 5:14). The verb **became** in the perfect tense connects the consequences of Eve's situation with the troubles facing women in Ephesus. They needed to be careful not to be deceived by false teachers, disqualifying them even to teach children and other women (2 Tim 1:5; 3:14; Titus 2:3-4).

Interpretive Options

This passage has created much dialogue among interpreters. The major (overlapping) positions are summarized as follows:

1. *Complementarian view.* This traditional hierarchalist position emphasizes that Paul viewed men and women having different roles, based on his reading of Gen 2. First Timothy 2:13 gives the reason why women should not teach men: Adam was created first, then Eve. Women are not inferior to men, but they have different roles in the family and in society. Men are natural leaders; women, followers. Paul's appeal to the creation narrative makes his directives here universally binding.

2. *Contextual view.* The reason Ephesian women could not teach men is because they were promulgating heresy or were uneducated. They may also have fallen prey to either an early form of Gnosticism that emphasized the feminine principle or the feminist influence of the Artemis cult.

3. *Temporary ethic view.* Paul accommodated to the needs of the Ephesian culture and gave directions that fit the needs of that place and time. The directions are only temporary until the optimism expressed in Gal 3:28 can be fully realized. As 1 Tim 2:14 reminds us, the curse of Gen 3:16 was still in effect. In 1 Tim 2:11 Paul does not say that educated women must remain silent.

4. *Feminist reconstruction view.* This text lacks authority because it interferes "with the actualization of human liberation" (Towner 2006, 199) and stands in opposition to the goal of equality expressed in Gal 3:28.

5. *Emerging ministry view.* This passage must be read in light of other passages that discuss the fuller involvement of women in ministry and the larger trajectory of Paul's mission. Thus, this deals with local problems in Ephesus and not other churches.

6. *Pseudonymous authorship view.* This letter was not written by Paul but by an unknown author writing in Paul's name. It attempts to return to the patriarchalism that Paul tried to challenge in Gal 3:28.

■ **15** This marks the climax of the discussion begun in 1 Tim 2:11 and functions as the focus of the whole section. It returns to the theme of salvation mentioned in v 4, applied to the challenges facing women in the Ephesian church. The adversative conjunction **but** (*de*) links v 15 with vv 13-14. There is some connection between Eve's situation and that of the Ephesian women. It ends the paragraph with a positive note of encouragement. But it raises several challenging issues:

The verb **will be saved** (*sōthēseta*) lacks a clear subject. The NIV supplies the word **women** to resolve this ambiguity, but this is not found in the Greek. The verb is singular. The closest singular noun antecedent is "the woman" of v 14. Is this "woman" Eve, a hypothetical "woman" in the Ephesian church, or a generic reference to "women," as the NIV takes it?

How are we to interpret the idea that a woman will be saved **through childbearing** (*teknogonia*)? The only other appearance of this word in the NT in 1 Tim 5:14 refers to the act of physical childbearing (its literal meaning). Several questions need to be resolved: (1) In what way is a woman **saved**? (2) How does **childbearing** relate to salvation? Similar to the challenges of earlier verses, there have been multiple answers to these questions (see Gritz 1991, 141-44):

First, a messianic interpretation takes childbearing as a reference to Mary's birth of *the Child*, Jesus. The preposition **through** (*dia*) can show agency. **Childbearing** here has the definite article and could refer to a specific event. Women will be saved through Eve's child, Jesus; Eve's sin is reversed through Jesus.

In Paul's thought, however, it was not the birth of Jesus that brought salvation but his death on the cross (1 Cor 1:18-25) as Mediator (1 Tim 2:6). The closest passage with a similar idea is Gal 4:4. There Paul refers to "Jesus, born of a woman, born under the law." But this passage quickly moves to the redemption Jesus provided (Gal 4:5). This view is possible, but unlikely within a Pauline context.

Second, this could refer to physical deliverance through the process of childbirth. Giving birth to a child was a dangerous experience for women in the ancient world and often led to death. Thus, this verse offers a reversal of the consequence of Gen 3:16, that women would suffer great pain in giving birth.

But not all godly women bear children. Although it is possible that Paul refers to family issues, giving birth is a new topic, remote from the broader community issues of this chapter.

Third, this verse may offer Christian women the hope of spiritual salvation from eternal judgment, despite their temporal judgment of pain in childbearing. The pain of childbirth as part of the penalty of Gen 3:16 does not disqualify one from salvation in Christ. Genesis 3:16 may lie behind this verse, since the sequence of Genesis 2 and 3 matches 1 Tim 2:13-14.

But there is no way to know if Paul is offering a commentary on the Genesis passage or responding to speculations on it from the false teachers (1:3-4, 8).

Fourth, although man was created first, woman has priority in giving birth (1 Cor 11:12). Childbearing is a form of reversing the deception of Eve. It brings life from the curse of death. Thus, women are freed from the condition that demands their silence. Childbearing remedies women's deception and transgression.

Elsewhere in the Pastorals, however, salvation is always focused on redemption from sin through God's grace and not directly related to egalitarianism within the church or society.

Fifth, a woman may experience salvation and her greatest fulfillment by accepting her God-assigned role as a submissive wife and mother. Her proper sphere is not teaching in the church but ruling in the home. Motherhood is not the means of salvation but provides purpose. When a woman embraces her role at home, she is kept safe from the temptations of the world.

But this perspective makes motherhood meritorious for salvation, which contradicts what Paul says elsewhere (Eph 2:8-9). **Through** (*dia*) can show the circumstances within which something happens; it is not necessarily instrumental (Marshall 1999, 470).

The obscurity of this verse makes any interpretation tentative. Motherhood may be part of what Paul wants Ephesian women to embrace. Perhaps, bearing children challenges the false teachers' extreme asceticism, which apparently rejected marriage and childbearing (1 Tim 3:4, 12; 4:1-5; Mounce 2000, 146).

Another possibility is that the rich and progressive wives had joined in the "new Roman woman" movement and had an aversion to having children (Winter 2003, 109). If these women were neglecting their culturally accepted role in the family, they may have been tempted to "elevate their religious functions to the neglect of the 'the drudgery' of home and family responsibilities" (Gritz 1991, 144).

The context of this chapter urges that this verse be read under the umbrella of salvation (see 2:4). Life in Christ is the heartbeat of Paul and must be worked out in one's daily life (Rom 2:6-10, 26-29; 1 Cor 6:9-11; Gal 5:21; Phil 2:12-13; 1 Tim 4:16). Women who embrace their responsibilities within the home and do not attempt to dominate when they are unqualified for leadership will experience salvation nonetheless.

How women may live out their salvation is given in a conditional clause at the end of the verse: **if they continue**. The last statement of 2:15 clarifies that childbearing is not sufficient for salvation. The verb **continue** (*meinēsin*) shifts to the plural. This raises the question: Who is its subject? The closest previous plural word is "women" of v 9. The plural shifts the focus from the generic "woman" of Paul's example to the plural "women" in direct application to the Ephesians. He hopes that these women will experience all he hopes for them.

The virtues they are to continue in are **faith, love and holiness with propriety**. The preposition **in** (*en*) in the Greek can show the "sphere" or type of life in which an action occurs. These three terms are related theologically and experientially. Faith is the open door to love. Holiness is the expression of faith and love in how we live. The phrase **with propriety** recalls the use of the same term (*sōphrosynēs*) in v 9 and brings the whole section to a close. Women will give evidence of God's mercy and grace in their lives by a godly and holy lifestyle (vv 2-3).

Faith involves the decision of accepting God's grace in Christ and allowing it to sustain us as we live out God's purposes for us in Christ. A "sincere faith" is one of the key ingredients for producing love (1:5).

Love is the result of the obedience of faith in response to the transforming work of the Holy Spirit (Gal 5:22; for the relation of faith and love, → 1 Tim 1:5, 14).

The important scriptural concept of **holiness** (*hagiasmos*) describes God's character and our experience of coming into a committed relationship with him. It has a moral connotation that shows a lifestyle of separation from sin and submission to the supremacy of Christ. Holiness is the work of the Holy Spirit (2 Thess 2:13) who cleanses the heart from sin (Rom 6:19, 22) and helps us grow into Christlikeness (2 Cor 3:18; see Towner 2006, 236). Paul insisted that women's holiness should be visible in how they dressed (1 Tim 2:9-10) and lived out their faith in their cultural context.

FROM THE TEXT

Though this passage has many ambiguities, several important themes emerge that can significantly influence the effectiveness of the church and those who minister through it.

A lesson on methodology. This passage provides the interpreter with plenty of opportunity to expand his or her skills in biblical exposition. The myriad of contextual issues related to social background, language usage, and literary connections test one's ability to bring together the complex into something both simple to understand and authentic to biblical faith. What has proven most difficult is how to preserve the authority of this text and at the same time apply it to contemporary settings. If Paul wrote this letter, then he is blamed for giving his patriarchal biases on the subject of women in ministry. If he did not write the letter, then he may be exonerated. But this historical judgment should not affect the inspiration and authority of the canonical text.

One of the crucial questions confronting readers is whether the directions given here are for all times and cultures or more for the specific situation in Ephesus. By using basic interpretive principles, we can diminish the ambiguities that we find. As an ad hoc letter, this text addresses issues facing the men and women of the Ephesian church. Something prompted the author to write this letter. Discovering this "something" allows us to listen in to this conversation, realizing that it was not written *to* us, although there is still a message *for* us. The principles we use with this passage can be used with other obscure passages in the Bible.

Fulfilling God's call, in whatever location one is. One of the most obvious messages of this passage recalls Paul's words to Timothy in 1:19 to be faithful to his calling by "holding on to faith and a good conscience." Unfortunately, this text has been read without consideration of the historical context and used to silence well-educated women in the contemporary church. The careful interpretation noted above shows that, rather than silencing all women, Paul is giving directions for how the men and women in the Ephesian church could live out their salvation with integrity and witness. Because of the false teachers, the roles, freedoms, and spiritual gifts of women within the community were being limited and distorted. Two dangers exist with this passage:

First, in an age preoccupied with political correctness, individual liberty, and egalitarianism, the nuances of Paul's argument can be missed or simply rejected. Thus, we lose out on a crucial message about effective witness.

Second, this text has been used by some to silence women in the church, with various positions represented across the theological and denominational spectrum. Paul is using "practical logic" in this passage that could be easily misunderstood if removed from its historical setting.

Many other texts both in the Pauline literature and outside support the idea that God calls both men and women to specialized ministries within the church. A useful place to begin is Gal 3:28 where "male and female" are partnered in powerful and united service and fellowship "in Christ" (1 Cor 11:12-13; Col 3:11). When the Holy Spirit comes with empowering presence, both men and women speak forth in prophetic message (Acts 2:17-18). Both are given spiritual gifts for service within the church (1 Cor 11:5; 12:4-7). Evidence for how the Spirit called and empowered women in the early church abounds throughout the NT: A partial list in Rom 16 includes Phoebe, a deacon in Cenchreae; Priscilla, the wife of Aquila; Mary; Junia, a fellow prisoner with Paul whom he calls an apostle; Tryphena, Tryphosa, and Persis, who work hard in the Lord; the mother of Rufus; and Julia, the sister of Nereus. Chloe had a church meet in her house (1 Cor 1:11), and Priscilla is mentioned in 1 Cor 16:19. Euodia and Syntyche were ministers who worked side by side with Paul (Phil 4:2-3). Apphia was a fellow worker with Paul (Phlm 2). Lois and Eunice importantly influenced young Timothy (2 Tim 1:5). A Claudia is mentioned in 2 Tim 4:21. The list could be continued with the many female disciples of Jesus.

The bottom line is that God calls both men and women to places of service in the church, where their gifts are vitally needed to move the church forward in its mission of proclaiming the good news of Jesus Christ. No two callings are the same because every person and every setting is unique. The Ephesian crisis required specific answers. Paul used his apostolic authority and ministry insight, giving directions to help turn these crises into opportunities for salvation.

Accepting roles within a culture. Related to the above, each of us is located within a particular cultural setting. We need to balance two concepts that do not necessarily oppose each other. Every culture has accepted roles for men and women, though these roles will change over time and within specific sub-groups within the culture. This passage encourages each person to live in the obedience of faith in whatever social situation one is in. Our Christian identity is not determined by our setting in life. But our social location ought to guide the particular ways we express the love that God pours into our hearts (Rom 5:5; 1 Tim 1:14). Our self-worth is found in Christ, not in any particular role in life. These roles, whether imposed by others or ourselves, provide the avenue by which we can express our faith in Christ (1 Cor 7:17, 20, 24).

This perspective should to be balanced with a willingness to critique culture. The gospel always calls us forward and upward into conformity to the image of Christ. What Christ does in us through the Holy Spirit leads us to experience a new life that constantly urges us and conforms us to the purpose for which we were created (Gen 1:27; 2 Cor 3:18). The church must not be afraid to confront any inequality or social injustice that diminishes the image of God in people. Love for God and love for others ought to compel us to "become all things to all people" so that we might win some to Christ (1 Cor 9:22). At the same time, we can live with integrity and holiness before the church and the culture as ambassadors of reconciliation (2 Cor 5:20).

C. Qualifications for Overseers (3:1-7)

BEHIND THE TEXT

In ch 3, Paul continues to advise Timothy on dealing with false teachers in the Ephesian church (1:3). The answer for heresy is for the church to appoint respectable and qualified leaders. Paul offers specific character qualities leaders needed to set the Ephesian church on course. Almost every character trait listed here counters the opponents in Ephesus (see Mounce 2000, 156-58). The emphasis is on the character and spiritual maturity of the leaders—their blameless lifestyle, not on their specific activities. The issues of this chapter are not doctrinal but missional.

Contemporary readers should proceed with caution: We must be careful to interpret ch 3 in its historical context, and not impose later church structure upon the leadership positions and polity mentioned. The chapter does not give a manual for church organization but deals with the pressing issues facing the Ephesian church.

The organization of the church was evolving in the first century, and there was no universal structure or clearly defined offices. The early church soon realized that fulfilling its mission required some division of labor (see Acts 6:1-7). They selected mature believers to serve pressing needs as they emerged. Formal institutional hierarchy seems first to appear during the second century in the letters of Ignatius of Antioch. His three-tiered structure included the "bishop" (*episkopos*) as the single leader, a college of presbyters or "elders" (*presbyteroi*) beneath him, and "deacons" (*diakonoi*) serving him and the church.

Chapter 3 shifts from the topic of prayer and corporate worship in the previous chapter to the qualifications for overseers. The broader theme of the behavior of God's people continues. Interpreters divide the chapter in various ways. It focuses on two types of leaders: those who give oversight and those who assist through service. It addresses three groups: overseers (vv 1-7), deacons (vv 8-13), and within the section on deacons, one verse addresses women (v 11). The chapter ends with the theological foundation for all church life and the core belief required of all leaders (vv 14-16).

Leadership in the NT

The NT was written during a period of development in response to the growing needs of the church. This entailed a movement from Spirit-gifted, charismatic leadership to a more hierarchical structure. Cultural expectations also determined the needs of a local situation. Both Jewish and Greco-Roman culture provided models for leadership and authority for the early church (Johnson 2001, 218-19; Towner 2006, 242-43).

Paul uses a number of descriptions for leaders within his letters, summarized briefly here:

- **Elder** (*presbyteros*): This word in Jewish usage applied to synagogue leaders. It literally describes an older person and the prestige and seniority that came with age and experience in that culture. In Acts 20:17 and 28 "elder" (see 1 Tim 5:17, 19; and Titus 1:5) and "overseer" are used interchangeably for leaders in Ephesus. "Overseer" describes the function of leaders while "elder" describes their status (Towner 2006, 246).

- **Overseer** (*episkopos*): This word in the Greek world was used for those officials who supervised the affairs of others. The term is used for Jesus in 1 Pet 2:25 as the "Shepherd and Overseer of your souls." Those who follow him as church leaders are to watch over the flock of God (1 Pet 5:2-4).

- **Deacon** (*diakonos*): In secular culture, a deacon (or minister) was a lowly servant who waited on others (Luke 10:40). Jesus' exemplary service reversed this evaluation (Mark 10:45; Luke 12:37; 22:27). Acts 6:3 describes seven men set aside to serve the practical needs of the growing church. Romans 12:7 identifies serving others as a spiritual gift.

- **Apostle** (*apostolos*): In the NT, "apostle" carries a sense of authority and function: Apostles were Christian leaders on a mission (2 Cor 8:16-24; Phil 2:25) from Christ (1 Thess 2:6). They helped build up the church through preaching like other leaders (Eph 4:11). They were a select group of people with recognized authority (1 Cor 12:28; 15:5-11), who preserved orthodoxy (Rom 16:25-26; Eph 3:1-9).

- **Prophet** (*prophētēs*): Prophets were messengers of special revelation from God. Typically, this revelation focused on the clear proclamation and application of the gospel (1 Cor 14). Prophecy is a spiritual gift (Rom 12:6; 1 Cor 12:28) used to build up the church (Eph 4:11-16).

- **Pastor** (*poimēn*): This term literally means "shepherd," a guardian and leader of people. Pastors cared for the spiritual welfare of believers. The term is used as a title for church leaders only in Eph 4:11 (although the idea can be found in John 21:15; Acts 20:28; and 1 Pet 5:2).

- **Teacher** (*didaskalos*): Teachers shared the same responsibility of other leaders: to help believers reach maturity. "Pastors" and "teachers" in Eph 4:11 may refer to the same group. Jesus is the teacher par excellence. Teaching is a vital theme in this letter. Teachers worked out the implications of the gospel for people and helped them know how to apply its truths.

- **Evangelist** (*euangelistēs*): Evangelists proclaimed the "good news," especially in local church settings (Eph 4:11). Like apostles, they often went to new territories. Philip was known as an evangelist, possibly because of his reputation of bringing the gospel to new places (Acts 21:8). Timothy was to do the work of an evangelist (2 Tim 4:5).

- **Leader** (*proistamenos*): Leadership is a gift of the Holy Spirit (Rom 12:8). Leaders directed the affairs of the church (1 Tim 5:17). Their responsibilities could include some of the activities described above, especially in spiritual matters.

- **Administrator** (*kybernēsis*): This is another spiritual gift (1 Cor 12:28) and refers to someone who governs or gives direction to a group. Again, this term could be inclusive of other types of leadership listed above.

IN THE TEXT

■ **1** Here appears the second **trustworthy saying** in the letter (→ 1:15; 4:9; 2 Tim 2:11; and Titus 3:8). It is unclear whether the **trustworthy saying** refers backward to 1 Tim 2:15 or forward to 3:1.

If it reflects back, the saying focuses on the salvation of women. The argument for this is that all the other sayings somehow deal with salvation. The other option assumes the word order and that Paul is stressing an important point for the continued vitality of the church and to help them deal with heresy (→ 1:3).

Assuming the latter, the saying is a conditional sentence with an inclusive invitation, *if anyone*. The sentence construction assumes the condition will be fulfilled. The verb **aspires** (*oregetai*) literally means to "stretch oneself, reach out one's hand," and figuratively "to aspire to, strive for, desire" (BDAG 2000, 721). The second verb, **desires** (*epithymei*), describes a heartfelt, strong longing. The word has a mostly negative connotation elsewhere in the NT. But here, it refers positively to a deep inner compulsion to be an overseer with a "decisive sense of call" (Guthrie 1990, 95).

The key word in this section is **overseer**. In v 1, the word *episkopēs* refers to the office or position. The word *episkopos* in v 2 refers to the one who holds the office. Both words are singular, suggesting this was a general principle for church life (→ ch 2).

The KJV translation of the key word as "bishop" carries too many anachronistic connotations of ecclesiastical hierarchy from centuries after the NT. The translation "overseer" literally renders the Greek. It implies some type of supervision, care, or responsibility. It was used in the ancient world for both people and deities. In Acts 1:20 (quoting Ps 109:8) the word refers to the replacement for Judas among the apostles. There it has the sense of "office" or "responsibility" (NIV: "leadership").

Interpreters have puzzled over the relation of overseers to elders. Titus 1:5-9 suggests many similarities between the two. Paul addressed the "elders" of Ephesus in Acts 20:18-35, charging them to give "oversight" to the church in v 28. First Timothy 4:14 and 5:17 indicate that a group of elders directed the affairs of the church.

It is not clear whether there was one overseer or several, since this verse seems to present a general principle. The overseer was particularly gifted with teaching, never mentioned as a qualification for deacons. Apparently, a council of elders was to govern the church with a division of labor.

The situation is ambiguous since the NT does not say much about who rose to leadership positions in the church. Such leaders and councils were not unusual for the time, especially among Jews. Each synagogue was led by a council of elders. The Qumran community had a teacher, called the *mebaqqer* in Hebrew, with responsibility for leadership within the community (Barrett 1963, 57-58). When Paul wrote to the Philippians (1:1), he included the "overseers and deacons" in the salutation. Since household language is strong here (1 Tim 3:4, 5, 12, 15), overseers (and deacons) may have been the heads of households where communities gathered (see Acts 14:23; 1 Cor 1:16; 16:15-16).

The desire to be an overseer is a **noble task** (lit. ***good work*** [*kalou ergou*]). The word **task** is singular, which distinguishes it from the plural form used for one's lifestyle of "good works" (1 Tim 2:10; 5:10, 25; 6:18; Titus 2:7, 14; 3:8, 14). The early church fathers understood the ministry of the overseer to be one of work and not an exalted status. "Work" describes the ministry to which Paul and his companions were called as they took the gospel to new areas (Acts 13:2; 14:26; 15:38). Timothy was to be involved in the "work" (ministry) of an evangelist (2 Tim 4:5). The work of leading God's people is **noble** because it "requires those who have the highest moral and spiritual character with the appropriate qualities" (Marshall 1999, 477).

■ **2-3** Now (*oun*) connects the position of overseer in v 1 with the characteristics listed in vv 2-7. The verbal construction **is to be** (*dei . . . einai*) shows what is fitting or necessary. It guides the sentence structure through v 11. Titus 1:7 has a similar structure, which suggests that Paul may have had a common set of instructions for both situations (Towner 2006, 249).

There are two general qualifications to be an **overseer**: (1) self-discipline and maturity, and (2) the ability to relate well to others and to teach and care for them. Acts 6:3 gives these twofold requirements as "'full of the Spirit and of wisdom,' the personal, and 'of good reputation,' the interpersonal" (Knight 1992, 156).

The listed qualities are common leadership characteristics, but especially fit the needs in the Ephesian church. There is nothing distinctly Christian about the list. All appear in the moral philosophers of Paul's time and describe familiar virtues and vices. First-century philosopher Onasander gave a similar list for a general, with two exact and three similar words (1.1-4.8, in Dibelius and Conzelmann 1972, 158-60). Characteristics of the overseer are what good people did in that time.

What is unique about this list is its context and purpose. Christian leaders differ only in that their source of strength is the Holy Spirit (Gal 5:22-23). The early church adopted the highest virtues of the surrounding culture and reinterpreted these through God's saving activity in Christ (→ 1 Tim 3:16). Christians were to be models of virtue in a culture. The list begins with the positive qualities overseers should possess.

First, they should be **above reproach** (*anepilēmpton*). They should not be open to attack or criticism since they have unblemished personal integrity.

The word *anepilēmpton* describes observable behavior that begins from one's inward character. Paul uses the word in 5:7 to instruct widows so that "no one may be open to blame." He also uses it in his final charge to Timothy in 6:14. As the first in the list it serves as the essential requirement. The rest of the list defines what this involves. The idea is repeated again at the end of the list in 3:7. Leaders are to be models for the rest of the church.

An overseer must be above reproach, first, by being **faithful to his wife**. The phrase is literally *a one-woman man*. This difficult phrase has four major interpretive options (Knight 1992, 157):

a. The overseer must be married. Paul counters false teachers who forbid marriage (5:14). This is problematic, since both Paul and Timothy were probably unmarried (1 Cor 7:7-8, 25-38; see Matt 19:10-11).

b. The overseer must have only one wife his entire life ("married only once" [NRSV]). He could not divorce his wife and marry another or remarry if his spouse died. The early church viewed remaining single after one's spouse died as a more honorable choice (Clement of Alexandria, *Strom.* 3.1). Paul says elsewhere, however, that if one's spouse dies, one is free to remarry. But he recommends remaining single as the better option (Rom 7:1-3; 1 Cor 7:39). Later in this letter, Paul encourages young widows to remarry in order to avoid temptation (→ 1 Tim 5:14).

c. The overseer must be monogamous. Some Jews of the first century were polygamous (Josephus, *Ant.* 17.1.2.14), but the general practice for both Romans and Jews was monogamy. There is no evidence that Christians were ever polygamists. In AD 212, the *lex Antoniana de civitate* made monogamy the law for Romans. In AD 393, Theodosius required Jews to be monogamous.

d. The overseer must be faithful in the marital and sexual realm. Marital infidelity was common in that time. It seems likely that Paul here urges the leaders of the church to be good role models of committed relationships. He is not commanding that an overseer be married, but that if he is married, he must be faithful to his wife. The emphasis is more on moral character than marital status. One's marriage reflects one's character.

Second, overseers must be **temperate** (*nēphalion*), "sober in the sense of clear-headed, self-controlled" (BDAG 2000, 672). They were to be aware of their surroundings and keep their heads on straight (→ 2 Tim 4:5). This called for more than avoiding alcoholic beverages. It included anything that can control a person when used in excess. One way to do this is by not being addicted to wine, which is listed separately.

Third, overseers must be **self-controlled** (*sōphrona*) by being prudent and thoughtful (BDAG 2000, 987). Discipline over one's impulses is vital in self-control. Self-control is not done exclusively by human effort but in cooperation with the Holy Spirit, who gives freedom from the passions of the flesh (see Gal 5:19-23, with a different Greek word in v 23 for "self-control": *enkrateia*). This is a virtue expected of all believers, but especially those who lead the church (1 Tim 2:9, 15; Titus 2:2, 4, 5, 6).

The inner discipline of self-control leads to being **respectable** (*kosmion*). Respectability results when one's behavior is viewed as honorable or virtuous by others. Both "self-control" and "respectability" are qualities of the modest dress expected of women in 1 Tim 2:9.

In addition, overseers are to be **hospitable**, a compound with two parts: "love" (*philo-*) for the "stranger" (*xenon*). Hospitality was an important virtue among both Jews and Greeks. The word, its synonyms, and the concepts behind them occur frequently in the NT. Hospitality is an extension of Christian love and a virtue commanded of all Christians (5:10; Rom 12:13; Heb 13:2; 1 Pet 4:9). Difficult and dangerous travel conditions made hospitality important for traveling apostles and evangelists (3 John 5-8). Overseers as householders (*paterfamilias*, → 1 Tim 3:4-5) served as role models for the entire church (Titus 1:8).

The next quality is the only skill listed: being **able to teach**. This skill is unique to overseers and not mentioned of deacons. The topic taught is unstated here. Teaching involves more than oratorical ability. Knowledge of sound doctrine is more crucial.

In describing the qualities of the elder, Titus 1:9 states that teaching should involve encouraging and refuting. Knowledge of the truth will enable church leaders to silence the ignorance of false teachers (→ Titus 1:11, 13). Teaching and preaching should be highly respected and deserve "double honor" (→ 1 Tim 5:17). Teaching is a gift of the Holy Spirit (1 Cor 12:28; Eph 4:11). But competence in teaching can be developed with study and practice. The strength of the church depends on the knowledge and skills of its teachers.

The list takes a negative turn, continuing with a series of vices to avoid. The first two are negated with the Greek word *mē* and the last two with *alpha* (*a-*) privatives. Overseers were not simply to avoid these actions, but to embrace their opposites.

Overseers should **not** be **given to drunkenness** or "not addicted to wine" (NASB). The Greek word is a compound of the preposition "alongside of" (*para*) and "wine" (*oinos*): They should not spend too much time sitting next to wine (Mounce 2000, 175). Deacons likewise should not be devoted to excessive wine drinking (1 Tim 3:8). This verse does not require total abstinence from wine, but from the excess that leads to the loss of control. The Bible does not prohibit drinking fermented drinks, but drunkenness is always viewed as evil (Deut 21:20; Prov 23:20-21, 29-35; 31:4-7; Isa 5:11-12; 19:14; 28:7-8; Jer 13:13; 25:17; Ezek 23:33; Hos 4:11, 19; Amos 6:6; Matt 11:19; Acts 2:15; 1 Cor 11:21; Eph 5:18; 1 Thess 5:7). Drunkenness impairs the senses and leads to poor judgment. Intoxicating substances can cause a loss of self-control and emotional instability. Too often, the result is not only physical harm to the participant but also violence toward others.

Paul perhaps had this problem in mind because the second attribute he urged overseers to avoid was violence. Someone who is **violent** (*plēktēs*) is an aggressive bully. Violence is not always physical. Words can inflict as much damage as fists. The false teachers were involved in quarrels (1 Tim 6:3-5; 2 Tim 2:22-26).

The negatives are interrupted at this point with a sharp contrast (the strong Greek adversative *alla*) to violence: being **gentle** (*epieikē*), the only positive word in this verse. Those who are gentle are courteous, kind, and tolerant toward others. They forgo their rights to preserve cordial relationships (Phil 4:5; Titus 3:2; Jas 3:17; 1 Pet 2:18). Skills in conflict management are important for church leaders. Overseers need to be considerate of the desires and dreams of others. Cultivating gentleness will eliminate the negative vices in this verse.

Third, overseers should avoid being **quarrelsome** (*amachon*) by being "peaceable" (NASB). There are many causes to quarrels—such as misunderstandings or differing opinions, but the outcomes often are hurt feelings and broken relationships. Peacemakers are blessed (Matt 5:9; Rom 12:18). By healing arguments, leaders can bring unity to people. By quarreling, the false teachers threatened the unity of the Ephesian church and hindered the effectiveness of its mission (1 Tim 1:4; 6:4-5). Quarrels can destroy relationships vital to a growing church.

Fourth, overseers should **not** be **lover[s] of money**. The NIV translation is a literal rendering of the Greek word *aphilargyron*. The KJV adds some flavor to the basic reading: "not greedy of filthy lucre." The pursuit of wealth can be a temptation for people of all walks of life, rich and poor. Money and the love of it can be a trap that takes one's attention away from spiritual matters (Matt 6:24, also 25-34; Luke 16:14; 1 Tim 3:8; 2 Tim 3:2; Titus 1:7).

In Greco-Roman society, the upper class comprised a small minority of the population; most people were in the lower class. The rich and the poor were separated by a vast social and economic gulf (Verner 1983, 47). The upper class was concerned about retaining wealth and the lower class about trying to get out of poverty. Although some church leaders may have been home owners, wealth and social status were not enough to qualify them for leadership. Compensation in ministry is often inadequate, which opens the door to temptation (1 Pet 5:2). Later in the letter, Paul urges the church to care adequately for its leaders (1 Tim 5:17-18). In Acts 20:33-35, Paul left the Ephesians with an example of hard work, self-support, and generosity.

The answer to greed is being content with what one has (Heb 13:5). Greed was one of the problems of the false teachers (1 Tim 6:5-10; 2 Tim 3:2; Titus 1:11). *Didache* 11.6, an early Christian document, identifies as false prophets any who ask for money for their ministry. Satisfaction should be found in God and God's care (→ 1 Tim 6:6).

■ **4** The grammar shifts here from adjectives to descriptive phrases. All these continue the Greek sentence begun in 3:2. The focus changes from the personal qualities of overseers to how they manage their own household. The family and household were central to the Greco-Roman urban culture. The basic point of this verse is that overseers will likely care for the church as they do their households.

The overseer is to **manage his own family well**. The adjectival participle translated **manage** literally means ***standing before***. It has the metaphorical sense of ruling, leading, or governing, with the nuance of protecting and caring for their home and family (→ v 12). The same word is used for leading the church in Rom 12:8; 1 Thess 5:12; 1 Tim 5:17. The adverb **well** (*kalōs*) describes something that is done in a fitting, appropriate, and correct way (BDAG 2000, 505). The word for **family** (*oikou*) can be interpreted as both the people who make up the household or the building in which they live. Since children are mentioned in this verse, clearly the people of the household are in mind (compare 3:12, 15; 5:4; 2 Tim 1:16; 4:19; Titus 1:11). Most churches met in homes in the first century. Since marriage was expected and typical in that culture, most of those appointed to leadership positions were old enough to be married and have children.

The Oikos

The basic sociopolitical unit of Mediterranean society was the household. The *oikos* provided the primary model for early church life. John Chrysostom (ca. AD 347-407) compared the church to a house, with its women, children, and servants (*Hom. I Tim.* 10).

The father (*paterfamilias*) was considered the head of the house. At his death, this duty was passed on to the oldest son. The head of the house had authority over his wife, children, and slaves. He had three primary roles: master (*kyrios*), husband (*despotēs*), and father (*patēr*). The father had complete control over all matters of the house, even the life and death of its members.

Mothers were involved in the education of youth until they were six years old. Daughters were given in marriage through agreements between fathers and husbands-to-be. Once married, the primary job of women was to manage the household. In ancient Athens, women were not allowed to own property without male oversight. But by the first century, they could own and manage businesses (e.g., Lydia in Acts 16:14-15). Women could appeal to their fathers for help in their marriage or to divorce.

Households usually comprised several generations. Everyone in a house adopted the same religion (e.g., Cornelius in Acts 10:44-48 and the Philippian jailer in Acts 16:32; Verner 1983, 28-35).

There are two ways an overseer can manage his household well, both related to how he treats his children and their response to him.

First, he must **see that his children obey him**. The ESV and NRSV are literal readings: "keeping his children submissive." The key word in this phrase is *hypotagē*, which can mean subjection, subordination, or obedience.

Both Greco-Roman and Jewish cultures were patriarchal, with the father as the key authority in the family. Children were expected to submit to their father's authority (Eph 6:1). The NIV's **see that** renders the participle *echonta*, **having**. Because the voice of this participle is active, the implication is that overseers were responsible for how well their household operated. The measure of this leadership could be seen in how their children treated them. The children's obedience was not to be forced but arise naturally from respect for their parents.

Second, the overseer must manage his children **in a manner worthy of full respect**. **Respect** (*semnotētos*) is "a manner or mode of behavior that indicates one is above what is ordinary and therefore worthy of special respect" (BDAG 2000, 919).

There are two ways to interpret this phrase: "the demeanor expected of the overseer's children (NIV; NRSV) or the way in which the father is to exercise the authority necessary to maintain his children in submissiveness (TNIV; REB)" (Towner 2006, 255). There is a reciprocal relationship between parents and children. "The subjection shown by the children must reflect the character of their father's leadership" (Knight 1992, 161). Children are more apt to obey parents who are good and loving role models.

Full ("all") suggests a consistent response of admiration that comes with good parenting. Good family relationships and spiritual leadership are also important for deacons (vv 8, 12) and elders (Titus 1:6).

■ **5** Here is the reason for the last part of v 4 (connected with the untranslated *de*, **and**). Several observations can be made about the structure of this verse.

First, the style of argumentation is from the lesser to the greater: If the overseer cannot manage his house, he cannot take care of the church. He lacks an essential quality in his leadership that should be evident in all he does. The principle is similar to what Jesus illustrated in Matt 25:14-30: The one who is faithful in a few things will be put in charge of many things.

Second, this is a rhetorical question with the expected answer of "no" (indicated with the *ouk* in the Greek).

Third, the verse functions as a parenthesis in the paragraph. It connects overseers' private and public lives. The NIV shows this with the appropriate punctuation.

The first half of the verse sets the condition: **If anyone does not know how to manage his own family**. The verse has the form of a general truth, marked by the inclusive **anyone**. The verb **know** (*oiden*), followed by an infinitive (here **to manage** [*prostēnai*]), refers to knowing how to do something (Knight 1992, 162). Practical knowledge in leading at home prepares one for service in the church. The same word for **manage** occurs in 1 Tim 3:4 and later for elders in 5:17. The word is further characterized in the second half of the condition as **care**.

Care (*epimelēsetai*) appears elsewhere in the NT only in Luke 10:34. There it describes the compassion of the Good Samaritan toward the injured man, involving bandaging his wounds and taking him to an inn to recover. This concern is resourced by love (*agape* [Luke 10:27]).

An overseer should show the same type of compassion to the church as he does his own family (Luke 11:11-13). This was not to be exceptional. It was the rule for anyone desiring the noble task of supervising the spiritual growth of others.

That this is a general principle is indicated by the article missing before the Greek word for **church** (*ekklēsia*). The word throughout the NT identifies the redeemed people of God. The church is defined primarily in its relationship to Christ and what he has done through his death and resurrection. Christ is the foundation of the church and the basis for its existence (1 Cor 3:11; Eph 2:20). But the church here is described as **God's**. It exists to praise God through Christ (Eph 1:11-14; 1 Pet 2:4-10).

This is the first time *ekklēsia* appears in the letter. The only other occurrences in the Pastorals are in 3:15 and 5:16. Despite the few uses of the specific term, Paul applies his ecclesiology to issues faced by the Ephesian church. He has two concerns: (1) how the leaders care for the church and (2) the reputation of the church in the community.

■ **6** The list of qualities for an overseer continues with another negative followed by a clarification. There is a shift from the theme of family management to spiritual maturity. The NIV continues the exhortation by adding **he must** (*dei* → 3:2 and 4). The overseer must not be **a recent convert** (*neophyton*) (lit. "newly planted"). In Christian literature, it refers to new converts to the faith (BDAG 2000, 669).

Spiritual maturity is expected of church leaders. This maturity is not dependent upon chronological age. For example, Timothy was a significant leader in the early church, despite his comparative youth by prevailing cultural standards (→ 4:12). When Paul wrote this letter, the church in Ephesus was well established and had several potential candidates for overseers.

At times, leaders must be chosen quickly, as Paul did in some mission situations (Acts 14:21-23). But these leaders should always be grounded firmly in their faith in Christ. The reason for this qualification is given in a negative result clause (*hina mē*). Two unfortunate outcomes may be avoided by not appointing a spiritually immature believer as an overseer.

First, he **may become conceited**. The word **conceited** (*typhōtheis*) is related to the word for smoke and portrays something clouded, deluded, and puffed up. There are three interpretations of this difficult word: (1) puffed up and conceited, (2) blinded and foolish, or (3) mentally ill (BDAG 2000, 1021). It occurs in the NT only here, in 6:4 for the foolishness of false teachers, and in 2 Tim 3:4 for the conceit of people in the last days. Most translations treat this word as if it were a finite verb (except the KJV). But it is actually an instrumental participle that emphasizes the most serious danger: falling into judgment.

Making new converts church leaders may make them feel excessively confident in their abilities and the power of their position. As a result they would lack the concern and humility necessary for nurturing healthy relationships within the fellowship. One must be a disciple of the Lord before one can lead other disciples.

Second, new converts should not be made overseers because they may **fall under the same judgment as the devil**. The **fall** is not an accidental stumbling but results from misplaced priorities (→ 1 Tim 6:9). The grim outcome of the fall is **judgment**. The interpretation of this judgment depends on the force of the genitive phrase, *of the devil*.

The subjective sense makes the devil into the judge who condemns the overseer for his pride (→ 1:20, where the devil teaches Hymenaeus and Alexander not to blaspheme). The devil accuses believers, mocking them when they fall into sin (Rev 12:10).

The objective reading is that the conceited overseer will suffer the same condemnation as the devil (NIV). The NASB makes this even clearer: "the condemnation incurred by the devil." The devil's pride led to his downfall (Gen 3:14-15; Matt 25:41; Rev 12:10).

Both interpretations are possible. The point is that those who get conceited in ministry leadership will face the same fate as the devil. Pride was a problem of the false teachers. Perhaps they were newer converts who did not know sound doctrine (1 Tim 6:4; 2 Tim 3:4). Humility is a crucial quality for overseers because it keeps the perspective on the needs of others.

3:6

■ **7** The final qualification for overseers summarizes the entire paragraph. It explains how they can be "above reproach" (v 2). The Greek begins a new sentence with **he must** (*dei*) as in v 2.

This verse is linked with v 6 in several ways: Grammatically, the verses are joined by the untranslated conjunction *de* followed by *kai*, meaning **and also**. Structurally, they have a similar construction: Necessary qualifications (v 6: "not . . . a recent convert"; v 7: **a good reputation**) are followed by potential outcomes to avoid (preceded by *hina mē* in both verses). Finally, the outcome to avoid in both is falling into the troubles of the devil.

As leaders of the church, overseers must have **a good reputation with outsiders**. **Reputation** (*martyrian*) is translated elsewhere in the NT as "witness" or "testimony" (Matt 8:4; John 19:35; Acts 22:18; John 1:7). The verbal form of the term in 1 Tim 5:10 describes the good works by which a widow can be "well known."

The **outsiders** are unbelievers who are not part of the church (1 Cor 5:12-13; Col 4:5; 1 Thess 4:12). These should be able to look at the leadership of the church and see people whom they may respect. Public office puts an overseer's character on display, within the church and before the world.

The last half of the verse warns leaders. Maintaining a good reputation is vital so that overseers might not **fall into disgrace and into the devil's trap**. The same word for **fall** is used here and in 1 Tim 3:6. This fall is not accidental and can be avoided by not letting one's reputation deteriorate because of poor character. There are two ways leaders fail, both governed by the same preposition **into** (*eis*).

First, a poor reputation can result in **disgrace** (*oneidismon*), reproach, insult, or shame. This strong term expressed a powerful social force in its first-century context. From the earliest years of life, people were taught to seek the honor and respect of others and to avoid disgrace at all costs. Honor is "the status one claimed in the community, together with the all-important public recognition of that claim." Public acclaim "meant access to power and privilege that could be gained no other way" (Rohrbaugh 2010, 111). Honor was obtained by conforming to the standards or expectations of a particular group (deSilva 2000, 243). Ancient people evaluated others socially by the degree of honor or shame they received. This was shown through praise or blame.

Early Christians, as evidenced in this passage and others, developed a code of ethics and marks of spiritual maturity that defined what they considered honorable. Paul is particularly concerned in this chapter that the church leaders in Ephesus should be honorable not only before other Christians but before **outsiders**. The credibility of the church and its message could be devalued if its leaders were shamed before unbelievers.

Second, the overseer might fall into **the devil's trap**. This **trap** (*pagida*) is like a snare used to catch animals, which brings sudden or unexpected danger or death (BDAG 2000, 747). It is not clear whether this is a trap set by the devil or the trap the devil himself is in.

Verse 6 implies that one of the problems of the devil is pride, which can be a temptation for church leaders. Pride can lead to hypocrisy—posing as something one really is not. This is difficult to hide from others for long. When the true character of hypocrites is exposed, it brings them disgrace, spiritual defeat, and ineffective mission. The devil attempts to ruin the reputations of Christian leaders by enticing them into the vices Paul lists (vv 1-6; see 6:9; 2 Tim 2:26).

Paul not only strongly warns church leaders but also encourages them to pursue a good reputation and effective witness. The church must be protected internally and externally by qualified and exemplary leaders. Leadership is not dependent upon wealth or social status but upon integrity. This honors God, the church, and the message the church proclaims.

FROM THE TEXT

Although Paul instructed Timothy on how to find qualified leaders in ancient Ephesus, his words have guided the church throughout the centuries since then. All Christians are called to serve, but some are gifted and called for specialized ministry as leaders. These must set an example and influence the rest of the church by the way they live their lives.

First, *ethical integrity.* How people act outwardly reveals who they are inwardly (Matt 15:17-19). The moral integrity of spiritual leaders will influence how they lead. They may fulfill their job duties with excellence. But unless they have godly integrity, their influence may eventually destroy the mission of the church. Moral compromise will lead to an unstable church.

The character of church leaders directly impacts the public image of the church. The world is always watching to see if Christians are living consistently with the message they proclaim (Eph 4:1). It is vital for those in ministry leadership to avoid any situation that compromises their character and reputation.

Scripture calls upon all believers to be blameless before God (Gen 17:1; Deut 18:13; Pss 19:13; 37:18; 119:1; Prov 2:21; Eph 1:4; Phil 1:10; 2:15; 1 Thess 3:13; 5:23; 2 Pet 3:14). Blameless does not mean faultless (Gould 1965, 579). It is important to realize that we are all on the same highway of holiness (Isa 35:8). We must honestly echo Paul: "Christ Jesus came into the world to save sinners—of whom I am the worst" (1 Tim 1:15). But we celebrate not our sinfulness, but our redemption. And we must jealously guard the irreproachable character God has graciously given redeemed sinners.

Second, *strong family relationships.* It is noteworthy that in second place in Paul's directions to Timothy is the call to be faithful in marriage (v 2). Two verses out of six (vv 4-5) are devoted to the family. Maintaining strong family relationships is crucial to effectiveness in ministry leadership.

Traditional family structures are being eroded in many cultures today. Especially disheartening are the numbers of divorces among Christians and even ministers. Although the reasons for the breakup of marriages are numerous and sometimes unavoidable, a failed marriage can hinder and even destroy one's ministry. Ministers must work especially hard to preserve their marriages.

How to interpret the phrase "a one-woman man" has been especially difficult in places in the world where polygamy exists. At the heart of polygamy is male-domination over women. "Serial polygamy" through divorce and remarriage results in many of the same issues (Lilema and Reed 2011). Wisdom must be used for those who have been divorced and remarried (Deasley 2000). The best wisdom of the church must be used to determine the qualifications of its ministers. Culture must not be the ultimate determining factor, but Scripture. The church and its leaders must look at the life of those called to ministry beginning when they were converted and see how they have been faithful in marriage and sexuality (Knight 1992, 159). In some cases, the mission of the church may be hindered by allowing such people to serve in leadership.

Paul nowhere says that ministry leaders must be married. He himself was single and saw this as a gift for more effective service for the Lord. It still can be, if one has the gift of celibacy (1 Cor 7:7-8, 32).

Church leaders who are parents ought to have good relationships with their children. This will surely involve not making them resentful or angry for the time their parents devote to the ministry (Eph 6:4). The children of ministers often face additional pressures because they are "on display" before others in the church. Letting children know their value to parents through loving-kindness modeled after God's own covenantal love may be a helpful protection and build proper self-worth in them.

Parents are not always responsible for the behavior of their children. There comes a point when children mature and make their own choices. Parents must do everything possible before that point to set a solid foundation so their children will choose the right path. The same qualities needed in ministry in the church are needed for ministry in the home: love, prayer, patience, firmness, and discipline. The patterns by which one lives can repel or attract children to the Lord.

Third, *spiritual maturity.* The early Christian document, the *Didache,* echoes the call of the Pastorals: "[Choose] overseers and deacons who are worthy of the Lord" (15:1). It is crucial that ministers of the gospel experience the transformation of the gospel. Those who lead the church must know doctrine well in order to preserve the gospel against the attacks of heresy. They must also be able to teach the truths of the gospel and live out what they preach. "Integrity and spiritual maturity are more important than ability" in Christian leadership (Black and McClung 2004, 67). Churches should avoid rushing to fill leadership positions just because there is a need.

Fourth, *dangers while ministering.* Overseers, pastors, or leaders in the local church will face many temptations. *Compromise* with culture can confront those who seek to reach out effectively to their community. Paul accommodates to a number of cultural expectations in this letter. But we must never compromise the message of the gospel in our effort to be all things to all people through creative ministry methodologies (1 Cor 9:22).

The temptation of money can be a problem in ministry, especially when there is a lack of resources and needs are not met, or when there is plenty and "no one will miss it." The amount of compensation should not determine one's service to God. Churches should work with their leaders to set up careful accountability and do their best to support these leaders so they can more effectively devote their time to the ministry. Money cannot be the motivation for ministry.

Pride is always a danger for leaders who work hard and whose ministries grow. Leadership in ministry should not be viewed as an achievement, reward, or career advancement. The disciples had to learn a hard lesson about pride in Luke 10:17-20. Jesus warned them to be humble and avoid pride, which caused Satan to fall from heaven. Leadership cannot be a matter of popularity. The early church warned against seeking the position of a "bishop" for the name, authority, power, or prestige and not for the work (Chrysostom, *Sac.* 3.11; *Hom. 1 Tim.* 10; Augustine, *Civ.* 19.19).

Fifth, *servant leadership.* Ministry must not be done out of selfish ambition. It is a privilege to lead God's people. There are many models of leadership today. The business world is realizing a truth that is at the heart of biblical leadership: the leader must be a servant. Jesus provides the ultimate example of servant leadership by considering others first, taking the form of a servant, and humbling himself even to death on a cross (Phil 2:1-11).

D. Qualification for Deacons (3:8-13)

BEHIND THE TEXT

The theme of leadership in the church continues with the introduction of "deacon," designating another group of leaders in the church. This passage, like the one for overseers, contains a list of qualifications required by those who assume this specialized ministry. There are two notable omissions in this new list: deacons apparently do not teach (→ 3:2) or care for the church of God (→ 3:5). This omission could suggest that only overseers serve in these special capacities. But the text does not allow us to be certain. Deacons may not have been primarily teachers, but they needed to know the "deep truths of the faith" (v 9) and be "tested" (v 10). So they must have had some responsibility for the spiritual growth of the church. The list is probably not exhaustive but created ad hoc for the Ephesian situation. The emphasis is on the character qualities and not on the deacons' job description.

This section can be divided into three smaller units: (1) the virtues of deacons (vv 8-10), (2) the virtues of "women" (v 11), and (3) the faithfulness of deacons to their wives (v 12). The unit ends with a note of praise in v 13. The major question about this sequence is the place of v 11 and who the "women" were.

The work of deacons is assumed in the title itself. "Deacon" transliterates the Greek *diakonos*, "servant" or "helper." In secular literature, it refers to those who assist superiors or represent higher authorities. Often slaves performed such service (Marshall 1999, 486). In some contexts, it refers to the menial job of waiting on tables (Luke 17:8; John 12:2). The plural form of the word here suggests that Paul addresses a group of ministers in one church. The gender of the Greek word is masculine, but not all deacons were male; there is no feminine word for "deaconess" in Koine Greek (→ 1 Tim 3:11). Acts 6:1-7 reports that the Jerusalem church chose seven Spirit-filled men "to serve" (*diakonein*) in the distribution of food. This specialization of ministry responsibilities was necessary for the church to grow.

Various people in the NT are described as deacons or have the role of serving others. Paul uses the word to characterize his own ministry and that of his coworkers (1 Cor 3:5; 2 Cor 3:6; Col 1:23; 4:7; Eph 3:7; 6:21; Col 1:23, 25; 4:7; 1 Tim 1:12; 4:6; 2 Tim 4:11). Jesus came "to serve" and showed the prime example by giving his own life (Matt 20:28; Mark 10:45). Deacons were not second-class ministers but people willing to follow in the footsteps of the Lord.

The relationship of the deacon to the overseer is difficult to determine based on this passage. Perhaps they assisted the overseers. Jewish synagogues had "servants of the synagogue" who assisted the leaders (Beyer 1964, 91).

IN THE TEXT

■ **8** In the same way (*hōsautōs*) introduces another type of leader in the church. Although there are some similarities in the characteristics of deacons and overseers, the logic of the passage implies that two different groups are in mind.

This passage gives the most detailed description in the NT of **deacons**. First, deacons are to be **worthy of respect** (*semnous*). That this quality stands

144

first in the list is significant. As in 3:2 and the "noble task" for overseers, **worthy of respect** summarizes and incorporates all that follows in vv 8-9. It describes people who are dignified and deserving of respect, leaders who stand above the mundane around them (Foerster 1971, 191-96). *Semnous* "is an inward quality with an outward expression which the author understands to have a theological origin" (Marshall 1999, 489). The same word in v 11 describes women and in Titus 2:2, older men. A related word describes how children of overseers should respect them (1 Tim 3:4). The important word "godly" or "reverent" (*eusebeia*) shares the same root (→ v 16; 2:2). Deacons ought to be outstanding in their qualifications. To be worthy of respect, deacons must avoid three negative vices:

First, the NIV puts this in a positive way: Deacons should be **sincere**. But this compound word literally means **not double talkers** (*dilogous*, "of two words"; **duplicitous**). Insincere people say one thing but mean another. They cannot be trusted because two different things come out of their mouths (Prov 11:3). It is difficult to respect people who do not keep their word.

Second, deacons should **not** be **indulging in much wine**. The participle **indulging** (*prosechontas*) refers to being devoted or giving attention to something. Like the overseers (→ 1 Tim 3:2), deacons should be temperate and avoid addictions. This verse does not explicitly prohibit drinking wine. Nevertheless, to avoid the dangers of addiction and excess, church leaders may do well to stay away from it altogether. Other dangers of alcohol indulgence include a loss of self-control and of witness before others, and even physical bondage (→ v 3; Titus 1:7; 2:3).

Third, deacons can be worthy of respect by **not pursuing dishonest gain**. Being "greedy for money" (NRSV) is another addiction that can ruin the reputation of church leaders (→ 1 Tim 3:3). "Shame" (*aischro*) is the root meaning of this word. Being too focused on money brings shame to the gospel because it usually exposes one's selfishness and pride. Greedy people are shameless because all they think about is how they can come out ahead, even if it means taking advantage of other people along the way. The use and abuse of money is mentioned also in the qualifications of overseers (v 3) and elders (Titus 1:7).

■ **9** Dangerous false teachers in the Ephesian church required the leadership to be grounded in sound doctrine (1 Tim 1:3). This explains the requirement that deacons **keep hold of the deep truths of the faith**. The grammar of this verse links this requirement to the idea of being "worthy of respect" in v 8. The instrumental participle (*echontas*) probably describes how deacons may maintain a good reputation: *by keeping hold of*. The word implies a "solid commitment to the true gospel" (Mounce 2000, 200). This verse connects the faith and character of deacons.

The phrase **the deep truths of the faith** is literally *the mystery of the faith* (*to mystērion tēs pisteōs*). The word "mystery" in the Pauline Letters is usually associated with the gospel (1 Cor 2:7; 4:1). It describes God's plan of salvation that was hidden for long ages (Rom 16:25; 1 Cor 2:7; Eph 3:9) but has now been revealed in Christ Jesus (Rom 16:25-26; Col 2:2). It is "God's pre-temporal counsel which is hidden from the world . . . and has been eschatologically fulfilled in the cross" (Bornkamm 1967, 821). Paul believed he had special insight into this mystery (Eph 3:4). It brings Jews and Gentiles together into one new entity (Eph 3:6). This mystery is more than a cognitive realization of God's eternal plan. It is personal and relational, since "Christ in you [is] the hope of glory" (Col 1:27). Paul's primary way of referring to the relationship between Christ and believers is being "in Christ." Being "in Christ" impacts every aspect of life. Believers experience Christ's inward presence through the Holy Spirit.

The *mystery* is qualified by a genitive modifier: **of the faith**. The genitive could explain that the mystery of the gospel is known only *through* faith. The context suggests, however, that the genitive is descriptive: The mystery is *about* the Christian faith that will be outlined in 1 Tim 3:14-16, where "mystery" is repeated. This mystery is the content of the message believed by the church. A firm grounding in the gospel is crucial for every local church leader. Like the overseers, who must not be recent converts, deacons must know the gospel so their leadership may be effective, uncompromising, and worthy of respect.

Deacons can fulfill this goal by having a **clear conscience**. **Clear** (*kathara*) means pure or free from guilt. The **conscience** is the awareness one has of truth and falsehood, of what is correct and what is to be avoided (→ 1:5). In 1:5 and 19, "conscience" is modified by "good." "The clean conscience is one that has been purified by the action of God and is not conscious of having done wrong, whereas the 'good' conscience is more one that works effectively" (Marshall 1999, 491). Here, a pure conscience is one that knows the truth of the gospel in a relational way, has not compromised this truth, and lives it out with deep conviction. A purified conscience, free from defilement, is able to comprehend the Christian faith. A purified conscience requires faith. "Belief determines the conscience which, according to the norm supplied by the content of belief, determines conduct" (Marshall 1999, 491).

This verse serves as a strong warning to potential leaders: They should not follow the course of the false teachers who rejected a good conscience and shipwrecked their faith (1:6, 19). The way the deacons live should be consistent with the mystery of the faith. "Without the life the profession is empty" (Knight 1992, 169).

■ **10** The qualifications of deacons continue with mention of a necessary test. The grammar shifts with a new sentence and the use of two third-person plural commands. This creates a sense of urgency and necessity.

The verse begins with an untranslated "also" (*kai*; included in the NASB and ESV). This conjunction links this verse with its context. How much this connects is a matter of interpretation. It could be simply another requirement in addition to those listed in 3:8-9. Or, it could indicate that the overseers were also to be tested ("no less than bishops" [NEB]). But testing is not mentioned as a specific qualification of overseers in vv 1-7. Some type of community discernment is, nonetheless, implied in the list of required character traits for any church leader.

It is unclear who is to do the testing, since the imperative verb uses the passive voice, leaving the actor anonymous. Since ministry leaders must gain the respect of the church and serve the public, it is likely that the community of faith is presumed to exercise this discernment. All the members of the Jerusalem church—the "brothers and sisters"—were involved in setting aside the seven who served in Acts 6:3. Something similar may be involved in the testing and examination here (see 1 Cor 16:3; 2 Cor 13:5). The word **first** indicates a sequence: deacons must first pass the test before they can serve.

The object of this vetting process is to assure that they have **nothing against them**. Paul specifies no explicit criteria for testing. But the qualities listed in 1 Tim 3:8-14 probably offer a good starting point. A literal translation of this phrase is *if they are blameless*. The word for "blameless" (*anenklētoi*) is synonymous with the requirement of being "above approach" for an overseer (v 2). They must be free from any impropriety or accusation of wrongdoing (with "holy" and "without blemish" in Col 1:22). There is a strong sense of personal responsibility in being "free from accusation" (Col 1:22; see 1 Cor 1:8; Titus 1:6, 7).

Only if the test is passed does the second command become operative: **Let them serve as deacons**. This English phrase translates one word in Greek—the present imperative form of the verb related to "deacon." The verb summarizes all the activities of service and ministry implied by the office of deacon.

This test and the appointment of leaders should not be rushed. Paul later instructs Timothy to take his time (1 Tim 5:22). People cannot be rushed into leadership (→ 3:6). The necessary character qualities must be recognized by everyone.

■ **11** This verse makes a simple assertion about the qualifications of **the women** in the Ephesian church. One of the biggest questions is how the verse fits into the context of vv 8-10 and 12-13 and the relationship of these "women" to the deacons. Why are women mentioned in the middle of the discussion of deacons requiring similar qualifications? There have been four major approaches to this issue (Knight 1992, 171): (1) These women were part of the group called "deacons." (2) They were a new group called "deaconesses." (3) They were female assistants to the deacons. Or (4) they were the wives of the deacons. The context argues against this being directed to women in the church in general.

Grammatically, like v 8, this verse begins a new Greek sentence with the word *hōsautōs*, **in the same way**. This sentence once again (like v 8) has the implied "it is necessary that" (*dei*, NIV: **are to be**), assumed from 3:2. This parallel suggests that Paul has in mind a third group of church leaders. He lays out the requirements for overseers, deacons, and **women**.

Another challenge is with translation. The Greek *gynaikas* can mean either "wives" (ESV, NKJV) or "women" (NASB, NIV, NRSV). Is Paul addressing the wives of the deacons or women deacons? If they are the wives of deacons, their mention in the middle of the discussion on deacons implies that they fulfill an important role in their husbands' ministry. But if this is what Paul meant, it seems odd that there is no mention of the duties of overseers' wives in the earlier passage (Kelly 1963, 83). Was there something unique in the ministry of deacons that was socially acceptable for women to do?

Verse 12 turns to the marriage and domestic life of deacons. If deacons were to have female assistants, Paul's first choice would likely have been their wives, so as to avoid sexual temptations (see 2:9; 5:6, 11, 15; Knight 1992, 171). But taking **women** to refer to the wives of deacons is not persuasive.

The other major choice is to see these **women** as the designation of a special group of female ministers within the church. There was no Greek word for a female deacon, like the English "deaconess." Paul may have used **women** to designate a subgroup within the larger group of deacons.

If Paul meant the wives of deacons, he could have used some possessive pronoun or close association between the deacons and "their" wives, but there is no indication of this in the text. Rather, he makes a generalized reference to "women" with no article in Greek.

The characteristics required in this verse likely address the particular needs of first-century women in ministry. The persuasiveness of this interpretation depends on how one reads 2:11-15 and the role allowed for women to serve in leadership in the local church (→ From the Text for 2:11-15).

The qualifications listed here are similar to the virtues expected of deacons. So it seems that Paul refers to a third group. These women were "ministering," so they could be called "deacons" in the basic sense of the term.

The ambiguities of this biblical text cannot be resolved with certainty. Christian interpreters have been divided throughout the ages about how to interpret this passage. At the least, these **women** had some special role in the church. Only this explains why Paul lists these qualifications. Since the rest of the chapter deals with church leaders, these women were apparently involved in public service and needed to act in a way that would attract people to the gospel and not repel them.

The specific characteristics listed here are similar to those for deacons in 3:9-10. At the head of the list is that these women should be **worthy of respect** (→ of deacons in v 8). This first requirement is again broad (→ 3:2, 8) and encompasses how the public would regard these women. Female leaders should be recognized as people of honor and respected by others. One way to preserve their honor would be to clothe themselves with good deeds and dress with decency (2:9-10). This verse provides other ways they may gain the respect of others.

The women should **not** be **malicious talkers** (*diabolous*). The Greek word behind this negative requirement is elsewhere translated "devil" (see 3:6 and 7). Here it has its broader meaning of "slander." Satan is called the "devil" because he bends the truth and entices people away from God's commands. A malicious talker is deceitful and cunning. One way to do this is through gossip (Louw and Nida 1996, 33.397). To avoid this, women must be honest, open, and speak the truth in love (Eph 4:15). Truthful speech is a crucial part of personal integrity.

Next, the women should be **temperate** (*nēphalious*; → of overseers in 3:2; of deacons in v 8). Temperance is maintained by self-control. This grows in a person's life in cooperation with and submission to the Holy Spirit (Gal 5:23). Paul also urges temperance of the older men and women on Crete (Titus 2:2-3). The dangers of addiction are real in any society and can lead to dishonor and ruin one's ability to serve others.

Finally, women should be **trustworthy in everything. Trustworthy** is the adjective form of *pistis*—faithful and dependable. It may be simply a mark of personal integrity. But there is a potential link to "faith." One's outward behavior is significantly influenced by one's commitment to Christ. Faithfulness to the gospel leads to faithfulness in other areas of life (contrast 2 Tim 3:6-7).

■ **12** Here Paul returns to the qualifications of deacons and their relationship to their wives and children. The two main points of this verse are abbreviations of the requirements of overseers in 3:2 and 4. Is this verse an afterthought prompted by his discussion of **women** in v 11? Or, is it a return to the qualifications of deacons briefly interrupted by the discussion in v 11?

If Paul is speaking about the wives of deacons in v 11, it is natural that he would address their relationships in v 12. But it is also possible that the issues related to women in v 11 prompted Paul to reiterate one more factor important for church leaders (see vv 4-5 of overseers). In either case, the verse makes the important link between home and public life of church leaders.

The opening phrase of this verse is (lit.): *Let deacons be husbands of one woman* (→ 3:2). The word for **manage** (*proistaenoi*; → 3:4) connotes caring concern in leading the affairs of the household. Typical households of the time included **children**. The ability of deacons to serve in the church would be evidenced by their ability to care for their own families (→ 3:5).

■ **13** Paul ends as he began in v 1, with a general statement of encouragement that can apply to all three groups. The substantival participle **those who have served** (*hoi diakonēsantes*) could encompass all three groups. It shares the same root as the "deacons" of vv 8 and 12. The important qualification for this service is that it be done **well** (*kalōs*)—"commendably" and "in the right way" (Knight 1992, 173). There is a two-part reward for good service:

First, these ministers will **gain an excellent standing**. The Greek includes the reflexive pronoun *themselves* (untranslated in the NIV). The middle voice of the verb points the action back to the subject. These two factors put the responsibility on the deacons (or all three groups of leaders) to strive for excellence in their service.

Standing (*bathmon*) designates rank or grade and figuratively refers to influence and reputation (BDAG 2000, 162). The question becomes, before whom is this standing, God or the church? Three major interpretations of this standing vie for consideration (Guthrie 1983, 100): (1) a step in promotion, (2) influence gained in the esteem of the Christian community, and (3) standing before God.

Concerning the first, nothing in this passage refers to advancement to a higher office or indicates that deacons were subordinate to overseers. Both overseers and deacons had vital ministries in the church, and the diaconate was an honorable office, not merely a stepping-stone on a career path.

The idea of reputation has been a steady theme throughout the letter so far. Paul has particularly emphasized the vital role of one's reputation in effectively representing the gospel (→ 2:3). In the Hellenistic culture of Ephesus, those who did well in public service gained increased honor (Verner 1983, 155-60). By serving well, deacons and other leaders brought honor to themselves and God. Those who did not serve well were disgraced, thus hindering the effectiveness of their message.

The second reward for serving well is that deacons gain **great assurance in their faith in Christ Jesus**. The key word here is **assurance** (*parrēsian*)— "confidence" and "boldness," especially in a public setting. In the NT, confidence is expressed before God and comes through Christ (Eph 3:12; Heb 10:19, 35). It can include boldness before other people (2 Cor 3:12; Phil 1:20; Phlm 8). The prepositional phrase **in their faith** focuses this confidence on the core issue of the deacons' relationship with God. The object of their faith is

Christ Jesus, who gave Paul confidence and assurance in his own calling and ministry among Gentiles (1 Tim 1:14).

The opposite can be seen in the false teachers who abandoned their faith (1:5, 19), and as a consequence, had ruined the effectiveness of their message. By being faithful in service, church leaders grow stronger in their relationship with Christ, resulting in more effective ministry.

FROM THE TEXT

Like overseers, those who are called by God and set aside by the church for the special ministry of service must be models to others of godly living. At the top of the list, deacons must have *moral and spiritual integrity.* Commitment to "sound doctrine" (1:10) will help ministers grow in their relationship with Christ and develop a good reputation with the church and unbelievers (3:13).

Vital to ministerial effectiveness will be the ministers' relationships with others. Many of the qualities called for in this passage deal with getting along with other people. Ministry is always relational. People appreciate sincere concern evident when ministers serve with authentic faith in Christ.

Accountability is important in any organization. In this passage, Paul sets the groundwork for ministerial accountability to the church. All church leaders should go through a process of testing (see Acts 6:1-6). Those led by God to serve in official leadership capacities should prove over time by their personal character and faith in Christ that they are "worthy of respect" (3:8). People should not be rushed into places of service simply because there is a need (→ 5:24-25).

If anyone should be *a model of servant leadership*, it should be deacons who by their very name are to "serve" in the church. "They should *be* deacons before they are *named* deacons" (Liefeld 1999, 139). What will guide them will be their relationship with the greatest servant of all, Jesus Christ (1 Pet 2:25). The greatest honor is to follow in the footsteps of their Lord. They can do this by growing in their convictions about the gospel and vision for others. Ministry must be intentional, not accidental.

E. The Theological Basis for Being the Family of God (3:14-16)

BEHIND THE TEXT

A new subunit begins with v 14, which clearly marks a change of topic. There is a noticeable shift from the third person to the first and second person. Paul turns from a discussion of various leadership positions in the church to a more personal correspondence between himself and Timothy.

Each time Paul has addressed Timothy directly in the letter so far, he has hinted at his purpose for writing and what Timothy must do in Ephesus. This section gives three key insights into the letter as a whole. First, Paul states his reason for writing: he has been delayed and could not be there in person to deal with the rising problems. Second, he expects Timothy to use this letter to show the church how to behave as the people of God. Third, he reminds Timothy and the church of the core Christian convictions about Jesus Christ.

This section comes at an important juncture in Paul's directions and is more or less the literary center of the letter. It reflects back and provides the core conviction Paul came to realize after his vision of Christ on the road to Damascus (→ ch 1). It also reminds all those who lead the church that their primary job is to uphold the core of the gospel found in 3:16 (→ chs 2—3). The passage also looks forward to the discussion in ch 4 about those who have abandoned the faith by clearly stating from what they have departed. It echoes some of the themes in the brief confessional statement of 2:5-6. By doing this, it helps define orthodox doctrine over against false teachings that were infiltrating the Ephesian church (6:3-5).

The middle part of the passage—3:15—hints at Paul's doctrine of the church. Although many have disputed the authorship of this letter, nothing in this passage is inconsistent with statements or allusions Paul makes in other letters about the nature of the church. The church as God's household expresses the adoptionist language of passages such as Rom 8:15-17 and the many places where Christians are called brothers and sisters in Christ. Household language is a key way Paul describes his vision for the church in Ephesus (2 Tim 2:20-21; see Eph 2:19). The emphasis in this passage is on proper behavior in response to the truth of the gospel. This behavior ought to be anchored in the person of Christ.

The passage ends with a hymn of praise about Jesus Christ. There is no way to determine if Paul wrote this hymn for this occasion or another, or if he is quoting one used by the early church in its worship or catechism. Its purpose in this letter becomes more apparent with its location in the context. It hints at Paul's missiological emphasis in 1 Tim 2:1-7. For him, it is crucial that piety be wedded to belief. The hymn is introduced as "the mystery of godliness" (3:16 [ESV, KJV, NASB]) and clarifies the "mystery of the faith" mentioned in 3:9 (ESV, KJV, NASB, NLT). Thus, it links ethics with theology, behavior with belief.

IN THE TEXT

■ **14-15** Paul continues the dialogue with Timothy from 1:18 by addressing him directly. Timothy serves as Paul's representative to bring leadership and change to the Ephesian church. These two verses express the reason Paul wrote this letter instead of going in person to resolve the problems in Ephesus. The problem is that he could not get to Ephesus at this time. In fact, he might be delayed longer. He writes that his intention is to come to see Timothy **soon** (*tachei*, quickly or in a brief time). There is no way to know how soon Paul intends to visit, but there is an obvious sense of urgency. He states his plan to visit again in 4:13. But by that point in the letter he may realize that the delay is immanent. If he is delayed, he hopes his instructions will get Timothy started in resolving the issues in Ephesus.

If the letters were written in the canonical order that we have them today (which is likely), there is no evidence Paul was ever able to join Timothy. Second Timothy, rather, appeals for Timothy to come to Paul (2 Tim 4:9).

Verse 15 of 1 Tim 3 begins with a conditional clause that indicates Paul **may be** delayed. The form of this condition (*ean* followed by a subjunctive verb) indicates that delay was probable. This "heightens the sense of the writer's absence and the importance of the instructions" of this letter (Marshall 1999, 506).

Paul describes what he writes to Timothy as **these instructions** (lit. *these things*). This phrase translates one word in the Greek: *tauta* is a vague pronoun with an unclear antecedent in this context. Such demonstrative pronouns often refer backward, perhaps to what Paul had just written in 2:1—3:13. But here, the pronoun could point ahead, to what Paul was about to say in v 16. The basic thrust of this statement is that in this letter as a whole and as he composed it, Paul was giving essential instructions for how Timothy could deal with the challenges facing the Ephesian church. The NIV (and NRSV) attempts to avoid confusion by adding **instructions** so that modern readers may understand what Paul means.

The reason Paul writes *these things* is given in a purpose clause (*hina*): **so that . . . you will know how people ought to conduct themselves in God's household.** The key word in this clause is the infinitive **to conduct** (*anastrephesthai*), which describes "manner of living" or "way of life" (2 Cor 1:12; Eph 2:3; BDAG 2000, 72), and how Christians ought to live as God's holy people (1 Pet 1:15). Ethical behavior for Paul arises in response to theology. One ought to live in a certain way because of what God has done in Christ Jesus.

Paul's concern is simply given in the word **how** (*pōs*). "Paul writes to communicate not theoretical knowledge but 'how to' knowledge" (Knight 1992, 179). The specific contents of this **how** are given throughout this letter as Paul addresses different groups: men, women, overseers, deacons, widows, elders, slaves, and others who fit in multiple groups. The necessity of this behavior is emphasized with the word **ought**. This is the same Greek word used at critical points in the list of qualities overseers and deacons should have (*dei*; → 3:2, 6, and 8). This clause represents the motive behind all Paul's instructions in this letter. He is concerned that the Ephesian church be the faithful household of God.

The metaphor of the church as **God's household** (*oikōi theou*) would have been familiar to the Ephesians, most of whom would have been a part of a household structure. The household was the center of Greco-Roman culture. The Greek word *oikos* can mean either the house (the building) or household (the family that lives in the building). Although most early churches met in homes (Rom 16:5; 1 Cor 16:19; Col 4:15; Phlm 2), Paul refers here not to the place where the people assembled but to the assembled people. Where the church meets is irrelevant. The household image stresses the close bond of kinship: God is the father and Christians are brothers and sisters who are to care for one another (Gal 6:10; Eph 2:19).

Being part of this household gives a particular identity to its members. The imagery of the church as the household of God was introduced in 1 Tim 3:5. It emphasized the care leaders ought to show members of this household. In v 15, the stress falls more on the ethical conduct of those who are part of this fictive family. Each family has its own unique traits or patterns of behavior. The same is true for God's family. Those who are part of this family should be distinct from unbelievers on the outside. The emphasis in this letter is not on behavior when people get together in a building called "the church," but on how the family members ought to live out their faith in community before the world around them (Fee 1988, 92).

The family of God is further described in a relative clause: **which is the church of the living God**. This is the second time Paul has used the word **church** in this chapter and letter to indicate the people of God (→ 3:5). The church is that special assembly of believers who have been redeemed by Christ's death and resurrection. Through the abiding presence of the Holy Spirit, this group becomes a cohesive unit, fit to do the will of God (Eph 2:19-22).

The church belongs to **the living God**. God as "living" is a common image in the OT (Josh 3:10; 2 Kgs 19:4, 16; Ps 42:2; Isa 37:4; Dan 6:20; Hos 1:10). It indicates that God is the only God in existence compared to the many worthless idols fabricated by people (1 Cor 8:4-6; Eph 4:6; 1 Thess 1:9). Visible evidence of his involvement in creation can be seen all around us (Rom 1:20). It also shows that he is the only true source of life. This phrase used with the imagery that follows emphasizes God's presence in the midst of his people.

The fulfillment of God's covenant-promise to Israel that he would dwell among them was most vividly evident in the wilderness tabernacle and later the temple (Exod 25:8; Lev 26:11-12; Ps 114:2; Ezek 37:27). But Paul builds on the OT tradition, which stresses that God's presence cannot be confined to any earthly temple (e.g., Deut 10:14; 1 Kgs 8:27; Neh 9:6; Pss 115:16; 148:4; Isa 66:1; Jer 23:24). His temple imagery emphasizes God's presence in the church through the Holy Spirit (1 Cor 3:16). What makes the church different from any other organization is that God dwells within it (2 Cor 6:16).

Wherever God's presence dwells must be holy and cleansed from all impurities (Lev 11:45; 1 Pet 1:15-16). The ethical tone of this verse, represented in the word **conduct**, calls the church to live differently than the fallen world around it. Because it is the dwelling place of God, the church is called to holiness as the core requirement to be in God's presence. Each of the words in this clause lacks the article in the Greek. This type of construction makes this statement more of a general principle that applies to every local congregation. Each church is part of the people of God and must make a fundamental choice: Will we allow the mercy and presence of Christ through the Spirit to transform us corporately into his likeness (1 Tim 1:16; 2 Cor 3:16)? Holiness for the people of God can only be lived out as a local community of faith.

The imagery then shifts to a building, with the church being called **the pillar and foundation of the truth**. Pillars (*stylos*) were the columns that supported the roofs of the temples of that time. When the Ephesians heard this word, they may have thought of the temple to the goddess Artemis in their city. This significant structure had one hundred ionic columns, each sixty feet (eighteen meters) tall. These supported a massive marble roof.

The meaning of the word translated **foundation** (*edraiōma*) is unclear. It refers to whatever gives "support" (NASB; "buttress" [ESV]; "bulwark" [NRSV]) to a building. Together the words **pillar** and **foundation** stress a single idea (employing the literary device hendiadys), symbolizing stability and strength. Both words refer to a temple, which represents the church as the dwelling place of the living God. Paul calls the church the temple of God in other letters (1 Cor 3:16-17; 2 Cor 6:16; Eph 2:21).

The genitive phrase **of the truth** probably modifies both **pillar** and **foundation**. **Truth** occurs fourteen times in the Pastorals (→ 1 Tim 2:4, 7; 3:9) and indicates "the content of Christianity as the absolute truth" (BDAG 2000, 42). The phrase indicates a dual responsibility of the church. First, as the **pillar**, the church must hold the truth of the gospel high for all to see. The church is the stabilizing repository of the truth, built on the foundation of apostolic teaching (Eph 2:20). Second, as the **foundation**, the church maintains the truth of the gospel over against encroaching heresies.

Paul opens this letter with directions for Timothy to deal with teachers of false doctrines who have abandoned the truth (1 Tim 1:3 6:5; 2 Tim 2:18; 3:8; 4:4). One function of the church is to safeguard orthodoxy. The church has been the custodian of the gospel truth throughout the ages by protecting it from compromise and clearly communicating it to unbelievers.

■ **16** The theological high point of the letter is reached with this verse. The untranslated *kai* ("and") at the beginning of the verse brings to a close the smaller unit of 3:14-15, the list of qualifications for overseers and deacons in this chapter, and the directions about men and women of ch 2. It returns readers to some of the key points Paul makes in ch 1 about the grace, faith, and love found in Christ (1:14). The faith the church must uphold is "the pillar and foundation of the truth" (3:15). Furthermore, this verse comes at the literary center of the letter. It includes a hymn to Jesus Christ and traces his appearance as a man from his birth to ascension.

Beyond all question (*homologoumenōs*) stresses the importance of what is to follow. This Greek word occurs only here in the Bible and expresses that what follows is beyond dispute and "without any doubt" (NRSV). There must be absolutely no compromise on this assertion. It is accepted by all true believers and confirmed in the church. The word is related to one's profession of faith. The opening line of this verse may have been used by the early church to introduce the confession of faith that follows (Michel 1967b, 213). This is a strong affirmation of a core belief the Ephesians ought to know and accept. If anyone is teaching something other than this, that person is unorthodox—unfaithful to the gospel of Jesus Christ (see Gal 1:6-9).

The core doctrine to confess is **the mystery from which true godliness springs**. This is the second time Paul has used the word **mystery** (*mystērion*) in this chapter. In 1 Tim 3:9, he refers to the "mystery of the faith" (ESV, NASB, NRSV). This second occurrence clarifies the first.

A mystery as understood in both Jewish (translating the Aramaic *raz* in Dan 2:18, 27, 28, 29, 30, 47) and Greek thought (a specialized word in contemporary "mystery religions") is something hidden that must be revealed to be known. Unlike the secretive mystery religions, Christianity was not a secret concealed but a secret revealed in Christ (Col 2:2-3).

In this verse, **mystery** is qualified by the genitive *of godliness* (*tēs eusebeias*). **Godliness** (*eusebeia*) is an important word in the Pastoral Epistles (→ 2:2). It is an ethical term that denotes religious piety, which leads the faithful to ethical behavior. Godliness as an observable behavior (the doing) springs from the inner life devoted to the truth of the gospel (the being). This verse has the effect of joining *being* and *doing*. The opposite is implicit: rejecting the mystery leads to faulty piety (see 1:19-20).

The mystery of godliness is called **great** (*mega*), **important**. This phrase recalls the pagan Ephesian confession, "Great is Artemis of the Ephesians!" (Acts 19:28, 34). Paul may have intentionally hijacked the idolatrous rhetoric to show that there is a new mode of existence in Christ (Towner 2006, 277). This verse sets the foundation for the following six occurrences of *eusebeia* in this letter (4:7, 8; 6:3, 5, 6, 11).

The content of this mystery is described in a hymn of six lines. There is no way to know if Paul wrote this himself or if he is quoting a hymn from the early church. Every element in the hymn was a core belief of early Christians. The hymn begins abruptly with a relative pronoun (*hos,* **who**) translated **he** in the NIV. There is no clear contextual antecedent for this pronoun, but the hymn makes it clear that Jesus Christ is the subject. The pronoun may point back to the word **mystery** and equate it with Christ (Marshall 1999, 523).

The grammatical structure of the hymn is symmetrical. Each line has first an aorist verb used historically for a past event. Each verb ends with the rhythmic *-thē* (third-person singular passive voice), simply translated *he was.* After the verb comes the preposition *en* ("in") followed by a noun in the dative case (*en* always takes dative objects). However, there is no preposition in line 3, although the dative case may assume the word "in" as part of its meaning. All this indicates carefully constructed poetry.

The division of the hymn is debated. Major modern translations give the following approaches: three stanzas of two lines each (NIV, NLT, UBS[4]), one stanza with six lines (JB, NASB), or two stanzas with three lines (ESV, NRSV). Commentators are similarly divided in their analyses. The relationship of each line is difficult to assess. There appears to be a basic thematic chronological organization recounting the life of Jesus Christ (Barrett 1963, 64-66). Line 6 poses a problem with this chronological understanding since the ascension happened before the birth of the church, which seems hinted at in lines 4 and 5 (→ 3:16). A two-stanza division breaks down as follows:

Stanza 1: *Earthly Ministry*

> Line 1: Incarnation
>
> Line 2: Resurrection
>
> Line 3: Exaltation

Stanza 2: *Exalted Ministry*

> Line 4: Christ's ministry through the church
>
> Line 5: The reception of the gospel in the world
>
> Line 6: Ascension or final glorification, possibly the second coming

Another approach breaks the hymn into a triplet with two lines, each with a rough chronological flow. Each pair has a contrast: body/spirit, angels/nations, and world/glory. The three couplets could have antithetical nouns influenced by Hebrew poetry (Dibelius and Conzelmann 1972, 63). Liefeld sees an alternating chiasm based on literary style (1999, 142-43):

Earthly	*Heavenly*
He appeared in *a body*	**was vindicated by the Spirit,**
Heavenly	*Earthly*
was seen by angels	**was preached among the nations,**
Earthly	*Heavenly*
was believed on in the world	**was taken up in glory**

Again, the hymn may simply have six parallel lines with no intended pairing. The main purpose of the poem appears to be to offer a brief historical outline of the life of Christ with the application and explanation of each line left to the local church and its leaders either in worship or catechism.

The first line claims that Christ **appeared in the flesh**. The word **appeared** (*ephanerōthē*) refers to something that has been revealed that was previously hidden—a "mystery" (Rom 16:25-26; Col 1:26; → 1 Tim 3:9, 14-15). The term as used in this line presupposes that Christ existed before his incarnation (→ 1:15; Mounce 2000, 227). The word **flesh** (*sarki*) is the same term used in John 1:14, "The Word became flesh," and Rom 1:3, "who was descended from David according to the flesh" (NRSV). The English "incarnation" comes directly from the Latin for "flesh" (*incarnatio*).

The implied emphasis is on what Christ did subsequent to becoming human. References are general, not specific. In early Christian thought, the ultimate reason Christ came in the flesh was to give himself as a sacrifice for sin (Rom 8:3; Eph 5:1-2; Phil 2:7-8). This line could also refer to Christ's postresurrection appearances that proved the validity of his death on the cross (Rom 1:4; Schneider 1967). The early church unanimously agreed that "the incarnation found its ultimate purpose/climax in the crucifixion" (Towner 1989; Rom 8:3; Phil 2:7-8). Christ's epiphany is a common theme in 1 Tim 6:14; 2 Tim 1:10; 4:1, 8; Titus 2:11, 13; 3:4. A confession like this in the early church would combat growing heresies, such as Docetism, which denied Jesus came in actual human flesh (see 1 John 4:2-3). Such heretics reject the claim that he was born, suffered, or died.

The second line is that Christ **was vindicated by the Spirit**. This line responds to line 1 and expresses his victory through death and resurrection. The verb **vindicated** (*edikaiothē*) indicates something that is "declared right" or proven true. Christ's resurrection proved him to be the innocent Messiah and Son of God.

Interpreters disagree as to how to interpret **Spirit** here. In the Greek, this word has no article and could simply mean "in spirit" or "by spirit" (*en pneumati*). There are two major approaches to interpreting this. One is to see a flesh/spirit antithesis between lines 1 and 2, the natural sphere vs. the supernatural. Although Jesus suffered in the flesh, he was proven right in the spiritual realm. After his resurrection, Jesus entered the spiritual realm as the firstfruits of those to follow (1 Cor 15:20). Hence, "the Christ-event was both a pattern for believing humanity . . . and the content of the gospel by which people enter into that pattern" (Towner 2006, 281).

The other alternative, followed by the NIV, is to see this as a reference to the Holy Spirit. Romans 1:4 states that the gospel is about God's Son, "who through the Spirit of holiness was appointed the Son of God in power by his resurrection from the dead." It was through the Spirit that Jesus was raised from the dead (Rom 8:11; 1 Pet 3:18). It was through the cross and resurrection that Jesus revealed the power of God (1 Cor 2:2-4). God exalted Christ because of his sacrifice and power over sin and death (Phil 2:5-11). Jesus sets the pattern for all who put their faith in him.

This second line is "the completion of Jesus' humanity, as through resurrection the limited authority of death is overcome by resurrection power and the destined Spirit-abode of humanity is entered" (Towner 2006, 281). If this is a reference to the Holy Spirit, then this is the first mention of the Spirit in the Pastorals (→ 1 Tim 4:1; 2 Tim 1:7, 14; Titus 3:5).

Third, he **was seen by angels**. **Seen** (*ōphthē*) is the same verb used for Jesus' resurrection appearances (Luke 24:31; Acts 9:17; 13:31; 1 Cor 15:5-8) and has the effect of verifying his resurrection. It gives experiential proof: people actually saw and touched him. The alliteration of sound is broken in this line with the missing "in" or "by" (*en*) in the Greek. The instrumental use of the dative case of **angels** (*angelois*) implies the word **by** and essentially has the same force of the preposition *en* of the other lines.

Interpreters are divided on the force of the word **angels**. It could be taken in the general sense of messengers or in a more specific way as supernatural beings. Jesus appeared to the early messengers of the gospel (Acts 2:32; 3:15; Barrett 1963, 65). In addition, angels were present at the resurrection (Matt 28:5-7; Mark 16:5-7; Luke 24:23; John 20:12-13). The most common use of this word in the NT, however, is for heavenly beings (Mounce 2000, 229). These heavenly angels could be contrasted with "the world" of the fourth line. If this line does refer to angels, at what point did Jesus appear to them? The Gospels assert that angels were present at his resurrection. There are some obscure references of Jesus appearing before spiritual powers in Eph 3:9-11; Col 2:15, 20; and 1 Pet 1:12. But these passages could be interpreted in other ways. The book of Revelation indicates that early Christians believed angels worship the exalted Christ (Rev 4—5; see Rom 8:34; Heb 2:9). "The point of the line is that the triumph of Christ over death was announced in the spiritual realm (just as it was/is in the human realm)" (Towner 1989, 92).

Lines 2 and 3 provide the basis for line 4: he **was preached among the nations**. The church's mission is summarized in the verb **was preached** (*ekērychthē*). The message preached occupies the first two lines: Jesus became one with humanity and expressed his love by dying on the cross. His resurrection proved the depth of this sacrificial love and opens the door of salvation for all people. The foolishness of preaching is the way the Christ event is made known to the world (1 Cor 1:21; 15:12). Paul believed in the need to proclaim the gospel accurately, fervently, and relevantly (Rom 10:14-15; 1 Cor 9:15-18).

We should not narrow the force of the term "preaching" to a twenty-minute, three-point address preached from a pulpit on Sunday morning. For Paul, preaching was much more dynamic. Acts implies that Paul took every opportunity to share the gospel (e.g., 17:16-34).

Although the tense of the verb **preached** is aorist, like the others in this hymn, the time period involved here began on the day of Pentecost in Acts 2 and continues to this day. The whole hymn reflects back on the events of Christ from the perspective of the postresurrection church. But this fourth line is open-ended, because the task is unfinished.

The reason for this is because the message must go out to all **the nations**. Nations (*ethnesin*) is inclusive. It is often translated in the NT as "Gentiles," as in 1 Tim 2:7. Paul's mission, however, was to both Jews and Gentiles. He never gave up on his own people. His vision compelled him to go to the "uttermost part[s]" of his world (Acts 1:8 [KJV]; see Matt 28:19-20). In his thinking, Christology should lead to mission (→ 1 Tim 2:1-7).

The fifth line indicates that Christ **was believed on in the world**. This indicates how the world received the message of lines 1-2 and preached in line 4. The verb **was believed** shares the same root as "faith." The object of this faith is the subject of the verb, Jesus Christ (→ 1:16).

In the world parallels **among the nations** of line 4. **The world** (*kosmōi*) is what Christ came to save and where the church is to minister (1:15). The world as human beings is capable of responding in faith, not the cosmos as the created order (6:7). Paul's underlying emphasis is again the mission of the church. He assumes that the church has carried out its mission of proclamation and that people have received it with faith. The church has this ongoing task: to carry out and complete what Christ began (Eph 3:7-12). Paul's inclusive vision expands beyond Gentiles or **the nations** to include the whole world (Gal 3:28). Christianity must be missional by definition and intent. The gospel is good news that must be proclaimed so that people can respond.

The last line states that he **was taken up in glory**. This line presents an ambiguity: To what point in Christ's life does this refer? Two major possibilities have been offered.

First, this could refer to the ascension of Christ recorded in Acts 1. The verb **was taken up** (*analambanō*) is used a number of times for Christ's ascension (Mark 16:19; Luke 9:51; 24:51; Acts 1:2, 11, 22). But this understanding destroys the chronological sequence of the hymn. The historical order would require this line to be inserted between lines 3 and 4.

Second, this line does not necessarily speak of Christ's ascension nor must this hymn follow a chronological order. It could refer to Christ's second coming when he lays the kingdom at the feet of the Father in the final sign of complete triumph (1 Cor 15:24-28; Phil 2:10-11; Barrett 1963, 66). The latter option stands beyond the experience of the early church and still exists in the realm of hope. The first option confirms one of the key affirmations of the church. **In glory** reaches the climax of the incarnation. Christ is seated at the highest place of honor in heaven, symbolized as at the right hand of the Father (Eph 1:20-23; Phil 2:9-11). Christ the glorified one is at work in his body, the church. This line may seem out of place in the chronology of the hymn, but it ends with the permanent location of Christ.

FROM THE TEXT

This revealing section of the letter offers significant insights into how Paul used Christology to deal with pressing leadership problems in the Ephesian church. In looking back, it confirms the "mystery" that the overseers and deacons were to uphold in their ministry. Looking forward, it censures the false teachers who were causing problems in this church. It draws the attention of modern readers back to the "one mediator between God and mankind, the man Christ Jesus, who gave himself as a ransom for all people" (1 Tim 2:5-6).

Upholding the truth of the gospel. The goal of all the directions Paul has given so far, and will continue to give in the remaining chapters, is "to preserve the integrity of the gospel message" (Mounce 2000, 231). The church as the pillar and foundation of the truth must preserve the truth by (1) knowing and confessing the essentials of the life of Christ and (2) living out this faith in godliness.

This hymn bears witness to the action of Christ seen in the passive verbs. God revealed his plan through the incarnation of Christ (Heb 2:14, 15, 17). Pope Leo the Great wrote, "For, the grace of God—by which the entire assembly of saints has always been justified—was not initiated at the time that Christ was born but augmented" (*Serm.* 23.4, quoted by Gorday 2000, 179). The church has been the key witness of this plan by upholding the message received from the apostles and preserved in the Scriptures. The truth claim of this hymn cannot be compromised. Any teaching contrary to this must be rejected.

Living out the truth in godliness. This section is a pause in the letter and allows Paul to put the expected behavior of those in the church in the proper perspective. It gives the basis for the behavior of believers (1 Tim 3:15). The TNIV acknowledges this by giving a major division that continues until 5:1. This passage functions as a pivot between how people ought to live in the church and the heresy to be discussed in ch 4. Paul continues in ch 4 by exposing the opposite behavior of what he expected in the church.

The Christ-hymn here directly confronts the speculative meanderings of the false teachers (→ 1:3-7). Theology is the crucial foundation for ethics in Paul's thought. This passage makes that clear with the word "godliness" (*eusebeia*). Godliness should result from a clear understanding of who Christ is and what he has done. Since we have been redeemed, we ought to live as redeemed people (1 Cor 6:19-20). If we walk in the obedience of faith, the Spirit will transform us into the likeness of the one who has saved us (2 Cor 3:18). The "mystery of godliness" is that God can sanctify us completely. The one who calls us "is faithful and he [can and] will do it" (1 Thess 5:23-24).

The mission of the church. Why does Paul quote this hymn at this point in his letter? One reason may be that the hymn essentially reminds the church of its core mission, which is anchored in the person of Christ Jesus. Christ ought to be at the center of all we do as the people of God. It does not take "eloquence or human wisdom" (1 Cor 2:1) but simple obedience in faith to the message embodied in the one who became one of us.

IV. INSTRUCTIONS TO TIMOTHY ABOUT THE FALSE TEACHERS: I TIMOTHY 4:1-16

Descending the theological summit of the letter in 3:14-16, Paul returns to the crises created by the false teachers in the Ephesian church. Fundamental to both Paul's theology and ethics is that Christian doctrine impacts practical living. Poor theology leaves a shaky foundation for godliness (*eusebeia*).

Paul first mentions the teachers of false doctrine in 1:3. There is a similar pattern to chs 1 and 4. In 1:3-17, Paul uses polemical language to reveal the erroneous position of the false teachers. In 1:18-20, he reminds Timothy of his calling in order to help him deal with these people. In 4:1-5, Paul again warns of the false teachers. This is likewise followed by a reminder of Timothy's divine calling and equipping to deal with this situation in 4:6-16 (Mounce 2000, 233).

Timothy is the primary person to confront these people, but he must do this by making sure the church is firmly grounded in *eusebeia*. The basis for this is given in the hymn of 3:14-16. What the opponents were teaching stands in stark contrast to this core confession of faith. The letter displays a strong unity as it revolves around the central theme of godliness. Chapters 2—3 show how members of the church ought to act; ch 4 compares the false teachers to this ideal.

The last half of the letter can be divided into two major sections: (1) personal reminders to Timothy about his ministry in Ephesus and his task of dealing with false teachers (4:1-16), and (2) how Timothy should deal with the various groups and leaders in the Ephesian church (5:1—6:2a). The latter part of the letter is marked by specific directions to Timothy (4:6, 11, 16; 5:23; 6:2, 17). Two passages deal particularly with the opponents: 4:1-5 and 6:3-10. The letter ends with further personal exhortation to Timothy about avoiding temptations about material things (6:2b-21; Marshall 1999, 530). Paul encourages Timothy to model to the Ephesians what Christians should believe and how faith should express itself in holy living.

There are three key movements of this chapter: (1) Verses 1-5 summarize how false teachers threaten the Ephesian church. Paul refutes their erroneous theology and flawed understanding of the Law, appealing to creation theology. (2) Verses 6-10 highlight Timothy's need for sound doctrine. Paul reminds him that God has called and equipped him to deal with this situation. Second-person singular imperative verbs create a noticeable shift in tone. (3) Verses 11-16 personally exhort Timothy to remain steadfast in sound doctrine (3:14-16) and godly living.

A. The Nature of the Heresy (4:1-5)

BEHIND THE TEXT

The church must be the guardian of the truth of 3:14-16, yet there were some people in Ephesus who had rejected this truth. These false teachers, first mentioned in 1:3, are reintroduced in 4:1, their activities described in v 3a, and their position refuted in vv 3b-5. The cause of their error is given in vv 1-2: They have abandoned the truth. The proof that this error is present in the church is shown in vv 3-10.

This section provides more information about the nature of their false teachings. These people wanted to be teachers of the Law but got caught up in genealogies and empty speculations (→ 1:3-7). Part of their faulty interpretation of the Law had to do with marriage and what types of food could be eaten. The church can be prepared to resist this heresy by the Spirit's warning. The answer to these opponents is found in creation theology: everything God created is good.

Timothy must strongly resist the opponents because the existence of the church and the vitality of its mission are at stake. He must watch his own life, set an example, and be active in his spiritual formation. This section accomplishes three things in the letter: (1) it reflects back on ch 3 and the need for strong leadership within the church, (2) it deals with the core issue of why Paul wrote the letter, and (3) it prepares for the discussion that follows about Timothy's character.

The verb tense shifts in 4:1 from the present to the future: "The Spirit . . . *says* . . . some *will* abandon." The present problem in Ephesus matches what will be evident in the last days. The source of this revelation is the Spirit, who is mentioned only rarely in this letter.

Verses 1-5 form one long sentence in Greek. Numerous ambiguities in its syntax necessitate choices about punctuation and translation. The section poses further questions about Pauline authorship with a significant number of words that occur only here in the NT. As with other parts of the Pastoral Epistles, this unusual vocabulary may have been shaped by the polemical language against the opponents in this section. It does not necessarily mean Paul is not the source behind the letter (Johnson 1996, 159).

The language of this section is polemical, with several explicit and implied contrasts.

Positive (Paul's Position)	*Negative* (The Opponents' Position)
Holy Spirit (4:1a)	Deceiving spirits and demons (4:1b)
Truth (3:15; 4:6)	Liars, hypocrites (4:2)
The faith (4:1)	Things taught by demons (1:1b)
Everything is good (4:4)	Certain foods should be rejected (4:3)
Godliness (4:6-11)	Faulty ethics (4:1-5)

IN THE TEXT

■ **1** The Greek sentence begins with an untranslated *de* ("but" or "and"), linking this chapter to the previous one, and in particular, the hymn of 3:14-16. Paul's polemical language should isolate the false teachers and help the Ephesians see that they do not align with "sound doctrine" (1:10-11) and "the mystery of godliness" (3:16 [ESV, KJV, NASB]).

God has intervened to resolve the problems in Ephesus with a prophetic warning—his Holy **Spirit clearly says** (→ 2 Tim 1:7). The Spirit of God is mentioned in this letter only here (and possibly in 3:16), and elsewhere in the Pastorals only in 2 Tim 1:7, 14; and Titus 3:5. The Spirit is the source of revelation

165

(Acts 20:23; 21:11) and gives warning through prophets of coming danger (Acts 11:27-28; see "the Spirit says to the churches" in Rev 2:7, 11, 17, 29; 3:6, 13, 22). The Spirit makes the mysteries of God known (Dan 4:9; 1 Cor 2:6-10).

Paul does not say how the Spirit reveals the coming apostasy, directly to Paul (see 1 Cor 7:10-12, 40; Acts 20:28-31; → 2 Tim 3:1-9; 4:3-4) or through an unnamed Christian prophet (Collins 2002, 112). The tense of the verb **says** (*legei*) indicates the present activity of the Spirit. Rhetorically, this strengthens Paul's ethos of authority (Campbell 1997, 193-94). That the Spirit is the source of this warning indicates that it should be heeded.

The Spirit gives this warning **clearly** (*rhētōs*), an adjective used only here in the Greek Bible. It guarantees the accuracy and certainty of what follows (Knight 1992, 188). It could be translated "unambiguously," "precisely," "explicitly" (NASB), or "expressly" (ESV, KJV, NRSV). Paul does not say how the Spirit is heard, but his message is clear.

That (*hoti*) introduces the general contents of the revelation. The Spirit speaks of events to come **in later times**. **Later** (*hysterois*) is a comparative adjective used superlatively. The phrase is unique in the NT (but compare 2 Tim 3:1 and Heb 1:2: "in the last days").

The question for Christians has always been, When are the "last days"? In Paul's thought, these are "the days inaugurated by the Messiah and characterized by the Spirit's presence in power, the days to be consummated by the return of Christ" (Knight 1992, 188). The "last times" are marked by the continued struggle with sin and fleshly desires but with the promise of victory through the Holy Spirit (Rom 8:1-11).

The "present evil age" is characterized by love of self, money, and pleasure (2 Tim 3:2-4). But the death and resurrection of Jesus Christ broke the hold of this "present evil age" (Gal 1:4; see 1 Cor 15:56-57). The exalted Christ's gift of the Holy Spirit inaugurated the new age for all who believe (Joel 2:28-32; Acts 2:17-21). But believers still face opposition from scoffers loyal to the defeated powers of the old age (2 Pet 3:3; Jude 18). Jews and early Christians expected the transition to the last days to be marked by difficulties and people rejecting God (Dan 12:1; *1 En.* 80:2-8; 1QpHab 2:5-6; 1QS 3:22; *T. Dan.* 5:5-6; Matt 24:24-25; Mark 13:22-23; Acts 20:29; 2 Thess 2:1-12; 1 John 2:18; Rev 13:11-18). The early church believed there would be a falling away in the last days (2 Pet 3:3-7; Jude 17-18), and the situation in Ephesus illustrates this. The Spirit predicted two events for the last days.

First, **some will abandon the faith**. The verb *apostēsontai* means going away, withdrawing, deserting, falling away, and apostatizing. In the LXX, it refers to rebellion against God (BDAG 2000, 157-58; Schlier 1964b, 512-13). In the present context, it means forsaking God. It is the opposite of repentance, which is turning toward God. What **some** "renounce" (NRSV) is **the**

faith. The faith is used in this letter for the truth of the gospel (→ 3:9). This apostasy is not simply an unfortunate falling away or innocent misunderstanding; it is a deliberate departure. The future tense refers to the present crisis in Ephesus. The situation is an expression of the apostasy of the last times.

The generic **some** (*tines*) has no direct reference to anyone, but the context implies that it refers to the false teachers in Ephesus and those they are leading astray. The vague reference could be "an intentional expression of disrespect" (Towner 2006, 289). These people are also a concern in the second letter (2 Tim 2:16-18; 3:13; 4:3-4). That they **abandon** the faith indicates that they were once part of the believing community. They rejected something they once had.

Second, the Spirit predicts that the apostates will **follow deceiving spirits and things taught by demons. Follow** is the translation of the participle *prosechontes*, paying attention or giving heed to something, leading to devotion (BDAG 2000, 881). The instrumental participle shows *how* these people abandoned the truth of the gospel. The sequence is noteworthy: By abandoning one set of values, they have embraced another. The participle has two objects:

First, the apostates have followed after **deceiving spirits**. The adjective **deceiving** (*planois*) indicates that the false teachers actively led some astray (Braun 1968, 249-50). The word in 2 Tim 3:13 describes "evildoers and impostors" who descend into immorality by deceiving and being deceived. Jesus warned of false messiahs in the end times who would try to deceive believers (Matt 24:4-5, 11, 24). Jews had a similar belief (*Sib. Or.* 2:154-73; 7:120-38; *T. Jud.* 23:1-5). Deceitfulness results when people reject God and become consumed by their passions (Rom 1:27).

The last days will be characterized by Satan's deceit as people reject the truth (2 Thess 2:9-12). The Holy Spirit has clearly revealed that these **deceiving spirits** are the cause of the apostasy. The close association with **demons** here indicates that these are evil spirits.

Second, those who have abandoned the faith have followed after the teachings of demons. The plural **things taught** (*didaskaliai*; → 1:10) contrasts with the singular truth; the deceived were confused about true doctrine (Collins 2002, 113). The NIV translates the genitive "of demons" instrumentally (**by demons**), but it could be interpreted as a genitive of source (*from demons*). In either case, demons sponsor these false teachings.

Demonic forces blind people to evil, making it palatable and easier to swallow. Paul does not indict the false teachers as demon-possessed (Mounce 2000, 237). He merely attempts "to 'locate' the heretical movement within the eschatological demonic opposition to God" (Towner 2006, 290). In 2 Cor 11:15, he maligns his opponents as Satan's "servants" (John 8:44; 2 Cor 2:11; Eph 2:2; 2 Thess 2:9-10; Jas 3:15; 1 John 4:6; Rev 16:14; 18:2).

The starkly polemical language here prepares for the clear contrast between the two positions, which occupies the remainder of the chapter. Paul characterizes the opponents using strong rhetoric, clearly warning Timothy and the Ephesians of the danger they represent. This style is typical of prophetic and eschatological texts (Mark 13:11; Acts 8:29; Rev 3:6; Saarinen 2008, 75-76).

Because the church is part of the new age inaugurated by Christ's resurrection, it ought to live under the influence of the old age dominated by the forces of evil. The second coming of Christ will bring the old age to a close (1 Tim 6:14-15; Ladd 1993, 360-75). Meanwhile, the church must heed the Spirit's warning about false teachers.

■ **2** Here, Paul gets to the cause of the problem: Because the false teachers and those who followed them had abandoned the faith, they had rejected the leading of their consciences. The phrase at the beginning of the verse in the NIV, **such teachings come**, is not found in the Greek. It seeks to show the connection between 4:1 and 2. Verse 2 continues v 1, clarifying further the effects of the demonic forces.

A literal reading of the two verses is: *Some have abandoned the faith by being devoted to deceitful spirits and the teachings of demons, by the hypocrisy of liars whose consciences are seared.* Verse 2 shifts its focus from the demonic forces to their human instruments. The teaching of the demons comes **through** the agency of (*en* with the dative) human **liars**. The preposition *en* has an instrumental force ("by means of" [NASB]), but there is the nuance of "in association with" (2 Tim 1:13; Marshall 1999, 539). The demonic forces have no power except through the lies and hypocrisy of those who allow them (Saarinen 2008, 76). Paul describes the deceived deceivers in Ephesus using three vivid images: they were hypocritical, taught lies, and lacked a conscience.

First, *hypokritēs* describes an actor who assumes a false identity by wearing a mask. The word has a negative connotation of deception in the NT (Gal 2:13): it is an outward show without inner correspondence. Jesus criticized those who look righteous on the outside but inwardly are evil (Matt 23:28; Mark 12:15; Luke 12:10). The opponents were like wolves dressed as sheep (Matt 7:15). Their teachings looked good on the outside but were really devoid of any truth. They had majored on minors, and their lifestyle betrayed them. It is not clear how they were hypocrites. Marshall offers three possibilities:

(a) They deliberately pretended to be Christian teachers and to be speaking the truth in order to deceive people.

(b) They put up a show of asceticism, which others regarded as an indication of their good character.

(c) They were self-deceived, mistakenly claiming to be Christian teachers. (1999, 540)

That Paul called them hypocrites suggests that their deception was intentional. They knew their message was wrong and pulled others down with them. The nature of their hypocrisy becomes more evident in 1 Tim 4:3.

Second, they were **liars**. This word occurs only here in the NT. It is made of two parts: *pseudo* ("false") and *logos* ("word"). The meaning is close to hypocrisy. Their lies stood over against the truth of the gospel. They had intentionally deviated from the message given in 3:16. "They do not utter these falsehoods through ignorance and unknowingly but as acting a part, knowing the truth but 'having their conscience seared'" (Chrysostom, *Hom. 1 Tim.* 12).

Third, their underlying problem is that their **consciences have been seared as with a hot iron.** The conscience is where decisions are made based on some criteria. It guides a person to differentiate between right and wrong ($\rightarrow$ 1:5).

There is a strong contrast in this letter between a good conscience and one that no longer works properly. A good conscience keeps the faith (1:5, 19; 3:9). By rejecting this faith, the conscience will follow another guide. The way the conscience goes, so does one's lifestyle. By departing from the faith, the opponents were following their own standards of behavior.

As a consequence, their consciences had become seared. **Seared** (*kekaustēriasmenōn*) is a rare participle, used only here in the NT. Its perfect tense implies that this scorching began in the past and continues in the present crisis. The word graphically refers to the burning done by a red hot iron. The phrase **with a hot iron** is implied by the Greek verb but added to the translation to relay its intended force. There are two ways to interpret this searing:

First, it could refer to being marked as with a branding iron. Branding was used in the ancient world for animals, convicts, fugitive slaves, and military deserters. The opponents bore the mark of Satan and belonged to him and did his will (Fee 1988, 98). Their seared consciences no longer worked and they lived the opposite of what they taught (Theodore of Mopsuestia, *Com. 1 Tim.*).

Second, it could mean being deadened as in cauterization, a medical procedure by which the flow of blood is stopped. The result of this is hardened flesh and a loss of feelings in that part of the body. The nuance of this word indicates that the false teachers and their followers had become insensitive to the leading of the Holy Spirit. They could no longer recognize the truth of the gospel. A similar situation may lie behind Paul's strong warnings in Rom 1:18, 28-32.

The outward evidence of this searing is hypocrisy. They attempted to hide their inner loss of spiritual life. The root cause was the rejection of the gospel. When the conscience no longer functions as a moral guide, one's lifestyle deteriorates to fleshly living (Rom 8:5-8; Gal 5:19-21); one is unable to make right decisions.

How deliberate was the apostasy of the false teachers? Their seared conscience suggests that they actively rejected the truth to the extent that they did not care anymore. False teachings can originate from curious people who become so enticed by more interesting ideas that they no longer see their error.

■ **3** Here Paul presents the evidence for his accusations against the false teachers in the previous two verses. He offers two tests against these teachers: (1) a theological test in 1 Tim 4:3-5 and (2) an ethical test in vv 6-10. These give us further insight into the heretical teachings of the false prophets and their followers.

The "liars" of v 2 were practicing a form of asceticism **by forbidding** [*kōlyontōn*] **people to marry** and **to abstain from certain foods**. It is difficult to determine whether the first prohibition entailed opposition to marriage in general or only certain marriages. The teachers may have influenced younger widows not to remarry (→ 5:11-14). Their idleness led these widows into relational and possibly even moral problems. Paul faced similar issues in Corinth. In response there, he insisted that marriage was not wrong but only that being single may allow some people more time to serve the Lord (1 Cor 7:32, 35). He affirms marriage in 1 Timothy in 3:2, 12, and will deal with the marriage of widows in 5:14.

There is no specific indication what **certain foods** they prohibited. The OT directed the people of Israel to abstain from certain unclean food (Lev 11; Deut 14:1-21). But Jesus declared all foods clean in Mark 7:19. Paul echoed this teaching in Rom 14:14. Meat sacrificed to idols created a knotty problem in Corinth (1 Cor 8—10). The Jerusalem Council of Acts 15 concluded that Gentile converts ought to avoid blood, food sacrificed to idols, and animals that had been strangled (15:20). Eating certain foods complicated relationship between Jewish and Gentile converts (Col 2:16).

Verse 3 of 1 Tim 4 ends with a theological explanation as to why the prohibition was wrong: **God created**. The relative pronoun **which** (*ha*) grammatically refers back to **foods** as its antecedent. God also created marriage, but as an infinitive (*gamein*), it seems to be an unlikely antecedent. The basic point is that all food is acceptable because it comes from God. The first teaching about marriage gets no further elaboration at this point, but in 5:14 Paul will direct young widows to remarry in order to avoid temptation and scandal.

The false teachers' prohibitions were essentially denying God as Creator. Their basic problem was a fundamental misunderstanding of the nature of God. They misinterpreted the first commands in Gen 1:28-30: Be fruitful and multiply, and care for the garden and eat from it. They may have had an overrealized eschatology and believed that they were already living in paradise (Towner 1989, 33-42). They may have confused physical resurrection with spiritual resurrection and thought that the end had already arrived in its fullness (Lane 1965). Some of the Corinthians apparently had similar ideas (1 Cor 15:12). The opponents' views hint at some form of dualism. But there is not enough evidence to say that they were gnostics or that they believed the material world was inferior to the spiritual realm and created by an inferior deity—the demiurge. Whatever else they believed, Paul confronted their dualism with the clear affirmation: **God created**. He based his response on creation theology, appealing to divine commands given long before the Torah and its food restrictions were decreed. He reasons: if God created it, it must be good.

What makes all food fit to eat is that God created it **to be received with thanksgiving**. The essential condition for eating any food as a Christian is thankfulness (*eucharistias*) because it expresses one's total dependence upon God. "Believers are indeed free in Christ to make use of all foods, but this is done within a relationship in which the gift nature of food is acknowledged by the recipients' response of gratitude" (Towner 2006, 298).

Prayers of thanksgiving were part of both Jewish and Christian practice. The Jewish custom can be seen when Jesus gave thanks before feeding the four thousand and five thousand (Matt 14:19; 15:36; Mark 6:41; 8:6; Luke 9:16; John 6:11). Jesus also gave thanks before his last Passover with his disciples (Matt 26:26-27; Mark 14:22-23; Luke 22:17, 19). Christian prayer is to be filled with thanksgiving (Phil 4:6), and food is to be received with a thankful heart (Acts 2:46; 1 Cor 10:30). The open door to knowing God is the attitude of gratitude. This puts God in the right place of honor and connects daily activities with worship. Prayers of thanksgiving acknowledge what God declared: all food is good.

To be received expresses the purpose for God's creation of food. It a Greek preposition (*eis*) followed by the accusative *metaēmpsin*, found only here in the NT. It carries the connotation of enjoying what one receives. God created food not simply as a necessity for human survival but as a blessing for people to enjoy (Gen 1:29; 2:9, 16; 3:2; 9:3).

In summary, marriage and food are consecrated in two ways:

First and foremost objectively in themselves, since God made or instituted them, gave them to us to enjoy, and has said so in Scripture. Then, secondly they are consecrated to us subjectively when we recognize their divine origin and receive them from God with gratitude. (Stott 1996, 114)

This thanksgiving is expressed **by those who believe and who know the truth.** This statement directly confronts the false teachers, who had rejected the truth. Those who know the truth will act accordingly. They realize that God is the Creator of all things and are aware of how their faith in Christ impacts their daily living. The opponents were using marriage and food as wedge issues to divide the church in Ephesus. They elevated their views to the level of law. Food should not be a basis for judging others (Rom 14:3; 1 Cor 10:29-

30). "One may do as one wishes before God, but one may not impose those 'wishes' as regulations for others to follow" (Fee 1988, 100).

Asceticism in the Early Church

There is no clear or direct link between the false teachers in Ephesus and the full-blown Gnosticism that developed a century later. Nevertheless, many elements of the later movement seem to have existed in seed form when the Pastorals were written. At the least, the two groups shared in the general Platonic milieu that had infiltrated much of the Hellenistic world. Gnosticism developed out of the same thinking that influenced the opponents in Ephesus.

One characteristic of some gnostic groups was an ascetic ethic. This stems from Platonic dualism, which considered the material world evil or inferior to the ideal, spiritual realm. Gnostics followed this thinking and taught that this world was created by an inferior god called the demiurge. Their goal was to reject any influence of the flesh and its passions. This led them to the practice of sexual continence and the prohibition of marriage.

Self-control is not a bad thing in itself. Paul warned of the dangers of basing one's life on the flesh vs. the Spirit in Rom 8 and Gal 5. The mistake of the gnostics, as with the opponents in Ephesus, was to forget that God created the world and pronounced it good. Paul found his answer to this challenge in the freedom that Christ brings (Gal 5:13).

The NT bears witness to the growing controversies and misunderstanding about food and sex in a number of situations (Acts 15; Rev 2:14-15, 20-25). Paul was compelled to deal with these topics often (see Rom 14:13-21; 1 Cor 7:12-16; 8:1-13; 10:25-31; Gal 2:11-14; 1 Thess 4:3-6).

There are some noteworthy similarities between the situations in the Ephesian and Corinthian churches. In both, groups within the church advocated special knowledge, spiritual elitism, the avoidance of sexual immorality, and the rejection of certain foods. In both settings the result was a dualistic disconnection between religious piety and daily life (Towner 2006, 295).

The issues faced in these churches and others developed in unfortunate directions in the following centuries. One such heresy, Encratism, is evident in the second-century apocryphal document *The Acts of Paul and Thecla*. It recounts the story of a young virgin named Thecla who, after hearing Paul preach, refused to get married because of her new devotion to Christ. Only abstinence from marriage allowed her to be faithful to the gospel Paul preached.

■ **4-5** Paul expands the theological basis for his rebuttal in 1 Tim 4:3, further explaining (**For** [*hoti*]) the implications of the affirmation of God as Creator. The logic is simply that:

1. What God created is good.
2. What God created should not be rejected because it is good.
3. How a person experiences this goodness is through thanksgiving, the promises of Scripture, and prayer.

The false teachers had rejected the good God had created. Paul affirms the goodness of food (and marriage) they had rejected (Collins 2002, 114). He reverses their designation of certain things as "unclean" and shows that these are, in fact, holy.

Verse 4 begins echoing Gen 1:31—**everything God created is good** (lit. "everything created by God" [NRSV]). Since the teachers wanted to teach the Law (1:7), Paul again uses the Scripture against them (→ 2:11-15). The predicate adjective **created** (*ktisma*) recalls God's activity in giving form, life, and purpose to all creation. All things came into existence simply **by the word of God**—"let there be . . . and there was" (Gen 1; see John 1:3; Col 1:16).

Any deviation from God's original plan for creation is bad. Sin entered the world through Adam and Eve's disobedience. This was the catalyst for the suffering of creation (Rom 8:20-22). To reject the created order is to reject the Creator. Paul counters claims of emerging gnostic thinking that despised creation as inferior and evil.

The second clause offers the implications of the first: **and nothing is to be rejected**. The rare adjective **rejected** (*apobleton*) can refer to something that is "taboo" (Guthrie 1990, 107). The false teachers considered taboo what God declared acceptable (Gen 2:9; 9:3).

The conditions under which nothing is to be rejected appear in a conditional participial phrase: **if it is received with thanksgiving**. This repeats the key idea of 1 Tim 4:3. "The antidote to rejection is not mere reception but rather reception with thankfulness to God as the acknowledged giver of these good gifts. It is God's goodness more than human freedom that Paul defends here" (Knight 1992, 192). "Thanksgiving" (*eucharistias*) is the same word used for the Lord's Supper in 1 Cor 10:16. But there is no obvious connection here. The focus is on daily meals in the routines of life.

Nevertheless, Paul essentially makes every meal sacramental. Eating food with thanksgiving allows believers to experience daily God's grace and goodness in new ways. Food is sacramental **because it is consecrated by the word of God and prayer**. The verb **consecrated** (*hagiazetai*) can also be translated as "sanctified." This relational term refers to something set aside for God's use. Common food becomes holy **by the word of God and prayer**.

For Paul, food itself is innately neither clean nor unclean. It can become holy, but it can also become unclean for those whose consciences speak against it (Rom 14:14). Food itself does not need to be "cleansed" from defilement, because it is intrinsically good. What makes food holy for the one who views it as unclean is prayer (Marshall 1999, 545). Through prayer, believers acknowledge the source of the food and respond in worship and thanksgiving. Expressing thanksgiving to God is the open door to experiencing more of God's grace.

To what does **the word of God** refer? **Word** has no article, so it could be taken generically as "a word." And how are we to take the genitive **of God**: "a word *about* God" or "a word *from* God"? Does this refer to Scripture, the teachings of Jesus, the gospel message, Jesus as the living Word, or a prophetic oracle? It could be narrowly interpreted as a reading from Scripture, a reference to God's blessing of all things good in Gen 1, or more broadly as a liturgical blessing. There is no way to know for sure what Paul intended here.

This much is clear: the freedom Christ brings allows believers to assert the goodness of creation. We confess God's goodness and grace while enjoying the food God created through some expression of thanksgiving and prayer.

The root for **prayer** (*enteuxeōs*) has the basic meaning of meeting or conversing with someone. "In effect, to receive God's gifts with thanksgiving is to have an encounter with God. God has spoken through his creation; humans respond with a prayer of thanksgiving" (Collins 2002, 118). This prayer should acknowledge God as Creator and Provider of all we need. Prayer does not magically change the food. It merely recognizes the one who created it. Through prayer, "the community acknowledges and activates what God has declared to be true" (Towner 2006, 299). Prayer internalizes what the word of God expresses. It takes the good news of the gospel seriously.

FROM THE TEXT

4:1-5   Paul clearly offers here a powerful critique of the false teachers in Ephesus. He shows how their rejection of the truth led to theological error, which resulted in their misguided behavior. The same problems are not far from modern Christians.

First, *God's Spirit and inspired messengers warn about potential false doctrines.* We join with Paul, Timothy, and the early church in living in the "latter days." Heresies still arise as the church awaits the coming of Jesus. Jesus warned his disciples about apostasy (Matt 24:10-11; Mark 13:22). We should not be surprised that some people turn away from the faith, but we should be prepared. The false teachers were preoccupied with speculation—fascinating but uncertain ideas about the Bible and theology. Many things we can know for certain, and for which we should even be willing to die. Others may be interesting but fruitless and futile. These have often become the seedbed for heresy.

Second, *we need to take seriously satanic and demonic oppression and possession.* In his *Screwtape Letters*, C. S. Lewis offers two traps for Christians concerning Satan: (1) ignoring his threat or (2) becoming obsessed with it (referred to by Black and McClung 2004, 89). Spiritual warfare is a reality though it is often veiled behind many aspects of modern life, addictions, and lifestyles. Paul warns Timothy and the Ephesians of how false teachings and those who advocate them especially open people to demonic forces. Falling

174

into temptation is the first step in this downward spiral. The specific temptation in this passage is to become insensitive to the truth of the gospel (Eph
4:19) and easily enticed by other teachings.

Martin Luther said, "It is the nature of all hypocrites and false prophets
to create a conscience where there is none, and to cause conscience to disappear where it does exist!" (quoted by Oden 1989, 59). Again, the antidote is
knowing the truth.

Third, *we must maintain a holistic and healthy view of the body as the
temple of God* (1 Cor 6:19-20). Two natural appetites can be abused or blessed:
sex and hunger. God created and blessed both to advance and preserve life in
this world.

Sexual intercourse is to be reserved for those committed to lifelong, monogamous marriage. God's plan was for a man and woman to join together in
mutual edification and procreation. Homosexuality, polygamy, and multiple
marriages are not God's plan. God can redeem through Christ those who have
deviated from his plan.

Food is a necessary part of life but can easily be abused. At times, it can
be good and even healthy to avoid certain types of foods, but this should be
done carefully, intentionally, and in consideration of others (see 1 Cor 8—10).

God blesses those who remain single (1 Cor 7) or who deny themselves
food for the sake of fasting (see Acts 13:2-3; 14:23). Whether a person marries
or abstains from certain foods should be done in light of a clear understanding
of God's creative purposes, with urgency to get the gospel to the world, and
in thoughtful prayer.

One way to celebrate the glory of God's creation is with thanksgiving
(1 Tim 4:4). Christians from the earliest times have offered thanks at their
meals. The reference to thanksgiving and eating in this passage is the first
textual evidence that Christians prayed before their meals. Gorging ourselves
without taking time to give thanks takes our eyes off of the one who blesses
and focuses on satisfying our own wants. Cultures of consumerism lose the
sense of creation as a gift of God.

In affluent cultures plagued by obesity and related health problems,
Christians may need to assess whether their eating practices have perverted
God's good gift of food into an idol of self-destruction.

B. The Vital Connection of Godliness to Timothy's Mission (4:6-10)

BEHIND THE TEXT

There is a noticeable change of tone in the letter at this point. In the previous section (4:1-5), Paul refutes the false teachers' erroneous position. They

were telling the Ephesians not to marry and not to eat certain foods. Their legalistic, ascetic doctrines were leading to relational and missional problems for the church. Paul wrote this letter so that Timothy would have the authority and knowledge to deal with these problems (3:15).

This section becomes more personal as Paul gives specific directions for how Timothy can be better prepared to deal with these aberrant leaders. The "voice" Paul uses shifts to the second-person singular "you." Verse 7 gives the first of the second-person imperatives in the whole letter. There are twelve present imperatives in this section, giving a sense of urgency to Paul's instructions (Mounce 2000, 346). Paul's personal exhortations to Timothy continue through v 16. Behind his direct language stands his close relationship with Timothy (→ 1:2). Chapter 5 changes the object of the exhortations to groups within the church. Timothy must make sure that his own life is firmly planted in "the mystery of godliness" (3:16 [ESV, KJV, NASB]) before he deals with others in the church.

Paul follows a pattern in the letter of discussing the Ephesian heresy (1 Tim 1:3-17; 4:1-5; 6:2b-10) and then encouraging Timothy to be forceful in correcting this heresy (1:18-20; 4:6-16; 6:11-16; Mounce 2000, 245). This section serves as a warning to Timothy not to fall into the opponents' traps. He had not abandoned his ministry in Ephesus. But Paul wants to preempt any potential problems in the future.

This section begins with a conditional statement that transitions into the qualities Timothy must embrace and avoid in order to be a "good minister of Christ Jesus." Verse 7a of ch 4 gives a clear contrast between the "godless myths and old wives' tales" the opponents were caught up in and the true godliness to which Timothy must devote himself. The two different approaches are compared further in v 8. Verse 9 affirms v 8, citing the third of five "faithful saying[s]" (KJV) that should direct Timothy's ministry. The resource for the lifestyle of godliness is "hope in the living God" (v 10).

Verse 11 begins a new paragraph in the NIV. It focuses on Timothy's personal responsibility. Verses 15 and 16 begin with imperatives and end stressing the favorable outcomes of keeping Paul's commands (Van Neste 2004, 53).

One of the major themes is that Timothy must serve as an example to the leaders in the church. The behavior he must have is compared to that of the heretics. Of utmost importance is Timothy's character, a theme also in 6:2, 11-14, 17, 20; 2 Tim 1:6; 2:1, 4-8, 14-16, 22; 3:10; 4:1-5 (see also Titus 2:1, 15; 3:8). The section, as with the letter, is intended for a larger audience than one person. How Timothy responds to Paul's letter will impact the future status of the Ephesian church.

IN THE TEXT

■ **6** This verse introduces the major theme for the next unit of the letter. There is a noticeable rhetorical shift from negative polemic to positive instructions. Timothy serves as a positive role model to the Ephesians compared to the negative examples of the opponents. Although Paul writes to Timothy, his words are ultimately intended for the Ephesians.

Paul begins his exhortation with a participial phrase. The NIV interprets *hypotithemenos* as a condition, **if you point . . . out**. The NASB interprets it instrumentally, "in pointing out." Both make sense in this context. By following Paul's instructions, Timothy will also prove himself a good minister. The verb's basic meaning is to teach or give instruction (BDAG 2000, 1042 s.v. 2). This is its only NT occurrence in the middle voice, which makes determining its meaning difficult.

Paul begins with a personal touch. Chrysostom comments, "He did not write 'ordering,' he did not write 'instructing,' but 'suggesting,' that is, as if giving advice" (*Hom. 1 Tim.* 12, quoted by Mounce 2000, 249). Paul will use stronger language in v 11, where he uses "command and teach." Timothy is not to approach the Ephesians with any timidity or hesitation. The problems are serious. Rather, his demeanor should be one of authority filtered through "love, which comes from a pure heart and a good conscience and a sincere faith" (1:5).

Timothy should give these instructions to the **brothers and sisters**. This inclusive term may refer to leaders (elders and deacons of ch 3) or the entire congregation. Jesus used "brothers" to refer to his disciples (Matt 12:50; Mark 3:35); early Christians, to fellow believers (Acts 6:3; 9:30; 10:23). Paul "juxtaposes the community and the anonymous 'some' of the previous pericope. 'They' are anonymous; believers are a family" (Collins 2002, 121).

Kinship Terms in the NT

Paul and other NT writers used kinship terms when referring to their readers. The most common is "brothers," as in 1 Tim 4:6. This designation is not unique to Christianity, but a common attribute of close human relationships. Anthropologists identify such close relationships outside of blood relatives as "fictive" (Aasgaard 2004, MacDonald 2010, Moxnes 1997, Osiek and Balch 1997, Parkin 1997).

The theological basis for the use of kinship terminology in the church is God's adoption of believers *in Christ* into his family as his sons and daughters (Rom 8:15; Gal 4:6). Adoption gives a new identity with God as Father. The cultural basis for fictive language in Paul's writings was the Greek household and various associations common in the first century (Hodge 2007). Paul uses fictive kingship terms to describe Timothy as his "true son" (1 Tim 1:2) and "my son"

(1:18). Paul obviously had a close bond with Timothy that transcended bloodline and distance.

The church as "God's household" creates a place of belonging, identification, support, and fellowship. The relationships shared within this fictive family can become even closer than those shared between actual family members. Their common faith in Christ and the presence of the Holy Spirit bind "brothers and sisters" together (Eph 4:3; Phil 2:1).

The main verb and clause of the sentence, and thus, Paul's key desire for Timothy, is that he **will be a good minister of Christ Jesus**. The verb **you will be** is a "logical future" (Marshall 1999, 549). Paul's wish will be fulfilled as Timothy completes the condition given in the opening phrase. The word for **minister** (*diakonos*) is the same used throughout the letter for those who serve. Here, it has the sense of a "servant of Christ Jesus" (Col 4:12) as simply a Christian, not as an officeholder in the church (as in 1 Tim 3:8-13).

Timothy can be equipped for this task by *being brought up in the words of the faith and of the good teaching which you have followed*. The passive participle *entrephomenos* translated here has an instrumental sense. Timothy will be a good minister *by* being nurtured in his knowledge of the gospel. The present tense shows that this should be Timothy's constant experience. This word is rare in Greek and used only here in the NT. It refers to bringing up as in rearing or training a child (BDAG 2000, 341). This may adapt Stoic terminology for education (Epictetus, *Diatr.* 4.4.48; Hanson 1966, 89).

The participle has one dative object, **on the truths** (lit. *the words* [*tois logois*]), modified by two genitives. The first, **of the faith**, likely refers to the gospel message—the core beliefs of the gospel (1:19; 3:9; 4:1) summarized in the creedal statements of 1:15, 2:5-6, and 3:16. Timothy's ministry will be strong and effective if he focuses on the gospel of Jesus Christ.

The second genitive, **of the good teaching**, refers to the doctrinal development that comes from the study of the gospel. In this letter Paul distinguishes between preaching the gospel and teaching its doctrinal implications (4:3; 5:17; 6:3). Clear understanding of the gospel and proper teaching of it are central concerns because the opponents were propagating false doctrines (1:10-11). "A reading of the gospel should always be accompanied by the correct interpretation or doctrinal understanding of the gospel" (Mounce 2000, 149-50).

The perfect-tense verb *parēkolouthēkas* in the last phrase, **that you have followed**, indicates that Timothy had faithfully pursued the gospel for some time. The verb means to "follow with the mind, understand, make one's own" (BDAG 2000, 767). Timothy's training in the Scripture began when he was young under the tutelage of his grandmother Lois and mother Eunice (→ 2 Tim 1:5; 3:14-15). He was mentored later by Paul (Acts 16:1-3). He also had significant opportunity for on-the-job-training as Paul's emissary. Timothy made a firm decision at some point to be a follower of Christ and stuck with it through all the challenges he faced in ministry. His effectiveness in Ephesus was directly connected to the depth of his appropriation of the gospel.

■ **7** After the positive reminder of v 6, Paul now warns Timothy that he should not be caught up in the preoccupations of the opponents. Paul contrasts (*de*) the gospel (v 6) with the heretical teachings of the opponents (v 7a). His warning implies a negative characterization of the opponents. They were not being "good minister[s]" (v 6) because they dabbled in "myths and endless genealogies" (1:4) and neglected the more important "godliness."

Have nothing to do with (*paraitou*) is a strong verb that means to refuse, reject, or avoid (BDAG 2000, 764 s.v. 2). The *par-* prefix gives the word "a nuance of aversion or repudiation" (Stählin 1964, 195). This word occurs three other times in the Pastorals (5:11; 2 Tim 2:23; Titus 3:10). The present imperative denotes "the continual need for Timothy's attention" (Mounce 2000, 250). Timothy should not get involved in such speculation at all. It would be a waste of time to debate the opponents. The verb comes last in the Greek, drawing the readers' attention to the **godless myths and old wives' tales** at the beginning.

The NIV's paraphrase, **godless myths and old wives' tales**, conveys the basic idea of the Greek, but it is not literal. The only direct object of the verb is **tales** ("myths" [*mythous*] in 1:4). This noun is modified by two adjectives.

The first is **godless** (*bebēlous*)—"profane" (NRSV), "worldly" (NASB), or "irreverent" (ESV). Something thus lacking divine character had to remain outside the precinct of a sacred temple (Liefeld 1999, 158).

The other adjective is contained in the NIV's **old wives' tales** (*graōdeis*) and adds additional negative effect to the first. In philosophical circles the word had a derogatory sense (Marshall 1999, 550 n. 71) arising from stereotypical cultural prejudices against gossipy old women. This is the only place this word occurs in the NT. Paul sarcastically compares the teachings of the opponents to the empty tales of chattering old women (Fee 1988, 103).

Instead of falling prey to empty speculation, Timothy should **train** himself **to be godly**. The word **train** (*gymnaze*) introduces an athletic image that will be further developed in 4:8. Paul's argumentation here is a fortiori, from the lesser to the greater. If physical exercise is good for the body, how much more is training in godliness beneficial for one's spiritual life and ministry?

Paul also employs the method of deliberative rhetoric, persuading Timothy to do what is to his own advantage (Collins 2002, 122). It is in Timothy's best interest to focus on godliness, not myths. Exercise is never easy. It takes rigor, self-discipline, and passion. The reciprocal pronoun **yourself** (*seauton*) emphatically applies this to Timothy.

One of the key words of the letter, "godliness" (*eusebeian*), is repeated as the goal of Timothy's training (→ 2:2; 3:16; 6:3, 5, 6; 2 Tim 3:5; Titus 1:1).

Devotion to God is the response of a holy lifestyle empowered by one's inward relationship with Christ. It directly impacts relationships with other believers and one's testimony to unbelievers. How Timothy can specifically train himself in godliness will be detailed in 1 Tim 4:11-16.

Athletic Imagery in Paul's Letters and the Ancient World

Athletic imagery was widely used in the ancient world as an illustration for training or growth in virtues (Epictetus, *Diatr.* 2.18.22; Seneca, *CS* 2.2; *Ep.* 78.16). Various athletic competitions were held in major cities throughout the Roman Empire. The better known were the Olympic Games in Greece and the Isthmian Games in Corinth. Ephesus was also one of the great centers for athletic contests. The Ephesia festival, held every four years, featured athletic competitions. Ephesus also hosted the Common Games of Asia.

Paul used athletics as a rhetorical tool to inspire the readers of his letters (see Pfitzner 1967; Williams 1999, 257-91). Numerous references to such imagery are scattered throughout his letters (see esp., 1 Cor 9:24-27; Gal 2:2; Phil 2:16; 3:12-14). The Christian life, like athletic training, takes discipline and self-control. The prize for which believers strive is the crown of eternal life (1 Cor 9:25; Phil 3:14). Romans 5:3-5 gives the typical sequence an athlete goes through from suffering to hope. Perseverance in one's faith and controlling the appetites of the flesh by embracing the way of the cross lead to strengthening one's hope and assurance of resurrection life.

■ **8** The conjunction **for** (*gar*) shows that this verse is the basis or explanation for the command in 1 Tim 4:7. This is why Timothy is exhorted: "Train yourself to be godly." Timothy's training can be compared to the intensity of physical exercise. The parallelism forms a proverb comparing two types of exercise:

> *For*
> *bodily exercise is beneficial for a little,*
> *but*
> *godliness [is beneficial] to all things.*

Like the previous verse, the comparison is from the lesser to the greater, placing the emphasis on the second clause.

The first half of the verse is self-evident: **Physical training is of some value**. The English word "gymnasium," a place for exercise, has its roots in the Greek word for **training** (*gymnasia*). **Some value** (lit. *little*) could be interpreted in regards to long-term usefulness. Exercise has value to the physical body, but over time, even a healthy body succumbs to age. The resurrected body will be immortal and, therefore, will not need exercise (1 Cor 15:42-44, 53). The point is not that physical exercise has no value, but the health and strength it provides pales in comparison to the effects of godliness.

Paul recognized the value of keeping control of the body (1 Cor 9:24-27). His missionary travels and work as a tentmaker probably required him to be quite physically fit. He is not telling Timothy either to pursue or neglect physical exercise. He is merely reflecting on the metaphor. Exercise is only good for this age; godliness is part of the eternal order (Fee 1988, 104). Physical training does not compare to spiritual growth. Paul offers an alternative to the asceticism of the opponents: rigorously engage the world through godly living. The asceticism of the opponents in 1 Tim 4:3 was a misuse of the body.

Paul's key point is that **godliness has value for all things. All things** (*panta*) "involves a promise that encompasses life now and in the future" (Knight 1992, 199). **Godliness** (*eusebeia*) offers "a virtuous mean between excessive radicalism and lazy accommodation" (Saarinen 2008, 82). It rejects the excesses of legalism while avoiding the apathetic abuse of freedom in Christ from bondage to the Law (Gal 5:13).

The participle **holding** is causal in force. It indicates why godliness has such great value: *because it holds promise of life.* The word **life** occurs only once, but Paul modifies it in two ways: it is one life experienced now and in the future. God is the source of life. In Paul's understanding of the "two ages," **the life to come** refers to "eternal life." What **the present life** and **the life to come** share is new existence *in Christ.* Believers are able to participate in new life now through Christ (→ 1 Tim 1:15-16; 2 Tim 1:1; Rom 6:4-11). The present life is a foretaste of eternal life because of our relationship now with Christ through the Holy Spirit. **Godliness** is the mark that eternal life is unfolding in the temporal life.

Apocalypticism and Eschatology in Paul's Letters

Scholars generally agree that Paul shared thought patterns with Jewish apocalyptic eschatology. There are three motifs typical of Jewish apocalyptic thought: (1) the idea of two ages, the present evil age and the blessed age to come, (2) the expectation that the sovereign God will intervene in history, and (3) the revelation of an imminent end to the world (Sturm 1989, 36; Beker 1980, 136).

For Paul, Christ's death and resurrection inaugurated the new age. We still live in this present evil age until either we die or Christ comes again (1 Thess 4:13-18). But we can do so with increasing victory because of the indwelling Holy Spirit (Rom 8:23; Eph 1:13-14). Believers experience new life now in Christ (2 Cor 5:17) with the goal of being transformed more fully into his likeness through the Holy Spirit (2 Cor 3:18; Eph 4:23-24; for further study, see Dunn 1998, 461-72; Ridderbos 1975, 205-52; Ackerman 2006, 98-101).

■ **9-10** The third **trustworthy saying** of the letter is now mentioned (→ 1:15; 3:1). The wording of 4:9 is exactly like the introduction of 1:15 (→). These sayings are a call to accept Paul's authority and follow his directions. Interpreters have been divided over to what verse, phrase, or clause this saying refers. The context suggests either to v 8 or v 10.

If v 9 looks backward, it concludes the proverb of v 8 (so Marshall 1999, 554). The saying could be the entire proverb or the second half, which speaks about godliness having great value for eternal life. Breaking the proverb into two parts, however, diminishes its rhetorical force. The key idea of godliness is still in Paul's mind, but godliness is only a subtheme to the larger concern about salvation, which is mentioned in v 10.

More likely, the saying looks forward to v 10, because it emphasizes God as Savior, an important theme in 1:1 and 2:3. Each **trustworthy saying** reflects on salvation, as does this one. Thus, it is likely that 4:9 introduces the "faithful saying" (KJV). Verse 10 reflects back on the proverb of v 8, and the proverb illustrates v 10 by connecting it to the specific needs in Ephesus. Consequently, v 10 serves as the climax and theological basis for the proverb and all that Paul has written thus far in the chapter.

The question then becomes, which part of v 10 is the "faithful saying"? Punctuation can be a challenge in interpreting the Bible since the original manuscripts contained none. In this case, translations and critical texts differ in their efforts to indicate the relationship of the phrases and clauses of vv 8-10.

Verse 10 begins in the NIV without translating *for* (*gar*), which introduces an explanatory clause and adds emphasis to what follows. The Greek almost necessitates a repetition of *for*, as the NASB has translated: "For it is for this." **For this** (*eis touto*) looks forward to the heart of the saying, which begins in the clause after **that** (*hoti*) in Greek.

There are three key elements in the saying: human struggle, hope in the living God, and God's gift of salvation (Collins 2002, 126). Paul's passion is summarized with the hendiadys, **labor and strive**. **Labor** (*kipiōmen*) describes hard work, wearisome toil, or struggle (BDAG 2000, 558). **Struggle** (*agōnizometha*) is used in athletic contexts (1 Cor 9:25) and for fighting (1 Cor 15:10; Phil 2:16; Col 1:29). It means "to strive to do something with great intensity and effort" (Louw and Nida 1996, 68.74). The same two words in Col 1:29 identify Paul's source of strength: "To this end I strenuously [*kopiō*] contend [*agōnizomenos*] with all the energy Christ so powerfully works in me."

This **trustworthy saying** was the focus of Paul's ministry and the cause for much suffering (2 Cor 11:23—12:10; Phil 1:21). The first-person plural **we** would include Paul and his coworkers, one of whom was Timothy. The present tense of both verbs indicates the ongoing challenge Paul and his companions face. Interestingly, "both words are derived from roots (*kop-* and *agōn-*) that early Christians used to describe the work of evangelization" (Collins 2002, 127). These words express the challenges believers face in living out their faith. Godliness does not come easily but takes discipline, struggle, and faith (Matt 5:11; 1 Thess 1:3). The variant reading in some manuscripts that replaces **strive** with "we are reviled or mocked" (*oneidizometha*) destroys the athletic imagery of the verse and is not preferred.

Paul gives the reason for striving in the last part of 1 Tim 4:10, which is the heart of the saying: **We have put our hope in the living God**. The verb **we have put** (*ēlpikamen*) is in the perfect tense, indicating decisive and ongoing trust in God. Paul could labor on knowing that God was with him. Jesus is called "our hope" in 1:1. Here, the object of our hope is **the living God**. The phrase "living God" is used twenty-nine times in the Greek Bible. This sets the one true God over against the lifeless idols of the Greek world (Acts 14:15; 1 Thess 1:9). Why did Paul choose this description here? It may be because God is active in history and this is seen in saving those who believe. The living God unites those engaged in the "mystery of godliness" (1 Tim 3:15-16 KJV).

The last phrase of the **trustworthy saying** focuses upon how we can know God is indeed living: he is **the Savior of all people, and especially of those who believe**. This repeats the affirmation that began the letter (→ 1:1) and assures us in our prayers for others (→ 2:3). Salvation is intended for **all people** (→ 2:4, 6), yet access to salvation is qualified by the last phrase. The key to interpretation here is the word **especially** (*malista*). This word has a range of meaning, including "most of all, above all, especially, particularly" (BDAG 2000, 613). It indicates "a very high point on a scale of extent" (Louw and Nida 1996, 78.7). It can distinguish what follows from what was before, or it could give further definition to what was before (Knight 1992, 203).

Paul is not advocating some form of universal salvation here. There is no **and** in Greek before **especially**, despite the NIV insertion. Rather, the substantival participle, **those who believe,** stands in apposition to **all people**. A better translation would be, *who is Savior of all people who believe*. All people are potentially saved; this is God's desire (2:4). But it is only those who believe who actually experience salvation. Salvation, then, is conditioned upon faith. This is not universal salvation but universal grace. God's desire that all be saved through Christ is universal (2:6) and the invitation goes out to all, but the required response is faith in the source. "All people are potentially believers" (Marshall 1999, 557). The whole tenor of Scripture asserts that God is the Savior of all people, but only those who believe take advantage of God's offer of salvation (2 Cor 6:15). This is the mission for which Paul and Timothy had committed their lives. The way to work out this salvation "with fear and trembling" (Phil 2:12) is through growing in godliness (1 Tim 4:8).

FROM THE TEXT

Paul urges Timothy to stand strong in the face of controversy and heresy. His message to his younger protégé is relevant to many who find themselves in leadership positions in the church and for all Christians as we seek to be faithful to the truth of the gospel. Paul sets out some essential qualities of a good minister. But this is not for pastors only, but for all fully committed believers.

At the core is *the need to know the "truths of the faith and of the good teaching"* (v 6). Those who serve as leaders in the church must know the gospel well before they can teach it to others. In order to feed others, one must feast first on the source of nourishment. Good ministry should be defined not by a business model but by diligence with learning and teaching the Scripture. It takes wisdom to distinguish the interesting but trivial from the important and nonnegotiable.

Good ministers will make godliness their goal. The reason people exercise is for health and to obtain a certain quality of life. The gathered church is the "gymnasium" for godliness, where believers are trained by competent teachers in the truths of the gospel. The "playing field" where we put our training to use is the life we live before others in the everyday world. Paul is concerned in this letter that the Ephesian Christians were receiving inferior and misguided training, which would adversely affect their witness before unbelievers.

The motivation for this pursuit springs from the hope we have in God as Savior. The prize for winning the "game of life" will be the salvation offered in Jesus Christ (1:1; 2:6). What will guarantee the outcome of life's race is faithfulness to God summed up in the word *eusebeia*. Have we lived out our profession of faith by our total commitment to God? Does our life give evidence of sincerity, integrity, and dependence upon God? Paul's fervency for embracing Christ often seen in his other letters inspires his desire for Timothy to be faithful to what God had called him in Ephesus (1:18; 4:6; 6:11-12).

C. Timothy's Personal Qualifications for Effective Ministry (4:11-16)

BEHIND THE TEXT

Paul continues to call Timothy to action and give him directions for effective ministry in Ephesus. Before Timothy can deal with the problems in the church, he must make sure he himself is spiritually and morally prepared. The danger of deceit is real, and he should be ready to face it. Behind the whole chapter lay the problems with false teachers who were dabbling in controversial and marginal doctrines, especially their urging the Ephesians to avoid marriage and certain foods (4:1-5). There is here a noticeable grammatical shift to second-person singular imperative verbs. This is Paul's personal advice to Timothy. The grammar also hints at the importance of this advice and has the tone of authority and urgency.

The key theme of these verses is Timothy's gift from God. God has equipped him for the task ahead, so he can face any obstacle with confidence.

This section also anticipates ch 5, where Paul gives specific directions for how certain groups in the church ought to behave. Timothy must be well prepared to deal with potential problems dealing with the aftermath of the false teachings.

IN THE TEXT

■ **11** Two imperatives here arise from the previous section. Timothy is to do two things: **command and teach**. One deals with the problem and the other offers the solution. **Command** (*parangelle*) is a strong term with military overtones (→ 1:3, 5, 18). Timothy must speak with authority (Kelly 1963, 103), giving orders to the heretics concerning their false teachings (Mounce 2000, 257).

Teach identifies Timothy's positive assignment. He must make sure that the faithful Ephesian believers are firmly grounded in sound doctrine. The best defense against heresy is the truth. Paul urges Timothy to **teach** Paul's commands (see also 5:7; 6:2*b*; see also 2 Tim 2:2, 14; Titus 2:15).

Timothy is to serve as the catalyst for the truth by living as an example to others. He is not alone in this and has Paul's authority behind him. Paul's commands give him confidence to deal with the challenges before him.

■ **12** Paul now preempts any reluctance from Timothy to carry out his instructions from v 11 by encouraging Timothy: **Don't let anyone look down on** [from *kataphroneō*] **you because you are young** (→ Titus 2:15—from *periphroneitoe*). The third-person imperative *kataphroneitō* carries the connotation of having contempt for someone or viewing the person as having little value (BDAG 2000, 529 s.v. 1). A lack of respect from those one leads can result in ineffective ministry. Sometimes, as in Timothy's situation, age can be a factor in this. The social custom was for those younger to listen to those older. Paul is reversing that here. Even as a young man, Timothy could serve as an example to the church and be an effective leader.

Timothy was **young** when Paul wrote this letter (→ 2 Tim 2:22). *Neotēos* in the ancient world applied to anyone less than thirty (or even in their thirties). In the Mediterranean world, men under forty were considered young (Roloff 1988, 251-52; Irenaeus, *Haer.* 2.22.5). By comparison, Paul was an "old man" (in Phlm 9), likely in his late fifties or early sixties. Timothy was probably younger than the elders in Ephesus (Acts 20:17). This may account for Paul's encouragement. Timothy represents the second generation of Christians who were beginning to take positions of leadership.

This verse could have had the rhetorical effect of giving more authority to Timothy as he dealt with the Ephesian problems. This statement and letter remind the church that Timothy came with the authority of Paul. His words were not his own. The false teachers who were not qualified for leadership might have challenged Timothy's authority and used his age as a weapon against him.

Strong words or signed letters are not always sufficient to resolve church issues. The negative statement at the beginning of the verse is countered with a positive one in the last half. The way not to be despised by others is to be a positive role model to them. As with the overseers and deacons of ch 3, Timothy could be above criticism by impressing people by how he lived. He needed to **set an example for the believers in speech, in conduct, in love, in faith and in purity.** The word **example** (*typos*) describes the imprint something makes into clay or how metal fills a mold. The image that results resembles the original. Paul had set an example for Timothy and now Timothy must set an example for others. Christ imprinted his image on Paul (1 Cor 11:1), Paul had imprinted his image on Timothy (1 Cor 4:16), and now Timothy must pass this image on to the Ephesians. If Timothy could live with integrity, no one would be able to say anything against him. He would lead by example, not by force. Paul lists fives areas in which Timothy could set an example:

First, Timothy should lead **in speech**. The Greek word *logos* is broad and used for many types of communication, including both written and verbal. In this context, the NIV is likely correct that this was verbal communication, which would have been Timothy's primary way of dealing with the issues in Ephesus. In the NT, how people should talk is often part of moral exhortation (Eph 4:25, 29, 31; 5:4; Col 3:8-9).

Second, Timothy should be an example **in conduct**. *Anastrophē* reflects one's "way of life" (Gal 1:13) based on a set of principles (BDAG 2000, 73). Through Christ, the old, corrupted lifestyle can be transformed into a righteous and holy one, beginning with a fundamental change of mind-set (Eph 4:22-24). Word and deed went together for Jews and Christians. James reminds his readers that their lifestyle must match their profession (Jas 2:14-26). Harmony between words and actions was also important to Philo (*Moses* 2.48).

The next three items in this short list reflect Paul's earlier comments in 1 Tim 1:5. Timothy should be a model **in love**. Love is the key attribute of believers and should mark all that they do (Rom 12:9; 13:9-10; 14:15; 1 Cor 8:1; 13; 16:14; Gal 5:6, 13; Eph 4:2; Phil 1:9; 2:1-2; Col 3:14; 1 Thess 3:12; 2 Thess 1:3). Timothy would be able to communicate the necessary changes effectively in Ephesus, if he approached the troubles with an attitude of love supported by a holy lifestyle.

Linked to love is **faith**. This word refers not simply to cognitive assent of belief but the result of trust and faithfulness. It is often connected with love in Paul's letters (1 Cor 13:13; 1 Thess 3:6; 5:8; 1 Tim 1:14; 2 Tim 1:13; Phlm 5). Timothy's faith in Christ would sustain him through hardships, allowing him to be a model to strengthen any weak faith among the Christians in Ephesus.

Finally, Timothy should be a model **in purity**. *Hagneia* is a cultic term in the OT and is used in the NT for moral integrity or chastity. It describes how

Timothy should behave toward younger women in 1 Tim 5:2. There should be no reason for anyone to accuse him of impropriety with the opposite sex.

Faithfulness and integrity were used together in Roman imperial times as words of praise for judges and civic-minded citizens (Montague 2008, 100). The phrase "in spirit" in the KJV is not found in the most reliable manuscripts and adds nothing significant that is not contained in the more accepted reading.

Sound doctrine goes with right conduct (→ 1:9-11). These five words describe the core ethical-spiritual qualities Timothy needed to deal with the false teachers. This list is similar to what Timothy observed in Paul's life (in 2 Tim 3:10). The next two verses describe how he could nurture these qualities.

■ 13 This verse marks a shift from the private to the public forum. The time reference, **until I come**, indicates that when Paul arrives, he will have further input to offer. Either he will engage himself directly in solving the problems or give further directions to Timothy.

Paul often mentioned in his letters his desire to see those to whom he wrote (Rom 15:22, 29, 32; 1 Cor 16:5; 2 Cor 13:1; 1 Thess 2:18; 3:10; Phlm 22). There is no indication when he planned to come or what was delaying him, though this is the second mention of a delay (→ 1 Tim 3:14). The phrase creates a sense of urgency in Timothy's task. He should not wait for Paul but begin right away. Even though Paul is far away, he could still deal authoritatively with the situation in Ephesus through Timothy. Timothy is to be involved in activities that Paul will continue once he arrives.

Timothy should focus on three public activities in Paul's absence. **Devote** (*proseche*) entails paying attention to or being occupied with something. It is used in 1:4 for the devotion the false teachers had for their own teaching. The present tense implies that this is something Timothy should do regularly (Marshall 1999, 563; → 4:15-16). These activities are grounded in the personal qualities listed in v 12. Each of these has an article in Greek, denoting specific activities that were part of the church's life. This verse offers one of the earliest references to liturgy in the early church.

Public Worship in the Early Church

Christians from the earliest recorded days of the church gathered for worship. Before and on the day of Pentecost, the gathered believers were in earnest prayer, waiting upon the coming of the Holy Spirit. Later, "they devoted themselves to the apostles' teaching and to fellowship, to the breaking of bread and to prayer" (Acts 2:42).

As the church continued to grow, their worship was marked by (1) "the public reading of Scripture" (1 Tim 4:13), (2) proclamation and exhortation (1 Cor 2:1-5; 15:11), (3) prayers (1 Cor 11:2-16; 1 Tim 2:1-7), (4) singing and possibly reciting of creeds (1 Cor 14:26; Phil 2:5-11; Col 3:16; 1 Tim 3:16), (5) prophecies

(I Cor 11:2-16; 12—14; I Thess 5:19-22), (6) baptism (I Cor 1:13-17; Rom 6:1-14; Col 2:12), and (7) sharing in the Lord's Supper (I Cor 11:17-34).

As far as the evidence shows, much of this was not in a fixed form during the decades in which the NT was written. Paul's letters hint at the activities of the early churches and attempt to give guidance on how to keep worship orderly (I Cor 14:26-38).

In the second century, Justin Martyr wrote,

And on the day called Sunday, all who live in cities or in the country gather together to one place, and the memoirs of the apostles or the writings of the prophets are read, as long as time permits; then, when the reader has ceased, the president verbally instructs, and exhorts to the imitation of these good things. Then we all rise together and pray. (*I Apol.* 1.67.186)

Some helpful resources on worship in the early church include:

Borchert, Gerald L. 2008. *Worship in the New Testament: Divine Mystery and Human Response.* Atlanta: Chalice Press.

Cullmann, Oscar. 1973. *Early Christian Worship.* London: SCM.

Hahn, Ferdinand. 1973. *The Worship of the Early Church.* Philadelphia: Fortress.

Martin, Ralph P. 1974. *Worship in the Early Church.* Grand Rapids: Eerdmans.

Moule, C. F. D. 1977. *Worship in the New Testament.* Bremcote: Grove.

Timothy should devote himself **to the public reading of Scripture.** This entire phrase comes from one word in Greek, *anagnōsei,* which simply means **reading.** The word **public** is added in translation since that is how Scripture was read then. Few people owned personal copies of any part of the Bible until the invention of the printing press because of the high cost of manuscripts. So copies were shared and read mostly in public worship. Even private reading was done aloud in the first century.

Ancient manuscripts had no spaces or punctuation, so it took considerable practice to read them well before people. The public reading of Scripture was one of the central acts of worship for Jews of the first century. Christians followed this practice in their own worship (Deut 31:11-12; Neh 8:7-8; Luke 4:16; Acts 13:15; 15:21).

Scripture is an addition in translation and assumed from the one Greek word *reading.* In the NT, the term *anaginōskō* often refers to the public reading of sacred writings (Acts 15:21; 2 Cor 3:14; Eph 3:4; Col 4:16; 1 Thess 5:27; 2 Thess 3:14). **Scripture** would have minimally included our OT, but by the time 1 Timothy was written, it could have included some early Christian writings (→ 2 Tim 3:16-17). Paul's letters had begun to be circulated and read publicly by the time 2 Pet 3:15-16 was written.

In order to deal effectively with the heresies in Ephesus, Timothy's ministry must be firmly based upon the truths of Scripture. This would allow him to teach, rebuke, correct, train in righteousness, and equip the Ephesians for good work (2 Tim 3:16-17).

The reading of Scripture served as the basis for preaching and teaching. **Preaching** is literally "exhortation," as many translations render the word *paraklēsei*. The word has three major meanings: to ask for help in prayer, to exhort or encourage, and to comfort (Schmitz 1967b, 793-99). Exhortation offers encouragement to embrace a particular belief or course of action (BDAG 2000, 766 s.v. 1). In the setting of public worship, this would have included the application of scriptural truths to the needs of the listeners.

Teaching (*didaskalia*) comprises catechetical instruction and further explanation of what is preached (Acts 13:15). Paul believed teaching was a gift of the Holy Spirit (Rom 12:7; 1 Cor 12:28-29), and, therefore, a Christian teacher ought to be filled with the Spirit and obedient to the leadership of the Spirit.

Both preaching and teaching are needed in the church. Teaching involves explaining sound doctrine and right conduct; exhortation involves giving hope and encouragement (Saarinen 2008, 84). "If teaching without exhortation may fill the head without warming the heart, exhortation without teaching will eventually evaporate" (Montague 2008, 101).

By doing these three things, Timothy would help the Ephesians focus on the truth of the gospel and not be swayed by false teachings. The result would be theological and social unity. Timothy must help them answer these essential questions: who are we, where did we come from, how are we to behave, and what arc wc to do? "Reading / hearing significant texts influences the formation, shaping, defining, and redefining of individual and corporate identity" (Towner 2006, 318).

■ **14** Verses 14-16 serve as the peroration or recapitulation of the key theme of Timothy's faithfulness to the job of confronting the false teachers. Three additional imperatives mark the key activities that would help him effectively accomplish this task. These commands put the responsibility on him.

The first command, however, reminds Timothy that he was not alone but had God and others with him. **Do not neglect** (*mē amelei*) implies that he had a part in using his gift and calling. He was not simply passive but had to be actively engaged in fulfilling God's calling on his life. **Neglect** describes being unconcerned about something that one ought to be doing, or shirking one's responsibilities.

Timothy was given a **gift** (*charismatos*) that he must put to use in his mission in Ephesus. There is no clear indication what this gift was. In other letters of Paul, there is a close association between gifts and the Holy Spirit (Rom 1:11; 1 Cor 1:7; 12:4). The word *charisma* shares the same root as "grace." A gift is a "gracing" of God through the Holy Spirit who enables believers to do something for the benefit of the church. A gift of the Spirit is not a natural talent but may enhance natural abilities.

Timothy's **gift** would help him be more effective in ministry. The Holy Spirit would use this gift to empower him for the task ahead (2 Tim 1:14). It is Timothy's responsibility to "fan into flames" this gift (→ 2 Tim 1:6). Part of this fanning involved the study of Scripture so that he could be prepared for the challenges before him (1 Tim 4:13).

Timothy received this gift in two ways, shown in an attributive participial phrase: **which was given you through prophecy when the body of elders laid their hands on you.** *Ho edothē* is an aorist passive participle with God as the presumed source of the gift. There is no indication of when Timothy received this gift, but possibly when Paul first took him as a travel partner in Acts 16:1-5 (→ 1 Tim 1:18).

The first way Timothy received this gift was **through prophecy.** Someone was moved by the Holy Spirit to speak a word about him. This prophecy gave external verification to his spiritual gift.

Second, the gift was mediated in part through the council of elders who recognized the gift and confirmed it by laying their hands upon Timothy. The laying on of hands is the human response, confirming what the Spirit had already given. "Mere 'digital contact,' as someone has called it, the laying on of the elders' hands, has no meaning apart from the antecedent work of the Holy Spirit" (Gould 1965, 600). It is the agreement with God's grace, not the means of this grace. Formal ordination into ministry did not yet exist, but acts such as this shaped what later came to be practiced in the church.

Those who **laid their hands** are described as **the body of elders** (one word in Greek [*presbyteriou*]), likely a group of mature believers in the church (→ 1 Tim 5:1; Luke 22:66 and Acts 22:5 refer to Jewish elders). When Paul left Ephesus, there were already elders in the church (Acts 20:17-38). In 1 Tim 4:14 and 5:17, the word seems to refer to church leaders. Beyond this, not much is known about these people. We are not told where they were when they laid hands on Timothy or when the event took place. We can assume that Paul and Timothy both had the event firmly in their memories. Recalling it here has the nostalgic and emotional effect of reminding Timothy that God was with him.

There is a different reference to Timothy's commissioning in 2 Tim 1:6. There Paul is the one who lays hands on Timothy. This could refer to a different event or could describe the same event in different ways. The differences may be due to the public intention of 1 Timothy—to be shared with the Ephesians, versus 2 Timothy's more personal and private character. In both cases, there is recognition of what God had already done, the human involvement of affirmation, and the channel by which this grace was received.

■ **15** Here Paul summarizes his previous exhortations and connects Timothy's commissioning to the present situation in Ephesus. Timothy must be a faithful steward of God's gift. He was responsible to preserve and use this gift. The verse contains two related commands: **be diligent** and **give yourself wholly**.

There is a wide range of nuances to the first command, **be diligent** (*meleta*): "practice" (ESV), "put . . . into practice" (NRSV), "meditate" (KJV), "cultivate" (TM), "take pains" (NASB), and "give . . . complete attention" (NLT). Together, these translations summarize the main idea behind the word. Wesley describes this as nothing "other than faith, hope, love, joy melted down together . . . by the fire of God's Holy Spirit; and offered up to God in secret" (1813, 227).

Timothy is to give his attention to **these matters** by *continuing* (present linear) "to perform certain activities with care and concern" (Louw and Nida 1996, 68.20). It would be tempting for anyone in Timothy's situation to give up when the stress increases. It will take discipline for Timothy to remain focused on **these matters**. He should make it his habit to carry out the preceding instructions, especially the need to pursue godliness (4:7), and to live them out as an example to others (v 12). This pursuit should be supported by reading the Scriptures and encouraging people by them (v 13).

The next command must have a similar force. The Greek verb is simply the present imperative *be into these things*. Such idioms call for an apt paraphrase: **give yourself wholly to them**, "devote yourself to them" (NRSV), "be absorbed in them" (NASB), or "immerse yourself in them" (ESV). This phrase fits the exercise imagery in vv 7-8 and reemphasizes the intensity Timothy should give his calling in Ephesus.

The outcome of such intense devotion to spiritual growth and godly living has the intended result: **so that everyone may see your progress.** People should be able to see the growth and change in Timothy's life because of his faithfulness to the leading of the Holy Spirit in using his gift. Stoics used the word **progress** (*prokopē*) for one who advanced in philosophy or ethics (Stählin 1968, 706-7). Growth is the natural result of someone totally committed to God (Luke 2:52; Phil 1:12, 24). Timothy should not remain static but grow in his walk with the Lord. He must avoid the path of the false teachers who were descending into godlessness (2 Tim 2:16). This will take personal discipline, but progress can only be made by cooperating with God's grace. Because Timothy is a public figure, people will see the results of his devotion. Positive growth will lead to more effective ministry leadership.

■ **16** Paul's final exhortations in this chapter continue the idea of Timothy's need to be faithful to his calling. The theological reason for his faithfulness is given as the salvation of himself and the Ephesians. This reason creates a sense of urgency and importance in how he should develop in godliness and devotion to the truth of the gospel.

The first charge is that he must **watch** his **life and doctrine closely. Watch** is used figuratively here for giving attention to something by holding fast to it (Phil 2:16). Timothy must be mindful of two essential matters: (1) his **life** and (2) his **doctrine** (→ 1 Tim 4:6-7). **Life** summarizes how he is to live, so as to develop his inner character so it may be seen in outward godliness (*eusebeia*). **Doctrine** is literally *teaching* (*didaskalia*). What should be taught is "sound doctrine" based on the truth of the gospel (1:10-11).

Paul will encourage Timothy to be a faithful teacher again in ch 6 and warn him about false doctrine. Timothy must keep in mind that the source of his doctrine is Jesus Christ and that these teachings should result in godly living (6:3). Paul exhorted the Ephesian "elders" with two similar ideas in Acts 20:28.

The second charge is closely related to the first and is given for emphasis: **Persevere in them**. The imperative *epimene* is the emphatic form of the verb "to remain." It has the figurative sense of staying involved in an activity. Timothy must have a "persistent fidelity to the teaching and a constant urging of it upon his hearers" (Knight 1992, 211). Weariness from confronting false teachings could tempt Timothy to get preoccupied with trivia and miss the more important matters related to salvation and godly living. The best way to avoid any compromise is to remain steadfast in his spiritual growth.

The explanatory *gar* (**because**) at the beginning of the last clause gives a sobering reminder that Timothy's salvation and the salvation of his hearers depend on his faithfulness to his call. The NIV interprets the participle *poiōn* as conditional, **if you do**. But there is also a sense of instrumentality: ***by doing this***. By his diligence in preaching the truth of the gospel and living it out in godliness, Timothy would help assure his own salvation and help the Ephesians not to compromise their faith in Christ. He was responsible to "continue to work out [his] salvation with fear and trembling" (Phil 2:12).

FROM THE TEXT

Paul's advice to Timothy continues to have relevance for twenty-first century Christians, especially those who are church leaders and ministers.

Age and example. Timothy was probably younger than the elders in Ephesus. Paul warns of the challenges young people may face as they enter ministry or lay leadership positions. People are often called and trained for ministry at young ages. Stress results in some cultures and settings when these young people finish their training and seek to enter ministry at twenty-two or younger. In some denominational polities, even teens can serve on church boards.

Younger people are known for being energetic, idealistic, and full of new ideas. Youth is also characterized by rushing hormones and lack of mature judgment. Temptations often accompany the excesses of youth. Younger people may be more likely to succumb to certain temptations associated with inexperience, cultural shifts, and peer pressure. Sexuality, entertainment, and eating or drinking habits confront them differently than they do older people. There are many things—even important things like work and family—that can distract young people from fulfilling their calling into ministry.

Wise young leaders will earn the respect of their elders or the "power holders" in their fellowship. Developing trust is vital for discipleship. A certain freedom results from accountability. The most critical area of trust young leaders must nurture is competence in the message. Their actions will speak louder than their words, but their words will be ineffective if no actions back them up. A good reputation takes time to develop.

Confirmation of gifts. Passing the mantle of leadership on to the next generation is often difficult for those who have carried it for a generation. However, if responsibility is not passed on, the church (or any organization) will eventually die from exhaustion and old age.

Paul reminds Timothy of the time when the elders laid hands on him (1 Tim 4:14). We do not know all of what this entailed, but it surely included some degree of commission and recognition of Timothy's gifts. His spiritual growth and maturity were evident to the group, and they added their blessings. It is vital that the church and mentors of young people give their affirmation and blessing to young leaders and release them for service to God. Community confirmation is crucial in a call to ministry.

Life and doctrine. Paul urges Timothy to watch how he lives and what he teaches. Personal care is vital for ministry leaders. It is far too easy to get caught up in the doing of ministry and forget the most important element of personal soul care (consider Luke 10:39-40).

4:11-16

V. HOW TO DEAL WITH VARIOUS GROUPS IN THE CHURCH: I TIMOTHY 5:1—6:2

BEHIND THE TEXT

Chapter 5 marks a change in topic and tone. But it is still connected to relational and ethical issues mentioned earlier in the letter. The key recurring theme is the need for the church to live out its devotion to God (*eusebeia*). Timothy may have needed extra encouragement to deal with the challenges of the negative influence of the false teachers. The situation in the church required wisdom, discernment, and strong authority. The call of God, confirmed by the church, had prepared him for the task (4:14). This ought to be exercised with "love, which comes from a pure heart and a good conscience and a sincere faith" (1:5).

Chapter 5 opens instructions as to how Timothy ought to deal with various age-groups within the church. The chapter has three sections: Verses 1-2 function as the general thesis statement for 5:1—6:2. Verses 3-16 discuss needy widows. Verses 17-25 treat elders, especially those who preach and teach. Finally, 6:1-2 gives instructions about slaves. It is likely that real or potential problems in the Ephesian church stood behind each of these treatments.

195

The unifying theme of these sections is the need to honor certain people and to avoid shame before the world. The word "honor" (*timē*) is repeated in 5:3, 17, and 6:1. At least three goals lie behind Paul's instructions. First, the church ought to live out compassionate godliness by caring for the needy. Second, the potential or actual influence of the false teachers should be stopped before further harm is done. Perhaps, some elders or young widows had succumbed to their teachings. This would have affected the mission and effectiveness of the church. Third, Timothy must not misunderstand the authority he had from Paul (4:11, 13). Timothy is to pass Paul's directions on to those in leadership in the Ephesian church. There is a sense of critical urgency to resolve these problems because the church was developing a bad reputation and some were following after Satan (5:15) and acting worse than unbelievers (v 8).

The key directive in the first major section is simply, **honor widows who are genuine widows** (v 3). "Widows" (*chera*) is the hinge word for the section, repeated eight times (vv 3 [2x], 4, 5, 9, 11, 16 [2x]). The phrase *hai ontos cheria*, translated in the NIV as "widows who are really in need," forms an inclusio (literary bookends) with vv 3 and 16. Paul puts qualifications on who needy widows are and whom the church should help.

Behind this passage stands the ancient sociological assumption of limited goods: There is a limited amount of goods that can be divided among people or groups. If some get more, others will get less.

The church has limited resources. Providing for the needs of every widow is impossible, because the needs of some widows might not be met. Other means must be found to meet their needs: Families with the means to do so should care for their own widows. Younger widows should remarry.

The goal is for those who really need help to get it. Those who have other resources must accept personal responsibility. A sharp contrast exists between the ideal widows of vv 5-7 and 9-10 and the younger widows of vv 11-15. The passage is to distinguish those who truly need help and those who do not.

Qualities of *Deserving Widow*	*Descriptions of* *Undeserving Widow*
"Left all alone" (v 5)	Has family to help (v 4)
"Hope[s] in God" (v 5)	"Lives for pleasure" (v 6)
	Some have turned to Satan (v 15)
Prays "night and day" (v 5)	Uncontrolled "sensual desires" (v 11)
"Over sixty" (v 9)	Young (v 11)
"Faithful to her husband" (v 9)	"Broken . . . first pledge" (v 12)
"Known for her good deeds" (v 10)	"Habit of being idle" (v 13)
Brought up children (v 10)	Go "from house to house" (v 13)

Shown hospitality (v 10)	"Busybodies who talk nonsense" (v 13)
Washed "feet of the Lord's people" (v 10)	Will be judged (v 12)
Helped "those in trouble" (v 10)	

Several issues have challenged interpreters: First, to what extent have false teachers influenced the women in the Ephesian church? It is possible that the teachers were causing women to reject their culturally expected roles (→ 2:8-15; 2 Tim 3:6-7). This would have brought shame on them and the church in the eyes of unbelievers.

Second, does the passage speak about an *order of widows*, which existed in the second and later centuries? Such a position is not necessary to interpret this passage. The letter is more ad hoc than paradigmatic and applies wisdom to resolve a growing crisis.

Third, the vocabulary poses challenges about Pauline authorship. There are fifteen words that occur only here in the NT and another eighteen words not found in the undisputed Pauline Epistles. The unique subject matter of this chapter can account for most of these words.

A. Honoring Those within the Family of God (5:1-2)

IN THE TEXT

■ **1-2** This chapter opens without any transition from Paul's personal exhortations to Timothy in ch 4. It continues the personal tone of the letter with a general statement of how Timothy should respond to various age-groups within the Ephesian church.

These two verses function as the proposition for 5:1—6:2. They provide a general guideline for how Timothy should respond to each of the groups discussed in the rest of the unit. Although Paul addresses Timothy specifically, the whole church is the intended audience.

Paul uses familial terms to describe four age-groups within the church. He appeals to fictive kinship (indicated with the adverbial comparative *hos*, "as," before each group) as the motivation for dealing well with each. Behind this appeal stands the early Christian belief that the people of God become one family (→ 3:15). Within this family, each member should live by certain household codes (→ 2:8). Jesus incorporated his followers into family by calling them his mother and brothers (Matt 12:49-50). As one united family, believers are bonded together with a love that surpasses even the love shown in human family relationships (Col 3:14). The family of God ought to be marked by relationships that mirror the respect, care, and concern shown in human families at their best.

Paul begins with a prohibition (in the subjunctive): **Do not rebuke an older man harshly.** The word for **rebuke** (*epiplēxēs*) is found only here in the NT. This strong word connotes rough treatment—scolding sharply, reproving, striking, or doing violence. It could mean "castigate" (Johnson 2001, 259-60). Timothy ought to treat others "on the basis of love" (Phlm 9).

Older man (*presbyterōi*) describes a male of advanced years. In the plural in Acts (11:30; 14:23; 15:2, 4, 6, 22; 16:4; 20:17; 21:18) and the Pastoral Epistles (→ 1 Tim 4:14, 5:17; Titus 1:5), it refers to a group of leaders in the church. The NIV and most modern translations assume a different use here, in keeping with the other three age-groups mentioned in 1 Tim 4:1-2. Because of the respect for age shown then, it is still possible that the older men were leaders in the church.

These older men may have been influenced by the false teachers and needed correction. If Timothy's actions were wrongly interpreted, the older men might reject his correction. The age difference implied in 4:12 (→) becomes more apparent when Timothy had to discipline his seniors.

Rather than harshness, Timothy should treat older men as he would his own father. Instead of rebuking (the two verbs are separated by the strong adversative *alla* ["but"]), he should **exhort** (*parakalei*). This word refers to a softer appeal, admonishment, correction, encouragement, consolation, or comfort (→ 1:3). In 4:13 and 6:2, the noun is used of "teaching." Timothy should put relationships above his need to be right or prove lines of authority (Towner 1994, 114). This verb, given only once in this verse, governs how Timothy is to approach all four groups. The NIV tries to capture this nuance by adding the word **treat,** which is not in Greek.

The **father** was treated with respect in both Greco-Roman and Jewish families. Paul may have in mind the fifth commandment, "Honor your father and your mother, so that you may live long in the land the LORD your God is giving you" (Exod 20:12; Deut 5:16; Knight 1992, 214). The seriousness of respecting those older is clear in Lev 19:32: "Stand up in the presence of the aged, show respect for the elderly and revere your God. I am the LORD." This verse connects worshipping God with honoring the aged (see the apocryphal Sir 3:12-16; *Spec. Laws* 2.237). In the Greco-Roman world, Cicero wrote,

> It is the duty of a young man to show deference to his elders and to cling to the best and most approved of them, so as to receive the benefit of their counsel and influence. Let everyone among us revere in deed and word whoever is older. (*Off.* 1.34.122, quoted by Montague 2008, 106)

These traditions also stand behind the later passage on widows in 5:3-16. Timothy must balance the need to correct error (4:11; 5:20) with the social constraints of respect for those older. The best way to do this would be in love (1:5).

Timothy should exhort **younger men as brothers** in the same way. These would have been men younger than the elders, probably Timothy's own age or younger (Mounce 2000, 270). Brotherhood ought to be saturated with self-giving love (Rom 12:10; 1 Thess 4:9). Brothers treat one another as friends and comrades. In this case, brothers share the same goal of eternal life (1 Tim 4:6-8).

Next, Timothy is to admonish **older women as mothers**, following the same principle he should use with older men. The Greek word behind **older women** (*presbyteras*) is the feminine form of the word in v 1 for "older men" and is found only here in the NT. Timothy should not ignore age differences but should acknowledge them by showing respect. In a culture where women had few rights, a young man might be disrespectful to an older woman. Timothy had good role models in his mother, Eunice, and grandmother Lois (2 Tim 1:5) who taught him the Holy Scriptures (2 Tim 3:15) in his youth. He now has the opportunity to reverse this influence by showing the same kind of spiritual care to the older women of the Ephesian church.

The final group to whom Timothy should appeal is **younger women,** who are to be approached **as sisters.** It will take special care for Timothy to relate to the young women in the church. So Paul adds, **with absolute purity** (*agneia*)—connoting sexual chastity (BDAG 2000, 12). Timothy must maintain high ethical standards to avoid temptation or any hint of impropriety in his relationships with women. There is no indication that Timothy ever married, making him even more vulnerable. Sexual purity and holiness are linked in 1 Thess 4:3.

Absolute (or **all** [*pasē*]) emphasizes Paul's warning. This is a strong call for integrity in ministry. Paul is concerned in this letter to preserve the reputation of the church. One way to do that is by making sure the leaders, including Timothy, maintain the highest standards of conduct. Apparently, the false teachers were taking advantage of some women (2 Tim 3:6). Good brothers take respectful care of their sisters.

FROM THE TEXT

Dealing with problem people in a church is always difficult. Timothy faced a number of obstacles in his mission to strengthen the Ephesian church and set it on the right course. The false teachers were causing a number of doctrinal and ethical problems, some more obvious than others. By the time Paul wrote this letter, the church was complex, multigenerational, and socially stratified. Paul offered Timothy a simple approach that could be used in many situations in ministry and life in general.

First, Timothy must *show respect in appropriate ways to everyone in the church*. As a "young" man (→ 1 Tim 4:12), Timothy needed to be careful how he worked with older believers. Young ministers often begin their service at a new church with new ideas and have to help change old attitudes. Generational differences compound this challenge. This becomes even more difficult in cultures where honor and shame are significant social forces. Overcoming generational differences can create stress and misunderstanding.

Timothy must also *avoid compromising situations*. It is not difficult to find oneself in a vulnerable situation in our modern cultures. Men and women often work together in ministry, business, and education. Temptation abounds, and so one must stay vigilant and maintain propriety with the opposite sex. We must give no reason for rumor to start. False accusations can destroy a person's ministry and leave pain in the lives of the other accused person (→ 5:19). Boundaries of purity must always be maintained (Matt 5:27-30).

Pastors must *be personally vulnerable and accountable*. Working with people necessitates that leaders be humble and willing to learn from and be corrected by those they lead. Leaders must show authority. But it must be in imitation of Jesus' words of caution to his disciples, "Whoever wants to become great among you must be your servant" (Matt 20:26; see vv 25-28). People are not steps in the ladder to higher office.

B. Advice about Widows (5:3-16)

1. Widows in Need (5:3-8)

IN THE TEXT

■ **3** This verse gives the central theme of this section. One of the groups from v 2 needs special attention—**widows who are really in need**. Two key questions guide this section: Who should care for the widows? and, Which widows qualify for support? (Stott 1996, 130). Paul will answer these questions by giving examples and setting up conditions to be met. There are three types of widows in this passage: (1) those over sixty who are in need, (2) those who have family to help them, and (3) young widows of marriageable age. Three groups are mentioned three times (Marshall 1999, 581):

1. The families of widows	4	7-8	16a
2. Pious widows	5	9-10	14-15
3. Impious or young widows	6	11-13	14-15

Apparently, too many widows were seeking church assistance and draining its resources. Young widows were abusing the assistance by becoming entangled in unproductive habits. Paul emphasizes the character, not the duties of widows. He sets out conditions for determining who should be helped.

These conditions are general principles, not a checklist. Not every situation or widow is identical. Paul uses pastoral wisdom to deal with an ad hoc situation. Although he continues to use the second-person singular imperative, he instructs not only Timothy but also the whole church. Therefore, everyone, especially leaders and widows, are his intended audience.

The basic instruction for this unit is to **give proper recognition to those widows who are really in need.** The imperative *tima* means to respect, honor, value, revere, and have high regard for these (BDAG 2000, 1005-6). The same verb appears in the LXX of the fifth commandment in Exod 20:12 (Deut 5:16)—"Honor your father and your mother" (see Eph 6:2).

This *honor* can be shown in many ways, depending on the situation. The text does not yet specifically state how to honor these widows. The balance of the passage suggests that this should include some type of material support (Schneider 1972, 178-79). The noun form of the word—"honor" in 1 Tim 4:17 and *deserving* in v 18—clearly connotes financial support. In 6:1, the verb "respect" describes how slaves ought to respect their masters. The command is directed toward Timothy as a leader. He must pass on the information and help decide how widows should be cared for.

Widows (*chēras*) refers to women whose husbands have died, but it could include celibates, virgins, and abandoned wives (Stählin 1974, 445). The reference to husbands and children in 5:9-10 narrows this to the wife of a deceased husband. The *real widow* is one who is (lit.) *truly* [*ontōs*: "indeed" (NASB), "really" (NRSV)] *a widow* (in vv 4, 5, 16). Paul will define them as those who have no relatives to support them and who have met the qualifications of vv 5 and 9.

Widows in Judaism and the Early Church

The plight of single women in the ancient world was difficult in most situations, since they had few ways to support themselves. The life expectancy of men was short, leaving about 40 percent of women between forty and fifty as widows (Winter 2003, 124). Caring for widows was a key obligation in both Judaism and the early church.

Widows are special objects of God's love in the OT. God is the advocate of and defender for widows (Pss 68:5; 146:9) through his justice (Prov 15:25). God's people should do the same (Isa 1:17, 23; see Exod 22:22-23; Deut 10:16-20). They were to collect tithes and store them for widows (Deut 14:28-29). A curse awaited those who deprived widows of justice or failed to provide for their needs (Deut 27:19; Job 24:3, 21). Neglecting widows was one cause of the exile (Jer 7:6; Ezek 22:6-8). Widows, like foreigners, the fatherless, and the poor, were economically helpless people (Jer 22:3; Zech 7:10).

Intertestamental Judaism continued the concern for the poor, orphaned, and widowed. After Judas Maccabeus and the Jews had defeated their enemies, they gave some of the spoils of war to care for the needs of widows (2 Macc 8:28).

God steps in to replace the care a husband provided (Philo, *Spec. Laws* I.310). Philo allegorized the plight of widows and compared it to the soul apart from God (see Stählin 1974, 447-48).

Looking out for widows became a key act of compassion for early Christians. In Mark 7:9-13, Jesus accused the Pharisees of neglecting to care for their parents. Jesus condemned scribes who walked around looking important yet devoured widows' houses (12:38-44). One of the marks of the earliest Christians was their care for one another by sharing together their resources and giving to anyone in need (Acts 2:42-47; 4:32-37). This continued to the point where the Jerusalem church had to develop specialized ministries. Acts 6:1 states, "In those days when the number of disciples was increasing, the Hellenistic Jews among them complained against the Hebraic Jews because their widows were being overlooked in the daily distribution of food." James 1:27 merges the compassionate care of widows with genuine faith in God: "Religion that God our Father accepts as pure and faultless is this: to look after orphans and widows in their distress and to keep oneself from being polluted by the world."

First Timothy hints at increasing social stratification in the early church as both poor and rich became believers in Christ. The needs expressed in I Tim 5 continued to exist as the church grew. The church had to find ways to minister to widows and at the same time provide for ministry within the church.

At some point in the second or third century, an "order of widows" emerged in the church (Ign. *Smyrn.* 13.1; Ign. *Pol.* 4.1; Pol. *Phil.* 4.3; Tertullian, *Virg.* 5.9). Scholars debate whether such an order existed when I Timothy was written. It may be anachronistic to say that an official office of widows with specific duties in the church was present in the Ephesian church (see Thurston 1989; but see Bassler 1984).

■ **4** Not all widows require the same attention and care. Paul puts several qualifications on those who do not need the help of the church. The first is given in this verse and others in vv 9-10. This qualification is set off by the conjunction **but** (*de*), showing an exception or antithesis to the proposition of v 3.

The first limit is given as a conditional statement in the form of case law marked by "if anyone" (the same as vv 8, 16). The protasis assumes that some widows were part of larger families with living children or grandchildren. The apodosis lays out what these descendants should do in caring for their widowed loved ones. The verb is the present imperative **let them learn** (*manthanetōsan*), implying that this is a growth process that, if not done yet, should be started and continued. **First of all** emphasizes the priority of this process.

The subject of this verb is unclear. John Calvin assumed "widows" from v 3 was the subject, which makes grammatical sense, and that they should put their faith to practice by caring for their children (Marshall 1999, 584). But most modern interpreters assume "children and grandchildren" are the subject, the closest plural nouns to the verb. That the passage goes on to describe how the family should be the first to care for widows and not burden the church supports the latter view. Paul reminds reluctant families that they must assume responsibility first, not the church (Knight 1992, 217).

Two infinitive clauses complete the action of the imperative verb, explaining why the family should care for its widows. The first infinitive (*eusebein*), **to put their religion into practice**, is one of the key words of this letter (→ "godliness" in 2:2). It describes piety, devotion, and consecration to God lived out in practical ways in relationships with others.

The first place believers ought to learn to live out their devotion is in *their own household* (*oikos*, the family unit, not the building in which they live; → 3:4, 5, 12). "For Paul, Christianity begins at the home; and one's conduct in the microcosm of the home shows one's abilities, or lack of abilities, in the macrocosm of the church" (Mounce 2000, 280).

The second infinitive clause is interpreted in the NIV as a result of the first: **so repaying their parents and grandparents**. Caring for them is one way children and grandchildren can show their devotion to God. The infinitive *apodidonai* means to give back what is due (BDAG 2000, 109-10). This is a "recompense" or "repayment" (*amoibas*, only here in the NT). Children should not take their mothers' love for granted.

The Greek for **parents and grandparents** (*progonois*) could include more than one generation. Many widows would have been part of multigenerational households. Descendants can express their gratitude by caring for women in their family who become widows.

The ultimate motive for both actions is stated in the last clause: **For this is pleasing to God.** It pleases God when a family honors its needy elders by caring for them (Eph 6:1-2). God's will for the family is given in the fifth commandment, which lies behind this whole passage. The promise is that life will go well, needs will be provided, and people will grow closer to God.

This verse shifts the responsibility for elder care from the church to the family. The burden of providing for the needs of a widow falls on her family first. The church should be used as a last resort when widows have no family to help them. Three basic reasons are given in this passage why families should care for their widows:

1. Positively, it pleases God (1 Tim 5:4).
2. Negatively, not doing so denies the faith (v 8).
3. Practically, so the church is not burdened (v 16*b*). (Mounce 2000, 279-80)

■ **5** This verse lays out the first qualifications for widows who should be helped by the church and clarifies further the opening exhortation in v 3. It gives directions to Timothy and other church leaders. But it also provides a subtle motivation for younger widows and a reminder to older widows of how they ought to live. Two essential qualifications apply: (1) a widow must have material need, and (2) her spiritual life ought to show that she relies on God to provide for her needs.

A widow **who is really in need** is one who has been **left all alone** in a permanent state of destitution (Mounce 2000, 281). **Left . . . alone** is a perfect passive participle found only here in the NT. The needy widow has no family to help her. If a believing widow has children who refuse to care for her as they should (→ v 4), she is still essentially **left all alone**. Being alone could be expanded to include "forsaken."

A widow deserving the support of the church is also one who has put **her hope in God**, shown by constant reliance upon God in prayer. The verb **puts her hope** is in the perfect tense. This widow has trusted God for some time and continues to do so. Her hope for the future gives her assurance for the present. The tense indicates "the unique Christian posture of confident anticipation of God's intervention and provision" (Towner 2006, 341). There is a sense of finality and certainty of her decision to rely fully on God. She is following after "the holy women of the past who [also] put their hope in God" (1 Pet 3:5). This type of widow has learned to look to God in her difficult situation. Such hope is "a hallmark of the believer" (Knight 1992, 219).

Growth in her reliance upon God has been developed through constant prayer (1 Thess 5:17). She **continues night and day to pray and to ask God for help. Continues** (*prosmenei*) in the present tense treats prayer as her habitual lifestyle.

Paul uses two words for prayer here (→ 1 Tim 2:1). **To pray**, a noun in the Greek (*deēsesin*), refers to supplications and petitions for others—***intercessions***. **To ask**, another noun (*proseuchais*), is the more general word for prayer, often used in the context of devotion and worship. The order **night and day** is Jewish, since the new day begins with sunset (Gen 1:5; 1 Thess 2:9).

Many older women are not capable of physically rigorous ministries in the church, but they can pray. In his letter *To the Philippians* (4), Polycarp calls widows who pray, "the altar of God." Luke 2:36-38 records the story of the eighty-four-year-old prophetess Anna who "never left the temple but worshiped night and day, fasting and praying" (v 37). Her prayer life gave her keen insight into the significance of the infant Jesus.

■ **6** Paul now gives an exception to his previous direction. This verse stands in sharp contrast to the praying widow of v 5. **But** (*de*) marks a comparison between two types of widows. The second type of widow is one **who lives for pleasure**. This phrase comes from the present participle *spatalōsa*, a rare word for someone who is self-indulgent, worldly-minded, focused on the luxurious, or given to pleasure (see Jas 5:5).

The outcome of the pursuit of pleasure is that this widow, ***even though she is living, has died***. The concessive participle *zōsa* is in the present tense.

The verb *tethnēken* is in the perfect tense (lit. "has hope" in v 5). Although this widow is alive physically, she has died spiritually and is already cut off from the source of divine life. She is too self-absorbed to recognize her need (see Rev 3:1). The imagery in this verse was used by other moralists to warn about excessive pleasures (e.g., Philo on Deut 30:15—"Goodness and virtue is life, evil and wickedness is death" [*Flight* 58], quoted by Collins 2002, 138).

There is no indication of the social or economic status of this type of widow. Was the Ephesian church supporting widows who did not need the help, enabling them to pursue unchristlike passions (1 Tim 5:11) and get involved in counterproductive activities (v 13; → 2:9; Winter 2003, 129-31)? In 6:10, Paul will discuss the dangers of wealth. Although wealth may contribute to a self-indulgent lifestyle (Johnson 1996, 174), one does not need to be rich to be self-absorbed. Even women living with few material resources can get caught up in pleasure.

The contrast between the types of widows illustrates the fundamental human predicament:

The widow of v 5	The widow of v 6
Living for God	Living for self
Relying on God	Relying on self

A different type of death is necessary, even for widows: a death to self. This is the surest way to experience true life (Rom 6:2-11).

■ **7** Paul next exhorts Timothy to **give the people these instructions**. **Give** (*parangelle*) in Greek might be better translated "command" (ESV), as in 4:11. **These instructions** (*tauta*) are probably the directions Paul just gave in vv 3-6. But they could include all his other directions in this section. He offers a policy for the church to follow to help it care for widows and preserve a good reputation before unbelievers.

The people would include especially those family members responsible for the care of widows (vv 6, 8), the widows themselves as they seek to put their hope in God (v 5), and the leaders who work with individual situations within families and the church. Everyone must assume responsibility to "learn" to practice godliness (v 4).

The purpose for these instructions is **so that no one may be open to blame**. This phrase echoes one of the concerns and intended outcomes of this letter: to improve the conduct in the church in socially acceptable ways by appealing to the best ideals of the culture. Christians ought to be shining examples of devotion to God (*eusebeia*) that surpass the best in the culture around them (→ 3:7; 5:14; Titus 2:5, 8).

Not only overseers (→ 1 Tim 3:2), but **no** Christian should be **open to blame** (*anepilēmptoi*: "above reproach" [NRSV]). A community or culture determines what is "blameless." Verse 8 of ch 5 will assert that even unbelievers care for their family members. Christians who do not take care of their elderly relatives bring shame on the church in the eyes of those around them. Shame as a powerful social force would hinder the mission of the church and prove detrimental to proclaiming the gospel.

■ **8** A second conditional clause reflects the principle of v 4 (→) and addresses the problem of some people not following the command of v 7 (→). The verse gives the negative outcome of not following Paul's instructions. This repetition "may underline his exasperation at the selfishness of some families in the Ephesian church" (Kelly 1963, 115). The indefinite **anyone** shows that this is a general principle to be applied in the church (Knight 1992, 221).

For emphasis the verb **does not provide** comes last in its clause. What the family should provide is "honor" or "support" (→ v 4). **Provide** (*provoei*) is made of two parts that mean to think about something or someone beforehand. It describes how superiors consider those under their leadership. It "combines forethought with the appropriate material provision" (Towner 2006, 344).

There are two parts to the protasis of the condition that involve two sets of people: **their relatives, and especially . . . their own household**. These comprehend both the extended family and those who live under the same roof (*oikeiōn*). This could include several generations.

The two-part condition is matched by a twofold consequence for families who neglect their widows. Both consequences link lack of provision with rejection of the Christian faith. The first is rather direct: **denied the faith** [*tēn pistin*; → 3:9]. They are not really Christian believers. **Denied** (*ērnētai*) in the perfect tense implies that at some point, these people had rejected core Christian values and teachings and continued to do so. Spurning apostolic teaching was a problem in Ephesus, and it apparently affected even critical family obligations (→ 2 Tim 2:12-13; 3:13; Titus 1:16).

The second outcome is closely related to the first: These people have become **worse than an unbeliever.** Even pagans care for their families. God's light has shone in their culture, revealing the importance of caring for the elderly (Rom 2:14-15). Because believers have even more light and have experienced God's revelation of love in Christ, they should know better. Believers who neglect widows are worse than unbelievers because they have deliberately broken God's law.

Both of these statements show the seriousness of the situation. All the Ephesians should be ashamed for any who are neglecting their families. Christian love is stronger than family ties, but should include them. Apparently, some in the Ephesian church were not even fulfilling this basic social responsibility, although they had sufficient wealth to care for their widows. Even those with little means should seek to provide for the basic necessities of impoverished widows. Paul is shaming the Ephesians into action (Witherington 2006, 268) and intimately connecting faith with action. This verse functions in this passage as a strong wake-up call to the seriousness of neglecting those in need.

2. Instructions for Young Widows (5:9-15)

■ **9-10** Paul now addresses the pastoral question, What determines a needy widow to whom the church should provide assistance? The verb **put on the list** (*katalegesthō*) is used only here in the NT. In other literature, it refers to compiling a list or enrolling onto a registrar (Balz and Schneider 1993, 2:261). Paul gives specific directions for which widows should be listed. The "list of widows" was not a particular order within the church, but a record of those desperately needing help (→ sidebar "Widows in Judaism and the Early Church" with 5:3). Here are the conditions and qualifications of widows the church should assist:

The first condition is *age*: a widow should be **over sixty.** Sixty was considered the age when someone became "old" in the ancient world (Kelly 1963, 115). Plato (*Leg.* 6.759c-d) said that sixty should be the minimum age for becoming a priest and is a good time for retiring for contemplation. Sixty was also a special age for those who wished to dedicate themselves to the Lord according to Lev 27:7.

Sixty marked a point in life when it would have become difficult for a widow to care for herself. Life expectancy then was not nearly what it is today. A widow of this age would not likely be on the list long; and few attained this life span. This considerably shortened the list of those who should receive church assistance.

The second qualification is *marriage*: A widow must have been **faithful to her husband.** This phrase is (lit.) *a one-man woman* (only here in the NT; but → 1 Tim 3:2, 12; Titus 1:6). This could mean that: (1) the woman had been married only once, or (2) she had been faithful to her husband. Women at that time and culture did not have multiple husbands (Knight 1992, 223)— this was not intended to exclude polyandrous women. The first possibility can be rejected since nowhere does Paul specifically prohibit remarriage after the death of a spouse. He actually encourages it for young widows (in 1 Tim 5:14). The NIV probably correctly chooses the second option, since the similar phrase in 3:2, 12 probably refers to faithfulness to marriage vows. Being faithful to one's husband was an admired virtue for women and the standard especially for believers (Eph 5:22-24; Col 3:18-19; Titus 2:5; 1 Pet 3:1-6).

The third qualification is that a widow should have a *good reputation* and be **well known for her good deeds** (v 10). These should display her extraordinary character and emanate from her life of faith. **Good deeds** describe "the observable, horizontal facet of the Christian life" (Towner 1989, 154). Doing good is important in the Pastoral Epistles (1 Tim 6:18; Titus 2:14; 3:8; 3:14), and leaders are to set an example in it (Titus 2:7).

This qualification is subdivided into examples that fit the first-century context. Each is given in the historical aorist tense to show "Christian character attested by service rendered in the past rather than a list of duties to be performed for the future" (Marshall 1999, 594). These characteristics appear in five conditional clauses, which assume the condition will be met in order for a widow to be added to the list. The first two are domestic in nature; the second two focus on service to the church; the last is inclusive of **all kinds of good deeds.**

The first is **bringing up children.** This quality comes from a Greek word that combines "child" (*teknos*) and "provide for" or "bring up" (*trephō*). It includes caring for a child both physically and spiritually (BDAG 2000, 995). The unstated emphasis is on how the woman cared for her children: Was she a good mother? The primary place of service for women then was the home (see 1 Tim 2:15; Titus 2:4). But bringing up children was not the sole responsibility of women (see Deut 6:7; Eph 6:4; 1 Tim 3:4).

If an otherwise qualified widow has children, they should care for her. So why does she need the church's help (→ 5:4)? Perhaps the children she raised well rejected her or are deceased. Surely a childless widow would not be excluded from the list. Later, official widows had responsibilities outside their own families and cared for orphans (Kelly 1963, 117; see *Herm. Mand.* 8.10; *Apos. Con.* 3.3.2). The simple conclusion must be that a widow must have been faithful as a caregiver to children and that her reputation has not been sullied by her past misconduct.

The second indicator of a good reputation is that a widow has shown **hospitality.** The verb here (*exenodochēsen*) is different from the one translated hospitality in 3:2 (*philoxenia*). It refers to consideration (*dokeō*) of the needs of a stranger (*xenos*). Hospitality was an important part of early Christian life (Rom 12:13; 16:23; Heb 13:2; 1 Pet 4:9). Hospitality in the early church was not merely a culturally determined virtue. More significantly, it was motivated by the teaching of Jesus (Matt 25:31-46; see Stählin 1967b, 1-36).

Travel was difficult in the first century. Inns had a bad reputation and were often unsafe places to stay. Hosting traveling missionaries created a bond and brought unity to various parts of the early church. But hospitality was not limited exclusively to travelers. Even destitute widows should evidence lives marked by kindness to others. Hospitality does not need to be costly; it simply involves receiving someone as if receiving Christ himself (Chrysostom, *Hom. 1 Tim.* 14). Being hospitable takes compassion, commitment, and sometimes sacrifice, all of which show the inner quality of a hospitable woman. There are several examples of such women in the NT (e.g., Tabitha in Acts 9:36-39 and Phoebe in Rom 16:1).

One tangible way to show hospitality is the third reputation builder—**washing the feet of the Lord's people.** Washing the feet of visitors was a sign of humble hospitality in Eastern cultures. Even though servants were usually the ones to do it, Jesus washed the feet of his disciples, leaving them an example to follow (John 13:14).

The Lord's people is literally "holy ones" (*hagiōn*), a term regularly used in the NT for believers (Rom 1:7; 1 Cor 1:2; 2 Cor 1:1; Eph 1:1; Phil 1:1; Col 1:2; Phlm 5). Here, washing the feet of other believers was an act of hospitality to visitors, showing a woman's willingness to serve others, "performing all manner of humble tasks for the benefit of others" (Towner 1994, 119). Foot washing as a ritual act was slow to catch on in many parts of the church. The first clear reference to it appears in Augustine, *Epist.* 55.33 (late fourth to early fifth century; Fee 1988, 125).

Another sign of **good deeds** is **helping those in trouble** (*thlibomenois*), those afflicted by outside forces or persecuted for their faith (2 Cor 1:4-5; 4:8-11; Col 1:24; 1 Thess 3:3-4). The verb "help" (*epērkesen*) means giving assistance or aid. A worthy widow demonstrated kindness by providing for the tangible needs of those suffering hardships. Helping the needy should characterize followers of Christ (Matt 25:35-40).

The last quality is inclusive of many others and leaves the list open-ended. It is not exhaustive but illustrative. A reputable widow has devoted **herself to all kinds of good deeds. Devoting** (*epēkolouthēsen*) means actively seeking. The whole phrase summarizes "the visible outworking of faith" (Towner 2006, 348). A worthy widow may not meet every criterion in the list, but her life will have been marked by concern for the needs of others.

The church should honor and offer financial support to the widows who have the reputation of helping others in the church and in their homes. They have lived out godliness in all areas of their lives.

■ **11-12** Verse 11 opens with an emphatic *refuse younger widows*. **Younger widows** should **not** be **put . . . on such a list** (not in the Greek, but assumed in the NIV from v 9). Their precise age is unclear. But they were young enough to remarry and have children.

The reason for this is more than limited resources in the local church treasury. There are moral and spiritual issues that require careful consideration. Paul's commonsense pastoral advice mentions two reasons why young widows should be denied church assistance. The first is given here; the other, in v 13.

This directive presumes that some younger widows took advantage of the church's generosity and became involved in unhealthy activities. Paul attempts to put a stop to that here. The rhetorical effect of these directions should shame any engaged in these activities. The argument proceeds as follows:

1. *Prohibition*: Exclude young widows from the list (v 11*a*).
2. *Problem one*: Since they are young, their passions may lead them into sin (vv 11*b*-12).
3. *Problem two*: Unemployed, they have become involved in time-wasting activities (v 13).
4. *Solution*: They ought to remarry to avoid these two problems (v 14).

The seriousness of the situation becomes apparent with the first problem: **their sensual desires overcome their dedication to Christ.** The attention of these younger widows shifted from Christ to their passions. The word translated **sensual desires** (*katastrēniasōsin*), only here in the NT, denotes strong physical cravings (BDAG 2000, 528; see Rev 18:3)—"to become self-indulgent in opposition to" their commitment to the Lord (Mounce 2000, 290). This may include more than sexual desires. The deeper problem is what happens to their Christian walk. **Their dedication** in the NIV is not in the Greek. The ESV provides a more literal reading: "Their passions draw them away from Christ." Their lifestyle contradicted their profession of faith. They replaced their passion for Christ with self-seeking pleasures.

Because these widows have been **overcome** by desire, **they bring judgment on themselves**. This judgment could come from two sources: (1) the court of public opinion, bringing shame to a widow and the church, and (2) ultimately from God. The extent of this judgment is implied in the following causal clause: **because they have broken their first pledge.**

Broken (*ēthetēsan*) means to reject, nullify, or ignore (BDAG 2000, 24). The word translated **pledge** in the NIV is difficult to interpret. It is the common word *pistis* (**faith**). In this context, it seems to refer to a solemn vow (BDAG 2000, 818 s.v. 1b). Scholars have offered several possible explanations of this pledge (Knight 1992, 226-27; Mounce 2000, 291):

1. to be faithful to a first husband
2. to remain celibate once one is in the order of widows
3. of faith in Christ; remarriage would be abandoning Christ
4. to serve Christ as an enrolled widow; widows were enrolled in the list to be supported by Christ's church

There is insufficient evidence for an "order of widows" at that time. So, the more likely meaning is that young widows were abandoning their total commitment to Christ when they followed their desires for remarriage. Marriage takes time and commitment (see 1 Cor 7:34-35). This problem could become more severe if widows married non-Christians who might pull them away from their faith commitment (Towner 1989, 121).

Not only Christians but also Roman pagans considered it virtuous for widows to remain unmarried (*univira*; Roloff 1988, 293-96). Since the church was small in the first century, finding suitable Christian husbands for young widows may not have been easy. Paul encouraged the Corinthian widows not to remarry (1 Cor 7:39-40). But if they could not control their passions, they should remarry to avoid sin. Both 1 Cor 7 and 1 Tim 5 make essentially the same argument:

1. The best option is to be totally committed to Christ as a single person. God will give special grace for this.
2. If a person is tempted by physical passions, that person should (re)marry.
3. If a person does get (re)married, he or she should marry a believer.
4. There is nothing wrong with (re)marriage.

■ 13 The second potential problem widows face is that they waste their own time and that of others. The NIV attempts to bring out the habitual nature of this in the translation **they get into the habit of.** The root of this present tense verb is **they learn** (*manthanousin*).

The bad habit they are learning is stated in an infinitive translated **being idle.** That this word is repeated again suggests that this was a key issue. **Being idle** (*argai*) leads to being lazy, ineffective, and unproductive (Titus 1:12). Paul's expression is ironic: "At the same time that they are turning against Christ, they are also studying hard to learn how to be idle" (Mounce 2000, 292).

An instrumental participle (*perierchomenai*) follows the infinitive. They are being idle **by going about from house to house.** Wandering to the homes of others implies that they are neglecting their own homes and the needs of the church (Fee 1994, 122). They are wasting time and causing further problems.

And not only . . . but also shows the worst aspect of the situation (Marshall 1999, 603). They have become **idlers** and **busybodies, saying things they ought not to.** They were speaking **nonsense** and meddling in the affairs of others. The word for **busybodies** (*periergoi*) in Acts 19:19 is translated "sorcery." This nuance may not be intended here (see 2 Thess 3:11).

These widows were actively talking about things they should not have been. Note the similarity between the widows' speech and that of the false teachers: foolish (1 Tim 1:6), empty (6:20), and showing they did not know what they were teaching (1:6-7; 4:7; 6:3-4; Fee 1984, 122).

The widows could have been spreading false teachings as they went from house to house (Marshall 1999, 603), under the influence of the false teachers (2 Tim 3:6), consciously or unconsciously.

One of the false teachings of the opponents was the rejection of marriage (→ 1 Tim 4:3). These young women were avoiding marriage, thus bringing potential harm to themselves and to the witness of the church in the eyes of their contemporaries. Their gossiping could have included "old wives' tales" (4:7). "When the proper structure of households is disturbed, false teachings begin to find supporters" (Saarinen 2008, 90).

The rhetoric of this verse puts the responsibility on young widows to change their behavior. Timothy, the church leaders, and the whole fellowship could facilitate this change by making careful decisions about whom they should and should not help. The preferred option for young widows appears in the next verse.

■ **14** Paul now gives positive instructions after the negative descriptions of 5:12-13. Remaining unmarried is not in the best interests of young widows or the church. It creates moral temptation and stewardship problems. The only reasonable solution is for the young widows to return to what is socially acceptable and to lead productive lives in their homes. Devoting their time to marriage, family, and home would make better use of their time and energy. Marriage would give their lives focus and provide for their material needs. This new course of action imitates the godliness of the older women described in vv 9-10.

Paul offers his **counsel** in these directions. *Boulomai* is used also in 2:8 with the force of authoritative judgment and can mean, "I want" (NASB). Paul's directions here are part of the larger policy about who should receive help from the church:

First, they should **marry**. This comes as a direct affront to the opponents who were against marriage (2:15; 4:3; → 5:12). The assumption behind this is that marriage is God's plan for procreation and the only acceptable situation for sexual union. Paul's primary motive is to keep the church and believers above reproach. The problem of temptation could be intensified because the widows had already been married (Knight 1992, 228). Therefore, remarriage is the better option to keep widows from falling into the trap of the **enemy**.

Second, they should **have children**. Raising children was the normal role for women in that culture (→ 2:15). Spending time raising a family would deter young widows from wasting time, getting into counterproductive talk, and promoting heresy.

Third, young widows should **manage their homes**. The infinitive behind this phrase (*oikodespotein*) comes from the same word used for those authorized to care for the household (Matt 13:27, 52). Women had significant management roles in Greco-Roman households. Several wealthy female Christian householders were involved in Paul's ministry (e.g., Lydia in Acts 16:14-15, 40; Phoebe in Rom 16:1-2; Chloe in 1 Cor 1:11; Priscilla in 1 Cor 16:19; and Nympha in Col 4:15; Witherington 2006, 272). Women oversaw daily activities around the home.

If the first three directives are performed, the fourth will automatically result: **The enemy** will have **no opportunity for slander**. There is no clear indication who **the enemy** (*antikeimenō*) might be. When this word occurs as a plural in the NT, it refers to people (Luke 13:17; 21:15; 1 Cor 16:9; Phil 1:28). In the singular, as here, if typically refers to God's endtime adversary (2 Thess 2:4; BDAG 2000, 89).

Since Satan is mentioned in the next verse, **the enemy** here could be Satan. Falling into disgrace or slander is linked to the devil in 1 Tim 3:7. It may be better not to attempt to designate specifically who this adversary is in this verse, since Satan was behind the human opponents in Ephesus (4:1-2).

Opportunity refers to the starting point or base of operations for an expedition or the resources needed for a mission (BDAG 2000, 158). If something is not done to guide young widows, the enemy will have a starting point in the church to cause further problems. The most obvious result will be **slander** (*loidorias*) by others. The unstated premise behind this directive is that the church will be given a bad reputation because of the activity of these women (→ 3:7; 5:7; 6:1; Titus 2:5, 10). This shift to polemic provides another strong motivation to young widows. Respectability "is a necessary component of the Church's missionary operation in that it allows the Church to maintain a redemptive interface with the observing world" (Towner 1989, 189).

■ **15** The situation in Ephesus had reached a crisis point because **some have . . . already turned away. Already** (*ēdē*) shows that the situation was not just hypothetical. The actual misconduct of some young widows made the issue urgent (Fee 1988, 123).

For (*gar*), untranslated in the NIV, makes the logical connection with the danger of 1 Tim 5:11-13 and reinforces Paul's point. **Some** in the context refers to young widows. There are two options for the young women: the safety of Paul's advice or the danger of Satan's trap.

To what extent the young widows are following Satan or what they have done is unclear. The letter as a whole hints that they have been deceived and surrendered into ungodliness (1:6; 4:1-2). They may have been influenced by the false teachers and their doctrines. Sadly, these women have **turned away** (*exetrapēsan*) from the truth of the gospel and embraced a lie (→ 2:5; 3:15; 4:3, 6). This is not merely an issue of social relationships or community cohesiveness, but of eternal life.

3. Women's Responsibility for Widows (5:16)

■ **16** Paul offers an alternative behavior to the dangerous course of some young widows described in vv 11-13. This verse functions as the conclusion to the section in the form of a proverb. It returns to the theme of v 3, making the point of the passage explicitly clear: families should care for their widows, and the church should care for widows without families.

The verse begins with a condition: **If any woman who is a believer has widows in her care. In her care** is not in the Greek but is supplied from the context. These directions address a particular type of situation. The adjective translated **who is a believer** (*pistē*) is feminine. This means that the antecedent of the indefinite pronoun "if any" (*tis*) is **any woman**. The pronoun is inclusive and expands **woman** beyond the previous discussion about young widows.

The identity of these women is unclear. The NIV assumes they were women with widows in their families. But they could have been wealthy women managers of households able to care for other women. There were some wealthy Christian women in the early church capable of helping others in need (e.g., Acts 16:14-15, 40; Rom 16:1-2; 1 Cor 1:11; 16:19; Col 4:15).

Why is Paul so specific here? Because this was the most practical solution for that culture. It would have been inappropriate for a single man or widower to care for a widowed woman. It would have been the responsibility of the wife of a married man to care for other women (Kelly 1963, 121). That households often included several generations makes this option even more plausible.

The principle is broad enough to be applied to all believers. The principle shows up in the protasis (conclusion): ***then* she should continue to help them and not let the church be burdened with them.** Help (*eparkeitō*) has the connotation of providing financial aid for someone in need. This need not be the only way a woman may help widows in her family, but it is a tangible one that covers many other areas.

The verb for **help** appears earlier in 1 Tim 5:10, describing how older widows have assisted those in various kinds of trouble. In essence, Paul asks the women of the church to follow the pattern set by the older widows devoted to works of compassion.

The reason for this advice is to free up the resources of the church **so that the church can help those widows who are really in need.** The church should not be burdened with every need but only with those that cannot be met in any other way. It must focus its resources on helping those who really need help. Practically speaking, the church may need to step in to help these widows if the believing women neglect their duty, but families have the first responsibility to care for widows. Even in its function as God's family (→ 3:15), the church is not to take on all the responsibilities of the human family.

FROM THE TEXT

The hermeneutical principle that guides this passage can be summed up in the question: What is the appropriate way to live out godliness in families and cultures? Cultures have different expectations and provisions for caring for their elderly. Each of the groups addressed in this passage has a relevant message.

First, *older widows* who are in need may have lost their husbands and have no children, but they *still have God* (Chrysostom, *Hom. 1 Tim.* 13). Widows can model steadfast commitment to God through their lives of prayer. Widows "are not withered branches on a vine but preciously fruitful by their witness, prayer, and service" (Montague 2008, 112). Widows are not simply to retire in obscurity but to remain active in ministry. The primary ministry of widows in the early church was prayer. "The church believed that she was *receiving* from these widows as well as giving" (ibid., 111). Prayer opens the door for widows to rely on God and reject the temptations of the world.

Widows who have learned to trust in God are alive spiritually even though their bodies are dying (→ v 6). They have learned what it means to crucify the old self with its passions and desires (Rom 6:6; Eph 4:22-24). They can respond to whatever situation they find themselves by seeking God's kingdom first (Matt 6:33) through prayer and doing what good they can in the church.

Second, younger widows have their own difficult road to travel. At the top of their list is the *need to maintain personal integrity*. Paul's directions place young women in a difficult place. How can they remain faithful to Christ and not let their natural passions control them? First Corinthians 7:7 hints at a solution: God gives a spiritual gift to those who remain single. With God's help, it is possible to remain true to Christ and control one's desires. Paul also makes it clear in both 1 Cor 7 and 1 Tim 5 that it is not wrong for young widows to remarry. If they do choose to remarry, it is crucial that they marry believers.

Third, Paul has an equally strong message for family members of widows. *It is primarily the family's responsibility to care for its older members.* A number of challenges make this difficult for families today. In many nations, there is a growing challenge of people living longer with better nutrition and health care. Increasing life spans put pressure on families and governments to find ways to care for the elderly. Many families experience a reversal of roles with children becoming the caregivers of their parents. The breakup of families, especially in Western cultures, has created vacuums of need among the elderly. Unlike other generations that had large families and households, smaller family sizes today make it difficult to provide financial and emotional support for older family members. With societies becoming increasingly mobile, when family members move, the elderly may be left isolated.

These realities mean that we need to be creative in our care of vulnerable members of society. We must consider the seriousness of the commitment God asks of us: to give toward the care of our older loved ones may require a renewed sensitivity to their needs.

Paul shows this seriousness by connecting this care to one's profession of faith and godliness (v 8). The fifth commandment (Exod 20:12), to honor one's parents, is connected to worshipping the Lord and is a manifestation of loving God and loving others. This command is not just for younger children to their parents but for adult children to their elderly parents.

Fourth, there is a message for the church. *The church must be both willing to help and discerning about whom it helps, because it has limited resources.* There are many demands on a church's finances today, and careful consideration must be made to help the neediest. The neediest in our culture may not be widows, but orphans or single parents. Care for orphans is often grouped with care for widows in the Bible (Jas 1:27). It should be noted that the situations Paul describes in this letter about "widows" (women) may often be just as true for "widowers" (men). Men who outlive their wives may find themselves in desperate need.

C. Support of Elders (5:17-25)

BEHIND THE TEXT

This section continues the theme started in 1 Tim 5:1 of honoring particular groups within the church. As with widows, the church should honor elders in tangible ways. There is also a warning against honoring people who do not deserve it. Both sections deal with mostly older people in the congregation (Marshall 1999, 609).

The focus in this section is on the elders in Ephesus (on overseers and deacons; → 3:1; 4:14; and 5:1-2). Here, the concern is not with age, as in 5:1, but with the status of elders as leaders in the church. Paul appoints elders (Acts 14:23) to serve as a governing board to "direct the affairs of the church" (1 Tim 5:17; see Acts 15:2, 4, 6, 22-23; 16:4; 20:17). This council may have been modeled after Jewish synagogues that had a board of elders often called *presbyteroi* (BDAG 2000, 862 s.v. 2a). Advanced age alone was not enough to be on this council; a reputable standing in the Jewish community was essential.

The specific duties of elders are not described in detail in the NT. First Peter 5:2 urges them to "be shepherds of God's flock." First Timothy 5:17 shows that they administered the church, preached, and taught. Titus 1:5-9 mentions elders in the same context as overseers. The overseers may have been a select group of elders who, as their name implies, had special oversight of the church and its leaders.

This section opens without transition (asyndeton) from the previous. An authoritative tone is marked with eight second-person singular imperatives. These address Timothy specifically, but as the messenger to the Ephesians.

The first paragraph has two parts: concern for the support of elders (1 Tim 5:17-19) and rebuke of those who are sinning (vv 20-21). Interpreters disagree as to whether the discussion on elders ends with v 20, v 21, or v 25.

Chapter 6 clearly identifies a third group to be honored. So, this makes it likely that 5:17-25 deals with the general topic of how Timothy is to deal with the elders. As a leader, he must exercise discernment when he appoints leaders in Ephesus. At first v 23 appears to be a digression, but it actually fits with v 22 and Paul's call for Timothy to remain pure. Two proverbial statements conclude the unit, warning about harboring hidden sins.

Paul's rhetoric in this section may have been prompted by the rise in false doctrine hinted at in the letter and the need for strong leadership to deal with this. The problems in this letter are usually associated with the Ephesian leaders. False teachers were tearing the church apart with their speculative doctrines and empty asceticism. It is critical, therefore, that Timothy appoint leaders who will not abuse their positions. They must know well the truth of the gospel and set a high standard.

IN THE TEXT

■ **17** A second group mentioned in 5:1 now becomes the focus. Paul exhorts Timothy to make sure the church gives elders proper honor for their service. The term **elders** (*presbyteroi*) is used in this passage with a more specific application than in 5:1. There, the emphasis is on respect for their age. Here, the focus is on recognizing their leadership in the church. All elders would have had some degree of influence in the Ephesian church because of their age and the respect the younger were to give to them. But age is not necessarily the only qualification for honor. Paul is writing about a particular subset within the church that provides oversight and indoctrination.

These elders **direct the affairs of the church well**. The attributive participle **who direct the affairs** (*proestōtes*) gives the image of a supervisor who manages the affairs of a household. The KJV "rule" gives too much of a dictatorial nuance to the term. Paul attaches this term to church leaders in 1 Thess 5:12. One of the job descriptions of overseers and deacons concerns how they handle their own homes (1 Tim 3:4, 5, 12). Leadership is a spiritual gift that contributes to the strength of a church (Rom 12:8).

The participle is in the perfect tense, indicating that they have led for some time and have a proven track record. The adverb **well** "underlines proficiency and, given the context of heresy, faithfulness of service" (Towner 2006, 362). It should not be viewed in a pejorative comparison to others but as a measure of each person's performance (Knight 1992, 232).

Paul refers to a specific group of elders: **those whose work is preaching and teaching**. **Work** (*kopiōntes*) takes time and effort, can involve discomfort,

217

and eventually leads to weariness (BDAG 2000, 558). Paul used this term for ministry (Rom 16:12). God calls and empowers people to serve. But they must respond with effort, both physical (1 Cor 4:12; Eph 4:28; 2 Tim 2:6) and spiritual (1 Cor 15:10; 16:10; 1 Thess 5:12; 1 Tim 4:10).

The adverb *malista* can refer to a subgroup within a larger group—**especially**, or to the same group—***namely*** (1 Tim 4:10; 5:8; 2 Tim 4:13; Titus 1:10). But it is unlikely that all elders shared in the preaching and teaching ministry. These are specialized gifts, so **especially** is the appropriate translation here. There was a division of labor in the early church (see Acts 6:1-7). This smaller group of elders could have included the overseers who had administrative responsibilities in the church (→ 1 Tim 3:2). But the correlation between the two groups is not necessary (→ Titus 1:5-7).

Logōi, (lit.) ***in word***, here means **preaching** (as in 1 Cor 14:36; 2 Cor 2:17; 4:2; Phil 1:14; Col 1:25; 2 Tim 2:9; and Titus 2:5). In 1 Tim 4:12 it has the broader sense of "speech." Because this word occurs with **teaching** in 5:17, and teaching is focused on the truth of the gospel (→ 4:6), these elders probably had the special ministry of proclaiming a word from God related to the message about Jesus Christ. **Teaching** involves explaining and applying "the mystery of godliness" (3:16 [ESV, KJV, NASB]; → 3:16). What is taught is scriptural salvation (2 Tim 3:16). The elders were to join in proclaiming the gospel with Timothy and serve as the leaders among the people.

Elders who fulfill their calling well **are worthy of double honor**. This could refer to honor as recognition *or* as an honorarium—financial support. The assumption behind Paul's directions to Timothy in 1 Tim 5:1-2 is that Timothy would show respect to those older than himself, so honoring the worth and position of the elders could be assumed. Not all the leaders came from the wealthy classes, so some could have benefited from material support. Verse 18 implies the existence of some type of support for those who worked in the church. This support allowed more time to be devoted to ministry (compare 1 Cor 9:3-18; 1 Thess 2:7-9).

But what is **double honor**? Chrysostom (*Hom. 1 Tim.* 13.460) and later Calvin (1964, 262) interpreted this to mean that elders should receive double the stipend given widows. This is possible, but unlikely. It is also unlikely that these elders were to get twice as much financial support as elders who did not preach and teach. Apparently, not all elders should receive the same honor, just as not all widows needed assistance. The "second" part of this honor could have consisted of some type of financial support. *Diplēs* can mean "twofold"—both honor and honorarium (Fee 1988, 89).

This verse gives evidence of the beginning of a professional ministry, in which church leaders were supported by a church. Because there is evidence of this in other passages in the NT, it is too much to use this passage to support a late dating of the Pastorals. What we see here is more primitive and foundational for what was developed later in the church (most notably evident in the writings of Ignatius [d. 110]).

Support of Ministry Workers in the Early Church

How to support those who give themselves in ministry has never been an easy discussion for the church. There are four major approaches that Paul and the early churches used.

First, those involved in ministry could be self-supporting. Acts 18:1-3 indicates that Paul's sideline trade was as a tentmaker, by which he supported himself in Corinth and later in Ephesus (20:34-35). Scholars are uncertain what this "tentmaking" involved but likely the manufacture and repair of various leather-type goods including tents and awnings. Paul's work was not easy, as he testifies of toiling night and day, working with his own hands (1 Cor 4:12; 1 Thess 2:9). This trade took much of his time and energy (Hock 1978, 1980).

There are several reasons why Paul had this trade. One background reason is that as a former Pharisee, he was expected to learn a trade alongside of his religious duties ('Abot 2.12). Second, he did not burden the local churches with the need to support him financially (1 Cor 9:15-18; 2 Cor 11:7-9). This freed him up to be in a sense independent of patronage obligation, and it also allowed the churches to devote their resources to other needs (2 Cor 9:5). He made it clear that he was not in ministry for the money but because of a divine call. Money was never to be the driving force of ministry (1 Pet 5:2). He did not want to cause a hindrance to peoples' acceptance of the gospel and rejected any notion that he should be obligated to anyone or that anyone should be obligated to him (1 Cor 9:12; 2 Cor 2:17; 7:2). Third, he hoped that his self-giving lifestyle would be a model to others. Fourth, his trade put him in busy marketplaces, where there was much opportunity for evangelism (1 Thess 2:9).

Not all apostles and missionaries were self-supporting like Paul. A second major approach was to rely on the hospitality of churches and patrons. As Jesus directed his disciples (Matt 10:9-15), many early itinerant missionaries relied on the generosity of others for their support. A number of early Christian leaders traveled extensively throughout the Roman Empire. Hospitality was a vital quality of the first believers as they hosted traveling missionaries (Acts 9:43; 10:48; 17:4-5; 18:1-3, 7; 21:15-16; 28:14-15). The household was the crucial entity for much of this support. Paul and his colleagues maintained their mission through the generosity of private individuals and wealthy households (Judge 1960, 58).

A third approach was to support ministers from a distance. Paul especially needed such support while he was in prison (Phil 4:14-18). The major offering that Paul collected for believers in Jerusalem (Rom 15:25-32; 1 Cor 16:1-4; 2 Cor 8:1—9:15) brought a sense of unity between Gentiles and Jews. But this was not intended to support Paul. It was to be a gift from Paul's churches to the mother church in Jerusalem. Giving is a way of participating in the ministry of others.

Fourth, those involved in local ministry should be supported by those who benefit from their preaching and teaching. The precedence for this practice can be found in ancient Israel where priests were to be supported by offerings (2

Chr 31:4). As in I Tim 5:18, Paul appeals to Deut 25:4 in I Cor 9:9 in an a fortiori argument: if animals receive food from their work, so should God's servants. "The other apostles and the Lord's brothers and Cephas" (I Cor 9:5) had been supported by their ministry. The basic reason for this support is so that ministers can devote full time to ministry (I Cor 9:14; Gal 6:6). Paul refused this while he was in Corinth because he did not want to hinder the Corinthians' growth in the gospel by devoting their allegiance to Paul rather than to Christ.

I TIMOTHY

5:18

■ **18** For (*gar*) shows that what follows is used to support the directions in 1 Tim 5:17. Paul draws upon two quotations from **Scripture** to provide the reason why elders should be supported and respected. This forms an inartificial proof, "evidence cited from a previous recognized authority, not an argument made up by the speaker" (Witherington 2006, 275). **Scripture** here literally means "writing" (*graphē*) but is always used in the NT for sacred writings (BDAG 2000, 206 s.v. 2; Schrenk 1964a, 751-61).

The first quotation comes from the LXX of Deut 25:4, except the word order is changed. The quotation in 1 Timothy puts the verb **do not muzzle** first, which is last in the LXX. The quotation appears also in 1 Cor 9:9 but with a cognate word for "muzzle." The word order in 1 Timothy emphasizes the threshing ox.

This excerpt from Israel's agricultural laws referred originally to threshing, the process of separating the grain from the chaff. The ancient method involved having an ox pull a heavy sled over the grain. The ox was allowed to eat the grain as it worked, providing both energy and incentive for it to continue. Covering its mouth so that it could not eat deprived the animal from nutrition and would eventually diminish its ability to do its job.

Both 1 Cor 9:9 and 1 Tim 5:18 follow the rabbinic argument called qal wahomer, from the lesser to the greater. What is true for an ox must more obviously be true for those elders who serve the church through preaching and teaching (v 17).

The second citation exactly matches Jesus' saying preserved in Luke 10:7 (compare Matt 10:10). It is noteworthy that this quotation appears under the heading of **Scripture**. How did Paul know this quotation? (1) Did he have a copy of Luke's Gospel (so Knight 1992, 233-34)? (2) Did he know the saying from the oral traditions in circulation? (3) Was Luke instrumental in writing the Pastorals (so Quinn and Wacker 2000, 462-63; Wilson 1979; Witherington 2006; Spicq 1969, 543-44)? or, (4) Was this a commonly known proverb that both Jesus and Paul knew and quoted? Option two seems most convincing: Paul knew of the Jesus tradition and viewed it as the Word of God (Ellis 1957, 36). Clearly, there is an assumed authority behind the quotation.

Dio Chrysostom (*Or.* 75) gives an encomium on reciprocity—why benefactors should receive thanks for what they have done for others. He writes of three particular groups to whom tangible thanks should be given: to parents from children, to private benefactors from their beneficiaries, and to public servants from their cities. Such rewards could include crowns, public proclamations, and seats of honor (cited in Kidd 1990, 54-55). Reciprocity was "a currency that allowed the creation of social power through the investment of wealth and energy in return for honor and heightened status" (Kidd 1990, 55).

The implied conclusion to these two quotations from **Scripture** is that a worker should be supported for work accomplished. The way to honor elders for their challenging work of preaching the gospel and teaching is that their basic necessities should be met. The church ought to take care of those who devote their energies to edifying its members.

■ **19** This verse lays out the due process that should be followed when someone accuses an elder of doing wrong. Paul will develop three key points in the next three verses. Timothy must (1) determine the evidence behind an accusation and if it is validated by at least two witnesses, (2) rebuke publicly those who have sinned, and (3) judge impartially.

The relationship of these points to the earlier context about honoring and supporting leaders in the church is difficult to determine. There appears to be a change in topic from the positive of honor to the negative of dishonor. Perhaps Paul's thinking shifted from what should be done for the elders to what is actually taking place. Some have been rejecting the leadership of the elders, especially their preaching and teaching, and even accusing them without justification.

Paul's strong words of warning to Timothy should be passed on to the church: **Do not entertain an accusation against an elder.** Entertain (*para-dechou*) can mean to accept or acknowledge (BDAG 2000, 761). Accusing involves putting blame on people or charging them for a supposed wrong. There is no indication in here what the possible charges may have been. With the influence of false teachings, this church could have found itself divided among those who sided with the opponents and those who followed Paul. If the false teachers were strong enough in their influence (which is what prompted Paul to write this letter in the first place; → 1 Tim 1:3-4), they may have been causing problems for those who tried to stand up for the truth of the gospel. This possibility would not rule out other reasons for accusing elders of wrongdoing, but it fits the context of the letter.

The last half of the verse gives the one condition under which an accusation may be considered—if **it is brought by two or three witnesses.** This directive follows Jewish legal practice based on Deut 17:6 and 19:15 (adopted in Matt 18:16; John 8:17; and 2 Cor 13:1). The basic motive behind this law is that it protects the innocent from false accusation; "Church leaders should not be at the mercy of frivolous or ill-natured complaints" (Kelly 1963, 126).

If two or three honest people agree about a matter, then it likely happened as described. It is possible that some collaboration between the witnesses has taken place, so the accusations should be carefully considered before judgment is passed (→ 1 Tim 5:21).

It is not clear who should bring or hear the charges (→ Titus 3:10). The witnesses might include anyone in the church, although other elders would know the responsibilities and doctrines better. "It is a safe rule that private sins should be dealt with privately, and only public sins publicly. It is neither right nor necessary to make what is private public, until all other possibilities have been exhausted" (Stott 1996, 139).

■ **20** The second careful approach Timothy must make is to rebuke sinners publicly. The masculine participle **who are sinning** (*hamartanontas*) is most likely pluralized as a general principle. If the discussion about elders continues past 1 Tim 5:19, as is likely, the more logical referent to the participle are the elders of v 19. Restoring wayward elders continues to be the theme. The tense is present, implying that their sinning may have become habitual. Their sins have been exposed—not past sins that have been resolved, but something going on at the moment. "Sin" is a moral fault involving transgressing God's law through rebellion or unbelief (→ 1:9).

First Timothy 5:10 is the logical outcome of v 19: The allegation of sin has been proven true by two or three witnesses. If the witnesses confirm an allegation, then the elder needs public rebuke. **Reprove** (*elenche*) can be used negatively—penalizing or disciplining someone for wrongdoing. Or it can be used positively—helping someone feel convicted for sin (BDAG 2000, 315). It occurs four other times in the Pastorals (2 Tim 4:2; Titus 1:9, 13; 2:15) and summarizes how Timothy and Titus should deal with problematic people.

Public rebuke could have several outcomes. In that culture, public shame was a strong motivational force for correction (Malina 2001, 27-57). Since people try to avoid being shamed, public rebuke warns others not to sin. It also serves as a form of public accountability, since others have seen the rebuke and will be looking for changes in the sinner. The rebuking ultimately has a redemptive purpose (→ 1 Tim 1:20). To rebuke is a summons to repent and may require educative discipline (Büchsel 1964a, 474). To give and receive such a rebuke takes a great degree of love and acceptance by all involved. The goal is not humiliation but restoration. The unstated hope is that the sinner will indeed repent.

Paul attempts to distinguish between (1) those who lead well vs. those who do not, (2) those who preach and teach vs. those who do not, and (3) those who live godly lives vs. those who have sinned or failed to do their duties.

■ **21** The last charge related to correcting wayward elders is that Timothy must not show partiality. Although the larger theme of leadership development pervades this whole section, 5:21-25 forms a smaller unit in which Paul gives Timothy directions about Timothy's own approach to the problems. The seriousness of the requirement for personal integrity is stated at the outset: **I charge you** (*diamartyromai*). This strong, legal term from Attic law refers to testifying under oath (Collins 2002, 147). Paul reminds Timothy that his own actions are subject to judgment.

The gravity of this charge is seen by the three parties Paul calls as witnesses: **God, Christ Jesus,** and **the elect angels** (compare Matt 16:27; Mark 8:38; Luke 9:26; 2 Thess 1:6-7; and Heb 12:22-24).

God is the final and impartial judge (2 Chr 19:7; Acts 10:34; Rom 2:11; Eph 6:9; Col 3:25; 1 Pet 1:17). Timothy should strive to be a judge like God and show no favoritism.

Christ will be involved in the final judgment (John 5:22, 27; Acts 17:31; 2 Cor 5:10; 1 Tim 6:13; 2 Tim 4:1). This should reassure the faithful that they have "an advocate with the Father" (1 John 2:1).

Angels served as part of the divine court and would have a part in the judgment in the view of both Jews and early Christians (Dan 7:10; 2 Esd 16:67; Matt 25:31; Mark 8:38; Luke 9:26; Rev 14:10). Paul's similar charge in 2 Tim 4:1 makes no reference to angels.

Timothy is **to keep these instructions without partiality, and to do nothing out of favoritism**. These two actions are synonymous. **Without partiality** (*prokrimatos*: **prejudice**) is a Latinism used as a legal term for how witnesses are heard (Roloff 1988, 312). It is found only here in the Greek Bible. To avoid partiality, judges must wait until all the evidence has been presented and evaluated before reaching a verdict (see Deut 19:16-21).

Do nothing out of favoritism. To do so would be to reach "an unfair decision even after the facts have been heard. It happens when someone hears all the evidence, but then chooses to overlook some of it or twist it in order to please the stronger party or protect the person one favours" (Ngewa 2009, 131). Timothy is accountable for his leadership in Ephesus. "If Paul recognized the possibility of failure even in himself (1 Cor 9:27), he surely knew the possibility existed for Timothy as well" (Mounce 2000, 315).

■ **22** Three more commands outline how Timothy must carry out his mission in Ephesus. The first two relate to 1 Tim 5:21 and his responsibility to judge well. The last is inclusive enough to apply to his entire ministry there.

First, he must **not be hasty in the laying on of hands**. Laying hands on people was a common practice in the early church (→ 4:14). In this passage, two meanings are possible. Laying on of hands was a sign of healing and forgiveness in Jesus' ministry (Matt 9:5; Mark 2:9; Luke 5:23; see 2 Cor 2:6-11; Jas 5:15). After the third century, penitents were readmitted to the church by the laying on of hands (Cyprian, *Sent.* 74.12; Eusebius, *Hist. eccl.* 7.2; *Apos.*

5:22

223

Con. 2.18.7). Tertullian interpreted the verse in this way (*Bapt.* 18.9). With this option, the verse would mean that those elders who publicly confess and repent of their sins (1 Tim 5:20) should likewise be publicly reinstated. Paul could instruct Timothy not to delay in readmitting them into communion (Kelly 1963, 128).

The other possibility involves Paul making a shift in topic to the laying on of hands as a form of ordination to service. Timothy is to do to elders what was done to him (→ 4:14; 2 Tim 1:6). Paul is urging him to consider carefully those he appoints as leaders (→ 1 Tim 3:1-13 for the guidelines for overseers and deacons). Strong leaders were urgently needed in the Ephesian church, but Timothy must take time to be certain they know true doctrine and live godly lives. Sad consequences follow hasty decisions.

Second, Timothy must **not share in the sins of others**. If he is too quick to appoint leaders without testing them carefully, he could be held account-able for any problems or sins of these leaders in the future. By laying hands on a sinning elder, he would be saying that the sin did not matter. Paul's warning recalls 4:6-16 (→). In order to be an impartial judge, Timothy himself must be free from accusation.

The third command shows how Timothy could avoid participating in the sins of others. Paul urges him, **keep yourself pure.** The present tense verb has a reflexive pronoun as its direct object. This stresses Timothy's ongoing personal responsibility to do his part in his spiritual development and leader-ship implementation. Paul gets to the heart of the matter with his call to holi-ness. The adjective *hagnon* refers to things free of defect or moral impurities. Holiness enables them to be in relationship with God, the Holy One (Hauck 1964a, 122-24). Paul calls Timothy to rise above sin. He must not let himself become defiled by any of those he may need to correct. Unless he as a leader maintained a holy life, he would lose the respect of the church and not be a fit judge of other leaders. For him to ask others to live "above reproach" (3:2), his own life must be morally pure (→ 4:12).

■ **23** At first glance, this verse appears to be a parenthetical remark, out of place in this context. It has its own paragraph division in the NIV. Taken by itself, it is a simple statement about a common health practice in antiquity. However, the context forces deeper consideration. It may be a form of digres-sion based on v 22c and the call to be pure.

This exhortation takes on a more personal concern, that Timothy **stop drinking only water, and use a little wine.** The reason for this is given in the last half of the verse: **because of your stomach and your frequent illnesses.** The health concern cannot be missed. It appears that Timothy was having some kind of frequent digestive ailment that made it difficult for him to fulfill his mission.

Paul's prescription was for him to drink **a little wine** in moderation for a specific purpose. Because of poor water quality or food poisoning, stomach problems were common in the ancient world, as they are still in developing countries. Paul strongly condemns drinking wine excessively in other letters (Rom 14:21; Eph 5:18; 1 Tim 3:8; Titus 2:3). So his concession here should be carefully considered in light of his larger concerns.

That Timothy had **frequent illnesses** has led interpreters to imagine that he was sickly and timid. But the evidence falls short of supporting this. His stomach problems are not linked here to any of his leadership or personality qualities. They affected only his ability to carry out his task. As Chrysostom said, bodily infirmity no less than spiritual infirmity injures the church (*Hom. Tit.* 1).

Wine and Poor Water Quality in the Ancient World

Wine had a wide range of uses and abuses in the ancient world and was viewed both positively and negatively. Several Scripture texts speak of wine in positive ways (Ps 104:14-15; Eccl 9:7; Isa 55:1; Amos 9:14). Jesus saved a wedding feast by turning water into the best wine (John 2:1-11). Drinking wine on special occasions such as weddings (John 2:1-11) or festivals, like Passover (Luke 22:17-18), was a customary part of Mediterranean life.

Scripture, history, and experience demonstrate that drinking wine opens people to temptation and abuse. Scripture strongly condemns drunkenness (Prov 20:1; 23:29-35; 31:4-7; Eph 5:18). Too much wine allows one to lose control, which often leads to poor choices and pain (Gen 9:20-26; 19:30-38; 1 Sam 25:32-38). Some groups like the Nazirites (Num 6:1-4) and Rekabites (Jer 35:5-6) avoided wine altogether.

Scripture and other ancient literature recognized the positive, medicinal qualities of wine. Wine can function as a pain killer. Jesus was offered wine mixed with myrrh while he hung on the cross (Mark 15:23). The Good Samaritan poured oil and wine on the wounds of the injured man (Luke 10:34).

Poor sanitation and impure water sources caused many people to experience gastric problems. Without the aid of modern science, ancient people observed that wine could be used as a dyspeptic or tonic against impure water. They discovered that wine could provide a remedy. Because of modern science and the microscope, we know today that the reason for this is that the alcohol in wine kills harmful organisms.

What Paul says to Timothy in 1 Tim 5:23 is consistent with other ancient literature. Hippocrates, for example, instructed patients to use wine if water alone did not help them (*Vet. med.* 13). Plutarch wrote that wine is the most useful drink and pleasant of medicines (*Tu. san.* 19). The Talmud *B. Bat.* 58b states, "Wine is the greatest of all medicines: where wine is lacking, drugs are necessary."

Why did Paul bring this issue up at this point in the letter? One possibility is that Timothy was avoiding wine in response to some of the asceticism of the opponents described in 4:3. Paul did not want him to participate in the ascetic hypocrisy of these false teachers (Fee 1988, 132). The opposite could have been the case: drunkenness may have been a problem of some of the leaders (3:3; Titus 1:7), and so Timothy responded by abstaining from wine (Towner 2006, 376).

Paul's point may be that purity does not depend on forms of asceticism like avoiding wine to the detriment of one's health. "This verse shows Timothy as a person of strong convictions, willing to do what was the best for the Ephesian community even though it hurt him physically" (Mounce 2000, 319). This is one of the ways Timothy could remain pure and self-disciplined.

■ **24-25** These two verses summarize the whole chapter and the discussion about widows and elders. The section ends with a proverbial tone marked with a shift to the third person. Two statements contrast the options before the Ephesian elders and, through application, all the believers in the church. They could choose the way of sin and face judgment, or they could progress in good deeds. Timothy has to approach the situation carefully. It would be easy to misjudge people in an effort to guide them, so Paul offers some precautions.

The first proverb is negative in tone and warns of two types of sin: some sins **are obvious** and **others trail behind**. Sin is a recurring theme in the letter (1 Tim 1:9-10; 3:2, 8; 5:13, 15, 20, 22). Sin results from rejecting the truth of the gospel and becomes manifest in ungodly living. There is no indication what these **sins** may have been, but the verse is broad and inclusive.

Obvious sins are more public and often affect other people. The judgment for these sins may be in the form of public shame or castigation. Minimally, they ruin relationships and people's witness to unbelievers. Some potential sins the elders may have faced are listed in 6:3-10. Elders would be especially prone to public sins by the nature of their leadership in the church.

Other sins are private and may not be evident until the final judgment. Which **judgment** is not specified here. Since some sins are hidden from other people and known only to God, they will only be known at the final judgment at the end of the age (Matt 10:26; Mark 4:22; Luke 8:17; 12:2; 1 Cor 4:2, 5). Hidden sins may not be evident to others but cannot remain hidden forever.

Those gifted with prophecy may through divine help expose the sins of some people through clearly preaching the gospel that convicts of sin (1 Cor 14:24-26). God knows the secrets of every heart (Ps 44:21; Rom 2:16). The good news is that both types of sins can be forgiven. Paul himself is an example that no one is beyond God's grace (→ 1 Tim 1:15-16).

In the same way marks a noticeable comparison with the repetition of the term **obvious**. Just as some sins are unmistakable, **good deeds are obvious**. **Good deeds** are what one does for the benefit of others (5:10). One difference between **sins** and **good deeds** is that the good cannot be hidden for long. Doing good has a trickle-down effect that eventually builds up community and strengthens relationships.

Jerome wrote,

> Certain persons sin so deliberately and flagrantly that you no sooner see them than you know them at once to be sinners. But the defects of others are so cunningly concealed that we only learn them from subsequent information. Similarly the good deeds of some people are public property, while those of others we come to know only through long intimacy with them. (*Epist.* 54.8, quoted by Gorday 2000, 208)

FROM THE TEXT

Support for the basic needs of those in ministry. There is a reciprocal blessing for churches that support those who serve them. On the church side, it allows the whole church to participate with its leaders in the growth of the ministry. Giving serves as a spiritual discipline of thanksgiving and expression of unity in the faith.

On the minister's side, giving preserves leaders from living in poverty. The assumption that ministers should live "by faith" on a day-to-day basis and that their support is dependent upon their own spirituality is misguided. God will take care of his servants, but God places the obligation to do this on local churches. Churches that do not adequately compensate their leaders create temptation for them. Calvin wrote that Satan finds a "means of depriving the church of teaching, by frightening many by a dread of poverty and want, so that they are unwilling to bear this burden" (1964, 262).

Paul is getting to a deeper, more basic principle that stretches the contemporary Westernized church's professional clergy. In many places in the world, it is not possible to provide adequate salaries for church leaders. There are many ways a church can support its ministers, including the obvious—finances. But support may also come through gifts of food, clothing, and other necessities, vacation and personal renewal opportunities, and most significantly by cooperating in the mission and vision of the pastor. What "honors" pastors the most is when churches catch their vision and respond to their preaching and teaching through transformation. Ministers may be more willing to live by little support if they are in a ministry setting in which they can fulfill their call with effectiveness.

Church discipline. One of the most difficult things for a church leader to do is to discipline those who have sinned. Paul warns Timothy to "double-check" the evidence of any accusation by calling on two or three witnesses. We should not believe every rumor we hear. Gossip and false accusation can kill a church. Augustine warned of the dilemma: "If you punish a man, you may ruin him. If you leave him unpunished, you may ruin another" (*Epist.* 95, quoted by Gorday 2000, 205).

Paul saw church discipline as a means of restoration. In 2 Tim 2:25-26, he writes that

> opponents must be gently instructed, in the hope that God will grant them repentance leading them to a knowledge of the truth, and that they will come to their senses and escape from the trap of the devil, who has taken them captive to do his will.

This echoes the instructions about the sinner in 1 Cor 5:1-5. It is dangerous to let sin remain unchecked in a person's life because "a little yeast leavens the whole batch of dough" (1 Cor 5:6). This is especially true if leaders with influence have sinned in word or deed; they may pull others down with them. Those who are involved in the discipline process should cover their actions with much prayer.

Choosing worthy and gifted leaders. Timothy found himself in the challenging place of finding qualified leaders for the church in Ephesus. Paul gives directions for this specifically in 1 Tim 3. In 5:22 (→), the directions are simple: Take your time in appointing or restoring people to leadership. Saying one wants to be a leader or professing a call to a ministry position is not enough. Those who appoint leaders must carefully discern their faithfulness to the gospel in how they live and what they say. Church governing boards and credentialing committees carry a heavy responsibility because the future vitality of the church rests in their hands. Time is a key factor because the true person often does not appear except over a period of time (vv 24-25).

Personal care in ministry. Paul gives Timothy practical advice about his health (v 23). Timothy would be ineffective in Ephesus if he were incapacitated in bed. We are holistic beings; what happens to our bodies will influence our souls. Maintaining good health through rest, exercise, and good nutrition keeps the tool of self sharpened, tuned, and ready for the Master's use. Those who are worn out physically are more open to burnout, depression, and even to forsaking their calls. Ministry is usually not physically demanding, but the mental and spiritual strain can lead to physical problems.

D. Instructions to Slaves (6:1-2)

BEHIND THE TEXT

The next two verses continue the theme of "honor" that began in 5:3 and concludes with this section. The word "honor" (*timē*) appears in each of the three sections: the church should honor needy widows (5:3), elders who preach and teach should receive double honor (5:17), and slaves should honor their masters (6:1). Paul may follow Hellenistic household codes, which usually contain exhortations about how slaves should behave (Collins 2002, 151). Conspicuously absent, however, is a word to the masters (contrast Eph 6:9; Col 4:1).

Perhaps a social problem in the Ephesian church resulted from a theological challenge. Paul's message of equality for all in Christ (Gal 3:28) and restructured relationships within the "household of God" (→ 1 Tim 3:15) may have prompted Christian slaves to assert their spiritual freedom. If they did so in disrespectful ways, it probably would result in friction with their masters. Many slaves had become Christians, and some of them likely had non-Christian masters. Paul's concern is for balance and respect in the household (2:15; 3:4, 12; 5:4). If Christian slaves abandoned social protocol and defied their masters, they would bring dishonor to the church and the gospel (→ 3:6-7; 5:14). Slaves were free and equal in the church but still bound to obedience within the home.

Paul made no attempt to alter the social structures of the existing culture. Instead, he worked within them to bring new life and hope to people. He did not defend slavery as God's will, as he did marriage (Eph 5:31) or obedience from children (Eph 6:1-3). Rather, he encouraged slaves to leave bondage when possible (1 Cor 7:21) or for masters to free slaves (Phlm 10-21; Knight 1992, 242). He did not directly attack the institution of slavery, but he tried to create a positive relationship of love between masters and slaves.

Love fundamentally alters the nature of slavery. In this passage, he reverses the cultural norm by urging Christian slaves to serve their masters as their masters' benefactors. Slaves' service can be given "from a position of strength and nobility" that "brings honor on themselves, as well as on 'the name of God and the teaching'" (Johnson 1996, 192).

Slavery in the Roman Empire

Slavery was a significant social institution in the Roman Empire of the first century, deeply embedded in the culture. Slavery was not based on race. People became slaves as prisoners of war, out of desperate poverty, or being born of parents who were slaves.

Slaves were treated differently, depending on the amount of freedom and responsibility given by their masters. They had no legal rights and were totally under the control of their masters. Aristotle called them "living property" (Pol. 1.2.4-5, 1252b).

Slaves had an essential part in the economy. Most of the poor of the empire were slaves forced into menial jobs such as farm labor or domestic help. Others had highly skilled jobs as teachers, architects, doctors, and even city administrators.

Slaves were a common part of the extended Greco-Roman household. Some slaves were able to get an education, improving their social standing. In certain settings, slaves could earn or buy their freedom, which created a significant motive for good service (Ferguson 1993, 56-59; Bartchy 1998, 65-73; Harrill 2006).

Paul never explicitly opposed slavery, but his letters provide the seeds for slaves' eventual emancipation. His language against kidnapping for slave trade is quite harsh in I Tim 1:9-10. In I Cor 7:21-23, he encourages slaves to gain their freedom if possible and to remember that they are free as Christ's slaves. Because slaves could not always gain their freedom (v 24), Paul encourages them to be obedient to their masters. This would make their living situations more pleasant (Eph 6:5-8; Col 3:22-25).

The worst kind of slavery for Paul is slavery to sin (Rom 6:1-11). Even though slaves are bound on earth, they can be free spiritually. The relationship between slaves and masters can be a model of new life in Christ (Gal 3:28). Christian masters and slaves are one in Christ and should treat one another as brothers and sisters (Phlm 16).

IN THE TEXT

■ **1** The final group of this unit (5:3—6:2) concerns Christian slaves. The theme of honor continues: slaves should honor their masters. The setting of v 1 is the home but shifts to the church in v 2. Although slaves are free in Christ and even brothers and sisters with their believing masters (Gal 3:28), they should still show them respect.

The intended audience here is **all who are under the yoke of slavery**. The focus is on the word **yoke**. Yokes were used with domestic animals, especially oxen, for plowing and pulling. They symbolize command and control and are used in the Bible for oppression (2 Chr 10:4; Isa 9:4; Gal 5:1). Jesus spoke of two different types of yokes (Matt 11:29-30). His was light and easy; the other, heavy and burdensome.

Being a slave was a burden to bear. Some masters treated their slaves harshly, assigning them menial and unpleasant tasks, causing slaves to resent them. Not all slaves were mistreated, however. Some rose to high ranks and lived relatively pleasant lives. All slaves, however, suffered the burden of being owned by someone else. Subject to their masters' wills, they had limited freedom to choose for themselves.

Christian slaves should **consider their masters worthy of full respect**. The present imperative describes an ongoing duty to submit to their masters. Honor is the upside-down Christian response to the yoke of slavery. There is no qualification (yet) in the passage about the master being a Christian. The command here applies to all masters.

The verb **consider** is noteworthy; not all masters are, in fact, worthy of respect. It takes a conscious decision to submit to some masters. It takes humility, especially when they do not deserve respect. Christ set the supreme example of submission, even when it ultimately led to his death (Mark 10:43-45; Phil 2:5-11; 1 Pet 2:18-25). Paul understood this principle well, and tried to live it out in his own mission (1 Cor 9:19; Gal 5:13).

The motive for this unexpected directive is found in a two-part purpose clause: **so that God's name and our teaching may not be slandered** (see Isa 52:5, cited in Rom 2:24). Slandering **God's name** involves rejecting his sovereignty. **God's name** is his reputation in the world (Bietenhard 1967, 271-76; Marshall 1999, 630). **God's name** is connected with **our teaching**—the message Paul received from God (Gal 1:12), confirmed by the church (Gal 2:2-3), and passed on to new leaders (1 Cor 15:3-8). "For Paul, to blaspheme the gospel is to blaspheme the source of the gospel" (Fee 1988, 138).

The implied syllogism has three parts: By honoring their masters, slaves bring honor to God, making the gospel more credible. Paul is concerned in this letter about the reputation of the church (→ 1 Tim 2:2, 10; 3:7; 5:8, 14; see Titus 2:5). He urges Christian slaves, who potentially could create problems for themselves and the church, instead to live out their faith in socially acceptable ways. Their submission presents a positive witness to unbelievers.

■ **2** The thought of v 1 is clarified further here (connected with an untranslated *de*, **and**). It may address a specific problem in the church. It is structured around two third-person plural imperatives, each followed by the reason for the command. The subject of both verbs is the substantive participial phrase, **those who have believing masters**.

The first command centers on the verb translated in the NIV as **should not show them disrespect**. The Greek word for **disrespect** consists of two parts—*kata* ("against") and *phroneō* ("to think"). It is a mind-set against another person shown with "contempt or aversion, with implication that one considers the object of little value" (BDAG 2000, 529; → 4:12). Christian slaves show spite for their masters by rejecting their authority and not submitting.

Here, the specific reason for honoring their master is **because they are fellow believers** (lit. "brothers" [*adelphoi*]).

The broader reason is given at the end of v 1: tension in the household would not be a good witness of the gospel. **Fellow believers** should be given even better service because they share the same Lord (Eph 6:7-8; Col 3:23—4:1). This is the point of the second, positive command, which by contrast (*alla*, **instead**) affirms the negative first command: *Let them serve all the more*. The verb is intensified by *mallon*, **especially**.

The point is not that unbelieving masters should be served in a lesser way, but that brothers and sisters in Christ have a higher motive to guide their relationships with others. The imperative in the present tense indicates that this should be their normal practice.

The reason for their special service is **because their masters are dear to them as fellow believers and are devoted to the welfare of their slaves**. This makes a total of three descriptions of the masters in this verse: they are *broth-*

ers, **believers**, and ***beloved*** (*agapētoi*). Christian masters and slaves are bound together by more than concern to preserve the social status quo (see Gal 5:13).

Welfare (*euergesias*) refers to a beneficial act done on behalf of another. In the patron-client culture of the Mediterranean, it was usually those in the position of power or wealth who would give benefits to the socially inferior (Oakes 2010). The receiver developed a sense of obligation as a "client" dependent upon the "patron." The one giving would in turn receive honor and public recognition as the benefactor.

Paul advocates an ethic of subversion in this command. "Slaves serve, but in God's surprising [household] they do so from a position of power; nobility and honor, the rewards of benefaction, are accorded here implicitly to the slaves" (Towner 2006, 390). Their Christian masters are indebted to them.

Paul did not seek to overturn social structures but to transform them from within. The basis for respect is not the virtue of the masters; it is the slaves' dedication to Christ. Paul indirectly places the burden on Christian masters to respond in a reciprocal way. A Christian master must recognize a Christian slave as not simply a slave, but as a fellow believer. Better service by slaves brings kinder treatment by masters.

The final statement of this verse serves as a transition: **These are the things you are to teach and insist on.** Scholars disagree as to whether this summarizes the teachings that come before (1 Tim 5:1—6:2) or what follows. Paul has used similar statements in 3:14; 4:6, 11, 15; 5:7, 21 (→ 2 Tim 2:14; Titus 2:15). Perhaps this serves as a transition, reflecting on what was just said and anticipating the conclusion of the letter, which comes next.

FROM THE TEXT

Behind this timely message to ancient Ephesian slaves lay timeless principles that can apply to many situations today. Paul's words challenge us with a new way to live out earthbound relationships. The radical call to be a follower of Christ may lead to conflict with social institutions. The paradoxical Christian ethic means that love supersedes individual freedom.

The unresolved debate concisely posed by H. Richard Niebuhr in his book *Christ and Culture* continues: Should Christians challenge the institutions of our cultures in revolutionary ways or quietly transform culture through Christlike living?

Paul assigns the highest priority to the cause of Christ. He does not say that being a slave is good or that the institution of slavery should be embraced. His agenda is not personal freedom but the proclamation of the good news of Jesus Christ and the salvation of all people (→ 2:3-4). "The success of the gospel is more significant than the lot of any one individual" (Mounce 2000, 327). Montague offers, "The bond of justice, the covenant by which persons are bound with rights and duties, is crowned with another kind of bond—that of love, a love born of Jesus Christ, who showed that love by becoming a servant, by washing the feet of his disciples" (2008, 96).

Many believers in the world live in settings in which they cannot choose political or economic freedom. Their freedoms are severely limited; they are virtual "slaves" to someone. Their bitter taskmasters may be in a sweatshop, an abusive family situation, an oppressive political situation, or grinding poverty. Even here Christians should have a good reputation among nonbelievers by developing a good work ethic that pleases those around them and a Christ-like character that witnesses to the love of God. This motivation is echoed in Col 3:23-24: "Whatever you do, work at it with all your heart, as working for the Lord, not for human masters, since you know that you will receive an inheritance from the Lord as a reward. It is the Lord Christ you are serving." Christians ought to be the most trusted and respected workers in all situations, even as "slaves."

The voice of liberation in Christ continues to break the hold of human bondage. "Any focus on behavior in this letter is redemptive in nature; it aims at the accomplishments of the salvation already initiated in the individual and in the world" (Towner 1989, 177). Paul's exhortation calls us to active faith shown in godly (*eusebeia*) living.

VI. FINAL INSTRUCTIONS: I TIMOTHY 6:3-21

BEHIND THE TEXT

The next section of the letter shifts to a fourth group in the Ephesian church. But honor is no longer the unifying theme here. Rather, Paul seeks to distance the faithful Ephesians from the false teachers. He attempts to help the Ephesians realize the danger of following them. This section is the final denunciation of and warning about the false teachers (first mentioned back in 1:3-7 and again in 4:1-5).

Paul's language returns to the polemical tone of ch 1. In the process, he repeats earlier themes. The inclusio reference to these opponents at the beginning and end of the letter suggests that they were among the main reasons why this letter was written. We find out more detail in this passage about what these people were teaching. In 1:3-7, a number of descriptions of these people are given:

- They "teach false doctrines" (v 3).
- They "devote themselves to myths and endless genealogies" (v 4).
- They are caught up in "controversial speculations" (v 4).
- They have departed from the core command of love (v 5).
- They have become involved in "meaningless talk" (v 6).
- They purport to be teachers but do not know what they are teaching (v 7).

Then in 4:1-5:

- They have "abandon[ed] the faith and follow[ed] deceiving spirits and . . . demons" (v 1).
- They are "hypocritical liars" (v 2).
- Their "consciences have been seared" (v 2).
- In their asceticism they "forbid people to marry and . . . certain foods" (v 3).
- Basically, they have a profound misunderstanding of creation theology (vv 3-4).

The real danger is that their speculations and self-serving ways have distorted the gospel. Paul focuses here on their behavior and the outcome of their teachings. Their motive of greed becomes clearer. He predicts that their false teachings and speculations will ultimately lead to their destruction. Their deceit has infected the church with a fatal disease and coincides with the deception of the end times in 4:1-5.

The language of this passage is dense and unusual. There are eleven words that occur only here in the NT and another twelve unique to Paul's letters. Part of this may be due to the specific subject matter discussed.

Paul criticizes the false teachers in three primary respects: (1) their doctrine, (2) their interest in controversial subjects, and (3) their desire for financial gain. The rhetorical method is marked by *synkrisis*: the destructive behavior of the opponents (6:3-10) is set in sharp contrast to Timothy's better approach (vv 11-16).

A. Recognizing and Dealing with the Opponents' Love of Money (6:3-10)

IN THE TEXT

■ **3** Verses 3-5 are one complex sentence. They function as a moral maxim in the form of a first-class conditional sentence. This verse functions as the protasis ("if"-clause) and vv 4-5 are the apodosis ("then"—conclusion clause). This type of condition states what actually is happening at the time of writing—the premise as certain. The sentence could begin, "Since someone is teaching" (Knight 1992, 249).

At issue are the teachers of false doctrines, implicitly compared with Timothy's **sound instruction** (→ v 2*b*). Paul uses an ad hominem argument against an unnamed **anyone** (Collins 2002, 154). This is "a rhetorical ploy not to honor or dignify an opponent by naming them" (Witherington 2006, 283). The verb **teaches otherwise** (*heterodidaskalei*) means to "teach false doctrines" (→ 1:3). The standard of truth is the apostolic teaching passed from Paul to Timothy. Paul believed he spoke the words of Christ with the authority of Christ (2 Cor 13:3; 2 Thess 3:6, 12). The false teaching is defined in contrast to **the sound instruction of our Lord Jesus Christ and to godly teaching**. These two terms define orthodox teaching.

First, **sound instruction** (*hygiainousin logois*) has no article in Greek but the context makes these words specific in comparison to the false teachings of the opponents. This "good teaching" first appears in 1 Tim 1:10 and again in 4:6 (see 2 Tim 1:13; 4:3; Titus 1:9; 2:1). Paul was concerned that churches be firmly grounded in the truth.

Hygiainousin can mean healthy and prepares for the medical metaphor of the sickness of the opponents. There are a number of different descriptions in this chapter for ***healthy words***: "sound instruction" (1 Tim 1:3), "truth" (v 5), "faith" (vv 10, 12, 21), "command" (v 14), and "what has been entrusted" (v 20).

Two interpretations for the genitive phrase **of our Lord Jesus Christ** are possible: The phrase could be subjective and refer to words from Jesus. An objective genitive would refer to words about Jesus. There are few direct references to the actual teachings of Jesus in Paul's letters. But Paul was obviously aware of some (e.g., 1 Cor 7:10; 11:23-25; 1 Tim 5:18). The following section shows familiarity with some significant themes in Jesus' teaching about wealth (Luke 6:20, 24; 9:23-25; 12:22-34; 14:25-33; 16:13; Johnson 1996, 197).

This full description of Jesus appears frequently in 1 Timothy (→ 1:1, 2, 12; 5:21; 6:3, 14; Knight 1992, 250). Christ is the ultimate source of what Paul says and hands on to Timothy and the Ephesians, whether directly from him or mediated through apostles. The teachings of Christ are the supreme authority for believers.

Second, **godly teaching** follows **sound instruction**. Again, the key word (*eusebeia*) describes the practical outcome of faith in the good news of Christ (→ 2:2; 3:16; 4:7, 8). The teaching that leads people to Christ should produce godliness (Titus 1:1). Such teaching is firmly based on the orthodox proclamation of the gospel. It works out the practical implications of the gospel—how people ought to live in full devotion to God. It results in a closer relationship to God and stronger fellowship within the church. The opponents' teaching had just the opposite effect, which is made clear in 1 Tim 6:4-5.

■ **4-5** The apodosis of the complex conditional sentence shows the inferior quality of the opponents' character. Their greedy motives will be highlighted

237

further in vv 9-10. Paul's language is strongly polemic, forcefully warning the Ephesians about misplaced priorities. Most of the problems described in these verses have been stated already in the letter. They are characterized as **unhealthy** results of rejecting sound doctrine.

One symptom of the false teachers' sickness is being **conceited**. The perfect tense of the verb *tetyphōtai* refers to mental illness (BDAG 2000, 1021 s.v. 3). With the participles of v 5, the tense emphasizes this as their established and apparently "permanent condition" (Mounce 2000, 338). Conceit in 3:6 describes one danger facing new converts prematurely appointed to leadership positions (→ 2 Tim 3:4). The irony behind this term should not be missed. It describes "a person in terrible physical condition, almost repugnant to look at" (Collins 2002, 155). But these teachers do not see themselves as they are. They imagine they have "knowledge" (→ 1 Tim 6:20) but are actually clueless. Their supposed knowledge has left them spiritually blind.

The verb is qualified by two present tense participles showing the result. The opponents' conceit leads first to the illness of **understanding nothing**. They thought they had knowledge (1:7) but missed the most important truths of the gospel (→ Titus 1:16). The second participle is compared to the first with an untranslated *alla*: **but by growing sick over debates and word-fights.**

Unhealthy interest (*noseō*) is rare (only here in the NT). It describes unhealthy cravings that are part of a serious illness. The opponents' error is a form of spreading cancer (2 Tim 2:17; Oepke 1967b, 1095). Their sick craving stands in sharp contrast with the **healthy words** of 1 Tim 6:3.

The false teachers' craving is for **controversies and quarrels about words.** "Idle speculations" eventually lead to "quarrel about words" (Fee 1988, 141). They have "a morbid fascination for debates and controversies" (Johnson 2001, 292) that have no purpose and contribute nothing to the household of God. In fact, the opposite is true. Their "preoccupation with pseudo-intellectual theorizings" (Kelly 1963, 134) and appetite for "meaningless talk" (→ 1:4, 6; 2 Tim 2:23; Titus 3:9) only leads to more difficulties for the church. This is shown in a prepositional phrase (*ex hōn*) modifying the two words **disputes** (*zētēseis*) and **word-fights** (*logomachias*).

Within the prepositional phrase are five results of the opponents' sick craving. Their inadequate theology shows up in how they live. The list of words has some similarities to Paul's descriptions of fallen humanity in Rom 1:29-31. Noteworthy in this comparison is that in both the Roman context and this one, a rejection of the truth leads to the breakdown of relationships and the destruction of community.

The first result is **envy** or **jealousy**. Envy drives people to do things out of self-interest and pride (Matt 27:18). It is often joined with **strife** (Mark 7:22; Rom 1:29-31; Gal 5:20-21). Strife, discord, or dissension grows from comparing what others have, resulting in coveting. "It gnaws away at the inner person and provokes the hatred towards others that destroys relationships" (Towner 2006, 396).

Malicious talk is abusive speech or verbal attack. The Greek word *blasphēmiai* is used for blaspheming God (Rev 13:6) and deriding people (Eph 4:31).

Evil suspicions are imaginary threats, "opinion or conjecture based on slight evidence" (BDAG 2000, 1040). These imaginations spring from envy and lead to further distrust.

The final outcome is **constant friction,** wrangling, or irritation. Each of these outcomes is interconnected with the others. These sick inward thoughts and attitudes lead to outward symptoms, expressed in inappropriate words and actions. Behind all these is the main vice, being **conceited**. The empty pride of the false teachers has the potential of destroying the church.

Three participles describe **people** (*anthrōpōn*), a veiled reference to the false teachers in Ephesus. The first two are perfect passive verbs, describing what the false teachers have become. Their past decisions have led to their current sickly condition. The third is present tense and shows what they are at the moment. The three mark stages of degradation.

The first participle is translated in the NIV as **of corrupt mind**. This medical term refers to the final stage of a wasting illness, which can mean decay (*diaphteirō*; BDAG 2000, 239). The false teachers rejected the sound words of the gospel. This has left their minds, their "inner orientation" (Behm 1967b, 952), in such a state of degeneration that they are no longer able to discern how they should act. The **mind** (*nous*) in Paul's letters refers to "the constellation of thoughts and assumptions which makes up the consciousness of the person and acts as the agent of rational discernment and communication" (Jewett 1971, 450). Paul links one's *nous* directly to one's disposition toward the apostolic message (Towner 1989, 158). Their minds, as the seat of their conscience, have become so seared that they no longer understand the essence of the gospel (→ 1 Tim 1:19).

This depravity is shown in the second participle, translated as having **been robbed of the truth**. This passive participle shows that an outside force—the false teachers' own *corruption*—led to this loss. They are not innocent victims. **Truth** refers to the gospel (2 Tim 2:18; 3:7, 8; 4:4; Titus 1:14) and is what believers have come to know (1 Tim 2:4; 4:3; 2 Tim 2:25).

The final participle gives a specific example of what happens when one rejects the truth. Again, the theme of **godliness** (*eusebeia*) is the focus. But the false teachers have distorted its meaning: Their appearance of outward piety is for **financial gain**.

Paul presumes that there is link between **truth** and **godliness**. Because the false teachers distorted the truth, they misunderstood godliness. They expected to be paid for their pretended piety. They thought that *"eusebeia* consisted of knowledge of God or divine things, and apparently they (consciously or unconsciously) separated this knowledge from outward behavior or ethics" (Towner 1989, 149).

How the aberrant teachers exploited the rest of the church is unclear. Were they hypocritically pretending to be godly so as to appeal to people's good nature for support? Were they like the traveling sophists of the day, who wandered around giving speeches for money?

Contrary to Paul's instructions about support for preaching and teaching elders (→ 5:17-18), these teachers wanted more than their basic needs met. They desired wealth at the expense of the reputation of the gospel. Reimbursement for work is not a bad thing (→ 5:17; 2 Tim 2:6). Pursuing "dishonest gain" is the problem (→ 1 Tim 3:8). Aristotle said, "The life of money-making (*chrēmatistēs biaios*) is a constrained kind of life, and clearly wealth (*ploutos*) is not the good we are in search of, for it is only good as being useful, a means to something else" (*Eth. nic.* 1.5.8; cited by Collins 2002, 156). One's motive eventually affects one's lifestyle. Their selfish pursuit of wealth led to sickness and division in the Ephesian church. This prepares for the major discussion of wealth in 6:6-10.

■ **6** Paul answers the opponents' logic, that **godliness** leads to **great gain**, by adding the key word **contentment** to the formula. The word order in Greek makes the contrast emphatic: ***Great gain is godliness with contentment***.

Contentment (*autarkeia*) in the Cynic-Stoic tradition means self-sufficiency independent of circumstances (*Ep. of Diogenes* 28.8; Epictetus, *Gnom.* 33; Dio Chrysostom, *Or.* 30; Dibelius and Conzelmann 1972, 84; Fiore 2007, 119; Malherbe 1986, 112-14, 120, 145). For Christians, it involves "freedom from any claims made by possessions of any sort" (Johnson 2001, 294)—being satisfied with whatever God gives.

Paul qualifies and redefines the term in Phil 4:11-12. Contentment is something to be learned. Its secret lies in total dependence on Christ. Contentment does not comes from one's own efforts at being religious, but from relying on the mercies of God (→ 1 Tim 1:12-17). Christian contentment is "not *self*-sufficiency but *Christ*-sufficiency" (Fee 1988, 143). One learns to be content while seeking the will of God through a life of faith and a lifestyle pleasing to him (Job 1:21; Matt 6:25; Luke 11:3; 12:23). The pursuit of **godliness** for selfish reasons leads only to spiritual bankruptcy.

The return for contentment is **gain**, but not the kind the false teachers sought. That ends in only "envy, strife, malicious talk, evil suspicions and constant friction" (1 Tim 6:4-5). Rather, this gain is "righteousness, godliness, faith, love, endurance and gentleness" (v 11) in this world, and "eternal life" (v 12) in the world to come (→ 4:8). **Godliness** is "the inseparable companion of true, vital religion" (Wesley 1813, 230).

■ **7-8** Here, Paul gives two reasons **for** (*gar*) the contentment he described in 6:6. The subject switches to an inclusive and proverbial **we**, universalizing the statement for all people. Two ways of life are contrasted: the contented poor (vv 7-8) and the covetous poor (vv 9-10; Stott 1996, 150-54). Verse 7 is marked by an *ouden . . . oude*, **neither . . . nor**, construction. This negative statement is contrasted with a positive one in v 8.

The syntax of v 7 is difficult, but the basic meaning is clear. The difficulty turns on the translation of *hoti*—usually, "that" or "because." A literal translation is awkward with either alternative: *The reason we have nothing when we are born is because / that we have nothing when we leave*. Scribes and interpreters have noted this problem through the centuries and have supplied words such as "it is clear that" or "truly" to make the meaning clearer (Metzger 1994, 576).

The first reason for contentment is the reminder that we are born with nothing and take nothing with us when we die. The material possessions of this age are bound to this age. A similar thought appears in Job 1:21 ("Naked I came from my mother's womb, and naked I will depart") and Eccl 5:15 ("Everyone comes naked from their mother's womb, and as everyone comes, so they depart." See also Wis 7:6; Seneca, *Ep.* 102.25). The emphasis is on the last half of the verse, since death marks the entrance into eternity. The pursuit of godliness in this life prepares us for eternity (→ 1 Tim 4:8).

The sobering reality is that "we may gather much or little between these two events, but in that final hour we must leave it all behind" (Gould 1965, 616). Created things of this world are bound to decay and are not part of the eternal realm. "For possessions are only the traveling luggage of time; they are not the stuff of eternity" (Stott 1996, 150). Paul's creation theology teaches that God gives us all we need. Therefore, we should be content and thankful (4:4-5; 6:13).

Verse 8 gives the second basis for contentment in the form of a positive statement. Paul offers here the basic standard for contentment and how we should view the material life. The NIV and most modern translations make the participle *echontes* into a condition, **if we have**.

Paul measures contentment with two basic necessities: **food and clothing**. **Clothing** (*skepasma*) can refer to anything that provides covering as a protection, including clothes or shelter such as a house (BDAG 2000, 927). In some climates, good shelter is as important as clothing. The ancient world considered **food and clothing** core necessities (Gen 28:20; Deut 10:18). Jesus promised that

241

God would provide food and clothing for those who "seek first his kingdom and his righteousness" (Matt 6:33; see vv 25-34; Luke 12:22-32; Heb 13:5).

Verse 17 of 1 Tim 6 will show that wealth is not the problem. It is what we do with wealth that matters. The future passive verb, **we will be content** (*arkesthēsometha*), has the force of an imperative—**we *must* be content**. Paul calls for a decision about contentment. Let us choose to live by the eternal perspective.

■ **9** The proverbial tone of the passage continues with another generalized statement that begins with a generic substantival participial phrase: **those who want to get rich**. The negative effects of pursuing wealth now become the focus. After the brief diversion of the earlier proverbs, Paul returns to the problem of the false teachers and gives the sad outcome of using "godliness [as] a means to financial gain" (→ v 5). Covetousness is compared (with an untranslated *de*) to contentment. The desire for more can become a consuming force that devours a person. It is the manifestation of the power of sin within (Rom 7:7-11). Adam and Eve were the first to want something against God's will (3:6). A sad example of hoarding wealth is the story of Ananias and Sapphira in Acts 5:1-11.

The problem is not wealth but the desire for it that leads to ruin. Poverty and wealth are relative terms. Even the poor can pursue wealth to their detriment. The Bible has many warnings against the pursuit of wealth (Ps 49:10; Prov 28:20; 30:8; Eccl 5:10; Luke 12:15). There is no indication of the social status of the opponents, but their goal is clear: They wanted more money. Their love of money was leading to a downward path seen in the verb **fall**, resulting in three consequences. The present tense verb shows that this is what usually happens if wealth is pursued (Knight 1992, 255).

First, they fall into **temptation**. There is a possible wordplay with *porismos* (**wealth**) and *peirasmos* (**temptation**). "The only profit the opponents gain is the pain of temptation" (Mounce 2000, 335). Certain temptations arise with money. Money can buy many things that satisfy the desires of the flesh.

There is no objection to asking God for basic necessities, like daily food, and for his help to avoid temptation. These are, in fact, two key components of the Lord's Prayer (Matt 6:11, 13).

Temptation tests one's loyalties and involves "the danger of being totally at odds with God's salvific plan" (Collins 2002, 158). Satan may be the one who sets the traps that come with wealth (1 Tim 3:7; 2 Tim 2:26). He offered Jesus the whole world, if he would bow down and worship him (Matt 4:8-11).

Second, people who yield to temptation fall into a **trap**. Temptation itself is not a sin. But when it is added to the desire for wealth, it can be overpowering. The word *pagida* refers to a snare or figuratively to something that brings sudden danger (BDAG 2000, 747). People create opportunities for temptation by where they go and what they do. If they are not careful, the devil will use their desire for riches to set traps that lead to spiritual and moral problems (→ 2 Tim 2:26).

Third, people fall into **many foolish and harmful desires**. There is no indication what these desires are, but money opens the way for them. "For money is a drug, and covetousness a drug addiction. The more you have, the more you want" (Stott 1996, 152). *Epithymia* usually has a negative connotation in the NT, often referring to sexual lust. Sexual immorality is not discussed in this context, but it could be included in the word **many. Foolish** desires are linked to **harmful desires** in experience. Foolishness leads to harm (Pss 14:1; 53:1; Prov 1:32; 10:8, 10, 14, 21).

These desires **plunge people into ruin and destruction**. The repetition of two almost synonymous words adds intensity to the conclusion. The verb **plunge** (*bythizousin*) literally means to force under water (as to sink a boat [Luke 5:7]). Figuratively it describes moral decline (Johnson 2001, 295). **Ruin** has an eschatological association in Paul's letters (1 Thess 5:3; 2 Thess 1:9). If that is the sense here, then there may be a time difference between the two words. The desire for wealth leads to present problems and judgment in the end, "the complete moral and spiritual devastation that leads (among other things) to apostasy (v 10*b*)" (Towner 2006, 403). The irony of the situation is graphic: seeking gain leads only to total loss. "The desire for wealth is founded on an illusion. It is founded on the desire for security; but wealth cannot buy security. It cannot buy health, nor real love, and it cannot preserve from sorrow and from death" (Barclay 2003, 148). "Many have committed sin for gain, and those who seek to get rich will avert their eyes" (Sir 27:1 NRSV).

Social Stratification in the Early Church

Paul told the Corinthian church, "Brothers and sisters, think of what you were when you were called. Not many of you were wise by human standards; not many were influential; not many were of noble birth" (I Cor 1:26). This and other evidence has led scholars to argue that Christianity emerged among the poor of the Roman Empire (Deissmann 1927). This thesis has proven inadequate with further analysis.

The general consensus today is that the Pauline churches represented a cross-section of urban society (Malherbe 1977b, 61). There were a number of wealthy individuals and householders in the Pauline churches. Archaeological evidence has suggested that Erastus was the treasurer of the city of Corinth (Rom 16:23). Phoebe was a financial patron of Paul (Rom 16:2). Chloe likely owned slaves (I Cor 1:11). Other householders included Stephanas, Fortunatus, and Achaicus (I Cor 16:15-17). Philemon was wealthy enough to host a church and own slaves (Phlm 1-2). Social and economic stratification likely existed in most early churches in urban settings like Ephesus. This undoubtedly led to social tension within early churches (see I Cor 11:17-34; Theissen 1982, 145-74).

It is possible that the false teachers exploited this social tension. What Paul urges is a form of "love-patriarchalism":

> This love-patriarchalism takes social differences for granted but ameliorates them through an obligation of respect and love, an obligation imposed upon those who are socially stronger. From the weaker are required subordination, fidelity, and esteem. (Theissen 1982, 107)

The early church invited in those with wealth and social status and found places of service for them. It also received the poor who found new freedom in their association with those of higher status. Paul encourages the wealthy (v 18) to be good "patrons" by providing for the needs of others. Their motive should not be honor in this world but honor before God (see further Countryman 1980; Kidd 1990, 35-110; Meeks 2003, 51-73).

■ **10** This verse gives logical support (*gar*) to v 9 and is in the form of another proverb: **For the love of money is a root of all kinds of evil**. The idea expressed here was well known by both Jews and Greeks. Commonsense observations led to the conclusion that money brought with it many temptations. This verse serves as both a warning to the Ephesian church of what they should avoid and a call to repentance for the false teachers.

The uniqueness of this proverb as compared to similar ancient sayings is the word **root**. It stands in the emphatic first position in its Greek sentence. Since *riza* has no article in Greek, it is better rendered not "the root" (KJV, RSV) but "a root" (NASB, NIV). Money is only one source among many for evil. The word *riza* refers to that from which other things grow (BDAG 2000, 905 s.v. 1b), thus the basic or core cause of something else.

Money itself is not the problem; the **love** of it is. **Love of money** comes from one compound word *philargyria*. The "love" part of the word (*philos*) indicates what one desires. Loving money is a form of selfishness (→ 2 Tim 3:2-4). It is idolatry in violation of the great commandment—to love God completely and others as oneself (Matt 6:24; 22:37-40).

Money itself is not evil. It is merely a tool that can be used for both good and evil. What matters is the intention that drives the use of it. When viewed as a gift from God and as a tool to be used for the glory of God, money can accomplish many good things in this world.

The pursuit of wealth, however, opens the door to many temptations. Tertullian (*Idol.* 11) and Cassian (*Inst.* 7.7) linked this verse to Col 3:5: "Put to death, therefore, whatever belongs to your earthly nature: sexual immorality, impurity, lust, evil desires and greed, which is idolatry" (Twomey 2009, 97). Loving money and things of this world leads to an obsession to get more and more of it. The Bible has many warnings about the dangers of wealth (Pss 39:6; 49:6-10; 52:7; Prov 11:4, 16, 28; 23:4-5; Eccl 5:12-13; Jas 4:4; 1 John 2:15).

All kinds of evil is broad and inclusive, incorporating many types of wrong desires. This aphorism is a form of deliberate overstatement (hyperbole) to emphasize a point. Proverbs are often overstatements, not universal truths that fit all situations (Fee and Stuart 2003, 195-98).

The danger of pursuing money is emphasized in the last part of 1 Tim 5:10. The emphasis is not on the origin of evil but on how money causes spiritual and temporal problems. The last clause begins with an emphatic relative pronoun (*hēs*), referring back to **the love of money** (*philargyria*). The NIV captures this by repeating **money**.

It is not clear to whom **some people** refers, probably to some of the opponents in Ephesus, whom Timothy knew or would soon recognize. They do not simply love money; they are **eager** for it. Their motive is expressed in an instrumental participle, *oregomenoi* (aspire or long for; → 3:1). This participle sets the condition for consequences expressed in two aorist tense verbs in the last half of the verse. The meaning can be captured in a literal translation: ***By longing for money, some have been led astray from the faith and pierced themselves with many pains.*** The first verb leads to the second.

The first verb in the passive voice shows that they were deceived, possibly by Satan (→ 4:1; 5:15). But they were not innocent victims; they were culpable for accepting a lie. They became enticed by interesting speculations and motivated by selfishness. This created a fatal recipe for ruin.

Faith is used with the article, indicating the Christian faith (→ 1:2, 19; 3:9; 4:1; 5:8). "Those Paul is referring to have strayed from 'the faith' by straying from faith or trust in God and Christ as the central desire and love of their life (cf. 2 Tim 4:10)" (Knight 1992, 258). Jesus taught that one "cannot serve both God and money." One or the other will be master (Matt 6:24).

The second verb, **pierced,** provides a graphic image, (lit.) meaning ***impaled***. The reciprocal pronoun **themselves** (*heautous*) shows that this is a self-inflicted wound. The instrument of death is **many griefs**. The opponents have destroyed themselves with the weapons of emotional, relational, and spiritual brokenness. Rejecting the source of life leads to pain, decay, and eventual death.

Paul has essentially offered two options in this chapter:

Those who long to use their wealth in the service of others and who will promote sound doctrine aspire to a noble work. But those who see their money as piety's reward and as an entitlement to leadership in the church—especially if they are careless in their doctrine—are headed for trouble. (Kidd 1990, 97)

Wealth in Ephesus and the Broader Culture

Archaeological and cultural information supports the potential problems wealth presented in ancient Ephesus. The temple of Artemis dominated the social, economic, and religious scene of the city (Acts 19:35). The manufacture and trade in silver shrines of Artemis brought a good income to many (19:24-27). The temple was the primary bank and moneylender, "the common treasury of Asia"

(Aelius Aristides, *Or.* 23.24). It held on deposit "not only money of the Ephesians but also of aliens and of people from all parts of the world, and in some cases states and kings" (Dio Chrysostom, *Or.* 31.54; both quoted by Baugh 1995, 19-20). The temple also owned large tracks of land. Boundary stones have been found that mark 27,000 acres.

The Greek city was divided by a social hierarchy, determined in part by wealth, birth, and citizenship. Wealth provided people certain social rights and obligations. Early Christians came from every economic status and social order in the society. The wealthy had an important part in the early church as patrons by giving resources to the needy, which resulted in a tighter fellowship. Along with this generosity came the expectation that the wealthy as benefactors would be bestowed with places of honor. Public recognition was a strong motivation for giving. Giving not only benefited the poor but the wealthy as well.

The danger with wealth, however, is that those with it might presume positions of leadership based on their benevolence even though they are not qualified for such position. They could undermine those who are placed in authority because of their gifted leadership. This type of attitude could be detrimental both to Timothy's leadership and community cohesiveness (Countryman 1980).

The proper role of the wealthy is to support those in need within the church. Aristotle taught that wealth must be put to work to benefit others (*Rhet.* 1361a35-43).

This willingness to spend could fairly be called the liquid capital of Hellenistic and Roman communities. For the rich themselves this willingness was simultaneously the surest path to social power, the best form of social security, and the most concrete opportunity for immorality one had. (Kidd 1990, 124)

FROM THE TEXT

Money can be either a blessing or a curse. It promises comfort, but when used for selfish purposes, it often ends up in grief, emptiness, and craving. This pain results "from a guilty conscience, tormenting passions, desires contrary to reason, religion, and one another. How cruel are worldly men to themselves!" (Wesley 1813, 231). "If it is difficult for the rich to enter the kingdom of God, it is relatively easy for those who strive to be rich to turn away from it" (Towner 1994, 140).

The pursuit of materialism captures the hearts of many today. God seems to have given humans an innate desire to improve their lives. We are by nature beings of industry (Gen 1:28). The sin of selfishness distorts this drive to the point of using other people as objects to further personal agendas. Paul flips this over in this passage.

Be careful against the deceitfulness of wealth. Scripture speaks loudly about the dangers of wealth (Prov 15:27; Matt 6:24; Mark 4:19; Luke 12:13-15; Jas 5:1). Seeking wealth is a foolish endeavor and will become an obstacle to kingdom life (Mark 10:24-25; Luke 6:20, 24; 9:23-25; 12:22-34; 14:25-33; 16:13). History is full of painful stories of how the deception of wealth often ends up in destruction. The lie goes like this: "If I just had *this*, it would make me happy." This promise is futile (Eccl 2:1-11) in comparison to the hope we can have of eternal life with Christ.

The answer comes by *finding our contentment in dependence upon God*. Wealth and poverty are relative concepts. There will always be someone wealthier or poorer than we. Even those who may seem "poor" in one nation may in fact be the wealthy of another.

What is the focus of our lives? Are we living to glorify God or to please ourselves? Epicurus was asked the secret of contentment: "Add not to a man's possessions but take away from his desires" (quoted by Gould 1965, 615). There is a reason why money is one of the most common topics in the Bible: How we use or abuse it shows our heart's motives. Thus, Wesleyans should not be surprised that John Wesley published more sermons on money than on holiness.

In response, we ought to *use God's blessings to us to bless others*. Wealth can be a tremendous tool for building relationships or a dangerous weapon for destroying them by using people. Love is the root of all good (Augustine, *Serm.* 179A.5). Jesus showed the way by giving of himself through service (Mark 10:45; Luke 22:25-27).

> Godliness is not about acquiring better and more material things; it is instead an active life of faith, a living out of covenant faithfulness in relation to God, that finds sufficiency and contentment in Christ alone whatever one's outward circumstances might be. (Towner 2006, 399)

The drive to care for ourselves and our loved ones is not wrong in itself. The problem is when the law of love is violated and God and people are neglected.

Wesleyans would do well to spend some time perusing the sermons of John Wesley—for our edification, not our comfort. He published more sermons on the proper use of money than on Christian holiness! His summary of the Bible's teaching on the subject may be simply summarized in three maxims: Earn all you can. Save all you can. And give all you can. The challenge is to consider what that might mean in practical ways.

B. Encouragement to Timothy to Keep the Faith (6:11-16)

BEHIND THE TEXT

At first glance, this section seems to be a digression from the discussion of wealth in 6:6-10 and 17-19. But it serves two purposes in the letter. It provides the counterargument to the position of the opponents in 6:6-10, showing the better way Timothy should live. At the same time, it reiterates key exhortations Paul gives Timothy in the letter.

Once again, Paul addresses Timothy directly. Each of the three references to false teachers in the letter is followed by a personal exhortation to Timothy (1:3-7; 1:18-20; 4:1-5; 4:6-16; and here). This section functions as the letter's peroration. It concludes the letter with a summary of its main topics.

The closing lacks the "apostolic *parousia* [presence]" (Funk 1967, 249). This typically expresses Paul's desire to visit, his hopes to see the recipients, appeals to his authority as an apostle, or a comment about sending emissaries (Rom 15:14-33; 2 Cor 12:14—13:13; Gal 4:12-20; Phil 2:19-24; 2 Tim 4:9-18). The ending, however, still carries authority as Paul recalls how Timothy ought to respond to the problems in Ephesus.

The section begins with four solemn charges before God and Christ Jesus (1 Tim 6:11-14) followed by a doxology (vv 15-16) that echoes the letter opening in 1:12-17. In this short paragraph, Paul recalls the past and looks forward to the future in order to deal with the present.

IN THE TEXT

■ **11** Paul begins his final charge to Timothy with an emphatic rhetorical **But you**. This offers a strong contrast with the "people" who pursue wealth in 6:10. He addresses his son in the faith as **man of God**. This description is used for the servants of God in the OT, including Moses (Deut 33:1; Josh 14:6), Samuel (1 Sam 9:6), Elijah (1 Kgs 17:18), Elisha (2 Kgs 4:7), and David (Neh 12:24; Kelly 1963, 140). Paul will use this again for Timothy in 2 Tim 3:17.

The designation becomes paradigmatic for all believers who should follow Timothy's lead by appropriating the qualities that follow. "They are summoned to turn their backs on the sinful desires of the world and to cultivate spiritual qualities which will have practical expressions" (Marshall 1999, 657). The rhetorical effect of this description is to assign Timothy a prophetic role as the guardian of orthodoxy in Ephesus. He has the responsibility of spiritual leadership within the church. It also opposes him to the false teachers whose authority is disqualified by their lifestyle and teaching.

Paul exhorts Timothy to watch the direction of his life. First, Timothy must **flee** [*pheuge*] **from all this**. He must escape to a safer place (1 Cor 6:18; 10:14). The demonstrative pronoun **this** (lit. *these things*) reflects back on the previous discussion, including the dangers of loving money (1 Tim 6:9-10), dabbling in false doctrines and speculations (v 3), and the divisiveness that results from these (vv 4-5). The NIV's **all** is not in Greek but is supplied from the plural pronoun. Paul uses the verb *pheuge* again in 2 Tim 2:22, charging Timothy to reject the passions of youth.

Timothy must avoid the dangers of certain activities and embrace a lifestyle radically different from that of the false teachers. **Flee** is followed immediately by **pursue** (*diōke*) in Greek. The same pattern of rejecting one way and pursing another appears in Titus 2:12, although the words are different.

Both imperatives—**flee** and **pursue**—are in the present tense: There is a constant need to avoid the temptations that arise in ministry leadership. The verb **pursue** describes a deliberate journey unswervingly following a given direction, goal, or lifestyle. The same word in Phil 3:14 refers to Paul's quest for the heavenly prize of resurrection life in Christ. Timothy's unending pursuit is the necessary response of obedience to God's inviting grace and merciful forgiveness (→ 1 Tim 1:12-16).

Timothy is to **pursue** six qualities that all reflect the transforming gospel of Christ. Timothy will need these to be effective in his ministry in Ephesus, and they are what the church will need for spiritual vitality. They may be in partial response to the vices listed in 6:4-5. The terms are related as three pairs (Knight 1992, 262):

The first pair focuses on spiritual qualities in relationship with God reflected in practical ways. **Righteousness** (*dikaiosynēn*; → 1:9) is both a forensic term for being guilt free before God's law and an ethical term for living in integrity according to God's law. Behavior is the emphasis in this verse.

Righteousness is experienced through faith in Christ and lived out through the abiding presence of the Holy Spirit (Rom 8:3-4; 14:17; Phil 1:11; 2 Tim 2:22; 3:16). Zechariah and Elizabeth (Luke 1:6) were examples of people who lived according to God's will and did what pleased him (Schrenk 1964b, 198).

Godliness (*eusebeian*; → 1 Tim 2:2), one of the key themes of this letter (3:16; 4:7-8; 6:5-6), refers to piety, devotion, and commitment to God lived out in the life of faith. It is marked by total dedication to God (Mounce 2000, 354). One's vibrant relationship with God ought to influence how one lives in relationship with others.

The second pair of words describes "the animating principles of the Christian life." **Faith** and **love** often appear together in Paul's letters. They are paired in the Pastorals in 1 Tim 1:5; 2:15; 4:12; 2 Tim 2:22; and Titus 2:2. The words occur with **endurance** in 1 Thess 1:3; 2 Tim 3:10; and Titus 2:2.

Faith (*pistin*; → 1:5) is active trust in God. Wesley calls this faith "the foundation of righteousness, the support of godliness, the root of every grace of the Spirit" (1813, 231). Faith for the sanctified life is saying yes to God.

Love (*agapēn*; → 1:5) is based on God's love for us (1 John 4:19) and "involves both feeling (caring about other people) and action (participating in their lives)" (Ngewa 2009, 158). **Love** is "the glorious spring of all inward and outward holiness" (Wesley 1813, 231).

The third pair shows how to act in a hostile world. **Endurance** (*hypomonē*) is "the capacity to hold out or bear up in the face of difficulty" (BDAG 2000, 1039). It is often translated as "steadfastness" (ESV) or "perseverance" (NASB). It is the "divine assurance that fires indomitable perseverance" (Montague 2008, 127), or the "patience and constancy in the face of adversity" (Collins 2002, 162). It is concerned with "the attitude with which one endures, the actual perseverance, and one's confidence in the final outcome, all with a dependence on God's grace and a determination to serve Christ by means of the *hypomonē*" (Knight 1992, 262). Timothy faced considerable opposition. He would need fortitude and determination to complete his mission.

The Greek word behind **gentleness** (*praupathian*) occurs only here in the NT (but compare *praus* in 2 Cor 10:1 and Gal 5:23). It is formed from the combination of two words, "gentle" (*praus*) and "to suffer" (*pathos*). Together they mean the ability to remain gentle in a difficult situation.

Gentleness begins with an attitude and is shown in the strength of **endurance**. The person who shows this attribute is not quarrelsome (compare 1 Tim 6:4-5) but has a calmness that leads to reconciliation (Collins 2002, 162).

Paul is passing the baton to Timothy, giving him the authority to deal with the problems in Ephesus. Timothy may be tempted to become discouraged in the face of the opposition. Paul reminded him of his call earlier in the letter (1:18; 4:14) and reaffirms this call here. Timothy must be careful because of the deceptive dangers that had trapped the false teachers. By embracing these six qualities, Timothy could reverse the effects of the false teachers who were plunging "people into ruin and destruction" (6:9*b*).

There was to be no connection between wealth and position in the church. These six qualities, not wealth, ought to be the real status indicators in the church and the core qualifications for those who are teachers. The opponents' goal was material things. Timothy must make his goal the pursuit of qualities that confirm his new life in Christ (→ 1:18-19).

■ **12** Paul gives two further exhortations in this verse that continue the idea of "pursue" from 6:11. The imagery shifts with **fight the good fight of the faith**. Fleeing and pursuing are not always easy to do. Paul stresses the urgency and intensity with which Timothy must pursue the six attributes of v 11.

The imperative verb **fight** in the present tense shows that there must not be any relaxing in this pursuit. The noun form of the verb is repeated for emphasis. The noun **fight** denotes a competitive contest, whether athletic or military. It graphically portrays the intensity with which one must seek God's rule (1 Cor 9:25-27; Phil 2:16; 3:12-14).

The nouns **fight** and **faith** both have Greek articles. Paul had a specific goal in mind for Timothy. **The faith** most likely refers to the Christian faith (as in 1 Tim 6:10). It is from this faith that the false teachers have wandered (vv 10, 21).

Faith is the arena for the Christian life. "Faith, by its very nature, demands a struggle on the part of the believer" (Pfitzner 1967, 179). Paul testifies in 2 Tim 4:7, "I have fought the good fight, I have finished the race, I have kept the faith." Although Timothy is younger than Paul, he must make his goal like Paul's. The six qualities in 1 Tim 6:11 are necessary equipment for the battle. Victory will not come by accident but through discipline and with perseverance. The battle is against those who would rob the Ephesians of sound teaching. Timothy can use two sources in his fight: (1) his own life of integrity and godliness and (2) sound theology communicated through careful teaching.

The second command shifts attention to the prize for winning the fight: **Take hold of the eternal life**. The goal is not the fight but the prize for victory. The verb **take hold** in the aorist tense accents the decision to embrace **eternal life** in a permanent way. It conveys the idea of seizing in order to possess, to make it one's own (BDAG 2000, 373). This eternal life can be possessed in part now and someday in full (Phil 3:12-14). "Thus the Christian athlete can enjoy the prize while still engaged in the contest" (Gould 1965, 618).

Timothy was **called** to this eternal life **when** he **made** his **good confession in the presence of many witnesses**. This coordinate clause is interpreted temporally in the NIV, highlighting the human response to God's call. The clause may be parallel to the shorter clause *you were called*. Both are governed by the prepositional phrase *for which*.

The preposition *eis* followed by the accusative pronoun *hēn* refers back to **eternal life**. This is the goal of Timothy's calling and the object of his confession. Eternal life is a quality of life that matches the new age Christ began with his resurrection from the dead. Eternal life is the deep universal call of God to all humanity, but experienced only by those who trust in Christ (1 Cor 1:9; 2 Thess 2:14; 2 Tim 1:9; Titus 3:3-7). It comes from knowing Christ and accepting his offer of divine grace (John 17:3). It is the present experience and possession for those who believe (John 3:36; 5:24; 10:28; 1 John 5:11-12).

Timothy embraced this call at his public **confession**. Commentators are split in whether this confession accompanied his baptism or ordination (→ 1 Tim 4:14). **Good confession** has the definite article, giving it a recognized, official character (Kelly 1963, 142). To confess is to "agree with" (*homo*, "the same," and *logeō*, "to speak") someone about a matter. For early Christians, this agreement was that "Jesus is Lord" and was made when they were baptized (Acts 3:13-15; 4:27; 13:28; Ign. *Magn.* 1.11; Justin, *1 Apol.* 13.3). The reminder of the public setting of Timothy's confession should motivate him to remain committed to the faith. The possible grammatical connection to eternal life suggests that this was his confession of faith when he came to saving faith in Jesus as the Christ.

The call does not guarantee an easy road. The call to discipleship involves bearing one's cross and at times suffering (Luke 9:23-26; 1 Cor 9:24-27; Phil 3:8-14). Timothy's calling in the past confirms the fight before him. "It is possible to possess something without embracing and enjoying it" (Stott 1996, 157). Paul reminds Timothy here of this important moment in his life and the seriousness of living it out at the present moment. There are at least four reasons why Timothy should persevere (Mounce 2000 351):

1. He has been called to eternal life (1 Tim 6:12*b*).
2. He made a commitment before others (v 12*c*).
3. He should imitate the type of confession Jesus made (v 13*b*).
4. He serves a powerful God and with God's help, he can make it (vv 15-16).

■ **13-14** Verses 13-16 form one long sentence in Greek, making them a challenge to translate and interpret. **I charge you** comes at the beginning of this sentence, although the NIV attempts to make its translation more understandable by putting it last in v 13.

This is another solemn charge to Timothy, like the reminders in 1:9; 4:12, 16; and 5:21. It rings with apostolic authority confirmed by its creedal formulation. The charge is not given until 6:14. **You**, omitted in some manuscripts, makes sense, even if it is not original. The charge is further motivation for Timothy to remain true to his confession of faith and calling to serve in Ephesus.

Paul names two direct witnesses: God and Christ (see 5:21; 2 Tim 4:1). He modifies both with attributive participial phrases. Pilate serves as a third, indirect witness.

Paul gives his charge, first, **in the sight of God**. Beginning with reference to God places a strong sense of obligation upon Timothy. He should not retreat in fear but fight all the more vigorously, because God **gives life to everything**. The participle **who gives life** (*zōogonountos*) in the present tense stresses God's ongoing creative activity of sustaining life. All creation depends on God's power, which comes through Christ (Col 1:15-17). This compound word appears elsewhere in the NT only in Luke 17:33 and Acts 7:19. God will give Timothy life in the midst of the hardships he will face in Ephesus.

There is a dramatic contrast between the creative power of God and the description of Christ "in his moment of supreme earthly weakness and vulnerability" before Pontius Pilate (Towner 2006, 413). The preposition **before** can be interpreted temporally as "in the time of," either the moment of Jesus' trial before Pilate or his whole ministry (Kelly 1963, 143). The aorist tense of the participle *martyrēsantos* probably refers to the moment of his trial.

Pontius Pilate was the fifth Roman prefect of Judea. He ruled from AD 26 to 36. He was the one who ordered the crucifixion of Jesus (Matt 27:24; Mark 15:15; Luke 23:25; John 19:16; Tacitus, *Ann.* 15.44, 28). The name "Pontius" is mentioned in the NT only in Luke 3:1; Acts 4:27; and here. The late apocryphal book the *Acts of Pilate* enlarges upon the Passion traditions. The full name Pontius Pilate became part of early Christian creeds (Ign. *Magn.* 11; Ign. *Smyrn.* 1.1; Ign. *Trall.* 9.1; the Nicene and Apostles' Creeds).

It is unclear what Jesus' **good confession** before Pilate was. Pilate interrogated Jesus as part of his trial. Pilate asked Jesus, "Are you the king of the Jews?" to which Jesus replied, "You have said so" (Matt 27:11; Mark 15:2; Luke 23:3; see John 18:33-37). Even as king, Jesus was willing to lay down his life for others (John 10:11, 15, 17; 1 John 3:16). He did not compromise his reliance on the Father even though it meant his death. His death on the cross confirmed his total trust in the power and hope of resurrection. Timothy needed to remain faithful to this confession (→ 1 Tim 6:16; 2 Tim 1:10-11; 2:8) as he faced his own battles with opponents in Ephesus. This is the only (albeit remote) reference to the crucifixion of Jesus in this letter.

The specific charge to Timothy appears in 1 Tim 6:14: **Keep this command without spot or blame until the appearing of our Lord Jesus Christ**. The antecedent of **this command** is probably the imperative in v 12: **Take hold of the eternal life**. Timothy must sustain this confession with the same commitment with which Jesus kept his confession before Pilate (compare v 20: "Guard what has been entrusted to your care").

6:13-14

Paul explains how Timothy is to keep the command with two adjectives with an adverbial sense. They modify **command**, describing the degree to which Timothy is to keep the command. Both words have *alpha* privative prefixes, which negates the root word (**without**).

First, Timothy should keep the command **without spot**. *Aspilos* is a cultic term in the Bible used for unblemished animals fit for sacrifice (Lev 4:3). Christ is the perfect sacrifice as "a lamb without blemish" (1 Pet 1:19). From this usage, the word takes on the ethical quality of being morally "unstained" (ESV) by sin (2 Pet 3:14; Oepke 1964b, 502).

Second, the command must be preserved **without . . . blame**. *Anepilēmpton*, "above reproach," described the required character of an overseer in 1 Tim 3:2. No one should find fault in how Timothy lives out the six qualities of 6:11. His personal integrity should match the object of his desire.

Paul has already (4:12; 5:2) urged Timothy to remain pure. "Paul's command has moral overtones. It was not only a *charge* to do something, but a *mandate* to be something" (Liefeld 1999, 211). The God who calls believers to lives of holiness will provide the resources for the journey (1 Thess 5:23-24).

Another basis for keeping the command is the certainty of final judgment, with its rewards and punishments. The temporal phrase, **until the appearing of our Lord Jesus Christ** gives a time limit. It introduces the language of expectation, providing motivation for keeping up "the good fight of the faith" (1 Tim 6:12).

Appearing (*epiphaneias*) describes the self-disclosure of a god or semidivine being, when gods miraculously showed themselves, or a king returns from abroad (Bultmann and Lührmann 1974, 1-10). In the cultural context, the use of this term would have been a direct confrontation with emperor worship and prepares for the doxology of vv 15-16. The word is used only by Paul in the NT (2 Thess 2:8). It refers to Christ's incarnation in 2 Tim 1:10 and to his return in 2 Tim 4:1, 8; and Titus 2:13.

Paul lived with a sense of God's presence and in expectation of Christ's imminent return (Phil 3:20-21; "will judge" [2 Tim 4:1]). He saw the present as part of the unfolding of the new age. During the interim, believers ought to remain faithful and holy (1 Cor 1:8; Phil 2:15-16; 1 Thess 3:13; 5:23). In 1 Tim 6:14, Paul urges Timothy to remain faithful to the truth of the gospel until the end. The expectation is that the hope of Christ's return would influence Timothy's behavior. There will be a reward for those who remain committed to the message of truth that Paul preached.

■ **15-16** The language shifts to a doxology similar to 1:17 (→). Paul bursts forth in praise as he reflects on the immanent return of Christ. His thoughts shift to the one who brings it all about. The glorious description of God in these verses connects Timothy to the source of power that will enable him to carry out his mission in Ephesus.

Doxologies in the Pastorals are "pertinent to and apt expressions of that blend of doctrine and life" (Liefeld 1999, 215). This doxology contains six lines (UBS[4]) describing seven qualities of God that cover two core themes: God's sovereignty and transcendence. The doxology ends with a typical closing line of exaltation. Its structure suggests possible use as an early Christian hymn, although there is nothing explicitly "Christian" about it. Kelly describes it as "a gem from the devotional treasury of the Hellenistic synagogue which converts had naturalized in the Christian church" (1963, 146).

What prompts the doxology is the reflection that **God will bring about** Christ's appearance **in his own time**. This statement of God's sovereign determination of the **proper** or **appointed** (*kairois*) time (→ 2:6; Titus 1:3) of the Parousia should lead to confidence that God will work everything out for Timothy. God is in control of the end-time schedule (Matt 24:36; 1 Thess 4:16). God will provide all the resources Timothy needs "to keep this command without spot or blame" (1 Tim 6:14). The doxology is a poetic way of confirming this statement of confidence.

The first line of the doxology emphasizes God's uniqueness as **Ruler** using two adjectives: **blessed** (*makarios*) and **only**. This is the only time the word **Ruler** (*dynastēs*) is used for God in the NT, but his sovereign reign is a constant theme. This Jewish (see 2 Macc 1:24; 12:15; 3 Macc 2:3; Sir 46:5; *Sib. Or.* 3:719) description of God as **blessed** appears only here and in 1 Tim 1:11 in the NT. The designation "Blessed" was a title for emperors and famous generals in the Imperial cult, which was especially strong in Asia Minor (Johnson 2001, 309). Calling God the **blessed . . . Ruler** would have caught the attention of many residents of Ephesus as having political nuances.

God as the **only Ruler** confirms the core monotheistic confession of Jews found in Deut 6:4: "Hear, O Israel: The LORD our God, the LORD is one" (→ 1 Tim 2:5). This statement directly confronted the polytheistic environment of Ephesus. This particularly challenged the worship of Zeus, the most powerful Greek god, the sovereign ruler from Mount Olympus. Both adjectives draw attention to God's utter supremacy and confirm his sufficiency for all Timothy and the church required.

God's sovereign power is again emphasized with the second and third lines: **the King of kings and Lord of lords**. A more literal translation of the two substantival participles shows the emphatic rhetorical affect: "God is the possessor of the highest power over all who possess power and has full control over all who exercise control" (Knight 1992, 269). No human or so-called divine authority can challenge God's rule (Deut 10:17; Ps 96:4-5). The same descriptions are used for the risen Jesus in Rev 17:14 and 19:16.

It is noteworthy that Revelation was written to churches in the same part of Asia Minor as this letter. These churches may have struggled against the influence of the Imperial cult. It is possible that this confession arose out of the need to persevere in the face of growing opposition and persecution. Paul knew firsthand the personal cost of challenging Roman authority, suffered in his many imprisonments.

The fourth line shifts to the second major theme in the doxology—God's transcendence. Lines four and five contain two substantival participles governed by the same article: *the only one who possesses immortality, [and the one] who lives in unapproachable light*.

Immortal literally means "without death" (*alpha* privative before *thanatos*). God is life itself and gives life to all things (John 5:26). The NT does not accept the Greek belief in the immortality of the soul, as taught by Plato. Life beyond death is a gift of God (Hanson 1982, 113). Augustine wrote, "True immortality is unchangeableness; which no creature can possess, since it belongs to the creator alone" (*Trin.* 1.1.2). Our immortality is a gift from the one who is truly immortal. Resurrection makes it possible for believers to participate in immortality (1 Cor 15:53-54).

God's purity and transcendent holiness stand behind the next line: **who lives in unapproachable light**. There are significant scriptural precedents for this thought.

On the divine side, light represents the manifestation of God's glory, which is too overwhelming for humans to see (Job 37:21-22; Ps 104:2; John 1:18). Moses had to hide behind the cleft of the rock even to witness the "backside" of the fading glory of God (Exod 33:19-23).

On the human side, it is impossible for sinful humanity to stand in the presence of the holy God (1 Sam 6:20; Isa 6:5; Rom 3:19-20; Heb 12:14). No lamps are needed in heaven because of God's presence (Rev 21:23). In Eph 5:8-9, light refers to God's righteousness. One of the great messages of the incarnation is that God became human so that we might gaze upon him unimpeded (John 1:5, 18; 1 John 1:1). The light of God shows us the way of purity in which we should walk (1 John 1:5, 7).

The last line adds further emphasis to line five: **whom no one has seen or can see**. This thought comes as the logical outcome of the previous line. No one can see God's glory and survive his overwhelming presence. It is not that God is invisible or unapproachable. He is too holy for sinful humanity to see and live. The story of Moses in Exod 33 is a good example of this as well. This theme is repeated in the NT (see esp., John 1:18; 6:46; 1 John 4:12). God accommodates himself to human experience: we can only know about God through what God reveals to us. In the OT, this occurred through theophanies (Gen 16:7; 18:1; 32:2). In the NT, God becomes visible in the Son who is "the radiance of God's glory and the exact representation of his being, sustaining all things by his powerful word" (Heb 1:3).

The doxology ends with a statement of praise: **To him be honor and might forever. Amen.** This is the only fitting conclusion to a doxology that acknowledges the awesomeness of God. It is a restatement of God's sovereignty.

Honor is what one gives to one's master (→ 1 Tim 6:1). It refers to God's position of immortality and dwelling in light. God's eternal power and **might** reflect back to God's sovereignty as **King** and **Lord**. **Forever** is a statement of assurance to a community going through difficult times. The only fitting response to these descriptions of God is the confirmation **Amen**. The rhetorical goal of this doxology was to encourage Timothy as he dealt with the false teachers. It is a strong statement about the source of the gospel to the church in the polytheistic city of Ephesus, where many religions were clamoring for adherents.

FROM THE TEXT

Essential qualities of the people of God. Paul's message to Timothy as a "man of God" is succinctly summarized in the two words "flee" and "pursue" (v 11). This ethical appeal is grounded in the basic storyline of Scripture. Since creation, the choice has really only been between two options: whether or not to love God by following his commandments.

To say "yes" to God often leads to an ethic subversive to the cultural norms around us (Rom 6:6; Eph 4:22). Jesus put it this way: "Whoever wants to be my disciple must deny themselves and take up their cross and follow me" (Mark 8:34). To embrace the way of the cross requires running from the dangers of sin, as Joseph did in Potiphar's house (Gen 39:12). The people of God ought to "renounce impiety and worldly passions, and in the present age to live lives that are self-controlled, upright, and godly" (Titus 2:12 NRSV).

Endurance against opposition. Standing up for the truth of the gospel may lead to opposition from unbelievers and, sadly, from some people within the church. Timothy faced opposition from the teachers of false doctrine in Ephesus. Paul faced similar opposition throughout his ministry from "Judaizers" who troubled churches with their doctrine of circumcision and law abiding (Gal 5:7-12; → Titus 1:10).

Christian ethics must be rooted in a proper understanding of the nature of God. It is noteworthy that Paul closes a section reminding Timothy of this call with a doxology about hope in God. Good theology will lead to good ethics. Orthodox doctrine will lead to proper behavior. How people live will reveal who or what their "god" is.

Our hope as Christians must be anchored in God as Savior and Christ Jesus as Mediator (1 Tim 1:1; 2:5). Paul's statements about God in this passage subverted the imperialism of his day. "The potent language and symbols of the present 'empire' will need to be decoded, and then turned around, strategically filled with challenging new meaning and delivered in a message that opposes all false claims to power, authority, promise, and hope" in our time (Towner 2006, 423). How will the church respond to the pressures around it today? The hope we have in the second coming of Christ (6:14) should compel us to total commitment to live blameless and holy lives through the help of the Holy Spirit.

C. Commands to Rich Believers (6:17-19)

BEHIND THE TEXT

Even after the glorious doxology of vv 15-16, there is one more topic and one more group on Paul's mind. He returns to the theme of wealth from vv 3-10 but merges it with the hope in God from vv 11-16. Some Christians have been blessed with wealth, which is not wrong in itself. However, because their wealth is a blessing from God, the rich must in turn bless others by putting their money to good use by helping others. These closing thoughts give the wealthy a sense of purpose in the church and let them know that Paul is not trying to condemn them as he did the false teachers (vv 3-10). His eschatology leads him to see wealth as having a greater purpose than comfort in this world. It can actually lead to storing up treasures in the coming age. Riches are part of the present age and not the age to come. Only things related to the new age in Christ are for certain in this world. Riches in this world should be used in light of the new age in Christ.

Verses 17-19 form one sentence in Greek. Four forms of the word "rich" are used (in vv 17*a*, 17*b*, 17*c*, 18*a*), forming a paronomasia, a repetition of sound. The series of commands in vv 17-18 are followed by the result in v 19*a* and the reason to do these things in v 19*b*. There are three exhortations to the wealthy: "first, not to trust in their riches (17*c*); second, to trust in God instead (17*d*); and third, to engage in good works (18) so that one might build a solid foundation for the future (19)" (Kidd 1990, 125).

Paul makes two essential points: (1) God provides for our needs, (2) so we should use what we have to do good toward others. The danger to avoid is feeling too confident in wealth. Security can be found only in God.

IN THE TEXT

■ **17** This is the fifth time Paul has given Timothy a **command** in this letter (1:3; 4:11; 5:7; 6:13). The **command** is an indirect exhortation to the **rich** in the Ephesian church. Those with wealth could have included householders, their wives (→ 2:9), and possibly their children. It would have been unlikely, though still possible, for slaves to be rich. This is the only time Paul addresses the wealthy in his letters.

The scene changes from the unapproachable light of God to ***the present age*** (Rom 12:2; 1 Cor 2:6; 2 Cor 4:4; 2 Tim 4:10; Titus 2:12). This time frame is contrasted with "the coming age" in 1 Tim 6:19. Wealth is limited to and defined by the criteria of this age, which is passing away (1 Cor 7:31). There are two things for the rich to avoid and one to embrace. The two negatives are given in infinitive clauses.

First, they are **not to be arrogant**. This is a compound word from *hypslos*, "haughty, lofty," and *phronein*, "to think." Pride comes as a temptation to boast in one's wealth (Deut 8:14; Jer 9:23; Ezek 28:5). Chrysostom wrote that nothing produces pride and arrogance as much as wealth (*Hom. 1 Tim.* 18).

Second, the rich should not **put their hope in wealth, which is so uncertain** (lit. ***the uncertainty of riches***). Uncertain (*adēlotēti*) occurs only here in the NT. It refers to something that cannot be counted on. ***Riches*** is a genitive of quality. The sense is that "riches are not a proper foundation for one's hope because they are uncertain, and riches are uncertain because they are of this age" (Mounce 2000, 366).

Ethicists of Paul's time recognized that riches were precarious and could not provide a solid foundation for the future. Kidd notes that "the ruins of cities across the Mediterranean basin are littered with monuments to the anxiousness of the prosperous to exchange their money for something more lasting" (1990, 126). **To hope** (*ēlpikenai*) is a rare perfect tense infinitive. Hope looks to the future, but this tense moves the hope of the wealthy to this age. It is ironic that people put their hope in uncertainty (Dibelius and Conzelmann 1972, 91). Wealth can be lost in a moment of time (Prov 23:5; Matt 6:19).

The infinitive **to hope** has another object set in stark contrast with **wealth** by the Greek adversative *alla*. The rich in this world ought **instead** to put their hope **in God, who richly provides us with everything for our enjoyment.** The irony cannot be missed. The rich seek certainty in their wealth, which is temporary at best. But they should put their hope in the one who provides the good things (Jas 1:17). The perfect tense of the infinitive shows how placing hope in the right object **(in God)** in this life continues on into the age to come. The key word, **rich** (*ploutos*), now becomes an adverb for how God gives.

The concept of **enjoyment** requires careful consideration. Wealth is a blessing from God (Eccl 5:19-20), not for our self-indulgence but for contentment. God does not give everything we want but gives blessings beyond bare necessities as gifts to be enjoyed and to aid others (→ 1 Tim 6:18). Even food and clothing should be viewed as a gift (→ v 8). This is a subtle counterargument against the asceticism of the false teachers (4:3). The perfect tense infinitive fits well with this last clause: hope placed in God in this age will endure into the one to come.

■ **18-19** The thought of 6:17 continues with a positive command of what the rich should do with their money. The imperative **command them** is assumed from v 17 and governs three more infinitives in this verse. Thus, the rich are to do four things: to hope (v 17), **to do good, to be rich in good deeds, and to be generous and willing to share.** These commands appear in an emphatic position in the letter, just before the closing statement. One gets the sense that Paul is specifically addressing another leadership issue that would be more apparent to those in the church.

Their wealth is not only for their enjoyment but should be used for the good of others. Those blessed by God in turn bless others. **To do good** summarizes the next two infinitives. Paul defines a different type of wealth that is measured by **good deeds.** The wealthy should have a certain detachment from their wealth so that they can help others (Rom 12:8, 13; 2 Cor 9:6-15). The required attitude is given with two adjectives, **generous and willing to share,** which are almost synonymous and mutually interpreting (forming a hendiadys).

Generous is used only here in the NT. As a compound word, its parts literally mean "to give" (*didōmi*) "with" (*meta*) a "good" attitude (*eu*), thus, liberally and joyfully giving to others (Collins 2002, 171). "The resources and the hearts of the wealthy will be oriented toward giving" (Kidd 1990, 128).

Willing to share (*koinōnikos*) is based on the more familiar word usually translated as "fellowship." It involves "the corporate or public nature of the giving" (Kidd 1990, 128) and shows a concern for public welfare. The rich are to use their resources for the common good rather than for private gain. They are to function in the church as benefactors, as in any other political or social situation. They are to live out the Christian ideal expressed in Acts 4:32: "All the believers were one in heart and mind. No one claimed that any of their possessions was their own, but they shared everything they had."

Verse 19 of 1 Tim 6 gives the motivation and promise for using wealth for doing good. It functions as a peroration to the exhortation. The benefit of being rich is that money can be an aid in sharing the gospel. The rich should invest their lives and resources in others and not hoard things for their own pleasures. Wealth should not be an end in and of itself but a means to kingdom fulfillment. Paul puts this in the form of a promise: **They will lay up treasure for themselves as a firm foundation for the coming age**. Using wealth in this age for the good of others is a deposit for "wealth" in the age to come (→ Titus 2:13). Paul is urging those with money to have a different type of wealth, one that will outlast the uncertainties of this temporal age.

There is a mixed metaphor in this phrase. The imagery shifts from **trea-sure** to **foundation**. The clause in the NIV, **they will lay up treasure**, comes from one participle, which could be better rendered instrumentally, *by laying up for themselves*. The Greek *apothēsaurizontas* is a compound found only here in the NT (but there are cognates in Rom 2:5; 1 Cor 16:2; 2 Cor 12:14; Jas 5:3).

The root word *thēsaurizō* means storing something for the future (BDAG 2000, 456). What is stored in this case is a *themelion*, a foundation that can be built upon (Rom 15:20; 1 Cor 3:10-12; Eph 2:20; 2 Tim 2:19)—a stable reserve for the future (BDAG 2000, 449). The echo of Jesus' teachings found in Matt 6:20-21 is clear: "But store up for yourselves [*thēsaurizete*] treasures [*thēsaurous*] in heaven, where moths and vermin do not destroy, and where thieves do not break in and steal. For where your treasure is, there your heart will be also." Jesus warned about being rich in the world but poor in spiritual matters (Luke 12:21). What is most important is following him (Matt 19:21). He is our hope for eternal life (→ 1 Tim 1:1; Titus 1:2; 3:7).

Those with extra resources can have a different type of wealth. They can use their wealth within the church to help support its mission. They are not to compete with the leadership for status but to serve in humility with their gifts (Countryman 1980, 154).

A concluding purpose clause (*hina*) gives the motivation for laying up a foundation in the age to come: **so that they may take hold of the life that is truly life.** The longer phrase **the life that is truly life** in the NIV attempts to capture the intent of the adverb *ontōs* (**truly**) used with *tēs zōēs* (**the life**). This is an indirect way to say "eternal life," which is to be the goal for Timothy (→ 1 Tim 6:12) and all believers (→ 1:16; 4:8, 10).

The implied comparison is between the so-called pleasant life of riches in this world and the true life that lasts for eternity. This new life begins now *in Christ* and will outlast death. The rich cannot buy eternal life because it comes as a gift—the result of God's mercy and grace (→ 1:12-17). Rather, they must live out their faith commitment through "godliness" (*eusebeia*).

One caution should be noted. Paul's point is not about storing enough spiritual treasure to be given eternal life, a point made clear in 1:9. It is about living out, putting into practice, our hope of eternal life. The use of wealth in this verse is not a form of buying eternal life from God but creating new futures for others. The rich will receive the best return for their investment in the lives of others.

FROM THE TEXT

Develop thankful hearts dependent upon God. This paragraph echoes Israel's prophetic tradition that warned about the dangers of idolatry, seeking pleasure, and the neglect of the poor and needy. Paul warns Timothy in v 17 of the core problem of pride. Pride results from misplaced priorities caused by forgetting who we are before God (Deut 8:14). Wealth is a prime catalyst for pride in the heart (Ezek 28:5). The remedy for pride is thankfulness, which comes in recognizing that all we have is a gift from God "who richly provides us with everything for our enjoyment" (1 Tim 6:17; see Jas 1:17).

Our thanksgiving ought to be grounded in a strong doctrine of creation, since "everything God created is good, and nothing is to be rejected if it is received with thanksgiving" (1 Tim 4:4; → 4:4-5). Recognizing God as Creator of the universe should cause us to recognize that all we have to sustain our lives comes from God. The only proper response to this is humility and worship.

Determine to live by kingdom priorities. Temptation to accumulate more wealth has not changed in our day. It is a universal problem that does not depend on where people live or their economic status—they will always want something better. National and personal debts crush people under severe loads of obligation and economic stagnation. Earthly wealth can be lost in a moment. Jesus warned of the life of greed in the parable of the rich fool (Luke 12:16-21). "Life does not consist in an abundance of possessions" (v 15) but in being "rich toward God" (v 21). Abusing God's gifts cuts us off from the one who gives them. "Hope in wealth undermines trust in God" (Towner 1994,

147). Security can be found only by investing in eternity. How we spend our income in this age will determine our outcome in the age to come.

Devote "wealth" to eternal matters. God's gifts are not simply to be hoarded and used for selfish pleasures but for the good of others. Investing in others yields the dividend of participating in the life of God (Matt 25:31-46). Paul quotes—to Ephesian elders—Jesus' saying in Acts 20:35, "It is more blessed to give than to receive." This passage explains why.

Wealth can be a great tool for the kingdom of God. Much of the modern church and its mission and compassion program depend on the faithful giving of believers. We may need to expand our concept of the church. Compassion does not simply involve alleviating hunger. It is an investment in one another because we are part of community. Wealth should be used to strengthen this community. People are more important than wealth.

D. Final Charge to Timothy (6:20-21)

BEHIND THE TEXT

Words found in other places in the letter are repeated in this closing section and summarize many of its key ideas (Richards 2002, 147):

Guard the deposit (*parathēkēn* and *paratithēmi*)	6:20	1:18
Guard (*phylassō*)	6:20	5:21
Turn away (*ektrepō*)	6:20	1:6; 5:15
Worthless (*bebōlos*)	6:20	1:9; 4:7
Knowledge (*gnōsis* and *epignōsis*)	6:20	2:4
Promise (*epangellomai* and *epangelia*)	6:21	2:10; 4:8
Faith (*pistis*)	17 times	
Depart (*astocheō*)	6:21	1:6

IN THE TEXT

■ **20-21a** As in other letters, Paul ends this one with one final exhortation. These verses summarize two key themes of the letter: a positive "call to personal perseverance," and a negative "attack on the Ephesian opponents" (Mounce 2000, 370). The letter begins and ends with the same message, forming a thematic inclusio. It is in the form of a direct appeal to **Timothy** (1:18 and 6:11), using the vocative case along with an untranslated *O*. This form of address adds "solemnity and urgency" (Knight 1992, 276). These last statements of the letter should grab Timothy's attention. The brief ending shows the seriousness of the letter. This is not simply a personal letter, although it is addressed to Timothy. Rather it tackles pressing issues in the Ephesian church, and thus was intended to be more public than private. The closing lacks personal greetings to friends (compare Galatians). Thus, the letter is "all business," and this closing summarizes that business (Fee 1988, 160).

There is one final comparison between two different ways of life. The positive way is given first in the one imperative of the sentence: **Guard what has been entrusted to your care.** The Greek is simply ***guard the deposit.*** *Phylaxon* has the nuance of guarding in order to preserve and pass on something without changing it. It was used for watching over someone else's treasure to keep it safe and protect it from corruption.

Parathēkēn is a legal term for a deposit of money or valuables for safe-keeping. It is used only here and 2 Tim 1:12, 14 in the NT. It refers to "the sketch that an artist would fill out into final form or the outline of a fuller body of written material" (Towner 1989, 126). Paul entrusted Timothy with the gospel (1:18; 4:12-14), and Timothy must hand this message on to trusted teachers (2 Tim 2:2) and protect it from heresy.

The final statement refers back to the false teachers who have been a constant background problem throughout the letter. What the NIV translates as a command is actually an instrumental participle that answers how Timothy can guard the deposit: ***by turning from.*** The aorist tense of this participle and the earlier imperative verb, **guard**, on which it depends, brings out the decisiveness necessary. To preserve the truth of the gospel, Timothy must reject false doctrine (→ 1 Tim 1:6).

6:20-21a

First, he must avoid ***empty noise*** (*kenophōnias*). This "foolish talk" (Louw and Nida 1996, 33.376) is modified by the adjective **godless** (*bebēlous*), which can mean pointless, worthless, or a rejection of divine matters (→ 1:9; 4:7; 2 Tim 2:16).

Second, he must turn away from **the opposing ideas of what is falsely called knowledge.** *Antitheseis* is used in rhetoric for a counterargument in a debate (Aristotle, *Rhet.* 1410A). What these ideas oppose is the truth of the gospel (→ 1 Tim 6:4).

The phrase, **what is falsely called knowledge,** has raised much discussion over the past century. Some interpreters have seen this as evidence for a late dating of the letter and that the author is fighting Gnosticism or Marcionism. Even those who opt for an earlier date see the battle forming against incipient Gnosticism.

> But it is not clear from 1 or 2 Timothy that *gnosis* had come to mean a knowledge which released the soul from enslavement to the material world—salvation in the Gnostic sense—nor that heretics engaged in the aeon and archon speculation that was so closely related to *gnosis* in the later system. (Towner 1989, 30)

The opponents claim to have knowledge but their speculations have proven empty and counter to godliness.

The relative clause that begins v 21 serves as a warning about what happens to those who continue to reject the truth of the gospel and further motivation for keeping the "command" of v 18. **Some *persons*** is anonymous, but these would not be hard for Timothy and the church to recognize once they received this letter.

The participle *epangellomenoi* has the nuance of instrumentality and is dependent upon the verb **have departed**. The ESV notes this: "by professing it some have swerved from the faith" (compare NRSV). The aorist verb *ēstochēsan* implies a completed action. This is not a potential but is already taking place (→ 1:19). The verb repeats the thought of 1:6 and summarizes the key emphasis of the letter (→ 2 Tim 2:18). The word can be translated as "miss" a target or "deviate" from the truth (BDAG 2000, 146), which gives more of an intentional departure from the faith and not an accidental wandering.

Apparently the false teachers have been "boasting" or "proclaiming their expertise" (BDAG 2000, 356 s.v. 2) in the Law (1:5-7), knowledge about marriage and food (4:3), and their pursuit of wealth (6:10) and knowledge (6:20). The dire problem is that because they have continued to hold to their speculative agenda, they **have departed from the faith**. **The faith** refers to the gospel and one's belief in it (→ 1:2). They have missed the key point of the Christian life: "love, which comes from a pure heart and a good conscience and a sincere faith" (1:5), and "righteousness, godliness, faith, love, endurance and gentleness" (6:11).

■ **21b** The letter ends with a simple benediction of praise and blessing: **Grace be with you.** It functions as a final prayer-wish for Timothy and the Ephesian church. This is the shortest ending of any letter in the NT. The ending is abrupt like Galatians, where Paul also deals with opponents. "Apparently, the distress of the situation in both these churches makes the letters to them all business" (Fee 1988, 162). Paul does not include any mention of others who may have been with him (→ 2 Tim 4:19; Titus 3:15). The pronoun **you** is plural, hinting that the congregation has been in Paul's mind all along.

Although the statement is short, it is still significant. Timothy will need the extra strength of **grace** to carry out the instructions of this letter because "for the ongoing life of believers, the grace of Jesus is absolutely essential" (Knight 1992, 277). The source of grace is not mentioned but other letters add, "the grace of our [or, the] Lord Jesus Christ" (2 Cor 13:14; Gal 6:18; Phil 4:23; 1 Thess 5:28; 2 Thess 3:18).

FROM THE TEXT

This letter challenges us to "keep first things first." There are a lot of interesting ideas in the world. The false teachers in Ephesus had gotten caught up in some of the theories and speculations of their time. Paul urges Timothy in this

6:21b

letter to return to the essentials and to make his focus the truth of the gospel. The core values of God as Savior and Christ Jesus as Mediator of this salvation needed to capture the heart and thinking of the Ephesian Christians. From this center, they would be enabled to work out the implications through godly living. This would affect every area of their lives, including the social relationships within their households and their witness to the culture around them.

Paul is especially concerned that the church have strong leadership. The theological understanding and personal integrity of the overseers, deacons, and elders could either propel the church forward in mission or drag it down into controversy and needless speculation. Timothy was in a critical position as his apostolic representative to give general oversight to the church and plant a clear vision of the gospel within the believers.

There is no greater need in this age than a clear understanding of the person and work of Jesus Christ. The Christian life is not simply following a set of commands. At its core, this life is about relationship with God in Christ shown in love "which comes from a pure heart and a good conscience and a sincere faith" (1:5). Paul had learned by firsthand experience that our fundamental need is God's grace shown through Christ Jesus, who displays "his immense patience" to "those who would believe in him and receive eternal life" (v 16).

6:20-21

COMMENTARY

2 TIMOTHY

I. OPENING SALUTATION: 2 TIMOTHY 1:1-2

BEHIND THE TEXT

Second Timothy is a personal letter that reveals the inner Paul as he prepares to hand leadership over to Timothy. Two major problems are addressed in the letter: (1) Paul's imprisonment and desertion by certain people, and (2) the need for Timothy to persevere in his ministry despite continued problems from false teachers. Paul stresses the importance of Timothy's character to the continuation of Paul's mission. Although the letter addresses Timothy, the Ephesian church remains in the background (2:19-20; 3:1-4; 4:22).

Second Timothy resembles ancient paraenetic letters in genre. These gave "advice in the form of exhortation that encourages certain actions and discourages others." Such a letter typically "includes imitation of a model, establishes an antithesis between pursuing good and avoiding evil, and makes explicit a concern for good reputation (honor / shame) in the eyes of others" (Johnson 2001, 322; Malherbe 1986, 124-29; 1977a). Paul uses three strategies as part of the exhortation:

- *Memory*: Paul reminds Timothy of his spiritual heritage (2 Tim 1:5-6; 2:14—3:9; 4:3-4).
- *Model*: Paul offers himself as a model (2 Tim 1:13; 3:10-11).
- *Maxims*: Paul instructs Timothy about how he should act (2:14).

The structure of this can be seen in the letter:

1. The presentation of Paul as a model, together with other exemplars (1:3—2:13)
2. Maxims for Timothy as a teacher, presented in contrast to the false teachers (2:14—4:5)
3. The representation of Paul as a model (4:6-18). (Johnson 2001, 324)

Paul's circumstances had changed since he wrote 1 Timothy. As a free man involved in active ministry, he had expected to see Timothy again soon (1 Tim 3:14-15). In 2 Timothy, after an unsuccessful first defense (→ 4:16), he sits imprisoned in Rome awaiting a second trial (1:17; 4:6, 9). He does not want to encounter the colder climate in Rome during the winter without a coat, so he asks Timothy to bring one to him (4:13, 21). There is no indication as to where Timothy was, possibly still in Ephesus (2:2). Paul had limited freedom but could receive visitors (1:16; 4:21), study, and write (4:13).

Like 1 Timothy and other Pauline Epistles, 2 Timothy begins with the typical epistolary prescript and greeting that clearly mark it as a letter. It follows the standard letter opening of author, to recipient, greetings. As is typical of his other letters, Paul expands these elements with theological and personal reflections that hint at his reason for writing. The opening salutations of the two letters are so nearly identical that some interpreters raise questions of literary dependency and pseudonymity (Marshall 1999, 683-84).

The Last Days of Paul

As he wrote, Paul was imprisoned in Rome awaiting a trial of some type (2 Tim 1:17). Apparently, his first defense did not produce the freedom he had anticipated (4:16). He expected the likely outcome of his trial would be his execution (4:6). There is no indication how long he had been imprisoned.

Scholars hotly debate how 2 Timothy fits into the chronology of Acts. Walker (2012b) proposes that 2 Timothy was written soon after Paul arrived in Rome (Acts 28; → Introduction). Paul was desperate. His hopes for a quick release upon arriving in Rome were dashed; future plans of ministry into Spain, delayed. Prolonged imprisonment as he waited for his formal trial before the emperor seemed likely.

Few people knew Paul's whereabouts at that point. Onesiphorus expended considerable effort finding him to give him aid (1 Tim 1:16-17). Paul felt alone; everyone had abandoned him except Luke (4:11). Acts 28 ends with him under house arrest because Luke, its author, was with him during this time (Eusebius, *Hist. eccl.* 2.22.6).

On first arriving in Rome, Paul did not know how severe his situation would be. His loneliness and despondency come out in the letter. At this low point of his life, he writes to his closest friend and colleague, Timothy, urging him to come quickly. On his way, Paul asked Timothy to pick up his cloak and precious parchments he had left in Troas (2 Tim 4:14). The overall tone of the letter is somber. But this is more than balanced with a genuine confidence in God's ability ultimately to save Paul even through death (vv 7-8).

It is possible that after Timothy arrived, Paul's outlook was renewed. Upon receiving further news of the churches, he may have written the other Prison Epistles—Ephesians, Colossians, Philemon, and finally Philippians (Walker 2012b). After the two-year house arrest, Paul likely had his final and unsuccessful appeal before Caesar.

The NT is silent about what happened next. Persecution of Christians significantly accelerated under Emperor Nero in the AD mid-60s. Large portions of Rome were destroyed by fire in AD 64. Nero blamed it on Christians, leading to the first official persecution of the church. Nero had the reputation of increasing mental instability and cruelty. His bodyguards forced him to commit suicide on June 9, AD 68. The justice Paul hoped for likely became injustice as he faced the insane emperor.

Few details survive as to exactly how and when Paul was martyred. One tradition indicates that he was beheaded on the Ostian Way at a place called the Aquae Salviae (*Acts Pet. Paul*, 80). Fourth-century church historian Eusebius gives some clues: Gaius, at the end of the second century, identified Paul's burial place as on the Ostian Way (*Hist. eccl.* 2.25.7). Eusebius confirms the presence of a cemetery there during his day. Throughout Christian history, Paul's tomb was thought to have been on the Vatican Hill under the basilica built by Constantine in 324, now under the altar of the Basilica of St. Paul Outside-the-Walls (Tre Fontane). In 2002, archaeologists found a sarcophagus under a large marble slab inscribed "Paulo Apostolo Mart." In 2009, carbon dating the human bone fragments determined their date to be the first century. Pope Benedict XVI officially confirmed the place as Paul's tomb.

IN THE TEXT

■ **1** The letter begins with four key components: the author, his role or position, his relationship to God, and the reason for his ministry.

First, Paul begins with his "signature" as the author. **Paul** was the only name Saul of Tarsus used for himself in his letters (→ 1 Tim 1:1). There is sufficient evidence to accept this letter as authentic (→ Introduction), the position assumed throughout this commentary.

Second, Paul identifies himself as **an apostle of Christ Jesus**. This short statement of relationship to Christ reveals Paul's *self-identity* as an apostle, "one sent forth" on behalf of another (→ 1 Tim 1:1). It also hints at his *purpose and calling* to go specifically to the Gentiles (1 Tim 1:12-16; 2:7). From the moment he had the vision of Christ on the Damascus road and received his call to preach among the Gentiles (Acts 9:1-19), to the writing of his last letter, he remained faithful to this calling (→ 2 Tim 1:11). This phrase serves as an assertion of *authority*, which will be important later as he admonishes Timothy in strong terms to be faithful (1:6-8; 2:3, 11-13; 3:10-15; 4:1-5; Fee 1988, 219; Knight 1992, 363). Although written to a close friend, this letter communicates a sense of urgency and seriousness as Paul connects his ministry with Timothy's. **Christ Jesus** was the *source* of Paul's apostleship and a present reality in his life. Christ is mentioned three times in the first two verses. Christ continued to occupy Paul's thoughts as he sat in the Roman prison.

Third, **the will of God** was the source, agent, or cause (*dia*) of Paul's calling as an apostle (1 Cor 1:1; 2 Cor 1:1; Eph 1:1; Col 1:1). He became an apostle, not by his own choosing but because it was God's purpose for him. His ministry was based on a theological conviction that connected his letters to orthodoxy. The appeal to God's will was important in situations where the integrity of the gospel was at stake. This was the case in Ephesus, where false teachers had defected from the faith (2 Tim 1:15; 2:16-18; 3:1-9; 4:10, 16; Towner 2006, 441).

Fourth, Paul sets the theological context of the letter with a concise statement of his life's goal: **in keeping with the promise of life that is in Christ Jesus**. The phrase **promise of life** is found elsewhere in the NT only in 1 Tim 4:8 (but compare Titus 1:2 and Jas 1:12). The genitive **of life** is the content of **the promise**. Because of its association with Christ, this life is eternal.

Life in Christ has both present and future aspects to it (→ 1 Tim 1:16; 4:8). As Paul will say later in 2 Tim 1:9, life in Christ has been part of the divine plan since before time began. The prophets (= Scripture) looked forward to the revelation of God's mystery in the Messiah (Rom 16:25-26). This hope was fulfilled in the life, death, and resurrection of Jesus the Christ. Those who believe in Christ become participants with him in resurrection life (Rom 6:4-5). Paul bequeaths this fundamental eschatological conviction to Timothy in this letter.

The focus of this promise is life **in Christ Jesus** (see 2 Tim 1:1, 9, 13; 2:1; 3:12, 15; 1 Tim 1:14; 3:13). This prepositional phrase describes the personal and intimate relationship with Christ that results as one submits to his lordship. It is a new way of life that begins when a person comes to Christ in submissive faith (→ 1 Tim 1:1, 14). Paul's ministry focused on this new life in Christ. He saw his earthly life as bound in Christ and lived by Christ's resources (Gal 2:20).

Verses 9-10 of 2 Tim 1 will develop further the theme of Christ as the source of **life**. At the beginning of the letter, Paul draws Timothy's attention to the most crucial aspect of his ministry: proclaiming the new life that comes when one believes in Christ. This faith statement sustained Paul through his suffering and would sustain Timothy through whatever trials lay ahead for him.

■ **2** The recipient of the letter is identified as **Timothy, my dear son**. While written to a single person, the letter ends with the plural pronoun "you all" (*hymōn*; → 4:22). This suggests that the letter was intended to be more than a private letter between two friends. What Paul writes in this letter should directly impact Timothy and indirectly those under his spiritual care who would listen in on the conversation as the letter was publically read.

Son is a term of fictive kinship (Meeks 2003, 87, 225) that shows the close relationship between Paul and Timothy. It is intensified with the adjective **dear**, or more literally, ***beloved*** (*agapōtē*). ***Beloved*** is a relational term Paul used for believers (Rom 1:7; 1 Cor 10:14; 15:58; 2 Cor 7:1; Phil 2:12; 1 Tim 6:2; and Phlm 16). Paul took Timothy under his spiritual tutelage and became his spiritual father (Acts 16:3-4; 1 Cor 4:15; Gal 4:19; Phlm 10). The second-person singular pronouns and verbs throughout the letter heighten this intimacy.

Paul calls Timothy his "beloved son" in 1 Cor 4:17 (KJV) with the rhetorical purpose of legitimizing Timothy in the eyes of the Corinthians as his authorized representative. In 1 Tim 1:1, Paul calls Timothy his "true son," possibly as a way to give credibility to Timothy in the eyes of the Ephesian church. In this second letter, however, there is no need to legitimize Timothy before them (Fee 1988, 220).

Paul may have felt some degree of responsibility for his spiritual child. One of the primary focuses of the letter is passing on to Timothy the responsibility for the mission. Timothy's sonship is based on "the promise of life . . . in Christ" (2 Tim 1:1) that joins all believers together into one family. This promise is the primary legacy Paul is leaving Timothy. The letter can be interpreted as a testamentary letter of a dying father passing on his last will and testament to his beloved child whom he leaves behind (Collins 2002, 188).

The last part of the salutation is the short greeting, **Grace, mercy and peace from God the Father and Christ Jesus our Lord**. This greeting is identical to the one in 1 Timothy. Both greetings are in the form of a prayer-wish that combines the typical Hellenistic greeting "be well" (*chairein*), stated as **grace** (*charis*), with the typical Semitic **peace** (*eirēnē*).

Added to these typical Pauline greetings is **mercy** (*eleos*), used only in these two letters. It is unknown why **mercy** is added to the greetings here. Did Paul feel that his own experience of God's mercy could serve as a paradigm of hope for Timothy (→ 1 Tim 1:13, 16)? Mercy is a divine attribute shown in God's response to his people (Jer 3:12; 9:24). In the LXX, it translates the Hebrew *ḥesed*, which generally connotes God's covenantal love and faithfulness. God looks at his people in love in spite of their rebellion and sin.

The theological significance of Paul's greeting appears in its function in the context. Each of the words occurs later in the letter. **Grace** in Christ is the basis of salvation, which gives assurance in difficulties (2 Tim 1:9; 2:1; 4:22). **Mercy** is a divine attribute that can be modeled by showing compassion to others, such as what Onesiphorus and his household did for Paul (1:16, 18). **Peace** is an attribute of "a pure heart" (2:22). Each of these is a quality Timothy should emulate. **God the Father and Christ Jesus our Lord** are the sources of these three blessings.

FROM THE TEXT

On the surface this letter begins with a simple greeting to a close friend. But it hints at the primary motives that drove Paul's ministry. Those who join Paul's ongoing mission of proclaiming the good news of Jesus Christ become part of the conversation.

Paul invites Timothy to embrace *the promise of life in Christ*. This was Paul's central message and expresses his hope for Timothy. Genuine life is defined in relationship with Christ. All of God's promises are related to Christ (2 Cor 1:20; → Titus 1:2). Everything else is but a shadow or distortion of this life (Col 2:8). The promise of life that the world gives is not one it can keep. Jesus is the source of new life (John 3:16; 14:6). This life is for what we have been created and to which we will be fully restored when Christ comes again. We can become participants with Christ in new life now by our complete devotion to him and rejection of the old life symbolized in baptism (Rom 6:4, 5, 22; 1 Tim 1:16). This same hope was to capture Timothy's devotion (1 Tim 6:12).

Paul also reminds Timothy of *the presence of Christ with us*. Paul's mission to proclaim new life in Christ led to his suffering through beatings, ridicule, hunger, shipwrecks, and various imprisonments (2 Cor 11:23-28). In the midst of all these hardships, he would not give up his call but learned to rely on God's sustaining grace in Christ (12:9). Facing possible death, he could write, "For to me, to live is Christ and to die is gain" (Phil 1:21). Jesus came to give abundant life (John 10:10), not life free from suffering (John 15:20), but life with purpose. Paul imparts to Timothy a crucial secret for those in ministry. We serve not for our own glory or out of our own abilities. Rather, God gives us all that we need in Christ to do what he calls us to do.

II. THANKSGIVING FOR SINCERE FAITH: 2 TIMOTHY 1:3-5

BEHIND THE TEXT

It is typical of Paul's letters to begin with thanksgiving or the mention of prayer. Some form of thanksgiving typically introduced ancient Hellenistic letters. Second Timothy is the only Pastoral letter that has the more typical thanksgiving section. The thanksgiving functions as the exordium, which anticipates the message of the letter. In it, Paul appeals to the emotions of his audience to build good rapport. Here he attempts to inspire Timothy to continue on the apostle's mission.

Many of the key themes of a letter are hinted at in the thanksgiving (Witherington 2006, 308; O'Brien 1977, 56-104). Paul urges Timothy to remain faithful to his call to ministry, even if it means suffering. If Paul has suffered because of his faithful proclamation of the gospel, Timothy should expect the same. They share a common faith heritage.

Two key themes are introduced in the thanksgiving section that become significant throughout the letter: (1) the shared faith heritage of Paul and Timothy and their close association in ministry, suffering, and faith, and (2) Paul's desire to see Timothy and so be mutually encouraged in ministry. The body of the letter can be divided into three major parts that deal, more or less, with these themes (Bassler 1996, 127). The thanksgiving unit continues through 2:13 where Paul reminds Timothy of their shared heritage, exhorts Timothy to follow his example, and provides positive and negative examples, ending with a call for Timothy to embrace wholeheartedly Paul's gospel of Christ.

In the next section, 2:14—3:9, Paul urges Timothy to avoid certain people and behaviors. In the last major section, 3:10—4:8, Paul again appeals to his example and urges Timothy to be faithful in preaching the gospel. The letter's conclusion begins in 4:9 with final instructions about Timothy's coming visit, restatements of the letter's central themes, and various greetings to colleagues.

This section also has the form of an encomium, showing Paul's confidence in Timothy (Fiore 1986, 23). Timothy had positive role models in his mother and grandmother. Paul warns him not to abandon his heritage. He must validate his faith and Paul's confidence by completing the tasks assigned him. Looking to the past is crucial for dealing with present challenges. Three words for remembering are used in this section (*mneian* [v 3]; *memnēmenos* [v 4]; *hypomnēsin* [v 5]).

This section also "supplies encouragement—Paul prays for [Timothy] and affirms his faith; it implies obligation with a note of warning—there is a heritage that requires loyalty, and a confidence that must be validated" (Towner 2006, 447-48).

Three themes indicate that 2 Timothy is a paraenetic letter (Johnson 2001, 340):

1. Paul serves as Timothy's example through his prayer and worship of God, his loyalty to his ancestral traditions and colleagues in the faith, and personal attributes of sincerity and affection.
2. Timothy should imitate the qualities that Paul shows through sincere faith and inherited tradition.
3. The need for growth in character is expressed as "I trust it is in you as well."

These verses are one long sentence in the Greek. It is usually divided in English translations to assist understanding. The grammar clarifies the logic. The sentence begins with the main thought, "I thank God." "God" is modified by the phrase "whom I serve." Two prepositional phrases describe how Paul has served: "as my ancestors" and "with a clear conscience." An adverbial phrase next describes when and how Paul thanks God: "as night and day

I constantly remember you in my prayers." Two participial phrases describe the circumstances of Paul's thanksgiving: **while longing to see you** and **while remembering your tears**. The reason for his longing is stated in a purpose clause: "so that I may be filled with joy." Paul finally explains the reason for his thanksgiving in v 5 with another participial phrase: **because I remember your sincere faith**. The rest of the sentence describes this faith. The whole paragraph could be simply summarized: "I thank God for your sincere faith."

IN THE TEXT

■ **3** This thanksgiving section, like 1 Tim 1:12, references Paul's experience. But in 1 Timothy, Paul calls himself the worst of sinners (1:16). Here he claims to be faithful to the traditions of his ancestors. This apparent contradiction can be resolved if the different contexts and rhetorical purposes are kept in mind. In 1 Timothy, Paul connects his past opposition to Christ to the present opposition to Christ of the false teachers in Ephesus. In 2 Timothy, he emphasizes his faithfulness to Christ as a model for Timothy to imitate. First Timothy primarily warns the community. Second Timothy is primarily an encouraging personal reminder to Timothy.

Paul's thanksgivings typically employ the verb *eucharisteō*, **I thank** (1:3; see Rom 1:8; 1 Cor 1:4; Eph 1:16; Phil 1:3; Col 1:3; 1 Thess 1:2; 2 Thess 1:3; and Phlm 4). Here, it begins with the simple statement: **I have gratitude to God**. **Gratitude** (*charin*) is the same Greek noun translated "grace" in v 2. At the basis of this word is the idea of "a beneficent disposition toward someone" (BDAG 2000, 1079). In Christian theology, human thankfulness in the form of praise and worship (as a good feeling of admiration toward God) is a result of experiencing some aspect of God's grace (through material or spiritual blessings). The reason Paul thanks God here is not explained until v 5*a*.

The verb **serve** (*latreuē*) in the LXX describes Israel's worship of God and the ministry of its priests (Strathmann 1967, 59-63). This worship is carried forward to the NT (Acts 7:7, 42; Rom 1:9, 25; Phil 3:3; Heb 8:5). The verb represents how Christians should live in total commitment and service to God (Luke 1:74; Acts 24:14; 27:23; Rom 12:1). The present tense here emphasizes service as Paul's continual, unbroken habit (Knight 1992, 366). He reflects on his heritage and how he has continued in this tradition through faithful service.

Ancestors (*progonōn*) is ambiguous (→ 1 Tim 5:4). It can refer to Paul's parents or further back to his Jewish forebears of the pre-Christian era. This statement has several effects:

First, it shows Paul's credentials as a faithful follower of God. Even as a persecutor of Christians and unwitting sinner, he was sincere in his attempts to follow God. He claims in 1 Tim 1:13 that he "acted in ignorance and unbelief," not out of spite or rebellion toward God. Ambrosiaster writes, "When Paul persecuted the church, he did it for the love of God, not out of malevolence" (*Com. Sec. Tim.*, quoted by Gorday 2000, 231). Paul was a faithful Jew and found his identity in being a Jew (Acts 24:14; Rom 9:1-5; 11:1; 2 Cor 11:22; Phil 3:4-5). He never rejected Judaism or the Law, only the Law used as the means for justification.

Second, the statement links Paul's thought and ministry to OT faith. Significantly, it shows that he was not inventing a new religion but saw following Christ as the fulfillment of the Jewish faith (Barrett 1963, 92). There was one consistent and continuous faith in God shared between the Jewish ancestors, stretching all the way back to Abraham (Rom 4), and Paul. "The fundamental human response is always toward or away from the living God" (Johnson 2001, 342). Because Paul and Timothy share in the same heritage as spiritual father and son, Timothy should have encouragement through suffering and assurance when dealing with any claims of the false teachers.

The second prepositional phrase shows that Paul serves God **with a clear conscience**. **Clear** (*kathara*) can be translated "pure" or "sincere." It modifies "conscience" in the Pastorals here and in 1 Tim 3:9. In 1 Tim 1:5, 19, "conscience" is modified by "good" (*agathos*). The construction here can have a moral sense (as in 1 Tim 1:5, 19; and 3:9), or as "undivided attention" so as to affirm that Paul was single-minded in his service to the God of his ancestors (Collins 2002, 191).

The **conscience** is the awareness of right and wrong measured against a stated or unstated standard (→ 1 Tim 1:5). In Paul's case, God is the primary judge of sincerity. Paul had been faithful to the message given to his Jewish ancestors, which is a noteworthy testimony for one near death. The false teachers who opposed Paul's mission had seared their consciences by distorting the traditions inherited from the OT and fulfilled in the gospel of Christ (1 Tim 4:2; Titus 1:15).

The final clause of this verse describes how and when Paul thanks God for Timothy: **as night and day I constantly remember you in my prayers.** This clause contains two adverbial ideas that emphasize Paul's fervency in prayer for Timothy. **Night and day** signifies the beginning and ending of the Jewish day (→ 1 Tim 5:5). This is emphasized with the second adverb **constantly** (*adialeipton*), which actually comes first in the Greek clause. Constant prayer for the churches was part of Paul's habitual practice throughout his ministry (Rom 1:9; 1 Thess 1:2-3). He was committed to intercede for Timothy, who was at the top of his prayer list. This consistent prayer kept his memory of Timothy alive. "For Paul, to think of someone is to pray for that person (Phil 1:3)" (Montague 2008, 139).

The **prayers** (*deēsesin*) here are petitions in behalf of others (→ 1 Tim 2:1). There is no specific reference to what Paul prayed for, but minimally for Timothy's continued loyalty and perseverance (Mounce 2000, 469). As part of a friendly letter, the mention of prayer expresses the warm feelings of the writer for the recipient and builds a strong bond of camaraderie between them (Towner 2006, 451). The mention of prayer also assures Timothy that God is always watching out for him. Paul's prayer assumes that God can help Timothy remain faithful to his spiritual heritage.

■ **4** This verse functions as a brief aside. It reveals Paul's pathos, the strong emotions he felt when Timothy left and still feels in his absence. The Greek sentence continues with a present participle, *longing* **to see you.** This introduces a second key idea in Paul's prayers: he hopes to be reunited with Timothy before his impending death (see 2 Tim 4:9, 21). The verb tense indicates that Paul's longing and remembering are simultaneous. **Long** (*epipothōn*) is an intense, emotionally charged desire to meet again, experienced as he recalls his relationship with Timothy (see Rom 1:11; 15:23; 2 Cor 7:7; 9:14; Phil 1:8; 2:26-28; 4:1; 1 Thess 3:6).

The reason for Paul's longing is clarified by a second participial phrase, **recalling your tears. Tears** is a synecdoche for "weeping," a state of strong sorrow. After they left each other and up until the present, Paul keeps remembering their tearful parting. This participle highlights the personal concern behind this letter. Paul does not say when or why they got separated. It could have been Paul's imprisonment or earlier trial. If the Pastorals can be integrated into the history recorded in Acts (→ Introduction), there were tears expressed in Ephesus at Paul's departure (Acts 20:37; Kelly 1963, 156; Hanson 1982, 119-20). Timothy was likely present at that time (20:4-6). If Timothy is still in Ephesus, there remains a great distance between him and Paul in Rome.

The very personal reason for Paul's longing is expressed in a purpose clause: **so that I may be filled with joy.** From Paul's perspective, **joy** answers the **tears** from the previous clause. The implied source of this joy is the occasion of their reunion. **Joy** (*charas*) is a natural human response when longings are fulfilled.

> It is a state more than a feeling, the residue of the presence of the Spirit that is compatible even with conditions of suffering and affliction (Rom 14:17; 15:13, 32; 2 Cor 1:15, 24; 7:4, 13; 8:2; Gal 5:22; Phil 1:4, 25; 2:2, 29; 4:1; Col 1:11; 1 Thess 1:6; 2:19, 20; 3:9; Phlm 7). (Johnson 2001, 338)

Paul's statement could have the effect of creating a mutual longing in Timothy to see him, leading to a greater urgency in carrying out Paul's directions in the letter.

■ **5** This verse completes the Greek sentence that began in v 3. It offers the reason for Paul's thanksgiving in a third participial phrase: *I give* **thanks to**

God . . . because I am reminded of your sincere faith. Timothy's faith is the occasion of thanksgiving. The aorist passive participle may imply that Paul had recently received news about Timothy, perhaps from Onesiphorus (1:16) or a letter from Timothy (Mounce 2000, 470).

Sincere [*anypokriotou*] **faith** is unhypocritical, genuine, committed, and authentic (→ 1 Tim 1:5; see Rom 12:9). Timothy has some weaknesses, but faith is not one of them. Paul has been reminded of "Timothy's continual disposition of belief in Christ" (Towner 2006, 453-54). Timothy did not waver in his core belief in Christ, even when faced with false teachers, persecution, and isolation. In this way, he imitated Paul's own perseverance through trials. This description distinguishes Timothy from the opponents (2 Tim 2:17-18), who had departed from the faith (like Demas [4:10]). This verse subtly reminds Timothy of who he is as a believer in Christ.

Paul next draws Timothy's attention to his own faith heritage handed down from his **grandmother Lois** and **mother Eunice**. This is the only mention of Lois in the NT. We know little about either woman. Eunice was a Jewish believer in Christ, married to an uncircumcised Greek (Acts 16:1-3). Children of Jewish women with Gentile fathers were considered Jewish unless the women moved to Gentile territory. They were then considered Gentile. This apparently compelled Paul to circumcise Timothy to confirm his Jewish identity (Cohen 1986, 266). Timothy learned the Scriptures as a child (2 Tim 3:15). But we are not told from whom, presumably Lois and Eunice.

Faith . . . lived in these influential women. As a result, Timothy shared in Paul's Jewish faith heritage. At some point, he and his family became Christian believers, presumably before they met Paul on his journey to Lystra (Acts 16). The inceptive force of the aorist verb **lived** "suggests that this state had a beginning, and the reader is invited to see God as the initial cause" (Towner 2006, 454). Paul's intimate knowledge of Timothy's family is confirmed with the last statement **and, I am persuaded, now lives in you also**. Paul has seen evidence of faith in Timothy's life and has strong confidence in the sincerity he has seen there.

FROM THE TEXT

The opening of this letter reveals the significance of spiritual heritage. Timothy had a rich heritage passed on from his mother and grandmother and influenced by his on-going relationship with Paul. This heritage was not new but stretched back to Paul's ancestors in the Old Testament. Looking to the past should compel Timothy into the future. It should create a sense of obligation to be a full participant in God's unfolding plan.

Prayer is a critical means for passing on the faith. Paul's constant prayers kept his relationship with Timothy fresh and relevant even though they were separated by great distance. It was Paul's way of life and kept him connected with his churches. He expected the churches to model him in prayer (Rom 12:12; Eph 6:18; Phil 4:6; Col 4:2; 1 Thess 5:17). There is power in earnest and consistent prayer. This power comes not from the person praying but from the Holy Spirit (→ 2 Tim 1:6-7, 14). Paul learned that when nothing else in life is dependable, God is (2 Cor 4:16-18). When Paul could not be present with his friends and colleagues, he knew God was there and would offer encouragement through the Holy Spirit (Rom 15:13). Paul did not want Timothy to lose heart, so he went to God in Timothy's behalf.

Timothy models someone who *embraced this spiritual heritage with sincere faith.* One of the purposes of this letter is to encourage Timothy on his own spiritual journey. The stresses of life, both purposeful and accidental, can challenge the depths of one's faith. Timothy had his own challenges. Hardships can either deplete one's hope and lead to doubt or cause one to rely more on God (see Rom 3:3-5). Chrysostom observed, "Dangers in this life . . . make us ready for eternal life" (*Hom. 2 Tim.* 1, quoted by Gorday 2000, 230).

Finally, Paul reminds Timothy of *the importance of handing on this spiritual heritage.* Timothy's faith had its roots in his mother and grandmother. In some way and at some time, Timothy embraced this faith as his own. "To be brought up in the fear of God is a great blessing; and a truly religious education is an advantage of infinite worth" (Clarke 1831, 642). Training up the next generation was at the core of Israel's faith (Deut 6:4-9). The church faces the same challenge of passing on the faith to its youth today. In some parts of the world, young people are leaving the church in droves. The issues are complex, but at the center of it all is the need for young people to embrace their faith heritage as their own. With rapidly shifting cultures, it is important to remember that "a second- or third-hand faith, good though it is, is neither personal nor powerful" (Batstone 2004, 414).

III. EXHORTATION FOR TIMOTHY TO EMBRACE PAUL'S WAY: 2 TIMOTHY 1:6—2:13

A. Paul as a Model of Faithfulness (1:6-14)

BEHIND THE TEXT

The body of the letter begins with v 6, which functions as the propositio, the main point. Paul writes to make sure Timothy's faith is strong and that he continues in his ministry. Paul is imprisoned and limited in what he can do. He builds on their mutual faith and the bond of their relationship. Between the exhortations, he provides the theological bases that should guide Timothy's response.

- Key idea, expressed as an indirect command: Timothy is to renew the work of the Holy Spirit in his life (v 6).
- Theological basis: God's Spirit gives power, love, and self-discipline (v 7).
- Restatement of the thesis and practical application: Do not be ashamed of the gospel; suffer for it (v 8).

- Restatement of the theological basis: Paul gives the contents of the gospel at the strategic center of this section, forming a rough chiasm (vv 9-10).
- Positive example: Paul presents himself as a positive example for Timothy (vv 11-12).
- Exhortation based on the theology and example: Timothy is to emulate Paul (see v 7; vv 13-14).
- Antithesis: Examples of the opposite behavior are given, with the implied warning not to follow them (v 15).
- Contrasting positive example: The section ends with another positive example of traits to imitate (vv 16-18).

1. Let the Breath of God Inflame You (1:6-7)

IN THE TEXT

■ **6** Paul begins the body of the letter by offering a conclusion arising from the introduction to the letter in vv 3-5: **for this reason.** The prepositional phrase functions as a conjunction looking back to the memories of the faith heritage Paul and Timothy shared. The reason Paul writes is because not everything was going well for either him or Timothy. He faced possible execution; Timothy, potential discouragement in his mission.

This letter is a gentle reminder about an important matter that "draws on shared knowledge and experience and implies that past commitments are still in effect" (Towner 2006, 457). Paul attempts to refresh Timothy's memory about the main reason for their mission. This will encourage both Paul, as he sits in prison, and Timothy, as he faces opposition.

The first indirect exhortation of the letter comes as an infinitive: **I remind you to fan into flame the gift of God.** The infinitive *anazōpyrein* means to rekindle, to reignite, or to set aflame again. The embers of a fire can be reignited by blowing air on them. Here, as in Gen 45:27, the word takes a more figurative sense of "revive" (see also 1 Macc 13:7).

We can only guess what **the gift of God** was that Timothy had received. The word **gift** (*charisma*) is a particularly Pauline word (except 1 Pet 4:10; see Rom 1:11; 12:6; 1 Cor 1:7; 7:7; 12:4, 9, 28, 30-31). It is related to the word "grace" (*charis*). It comes as a result of what God has done in Christ. "The gift is accordingly an inward grace which affects the personality and manifests itself in outward actions" (Marshall 1999, 697). First Corinthians 12 especially points out that "spiritual gifts" come through the Holy Spirit for the purpose of building up the church (vv 4-11).

The gift mentioned here is singular and has the article. So Paul seems to have a particular gift in mind. The genitive **of God** is likely subjective: God is the source of the gift—*the gift you received from God*. Interpreters have offered three major options for what this gift was (Towner 2006, 458):

1. Timothy's ordination and office, which gave him the authority and ability to carry out his mission.
2. The various abilities God gave Timothy for ministry, his "spiritual gifts."
3. The Holy Spirit.

Of these options, the last is more likely, based on the context and biblical theology. This partially depends on how one interprets "spirit" in v 7 (→). Verse 7 starts with the statement, "God gave," connecting v 7 with the gift Timothy received at an earlier point. This gift is internal, **which is in you.** Thus, it is spiritual in some way. Verse 14 further hints that this gift was related to the Holy Spirit: Timothy should "guard . . . the deposit . . . with the help of the Holy Spirit who lives in us." The presence of the indwelling Spirit will enable Timothy to carry out his mission and is his primary requirement. Any other "spiritual gift" is derived from the Spirit. Thus, the clearest option is that the gift was not the gift of ministry but its source—the Holy Spirit (Fee 1994, 787).

Paul wants Timothy to depend fully on the Spirit and allow him to empower his mission. God's gifts must always be used to be realized. Chrysostom wrote,

> For it requires much zeal to stir up the gift of God. As fire requires fuel, so grace requires our alacrity, that it may be ever fervent. . . . For this grace it is in our power to kindle or to extinguish; wherefore he elsewhere says, "Quench not the Spirit" [1 Thess 5:19]. For by sloth and carelessness it is quenched, and by watchfulness and diligence it is kept alive. (*Hom. 2 Tim.* 1)

If the fire of the Spirit can be quenched, it can also be fanned into flames (Fee 1994, 787).

Since the earliest days of the church, fire has been a symbol of the presence of the Holy Spirit (Matt 3:11; Luke 3:16; Acts 2:3-4, 19). The present tense of the verb shows that ongoing effort is needed to keep the fire burning. Timothy's faith is not waning, nor is he tempted to shrink back from his duty. But positive reinforcement to continue on in the right way is always appropriate. "Just because people are encouraged by someone does not mean that they are failing. It can mean that they are being encouraged to continue despite the pressure" (Mounce 2000, 476). God had done his part of supplying the gift of his presence and grace in Timothy; Timothy needed to do his part in cooperation with the Holy Spirit.

The gift of God was confirmed in Timothy **through the laying on of my hands.** "Paul knows that Timothy has the gift within him (*en soi*) because he was one of the instruments through whom God bestowed it, and therefore he can rightly call on him to stir it up" (Knight 1992, 371). Paul encourages Timothy to recall their early days together in Lystra (Acts 16:1-5) when he confirmed Timothy's faith as he did that of the Ephesian elders (19:1-6).

Scholars debate the relationship between Paul laying his hands on Timothy here and the elders doing the same (→ 1 Tim 4:14). Paul probably condenses the occasion and emphasizes selected aspects of it here for rhetorical purposes. The two events may be actually the same event described differently.

One of the functions of the laying on of hands in the early church was as a symbol of receiving the Holy Spirit (Acts 8:17-18; 9:12, 17; 19:6; → 1 Tim 4:14). Whether one event or two, Paul assumes Timothy knows exactly what he means and will recall this shared experience.

■ **7** The rhetoric shifts in this verse by contrasting what God does and does not give believers. **For** (*gar*) introduces Paul's explanation of the personal benefits of the gift of the Holy Spirit (→ 2 Tim 1:6). How should we translate *pneuma* here, without the Greek article? The NIV[84], KJV, RSV, NRSV, ESV, and other translations prefer "spirit," implying that Paul is referring to a human disposition or character quality (as in Rom 8:15; 11:8; 1 Cor 4:21; 2 Cor 4:13; Gal 6:1; Phil 1:27). But the conjunction **for**, connecting vv 6 and 7, implies that the gift is the Holy Spirit. Thus, the 2011 NIV prefers **Spirit**. This change recognizes the Holy Spirit as God's foremost gift and the focus of this paragraph.

The Holy Spirit **does not make us timid** (*deilias*, only here in the NT). Timidity may refer to a "lack of mental or moral strength" shown as "cowardice" (BDAG 2000, 215). In the LXX (Ps 55(LXX 54):5; Sir 4:17; 1 Macc 4:32; 2 Macc 3:24; 4 Macc 6:20; and others), it can mean to be terrified. It is a "terror that overtakes the fearful in extreme difficulty" (Fee 1988, 227).

Earlier commentators assumed Timothy was a weak person and that Paul challenges him here to break out of his shyness. But there is little exegetical support for this (Hutson 1997). Rather, Paul appeals to Timothy's sense of shame. Acts and Paul's letters suggest that Timothy was actually a strong personality. He dealt successfully with a number of difficult churches and situations, most notably in Corinth.

Nevertheless, potential suffering lay ahead for Timothy in dealing with the crisis in Ephesus. This could cause fear to arise, even in an otherwise strong person (see 1 Cor 16:10). The word **timid** is simply a foil to contrast with **power** in the next phrase (Mounce 2000, 478-79). Paul's ultimate goal is not to shame Timothy but to encourage him.

The plural **us** makes Paul's statement far more proverbial than an indictment on Timothy's personality type. What he recommends here can apply to all believers who suffer because of their faith (→ 2 Tim 3:12).

The next phrase sharply contrasts (*alla*) with the negative foil. The focus is now on what the Holy Spirit actually **gives us**, not on what he does not give. The three positive endowments are **power, love and self-discipline**. These constitute Paul's key point and the intended application to Timothy's life (→ v 8). Each of these three descriptions is governed by **Spirit** in the earlier clause.

The **power** (*dynameōs*) of the indwelling Spirit helps believers fulfill God's purposes for them. The Spirit provides the wherewithal for believers to face suffering with courage (vv 8, 12). He enables them to live lives of godliness (3:15). He endows them with a knowledge of the will of God and how to proclaim it (1 Cor 2:4-5; 4:19-21; 1 Thess 1:5). He gives them the ability to live holy lives (Rom 14:17-18). He inspires hope for the future (Rom 15:13). He performs miracles through them (Rom 15:19). He sustains them with inner strength from knowing the love of Christ (Eph 3:16, 20). Jesus promised his followers the power of the Spirit (Acts 1:4-5, 8). His presence sustained Paul throughout his ministry and could do the same for Timothy.

The Spirit also gives **love** (*agapēs*). The gift of the Spirit validates to believers that God loves them without reservation and thereby enables them, in turn, to love others unconditionally (Rom 5:1-8). **Love** holds the key central position in this short list. It is the firstfruit of the Spirit from which all others derive (1 Cor 12:31—14:1; Gal 5:22-23). Love is an outward expression that affects relationships with others (Gal 5:13). Loves arises from faith in Christ (Gal 5:6). It is evidenced through obedience to his commands (John 15:10, 12). Love should characterize Timothy's approach to the challenges in his ministry (→ 1 Tim 1:5; 2 Tim 2:13, 22).

Finally, the Spirit enables **self-discipline** (*sōphronismou*, only here in the NT, but with cognates in the other Pastoral letters—*sōphroneō* [Titus 2:6]; *sōphronōs* [Titus 2:12]; *sōphronizō* [Titus 2:4]; *sōphrosynē* [1 Tim 2:9, 15]; *sōphrōn* [1 Tim 3:2; Titus 1:8; 2:2, 5]). It has the broad sense of right moral thinking. It refers to controlling one's actions by controlling one's thoughts. It involves prudence, balance, wisdom, and clear thinking. Timothy needs the Spirit's help as he stands firm for the gospel against increasing opposition.

When everything is coming unglued, this quality of "levelheadedness" will keep the Christian focused calmly on the power and love that the Spirit provides, and so it makes perseverance in life and ministry possible. (Towner 1994, 161)

Such thinking comes in the response of faithful obedience to the Spirit.

The Opponents' View of the Spirit

Towner (1994, 159) offers three points that may have characterized the faulty understanding of the Holy Spirit held by the opponents. This seems to have a modern counterpart in the "triumphalism" or "health and wealth gospel" of today:

For them (1) "Spirit" meant power in the sense of the completion of their spiritual life; (2) the gift of the Spirit at conversion meant transfer (resurrection) from this fallen world to a spiritual dimension of final triumph; and consequently (3) the Holy Spirit had very little to do with suffering and struggling, things that pertain to the physical, bodily existence. Suffering and struggling may have been viewed as indications of unspirituality.

2. Paul's Assurance in the Gospel (1:8-12)

■ **8** After the proverbial statement of 2 Tim 1:7, Paul speaks directly to Timothy in this crucial, two-part imperative. The next imperative comes in v 13, forming an inclusio (envelope structure) for vv 8-12. These five verses represent one long sentence of seventy-nine words in Greek.

So (*oun*) applies the theology of v 7 to Timothy's situation. The answer to any fear that Timothy may have is answered by the presence of the Holy Spirit (see Rom 8:15). The verse has two parts:

The first gives the negative command: **Do not be ashamed**. Honor and shame were significant social forces in the first century and a key motivation for certain types of behavior (→ 1 Tim 5:7). Honor and shame indicated the worth of a person. People would avoid almost anything that would shame them in the eyes of others. Paul uses an intense form of the word **shame** here (*epaischynthēs*). Two things could potentially cause Timothy shame, especially before unbelievers.

(*a*) **The testimony about our Lord** might cause Timothy to be ashamed. **Lord** is used from this point on in the letter without designation, clearly referring to Christ Jesus (→ 2 Tim 1:2; Knight 1992, 372). There are two ways to interpret the genitive *tou kyriou* (*of the Lord*). A subjective genitive would make the testimony the one Jesus gave. This is possible, but the earthly ministry of Jesus does not seem to be Paul's concern here (as it is in 1 Tim 6:13). The NIV interprets the genitive as objective—the testimony is *about* Jesus (as in 1 Tim 2:6). This would make it the equivalent of the gospel, which God called Timothy to preach.

The gospel was shameful in the eyes of the world. Its message focused on a condemned man, who died on a Roman cross—one of the most shameful forms of execution in that time. That he rose again was unbelievable. Paul acknowledged that this was "a stumbling block to Jews and foolishness to Gentiles" (1 Cor 1:23; Hengel 1977). He was confident, however, because the gospel contained the very "power of God that brings salvation" (Rom 1:16). He does not want Timothy to be ashamed of this message either since "shame is a feeling which leads to action which hides witness" (Marshall 1999, 703). Timothy has the choice of honor before God or shame before people (Mark 8:38).

(*b*) Paul, the Lord's **prisoner**, should not cause Timothy to be ashamed. Paul was bound in a Roman prison because of his testimony for the Lord. He was not a prisoner of Rome but of Christ. Rome had no control over him. Human chains kept him in custody, because of his "attachment" to Christ. But he was free in his spirit. The only prison that held him was his commitment to Christ (Eph 3:1; 4:1; Phlm 9). The Roman judicial system did not use imprisonment as a form of punishment but for those awaiting trial (2 Tim 4:16) or execution (4:6-8) (Collins 2002, 199). Paul had little hope of release. He bore the shameful stigma of a condemned criminal.

Prisoner (*desmion*) is a term often used for a chained criminal (see Acts 16:26; 20:23; 23:29; 26:29, 31). Paul was not ashamed of his imprisonment for Christ (Phil 1:20). Even though Timothy was not in prison, his close association with Paul could lead to shame in the eyes of the false teachers and those who were abandoning Paul and his mission. To be ashamed of Paul would be the same as being ashamed of the gospel.

"Faithfulness to Christ makes no sense apart from faithfulness to those appointed by him and suffering for him (1:11-12)" (Towner 2006, 465). The paradox of the gospel and the irony of Paul's rhetoric should lead Timothy to bold proclamation and courageous leadership. The letter attempts to encourage Timothy to stay true to the gospel even to the point of suffering like Paul.

The second imperative was the positive alternative to being **ashamed**. Paul links Timothy to his own situation with the invitation: **Rather, join with me in suffering for the gospel**. The verb here, *synkakopathēson*, is unique and may have been coined by Paul for this letter (again in 2 Tim 2:3). It is a compound of the preposition "together with" (*syn*) followed by "bad" (*kakos*) "suffering" (*pathos*). Suffering alone is difficult; suffering with others provides strength.

Preaching the gospel often led to suffering for early Christians (Rom 8:17; 2 Cor 4:7-15; Phil 1:12, 29; Col 1:24; 1 Thess 1:6; 2:14; 3:4; 2 Tim 2:9; 4:5). Paul invites Timothy to participate in the paradox of the cross. "To believe in the cross and to preach the cross is to share in its shame—and its power" (Montague 2008, 145).

Paul believed his suffering led to a deeper understanding of Christ's resurrection power (Phil 3:10). **For the gospel** (*tōi euangeliōi*) is a dative of advantage and shows for what Timothy should suffer. If he embraces the message of the cross, Timothy must be prepared to accept the scorn that comes with it (→ 2 Tim 4:5).

Timothy could endure suffering **by the power of God**. The word **power** here refers back to the "gift" in v 6. The power God will give Timothy is the gift of the presence of the Holy Spirit. "Timothy can rely upon 'God's power' because God's powerful Spirit is in him to give him that power" (Knight 1992, 373). In this verse, Paul points out two characteristics of suffering: (1) we are not alone in our suffering for the gospel because other believers face the same challenges; (2) we have the power of God with us through the indwelling Holy

Spirit. Suffering leads to stronger character, faith, and witness. "The ability to suffer for the sake of the gospel is a gift from God" (Collins 2002, 199).

Suffering for Being a Christian

Jesus warned his disciples that they would suffer for being his followers (Matt 5:11-12; Mark 13:5-23; John 15:18-20). It did not take long for the early church to begin to experience persecution (Acts 4). Suffering is inevitable for followers of Christ because we live in a fallen, evil world where flesh and the Spirit battle for allegiance (Rom 8:17; Phil 1:29-30). The darkness does not like to be exposed by the light and will attempt to put it out (John 3:19-20).

Suffering is a major theme in Paul's letters, not because he was a hypochondriac but partially because he experienced suffering repeatedly in his ministry (1 Cor 2:1-5; 4:9; 2 Cor 11:23-29; Gal 6:17; Phil 1:30). The risen Jesus had predicted Paul would suffer for his sake at the time of Saul's conversion call (Acts 9:16). Through suffering Paul experienced God's grace on a deeper level (2 Cor 12:9-10). It helped him share Christ's own suffering and resurrection (2 Cor 2:14; 4:11). His constant suffering left him feeling, "I die every day" (1 Cor 15:31 NIV[84]). He came to know Christ more deeply by suffering for him (Phil 3:10-11). He saw his suffering as an extension of the gospel that helped others come to know the depth of God's grace (Col 1:24). He called the early church to join him in suffering out of love for others (1 Cor 9:1-27).

Do we share Paul's unswerving conviction that God is working in all things to bring us to Christlikeness? Because we have God's grace to sustain us, we can approach suffering with joy because we know "all things God works for [our] good" (Rom 8:28).

■ **9** Verses 9 and 10 of 2 Tim 1 simply state the kerygma in the form of praise prompted by the appeal concluding v 8 and its mention of "the power of God." The rhetorical purpose is to lay a theological foundation from which Timothy can find encouragement. It is the common heritage he and Paul share. As Paul often does (→ 1 Tim 1:17), he bursts forth in hymnic language as he reflects on God's power, love, and grace.

These verses describe the power of God upon which Timothy can rely to get through the challenges he faces in his ministry. Although the verses have a hymnic quality to them, the grammar flows smoothly in continuation of the sentence begun in 2 Tim 1:8. The thought and vocabulary is fully Pauline, and there is no reason to assume that Paul is quoting a hymn here (Mounce 2000, 475, 481).

The verse begins with two attributive participles modifying "God" (v 8). Both aorist participles point to action prior to the "suffering" of v 8. God **saved** and **called** Timothy in the past (v 9). Therefore, Timothy already has received the resources to endure any suffering he may face (v 8). The participles point to the grace given at a point in history through Christ Jesus (v 10). The NIV changes the participles into finite verbs to make the English easier to understand.

First, **he has saved us** recalls one of the primary messages of 1 Timothy (→ 1 Tim 1:1, 15). Eternal life, the result of Christ's saving activity, ought to be Timothy's primary motivator (→ 1 Tim 6:12). The salvation of all people is the goal of preaching the gospel (→ 1 Tim 2:3-7; Rom 10:9-15; 1 Cor 1:21).

Second, he has "called us to a holy calling" (ESV). The word "call" is used twice, in the participle *kalesantos* and the cognate dative noun *klēsei* (see Rom 8:30; 9:12, 24; 1 Cor 1:9; Gal 1:6; 5:8; 1 Thess 5:24). God's call and purpose for us is our transformation into Christlikeness (Rom 8:28-30). The phrase "holy [*hagia*] calling" can be interpreted as a dative of means, "with a holy calling" (NASB, NRSV) or a dative of interest, **to a holy life**. Perhaps, Paul intended both possibilities.

The sequence Paul uses here is noteworthy. Holiness is the outflow of salvation. God through his Holy Spirit calls all people to holiness in its full relational and ethical meanings (Rom 1:7; 1 Cor 1:2; Eph 1:3-6; 1 Thess 4:7). Those who respond to this call experience the power of God's transforming grace. God calls believers to participate in his character of holiness (1 Pet 1:15-16; 2 Pet 1:3-4). Thus, "God's call is highly ethical: God does not just call believers; he calls them toward himself, toward holiness" (Mounce 2000, 482). "God has called us *to a holy life* because he himself is holy. His activities partake of his own character" (Guthrie 1990, 146).

Paul's next point is that God's salvation and call to holiness extend to all his people. This gift of grace does not depend on anything we do:

> "Not according to our works
>
> but
>
> according to his own purpose and grace." (KJV, NASB)

The first phrase is stated most succinctly in Eph 2:9. This may be a subtle challenge to any thought that we can make ourselves right with God by doing what the Law requires (see Romans and Galatians). Paul understood firsthand the futility of trying to overcome the power of sin through human effort (Rom 7:7-25). The only means of justification is relying on God's gift of grace through Jesus Christ (→ Titus 3:5). Human effort (*erga*) cannot save because no one can fulfill the Law perfectly. Everyone sins and therefore needs a Savior (Rom 3:23-24).

The second phrase highlights God's sovereignty and plan of redemption in Christ. Salvation and holiness come as a result of God's own purpose. This takes the pressure off of trying to earn salvation and places it with the author of salvation. The positive statement is the counterpart to the negative statement. **Purpose** (*prothesin*) refers to God's plan (BDAG 2000, 869), which has existed since **before the beginning of time.**

This phrase is significant theologically. This Semitic idiom literally could be read as *before times eternal*. The NASB captures the idea well: "from all eternity." *Chronos* means an expanse or period of time, and the intended meaning is this present age beginning with Gen 1:1 (Eph 1:4). God has always existed, dwelling in the realm of eternity (Eph 3:11; Titus 1:2; 1 Pet 1:20; Marshall 1999, 706). This veiled reference to eternity stands in contrast to the present moment—"now" of v 10. **Grace** focuses God's eternal plan on the context of salvation and counters the idea that there is something we can do to earn our salvation. It is all a gift, priceless but free.

The fulfillment of God's purpose came in the grace that **was given us in Christ Jesus** (see Eph 3:11) This phrase is introduced by another attributive aorist participle (*dotheisan*). It could refer to **purpose** or **grace** or both. Since we experience God's **purpose** in his **grace**, it more likely modifies **grace**. The participle is passive; God is the unnamed agent.

The participle's aorist tense points to the historical appearance of Christ mentioned in v 10. God's eternal plan became a reality in this present age; it will be completed at Christ's second coming. The eternal, divine plan entered history as the preexistent Christ came "at just the right time" (Rom 5:6; Marshall 1999, 707). The once hidden mystery of God has been revealed in time. Paul was one of God's key agents, called to make this mystery known (Rom 16:25-26; Titus 1:2-3).

God's saving plan came to us **in Christ Jesus**. Christ is the source of all grace (1 Cor 1:4; Eph 2:6-7). Almost every one of Paul's benedictions in his letters concludes with a statement of "the grace of our Lord Jesus Christ." This phrase should be interpreted as more than simply instrumental: Christ is the way God revealed his plan. It borders on Paul's mystical idea of new existence in intimate fellowship with Christ (→ 1 Tim 1:14). This transformative grace is not simply objective, resolving enmity between God and humanity (2 Cor 5:19). It is internal and spiritual, experienced existentially through the indwelling Spirit of Christ who transforms believers into Christ's likeness (Rom 8:9-13; 2 Cor 3:18).

In the background of this profound theological claim stands Paul's encouragement to Timothy. Paul found his source of strength in knowing Christ (Phil 1:21; 3:8-11). He now places the responsibility on Timothy to respond in similar faith. Although salvation is a gift, people must act on the gift and receive it in faithful obedience shown in holy living. The theology in this verse provides the certainty of victory through suffering.

Reading of Verse 9 as a Wesleyan vs. a Calvinist

Verse 9 poses some theological challenges for two major branches of Protestantism. This verse has been used to support the Augustinian/Calvinistic view of predestination, unmerited grace, election, and eternal security. John Calvin wrote, "By this confession we deprive man of all righteousness, even to the slightest particle" (*Institutes of the Christian Religion* 3.14.5, cited by Twomey 2009, 123).

The logic is that since God had salvation in Christ already planned before creation, and since we can only be saved by his grace, then those who are saved are saved by God's will alone. God "elects" or "predestines" those who will be saved arbitrarily—as he sees fit. Since God saves, those he saves he will keep securely his for eternity. If there is any good in a person, it comes because of God's grace. Calvin preached several sermons based on this passage in which he laid out his doctrine (1830, 34-59).

John Wesley shared much with Calvin at this point but differed in a significant way. Toward the end of his life, Wesley wrote to John Newton on May 14, 1765, that his understanding of justification came within a "hair's breadth" of Calvin. Like Calvin, Wesley taught that God is the one who initiates salvation and that people are totally unable to save themselves because of the depravity of sin. It is God through grace who enables us to choose to put our faith in him. Wesley wrote (1986, 7:285),

> Wherein may we come to the very edge of Calvinism?
> A. (1) By ascribing all good to the free grace of God.
> (2) In denying all natural free-will, and all power antecedent to grace. And
> (3) In excluding all merit from man, even from what he has or does by the grace of God.

Although there are similarities, there are also significant differences in Wesley's understanding of grace. Wesley replaced Calvin's doctrine of "predestination" with "prevenient grace." God's grace is universal to all, not just to some. God reaches out to all people and wants all people to be saved (2 Pet 3:9). This grace can be resisted, if there is no response of faith. In this sense, God leaves it up to the individual whether or not to choose Christ. Wesley had an optimism that God's grace can change anyone, even the worst of sinners like Paul (1 Tim 1:15-16), not just the elect. Wesley wrote (1986, 6:509, 512),

> Allowing that all the souls of men are dead in sin by nature, this excuses none, seeing no man is in a mere state of nature. There is no man, unless he has quenched the Spirit, that is totally void of the grace of God. No man living is devoid of what is vulgarly called natural conscience. But this is not natural; it is more properly termed preventing grace. . . . So that no man sins because he hath not grace, but because he doth not use the grace he hath.

■ **10** This verse shifts from eternity to the realm of time and connects God's eternal plan with the historical event of the appearance of Christ. A second participle describes the "grace" of v 9: This grace **has now been revealed** (*phanerōtheisan*). Like the first participle, "given," this second one is also passive, with God as the unnamed actor. Its aorist tense likewise points to the historical Jesus (→ v 9).

The temporal indicator **now** corresponds to the reference to eternity in v 9, expressing the relevance of the Christ event in Paul's thinking. The new age in Christ began with his resurrection from the dead. All of time and eternity has been altered because of it (→ 1 Tim 3:16; Titus 1:3).

1:10

Specifically, God's plan was fulfilled **through the appearing of our Savior, Christ Jesus**. Salvation is attributed to both God and Christ Jesus frequently in the Pastorals (→ 1 Tim 1:1; 2:3; 4:10; Titus 1:3, 4; 2:10, 13; 3:4, 6; see also Eph 5:23; Phil 3:20).

God desires all people to be saved and planned to show his grace through the "one mediator . . . , the man Christ Jesus" (→ 1 Tim 2:5). Paul expresses that idea here with the word **appearing** (*epiphaneias*), which he uses for the coming of Christ either in the incarnation (Titus 3:4) or second coming (1 Tim 6:14; 2 Tim 4:1, 8; Titus 2:13). This passage refers to what God *has done*. So the appearance here refers to Christ's earthly life, death, and resurrection, which should not be separated. Two parallel participles describe two ways Christ's first coming has altered the human situation.

The first participle, **destroyed,** from the root verb *katargeō*, means make something ineffective or powerless (BDAG 2000, 525 s.v. 2). Christ conquered the power of sin and death through his resurrection. Because he has been raised from the dead, all those who put their trust in him will also be raised (1 Cor 15:20-23). Death still remains as the last enemy every person must face (Heb 9:27), but it will be finally vanquished when Christ comes a second time (1 Cor 15:24-26).

Paul's point here is that believers can now be confident in their battle against the effects of death. Christ has already destroyed death in three ways: (1) the sting and pain of death beyond the grave (1 Cor 15:54-56); (2) death as the punishment for sin (Rom 5:12) since sin has been forgiven (Rom 8:1); and (3) spiritual death as the separation from God with the hope of eternal life (2 Tim 1:10*b*; Mounce 2000, 484).

The two aorist participles point back to Christ's resurrection from the dead. Although the future victory is certain, we continue to live in this "already but not yet" tension. Suffering shows that death is still a reality. Death reminds us that this age is not over. But the presence of the Holy Spirit in our lives guarantees that the new age in Christ has begun. He gives us confidence that we are "in Christ" and participants now in the coming age of resurrection.

In its original historical context, this affirmation is a strong testimony of faith from one facing execution in the near future (4:6-9). Paul's confidence in the gospel was to encourage Timothy to be bold, preaching the gospel even if it meant suffering or death.

The Suffering and Martyrdom of Timothy

The NT does not tell the fate of Timothy. According to Heb 13:23, he was imprisoned and released. But it offers no information about where or when. Church tradition has him returning to Ephesus and becoming the first bishop there. Supposedly, ca. AD 97, when Timothy was eighty years old, he was stoned to death by a mob because he opposed a pagan festival in honor of the goddess Diana.

In the fourth century, his relics were moved to the Church of the Holy Apostles in Constantinople. Today, he is venerated on January 22 by the Eastern Orthodox Church, on January 24 by the Roman Catholic Church and the Lutheran Church-Missouri Synod, and on January 26 by the Evangelical Lutheran and Episcopal Churches.

By conquering death (*katargēsantos*, an instrumental reading of the first participle), Christ **has brought life and immortality to light through the gospel** (taking the second participle *phōtisantos* as the result of the first). This statement is God's answer to the darkness of death. The root verb (*phōtizō*) of the second participle is used for shining a light or revealing something. Christ has revealed what already existed. "This life is not created by Christ. Rather, it already exists in the divine sphere, and what Christ does is to reveal its existence and the possibility of sharing in it" (Marshall 1999, 708).

The life Christ revealed is God's immortal life, which is eternal life. God extends his eternal existence, which stands outside of death to all willing to accept his free offer of salvation. Believers begin to experience this life now. It is "a present experience of the eschatological existence promised to the believers through Jesus Christ" (Mounce 2000, 485).

This new life is captured with the word **immortality** (*aphtharsian*; "imperishable" in 1 Cor 15:42, 50, 53-54). This is a different word than the one translated "immortal" in 1 Tim 6:16 (*athanasian*). It describes something not subject to decay, and thus immortal. Everything in this world is subject to the decay of death and is renewed only because of God's sustaining grace in Christ (Col 1:17). "Through Christ God reveals the existence of the alternative reality and opens it up as a human possibility (Titus 1:2-3)" (Towner 2006, 472-73). The Greek comparative *men . . . de* construction indicates that "death is conquered by death, eternal life is unveiled in resurrection" (Towner 1989, 98).

The new existence Christ made possible is offered **through the gospel**. The "good news" of Jesus' victory points the way to new life in him. "It is 'through the gospel' that the past event obtains (and retains) its present relevance" (Towner 1989, 99). God has chosen to reveal his eternal plan through what appears to be weak and foolish from the world's perspective, but actually reveals his power and wisdom (1 Cor 1:23-24). Paul believed preaching the gospel demonstrated the Spirit's power, not because of rhetoric (1 Cor 2:4-5), but because of changed lives (2 Cor 3:2-3).

Here Paul explains the reason why Timothy should not be intimidated or discouraged because of suffering. The appropriate response to this good news is allegiance and faithfulness. Paul models this response in vv 11-12.

■ **11** This verse is grammatically dependent upon v 10. It continues the Greek sentence that began with v 8. It refers back to the "gospel" mentioned at the close of v 10.

295

Paul was divinely appointed to preach the gospel (→ 1 Tim 1:12). The subject pronoun I (*egō*) is emphatic in Greek, since Paul is now setting himself before Timothy as an example of faithfulness. He gives three descriptions of his mission of spreading the good news. All three are given in the same order in 1 Tim 2:7 (→). The Greek article is missing with each of these descriptions, broadening the application—Paul was not the only person to proclaim the gospel (Marshall 1999, 708). Timothy could model all three of these in his own unique way.

A **herald** (*kēryx*) is someone who proclaims good news, usually of an important event or successful battle. Its position as first in the list implies the initial announcement of good news. Preaching was Paul's primary activity when he entered new territories (Acts 14:7, 21, 25; 15:35; 18:5).

Apostle (*apostolos*) speaks of Paul's authority and special mission, especially to the Gentiles.

A **teacher** (*didaskalos*) is one who reveals the truth by building up the church (1 Cor 12:28; Eph 4:11-12; → 1 Tim 3:2). Paul uses it for himself only here and 1 Tim 2:7. Teaching is given as a separate ministry of church leadership in 1 Cor 12:18-29 and Eph 4:11. The prepositional phrase "of the Gentiles" is added here in some reliable manuscripts. Despite the strong textual evidence for this inclusion, it is probably a gloss influenced by 1 Tim 2:7 (Metzger 1994, 579).

■ **12** The thought of the previous verses continues with the causal conjunction, **that is why**. Paul's appointment as a herald, apostle, and teacher led to his imprisonment. He considered his many hardships (see 2 Cor 11:21-33) opportunities for God's grace to work. It was only through Christ's power that Paul could endure his suffering (2 Cor 12:7-10). His faith in Christ set him on a collision course "against the rulers, against the authorities, against the powers of this dark world and against the spiritual forces of evil in the heavenly realms" (Eph 6:12). This same kind of conflict awaits all sincere believers in Christ (→ 2 Tim 3:12). **But** (*alla*) the gospel was no reason for Paul to be ashamed (Rom 1:16) and neither should it be for Timothy (2 Tim 1:8). This is one of the strongest and most confident confessional statements in the NT: **I know whom I have believed**.

Know (*oida*) is used both for knowing the facts about or character of someone, and for personal acquaintance with someone (Marshall 1999, 710). The perfect tense of this verb describes Paul's unswerving conviction, arising from his personal and experiential knowledge of God in Christ.

The antecedent of the pronoun **whom** is unclear—it could refer to either God (vv 8-9) or Christ (vv 9-10). The two are so closely related in Paul's thought that no decision is necessary. God's fullest self-revelation is in the Son

(Col 1:15-19). Paul trusts God alone, not any human teaching or practice. The pronoun is personal—Paul believes in a person, not a creed.

I have believed is also in the perfect tense, with the emphasis on the permanent state of Paul's faith. "Paul's knowledge of God has grown out of a steady experience of belief" (Towner 2006, 475). God has been faithful in the past and will continue to be with Paul while he is in prison.

Paul's faith is reiterated with another perfect tense verb: **I . . . am convinced**. He was persuaded that God was able to sustain him in all situations (Rom 8:28): *He has the ability to guard* [*phylaxai*] *my deposit* (→ 1 Tim 6:20). God would keep him safe and secure (→ 2 Tim 1:14). What was this *deposit*?

One option is that it was something God had first entrusted to Paul (GNT, NEB, RSV). In the present context, this would be God's calling to proclaim the gospel (v 11). God deposited the gospel into Paul's care. Whatever Paul faced in the future, as a faithful steward he would do his best to keep the deposit safe.

The second option reverses the first. Paul had placed the deposit into God's care (NASB, NIV, NRSV). Based on God's character, this deposit was safe and would never be lost. Thus, Paul made the deposit; God is its guard. This confidence in God is literally expressed as *I know in whom I have trusted*.

Either of these options is possible; they do not exclude one another. But the context favors the second option. Paul testifies that God has enabled and sustained his ministry through many trials and persecutions. Paul's confidence should encourage Timothy to entrust his own ministry to God, who will sustain him through whatever he may face.

Thus, the "deposit" is the gospel and the entire Pauline mission of proclaiming it (v 14; Towner 2006, 476). One way God will guard Paul's deposit is through the faithfulness of those who follow Paul, such as Timothy (2:2). By keeping Timothy strong through suffering, God will preserve Paul's message and mission in witness to the gospel.

Until that day marks the time period of this guarded deposit. **That day** is the future point of final judgment, when Christ will return (Rom 2:16; 13:12; 1 Cor 1:8; 3:13; 5:5; 2 Cor 1:14; Phil 2:16; 1 Thess 5:4; 2 Thess 1:10). Paul was convinced that the gospel message would go out throughout this present evil age and nothing would be able to stop it (Acts 1:8; 5:39).

Honor, Shame, and Rhetoric

Honor and shame were attached to certain beliefs and behaviors in the ancient Greco-Roman world. Decisions were often made based on honor and shame. Every group and culture determines what behavior it finds acceptable. Acting in certain ways brings esteem and value in the eyes of others.

Timothy had reasons to feel shame in the views of first-century Greco-Roman culture. The paradoxical message of the cross conflicted with the sensibilities of the culture (1 Cor 1:22-23), in particular the growing devotion to the Imperial cult (1 Thess 1:9). Timothy's mentor was in prison as an accused criminal (2 Tim 2:9). Paul was experiencing increased isolation as no one had come to his defense (4:16), and many people had abandoned him (1:15; 4:10). And Timothy was facing opposition from Paul's opponents (4:15; Johnson 2001, 358-59). The dangers of cowardice (1:7) and avoidance of suffering (1:8) were real.

Rhetoric or persuasive communication was a primary way to instill elements of honor or disgrace within a group or individual (Robbins 1996, 144-91). Paul's letters employ rhetoric to persuade his readers to see reality from his faith perspective.

In 2 Timothy, Paul attempts to create an alternative system of honor that Timothy should follow. The better course of action is honor before God (Gal 1:10; 1 Thess 2:4-6), especially on the day of judgment (2 Tim 4:1). Since the Holy Spirit gives honor not timidity (1:7), Timothy should not feel ashamed (1:8) of his association with Paul, the prisoner (1:12), or the message of the gospel (1:13). He should not feel ashamed of suffering for the gospel (2:1), since the gospel brings honor before God.

The underlying motive in suffering shame before others is that it leads people to Christ (2:10). The short catechism of 2:11-13 is all about honor before God rather than people. Holding to the truth of the gospel may bring conflict with the opposition. But faithfulness will be vindicated by God, who knows his own people (2:14-19).

One advantage Timothy had in embracing Paul's system of honor is that he was raised with a similar heritage to Paul's. He did not need to break a major group boundary to accept Paul's way of life, as did those from totally pagan backgrounds. When a new generation has been brought up with the values of the older generation, it is easier for it to absorb the values of its elders (deSilva 1999, 36).

Nevertheless, Timothy was raised as the child of a mixed marriage. His mother was Jewish, but his father was a Greek. And there were certainly pagan cultural influences that came from growing up in the Gentile city of Lystra. We do not know which was the more dominant culture in Timothy's childhood, Greek or Jewish (→ 1:5; 3:14-15). Timothy also faced difficult opposition from false teachers in the Ephesian church. He would have to win the hearts and minds of the church by preaching the gospel accurately and convincingly (4:2).

"When group members . . . experience insult, scorn and hostility at the hands of the members of the majority culture, they need to have ways of interpreting this experience positively from within the worldview of the group" (ibid., 41). This is in essence what Paul attempts to do in this letter. He reminds Timothy that his self-worth must be found in Christ and the gospel (1:9-10). Even though Paul was in prison and facing death, he had confidence that his work would continue through Timothy (1:13-14).

3. Imitate Paul's Example (1:13-14)

■ **13-14** The exhortation of v 8 continues in these two verses with two similar commands. Each verse issues a command, followed by the means by which to keep it.

(*a*) The Greek text begins with the first command, **keep** [*eche*] . . . **the pattern of sound teaching**. The present tense verb stresses the habitual course of action Timothy should pursue. This will involve "holding on to faith and a good conscience" (1 Tim 1:19), but also following the **pattern** set by Paul.

Pattern (*hypotypōsin*) or "standard" (NASB, NRSV) represents a prototype, guide, model, form, or norm one can follow (→ 1 Tim 1:16). It is the blueprint an architect uses in constructing a building, the outline of a speech, or the initial sketch of a picture (Goppelt 1972, 246-59). Paul had already given the template through years of mission work with Timothy.

Paul had in mind far more than mere style or methodology. His concern was the message. Timothy is to model and preserve **sound teaching**. **Sound** (*hygiainonōn*) refers to something healthy or free from error in the sense of correct (BDAG 2000, 1023; → 1 Tim 1:10; 6:3). Correct doctrine is an important theme in 1 Timothy, in which Paul wrote against the influence of false teachers in Ephesus. This problem must have continued, since he gives further warnings about such people in 2 Tim 2:18; 3:1-9. By knowing Paul's doctrine well, Timothy will be better equipped to deal with any false teaching.

What sets the pattern for Timothy is **what you heard from me**. Timothy had been around Paul, received his correspondence, and knew his message and way of life. They had spent many years of ministry together, sometimes side-by-side and at other times far apart. Timothy knew the gospel well. This letter functions to prepare Timothy to take over Paul's mission. Timothy must guard the faith by finding his confidence in God and imitating Paul's example.

How Timothy should follow Paul is **with faith and love *that are* in Christ Jesus**. This verse echoes 1 Tim 1:5, in which Paul instructs Timothy to approach the problems in Ephesus with love sourced by "a pure heart and a good conscience and sincere faith." Christ Jesus is the source and perfect example for Timothy. The whole existence **in Christ** is summed up in faith and love. One is vertical, expressed as faith in God, and the other is the outworking of this faith horizontally through love toward others. These two qualities ought to govern Timothy's life.

Paul will emphasize this point again in 2 Tim 2:22; 3:10, and 15. The opponents had distorted "the faith" (2:18) and lacked love (3:3). Timothy must pursue a different course, one that will ultimately lead to his final salvation and the salvation of those under his spiritual care.

(*b*) The second command is given in v 14: **guard the good deposit** (→ 1 Tim 6:20). The adjective **good** (*kalēn*) marks the quality of the **deposit** and can mean rich or beautiful. "'Rich' catches the nuance of endless wealth available in the tradition, while 'beautiful' suggests something that can be the source of endless contemplation" (Montague 2008, 152).

Good deposit is in parallel to **sound teaching**, implying that they are the same. The deposit is the gospel message as in 2 Tim 1:12 (→). It is not clear who made the deposit. Paul had commissioned Timothy to ministry. But behind Paul is God, who gives the message (1:9-10) to both Paul and Timothy. Thus, the deposit ultimately has divine origins.

Timothy can follow Paul because Paul follows Christ (1 Cor 11:1). The gospel and the mission to proclaim it have been **entrusted** to Timothy. The phrase **that was entrusted to you** is not in the Greek and is assumed in the NIV from the meaning of the word **deposit**. Behind the thought of this verse lay the threats against the gospel message from the opponents (2:14, 16-18, 25; 3:13-14; 4:3-4, 15).

Paul gives the theological foundation at the end of the paragraph. Timothy can keep the deposit through **the Holy Spirit who lives in us**. The full name **Holy Spirit** is mentioned in the Pastorals only here and in Titus 3:5. What makes the Spirit "holy" is that the Spirit is from God. He is God's presence among God's people.

This argues for reading "spirit" in v 7 as *the* Holy Spirit, and the "gift" of v 6 as the Spirit's assuring presence. The Holy Spirit in Paul's thought is the one who empowers God's people for holy living and ministry (Rom 8:1-17; 1 Cor 12; Gal 5:16-26).

The Spirit dwells **in us**, that is, in those who believe (Rom 5:5; 8:9, 11, 14, 16; 1 Cor 2:12; 3:16; 6:19; 12:13; Gal 3:14; 4:6). These verses return to the propositio of the letter: God is the one who guarantees the success of Timothy's mission; therefore, Timothy can move forward with confidence and a sense of honor.

FROM THE TEXT

Paul begins the body of the letter with strong words of assurance for Timothy. He is passing on the mantle of leadership to Timothy, like Elijah did to Elisha (2 Kgs 2). He gets down to the "fundamentals" to which Timothy should be devoted.

First, he must *have courage to preach the gospel of grace in Christ Jesus.* Paul defines grace in 2 Tim 1:9. The gift of grace has been God's plan before creation; it is the very nature of God to give generously. This grace initiates our salvation, since there is nothing we can do to save ourselves. The goal of grace is twofold: to restore fallen humanity's relationship with God, and to give them an eternal purpose for living on earth experienced as holiness of heart and life (→ 2:19).

God will work out his plans through human cooperation and obedience in response to his grace. The holy life is a matter of grace first and human response second. The fire of holiness requires the fuel of grace. Chrysostom wrote,

> As fire requires fuel, so grace requires our alacrity, that it may be ever fervent. . . . For it is in our power to kindle or extinguish this grace. . . . For by sloth and carelessness it is quenched, and by watchfulness and diligence it is kept alive. (*Hom. 2 Tim.* 1, quoted by Gorday 2000, 232)

Second, Timothy must *be prepared to suffer for this message*. Some people will not welcome this message. And they may take out their rejection of it on the messenger. Paul's experiences that stand behind this letter are good examples of the type of reactions to expect.

Suffering can take many forms. The most obvious is *physical persecution* like Paul experienced many times (2 Cor 11:23-29). There were more Christian martyrs in the twentieth century than at any other point in history. The twenty-first century will likely be no different (Barrett and Johnson 2001, 228-35).

Believers may also experience *emotional persecution* by feeling shamed by others and the rejection that occurs because of this. Shame will take different forms throughout the world. It may be the strongest force that keeps Christians from sharing their faith or living by their convictions. The gospel of Jesus Christ makes exclusive claims that battle an age of tolerance, political correctness, and pluralism. It is not easy to stand out from the crowd, when we are afraid of being labeled intolerant. Anyone who claims that Christianity points the way to "absolute truth" is ridiculed. When faced with opposition, we will be tempted to take the course of least resistance.

A closely related type of suffering is from *relational persecution*. The gospel may bring animosity from family members. Jesus spoke about how much it may cost those who wish to be his followers (Luke 14:26). It may put "a man against his father, a daughter against her mother, a daughter-in-law against her mother-in-law—a man's enemies will be the members of his own household" (Matt 10:35-36).

The church must have a strong theology of suffering, based in part on letters like 2 Timothy. Being a Christian does not mean that all of life's problems will disappear. Because we identify with the death and resurrection of Christ (Rom 6:3-5), we should expect to participate in his suffering. Jesus set the example for sacrificial love by suffering, so that we might have eternal life (Phil 2:1-11; → 2 Tim 2:11-13).

Third, Timothy should *not forget that he has the Holy Spirit with him to help him fulfill his mission*. The Holy Spirit is God's greatest gift to us (Luke 11:13; 1 Cor 2:12) and will give us courage to face life's battles. The Spirit connects us to the power of God and helps us overcome the temptations we may face because of the pressures to compromise our faith (Rom 5:5; 8:15; 1 Thess 1:6).

The Spirit will help us through trials but not necessarily keep us from trials. The Spirit is God's gift to us to help us fulfill his mission for us. "Every Christian worker engaged in however small a task requires assurance that God never commissions anyone to a task without imparting a special gift appropriate to it" (Guthrie 1983, 144). Paul offers his own life as a testimony to God's faithfulness to guard the gospel to which he had given his life. He remained confident in God's care, even though everyone was abandoning him and he was alone in chains.

B. Examples of Disloyalty and Loyalty (1:15-18)

BEHIND THE TEXT

This is the first of four autobiographical statements in the letter (3:11; 4:6-8; 4:16-18). This section is a brief digression, formally a narratio, which provides the facts behind a call to imitation in deliberative rhetoric. There is no direct appeal to Timothy here; the exhortation is implied through negative and positive examples. These function as a synkrisis, rhetorical contrast, showing Timothy both how not and how to behave (Witherington 2006, 322). Here we get a glimpse of Paul's emotions as he anticipates the exhortation in 2:1.

Timothy probably recognized the names Paul lists since they were from Asia and Ephesus. The three persons listed illustrate two types of responses. Phygelus and Hermogenes represent those who are ashamed of the gospel and have turned their backs on Paul. They did the opposite of what Paul urges Timothy to do in 1:6-14. Onesiphorus, however, functions as a positive example of courage and faithfulness in the face of opposition. He went out of his way to find and help the imprisoned Paul. The application to Timothy is obvious: follow the pattern of Onesiphorus. This repeats the theme of strength in loyalty (Johnson 1996, 61-62).

The section begins and ends with verbs of knowing. From the modern reader's perspective, there are some uncertainties about this passage: What is the relationship of the three persons named here to Paul's mission? Where did these events take place? Were these events recent—while Paul was in prison? Or, did they happen earlier while he was in Ephesus?

IN THE TEXT

■ **15** Paul follows up on his exhortation to Timothy to stay true to his preaching and mission (1:6-12) with an indirect warning. He mentions the negative example of people who deserted him and his mission. **You know** implies that

Timothy is aware of the situation. This accounts for the lack of details about the people mentioned.

Everyone . . . has deserted me is hyperbole, a deliberate overstatement for literary effect. In 4:11 and 21 (→) he will mention some who still actively support him. Timothy must have some idea who this **everyone** includes. These people were from **the province of Asia**. They may have been from Asia and visiting in Rome at the time of the letter, or they could have rejected Paul while he was still in Asia. The province of Asia included what is today western Turkey. Its capital was Ephesus, Timothy's likely location at the time.

Paul names only two from this group of deserters, **Phygelus and Hermogenes**. This is the only place in the NT that these men are mentioned. But they are named in the later apocryphal *Acts of Paul and Thecla* 3:1-7, which appears to be a reflection on this letter and some traditions about Paul.

The passive voice verb **deserted** (*apestraphēsan*) literally means **turned from** or **rejected**. In 4:4 and Titus 1:14 (→), the same verb in the active voice connotes apostasy. What the desertion here involved is unclear. Were they merely inhospitable to him at a point of great need? Did they (like John Mark in Acts 13:13) forsake Paul on a missionary journey? The apostle does not mention any false teaching or explicitly call these deserters apostates. But in 2 Tim 1:8 (→) he associates rejecting him as tantamount to rejecting the gospel he preaches. If v 8 is a clue, the deserters may have left Paul because they felt ashamed of the message he represented.

There is no time indicator here, but this probably happened after Paul wrote 1 Timothy (Fee 1988, 236). In 2 Tim 4:16, he laments about "everyone" forsaking him at his first defense. But this uses a different word for "desert" (*enkatelipon*). At some point, Demas, Crescens, and Titus also left him, leaving Luke his only companion (4:10-11). These others may have had legitimate reasons for leaving, but Paul was evidently lonely all the same.

What were the emotions behind Paul's words here? Was his language hyperbolic, or was he experiencing emotional pain? Was he suffering from the natural psychological depression typical of situations like his (Mounce 2000, 493; Kelly 1963, 169)? What is most remarkable is the confidence in God he communicated as he wrote this letter, chained and awaiting execution.

■ **16-17** Paul concludes this chapter, giving Timothy a positive example of others who did not abandon him. **The household of Onesiphorus** actually went out of their way to help him. The verse has the form of an indirect prayer, using the rare optative mood (compare Rom 15:5; 1 Thess 3:11; 5:23; 2 Thess 2:16-17; 3:16). "The wish is intended as a prayer expressed indirectly to the Lord (Jesus) but directly to the one or ones to be blessed, showing a sense of solidarity and immediacy of concern" (Towner 2006, 482). There are two prayer-wishes in the one Greek sentence that makes up 2 Tim 1:16-18; the first is in vv 16-17, and the other is in v 18.

Onesiphorus and his **household** are the focus of these prayers. The first prayer asks that **the Lord show mercy to the household of Onesiphorus**. Mercy, a part of the greeting in 1:2, is compassion toward someone in need (→ 1 Tim 1:2, 13, 16; 2 Tim 1:2, 16, 18; Titus 3:5). Whether Onesiphorus acted directly or through his agents, he showed mercy toward Paul, who now asks that this same mercy be extended to his household.

The thought echoes Matt 5:7: "Blessed are the merciful, for they will be shown mercy." Scholars speculate as to why Paul asks for mercy in behalf of Onesiphorus' household, not just Onesiphorus. One theory is that Onesiphorus had died, leaving the household without its breadwinner. But this is pure speculation, since there is no mention of his death. Was he away from his family, who remained in Ephesus (2 Tim 4:19; Knight 1992, 384)? Had he commissioned his slaves to assist Paul? Regardless, Paul asks God to bless his benefactor's entire extended family (→ 4:19).

Little is known about Onesiphorus. The focus is not on his identity but on his hospitality. Since Timothy is most likely in Ephesus at the point of this letter and is to greet the household of Onesiphorus there (4:19), Onesiphorus was likely from Ephesus. At some point, he (or some members of his household) went to Rome, either on business or specifically to seek out Paul. Paul prays for mercy because of three acts:

First, Onesiphorus **often refreshed me**. The verb *anepsyxen*, used only here in the NT, means "bring life" (*psych-*) "again" (*ana*), hence **revived** or **enlivened**. How Onesiphorus helped Paul is unknown, but it likely included some form of hospitality. Roman authorities did not provide food, drink, or other necessities to prisoners like Paul. So outside help was crucial to his survival (Fee 1988, 186). Onesiphorus' unspecified acts of compassion **refreshed** Paul **often**. They encouraged him as he awaited his second trial.

Second, he **was not ashamed of my chains**. **My chains** could refer to the actual method by which Paul was imprisoned (see Acts 28:20; Phil 1:13-14) or figuratively to his captivity in general. The theme of honor and shame continues with 2 Tim 1:16 (→ 2 Tim 1:8). Unlike those who abandoned Paul (v 15), Onesiphorus was not ashamed of Paul and Paul's faith in Christ. He was willing to experience shame before others rather than give up his association with the gospel. In the context of this chapter, Onesiphorus serves as a positive example for Timothy to remain faithful, even if it means great personal risk.

Third, **when he was in Rome, he searched hard for me until he found me**. Paul puts the example of Onesiphorus now in a positive way and refers to the actual historical situation. This is the only time in any of the Prison Epistles that Paul mentions the location of his imprisonment.

Paul's Imprisonments

The first description of Saul of Tarsus in the Bible is of him imprisoning Christians (Acts 8:3). This was ironically reversed by his being imprisoned numerous times during his ministry travels. He spent perhaps 25 percent of his ministry in prison. Not all of his arrests, beatings, and imprisonments are specifically known. There are references and allusions in both Acts and his letters (Eph 6:20; Phil 1:13-14; Col 4:3, 18):

- Briefly in Philippi (Acts 16:23-40)
- Briefly in Jerusalem (Acts 21:33-34; 23:16)
- Two years in Caesarea (Acts 23:35; 24:27)
- Two years in Rome (Acts 28:30)
- More imprisonments than his opponents (2 Cor 11:23)

Prison brought shame and often physical abuse to the imprisoned. Prison conditions varied, as Paul's experiences show, from being locked in stocks or chains to a more lenient house arrest. Some prisons were dark, cold, and damp. Prisons offered little or nothing to eat or drink. Prisoners often committed suicide or begged for death (McRay 2007, 146-48). That Paul survived his imprisonments intensifies his statements about relying on God's grace and strength (2 Cor 12:9; Phil 4:13; 2 Tim 4:17). No doubt, the assistance of friends on the outside helped save his life (Acts 24:23).

Prisons were not primarily for punishing criminals, but holding cells for those awaiting trials, as Paul's experience in Rome shows. He understood himself to be a "prisoner of Christ Jesus" (Phlm 1, 9; Eph 3:1; 4:1) rather than of Caesar. He used his prison experiences to encourage other Christians who were suffering various types of persecution. In 2 Timothy, he refers to his imprisonment as a rhetorical tool to motivate Timothy to remain faithful to his own calling despite the challenges he faced in Ephesus.

The adverb **hard** (*spoudaiōs*) shows how diligently, earnestly, and zealously (BDAG 2000, 939) Onesiphorus searched. It was probably not easy to locate Paul. It is possible that Paul was kept at the Campus Martius, a military camp for prisoners located on the edge of Rome (Witherington 2006, 324). It took considerable nerve—boldness, persistence, and risk—for Onesiphorus to find Paul and to help him. Timothy will need to show this same resolve with his own ministry and when he comes to Paul (4:9).

■ **18** Based on what Onesiphorus did for him, Paul offers a second prayer-wish similar to the one in 1:16. The repetition shows how deeply Paul felt about the help he received. The prayer is simple: **May the Lord grant that he will find mercy from the Lord on that day**. The prayer is basically the same as v 16, with the same optative verb *give* and focus on **mercy**. The addition of the infinitive **find** (*herein*) corresponds with "searched hard" in v 17. The prayer presumes that Onesiphorus found Paul and was able to be of assistance to him. This much is clear. But the verse raises several questions:

305

First, what are we to make of the awkward double reference to **Lord** (*kyrios*) in this prayer? **Lord** almost always refers to Jesus Christ in Paul's writings. The second **Lord** lacks the Greek article, as does the divine name Yahweh in the LXX (Quell 1965, 1058-59). The phrase **from the Lord** may have been such a cliché in Paul's Jewish religious language that he departed from his usual practice. The first **Lord** refers to Christ, who will be the Judge when he returns (4:1, 8); the second to God the Father.

Second, to what does **on that day** refer? If it echoes 1:12, it would seem to be a veiled reference to the day of judgment (Matt 25:31-46; 1 Cor 3:13). Why would Paul delay Onesiphorus' reward to a day that is still future? Some interpreters suggest that Onesiphorus had died and that Paul prayed for God to be merciful to him on judgment day (Holtzmann 1880, 401; Fee 1988, 236). Nothing in the text supports the assumption that Paul is praying for the dead. Even if he were dead, Paul is simply expressing his hope for a favorable outcome on the day of judgment (Knight 1992, 386).

As in 2 Tim 1:16, Paul again gives the reason for his prayer: Onesiphorus had **helped** him while he was **in Ephesus**. Ephesus was a key center for Paul's ministry in Asia (Acts 18—20; 1 Cor 15:32; 16:8; 1 Tim 1:3; 2 Tim 1:18; 4:12). Acts reports that he spent almost three years in ministry there, longer than in any other one place in his journeys.

Helped comes from the same word translated "minister" or "serve" (*diakoneō*) elsewhere. The plural **how many ways** is like "etcetera" in English: there are too many ways to list them all. This reveals the character of Onesiphorus. What he did in Rome was consistent with what he had done in Ephesus. Onesiphorus may have been one of the benefactors who allowed Paul to focus on preaching rather than laboring in the marketplace making tents.

You know very well implies that Onesiphorus had developed a reputation Timothy knew about. This brings Timothy back into the conversation. The type of courage Onesiphorus showed is precisely the kind Timothy needed in Ephesus.

FROM THE TEXT

Paul is not seeking sympathy from Timothy in this passage. He is using his situation to offer in Onesiphorus an example Timothy could imitate in his compassion, conviction, and courage:

Compassion. Onesiphorus' presence comforted Paul during one of the low moments in his life. This passage is brief, and we have no details as to what he did. Church leaders carry a heavy load of responsibility for the community. But they, too, need care and encouragement, especially from those they lead.

In 2 Cor 1:3-11, Paul reflects on the trouble he had in Asia and how God brought comfort to him. Was Onesiphorus God's agent in this? God is the author of comfort, but he "comforts us in all our troubles, so that we can comfort those in any trouble with the comfort we ourselves receive from God" (v 4). By sharing in others' sufferings, we become participants in their comfort (v 7).

Conviction. Onesiphorus was not ashamed of Paul or the message he stood for in a potentially dangerous situation. Although shame and embarrassment are strong social forces, believers do not need to fear because God is with them (Josh 1:9). At points in his ministry, Paul felt tremendous pressure that caused him to be afraid (2 Cor 7:5). But he also knew that God would provide strength to overcome his fear (Eph 6:19).

Fear of losing face may tempt us to compromise our convictions. Jesus warned, "If anyone is ashamed of me and my words . . . , the Son of Man will be ashamed of them when he comes in his Father's glory with the holy angels" (Mark 8:38). We should pray that the power of the Holy Spirit will give us "power, love and self-discipline" (2 Tim 1:7).

Courage. Onesiphorus was determined to find Paul in Rome—the capital of the empire and the largest city in the world at the time. He did not have the advantage of a city map, much less a cell phone, the Internet, or GPS.

Although we do not know the extent of his "hard" search, it must have taken perseverance and creativity. Courage is fueled by faith, conviction, and knowledge (see Josh 1:7). Courage is the antidote to shame. Paul testified from his Roman imprisonment, "I eagerly expect and hope that I will in no way be ashamed, but will have sufficient courage so that now as always Christ will be exalted in my body, whether by life or by death" (Phil 1:20).

C. Endurance in Suffering (2:1-13)

BEHIND THE TEXT

Second Timothy 2:1-13 continues the unit begun in 1:6 (→). This chapter specifically brings up some of the challenges Timothy faced in Ephesus. Onesiphorus' loyalty to Paul and the gospel (1:16-18) offers Timothy a positive example to imitate: he must be similarly "strong" and willing to endure "suffering" for the sake of the gospel (2:1, 3).

Paul's rhetorical strategy of inductive "invention" supplies both positive and negative examples that teach character (Harding 1993, 195-96). Paul repeats themes from ch 1 to be sure Timothy gets the point (Towner 2006, 488). This section has two parts: 2:1-7 and 8-13.

Verses 1-7 form an inclusio on the theme of the enabling grace of Christ Jesus. Grace will enable Timothy to imitate Paul in two respects: (1) by training leaders to carry on the mission in Ephesus and (2) by enduring hardships in his ministry. To do so, he must develop three core character qualities: strength (v 1), foresight (v 2), and endurance (v 3; Liefeld 1999, 245). Three examples illustrate his exhortation to hard work, endurance, and reward: a good soldier (vv 3-4), a competing athlete (v 5), and a farmer (v 6).

Verses 8-13 continue the themes of vv 1-7 with Christ as the prime example. Paul skillfully connects the gospel and his suffering to urge Timothy to face his trials with courage. The exhortation in this section is implicit only. The goal remains to show Timothy that he can carry out his ministry because he has been empowered by the Holy Spirit (1:14).

I. Three Examples of Dedication to a Cause (2:1-7)

IN THE TEXT

■ **I** The chapter again directly exhorts Timothy (1:13-14) with an emphatic **you**. **Then** (*oun*) connects this unit to 1:15-18 as its logical consequence. Its key theme is enduring suffering with God's help. Timothy should reject the bad example of the Asians who deserted Paul in 1:15 and instead follow the good example of Onesiphorus in 1:16-18. Other comparisons in this chapter drive home the same points of faithfulness and hard work. Paul will next move on to the opponents and remind Timothy that he cannot deal with such problems in his own strength. He will need the grace of Christ through the power of the Holy Spirit.

Paul calls Timothy **my child** (*teknon*; **son** in the NIV, as in 1 Tim 1:18). This term of fictive kinship shows the affection and personal attachment Paul had for Timothy. It also implies that Timothy should imitate Paul, his spiritual father (Chrysostom, *Hom. 2 Tim.* 4), and carry on his mission with the authority passed on from Paul (→ 1 Tim 1:2).

The first command is a call to **be strong** (echoing 1:6-7). The middle/passive imperative *endynamou* invites Timothy to allow God to strengthen him (Rom 4:20; Eph 6:10; Phil 4:13; 2 Tim 1:7-8, 14; 4:17). God is the source, but the command assumes that Timothy is responsible for his own spiritual growth. His response to God's provision is the key theme of this letter. What Timothy should do with God's help is stated in 2:2-3: Proclaim the message despite suffering.

The resource Timothy has for this task is **the grace that is in Christ Jesus**. The prepositional phrase has both a personal and instrumental force: "Be strengthened by the grace" (ESV), which has it source **in Christ Jesus** (→ 1:2; John 1:16). This grace has been part of God's plan since before time began (→ 2 Tim 1:9).

Paul has identified two divine sources of help for Timothy in the letter: the power of the Holy Spirit and the grace of Christ Jesus. The gift of grace is experienced through the power of God's presence. With these, Timothy has nothing to fear.

■ **2** Having Christ with us does not remove our problems. Echoing 1:13, Paul begins to offer solutions to the challenges Timothy faced in Ephesus by reminding him of **the things you have heard me say in the presence of many witnesses**. The plural pronoun **things** (*tauta*) includes every aspect of Paul's gospel. **Heard** points to the oral character of his teaching and preaching (1:13; Knight 1992, 389). Paul is clarifying further the "deposit" of 1:14 (→) and the heritage of 1:5 (→). Timothy is the vital link in a chain from past to future. Four generations of believers are implicit in this verse: Paul, many witnesses, Timothy, and new teachers.

Paul passed on his message to Timothy **in the presence of many witnesses**. The English **in the presence of** translates the Greek preposition *dia* ("through" [NRSV]). This seems to indicate that Timothy received the message through the agency of others. But the preposition *para*, untranslated in the NIV, indicates the source as Paul ("from me" [NRSV]). The witnesses were merely public confirmation of Paul's word. *Dia* thus shows attestation, "denoting the manner, attendant circumstance, or perhaps occasion of Timothy hearing the gospel repeatedly from Paul" (Mounce 2000, 506). The apostle identifies no specific time or context to indicate when the transfer occurred during their many years together in active ministry. **Witnesses** adds authenticity to the message and confirms that Timothy was not alone in his faith. He was part of a "living network" (Johnson 1996, 62).

The second command of this section urges Timothy to **entrust** (*parathou*) the message Paul gave him **to reliable people**. The verb refers to putting something in the care of another for safekeeping (→ 1:12, 14; 1 Tim 1:18). To keep the message pure and unadulterated from the falsehood of the opponents, Timothy must choose who satisfies two conditions: First, they are **reliable people**. Second, they are **qualified to teach others**.

First, **reliable** (*pistois*) comes from the word often translated "faithful" or "believing" (1 Tim 4:3, 10, 12; 6:2; Titus 1:6). **Reliable** people are **trustworthy** (2 Tim 2:11; → 1:5, 12, 13). The adjective assumes they are Christian believers. But it emphasizes their dependable character, which matches their confession of faith. The message cannot simply be handed on to those with power, position, or prestige, but to those who have proven the genuineness of their faith in exemplary ways.

People translates *anthrōpois* (→ 1 Tim 2:1). In some contexts, this might be translated "men." But it is too restrictive here (against Knight 1992, 391). In some cases in the early church, it would have been more strategic for men to be the teachers (→ 1 Tim 2:12). However, Paul allowed women to teach where it was socially acceptable (Acts 18:26). "Accommodating social custom is a strategy in service of the goal of gaining a sure foothold for the Gospel in the world it means to save" (Fiore 2007, 147). The issue in the present context is not gender but competency, character, and mission.

Second, these people should be **qualified [*hikanos*] to teach others**. They must know the truth and have the ability to teach it. The adjective **qualified** describes competence that meets a certain standard (BDAG 2000, 472 s.v. 2)—here, faithfulness. Behind this passage seem to stand the directions for choosing leaders in 1 Tim 3.

The heritage of 2 Tim 1:5-6 must be shared with others so that the gospel can continue to go out to the world (1 Thess 1:6-8). Timothy was a vital part in the chain of transmission. He could expend all his energy putting out the fires of the heretics. (Of course, some of this would be necessary.) Or, he could focus on strengthening the orthodoxy of the church by finding and training strong and competent leaders to guide the church into the future.

Commitment to this positive course will mean following in the footsteps of Paul. This requires a willingness to suffer shame in order to preserve the integrity of the message. The mission-minded Paul recommends his strategy of appointing leaders in each community (Acts 14:23). The practical reason in this instance is that he needs Timothy to come and help him in Rome (2 Tim 4:9, 21). Having qualified teachers was vital to the short-term and long-term health of the Ephesian church.

■ **3-4** Paul invites Timothy: **Join with me in suffering** (→ 1:8, *synkakopathēson*). This simple imperative gets to the heart of the letter. Paul assumes that if Timothy is faithful to the gospel, he can expect suffering. It is a shared experience for believers, because the world rejects their message. Timothy must be willing to pay the cost to get the message out (→ 4:1-5).

Paul uses three illustrations (introduced with *hōs*) from everyday life in the Roman Empire to emphasize that doing one's job takes discipline and may involve some hardship and pain. Each example shows "the Stoic-Cynic understanding of moral progress as a kind of struggle for self-mastery" (Johnson 2001, 371; Epictetus, *Diatr.* 3.22.51-69; 3.24.34-35; 4.8.35-40; Dibelius and Conzelmann 1972, 32-33, 108). Paul uses the same three examples of soldier, athlete, and farmer in 1 Cor 9 to compare his willingness to give up earthly rewards (ministry compensation) in order to win the eternal crown. The point is similar here, despite the different context. Each analogy calls for suffering with a reward for perseverance (Mounce 2000, 507):

Sharing in Suffering

Metaphor	Soldier	Athlete	Farmer
Call to suffer	Single-mindedness	To compete by the rules	To work hard
Reward	To please the one who enlists him	To win a prize	To share in a crop

The first illustration is of **a good soldier of Christ Jesus**. Paul used military metaphors in other letters (Rom 6:13; 7:23; 1 Cor 9:7; 2 Cor 6:7; 10:3-4; Eph 6:11-18; Pfitzner 1967, 157-86). He refers to his ministry colleagues as fellow soldiers in Phil 2:25 and Phlm 2. A **good** soldier here is one willing to suffer for proclaiming the truth of the gospel. The **commanding officer** is **Christ Jesus**. His soldiers battle against the forces of evil, so they must be prepared to suffer for his sake.

The Life of a Roman Soldier

Soldiers were a common sight throughout the Roman Empire, especially along frontiers and in troubled areas. One of their primary jobs was to be the police force of the empire and to protect the borders. Their experiences were typical of other soldiers in antiquity.

Roman soldiers were highly trained professionals, which made them difficult to overcome in battle. Rome was a mighty empire by the first century AD largely through the discipline of its armies. Commanding officers denied soldiers "creature comforts" to harden them for battle. The suffering and disciplined lives of imperial soldiers were legendary (Josephus, *J.W.* 3.7.28-29, 271-82; 3.10.9, 525-29; 3.72-108).

Being a soldier required total commitment to the emperor and commanding officers. Any soldier who stepped out-of-line or was derelict in his duty was severely punished or even executed. Those who did well and pleased their commanders were promoted and rewarded (Southern 2006, 145-48). A Roman soldier could not marry or be involved in secondary business (Dio Cassius, *Rom. Hist.* 60.24). The discipline of soldiers often served as an illustration in ethical discourse (Plato, *Apol.* 28; Epictetus, *Diatr.* 3.24.34-36; 3.26.27).

The point of the metaphor comes in 2 Tim 2:4: soldiers should focus on pleasing their commander and not get distracted with **civilian affairs**. **No one** (*oudeis*) gives this a proverbial tone that applies to all believers. **Entangled** (*empleketia*) describes how a soldier's weapon might get caught in his cloak. Figuratively, it refers to distraction or preoccupation with other things. In 2 Pet 2:20, it is used in a strong sense of getting caught up in the corruption of the world. Paul is likewise forceful, but his focus is on disciplined priorities, not moral failure. His concern is that Timothy not get caught up in ***the legitimate activities of life*** or the "business affairs or undertakings that concern material existence" (Johnson 2001, 366). Having a side business as a ministry leader may be a necessity; Paul was involved in tentmaking. Paul's concern is that Timothy avoid getting so caught up in everyday affairs that they compromise his commitment to Christ. A good soldier has a "single-minded devotion to duty" (Towner 2006, 492).

Soldiers should make their highest priority to please their **commanding officer**. **Commanding officer** translates an attributive participle (lit.): "the one

311

who recruited him to be a soldier" (*stratologēsanti*). Both Paul and Timothy were recruited into Christ's service (1:9). As his soldiers, they must follow his commands and be willing to suffer for his sake. They must *consecrate* themselves to the will of their commander (Gould 1965, 637-38).

■ **5** The second image of an athlete comes from a Greek context. The emphasis shifts from commitment to reward, although both ideas are present. Only athletes who compete according to the rules qualify to receive the victor's crown. The similar image in 1 Cor 9:24-27 stresses training and competition, which are only implied here. Athletic competitions were common in many Roman cities (→ 1 Tim 4:7).

The **victor's crown** (the verb *stephanoutai*), typically a laurel wreath, symbolized honor and achievement. Athletes devoted their lives to winning it. Christians hoped to receive the reward of eternal life awaiting the faithful in this life (1 Cor 9:25; Phil 4:1; 1 Thess 2:19; Jas 1:12; 1 Pet 5:4; Rev 2:10).

Paul adds to the typical imagery the idea of **competing according to the rules** in an exception clause (*ean mē*). Every sporting competition has rules winners must follow. How well an athlete skillfully follows these differentiates professionals from amateurs (Barclay 2003, 185). In the first century, there were severe penalties for cheating in a competition.

The imagery may allude to the preparatory work before a competition, but the stress is on the race itself (Fee 1984, 242). The difference between winners and losers is often the amount of work, discipline, and training that goes on before the competition. But Timothy is now ready for the race, so this seems to be the point of the metaphor here (Mounce 2000, 510).

What rules does Paul have in mind here? The context suggests a willingness to suffer for the sake of Christ by being faithful and not giving in to temptation. The ultimate goal is to eternal life. In this race, everyone who calls on the name of the Lord can be a "winner" (be saved; Acts 2:21; Rom 10:13).

■ **6** The final illustration of a **hardworking farmer** continues the theme of effort and reward. The adjectival participle **hardworking** (*kopiōnta*) shows again that suffering is in Paul's mind. Anyone who has worked a large garden or farm knows that the hard work involves physical pain and exhaustion. The word is grammatically in an emphatic position. Farmers must work hard—tilling, planting, watering, weeding, and fertilizing—before the harvest (1 Cor 3:6-9). The hard work (Rom 16:6, 12; 1 Cor 15:10; 16:16; Gal 4:11; Phil 2:16; 1 Thess 5:12; 1 Tim 4:10; 5:17) of farming was a ready illustration for pursuing moral and religious causes (Jas 5:7; Epictetus, *Diatr.* 4.8.35-40).

Their toil entitles farmers to **be the first to receive a share of the crops**. Timothy's hard work in the labor of ministry entitles him to a **share** in the harvest. Paul does not indicate what his **share of the crops** might symbolize. It is certainly not health, wealth, and prosperity in this world. This letter offers only the prospect of suffering for the gospel for the present. His future reward may be what Paul mentions in 1 Tim 4:16: "Watch your life and doctrine closely. Persevere in them, because if you do, you will save both yourself and your hearers." The irony of this passage is that suffering for Christ brings positive results. "Beyond warfare is victory, beyond athletic effort a prize, and beyond agricultural labour a crop" (Barrett 1963, 102).

■ **7** The letter returns (from 2 Tim 2:3) to direct exhortation with Paul's call for Timothy: **Reflect on what I am saying.** This peroration prepares Timothy for the example of Christ that follows.

Reflect (*noei*) means apprehend, understand, gain insight into, or think carefully about a subject (BDAG 2000, 674). In this case, **insight** comes from **the Lord**. There is special **insight** (*synesin*) that comes to those who seek the Lord's illumination (Ps 111(LXX 110):10; Prov 2:1; Sir 5:10; 34:11). **Lord** here may refer to God the Father or Christ Jesus. Which is not important to the argument (see 1 Cor 2:6-16). Paul may echo Prov 2:6: "For the LORD gives wisdom; from his mouth come knowledge and understanding."

The message of the three illustrations is simple enough. But to live it out requires divine help. Timothy needs to give his all for the cause of Christ. As he makes himself a living sacrifice, he can be assured that God will fill him with the Holy Spirit and empower him for his assigned task.

FROM THE TEXT

Paul calls Christians to endure in the face of adversity. Becoming a Christian, and particularly a Christian minister, does not exempt one from suffering. It may instead invite ridicule and rejection from others. Jesus warned his disciples that they would suffer because of their allegiance to him (Matt 10:22; 24:9; John 15:18). The choice is between accepting the world's praise and disowning Christ, which lead to his disowning us before the Father, or we must accept the way of the cross and risk rejection by the world (Matt 10:32-33; Mark 8:34). Paul believed suffering for Christ opens the door to resurrection life (Rom 8:17; Phil 3:10-11). He reminds Timothy here of three resources available to enable him to endure the suffering he might face in Ephesus.

First, *the grace found in Christ Jesus.* Paul lived out the conviction that "The Sovereign LORD is my strength" (Hab 3:19). His modus operandi was that he could do anything through him who gives strength (Phil 4:13). We experience the riches of divine grace through the indwelling Holy Spirit, who strengthens our inner being so we can deeply know the love of Christ (Eph 3:14-21). Paul knew that the Lord's strength enabled him to preach the gospel in the face of adversity (2 Tim 4:17). God's grace in Christ saves, sanctifies, and empowers believers for service.

Second, *personal discipline and hard work*. Christians take advantage of God's help by opening their lives completely to his purposes and direction. Authentic faith demands total obedience to God (see Rom 1:5). He has designed life so that we find our greatest pleasures walking in his righteousness. The task of ministry involves training others to obey: "To this end *I strenuously contend* with all *the energy Christ so powerfully works* in me" (Col 1:29, emphasis added).

Ignatius of Antioch expands on Paul's image of the well-disciplined soldier to help believers stay committed to their commander and not desert him (as Demas did [2 Tim 4:10]): "Let your baptism be your arms; your faith, your helmet; your love, your spear; your endurance, your armor" (*Pol.* 6.2, quoted by Gorday 2000, 241). Origen emphasizes the importance of orthodoxy: "The true soldiers of Christ must, in every way, form a fortification for truth and nowhere permit an opening for persuasive falsehood, so far as they are able" (*Comm. Jo.* 6.32, quoted by Gorday 2000, 240).

John Wesley suggested three primary "means of grace" to strengthen believers to live in obedience to Christ. These "means" are "outward signs, words, or actions, ordained of God, and appointed for this end, to be the ordinary channels whereby he might convey to men, preventing, justifying, or sanctifying grace." He recommends in particular prayer, searching the Scriptures, and receiving the Lord's Supper (1986, 5:185-201). Obedience through spiritual disciplines such as these and others has two effects: (1) we allow God's grace to transform us into Christ's image (2 Cor 3:18), and (2) we find the inner strength to endure trials and tribulations (2 Cor 4).

Finally, we must *keep the goal in mind*. Paul's goal was clear: to win the prize of eternal life with God (1 Cor 9:27; Phil 1:21; 3:10-14). There will be no greater reward than to hear from our Lord, "Well done, good and faithful servant!" (Matt 25:21). And "So we make it our goal to please him, whether we are at home in the body or away from it" (2 Cor 5:9). Keeping our eyes on the mountaintop helps us walk through the valleys along the way. If our eyes are focused on Christ, we will do what pleases him, even if it may mean discomfort and rejection. Paul and countless other Christians have faced such challenges throughout the centuries. Why should we expect to be exempt?

2. Jesus as the Great Example of Suffering and Endurance (2:8-13)

BEHIND THE TEXT

Paul reaches the climax of his appeal for Timothy to endure by providing Jesus as the greatest example to follow. Verses 8-10 are one sentence in Greek. They connect Paul's imprisonment to the gospel of the risen Christ.

The passage ends with an implied appeal for all believers to endure for their faith in Christ. The only imperative comes at the beginning. And it is simply a call for Timothy to remember. The major stylistic feature is a confession of core doctrines.

The key theme is simply that one must be willing to suffer like Christ in order to experience a resurrection like his. Paul does this by reducing his kerygma to several simple statements and quoting a four-line hymn. The whole section echoes the call to endure suffering in 1:8.

Verses 11-13 form a small unit that is a poetic restatement of vv 8-9. Their rhetorical function is to remind Timothy of the essential core of the Christian faith and to inspire him to remain faithful to the gospel. It is unclear whether this poetry quotes an early Christian hymn or is Paul's original creation. As a hymn, it could have been used in a baptismal setting (Beasley-Murray 1973, 207-8). But everything in the passage fits the context and could have been composed by Paul for this occasion (Fee 1984, 249; Towner 2006, 507).

The hymn is introduced as a "trustworthy saying," the only one in 2 Timothy ($\rightarrow$ 1 Tim 1:15). The hymn is organized into four pairs of symmetrical first-class conditional sentences. In this type of construction, the condition (= protasis) is assumed to be true for the sake of the argument. Each "if"-clause gives the human action in the first-person plural ("we"). Each apodosis ("then," conditional clause) gives the divine response.

God's response echoes that found in Mark 8:38—"Sentences of Holy Law." God reacts to human actions in a way that is equal and of the same kind (see also 1 Cor 3:17; 14:38; Käsemann 1969, 66-81). The symmetry is broken in the last line, which functions as an explanation to the fourth pair. The first two pairs are positive and the last two are negative.

Another noteworthy feature is the progression of verb tenses, from the past, present, to future, and a return to the present. This last may intentionally wrap up this section with an applied appeal for Timothy to endure.

IN THE TEXT

■ **8** Paul now draws Timothy's attention to what really matters—the message of hope in Jesus Christ. Timothy must avoid getting tangled up (2 Tim 2:4) in the futile and detrimental speculations of the opponents (v 16). Paul's answer returns to the basics in the form of a short creedal statement. Since the Lord gives further understanding (v 7), Timothy must now **remember Jesus Christ**.

The present tense verb here conveys a continual nuance: *Keep on remembering*—keep the message burning in your heart. This is not to be "a momentary recall, but a persistent and formative recollection" (Johnson 2001, 373). Memory is one of the key ways Paul attempts to motivate Timothy in this letter (1:3, 13).

The order of **Jesus** before **Christ**, unique in the letter (compare 1:1-2, 9-10, 13; 2:1, 3, 10; 3:12, 15; 4:1), probably emphasizes Jesus' humanity. This may be subtle polemic against the opponents' view on resurrection (→ 2:18; Towner 1994, 176). Jesus the anointed Savior is the focus of the gospel and the source of God's mercy and grace. Timothy should remember two specific things about Jesus:

First, he was **raised from *among* the dead**. He is the firstfruits of resurrection, the one who made the resurrection of others possible (1 Cor 15:20-23). The perfect tense of the attributive participle *egēgermenon* stresses Jesus' resurrection as a past event that has continuing consequences in the present— he is alive forevermore (see 1 Cor 15:4, 14). Christ's resurrection "is not just a historical event to be remembered but a truth holding promise for believers to be rehearsed over and over again (1:10)" (Towner 2006, 500). The passive voice of the participle presumes that God the Father was the presumed actor.

Jesus' resurrection is the crucial element of Christian theology because it shows his victory over the power of sin and death (1 Cor 15:55-56). Resurrection is what distinguishes Christianity from all other religions (Augustine, *Serm.* 234.3). Resurrection proved Jesus' messiahship and fulfilled OT prophecies (Acts 2:34). It is emphasized in 2 Tim 2:11-12*a*.

Second, Jesus is ***descended from the seed of David*** (compare Rom 1:3-4). Paul emphasizes Jesus' humanity and physical lineage. That the "anointed one" would come from the line of David was promised in the OT (2 Sam 7:12; Ps 89:3-4; Isa 11:1; Jer 23:5). The NT also emphasizes Jesus' Davidic descent (Matt 1:1, 6, 17; Mark 12:35-37; Luke 1:32; 3:31; John 7:42; Acts 2:29-30; Rev 5:5; 22:16). Paul stresses both Jesus' humanity and his position as sovereign King. He is able to help Timothy through whatever challenges he may face.

Jesus' resurrection and Davidic descent form the basis of the **gospel** that Paul preached (Rom 2:16; 16:25). He states the four key components of his message in 1 Cor 15:3-5*a*: "For what I received I passed on to you as of first importance: that Christ died for our sins according to the Scriptures, that he was buried, that he was raised on the third day according to the Scriptures, and that he appeared." This message that Paul received by direct revelation (Gal 1:11-12) agrees with the beliefs of the primitive church. He was merely a steward of this message (1 Cor 4:1), an instrument God used to get the message out to the world. In 2 Tim 2:9, Paul will claim that his **gospel** was the reason why he was in prison.

■ **9 For which** (*en hō*) marks a transition back to the topic of **suffering** and connects Paul's present situation to his gospel (v 8). He was **suffering even to the point of being chained like a criminal**.

The word **suffering** comes from a combination of "suffer" (*patheō*) and "evil" (*kakos*). **Chained** (*desmōs*) refers to bonds or fetters (Luke 8:29; Acts

16:26; 26:29). Paul may have been quite literally chained. But he may simply have been in prison. He sometimes uses chains as a synecdoche for imprisonment (Phil 1:7, 13, 14, 17; Col 4:18; Phlm 10, 13).

Paul was an accused **criminal** for supposedly breaking Roman law. Acts 26:31-32 reports that King Agrippa found nothing justifying his imprisonment. But since Paul had appealed to Caesar, Agrippa and Festus used this as an opportunity to get rid of him and send him to Rome for trial. The NT lists no formal Roman charges against Paul.

At some point in Paul's later years or soon after his death, Nero made it illegal to be a Christian (Tacitus, *Ann.* 15.44; Suetonius, *Nero* 16). The charges against Paul may have been associated with this decision by Nero. The word **like** (*hōs*) indicates Paul's innocence, comparable to the innocence of Christ, who also suffered (Fiore 2007, 149).

Paul reveals his optimism with the last phrase: **But God's word is not chained.** The stark contrast with Paul's situation cannot be missed. The perfect tense of the verb *dedetai* (**bound**) matches the tense of Christ's resurrection. The power of resurrection confirms the power of God's word, because they are linked. Paul believed his suffering and imprisonment were opportunities for God's grace in Christ to be revealed (Phil 1:12-18).

Paul's Roman imprisonment did not stop the gospel; it actually showed its power. Through his suffering he still speaks powerfully today to those who will listen. Chrysostom reflects, "Just as it is not possible to bind a sunbeam or to shut it up within the house, so neither can the preaching of the word be bound" (*Stat.* 16.5, quoted by Gorday 2000, 244).

■ **10** The connection between Paul's suffering and the message of the gospel continues. **Therefore** reflects back to indicate the reason why Paul endured suffering. The verb **endure** (*hypomenō*) restates the key theme of the letter and is one application of the command to "be strong" in 2 Tim 2:1.

Paul reminded Timothy in his first letter that endurance was one of the character qualities he should pursue (→ 1 Tim 6:11). Paul offers himself as an example of endurance in this second letter (2 Tim 3:10-11). Here, his motive for suffering is the salvation of others. In this, he follows in the footsteps of Jesus (Matt 26:59-60; 27:27-31; Mark 15:22-26; John 8:48) who, as the author of Hebrews writes, "endured the cross, scorning its shame" (12:2).

Endurance was a noble virtue among philosophers. The Stoics saw resistance against passion as an ideal of the ethical life. Rebekah became a symbol of endurance for Jews, with her name interpreted as "strong confidence" (Collins 2002, 225). For a Christian, endurance leads to character formation and the deepening of hope (Rom 5:3-4). Hope supplies the motivation for endurance. Hope is expressed in the last half of this verse.

The reason Paul endured suffering is **for the sake of the elect**. Who are the **elect**? Elsewhere he follows the OT (1 Chr 16:13; Pss 89(LXX 88):3; 105(LXX 104):6; Isa 65:9, 15) and uses the word to describe God's people—those who have put their faith in Christ (Rom 8:33; 16:13; Col 3:12; Titus 1:1; Towner 2006, 504-5).

Nothing in this passage supports the theological concept of "unconditional election" or that as once saved, they are always saved. Rather, the elect must endure to win the victor's crown (2 Tim 2:5). Election is not a guarantee of victory. The **elect** must endure suffering and avoid the deceit of the devil (v 26). Paul may use the word **elect** here to give further assurance about the need to persevere and the grace of Christ that will help (v 1).

The purpose clause (*hina*) that concludes this verse clarifies the prepositional phrase. It expresses Paul's hope for the people of God—**that they too may obtain the salvation that is in Christ Jesus, with eternal glory. Obtain** (*tychōsin*) can be translated as "experience" or "attain" (BDAG 2000, 1019). The goal is **salvation,** which is an "already but not yet" experience (→ 1 Tim 1:15; Phil 3:12-14).

Salvation can be obtained here and now. **Eternal glory**, however, belongs entirely to the future (Knight 1992, 400). This comparison may be why **eternal** is added to **glory**. In the biblical context, **eternal** is an unnecessary addendum to **glory,** since the eternal God is the source of glory (→ 1 Tim 1:11, 17; 3:16; 2 Tim 4:18). Its addition here connects the need to endure with God's purpose for humanity.

Sin leads to a loss of the glory of God's abiding presence for which we were created (Rom 3:23; 5:1-2; 8:19-21; 2 Thess 2:13-14). The goal of **salvation** is the restoration of this glory (2 Cor 3:18). There is an unfinished aspect to salvation, making endurance necessary. Endurance comes as the byproduct of growing faith and reliance upon **Christ Jesus,** the source of salvation (→ 1 Tim 1:1, 2, 15). The more we learn to trust, the greater our hope becomes. The epitome of hope must be the confession, "To live is Christ and to die is gain" (Phil 1:21).

■ **11a** The hymn is introduced as the fourth **trustworthy saying** in Paul's letters to his colleagues (→ 1 Tim 1:15; 3:1; 4:9; Titus 3:8; Knight 1979, 112-37). The adjective **trustworthy** (*pistos*) shares the same root as "faith" and refers to something that can be counted on because of the one who stands behind it. Each saying draws attention to what follows, but it also fits within the larger context. Here it could reflect back on the kerygmatic statement in 2 Tim 2:8. But vv 11b-13 build on the earlier verses. Verse 11a, therefore, functions more naturally as the introduction to the saying that follows.

■ **11b-13** Our comments treat each of the hymnic couplets in succession.

For if we died with him,

we will also live with him. (V 11bc)

The NIV leaves *gar* (*For*) untranslated. It connects the "faithful saying" (v 11a KJV) to Paul's suffering. The saying as a whole functions to support and explain what it means to identify with the gospel to the point of suffering. In the first and third couplet, the NIV supplies direct objects—**him**, not explicit in Greek. Here, the idea of identification with Christ is implicit in the two Greek verbs that have the *syn-* ("with") prefix. The implicit antecedent of **him** is Jesus Christ (from v 8).

The first couplet echoes Rom 6:3-8, Paul's answer to the sin problem. There Paul refers to spiritual death as the old way of life controlled by the power of sin. The aorist verb **died** in 2 Tim 2:11b, implies a decisive point of decision as a completed act. This metaphorical death represents the first vital step in spiritual growth. It refers literally to total submission to the supremacy of Christ (as in Gal 2:20).

New life with Christ comes only after "death." The future tense of the verb in the second line is a logical future, to be experienced in this lifetime. New life begins in earnest when one sincerely submits to Jesus as Lord (Rom 6:4, 8). This new life is essentially what it means to be "in Christ" (→ 1 Tim 2:1, 9). This new life marks the beginning of an ongoing process of being transformed into Christ's likeness (2 Cor 3:18). The future result will be eternal life (Rom 6:22).

Some believers suffering for the gospel may face physical death. What Paul writes in this line offers encouragement to those in similar situations. The same Holy Spirit who brings new spiritual life will supply the power needed to endure in the physical life (2 Tim 1:14; 2:1; Rom 8:9-17).

> **If we endure,**
>
> > **we will also reign with him.** (V 12ab)

The second line gives the practical application of the theology of the first line and speaks to the potential challenges Timothy may have faced. If the condition of endurance is met, there is a positive promise that follows. **Endure** recalls Paul's example of endurance in v 10. The present tense matches the meaning of the word: Enduring is an ongoing process, which if stopped ceases to be endurance. Endurance should not be hit and miss but continue throughout all of life (Knight 1992, 404).

The protasis (condition clause) summarizes the key idea of the letter to this point: endurance may lead to suffering if one is faithful to the gospel. This line assumes the divine resources for this endurance: the gift of God (1:6), the Spirit (1:7), the power of God (1:8), grace (1:9), God as the guard of the deposit (1:14), the Holy Spirit (1:14), grace of Christ (2:1), and God's word (2:9).

The second line (the apodosis, result clause) provides a promise and incentive. The result of endurance in this life is reigning with Christ in eschatological victory. Future reward is dependent on how we live in this life.

Endurance through suffering with Christ is the necessary prerequisite to reigning with him. "The one with whom Christians will reign is the one for whom they endure" (Knight 1992, 405).

The hope of eternal life is the compelling motive for enduring hardship for the sake of Christ in this life (Matt 5:11-12). Ambrose said that we will reign with Christ, "But we by adoption, he by power; we live by grace, he by nature" (*Spir.* 3.20.158, quoted by Gorday 2000, 245).

If we disown him,

he will also disown us. (V 12cd)

What happens when one does not endure because of shame for Christ and the gospel? The third couplet introduces the problem, and the fourth develops it further. These couplet pairs are the negative contrast to the second. They function as a strong warning about rejecting Christ.

Disown (*arnēsometha*) has the sense of repudiating or refusing to acknowledge a person because of the pressures of social rejection or persecution (Mark 8:34-38; Luke 9:23-26; Schlier 1964c, 470). The word is repeated in the last couplet of the hymn.

Fear of suffering or the shame of rejection causes people to deny Christ. Such denial is a form of rejection. "Denying a person implies refusal to admit one's prior relationship with that person" (Fiore 2007, 151). Peter is a good example of someone who gave in to the power of shame (Matt 26:69-75).

2:11b-13   Disowning Christ can be shown by denying his messiahship or unique relationship to the Father (1 John 2:22-23), rejecting his name (= **him** [Rev 3:8]), or abandoning one's faith in him (Rev 2:13). There are nonverbal ways to deny Christ or the gospel, including not providing for one's relatives (1 Tim 5:8) and disobedience (Titus 1:16). Denying Christ is the opposite of dying with Christ. One's perceived self-preservation outweighs one's desire to be one with Christ. It indicates that sin still has control and that one has not come to the point of total surrender.

The sad part comes when the condition of this statement is met, and, as a result, Christ rejects us. The **he** in the NIV is emphatic; it means (lit.) *and that one* (*kakeinos*). It refers to the unstated but assumed **him** in the compound verbs in v 11bc.

The apodosis of this couplet uses a future tense, which is rare in this type of conditional statement. It adds urgency and seriousness to the statement. This clearly echoes Jesus' teaching in Matt 10:33: "Whoever disowns me before others, I will disown before my Father in heaven." This couplet is a strong warning to the "elect" (2 Tim 2:10), who may be tempted to deny the gospel because of social pressure or the influence of the false teachers. Apparently, some had already done this, including Hymenaeus and Alexander (1 Tim 1:20).

> If we are faithless,
>
>> he remains faithful. (V 13*ab*)

The fourth couplet continues the tone and warning of the third about rejecting Christ. The verb **faithless** (*apistoumen*) has an alpha privative (*a*) prefix. This could indicate disbelief or a lack of faith. Since the subject of the verb is first-person plural (**we**), it is doubtful that Paul refers to disbelief (= atheism). The problem seems to be a lack of appropriating and living out one's faith in Christ. This is shown in a lack of trust, which the grace of Christ (2:1) can sustain through troubles. Weak faith subtly denies the power and presence of Christ. If Paul ended with this statement, it would indeed be bad news. But he continues the conditional statement with assurance: Christ **cannot disown himself** (v 13*c*).

The apodosis shifts to a positive statement about Christ's faithfulness. Even if our faith grows weak or fails, God's grace in Christ remains. Christ remains faithful no matter what people do. He will not go back on his word, in particular, the promises of the gospel. His faithfulness is not dependent upon our own lack of faith. Athanasius said, "He is ever the same and unchanging, deceiving neither in his essence nor in his promise" (*Apol. sec.* 2.10, quoted by Gorday 2000, 246). The dependability of God is a core claim of biblical theology (Num 23:19; Deut 7:9; Mal 3:6; Titus 1:2; Heb 13:8; Jas 1:17) and often stressed in Paul's letters (1 Cor 1:9; 10:13; 1 Thess 5:24; 2 Thess 3:3).

The covenantal overtones of this phrase are strong. Christ as the inaugurator and source of the new covenant guarantees the reliability of the gospel message and hope because of his resurrection from the dead (2 Tim 2:8). This is an encouraging word for Christians facing persecution or shame for their faith.

> **For he cannot disown himself.** (V 13*c*)

The fourth couplet adds an explanation (*gar*) that reinforces Christ's faithfulness from the previous statement. The break in the grammatical parallelism grabs the attention of readers. At stake is the very nature of the triune God. God cannot deny himself because his will is perfect. He makes no mistakes. God remains faithful no matter how unfaithful people are. This statement has two possible effects:

First, it gives assurance to those suffering for their faith that nothing "will be able to separate us from the love of God that is in Christ Jesus our Lord" (Rom 8:39). This is good news for any in Ephesus who faced Timothy's correction.

Second, for any who denied Christ in some way, there is hope of redemption, because his grace knows no bounds. "There is no limit to the divine compassion, and there is no sin too deep-dyed for the Blood to cover. Such is the magnitude of God's mercy" (Gould 1965, 641).

All of Paul's letters at some point reflect on the person and work of Jesus Christ. Paul's theology is always practical. What Christ has done for us (usually in the indicative mood in Greek) is the basis for how we ought to live (using the imperative mood).

First, *we can face suffering with confidence because Christ rose victorious over death and everything leading to it* (2 Tim 2:8-10). The paradox of the gospel is that God works through suffering and weakness to reveal his power (2 Cor 4:7-12). The power of the gospel is that it changes people and gives them the hope and assurance of eternal life. We must have a comprehensive theology of Christ's resurrection that inspires our hope. But the Christian hope is not just for our own bodily resurrection after we die. It propels us into hopeful living as we battle with our suffering in this present life.

The irony is that our suffering may be a form of ministry that leads others to salvation. Montague writes, "There are two ways a Christian, and especially a Christian minister, can promote the gospel and the kingdom: by work and by suffering" (2008, 163). If we do not endure, someone may not hear the gospel. And someone who looked to us as models of faith may follow our example of bad faith.

Second, *the way to new life comes through death to the old life* (2 Tim 2:11). This is a common theme in Paul's writings (Rom 6:1-11; 2 Cor 5:17; Eph 4:22-23; Col 3:3-4, 10), partially because it deals with the fundamental human problem of pride and self-reliance.

The first couplet shows that dying to self opens a person to the power of divine grace. Death negates any control of the world and frees us from concerns about self-preservation that may arise in the midst of suffering. Metaphorical death to self is not simply a suppression of natural urges, the flesh, or a subjection of self-indulgence (as in Buddhism or Gnosticism). It marks the beginning of a new kind of life *with the risen Christ*. He becomes our Lord, the supreme source and guide of our lives. Commitment to Christ entails consecration of self to his authority. The twentieth-century German martyr Dietrich Bonhoeffer, understood this well:

> Just as Christ is Christ only in virtue of his suffering and rejection, so the disciple is a disciple only in so far as he shares his Lord's suffering and rejection and crucifixion. Discipleship means allegiance to the person of Jesus, and therefore submission to the law of Christ which is the law of the cross. . . . To deny oneself is to be aware only of Christ and no more of self, to see only him who goes before and no more the road which is too hard for us. Once more, all that self-denial can say is: "He leads the way, keep close to him." (1959, 96-97)

2:8-13

Third, *because Christ is supreme, we can have victory through suffering* (2 Tim 2:12*a*). Christians are people of hope, and this hope sustains us through the ups and downs of life. Suffering can develop our hope if we endure it (Rom 5:3-4). Suffering has a way of clarifying and exposing what is in the heart. It often produces two types of responses: (1) it presses us deeper into despair and doubt, or (2) it drives us closer to God. The difference between the two depends in a large part on the focus of our worship. If Jesus is truly Lord of our lives, our focus shifts from our own strength to his. The entirely sanctified life finds the source for endurance in total dependency upon the strength of the Lord.

Fourth, we should be aware that *suffering may wear down our resistance to temptation* (2 Tim 2:12*b*). The attacks of Satan, the weakness of failing bodies, and persecution from unbelievers can chip away at our spiritual armor and tempt us to follow a road that seems to offer less stress. Peter experienced this challenge when Jesus was being interrogated by the Jewish leaders the night before his death. When the pressure of shame became great, after a busy and stressful week, Peter denied three times that he knew Jesus (Luke 22:54-62).

The good news is that grace is always available to help us through our failures. Paul makes the option clear, echoing the words of Jesus in Matt 10:33: What we do with Jesus in this life will determine what he does with us in the next. Being his followers may mean that we suffer to some degree. We may find this suffering increasing as we reject the world's influences and follow the way of Christ.

Fifth, *the last word is that God's grace is bigger than our failure* (2 Tim 2:13*a*). John 21:15-19 reports Jesus' reinstatement and reaffirmation of Peter after his denial. It is a good thing that we live by grace and not by our own efforts, because none of us measure up to God's standards (Rom 3:23; Eph 2:4-9). The Christian life is not a matter of developing the ability to endure hardship through self-discipline—even nonbelievers can do that. It is to become wholly dependent on God's grace. Eternal life is not determined by our faithfulness, but first and foremost by Christ's faithfulness.

Our endurance through trials and victory over temptations appropriate the grace of God and give us assurance of eternal life. Jesus offered this blessing: "Blessed are those who are persecuted because of righteousness, for theirs is the kingdom of heaven" (Matt 5:10). The difficult journey of persecution removes the dross from our lives and purifies our faith, resulting in the salvation of our souls (1 Pet 1:6-9).

IV. DEALING WITH THE OPPONENTS IN EPHESUS: 2 TIMOTHY 2:14—3:9

BEHIND THE TEXT

The letter makes a noticeable shift at this point to dealing with problem people in the Ephesian church. Evidently, many of the problems that occasioned 1 Timothy had continued. Timothy faced the ongoing and difficult challenge of correcting false teaching. Paul urges him to return to the core truths of the gospel (highlighted in vv 11b-13). Only when he knows his spiritual past will he be prepared to deal with present crises.

This section has three paragraph divisions in most modern translations:

- In vv 14-19, Paul gives instructions for how Timothy can deal with the false teachers.
- In vv 20-21, Paul offers an analogy of a house with vessels of various kinds.
- Finally, vv 22-26 return to how Timothy should deal with the opponents, through his own exemplary character and then gentle instructions.

All the imperatives are second-person singular and addressed specifically to Timothy. Timothy functions as the key warning for the opponents to leave their heresy and return to the truth.

Timothy *What to Pursue*	Opponents *What to Avoid*
Remind and warn (v 14)	Quarreling about words (v 14)
An approved worker (v 15)	Leads to ruin (v 14)
Unashamed (v 15)	Godless chatter (v 16)
Correctly handles the word of truth (v 15)	Leads to ungodliness (v 16)
Turned from wickedness and to the Lord (v 19)	Teaching spreads infection like gangrene (v 17)
Cleansed instruments for God's special use (v 21)	Departed from the truth (v 18)
Made holy and prepared for good work (v 21)	Belief that resurrection has already happened (v 18)
Flee youthful desires (v 22)	Destroying the faith of others (v 18)
Pursue righteousness, faith, love, and peace, pure heart (v 22)	Foolish and stupid arguments (v 23)
Not quarrelsome (v 24)	Quarrelsome (v 23)
Able to teach (v 24)	Captives of the devil (v 26)
Not resentful (v 24)	Goal: to come to their senses and avoid the trap of the devil (v 26)
Kind to everyone (v 24)	
Goal: to instruct the opponents gently about the truth (v 25)	

The focus is on Timothy and his personal preparation for dealing with heresy as God's instrument (v 21). The three imperatives in vv 22-23 adopt a chiastic pattern:

> *Negative*: "Flee the evil desires of youth"—a personal requirement.
>> *Positive*: "Pursue righteousness, faith, love and peace"—a spiritual requirement.
> *Negative*: "Don't have anything to do with foolish and stupid arguments"—a ministry requirement.

Paul gives various opposing forces (Towner 2006, 551) in order to show the better course for Timothy to take:

- Timothy vs. the false teachers
- Moses vs. Korah
- Implements of honor vs. implements for dishonor
- God vs. the devil

The ultimate struggle is between God and the devil for the souls of people. Timothy is the representative of God, and the teachers are the agents of the devil (→ 1 Tim 4:1-3). Paul attempts to show Timothy that he has the resources to win this battle.

A. Becoming Fit for the Master's Use (2:14-21)

IN THE TEXT

■ **14** There is a shift in topic with this verse, marked by a return to direct exhortation. All that follows should be read in light of the hymn in vv 11b-13 and the call to identify with Christ, even if it means suffering. The grammar of this verse is difficult to follow, making it necessary to supply several words in English translations.

The key idea of the sentence is given at the start: **Keep reminding *about these things*.** The NIV's **God's people** is not found in Greek, but it may be assumed from the context of 2:2 and 10. The present tense verb *hypomimnēske* has a continuous force, emphasizing the theme of memory (→ v 8). **These things** in the Pastorals refers to the Pauline tradition. In this context, it refers back to the trustworthy saying of vv 11-13. People forget the key points of the gospel when they get entangled in trivial matters. Christians should always emphasize the fundamental points of the gospel Paul mentions in vv 8, 11b-13.

How Timothy is to remind **God's people** appears in an instrumental participle: **by warning them before God. Warning** (*diamartyromenos*) is a word used in the courtroom. In this case, God is the judge and jury of whether or not believers have remained true to the gospel. As a present tense, the warning must accompany the continual call to remember the gospel.

Timothy must warn the Ephesians **not to fight about words**. This infinitive combines two terms: "word" (*logos*) and "wars" (*machē*). The earlier disputes and speculative teachings addressed in 1 Tim 1:4 and 6:4 had not been resolved. The opponents were entangled in foolish arguments that lead to quarrels (2 Tim 2:23). The as-yet unidentified controversial issue may have been one of the key doctrines mentioned in the "faithful saying" (v 11a KJV) or the heresy about the resurrection taught by people like Hymenaeus and Philetus (vv 17-18). Two reasons to avoid quarreling appear in two prepositional (*epi*) phrases:

First, fighting about words does no good (NRSV); it only creates controversies over trivial matters. **Value** (*chrēsimon*, only here in the NT) identifies something useful or profitable. **Quarreling** does nothing to build up the church. Studying the Scriptures does (3:16).

Second, **quarrelling** leads to ruin. The verb **ruins** appears in English in the word "catastrophe" (*katastrophē*). It is beyond useless; it is detrimental.

Elsewhere in the NT, it appears only in a textual variant of 2 Pet 2:6, describing the destruction of Sodom and Gomorrah.

Instead of "training in righteousness" (2 Tim 3:16), quarrelling tears down **those who listen**. "Splitting hairs" (BDAG 2000, 598) over trivial matters is a persistent temptation for those who lose sight of the crucial center of the gospel. Consequently, the church needs constant warning.

■ **15** Here Paul briefly shifts to a focus on Timothy's character and what he can do to stay clear of destructive conflict in the Ephesian church. He attempts to motivate Timothy to avoid shame before God by preaching the gospel without fear. As in 1 Tim 4:6-8, 13-15; 6:11-14, Paul urges Timothy to be grounded firmly in the truth of the gospel so he has the theological and spiritual strength he needs to deal with problems in the church. Timothy must not neglect his own spiritual health.

So Paul tells him, **Do your best to present yourself to God as one approved.** The word *spoudason* is difficult to translate. The most well-known is the KJV: "Study to shew thyself approved unto God, a workman that needeth not to be ashamed." *Spoudazō* typically means "hurry up" or "expedite." When used figuratively, as here, it can mean "to be zealous / eager, take pains, make every effort, be conscientious" (BDAG 2000, 939). The KJV "study" had that connotation in 1611, but not today. The NKJV comes closer to the modern understanding with "be diligent."

Timothy must "work hard" (NLT) to be competent before God. To **present** oneself before God through total commitment and consecration is a key Pauline idea (Rom 6:13; 12:1; 14:10; 1 Cor 8:8; Col 1:22, 28). In ancient moral teaching, "unless character is tested and proved, it cannot be considered fully formed" (Johnson 2001, 384). **One approved** has been tested and proven genuine (BDAG 2000, 256); such a person is prepared for the final judgment (Grundmann 1964b, 255-60).

Orthodoxy and orthopraxy are inseparable. Timothy's faithfulness to the gospel should be apparent in his "right interpretation of the gospel" and his "right behavior" (Mounce 2000, 525). Both prove that his work meets God's expectations:

First, he can be **a worker who does not need to be ashamed. Worker** (*ergatēn*) usually refers to agricultural laborers (2 Tim 2:6). Timothy labored in ministry, as did other early believers (→ 1 Tim 4:10; 5:17; Rom 16:12; 1 Cor 15:10; 16:15; Phil 2:16; 1 Thess 5:12). The avoidance of shame serves as a key motivator (as in 2 Tim 1:8, 12, 16). The rare word **ashamed** (*anepaischynton*) builds on the cultural norms of honor/shame. Timothy may present himself and his ministry before God, confident of his approval. The false teachers, however, have cause to be ashamed.

Second, Timothy will receive God's approval *by* **correctly handl[ing] the word of truth.** The participle combines two words: *ortho* ("right") and *tomein* ("cut"). In medical contexts, the verb described good surgeons who made precise incisions. It also describes straight roads and plow rows (see LXX Prov 3:6; 11:5). **The word of truth** refers to the gospel Timothy received from Paul (Gal 2:14; Eph 1:13; Col 1:5; 2 Tim 1:13; 2:9, 11; 4:2).

■ **16-17a** Paul contrasts Timothy and the opponents. He repeats the basic idea of 2:14, now with the motive. Rhetorically, the polemic of vv 16-18 serves as a warning and gauge for the truth stated in v 15 and developed in vv 8, 11-13.

Timothy must **avoid godless chatter** (see 1 Tim 6:20). The present imperative emphasizes something requiring constant attention: Always avoid the temptation to talk without thinking. **Godless** (*bebēlous*) describes something profane, impious, or worldly (→ 1 Tim 4:7). **Chatter** translates a compound word ("empty" [*kenos*] "sound" [*phēnē*]) meaning **nonsense.** This type of talk will not result in godliness or spiritual growth (→ 1 Tim 4:7; 6:20).

This describes the false doctrine in Ephesus. **Chatter** was more than preoccupation with trivia, as it probably started. Timothy should have nothing to do with their "foolish and stupid arguments" (2:23). Instead, he should gently instruct the opponents (v 25). Paul gives two reasons why Timothy and the church should avoid such "profane babble."

First, **because those who indulge in it will become more and more** [*prokopsousin*] **ungodly. Those who indulge in it** in the NIV supplies an antecedent missing in the Greek. The verb *prokopsousin* simply says: **They *will* progress *toward*.** Verse 17 implies that **they** refers to people like "Hymenaeus and Philetus, who have departed from the truth" (see 3:9, 13).

Ungodly (*asebeias*) is the opposite of *eusebeia*, one of the key concepts in the Pastoral Epistles (→ 1 Tim 1:9-10). The irony is that these people mistakenly thought they were becoming more religious and "godly." They were instead on a slippery slope leading to moral degradation.

Second, Timothy should avoid the heretical chatter of the opponents because **their teaching will spread like gangrene.** Paul uses two graphic medical terms in this clause (on such imagery, see Malherbe 1980, 19-35). **Spread** (*nomēn*) describes ulcers or disease. In other contexts, it describes how sheep eat away the grass in a pasture (John 10:9; BDAG 2000, 675). **Gangrene** (*gangraina*) is a disease that spreads like cancer and decays bodily tissue. It can lead to death if it is not cut away. The GNT translates this verse, "Such teaching is like an open sore that eats away the flesh" (2 Tim 2:17).

The Ephesian heresy that had slowly penetrated the church was insidious: If left unchecked, it would destroy the church. The diseased imagery in this verse starkly contrasts the healthy imagery for the gospel as "sound teaching" (1:13; 4:3; 1 Tim 1:10; 6:3; Titus 1:9, 13; 2:1, 2, 8).

Hymenaeus and Philetus are examples of those **who have departed from the truth**. **Hymenaeus** here is likely the same man mentioned in 1 Tim 1:20 (→). His rejection of his conscience led to his descent into heresy. Evidently Paul's handing him over to Satan did not have its desired effect. **Philetus** is an otherwise unknown fellow heretic with Hymenaeus.

Their problem is that they **departed from the truth** found in the gospel (→ 2 Tim 1:9-10; 2:8, 11-13). Paul's earlier catechetical statements may have been to set in starker contrast the false teaching of the opponents. The verb **departed** (ēstochēsan) means "to go astray by departing from moral or spiritual standards, miss, fail, deviate, depart" (BDAG 2000, 146).

The heretical duo had rejected the **truth** of the gospel (see v 15). "False doctrines," "myths and endless genealogies," and "meaningless talk" (1 Tim 1:3-4, 6) continued with "quarreling about words" (2 Tim 2:14), "godless chatter" (v 16), and "foolish and stupid arguments" (v 23). They were victims of the trickery of demons (1 Tim 4:1) and the devil (2 Tim 2:26).

The specific way the two had **departed from the truth** was *by saying* [an instrumental participle] **that the resurrection has already taken place**. This is one of the few references to the content of the heresy in Ephesus.

The article with the word **resurrection** is missing in some Greek MSS. If original, Paul referred to **the resurrection** of Christ. But this makes no sense; he defended the historical nature of Christ's resurrection. Without the article, his intent was to reject the opponents' belief in a **resurrection** that **has already taken place**. Their overrealized eschatology claimed believers already experienced spiritual fullness in this life. They misunderstood that the new life Christ's resurrection made possible in this life (2:11b) did not eliminate future bodily resurrection (see Rom 6:3-8; Eph 2:5; Col 2:12).

The heretical movement in Ephesus resembles the problems Paul addresses in 1 Cor 15. Perhaps there were some links between the heresy in Ephesus and Corinth; the two cities were on the same major shipping route, and ideas readily flowed between them. Some of Corinthians believed that the Holy Spirit had given them "spiritual" resurrection. Specifically *bodily* resurrection was unnecessary. There was no need for an end-times resurrection (1 Cor 4:8; 15; Thiselton 1978). There is not enough information about the Ephesian heresy to determine if this was the same problem, but the possibilities are intriguing.

Significant implications arise from the Ephesian heresy. Theologically, the opponents misunderstood one of the central tenets of the Christian faith. Christ's resurrection showed his victory over the power of sin and death (1 Cor 15:56-57). The possibility of new life for believers is connected to the reality of his resurrection. Paul does not say that or how the opponents misinterpreted Christ's resurrection. But he leaves no doubt about its importance (2 Tim 2:8, 11).

Theological error led to ethical degradation. The opponents may have spiritualized the doctrine of the future resurrection of the body. They may have thought that they had arrived at spiritual maturity. The body was inconsequential. They rejected the material world. If spiritual resurrection has already taken place, it does not matter what one does with the body. This could produce two opposite outcomes: either rejecting the world through asceticism (→ 1 Tim 4:3) or embracing the world and living in disregard for the danger of sin (1 Cor 6:12-20; 15:32-34). The threat of the neoplatonic dualism of Gnosticism may have already been infiltrating the Ephesian church, leading to these theological and ethical errors (→ 1 Tim 1:4).

Paul may also mention the false belief that **the resurrection has already taken place** because it detracts from the need to endure suffering. Chrysostom wrote, "If resurrection is past, retribution also is past. The good therefore have reaped persecutions and afflictions, and the wicked have not been punished. On the contrary, they live in great pleasure" (*Hom. 2 Tim.* 5, quoted by Gorday 2000, 251). Resurrection hope motivates believers to endure suffering in this life.

The outcome of this false doctrine leads to the destruction of others' faith (see 1 Cor 15:19). Human pride makes believing that one has already arrived at spiritual maturity appealing. But it causes us to take our eyes off the prize and put them on ourselves. The pronoun **some** (*tinōn*) is indefinite and shows that not everyone in the church had been infected with this disease.

Beliefs in the Afterlife in the First Century

Most world religions believe in some type of afterlife. Many ideas of this circulated during the first century among both pagans and Jews.

Generally speaking, Hellenistic religions believed in the immortality of the soul. Death freed the soul from the confines of the body. Death was a shadowy existence in Hades, where the dead awaited judgment. Those who lived exemplary lives went to the beautiful Elysian Fields. The wicked were confined to dark Tartarus.

There were variations on this basic belief structure. One modification influenced by philosophers was that the spirits of the good rose to live with the Supreme Being in luminous bliss, while the wicked descended to subterranean darkness and eternal chastisement. Between the two, purgatory was a place where those who had pardonable transgressions were purified and eventually allowed to ascend to bliss (Ferguson 1993, 145-46, 234-35).

Ideas of the afterlife were developing in the OT period. The earliest belief may have been that people returned to the dust at death (Gen 3:19; Ps 90:3) or descended to Sheol, the grave (Gen 37:35; 42:38). Popular beliefs about the ascent of Enoch and Elijah suggest that some Jews were developing a concept of some form of life with God after death.

331

The idea of resurrection began to develop especially with the prophets (Isa 25:8; 26:19; Hos 6:1-3). One of the key passages for belief in resurrection is found in Job 19:25-26; "I know that my redeemer lives, and that in the end he will stand on the earth. And after my skin has been destroyed, yet in my flesh I will see God." The most developed OT reference to resurrection can be found in Dan 12:1-3, 13.

Jewish belief in the afterlife during the intertestamental and postbiblical periods overlaps somewhat with Hellenistic ideas. But significant variations on this belief developed among the various sects of Judaism. The Sadducees rejected belief in resurrection, whereas the Pharisees accepted it (Acts 23:6-8; 26:8). Sheol or Hades was generally believed to be the gathering place of the dead (Sir 14:16-19; 17:25-32; 38:16-23). Fourth Maccabees refers to the immortality of the soul in Hellenistic fashion (4 Macc 10:15). Second Maccabees, however, refers to bodily resurrection (2 Macc 7:14). The *Sibylline Oracles* speak of the resurrected body being fashioned like the earthly body (*Sib. Or.* 4:176-82). Rabbinic Judaism referred to the afterlife as simply "the world to come" (Ferguson 1993, 519-20; Osborne 2000, 931-33).

The Christian heresy known as Gnosticism built upon Platonic dualism and merged various Jewish and Christian ideas into a complex eschatology. Details vary with the different gnostic sects.

Gnostics generally believed that the goal in this life is to gain secret, revealed knowledge that will lead to freeing the soul from the material world, including the body. Humans were essentially spiritual beings trapped in the material world. There was a tendency in Gnosticism to have an overrealized eschatology—spiritual enlightenment was equated with "resurrection." The initiated could experience spiritual resurrection in this life. This would lead to spiritual ascent to God after bodily death.

The author of the Nag Hammadi *Treatise on the Resurrection* 49 writes to Rheginos, that he has already received resurrection and should not live as if he is controlled by this world. Similarly, the *Gospel of Philip* 56 refers to the soul as trapped in a contemptible body. Our goal is to rise before we die: "If someone is not first resurrected, wouldn't that person die?" (Meyer 2007, 165).

The key difference between Gnosticism and Paul at this point is that the gnostics defined resurrection in spiritual terms and Paul in physical terms. The starting point between the two is vastly different, but the articulation is easily misunderstood. Paul believed that believers could live a new kind of life in this world by figuratively dying to sin (Rom 6:4). But he was not a dualist who rejected the material world or bodily life. He believed that Christians who enjoyed new life in Christ would eventually die. But they would be resurrected to transformed bodies in the future.

Some form of overrealized eschatology was making inroads in Ephesus (→ 1 Tim 4:3). But this problem was not unique to Ephesus (1 Cor 4:8; 15:12; 2 Thess 2:2).

The NT never holds out hope for the immortality of the soul, but only for the resurrection of the body. Eternal life is a gift of God. He alone has immortality (→ 1 Tim 6:15-16). Christians look forward to a resurrection of a transformed body that is not bound by anything that demands death. We can have hope in eternal life in this world through the assurance that comes through the indwelling Holy Spirit.

For further reading about the Christian hope of bodily resurrection, see:

Thiselton, Anthony. 2011. *Life After Death: A New Approach to the Last Things.* Grand Rapids: Eerdmans.

Wright, N. T. 2003. *The Resurrection of the Son of God.* Minneapolis: Fortress.

_____. 2007. *Surprised by Hope.* London: Society for Promoting Christian Knowledge.

■ **19** Paul responds here to the decay and destruction of the opponents. The contrast (**nevertheless** [*mentoi*]) should encourage those who have so far resisted the false teaching. And it offers a way of escape for those trapped by the devil (v 26).

The answer is in the metaphor **God's solid foundation**. What type of building Paul has in mind here is unclear. In other places, he refers to God's temple as the church (1 Cor 3:10-15; Eph 2:19-23). In 1 Tim 3:15 (→), he calls God's household "the church of the living God, the pillar and foundation of the truth," but with a different word for "foundation."

The point here is not the type of building but the strength of its foundation. A foundation is critical for the strength of a building (Matt 7:24-27). Strong foundations are especially important in the earthquake-prone Mediterranean area. **God's . . . foundation** is **solid** and **stands firm**. The NIV's **solid** and **firm** come from one Greek word, *stereos*. The double reference in the NIV attempts to capture the force of the perfect tense (→ 2 Tim 2:8) of the verb *hestēken*. This emphasizes the ongoing reliability of this foundation, which had a point of beginning. Perhaps, Christ's resurrection in 2:8 is the solid foundation for faith and hope Paul has in mind.

The second part of the metaphor is an **inscription** written on the foundation. Many ancient stone buildings had inscriptions on their foundations and walls. A seal of some type was a form of remembrance, authentication, ownership, or guarantee (Rom 4:11; 1 Cor 9:2; 2 Cor 1:22; Eph 1:13; Fitzer 1971, 948). Two quotations appear on the foundation:

The first gives further assurance and a subtle warning: "**The Lord knows those who are his.**" The source of this quote is the LXX of Num 16:5 (with *kyrios* [**Lord**] replacing *theos* ["God"]). Numbers 16 recounts the story of a revolt against Moses led by Korah. He and an assembly of leaders challenged the leadership of Moses and Aaron, so Moses set up a test to determine who were the Lord's leaders. The rebels were instantly incinerated. The Lord can tell the motives of people's hearts and distinguish those who are truly loyal to him from the frauds.

This story is directly analogous to the Ephesian situation. The opponents were challenging Paul's authority and message relayed through Timothy. They had rejected the truth of the gospel by their dabbling in false teachings. Those who accept the orthodox teaching of Paul's gospel (→ 2 Tim 2:11-13), however, can have the assurance that God is with them.

The second quotation gives the means of assurance and way of escape from the Lord's judgment: "**Everyone who confesses the name of the Lord must turn away from wickedness.**" The source of this quotation is uncertain. It does not match any particular OT reference. If Paul has in mind the story of Korah's rebellion, this quotation may paraphrase Num 16:26. There Moses warns the assembly to turn away from the wicked, rebellious people.

Confesses the name is (lit.) *names the name*. To use the Lord's name is to recognize and honor his supremacy and to call upon him for help. The first half of the statement has a possible background in Isa 26:13 or Joel 2:32. The NT uses a similar phrase several times (Acts 2:21; Rom 10:13; 1 Cor 1:2).

Those who call on the Lord must acknowledge his grace by turning from wickedness (see Josh 23:7; Job 36:10; Pss 6:8; 34:14; Prov 3:7; Isa 52:11; Matt 7:23; 2 Cor 6:17). To remain in wickedness is incompatible with naming the name of the Lord. **Turn away** (from *aphistēmi*) means withdraw from or avoid in a moral sense (BDAG 2000, 158). One cannot call on the name of the Lord and remain in sin. "Obedience to the ethical demands of the gospel [is] mandatory, not optional" (Mounce 2000, 529).

This quotation offers a strong warning to two groups in the Ephesian church: Those tempted by the speculative false teaching of the opponents must separate themselves from it, if they truly believe in Christ. The false teachers must stop their rebellion and return to the orthodox message Paul preached. The rest of the chapter expands on these two themes.

■ **20-21** The next two verses shift (marked by *de*) the metaphor from a foundation to articles within a large house. The image and application prepare for the commands that follow in 2 Tim 2:22-26. Paul builds his rhetorical argument with further "proofs" by example and analogy.

The setting for the illustration is **a large house**. The Ephesians would have thought of the mansions of the wealthy, upper social class found in every major imperial city. This was no typical dwelling, since some of the items are made of **gold and silver**. Common people had vessels of **wood and clay**. What distinguished the two kinds of items was how they were used. **Gold and silver** are for **special purposes** and **wood and clay** for **common use**. Dishes of **gold and silver** were used for special occasions or in the table settings of the wealthy. **Wood and clay** were the poor person's daily utensils or were used in the kitchen or for garbage. A modern comparison might be the difference between the fine china reserved for special occasions and the cheap plastic plates used on a daily basis. How a vessel is used determines its value. There are different levels of honor and shame for these vessels (Rom 9:21; 1 Cor 3:12). It would be shameful to use a gold or silver plate for common purposes (Knight 1992, 418).

The power of the illustration comes in 2 Tim 2:21, which reverses the logic of the last statement in v 20. Regardless of the material a vessel is made from, it can be cleansed and made holy for God's use. The Greek sentence has the form of a third class conditional statement. It denotes a hypothetical situation, with some uncertainty as to whether the condition will be met. If it is, mundane vessels become fit for the **Master**. This is an open invitation to anyone (*tis*). The condition to be met is to **cleanse themselves**.

Cleanse (*ekkatharē*) here is a rare word. It refers to removing something unclean (1 Cor 5:7). The root of the verb describes purifying something defiled that it may be in God's holy presence. The *ek* prefix adds the idea of thorough cleansing (Knight 1992, 418). Because God is holy, vessels used in the service of God must be holy. People experience God's holiness as moral righteousness. To be made holy, the vessel must have all defilement removed. "As the holiness of Yahweh acquires moral content, so the ritual purity demanded of believers becomes a symbol of inner moral purity" (Hauck 1965, 417). To cleanse oneself is not a self-improvement regimen. It requires total commitment to God (Rom 12:1-2). Whatever we give unreservedly to God, he can completely sanctify (1 Thess 5:23-24).

From what type of defilement should people **cleanse themselves**? There is no clear antecedent for *from these things.* The context offers several possibilities and could include anything in the "What to Avoid" chart in the Behind the Text section. Because this is an open-ended invitation, the fulfillment of the condition is up to the vessel. As Paul's own testimony in 1 Tim 1:12-16 shows, no one is beyond God's grace and transforming power.

If people call on God for mercy and put away evil, the result is that they **will be instruments for special purposes**. **Special purposes** (*timē*) is more typically translated as "honor." This honor corresponds to the shame of 2 Tim 2:15, the outcome for the opponents. The *vessel* (*skeuos*) is described in three ways:

First, it is *sanctified* (*hēgiasmenon*). This important biblical term refers to something ready for God's use. Sanctification is accomplished by cleansing from defilement. Anything in relationship with the Holy God must be **made holy**. The form of the word here is a perfect passive participle and modifies *vessel*. One becomes a "a vessel for honorable use" (ESV) *by having been made holy*. The passive voice points to God as the one who responds to the act of consecrating oneself wholly to him.

Second, cleansing makes one **useful to the Master**. This phrase shows the overall goal of Paul's statement—to be made fit for God's use. God is the **Mas-**

ter (*despotēs*; Gen 15:2, 8; Job 5:8; Jer 1:6; 4:10; Jonah 4:3; Dan 9:15; Tob 8:17) of his household, the church (1 Cor 3:9-17; 6:19; → 1 Tim 3:15). Everything in his house must be holy (Heb 12:14). The invitation to be holy is for all who consider themselves part of God's family (2 Cor 7:1).

Third, as a result these vessels will be **prepared to do any good work.** **Prepared** is a perfect passive participle modifying *vessel.* The implied exhortation behind this phrase is this: if one wants to be effective in service to God, one must be made holy by separating from sin. **Good work** will be the natural result of one who has been sanctified.

John Wesley's Covenant Service

The modern version of the prayer in John Wesley's *Covenant Service* (found in the Methodist *Book of Offices,* 1936, 57) captures well the attitude needed in consecrating ourselves as vessels for the Lord's use:

I am no longer my own, but thine.

Put me to what thou wilt, rank me with whom thou wilt.

Put me to doing, put me to suffering.

Let me be employed for thee or laid aside for thee,

exalted for thee or brought low for thee.

Let me be full, let me be empty.

Let me have all things, let me have nothing.

I freely and heartily yield all things to thy pleasure and disposal.

And now, O glorious and blessed God, Father, Son and Holy Spirit, thou art mine, and I am thine.

So be it.

And the covenant which I have made on earth, let it be ratified in heaven.

Amen.

B. Timothy's Character around Problem People (2:22-26)

IN THE TEXT

■ **22** After the examples of 2:20-21, Paul again exhorts Timothy directly. The Greek connective *de,* untranslated in the NIV, compares Timothy with the honorable vessel of v 21. The urgency of the situation demands Timothy's careful response, and at the heart of this response is his character. Paul gives him several specific ways for cleansing himself to be a *good worker* (v 15) fit to do *good work* (v 21).

The two key imperatives **flee** and **pursue** appear also in 1 Tim 6:11 and describe one example of the cleansing process of 2 Tim 2:20-21. Timothy must "seek safety in flight" (BDAG 2000, 1052) from **evil desires of youth.** *Epithymias* is a neutral term that simply means "desires" (LEB, TNIV) or "passions"

(ESV, NRSV). The context will determine whether these desires are for good or evil (→ 1 Tim 6:9; 2 Tim 3:6; 4:3). The NIV's **evil** is missing in Greek and is an unnecessary interpretation. Not all youthful desires are evil. Some may be mere distractions from more important goals. **Youthful** (*nōterikas*, only here in the NT) describes practices that are "modern in style, novel, or cravings for novelty" (Johnson 1996, 81). Paul may remind Timothy not to be caught up in the trivial pursuits that sometimes preoccupy young people. Or, he may hint that he should not be "uncontrolled, vehement, and aggressive" (Fiore 2007, 162) in dealing with opponents (→ 2:23-24).

The best defense is a strong offense. As Timothy rejects youthful impulses or temptations, he must **pursue righteousness, faith, love and peace**. **Pursue** (*diōke*) involves following after something with purpose and zeal (see BDAG 2000, 254). "Genuine Christianity is a positive pursuit" (Towner 1994, 187). The four qualities listed are all important Pauline words (→ 1 Tim 6:11).

Righteousness is a moral term describing right standing before God because of obedience to his will (→ 1 Tim 1:9; Schrenk 1964b, 198). Righteousness is impossible to gain by one's own effort; it comes in the response of faith in Christ's death and resurrection (Rom 3:21-24; 4:25). It marks the lifestyle of the believer in relationship with Christ (Rom 6:13-19; Eph 4:24) through the transforming work of the Holy Spirit (Rom 14:17). The believer's part is responding in obedience to the truths of the gospel especially as found in the Scripture (2 Tim 3:16-17). The only way to live right is to be right with God.

Faith is a key word in the Pastoral Epistles (thirty-three times). It involves a lifestyle of dependence and trust in God that is evident to others (→ 1 Tim 1:12; 3:11).

Love is another important word in these letters (1 Tim 1:5, 14; 2:15; 4:12; 6:11; 2 Tim 1:7, 13; 3:10; Titus 2:2). It should be the central goal of Christians (1 Cor 14:1). It results from the Holy Spirit's work (Gal 5:22). **Faith** and **love** often occur together (Gal 5:6; 1 Thess 3:6; Titus 2:2). There is no object for **love** given here, but loving God must be shown in loving others (1 John 4:10-11).

Peace describes harmony and rest from struggle. Like the other attributes in this list, there is a relational application to the word as it appears in one's attitudes and actions toward others. The use of it here counters the quarrelsomeness of 2 Tim 2:23. Peace with God leads to peace with others (Rom 14:19; 2 Cor 13:11; Gal 5:22; Eph 2:14-18; 4:3; Col 3:15).

Timothy is not alone in his pursuit of these qualities. He joins all **those who call on the Lord out of a pure heart**. **Pure** (*katharas*) comes from the same root as "cleanse" in 2 Tim 2:21 and links the two verses together. Believers develop these four qualities in their lives as a result of the sanctifying work of God.

The **heart** is the place of decision and intention; one that has been made **pure** produces **love** (→ 1 Tim 1:5). Calling on the Lord opens us to the working of God's grace (Rom 10:12-14). This phrase reflects the last quotation in 2 Tim 2:19 and is the positive response to rejecting wickedness. Cleansing oneself from impurity and calling on the Lord are two sides of the same coin.

■ **23** Another way (v 16) Timothy can cleanse himself (v 21) from wickedness (v 19) and avoid any youthful temptations (v 22) is to *avoid foolish and ignorant controversies*. Paul uses the same imperative (*paraitou*) in 1 Tim 4:7 to urge Timothy to reject "godless myths and old wives' tales." As Timothy engages the opponents and corrects their heresies, he must not get caught up in their preoccupation with empty speculation.

Foolish (*mōronas* [*moronic*]) describes something "frivolous and un-skilled because it produces nothing useful" (Towner 2006, 545). It is the opposite of God's wisdom seen in the message of the cross (1 Cor 1:27). The opponents' rejection of the truth of the gospel may lie behind this verse. **Stu-pid** (*apaideutous*, only here in the NT) refers to an ignorant, uninformed, uneducated person, who has not learned to think (Dibelius and Conzelmann 1972, 113; → 1 Tim 1:7).

The teaching of the opponents was not bringing people closer to Christ but driving them farther away. Their arguments **produce** only **quarrels**. Philo used **produce** (*gennōsin*) for a fruit crop (*Creation* 113). The fruit that the opponents bore led to division and ruined the faith of others. **Quarrels** (*machas*) simply means "battling" or "fighting"—"verbal conflict" (→ 1 Tim 6:4). This was a problem Titus had to face in Crete as well (→ Titus 3:9). The motive of the opponents is not clear, but such quarreling usually stems from some aspect of selfishness or insistence on one's views being the only correct ones.

■ **24-25** Verses 24-26 of 2 Tim 2 are one sentence in Greek. It states how Timothy should respond to the opponents in Ephesus. The shift to a third-person subject, **the Lord's servant**, gives it a proverbial quality applicable to anyone in ministry leadership. In his letters, Paul calls himself or other Christian leaders "servant[s] of [Jesus] Christ" (Rom 1:1; 2 Cor 11:23; Gal 1:10; Eph 6:6; Phil 1:1; Col 4:12) or "servant of God" (Titus 1:1). The specific designation here is unique to the NT. Since he distinguishes "God" from "Lord" in this chapter, "Lord" likely refers to Jesus. Timothy ought to approach the problems in Ephesus as Christ's servant with five characteristics:

First, he should **not be quarrelsome** like the opponents (v 23).

Second, he should instead (with the strong adversative *alla*) **be kind to everyone**. The same word (*ēpios*) is used in some MSS of 1 Thess 2:7 for a mother's gentle care for her nursing child (see Metzger 1994, 561-62). Kind-ness is not dependent upon the response of the other people but makes a significant difference in how people receive correction. A heated response will only lead to more problems.

Third, a servant should be **able to teach**. This is one of the qualities of an overseer (→ 1 Tim 3:2). A good teacher will show kindness and patience in seeking to guide people to a better perspective.

Fourth, a servant must be "patient" (NRSV) or "tolerant" (LEB). The word *anexikakon* (only here in the NT) is a compound of *anexomai* ("will endure") and *kakos* ("evil"). It has the sense of "bearing evil without resentment" (BDAG 2000, 77). The patient are long- (vs. short-) suffering in the face of opposition (Grundmann 1965, 486-87).

Fifth, a servant engages in *instructing in gentleness those who oppose*. *Paideuonta* refers to instructing or disciplining children, as "corrective instruction" (Knight 1992, 424). It is guidance intended to change behavior (→ 1 Tim 1:5). Timothy must approach the contentious situation in Ephesus *with humility*. This important qualifier may make the difference in how his instruction is received (see Prov 15:1—"A gentle answer turns away wrath, but a harsh word stirs up anger").

Paul's optimism in God's transforming grace appears in the final clause of 2 Tim 2:25. The goal is that the opponents will be restored and the church experience renewed health. The particle *mēpote* (**in the hope that** or "perhaps" [ESV, NKJV, NRSV, and others]) gives his statement a sense of contingency. He hopes the opponents are not beyond repentance.

At first, this phrase seems awkward and theologically contradictory. **Repentance** (*metanoian*) contains the word for mind (*nous*) and basically is a change of mind-set that should lead to a change of behavior. Negatively, one turns away from sin, and positively, one lives in righteousness according to God's will. Repentance comes in realizing that one is on the wrong path and that there is a better way.

The opponents need a fundamental change in their thinking, especially as it related to resurrection and other core doctrines. Paul does not use the word "repent" often in his letters. The verb appears only once, and the noun just four times. He views repentance as a gift of God's kindness (Rom 2:4), but it also involves the human response of sorrow (2 Cor 7:9-10) for sin (12:21).

Paul does not say that God overpowers human free will. But only God can make repentance possible. Timothy can do his part in disciplining the opponents. But only God can change their hearts through his grace.

The condition for this change is that the opponents turn from their wrong ideas and return to **a knowledge of the truth** (→ 2 Tim 2:18). Knowing the truth is a key theme in the Pastorals (1 Tim 2:4; 2 Tim 3:7; Titus 1:1). **Truth** represents the accepted orthodox interpretation of the gospel that Paul received and passed on to Timothy and the Ephesian church (→ 1 Tim 2:4).

Paul gives the opponents an opportunity to come clean and return to orthodox doctrine. As the representative of the truth, Timothy is the key person to encourage this change.

■ **26** This verse gives both the solution and the problem. To repent, the opponents must first **come to their senses**. This is the only place the verb *ananēspōsin* is found in the NT. It is part of the *sōphrōn* word group found several times in the Pastoral Epistles (→ 2 Tim 1:7). This word group denotes being clearheaded, aware, and of sound mind (4:5; Titus 2:2; Philo, *Alleg. Interp.* 2.60 on Gen 9:21).

The verb is in the subjunctive mood, continuing the contingency of 2 Tim 2:25. Repentance is possible only through God's grace and their change of mind. Neither can be taken for granted as a given. Repentance will bring a new awareness that might not otherwise happen. The problem with the false teachers is that they had become dull in their thinking. This may have started innocently enough with curiosity about obscure doctrines. But eventually it led them into heresy and the errant lifestyle it promoted.

The new awareness Timothy should bring to the opponents will help them appreciate that there is a way to **escape from the trap of the devil**. The verb **escape** is not in Greek. It is added in the NIV to show the result of coming to one's senses about the tricks of the devil.

A *pagidos* is a **snare** for catching animals or fish (→ 1 Tim 6:9). In 1 Tim 3:6-7 (→) Paul warned Timothy not to choose immature believers as leaders because they might become conceited and "fall into . . . the devil's trap." The devil catches those easily deceived by their curiosity about trivial matters (→ 1 Tim 1:3). Once trapped, their consciences become seared and they follow the devil (→ 1 Tim 4:1-2).

Apparently, 1 Timothy did not succeed in changing the situation. Second Timothy was written because the false teachers *have been taken captive* to do the devil's will. The perfect passive participle suggests that the devil had captured and firmly held these people (Knight 1992, 424). The verb *zōgreō* describes being captured alive. The devil had taken them captive and would not let them go.

One question about the last phrase of 2 Tim 2:26 is the antecedent for the pronoun *ekeinou* (*that one*). There are two options. The word could refer to God, who snatches away those trapped by the devil. In this interpretation, the participle has a more positive sense of *rescuing alive*. The possible translation becomes "once they have been snatched alive by God from the devil's snare, so that they can do God's will" (Johnson 1996, 82). The other option, implied in most modern translations (which simply translate the word as "his"), is that the pronoun refers back to the nearest noun, here, "the devil." The only possibility of rescue comes from the repentance God may grant (v

25). Neither option significantly changes the meaning of the sentence. The idea of being trapped by the devil and the potential rescue through God's help is clear.

Timothy's correction should sober him as to what the devil is scheming. Realizing the problem is half the solution. Paul offers a two-part suggestion: First, Timothy needs to rebuke the opponents gently, warning them of the danger they face. Second, the opponents must take the initiative and respond to God's gracious offer of repentance given through Timothy. "God's gift of repentance is in fact a kind of redemption; it is liberation from enslavement to the devil" (Collins 2002, 243). There is a sense of urgency. They must act quickly so the gangrene does not spread, leading to further problems in the church.

FROM THE TEXT

Paul wants Timothy to work on two areas: (1) his own character and (2) his approach to the opponents. Two important lessons emerge from this.

First, *character is crucial in leadership.* Strong character begins with (*a*) a clear conscience before God as leaders fulfill the mission to which God has called them (2:15*a*). One crucial way to do this is (*b*) by knowing the truth of the gospel in order to explain it clearly to others (v 15*b*). The personal devotion of leaders is important for filling up the well from which they can draw strength and insight to help others grow. (*c*) A leader will develop wisdom to discern what is most important and learn to avoid trivial opinions (vv 14*b*, 16*a*).

In theological and biblical study, it is particularly easy to become diverted over tangential matters that are open to several plausible interpretations. Church leaders must never deviate from the apostolic faith found in Scripture (→ 3:15-17) and preserved in the creeds. Apostasy arises, like it did in Ephesus, when leaders begin to dabble in minor or controversial doctrines that draw people's attention away from the gospel (2:18). Leaders should set an example to all believers by living a sanctified life of obedience (2:19-21). Spiritual growth does not happen by accident but through discipline and commitment.

Second, *good leaders will develop strategic compassion when dealing with church problems.* Correcting the wayward must be done from love and the purest of motives lest those who are being disciplined discern any hypocrisy or selfishness in the leader (2:22). As God's own example with Israel in the OT shows: sometimes love must be tough. Paul showed this when he directed the Corinthians to expel the immoral man from the church (in 1 Cor 5:1-5; → 1 Tim 1:20). Blatant sin must be corrected or removed.

Paul knew from experience that it can be difficult to dialogue with opponents who refuse to be corrected (1 Tim 1:20; 2 Tim 2:17). Kindness will go a lot further in correcting the wayward than harsh discipline. Good leaders will develop sensitivity to the personalities and unique needs of those under their care. One remedy for making sure the people of God are not seduced by false doctrine in the first place is with good pastoral care (Leo the Great, *Serm.* 16.3). This care should not be conditioned upon the response of the errant but be an extension of the love of God within the leader's heart.

C. The Folly of the False Teachers (3:1-9)

BEHIND THE TEXT

This chapter continues the section comprising 2:14—4:8. The section alternates between negative and positive examples and exhortation. Here, Paul shifts from the positive tone of ch 2. He is optimistic that God's grace can sanctify common vessels and make them fit for God's use (2:20-21, 25). But the behavior of his opponents in Ephesus raises questions about their willingness to change (v 19; 3:2-5).

The downward path of the Ephesian heretics will become more obvious over time. But the danger is that they will pull others down with them vv 6-9). Paul repeats the same theme found in 2:1—that Timothy must be strong in his faith and knowledge of the truth of the gospel (3:14). He should not let the teachings and behavior of the opponents influence him personally. And he should be the primary advocate for those in the church being deceived by the false teachers.

The most notable feature of this passage is the vice list. This list functions rhetorically as polemic against the deviant behavior of the opponents. It indirectly warns Timothy not to be fooled by these people and to persuade the church to reject their practices. Similar vice lists were common in Hellenistic moral discourse (McEleney 1974; Fitzgerald 1992, 858-59).

The passage begins with a negative example of evil people (v 1). This is followed by the vice list of attributes to avoid (vv 2-5a). Verses 6-9 characterize the tactics of the opponents. This section offers the last direct reference to the opponents in this letter. But the trouble their heresy has created lurks in the background to the letter's end.

Evidently, the situation in Ephesus had not changed much since the writing of 1 Timothy. This passage echoes 1 Tim 4 (→) and its mention of the deceitful heresy in the last times. What the opponents had been doing mirrors the general degradation of society expected in the last days. The passage has a prophetic style that "is meant to show that the occurrence of evil and apostasy is already known to God and therefore should not take the church by surprise or be regarded as something that is not under God's ultimate control" (Marshall 1999, 769).

342

■ **1** Paul continues to exhort Timothy (2:1, 8, 14, 22) and warn him about the false teachers infiltrating the Ephesian church. The optimism of 2:25—that the opponents may repent—is replaced with the reality of the current situation.

Paul grabs Timothy's attention with **but *know* this**. The pronoun **this** points ahead to the next clause (marked by *hoti*). Paul lays out evidence in the following verses justifying his warning about the seriousness of the situation. Timothy should be aware of the growing crisis and realize that he is not alone.

The warning is given in a simple statement. The future tense **there will be** gives this passage a prophetic tone. The future, however, has already arrived in Ephesus, as the present tense verbs in vv 6-8 demonstrate. The mention of **terrible times** creates a sense of urgency and need for vigilance.

Both Jewish and Christian apocalyptic writings predicted difficult (*chalepoi*) or "distressing" (NRSV) days in the end times (Dan 12:1; 1 En. 80:2-8; 100:1-3; 4 Ezra 5:1-12; Mark 13:3-23; 1 Cor 7:26; Jas 5:3; 2 Pet 3:3; 1 John 2:18; Jude 17-18). This would be partially due to moral collapse.

Paul believed he was living in the last days, which made his mission urgent (Rom 13:11-14; 1 Cor 7:29-31; 1 Thess 4:15-18). The last days began with Christ's resurrection and the outpouring of the Holy Spirit (Acts 2:16-21; Heb 1:2). Jesus' resurrection set in motion the close of history by inaugurating a new age, which began encroaching on the old age of sin and death. The "present evil age" (Gal 1:4) will end with his second coming—"that day" (2 Tim 1:18; 4:8). Between these two points, the forces of evil would wage an intensifying war against God's people. These forces oppose the victory of the cross and attempt to deceive people (→ 1 Tim 4:1; 1 John 2:18; Jude 18).

■ **2-5a** Paul here lists the evidence that the problems of the last days were already infiltrating the Ephesian church. This list of nineteen vices portrays how people will live in the end times. Paul offers a two-part strategy to help Timothy (1) identify the false teachers and (2) denounce their behavior (Towner 1994, 191).

Vice lists are common in Paul's letters (→ 1 Tim 1:9-10; Rom 1:29-31; 13:13; 1 Cor 5:10-11; 6:9-10; 2 Cor 12:20-21; Gal 5:19-21; McEleney 1974). The list in 2 Tim 3:2-5a resembles Rom 1:29-31 and 1 Tim 1:9-10. Like others, it is not exhaustive but representative. Its one sentence in Greek features a number of words unique to the NT (seven) and Paul's letters (five). These vices generally reject the Christian love ethic (Matt 22:34-40). They can be divided into sins against God and against people. Selfish love begins the list in emphatic position. It appears again at the end, forming a thematic inclusio. The first four qualities focus on misdirected selfish love.

(1) **Lovers of themselves** (*philautoi*) is an "inordinate self-regard" (Johnson 2001, 404). Egocentrism results in boastfulness, an unbalanced sense of self-importance. "Self-centeredness . . . usurps God's rightful role" (Mounce 2000, 545). Church leaders should avoid this attitude (1 Tim 3:6; 6:4, 17; Titus 1:7).

The first two vices both come from compound words using *philos* ("love"). This vice comes first because all the others are manifestations of it. Selfish pride is the fuel for sin. It results when God is not put first or something other than God is worshiped (see Rom 1:25). It is the opposite of the type of love believers ought to manifest (1 Cor 13:5).

(2) **Lovers of money** (*philargyroi*). Greed is a result of the first vice. Loving money is a source of all kinds of evils, opening the door for many temptations and taking advantage of others. It was one of the problems of the Ephesian opponents (→ 1 Tim 6:5, 10, 17) and should be avoided by church leaders (→ 1 Tim 3:8; Titus 1:7, 11).

(3) Another result of improper self-love is being **boastful** (*alazones*)—having too high an opinion of oneself. Arrogance and bragging can ruin relationships with others.

(4) The next vice of being **proud** (*hyperēphanoi*) is almost synonymous. Both words occur in Rom 1:30. Boastfulness is the behavior; pride, the underlying feeling (Mounce 2000, 545). Arrogance results from setting oneself up against God's sovereignty (see 1 John 2:16). It was another problem of the Ephesian opponents (→ 1 Tim 1:7; 6:4). God opposes such people (Prov 3:34; Jas 4:6; 1 Pet 5:5).

(5) The next two items further show how selfish love destroys relationships. The vice of being **abusive** comes from the same word for "blasphemous" (*blasphēmoi*). It describes slandering another person. In the Bible, God is often the one blasphemed (→ 1 Tim 1:13). But there is no object here. Since the general direction of this list is about relationships with people, most modern translations take this as speaking badly of another human. In Hellenistic thought, the word depicted antisocial behavior (Collins 2002, 247). Slandering others is a form of blasphemy against God's command to love one's neighbor.

The list makes a noticeable change at this point with the following eight words using alpha privatives (*a-*) to negate a root word. These show that "these end-time malefactors will lack the qualities to which each of these vices is opposed. The end-time evildoers are no good and will be up to no good" (Collins 2002, 244).

(6) Another quality that destroys relationships is being **disobedient to their parents**. Disobedience (*apeitheis*) involves exerting self above others, especially those in authority. Obedience to parents and other authority figures is an important topic in the Pastoral Epistles (→ 1 Tim 1:9; 5:4, 8, 16; 2 Tim

1:3-5; 3:15; Titus 1:16; 3:3; see also Eph 6:1-2; Col 3:20). The root cause is a rebellious attitude (Deut 21:18-21; Rom 1:30).

(7) The next two vices deal more specifically with one's relationship to God. Being **ungrateful** (*acharistoi*), as the root suggests, involves not recognizing the "grace" of God or the kindness of others. The good news is that God is still kind to such people (Luke 6:35).

(8) Being **unholy** (*anoisios*) refers to profanely disregarding and opposing God (BDAG 2000, 86; → 1 Tim 1:9). It results from a lack of relationship with God.

(9) **Without love** (*astorgos*) involves showing no affection, especially toward family members. It could be a reflection of "disobedience to parents."

(10) **Unforgiving** (*aspondoi*) characterizes a relationship that results from not loving others. Its opposite (*sponde*) "was a libation, an offering of wine poured out to the gods. Such offerings were frequently made prior to banquets celebrating a truce. Hence, the term came to be used of the truce itself. Those who are implacable are basically unwilling to make peace with others" (Collins 2002, 248).

(11) The vice list deviates from the alpha privatives here with **slanderous** (*diaboloi*). This word is used for the devil, who is the most slanderous of all. Malicious talk had become a problem in the Ephesian church (1 Tim 3:6, 11; 2 Tim 2:26).

(12) The alpha privatives continue with three more words. **Without self-control** (*akrateis*) depicts undisciplined people. This makes them more vulnerable to temptation or fits of anger. Self-control is crucial for church leaders (1 Tim 3:2; Titus 1:8; see Acts 24:25; Gal 5:23; 2 Pet 1:6).

(13) Those who are **brutal** (*anēmeroi*) "lack common politeness and gentleness" (Collins 2002, 248). They are uncivilized and behave like savage animals or criminals. Church leaders should be the opposite of this (1 Tim 3:3; Titus 1:7).

(14) **Not lovers of the good** (*aphilagathoi*) is a compound word unique to this passage in all ancient Greek literature. Perhaps Paul coined it for this situation. It is the opposite of how overseers should act (Titus 1:8). "The willful inward turn of the heart and emotions robs the individual of the capacity to love the good" (Towner 2006, 558).

(15) The next two words begin with the *pro-* prefix and are shared with Luke-Acts. Those who are **treacherous** (*prodotai*) lack loyalty. The word is used for Judas in Luke 6:16 and the Jewish leaders in Acts 7:52 who betrayed Jesus. The false teachers in Ephesus were being traitors to the truth of the gospel.

(16) **Rash** (*propeteis*) describes one who is "impetuous, rash, reckless, thoughtless" (BDAG 2000, 873). Such a person does something without thinking about the consequences. Rash behavior results from a lack of self-

control and can lead to injustice and violence. In Acts 19:36, it describes the mob in Ephesus.

(17) The next word breaks the grammatical pattern and is the only participle in the list. Those who are **conceited** (*tetyphōmenoi*) are puffed up and think they are important. This is one of the characteristics of the false teachers in Ephesus that should be avoided by church leaders (1 Tim 3:6). This behavior leads to the breakdown of community and is the opposite of self-giving love (1 Cor 4:6, 18-19; 5:2; 8:1; 13:4).

(18) The list ends as it began, with two words that begin with the *phil-* ("love") prefix. This attribute offers the crucial choice between being **lovers of pleasure** or being **lovers of God**. Loving pleasure (*philēdonoi*) involves gratifying oneself. *Hēdonē* is sensory pleasure, especially sexual lust (→ Titus 3:3; Luke 8:14; Jas 4:1). One prime example is sexual immorality. The better option is to love God (*philotheoi*; Rom 8:28; 1 Cor 2:9; 8:3; Eph 6:24). "When God is removed as the priority in life and is replaced with self, money, and pleasure, all the other vices naturally follow" (Mounce 2000, 547).

(19) The list concludes with the real danger facing the Ephesian church: **having a form of godliness but denying its power**. This phrase has two opposing participles. The first, in the present tense, describes the continuing problem of the opponents. They have denied the essence of the Christian faith by their lifestyle.

Godliness (*eusebeias*) is a core quality Paul desires for the Ephesian church (→ 1 Tim 2:2; 3:16; 4:7-8; 6:3, 6, 11). This attribute is evidenced in devotion to God shown in a lifestyle pleasing to him. People who are part of the last-days' lifestyle look "religious" on the outside, but their walk does not match their talk. The false teachers in Ephesus appeared to be smart and religious with their speculations (1 Tim 1:3-4) and ascetic practices (1 Tim 4:2-3). But, their supposed knowledge of God did not lead to faithfulness to God. They thought they were "obviously righteous because they were obviously religious" (Fee 1984, 270).

The deeper issue is that the opponents depended on the wrong power source in their own selfish ambitions. The perfect participle **denying** shows that they were in a guilty state resulting from apostasy (2 Tim 2:12-13; Towner 2006, 560). The true power source for godliness is the Holy Spirit (1:7-9).

Paul indirectly urges Timothy and the Ephesians to adopt a lifestyle that operates by a different standard and power source. "True Christianity consists not in the show of religiosity but in the powerful proclamation of the gospel accompanied by the life of obedience that conforms to the demands of the gospel" (Mounce 2000, 547). Paul takes the highest ethical ideals of his day and puts them through the filter of his hope for Christ's soon return. Living in

3:2-5a

the last days does not mean one must live according to the decadent lifestyle of the last days.

■ **5b** Paul here applies the vice list directly to Timothy and the Ephesian church. The present imperative *apotrepou* (**Have nothing to do with**) indicates that this matter requires urgent, ongoing attention. The rare word (only here in the NT) means "avoid them with horror" (Kelly 1963, 195). This is a different strategy than Paul advised in 2:25 (→): treat them gently, but keep them at arm's length. Timothy must not catch their "disease."

■ **6-7** Paul explains why (*gar*) Timothy should avoid the lifestyle of the false teachers. The opponents resembled the false prophets and teachers Jesus predicted would come in the last days (Matt 24:23-26; Mark 13:21-22).

The opponents spread their false teachings in the Ephesian church by taking advantage of weak people. The phrase **worm their way into homes** translates a rare verb (*endynontes*, only here in the NT) referring to creeping (ESV, NKJV), sneaking, or conniving (see 1 Pet 5:8). The early church typically met in private **homes**, so the method of the heretics seriously threatened the existence of the church. Contemporary philosophers and sophists also preferred to hold their classes in homes (Stowers 1984, 66).

The goal of the false teachers was to **gain control over gullible women.** The participle **gain control** is a military term for taking something captive (Luke 21:24; Rom 7:23). In this case, the teachers seduced vulnerable women. **Gullible** (*gynaikaria*) is a diminutive term that means (lit.) *little women*. In a male-dominated culture, uneducated women were particularly easy prey for charlatans. Not all women in the church were so easily victimized (→ 2 Tim 4:19-21; but see 1 Tim 5:13). Three characteristics show why some were particularly vulnerable.

The Deception of the Ephesian Women

The easy deception of some Ephesian women may be one reason why Paul did not want women teachers in the Ephesian church (→ 1 Tim 2:12). If opponents were leading women astray, this would explain some of the problems discussed in 1 Tim 2:9-15; 3:11; 4:7; 5:3-16 (→). Women were stereotypically more vulnerable due to their lower social status and lack of education.

What Paul says here

is not applied to the nature of women as a class of humans, but to the dilemma of women within a certain societal class in the Greco-Roman world. It is the dilemma posed, on the one hand, by the privileges of wealth, status, and the opportunity for education, and, on the other hand, by a lack of significant opportunities for expression in the larger world. (Johnson 2001, 412)

Paul is simply making observations here about social status at that time.

First, they were **loaded down with sins**, or "burdened with a sinful past" (NEB). This perfect participle indicates that their pre-Christian lives had left them scarred. These women continued to struggle with their sin, and the opponents took advantage of this struggle. Paul mentions no specific sins, but they may have been related to the second characteristic.

Second, they were **swayed by all kinds of evil desires**. The present tense of this participle points to a continuous struggle. *Epithymiais* has a negative connotation here (→ 1 Tim 6:9). In 1 Tim 5:6, 11, it describes sexual desires in particular.

Third, they were **always learning but never able to come to a knowledge of the truth**. Each of these problems builds on the previous one. Their sins and passions had blinded them to the power of the gospel—**the truth** in the Pastoral letters (→ 1 Tim 2:4; 2 Tim 2:25; Titus 1:1). **Knowledge** is evidenced in obedient faith that impacts how one lives. Like the opponents, these women were focusing on interesting but trivial religious ideas that did not move them closer to Christ. They appeared to learn but were missing the point. They had the wrong power source (*dynamena*) for genuine godliness (Johnson 2001, 407).

■ **8** Paul now (*de*) appeals to Jewish tradition for an example to support his point: **Jannes and Jambres** serve as antetypes for the opponents in Ephesus. Their names are not mentioned in the OT. But Jewish haggadic tradition identifies them as the Egyptian magicians who turned their staffs into snakes when Moses confronted Pharaoh in Exod 7:12—8:19. According to Eusebius (*Praep. ev.* 9.8.1), their names appeared in the work of the second-century BC writer Numenius of Apamea. Their names were also found in pagan (Pliny the Elder, *Nat.* 30.2.11; Apuleius, *Apol.* 90) and Jewish literature (*Tg. Ps.-J.* 1.3 on Exod 1:15; 7.2 on Exod 7:11; *Tg. Jer.* 1 on Exod 1:15; Num 22:22; CD 5.18). Traditions about them eventually appear in the apocryphal book of *Jannes and Jambres* mentioned by Origen (*Cels.* 41.51). Timothy was probably aware of this legend, so Paul had no need to elaborate further.

The key point is that these two characters opposed God's messenger of truth. **Opposed** (*anthestēsan*) is a strong word that indicates a mind-set against or in resistance to something. The false teachers were like (*houtōs kai*) **Jannes and Jambres** because they had set their minds against the truth that Paul had preached and Timothy represented (→ 1 Tim 6:5, 20). Two descriptions warn the Ephesian opponents of the danger of their present bad models:

First, **they are men of depraved minds** as a result of their heresy and Satan's deception (1 Tim 4:1; 2 Tim 2:26). **Depraved** (*katephtharmenoi*) describes something ruined or corrupted. The word in the Pastorals refers to moral corruption (→ 1 Tim 6:5; Titus 1:15; Harder 1974, 103). This comes through mental seduction, which makes it difficult to choose the right course.

Second, as a consequence of the first, ***they are rejected in regards to the faith.*** It is unclear whose faith is intended, the opponents' faith or the Christian faith. If one rejects the truth (= gospel), one has no faith. **Rejected** (*adokimoi*) modifies **men** who are "unqualified" or "not up to par." They do not meet acceptable standards (Collins 2002, 253). These teachers were unfit because they had rejected the gospel (Rom 1:28). This was evident in how they lived. Timothy must reject this way of life and offer a positive role model to the Ephesians (2 Tim 2:15).

■ **9** The situation was not beyond hope, as Paul ends this section with a note of optimism. **But** (*alla*) here offers a strong contrast to the negative conclusion of 3:8—**they . . . are rejected.** The opponents will not succeed in their deception, because people will see how they had lived.

What made the folly of Jannes and Jambres so obvious was the overwhelming power of the one true God. Likewise the true gospel will outshine the falsehood of the Ephesian heretics. Three major problems assure the defeat of the opponents: (1) They had rejected the truth of the gospel, especially as expressed through Paul's preaching. (2) They had an aberrant lifestyle that did not conform to godliness. And (3) they were enticing others to follow them.

Magicians in Ephesus

The practice of magic was widespread in the Mediterranean world of the first century. This was more than sleight-of-hand deception, what we call magic today in the West. This was a religion that attempted to manipulate spiritual forces for protection, altering fate, for selfish or evil reasons (Arnold 1993, 580-83). False teachers and religious charlatans were common in Ephesus, an infamous ancient center for magic (see Acts 19:13-20).

FROM THE TEXT

"Last days" behavior becomes more evident as the light of God's kingdom shines ever brighter. We learn from Paul that *our lifestyle must match the message we proclaim.* The opponents in Ephesus were headed down the wrong path with their teachings. Their deceit and error were opening them up to sin. There is a serious danger of trying to act religious while lacking the divine power to live it authentically. The situation becomes more destructive when this hypocrisy is fueled by selfishness.

We must *be vigilant against the dangerous influences of the last days.* The tendency of culture is to degenerate and decay unless there are times of spiritual renewal. Students of culture realize that every generation of Christians has felt it was living in the last days—including many early church fathers (see Gorday 2000, 259-60). The core problem—that people love themselves—is a perennial *human* problem (see Rom 1—2), not just a feature of the end times.

Therefore, *it is crucial to know the essential truths of the gospel*, regardless of the time on the eschatological clock. Rejecting or distorting the gospel truth leads to moral breakdown. The gospel is not open to debate and cannot be influenced by the latest theological fads. Fiore writes, "Compromise on essentials ultimately leads to the discrediting of the body of doctrine as a whole and of those who uphold and teach it" (2007, 172). If we are not firmly grounded in the gospel, we can be deceived by false teachings.

V. ENCOURAGEMENT TO TIMOTHY TO PROCLAIM THE GOSPEL: 2 TIMOTHY 3:10—4:8

BEHIND THE TEXT

The letter shifts from the negative warning in the previous section to a positive example using the rhetorical tool of *synkrisis*, a comparison by contrast (Witherington 2006, 356). This section is organized in an ABA' chiastic (X-shaped) structure (Marshall 1999, 781):

    A The pattern Timothy should follow (vv 10-12)

      B The contrasting pattern of wicked people (v 13)

    A' Call for Timothy to remain faithful (vv 14-17)

The two "A" sections begin with ***But you*** (*sy de*), directly appealing to Timothy. Both call for him to be loyal to Paul and his message (see Knight 1992, 438).

In vv 10-11, Paul responds to the negative influence of the false teachers by offering himself as a positive example to Timothy and the Ephesian church. A short catalog of virtues in reflection of Paul's ministry serves as the counterpart to the list of vices in 3:2-5a (→ 1:6-14). Its main theme is endurance through suffering (2 Cor 6:3-10).

The overall purpose of this section is twofold: to remind and encourage. It attempts to build confidence in Timothy so he will be better equipped spiritually and emotionally for dealing with the difficult people portrayed in 2 Tim 3:1-9. He has three resources to help him with this: his relationship with Paul as his inspiring model, his memory of his upbringing as a child, and Scripture. The passage ends with an implied three-part enthymeme (Donelson 1986, 86-87):

1. A man of God should do good works.
2. Scripture equips one for good works.
3. Therefore, study Scripture.

A. Three Resources for Endurance (3:10-17)

IN THE TEXT

■ **10-11** The emphatic **You, however** in Greek (*sy de* [see v 14]) marks a strong contrast between Timothy and the opponents (vv 6-9). The verb **know** (*parēkolouthēsas*) has the nuance of *follow as a disciple* (see Mark 2:14; Luke 9:23). The word means to accompany someone. Stoics used it to describe the close relationship between pupils and teachers (Kittel 1964, 215). As Paul's longtime ministry partner (→ Introduction), Timothy knows and should imitate Paul's way of thinking and living (→ 2 Tim 1:13; 2:2).

The virtue list here stands in sharp contrast to the vice list in 3:2-5. Each word has its own Greek article, reflected in the NIV with the repeated **my**. The list begins with a triad of what, how, and why Paul did what he did.

(1) **My teaching** is the "what" Paul did and comes in the emphatic first position. This may be because the primary problem and urgent need in Ephesus had to do with teaching (1 Tim 2:7; 4:6, 14; 6:2; 2 Tim 1:11; 3:10; 4:2). In the Pastoral Epistles, "teaching" in the singular, as here, refers to authentic teaching. "Teachings" in the plural refers to false teachings (Collins 2002, 255). The teaching that Paul passed on to Timothy was the apostolic tradition—the orthodox interpretation of the gospel. Timothy must be firmly grounded in the apostolic faith and faithfully preserve its integrity.

(2) Paul's **way of life** (*agōgē*) describes "how" he lived on a daily basis. People's lifestyle becomes evident over time to those who are closely associated with them. Paul focused his life on imitating Christ's example of self-giving love (1 Cor 4:17; 11:1). The balance of the virtue list portrays his lifestyle.

(3) Paul's life **purpose** (*prothesei*) describes "why" he lived as he did. His purpose was wrapped up in God's purpose of salvation in Christ (Eph 3:11; 1 Tim 2:4; 2 Tim 1:9-10). He believed that his part in this was to bring the message of salvation to the Gentile world (1 Tim 2:7). This word "expresses the ideas of commitment and firm resolve to carry out what he felt called to do" (Towner 2006, 571).

(4) The next three terms are key Christian virtues Timothy learned from Paul. **Faith** (*pistei*) often occurs with **love** in Paul's virtue lists (→ 1 Tim 1:14) and is an important word in this letter (2 Tim 1:5, 13; 2:13, 18, 22; 3:8, 10, 15; 4:7). The content of this faith is particularly summarized in the trustworthy (faithful) sayings in 1 Tim 1:15; 3:1; 4:9; and 2 Tim 2:11. Faith involves trust and reliance upon God (→ 1 Tim 4:12; 6:11; 2 Tim 2:22). Trust in God is the crucial human commitment required for all the other virtues. Paul had learned to trust God even in difficult, life-threatening situations (2 Tim 1:12).

(5) Faith in God provides the resource for **patience** (*makrothymia*). Patience is a divine characteristic (1 Tim 1:16) and an essential attitude for ministry (2 Tim 2:24-25; 4:2) and for dealing with difficult opponents (1 Tim 1:20; 2 Tim 2:21). Patience is a by-product of the indwelling Holy Spirit (Gal 5:22; Eph 4:2; Col 1:11; 3:12; 1 Thess 5:14). Patience helps one endure suffering because it is fueled by hope and trust in God.

(6) **Love** (*agapē*) is the supreme gift from God and the highest virtue to seek (1 Cor 13). It incorporates all other virtues and is possible only because of God's love for us (1 John 4:19) and the inward working of his Holy Spirit (Rom 5:5; Gal 5:22; 2 Tim 1:7). Love is expressed in and resourced by our relationship with Christ (1:13) and comes out of a purified heart (2:22). We express love for God by total dependence and trust in him, and for other people in affirming, edifying relationships.

(7) The next three virtues refer to Paul's sufferings. He probably included these here to encourage Timothy in his own struggles in Ephesus (→ 1 Tim 6:11). **Endurance** (*hypomenē*) involves "perseverance" (NASB, NJKV) and "steadfastness" (ESV, NRSV) in difficult situations. It is nearly synonymous with patience (see Col 1:11). But patience is more inward directed, while endurance deals with outward challenges (Collins 2002, 256). Endurance is empowered by courage and hope and prompted by suffering (Rom 5:3-4). The motivation for enduring suffering is that we will someday reign with Christ (→ 2 Tim 2:12).

(8) The next two plural words illustrate what Paul endured. **Persecutions** (*diōgmois*, only here in the Pastorals) are a form of physical pain and distress imposed by others because of one's faith.

(9) **Sufferings** (*pathēmasin*, only here in the Pastorals) are the traumatic human experience of discomfort caused by persecution. Jesus predicted that

his followers would experience suffering for their faith in him (Matt 5:11; Luke 6:22). The greatest cause for Christian suffering is preaching the gospel. Paul has already called for Timothy to share in suffering (2 Tim 1:8; 2:3, 12).

Persecutions allow the grace of Christ an opportunity to show its power (2 Cor 12:10). Knowing that persecutions cannot stop God's love in Christ should give believers hope and lead them to endure (Rom 8:35).

Before Paul met Christ, he caused many Christians to suffer (1 Tim 1:13). When he met Christ, he was called to suffer (Acts 9:16) and frequently did because of his missionary labors (Acts 13:50; 2 Cor 11:21-29). He refers to several places where he experienced persecution on his first missionary journey: Pisidian **Antioch** (Acts 13:13-52), **Iconium** (Acts 14:1-7), and **Lystra** (Acts 14:19-22). Timothy was from **Lystra** and would have known firsthand of Paul's experience there (Acts 16:1). As in 2 Tim 1:3-5, Paul reminds Timothy of the early days in his Christian life and of his spiritual origins.

Paul offers a bold statement of his confidence in God's protection: **Yet the Lord rescued [*errysato*] me from all of them.** Rescue entails salvation or deliverance from danger; God or Christ are always the agent (Kasch 1968, 1002; see Rom 7:24-25; 11:26; 15:31; 2 Cor 1:10; Col 1:13; 1 Thess 1:10; 2 Thess 3:2; 2 Tim 4:17). Paul was confident God would rescue him from his present situation (→ 2 Tim 4:18).

From (*ek*) "shows Paul's awareness that he is not so much kept away from persecutions and sufferings as that God keeps him safe in the midst of them" (Mounce 2000, 559). The rhetorical effect of this statement is powerful: just as God rescued Paul, God would rescue Timothy.

■ **12-13** Paul applies his experience of God's rescue (3:11) to the whole church. All believers will suffer (v 12). The sentence contains an indirect condition. The logic is clear: leading a godly life will lead to persecution. The reason why is implied in v 13.

Persecution will come if one **wants to live a godly life in Christ Jesus.** Godliness (here the adverb *eusebōs*) is a key theme in the Pastoral Epistles (→ 1 Tim 2:2). It is evident in a lifestyle of devotion and dependence upon God. Paul adds the important qualifier **in Christ Jesus.** Relationship with Christ distinguishes the piety of believers from the religiosity of those who dabble in false doctrines. Being "in Christ" empowers and compels one to holy living in dependence upon God's grace.

Why should being in Christ lead to persecution? Part of the reason can be found at the ending of v 13: **deceiving and being deceived.** The verb *planaō* (*deceive*) portrays misleading people with false information. In this case, **evildoers and impostors** are directly responsible, but they have themselves been deceived by Satan, the great liar (1 Tim 4:1-2; 2 Tim 2:26).

This may refer indirectly to the opponents in Ephesus. But it is inclusive enough to fit the general principle of 3:12. It matches the deception predicted for the last days (2 Thess 2:10-12). Deceivers entice others to reject true godliness (2 Tim 3:5).

Persecution does not happen simply because one lives by a different ethical standard. That would limit Paul's understanding of "godliness." Christians are engaged in spiritual warfare with the forces of evil (Eph 6:12). Standing up for the truth of the gospel may be costly. It takes constant vigilance to remain relationally and intellectually bound to the truth that is Christ Jesus.

Ironically, the false teachers thought they were making spiritual progress. But they were actually sinking deeper into corruption (→ 2 Tim 3:8-9). Paul predicts a different outcome for them than for the righteous orthodox. On the outside, the heretics looked religious, but they were **impostors** of genuine godliness. Because they rejected the truth of Paul's gospel, they were becoming progressively worse (→ 2:16; 3:9). The outcome for those who remained faithful, like Paul, would be "the crown of righteousness" (→ 4:8). These verses function as a warning to Timothy and the Ephesians. They should motivate them to remain faithful in spite of their suffering.

■ **14-15a** There is a noticeable shift, marked by **but . . . you** (*sy de*; → v 10), from descriptive language to direct exhortation and application to Timothy's life. The negative warnings (vv 1-9), the positive example of Paul's life (vv 10-11), and the general principle (vv 12-13) all serve to remind Timothy of the need to remain faithful to the gospel. Paul again uses the rhetorical tool of memory to motivate Timothy to **continue** in his ministry (→ 1:3-5). The present tense verb **continue** implies that this has been Timothy's way of life since he was a small child.

The relative clause **what you have learned and have become convinced of** contains two aorist verbs. These point back to prior events that influenced Timothy. **Learned** (*emathes*) involves cognitive understanding of the contents of the faith. **Convinced** (*epistōthēs*, only here in the NT) is an intensified form of the verb "believe." Conviction shows commitment to what one understands about the faith. It is a state of confidence about what one believes (BDAG 2000, 821). Paul asks Timothy to be faithful to what he has learned (Marshall 1999, 788). Here, the ***things*** (*hois*) Timothy believes is the gospel. Second Timothy repeatedly emphasizes the core elements of the Christian faith (→ 1:13-14; 2:2, 8, 14; 3:10; 4:2).

Paul devotes the rest of this chapter to the sources from which Timothy learned about the gospel. He stresses two in particular:

First, **those from whom you learned it**. He does not name these people here. But the next phrase mentions **from infancy**. This implies that they certainly included Timothy's grandmother Lois and mother Eunice (→ 1:5; Acts

16:1). But this phrase does not limit the influence only to Timothy's infancy; Paul had also been a significant mentor in his early life (→ 2 Tim 1:13; 2:2; 3:10). **Because you know** interprets the adverbial participle *eidōs* (lit. "knowing" [NASB, NRSV]). This personal element from Timothy's memory provides the motivation for continued faithfulness. Based on the character of the teachers, Timothy should know the quality of the teaching.

Second, the foundational source for Timothy's faith was the **Holy Scriptures** (*hiera grammata*, only here in the NT). *Hieros* is a rare word in the LXX and NT but more common in Hellenistic Judaism (Schrenk 1965, 221-30). Greek-speaking Jews used the expression to refer to the OT (Schrenk 1964a, 763). A different word (*graphē*) for "Scripture" appears in 3:16.

Mounce (2000, 563-64) offers two possible explanations of the force of *hieros*: (1) The phrase may stress the recognized sanctity of the OT, that it is from God and useful. Or, (2) it could comprehend more than the OT and include early Christian writings and teachings.

Acts gives no indication as to when Timothy's mother and grandmother became Christian believers or whether they had access to early Christian writings. Almost certainly they taught Timothy the Jewish Scriptures. Christians were convinced these writings pointed to salvation in Christ.

Whatever the extent of these writings, their goal is unmistakable: They point to salvation in Christ. Paul brings up Scripture as the source for the truth of the gospel, perhaps because the opponents abused Scripture in their speculation (→ 1 Tim 1:6-7).

Religious Education in Jewish Homes

The typical education of boys in the Roman Empire had three stages. Primary consisted of learning to read and write, music, social skills, morality, and practical mathematics. Secondary involved especially the study of rhetoric and grammar. Advanced included some type of apprenticeship in a specialized skill such as medicine, architecture, and teaching.

Depending on a family's geographical location and wealth, education generally included philosophy, grammar, rhetoric, and arithmetic. There was no free public education in most cities. Wealthy homes hired private tutors or secured educated slaves as teachers. The wealthy sent their children to schools in temples, forums, or gymnasiums. Those of more modest means taught them at home. Only limited educational opportunities existed for girls.

Jewish education followed similar patterns to the Greco-Roman. But its focus was on the Torah (Deut 6:4-9). The rabbinic tractate *'Abot* 5.21 (late first century) indicates that boys could begin to study the law at age five. They memorized considerable portions of the Scriptures. More advanced education involved learning how to interpret the Bible.

There were two primary settings for Jewish education: the home and the local synagogue. It was the father's responsibility to teach his sons the Scriptures.

Synagogues often had weekday schools attached to them for Jewish boys. Formal education ended at thirteen, when a boy began to learn a trade as an apprentice, usually from his father. Those who were especially gifted could study the Torah further under special teachers (Ferguson 1993, 100-103; Watson 2000, 308-13).

Many Jews of the Diaspora were schooled in Greco-Roman ways. Paul apparently received both a Greco-Roman education in rhetoric and an advanced Jewish education in Scripture and rabbinic interpretation. Timothy's education was probably similar. Since his father was not Jewish, his mother and grandmother were his primary religious influences.

■ **15b-17** Paul mentions five key characteristics of Scripture in these verses:

First, they **make you wise for salvation**. Scripture as a source of wisdom was a crucial part of the Jewish and later Christian faith (Pss 19:7-8; 119; Wilckens 1971, 527-28). This wisdom has a specific goal (*eis* followed by the accusative): the primary purpose of Scripture is to point the way to salvation (Rom 15:4). The saving wisdom of Scripture sharply contrasts the foolishness of the opponents (2 Tim 3:9, 13). Both Paul and the opponents appealed to the Hebrew Scriptures. But Paul found the major emphasis in Christ and not trivial matters, myths, genealogies, or speculations (→ 1 Tim 1:3-4, 7).

Second, the *holy writings* show that the source of this salvation is **through faith in Christ Jesus**. **Faith** opens the door to life **in Christ Jesus**. Early Christians interpreted the Jewish Scriptures christologically. They believed the OT prepared for and spoke about the coming Messiah and the salvation he would bring (Matt 26:56; Luke 24:44-47; John 5:46; Rom 1:2-4; 1 Cor 15:3-4; 1 Pet 1:10-12). The gospel of Christ fulfills the revelation of Scripture. "Life characterized by faith in Christ . . . releases the potential of the Scripture for the eyes of faith" (Towner 2006, 584).

Third, **all Scripture** is inspired—(lit.) **God-breathed** (*theopneustos*). The *pneu-* word group in Greek refers to both "air/breath" and "spirit." The "breath" of God through his Spirit moved people to write what we have in the Bible (Acts 1:16; 2 Pet 1:21). God's breath brings life (Gen 2:7), and this breath working through Scripture brings new life. This is the earliest known usage of the term, but it began to be used in other texts for God's activity in inspiring Scripture (Marshall 1999, 794). There are several challenging interpretive issues related to this phrase:

(1) The phrase lacks an explicit verb. **God-breathed** is an adjective. As a predicate adjective it could mean: "Every Scripture is God-inspired." As an attributive adjective it would mean: "Every God-inspired Scripture is useful."

The first option means that everything considered "Scripture" has been inspired by God. The second option implies that some supposed Scripture is not inspired, and thus not as useful for the church (the Protestant view of the

Apocrypha and Pseudepigrapha). The first reading is more natural and followed by most translations.

(2) Another question concerns the meanings of the words and their influence upon the grammatical issue above. The adjective **all** (*pasa*) is singular to match the singular **Scripture** (*graphē*). Is this a collective use of the singular to include the whole of Scripture (Fee 1984, 279), or does it refer to every passage in Scripture that speaks about salvation (Fiore 2007, 171)? That is: Is all of Scripture inspired or just certain passages? How we answer this question will affect our doctrine of inspiration.

The word for "scripture" in the NT is usually in the plural when it refers to the Hebrew Bible (except perhaps in Gal 3:22). *Graphē* is the generic word for "writing." But in the NT it refers specifically to "Scripture" (Schrenk 1964a, 751-55).

Jews used Scripture in synagogue worship to refer to the Tanak: the Law (Torah), Prophets (Nebiim), and Writings (Ketubim). When Paul wrote his letters, the OT was in the final stages of canonization. There was not clear agreement as to whether certain books were or were not Scripture. Until the invention of the printing press, the Bible was handwritten. So it typically could not be contained in a single book, but required several separate scrolls or codices. The development of codices (bound books) began in the first century AD. The plural form "Scriptures" applies more naturally to scrolls.

The word **Scripture** may be more inclusive than *grammata* (**Scriptures**) in v 15. In 1 Tim 5:18, the singular *graphē* refers to the words of Jesus. Second Peter 3:15 seems to refer to Paul's letters as "scripture." Paul himself expected his letters to be read (1 Thess 5:27), exchanged (Col 4:16), and obeyed (1 Cor 14:37; 2 Thess 2:15) because they contained the authoritative words of the gospel (Knight 1992, 448). All these passages strongly suggest that the whole idea of what constituted "sacred writing" was expanding in the early church to include the authoritative writing of the apostles or their close associates.

Theologians appeal to this passage to establish the inspiration of the Bible. Early church fathers quoted it more than one hundred times as they developed their doctrine of inspiration. There is certainly a basis for considering this topic here. But most discussions ignore the context:

Paul is writing to counter the influence of the false teachers who were selectively using Scripture to support their speculative doctrines. In a sense, they endorsed a canon within a canon, focusing on their favorite proof texts. Paul does two things in this passage. First, he identifies God as the source of Scripture. But he does not describe how God inspires. And second, he emphasizes the purpose of Scripture within the church (Johnson 2001, 420). His point is not how God inspired Scripture. He stresses the usefulness of Scripture for theology and ethics: Scripture points people to the truth of the gospel of salvation in Christ (1 Cor 10:11).

The Bible Paul Used

There are at least one hundred quotations of the OT in Paul's letters and just as many allusions. Paul's "Bible" was the Jewish Scriptures, the OT. Paul would not have had a bound Bible of thirty-nine books on his shelf from which he could easily quote. Scrolls were expensive, and few people owned them privately. Part of his formal education would have involved memorizing large portions of the Jewish Bible. He probably studied the Greek LXX growing up in Tarsus and the Hebrew text during his time in Jerusalem. Both of these would have been available as scrolls belonging to local synagogues or the temple complex.

Which version of the OT did Paul use when he quotes or alludes to Scripture in his letters? The answer is not easy. There are few times when what he writes exactly matches a Greek translation of a Hebrew text. Most of the time, he appears to use the LXX, which would have been the common translation of Diaspora Jews. In some places, he matches neither. Instead, he appears to be paraphrasing or interpreting a passage using standard rabbinic methods of the time. At times he freely inserts words directly into a quotation to fit his argument. He read the Scripture through the lens of Christ. He believed that the Scriptures contain the plan of God and foretold the coming of Christ (Rom 3:2; 16:25-26). There has been much debate about Paul's use of the OT represented in three generations of important studies:

Ellis, E. Earle. 1957. *Paul's Use of the Old Testament*. Grand Rapids: Baker.

Hays, Richard B. 1989. *Echoes of Scripture in the Letters of Paul*. New Haven & London: Yale University Press.

Moyise, Steve. 2010. *Paul and Scripture: Studying the New Testament Use of the Old Testament*. London: SPCK.

The fourth characteristic of Scripture is that it is **useful** in the church **for teaching, rebuking, correcting and training in righteousness** (see 2 Tim 2:5, 10; 4:2, 8). **Useful** (*ōphelimos*) as an adjective describes something that has a practical benefit. The logic is that since Scripture comes from God, it must be useful for salvation and anything that moves us toward the full experience of this salvation.

Paul shows the usefulness of Scripture by his many citations of it in his letters. Early Christians found the OT to be a source for spiritual growth. Paul writes in Rom 15:4, "For everything that was written in the past was written to teach us, so that through the endurance taught in the Scriptures and the encouragement they provide we might have hope."

Each of the four uses of Scripture are introduced with the preposition *pros* (**for**). They are similar to Timothy's ministry assignment (→ 2 Tim 4:2). The first two deal with doctrine ("orthodoxy") and the second two with behavior ("orthopraxy"; Mounce 2000, 570; Guthrie 1990, 182). They form a chiasm:

A **Teaching** (positive), a focus on education;

  B **Rebuking** (negative), dealing with sin;

  B' **Correcting** (negative), dealing with sin;

A' **Training** (positive), a focus on education.

"Scripture gives us not only God's *Yes* but also His *No*. Both are given for our benefit" (Black and McClung 2004, 179).

A. **Teaching** (*didaskalian*) refers to instruction in doctrine and conduct (→ 1 Tim 1:10). In the Pastorals, the focus of true teaching is the gospel. In the local church, such teaching is particularly the job of qualified elders (1 Tim 2:11-12; 3:2; 5:17; Titus 1:9).

B. **Rebuking** (*elegmon*, only here in the NT, but cognates appear in Titus 1:9, 13; 2:15; Heb 11:1; 2 Pet 2:16) involves correcting wrong ideas and interpretations. It is the negative side of the more positive **teaching**. The result should be a conviction of sin and the truth. Scripture sets the standard by which behavior and doctrine can be measured. We learn how to avoid judgment from the wrong choices reported in Scripture (1 Cor 10:11-12).

B'. **Correcting** (*epanorthōsin*, only here in the NT) is a way to censure behavior. It has a negative connotation when sin is the issue. It has a more positive connotation than rebuke with the goal of restoration and forgiveness. Its root (*orthos*) gives the word the sense of helping someone stand up straight again in a restored position. Its place between **rebuking** and **training** assumes that restoration has occurred (Preisker 1967, 451).

A'. **Training in righteousness** returns to the positive goal of education—**teaching**. **Training** (*paideian*) is instruction that may include discipline (Heb 12:5, 7-8, 11). It describes the training of a child (Eph 6:4; → 2 Tim 3:15). Scripture is the primary source for knowing how to pursue **righteousness** (*dikaiosynē*). God sets the standard for "right conduct" and relates this through his laws as recorded in Scripture (→ 1 Tim 1:9-10; Schrenk 1964b, 210). Scripture provides the knowledge for how one ought to live to please God and be used by God (→ 1 Tim 6:11; 2 Tim 2:22). This last element comes in the emphatic last position, preparing for the closing purpose/result statement of 3:17. Timothy could use Scripture in his strategy of correcting the false teachers in Ephesus (2:24-25).

The fifth characteristic of Scripture is that it has the purpose or result (*hina*) of **thoroughly** equipping believers **for every good work**. This is the practical outcome of salvation in Jesus Christ. The NIV's **servant of God** is (lit.) *man of God* (→ 1 Tim 6:11). The word is singular with clear implications for Timothy. But since it is proverbial, it applies to all believers.

Paul lists two purposes for Scripture in this passage. The primary purpose is to lead to new life in Christ (2 Tim 3:15). The consequence to this is that believers learn how to live out this new life through good works, which are detailed in Scripture. Scripture is the road map for how believers ought to live. The goal is that believers become *artios*. This rare NT word has the basic meaning of "being well fitted for some function, complete, capable, proficient" (BDAG 2000, 136). Here, it "denotes what is right or proper, and more particularly what is becoming to a Christian, obviously with a moral accent" (Delling 1964a, 476).

Christians know what is the right way to act based on the Bible. A different word based on the same root appears as a participle in **thoroughly equipped** (*exērtismenos*). The *ek* prefix at the beginning adds emphasis and shows that something has been completely prepared for service (BDAG 2000, 346). The perfect passive participle has Scripture as the implied resource.

Since God's Spirit is the source of Scripture, God's plan is for believers to become thoroughly prepared for his service through study and application of Scripture. "Good works" are an essential aspect of life in Christ (Eph 2:10). Scripture contains the authoritative word from God about Christ. Paul is concerned that the Ephesians learn how to identify and live out the truth of this good news properly (1 Tim 2:10; 5:10, 25; 6:18; 2 Tim 2:21; → Titus 2:7, 14; 3:1, 8, 14).

FROM THE TEXT

Endurance through persecution and opposition functions as the central theme of this section (2 Tim 3:12). Those who follow Christ should not expect the fallen world to receive them with open arms. Our efforts to live a godly life will bring persecution (Matt 5:10-12; 24:9; Mark 8:34; John 15:18; Acts 14:22; Phil 1:29; 1 Thess 3:4). The hope of eternal life can sustain us in our sufferings (Rom 5:3; 8:18, 35; 2 Cor 4:9; Gal 4:29; 5:11; 2 Thess 1:4). Suffering may teach us to rely more fully on God's grace (2 Cor 12:10) and be a source of blessing to others (Rom 12:14; 1 Cor 4:12; 2 Tim 2:10).

Paul offers Timothy three resources to help him through any difficulty he may face in Ephesus: (1) Paul's own example (3:10-11), (2) Timothy's rich Christian heritage (vv 14-15), and (3) Scripture (vv 15-17).

Hebrews 12:1 invites us to look at the great cloud of witnesses of ch 11 who persevered through suffering because of their faith in God. Some were tortured, ridiculed, flogged, imprisoned, stoned to death, sawn in two, and killed by the sword. Others were mistreated and had to flee out of desperation (11:35-38). Their hope in resurrection life sustained them through this suffering (11:16). Paul shared this hope with the author of Hebrews (Phil 3:10-11).

There is a two-part message with this: (1) Those who are experiencing suffering can lean on the strength of those who have remained faithful to God through their own suffering. And (2) those who are suffering should realize

361

that others will be influenced by how they respond to the challenges they face. God uses suffering to build up his church.

Timothy was raised by a faithful mother and grandmother (2 Tim 1:5). These two women planted seeds that would one day bear fruit in Timothy's life as long as he continued in this same faith. The formative years in children's lives can lay a foundation and set a trajectory that can sustain them through the trials of life (see Prov 22:6).

The greatest resource from which Timothy could draw his strength is the Scripture, because it points the way to salvation in Christ. Scripture contains the very oracles of God (Rom 3:1-2) and should be the foundational basis for all doctrine. This is because it is the primary witness to the truth of the gospel longed for in the OT and incarnated in Jesus Christ. The power of Scripture becomes evident when it is allowed to become the rule for faith and conduct. The Bible is a source for defense against heresy. But it is also a resource for offense by strengthening believers to live out their salvation.

John Wesley follows John Calvin's emphasis on the twofold inspiration of Scripture. He wrote on v 16 (1813, 239):

> The Spirit of God not only once inspired those who wrote it, but continually inspires, supernaturally assists, those who read it with earnest prayer. Hence it is so profitable for doctrine, for instruction of the ignorant, for the reproof or conviction of them that are in error or sin, for the correction or amendment of whatever is amiss, and for instructing or training up the children of God in all righteousness.

Scripture was to be the most significant source Timothy had to draw upon to correct those in error and empower those already on the right path. The study of Scripture is vital in spiritual formation since it bears witness to the incarnated Word, Jesus Christ. Jesus promised his disciples that the Holy Spirit would remind them of his words (John 14:26). If we do not study the Bible, of what can the Holy Spirit remind us? Renewal and revival come from the seeds of Scripture. Those who lead the church, especially elders who preach and teach (1 Tim 5:17), bear the important responsibility of making Scripture understandable and relevant to the church. But it is ultimately up to each individual to be engaged in Bible study. The study of the Bible serves as the foundation for preaching the gospel, which Paul takes up next.

B. Preach the Gospel (4:1-8)

BEHIND THE TEXT

Paul continues to remind and encourage Timothy to be faithful to his calling despite his hardships. This section functions as the peroration, the climax of the letter. It recapitulates and summarizes the key themes with an emotional appeal (Witherington 2006, 362). Timothy has all the resources he needs to fulfill his calling: the gift of the Holy Spirit (2 Tim 1:6, 14), Paul's example (1:13; 2:2-3), a rich spiritual heritage (1:5; 3:15), and the Scriptures (3:15-17). The threats of apostasy from the false teachers infiltrating the Ephesian church made Paul's appeal urgent. This tone is reiterated in this section with the use of five imperatives in 4:2 and four in v 5.

As part of a paraenetic letter, this section offers two contrasting examples: negative—the false teachers and those they have deceived (vv 3-4); positive—Paul who has faithfully completed his service to the Lord (vv 6-8). Between these two is an exhortation (in v 5) that restates the theme of the letter. The choice is clear for Timothy and the Ephesians.

The negative example justifies the strong language in this section. Paul's example is something like the last testament of one facing imminent death. He is passing the baton of leadership on to Timothy. Paul's thinking shifts to his heavenly reward, marked by eschatological language of Christ's second coming in vv 1 and 8 (inclusio—literary bookends). Paul's final charge has a chiastic structure (Smith 2006):

Charge Verb and Authority Phrase (4:1)
   Content of the Charge (4:2)
      Reason for the Charge (4:3-4)
   Content of the Charge (4:5)
Paul's Autobiographical Comments (4:6-7)
Implications of the Charge (4:8)

I. Timothy's Charge (4:1-5)

IN THE TEXT

■ **I** *I charge [you]* comes emphatically first in Greek. It has the form of a solemn oath: Paul speaks with full authority as Christ's apostle and Timothy's mentor (1:1-2). The calling of two divine persons as witnesses underlines the seriousness of the charge (→ 1 Tim 5:21; 6:13-14). The preposition **in the presence of** (*enōpion*) governs both objects and shifts the imagery to the heavenly court. **In the presence of God** is used in Scripture with a sense of judgment (1 Sam 7:6; Pss 56:13; 61:7; 68:3-4). To do something before God (Gal 1:20; 2 Tim 2:14) or before Christ (1 Tim 5:21; 6:13) makes one accountable to them.

The focus of the verse quickly shifts to **Christ Jesus, who will judge the living and the dead** (on Christ as Judge, see Matt 25:31-46; Mark 13:26-27; John 5:22, 27; Acts 10:39-43; 17:31; 24:25; Rom 2:16; 14:9-12; 2 Cor 5:10; 2 Thess 1:5-9; Heb 6:2; 1 Pet 4:5; 2 Pet 3:7; Jude 6; Rev 20:4). Incarnation makes Christ worthy to decide the final destiny of all humanity; as one of us, he knows our limitations (Heb 4:15). The belief that Christ will judge humanity when he returns became an important confession of faith in the early church

(*Barn.* 7.2; Pol. *Phil.* 2.1; *2 Clem.* 1.1). It was later codified in the Apostles' Creed: the risen and ascended Christ will come from heaven "to judge the quick and the dead."

Will judge (*tou mellontos krinein*) translates a Greek periphrastic future. The end is near; judgment is about to happen. Then Christ will judge **the living and the dead**. These words form a figure of speech (merism) in which opposites comprehend "all" (Collins 2002, 367). The statement is literally true because not all will be dead; some will be alive when Christ returns (1 Cor 15:51; 1 Thess 4:15-17).

Two other "witnesses" to Paul's charge serve to motivate Timothy and remind him that he must give an account to God. Paul reminds him of Christ's **appearing** (*epiphaneian*) and **kingdom** (*basleian*). The first word refers to Christ's second coming in 2 Tim 1:10, 2 Thess 2:8, 1 Tim 6:14, and Titus 2:13. The **kingdom** of God was a central theme of Jesus' preaching (Mark 1:15). Jesus' status as Messiah—Davidic king—is implied in 2 Tim 2:8. The kingdom of God is breaking into history because of the death and resurrection of Christ. Believers participate now in Christ's eternal reign, which will come fully at his second coming (1 Cor 6:9; 15:24-28; Gal 5:21; Eph 5:5; Col 4:11). Christ will intervene in history with two results: he will bring salvation to God's people and judgment to those who resist him (Towner 2006, 597).

These reminders serve as motivation for Timothy and the foundation for the following imperatives. Timothy, like Paul, should not fear earthly rulers. They can take away only his physical life; eternal life is determined by King Jesus, who gives endurance and hope to his servants.

■ **2** Paul lays out his charge in five concise imperatives.

First, **preach the word**. Preaching is to be Timothy's primary activity; all others are aspects of this. Preaching is what Jesus came doing (Matt 4:23; 9:35; 24:14; 26:13; Mark 1:14-15; 13:10; 14:9; 16:15), what his disciples were to do (Mark 3:14), and what the early church did (Acts 8:5; 10:42). Paul's highest priority was to proclaim the gospel (Acts 20:25; 28:31; Rom 1:15; 1 Cor 1:23; 9:16; 15:12; 2 Cor 1:19; Gal 2:2; 1 Thess 2:9; see Rom 10:14-15). As Timothy continues to do what got Paul imprisoned, he can likewise expect opposition.

The usual direct object of the verb **preach** is Christ, the word, or the gospel (2 Cor 4:5). **The word** (*logos*) is shorthand for the gospel, the "good news" of Jesus Christ (→ 2 Tim 2:9; 1 Tim 4:5; and 2 Tim 2:15). **The word** is set in strong contrast to the heretical teachings of the opponents in 4:3-4. Timothy should guard the deposit of the gospel (→ 1 Tim 6:20; 2 Tim 1:14) and proclaim it accurately.

Second, Timothy should always **be prepared** (*epistēthi*) to preach. The verb may mean to be "persistent" (NRSV) or "ready" (ESV, NASB) and urgent. "Grasp opportunities that offer themselves" (Marshall 1999, 800). When listeners provide the opportunity, preachers take advantage of it.

In season and out of season is another merism (→ v 1) with two opposite statements comprehending all between. The two adverbs show in what type of situation the preaching should be done. Both are based on the word for "time" or "opportunity" (*kairos*). They can be translated as in **good times** (*eu-* prefix) and **inconvenient times** (alpha privative *a*-prefix). Preachers should be ready *in all circumstances*, even if the audience will not listen (Malherbe 1984). The mention of "time" in v 3 implies that this was not a convenient time for Timothy to preach in Ephesus because of the false teachers.

Third, Timothy is to use his rhetorical skills in his preaching and appeal to reason, conscience, and the will (Johnson 2001, 429). He must **correct** people, helping them become aware of their sins (Büchsel 1964a, 474). *Elenxon* can mean **convince** or **reprove**. Correction received leads to conviction and repentance (1 Tim 5:20). Titus must also do this in his ministry on Crete (→ Titus 1:9, 13; 2:15).

Fourth, **rebuke** (*epitimēson*, only here in Paul's letters) is confrontational. Correction merely tries to persuade people that what they are doing is wrong; rebuking attempts to get them to stop their wrongdoing (Knight 1992, 454).

Fifth, **encourage** (*parakaleson*) is exhortation to pursue a positive direction. Paul's letters to Timothy and Titus were written with the express purpose of exhortation (1 Tim 1:3; 2:1; 4:13; 5:1; 6:2; Titus 2:6, 15).

The goal of all preaching is restoration (1 Cor 4:21). At times one must use different approaches. Benedict of Nursia wrote, "Use rigor with the irregular and the turbulent, but win to better things the obedient, mild and patient" (*Rule* 2, quoted by Gorday 2000, 270). Timothy should do all these preaching-related tasks **with great patience and careful instruction**. These two cover attitude and content (Towner 1994, 204).

Patience is a necessity in the task of teaching because people are slow to learn and to change their ways. Jesus is the greatest example of patience (→ 1 Tim 1:16). Paul offers himself as another model of patience (→ 2 Tim 3:10). Paul's letters, such as the Corinthian correspondence, illustrate how he patiently dealt with difficult churches that were slow to heed his teachings. **Great** and **careful** in the NIV translate one Greek word (*pasē*). Timothy's teaching is to be done with *full* commitment.

■ **3-4 For** (*gar*) introduces the reason why Timothy must preach the gospel effectively, accurately, and patiently (4:2). Paul intended this general statement to apply specifically to the Ephesian context. The threat of false doctrine infiltrating the Ephesian church was serious. Timothy needed to keep a clear head in such difficult situations (v 5).

These two verses begin with a prediction: **the time will come**. The negative traits of the last days were already present in Ephesus (→ 3:1-9; 1 Tim 4:6). **Time** (*kairos*) "depicts the apostasy as a single element in a larger eschatological scenario" and creates the specific need for Timothy to act (Towner 2006, 603). Two contrasting statements offer four characteristics of what people will and will not do in response to the preaching of the gospel in these last days:

First, **people will not put up with sound doctrine**. The verb *anexontai* means tolerate or bear (Schlier 1964a, 359-60). In Heb 13:22, it has the positive sense of willingly accepting a word of exhortation. **Sound doctrine** here (→ 1 Tim 1:10; Titus 1:9; 2:1) uses medical imagery (**sound** = **healthy** [*hygiainousē*]) to characterize orthodox teaching that agrees with the apostolic message. Deceptive teaching and opposition had hampered Paul's work in Ephesus from the beginning (Acts 19:9, 13). The problem had not resolved by the time he wrote this letter (2 Tim 2:17-18, 23; 3:1-9).

Second, people surround themselves with so-called **teachers** who say only what they want to hear. **Gather around** (*episōreusousin*, only here in the NT) means "accumulate" (ESV, NASB, NRSV) as in stockpiling (Lang 1971, 1094-96). The problem is not the oversupply of teachers but that their only qualification is their commitment to pleasing their audience—satisfying their **own desires**. **Desires** (*epithymias*) has a strongly negative sense in the Pastoral Epistles (→ 1 Tim 6:9; Titus 2:12; 3:3). Such teachers offer no challenge, only deceptive comfort. These people are enticed by false doctrine because it satisfies their **itching ears**. This metaphor illustrates a "curiosity that looks for interesting and juicy bits of information" (BDAG 2000, 550).

Third, people in these last days **will turn *the ear* away from the truth**. The verb *apostrephō* in 2 Tim 1:15 means "deserted." Thus, these people once professed to know **the truth** of the gospel (Knight 1992, 456; → 1 Tim 2:4; 2 Tim 2:15, 18, 25; 3:7-8). They are backslidden or apostate, former believers.

Fourth, the outcome (*de*) of rejecting the truth is that these people now go the totally opposite direction: they **turn aside to myths** (→ 1 Tim 1:4; 4:7; 2 Tim 2:14, 23). The myths of the false teachers did not edify the church or lead people closer to God. Instead, they drove them away in confusion. The opponents sounded religious, but their wrong motives showed up in their ungodly living (→ 3:5). They redefined "truth" to suit themselves. They craved novelty so much that they could no longer judge between truth and error (Towner 2006, 604-5). Truth is not decided by a popularity contest.

■ **5** Paul shifts to paraenesis (ethical advice) with a second series of imperatives (see 4:2). The emphatic ***but as for you*** (→ 3:10, 14 for the same Greek construction) contrasts Timothy with the confused end-times "people" of 4:3-4.

First, Timothy must **keep his head** [*nēphe*] **in all situations**. The verb literally means remain "sober" (NASB, NRSV). But here it has the figurative sense of being "self-controlled" (LEB) or maintaining a "clear mind" (NLT). Timothy must keep his thinking disciplined, keenly aware not only of the truth but also of error. In the ancient world, clear thinking was considered crucial for public service (Bauernfeind 1967b, 937) and a prerequisite for leadership (Plato, *Leg.* 11.918D). Paul echoes that sentiment, making critical thinking skills a requirement for church leaders (→ 1 Tim 3:2, 11; Titus 2:2).

Clearheaded leaders must be adaptable. **In all situations** shows their need for flexibility and ingenuity. In Ephesus, many were being deceived because they had grown lackadaisical. They had not grown in their knowledge of the gospel. Their fuzzy thinking made them vulnerable to heresy.

Second, Timothy must **endure hardship**. This command echoes a key theme in this letter (→ 1:8, 12; 2:3, 9, 12; 3:11, 12). Paul modeled such endurance (3:10-11). Persecution is not optional for sincere followers of Christ. Endurance depends on the resources from which one draws strength. Paul found his strength in Christ (Phil 4:13) and urges Timothy to do the same (2 Tim 2:1; → 4:17). The mention of *suffering misfortune* (*kakopathēson*; → 2 Tim 2:9) here prepares for Paul's testimony in vv 6-8.

Third, Timothy should **do the work of an evangelist** (*euangelistou*, only here and in Acts 21:8 and Eph 4:11 in the NT). The verbal cognate in Acts 8:4, 12, 35, and 40 describes Philip the evangelist's preaching of the gospel. At the heart of being an evangelist is preaching the gospel to both nonbelievers and those within the church. This is the type of ministry to which Paul devoted his life (1 Cor 1:17). He urges Timothy to continue his legacy (Phil 2:22; 1 Thess 3:2).

There is insufficient evidence in these passages to indicate that there was a special office of "evangelist" in the early church. Rather, preaching the gospel was a crucial activity for all church leaders (Campbell 1992).

Fourth, Timothy should **discharge all the duties of** his **ministry**. **Discharge** (*plērophorēson*) refers to fulfilling or completing a task with a sense of accountability (Col 4:17). Timothy's job was to continue what Paul had started. **Ministry** (*diakonian*) is a broad and inclusive term for the *service* Paul and Timothy were performing. The term can more narrowly refer to some leaders in the church who had the special calling as deacons (→ 1 Tim 3:1-7). Here, however, it refers more broadly to the preaching and church-planting ministry of Paul and Timothy (2 Cor 5:18; 1 Thess 3:2).

FROM THE TEXT

This passage has been traditionally featured in services of ordination for ministers. The idea of a "professional clergy" was foreign to the early church. As time went on, the division of labor increased. Many of Paul's thoughts here can apply equally well to lay leaders in the church today.

First, *leaders within the church should realize before whom and for whom they serve*. Paul was strongly aware of his accountability before God and Christ Jesus. This came from his loving and healthy respect for God ("the fear of the Lord") and his hope for eternal life. The eternal character of the Christian life should not be lost in the blur of earthly busyness. Scripture warns that all of us will give an account for how we have lived (Rom 14:12; Heb 4:13; 13:17; 1 Pet 4:5). Charles Wesley's hymn "A Charge to Keep I Have" invites us to recommit our service to God.

Second, *the highest priority in the church ought to be preaching the good news of Jesus Christ*. "Preaching" is not limited to a thirty-minute Sunday morning sermon. Rather, it speaks to the core value of living out the incarnational message expressed succinctly in John 3:16. Although "elders" (→ 1 Tim 5:17) have the particular responsibility of preaching and teaching within the church, all believers are called to witness (Acts 1:8). The ingredients to a good witness include preparation in prayer (Acts 1:14; 2:1), knowledge of the message ("careful instruction" [2 Tim 4:2]) and Scripture (→ 3:16-17), and adaptability to the context ("in season and out of season" [4:2]). A good illustration can be found when Philip, the "evangelist," met the Ethiopian eunuch in Acts 8:26-40. Philip, "full of faith and of the Holy Spirit" (6:5), was able to explain the connection of Isa 53 to Jesus (Acts 8:35), and took advantage of the opportunity to baptize the new convert (v 38).

Third, *clear and orthodox preaching will lead to quality spiritual growth*. One of Timothy's greatest challenges in Ephesus was correcting the wrong teaching of the opponents who set themselves up as teachers. People tend to be attracted to those who give a message they want to hear. The sharp message of scriptural truth is seldom pleasant to receive (see Heb 4:12). Other standards for truth besides the gospel (Gal 1:8-9) merely create a facade of relativism. Paul saw through this Ephesian error. God has chosen the foolishness of preaching to help his people know him better (1 Cor 1:21)—to be transformed and renewed, not conformed to this world (Rom 12:1-2).

Finally, *although ministry can be difficult, its rewards are out of this world*. Church people will disappoint and enemies will persecute, but we cannot give up our service to God. Timothy faced a serious challenge. He, like Paul, faced rejection, persecution, and imprisonment. Paul's sights were set on receiving "the crown of righteousness" (→ 2 Tim 4:8). Because we will face "the righteous Judge" (4:8), we must not give up the task laid out before us.

2. Paul's Final Testimony (4:6-8)

BEHIND THE TEXT

The next three verses continue the letter's conclusion begun in 4:1. We treat them separately here because they function as Paul's eulogy. Many people over the years have interpreted this passage as Paul's last recorded testimony before his execution. Although there are many unknowns about Paul's final days, from simply the perspective of the words of this letter, Paul expects an imminent end to his life.

Paul's historical setting drives the close of the letter. He had already experienced a preliminary trial, which turned out badly (→ 4:16-18). As he writes this letter, he awaits a second trial, which he fears will not go well. His hope is in Christ, so he does not fear for himself personally. Rather, he is concerned about Timothy and the mission in Ephesus and beyond. This closing reveals the reason why Paul wrote the letter.

The unit's most notable literary feature is the shift to the first-person singular. From 4:6 to v 18, there are twenty-two first-person pronouns in Paul's personal appeal to Timothy (Witherington 2006, 367). Paul's vivid images offer his own example for Timothy to follow. He had faithfully kept his charge to preach the gospel. He implicitly urges Timothy to follow his example. His testimony should motivate his younger protégé and make clear why Timothy must diligently follow the instructions in this letter. They reflect what Paul considered most important in his ministry.

This passage has several interesting similarities to Phil 1:23 and 2:17. If this letter were pseudonymous, it would indicate some knowledge or literary dependence of the author upon Philippians (Dibelius and Conzelmann 1972, 121). But this is tenuous and highly subjective. Another possibility is that the same author—Paul—wrote them both within the same time period. This would have implications for dating both 2 Timothy and Philippians. Of course, it is also possible that facing the possibility of execution prompted Paul to draw from the stock imagery of condemned prisoners. In both cases, he sees his life as a sacrifice given to Christ in behalf of others. He desires to be with Christ but knows the churches need strengthening in their faith.

IN THE TEXT

■ **6** There is a noticeable shift from Timothy's situation ("but you" in v 5) to Paul's situation. This is marked in Greek with an emphatic **I** (*ego*), which comes first in the sentence. There is a secondary contrast between Timothy's future struggles and Paul's finished race (Bassler 1996, 171). **For** (*gar*) links the two sections, explaining why Timothy must continue the ministry. Paul will not be there to help. All he can do is only explain how he fulfilled his own calling.

Paul has a sense that his life will soon end. He uses the cultic imagery of **being poured out like a drink offering**. The present tense verb **I am . . . being poured out** (*spendomai*) indicates that the process that will lead to his death is **already** underway (Knight 1992, 458). He does not think it will happen immediately, since he expects to live through the winter and wants Timothy to bring his cloak (vv 9, 13, 21). The imagery of a **drink offering** would have been understood in both Greco-Roman and Jewish contexts.

Libations in the Ancient World

In Greco-Roman culture, a common religious practice involved pouring out a libation of wine to the gods before drinking or after a meal. Collins notes, "In the solemn meals of religious associations and trade guilds, a libation was usually offered to the divine patron between the meal itself and the discourse, the *symposium*, that followed" (2002, 273). It was also customary to pour out a drink offering before the moorings of a ship were loosened for departure (Spicq 1969, 2:803-4). Wine was sometimes poured out in honor of the Olympian gods (Homer, *Od.* 12.363; Plutarch, *Def. orac.* 49).

In ancient Jewish cultic practice, wine was poured out at the foot of the altar as an offering to God (Num 15:5, 7, 10; 28:7; 2 Kgs 16:13; Jer 7:18; Hos 9:4; Sir 50:15), especially on the Day of Atonement and Passover (Exod 29:40-41; Lev 23:13; Num 15:4-10).

It is impossible to determine from which cultural context Paul drew his imagery. The race metaphor in the next verse fits well the Olympic context. But Phil 2:17, which is similar, strongly implies the Jewish cultic practice.

Paul writes in a somber tone: **and the time for my departure is near**. The perfect tense of the verb **has come near** (*ephestēken*) indicates that his fate has already been settled; his death is imminent. The process that will lead to his execution has begun. He gives no time indicator, but he was aware of the probable outcome. The letter's content does not sustain the traditional theory that 2 Timothy must have been the last letter Paul wrote, only that he expects things to go badly in the near future. He could have written other letters after this (→ Introduction; Walker 2012b, 125-27).

Departure (*analyseōs*) was used for dismantling a tent or loosening the lines on a ship in preparation for leaving. Here it refers figuratively to his death (as in Phil 1:23). But it should be noted that Paul does not use the word "death." Death for him was only a temporary interruption of passing from one mode of existence to another. Believers cannot be defeated by the fear of death because Christ has already defeated death, "the last enemy" (1 Cor 15:26). To live in this present world is to experience the presence of Christ now through the Holy Spirit. To die is to gain the hoped-for experience of unhindered fellowship with Christ (Phil 1:21; 1 Cor 13:12; 2 Cor 5:1-9).

Paul viewed his death positively because it would open the way for him to receive his reward. Furthermore, his death would have a positive impact upon others as a model of faithful service. "He sees himself as having lived a purposeful life, now living a purposeful death" (Oden 1989, 171). He endures suffering as a "living sacrifice" (Rom 12:1-2) because he hopes in "the promise of life that is in Christ Jesus" (2 Tim 1:1).

■ **7** Three grammatically parallel clauses show how Paul remained faithful to his calling. In each, the direct object precedes a perfect tense verb. These completed actions had ongoing consequences. Paul's intent was to encourage Timothy, not to boast. His confidence was in the Lord, not himself. The theme behind each statement is Paul's faithfulness to his calling. To inspire Timothy to fervent faithfulness, he draws upon military or athletic imagery (→ 1 Tim 1:18; 6:12; 2 Tim 2:3-5; see 1 Cor 9:7, 24-27; 1 Thess 2:2; 5:8).

First, Paul draws upon the *agon* (= agonizing struggle) motif (Pfitzner 1967; → 1 Tim 6:12): **I have fought the good fight. Fight** (*agōna*) could refer to an athletic boxing competition (Kelly 1963, 208), race (Pfitzner 1967, 183), or a military engagement—which does not impact the overall meaning. The adjective **good** (*kalon*) modifies **fight.** Paul is not boasting in his fighting prowess, but of his devotion to a noble cause. He has been a participant in the greatest race of all. The perfect tense of the verb emphasizes his enduring commitment to the mission God gave him in spite of opposition, desertion, suffering, and persecution. The joy of the journey has been worth it all.

Second, Paul declares: **I have finished the race. Race** figuratively depicts the course of his ministry. He has a sense of accomplishment—his ministry has been worth it; he has fulfilled his calling. He awaits only his final goal—his heavenly **crown** (v 8; 1 Cor 9:25-26; see Acts 20:24).

Third, the only basis upon which Paul could make the two previous claims comes last: **I have kept the faith.** This phrase reveals his primary motive. **The faith** refers to his sustained personal trust in Christ and his faithful adherence to orthodox doctrine (→ 1 Tim 6:20; 2 Tim 1:14). The two cannot be separated. His personal faith in Christ is wrapped up in faithfully carrying out his duty as Christ's witness. Since this clause parallels the other two, which stress Paul's call, he may refer to his faithfulness to Christ's call on his life (Acts 9:1-19; 22:1-22; 26:1-32). He can look back on his life confident that he fulfilled his calling.

■ **8** "From now on" (*loipon*; NRSV) marks a shift in Paul's thought from his past and present trials (2 Tim 4:7) to his hope of eternity with Christ. He looks forward to receiving **the crown of righteousness.** A crown or wreath of olive leaves was used to honor the victors in ancient athletic competitions. This fits well with the imagery of v 7 (→ 1 Tim 4:7; 2 Tim 2:5; 1 Cor 9:25; Phil 4:1; 1 Thess 2:19).

The genitive **of righteousness** (*dikaiosynēs*) describes the figurative nature of **the crown** awaiting believers. Righteousness is a moral and forensic term describing harmonious relationships with God (→ 1 Tim 1:9). Those who are made right with God enjoy peace and reconciliation with God in the present (Rom 5:1-11). One becomes right with God through God's forgiveness, offered freely by the grace of Christ to all who will receive it (Rom 3:24).

But righteousness must also be expressed in a life of faithful obedience to God (Rom 6:17-19).

Righteousness is not only a present reality but also a future hope (Gal 5:5). Its fullness comes only **on that day**—at Christ's second coming, **his appearing** (*epiphaneian*; → 1 Tim 6:14; 2 Tim 1:10, 12, 18; 4:1; Titus 2:13; see Gal 5:5). Then we will know God fully as we are now fully known by God (1 Cor 13:12). The crown of righteousness is not an extrinsic reward, unrelated to the life of righteousness. For Paul, it would be the intrinsic reward of the vindication of his message and way of life.

Paul has confidence in this hope of reward because **the Lord** is **the righteous Judge**. The reference to **his appearing** indicates that **the Lord** is Jesus. This repeats the theme of Jesus as Judge from 2 Tim 4:1. The adjective **righteous** (*dikaios*) can also be translated as *just* in the sense of fair (BDAG 2000, 246-47 s.v. 1.b). Jesus is an impartial **Judge** because he is the incarnation of righteousness; he bridges the separation between the holy God and unholy humanity (→ 1 Tim 2:5).

The righteous Judge will grant righteousness to those who persevere like Paul and **have longed for his appearing.** The perfect tense of the substantival participle (*ēapēkosi*) matches the perfect tenses that express Paul's faithfulness in 2 Tim 4:7. The nuance of the base verb *agapaō* expresses more than simply a *desire*, but a genuine devotion and continuing commitment to act on this devotion. Paul's last testament should motivate Timothy and the Ephesians to share in his journey of faithful commitment in the midst of difficulty. His life sharply contrasts with that of Demas who loved the world (→ 4:9-10; Fee 1984, 290).

FROM THE TEXT

This short passage reveals a great deal about Paul. It should encourage us to continue walking faithfully with Christ no matter what happens around us.

We can aspire to the goal of coming to the end of our lives with a sense of completion and no regrets. No one wants to come to the end of life full of regret for wrongs done or missed opportunities. Paul had no shame for how he had lived his life. The Christian race is no competition because all can be winners. We may enjoy a right relationship with God now and the culmination of that in the world to come.

Second, *we can find our motivation for the present by looking to the future.* Knowing that we must give an account to God should be a strong motivation for how we live. We can be motivated by an *unhealthy fear* of punishment. We may obey God's laws because we are afraid that he will punish us if we fail. Or we can live with healthy *reverence*—we obey God because we love God. As 1 John 4:18 states, "There is no fear in love. But perfect love drives out fear, because fear has to do with punishment. The one who fears is not made perfect in love."

John Wesley distinguished between the faith of a slave and the faith of a son in his sermon "The Spirit of Bondage and of Adoption." The slave is bound "under the law" and is unable to keep the Law because of the power of sin. The son is "under grace" and finds freedom in serving God out of love. Joy and peace are promised for those who serve God out of love. We can seek to receive "the crown of righteousness" by loving God completely and loving others unselfishly (Luke 10:27).

Third, *Jesus' second coming should be something to look forward to, not fear.* There have been many gloomy apocalyptic predictions of the end of the world over the centuries, especially in recent decades. Even Christians fear going through a period of great tribulation. For those who love Christ, his second coming and any events that may happen related to it should bring hope, not discouragement. Fear results when we give too much importance to this world and our own physical well-being. What sustained Paul through his trials and final imprisonment was his hope of eternal life. That Jesus will come again should bring us encouragement (1 Thess 5:4-11).

VI. LETTER CLOSING: 2 TIMOTHY 4:9-22

BEHIND THE TEXT

Having looked at the past and future, Paul now returns to his present predicament (Stott 1973, 177). The perspective shifts again from the first (→ 4:6) to the second person (vv 9, 11, 13, 15, 19, 21, 22) as Paul gives Timothy specific personal instructions. Nevertheless, first-person pronouns or verbs appear in every verse except vv 13, 19, 21, 22.

One of the key themes of the letter lies behind this closing section: because of his imprisonment and the desertion of "everyone" (v 16), three times Paul urges Timothy to come quickly to Rome (vv 9, 11, 21). This highly personal passage reveals the difficulty Paul faced and how he handled it. Despite being abandoned by people, he was confident of God's presence and strength. One reason he wrote this letter was so that he could see his "son in the faith" (→ 1 Tim 1:2; 2 Tim 1:2).

The historical setting that occasions this letter becomes apparent in its closing: Paul's impending trial and death. His first defense did not go well, and he did not expect a quick release. Uncertainty about the outcome of his next trial or its time frame creates a sense of urgency.

Historical questions about the closing of the letter have led some scholars to question its authenticity (notably Dibelius and Conzelmann 1972, 122-28). However, the details, names, and historical setting add weight to Pauline authorship and are more useful for a canonical reading of the letter (Towner 2006, 620).

Paul reveals some of his personal needs. These include having colleagues desert him (4:10-11, 16), not having his precious writings (v 13), opposition (vv 14-15), having no warm clothes for winter (vv 13, 21), and his impending execution (v 18). Although the tone of this unit is somber, Paul anticipates God's salvation (v 18).

The passage has three sections (Knight 1992, 463): (1) request for Timothy to come soon (vv 9-13), (2) warning about Alexander the coppersmith (vv 14-15), and (3) Paul's situation (vv 16-18). The letter closes with personal greetings, like other Pauline letters (Rom 16:1-23; 1 Cor 16:19-23; Col 4:7-18; Titus 3:12-15).

Letter closings had several functions (Johnson 2001, 446): (1) They addressed the complex business of the Pauline mission. Over forty known people were associated with Paul's work, and he did his best to keep up his administration of them while in prison. (2) They reinforce the networks of communication essential to the success of the mission. (3) They reinforce points made earlier in the letter.

A. Personal Instructions (4:9-15)

IN THE TEXT

■ **9-10** As Paul begins to close the letter, he urges Timothy: **Do your best to come to me quickly** (see 2 Tim 4:11, 21; → Titus 3:12). The adverb **quickly** (*tacheōs*) indicates urgency. But it is a relative term, considering how long it would take for the letter to get to Timothy, for him to resolve the Ephesian situation, and travel to Rome. Paul likely knew his appeal and trial would take a while, because of delays in the Roman court system.

Timothy's trip to Rome to see Paul would entail two risks: First, he would put himself in possible danger with authorities by associating with the imprisoned Paul. Second, he would have to leave a difficult situation in Ephesus that needed spiritual and administrative guidance. This may explain 2 Timothy's two major themes: how to deal with the false teachers in Ephesus, and encouragement for Timothy to be strong against persecution.

Verse 10 of ch 4 offers the reason (*gar*) why Paul needs Timothy: he feels that everyone has left him! First in the list is **Demas**, who left for **Thessalonica**. In other letters, Paul mentions Demas as a faithful coworker with Luke and Mark (Col 4:10, 14; Phlm 24; see Barrett 1963, 120). **Demas** is a nickname for Demetrius (Fiore 2007, 183), who should not be confused with the Ephesian silversmith mentioned in Acts 19:24, 38.

Paul was disappointed with Demas for two reasons: (1) he **deserted** Paul, and (2) **because he loved this world**. **Deserted** (*enkatelipen*) is a strong word of personal abandonment when a person is forsaken and uncared for (Louw and Nida 1996, 1:464). Paul offers no information as to why Demas left for **Thessalonica**.

Loved translates an adverbial participle (*agapēsas*) causally, as the reason why Demas deserted Paul. He loved the wrong object, like the false teachers in Ephesus (→ 3:2, 4). His love preferred *the present age* (see 1 John 2:15) to God and people. **This world** is dominated by the power of sin and the evil desires of the flesh. It offers a false promise of comfort and ease. Those who live by its value system reject the way of the cross (Towner 1994, 209). Something in Thessalonica must have diverted Demas' focus from the mission of Christ. Demas chose immediate comfort over struggle for greater reward (Towner 2006, 622).

We do not know what happened to Demas after he left Paul. If Colossians was written after 2 Timothy, he may have returned to Paul after he cared for "worldly affairs" in Thessalonica. Because his friend Aristarchus (Phlm 24) was from Thessalonica (Acts 20:4), Chrysostom (*Hom. 2 Tim.* 4.10) assumed that Demas returned to his hometown. The apocryphal *Acts of Paul* (3.14) characterizes him as a hypocrite; Epiphanius (*Pan.* 51.6), as an apostate. We cannot be certain (Marshall 1999, 816).

Two others left Paul, but Paul's syntax does not indicate that they abandoned him for the same reason Demas did. He is the only subject of the verb **deserted**. **Crescens** appears only here in the NT. The apostle gives no reason why he went to **Galatia**, perhaps on a mission for Paul (see Acts 16:6; Galatians; 1 Pet 1:1). Galatia was a Roman province in Asia Minor and the home area of Timothy (Lystra [Acts 16:1]). An Alexandrian textual variant identifies the location instead as "Gallian" (Metzger 1994, 581). Eusebius follows this tradition, writing centuries later that Crescens went to Gaul (*Eccl. hist.* 3.4.8).

Titus also left Paul and went on to **Dalmatia**. Titus was a Gentile by birth (Gal 2:3), an important emissary for Paul, and his coworker in ministry (2 Cor 2:13; 8:23). He helped Paul reconcile with Corinth (2 Cor 7:6, 13-14; 8:6, 16, 23; 12:18) and was later sent to Crete (→ Titus 1:5). He accompanied Paul and Barnabas to the Jerusalem Council (Acts 15; Gal 2:1, 3). Paul considered him a son in the faith, like Timothy (Titus 1:4). There is no other mention of a mission to Dalmatia in the NT. Dalmatia was part of the Roman province of Illyricum (Rom 15:19), located on the Adriatic coast of modern-day Croatia, Albania, and Bosnia and Herzegovina.

■ **11-12** Paul continues with personal references to other coworkers in the ministry (see Col 4:14; Phlm 24). He painfully notes, **Only Luke is with me.** **Luke** was a travel companion of Paul who apparently joined him on his second missionary journey (note the "we" statements in Acts 16:10-17; 20:5-15; 21:1-18; 27:1—28:16). He is the traditional author of the Gospel of Luke and the Acts of the Apostles. Paul identifies him in Col 4:14 as a physician and beloved friend. If Luke was incarcerated with Paul, he may have helped Paul write the Pastoral Epistles. This would account for the linguistic similarities between Luke's writings and the Pastorals (→ Introduction).

Paul directs Timothy to get **Mark** and bring him to Rome. John Mark was the cousin of Barnabas (Col 4:10). His mother Mary hosted a house church in Jerusalem (Acts 12:12). Mark is known in tradition as protégé of Peter (1 Pet 5:13), who was the source behind the Gospel of Mark (Eusebius, *Eccl. hist.* 3.39.15). He accompanied Barnabas and Paul on their first missionary journey (Acts 12:12, 25; 15:37, 39), but abandoned them at Perga and returned to Jerusalem (Acts 13:13). The dispute resulting from this led to the parting of Paul and Barnabas (15:37).

Sometime later, Mark again became a ministry partner with Paul, Luke, and others (Col 4:14; Phlm 24). It is unclear where Timothy was to find Mark. The mention of him in Col 4:14 may suggest that he was somewhere in Asia Minor. The reason Paul wants Mark is **because he is helpful to me in my ministry** (*diakonian*). **Ministry** has the broad sense of gospel service (→ 1 Tim 1:12; 2 Tim 4:5; 1 Cor 3:5; Eph 3:7; 6:21; Col 1:7, 23, 25; 4:7). **Helpful** (*euchrēstos*) describes someone who is "useful" or "beneficial" in some type of service (BDAG 2000, 417). Paul gives no specifics as to how Mark will serve him, perhaps with Paul's personal needs or in the mission in Rome. This verse testifies to the reconciliation of differences between Paul and Mark and renewed partnership in purpose-driven ministry.

Paul may need Mark because **Tychicus** had left for **Ephesus**. Tychicus appears with Trophimus in Acts 20:4. He went with Paul to Jerusalem with the collection for Jewish believers there. Paul calls him "a dear brother, a faithful minister and fellow servant in the Lord" in Col 4:7. Here and in Eph 6:21, he brings news of Paul to the churches, so he could have been the one who delivered Ephesians and 2 Timothy. Tychicus was one of Paul's key apostolic emissaries.

The aorist verb **sent** can be taken in an epistolary sense. This describes the action of the verb as in the past for the benefit of a letter's readers. But from its author's perspective, it has not happened yet. Thus it could mean, "I am sending this letter along with Tychicus." Two possible reasons may explain why Paul was sending Tychicus to Ephesus—to deliver this letter to Timothy and to take temporarily Timothy's place of leadership there (→ Titus 3:12, in which Artemas or Tychicus is to replace Titus in Crete).

■ **13** Personal remarks here add to the historical verisimilitude of this letter. Paul asks Timothy to bring two or three things with him. First, **the cloak** Paul **left with Carpus at Troas.** A **cloak** (*phailonēs*, its only NT occurrence) was a sleeveless, heavy outer garment of heavy cloth, like a poncho. Such cloaks were valuable, with people typically owning only one (Towner 2006, 628-29). With winter coming (2 Tim 4:21), such a garment would have been needed by the imprisoned Paul. Beyond this reference, **Carpus** is unknown.

Troas was an important launching point for Paul's ministry in Europe (Acts 16:8-11; 20:5-13). It was a seaport north of Ephesus along the coast of Asia Minor (Quinn and Wacker 2000, 817), which made it a strategic place for preaching the gospel (2 Cor 2:12-13). Paul passed through Troas at least three times (see 2 Cor 2:12). There he received his vision of a man from Macedonia urging him to bring the gospel to Europe (Acts 16:8-10). He later stopped in Troas for a week on his way to Jerusalem with the collection (20:6-12).

Paul may have left these valuable items with Christian friends in Troas on his way to the warm climate of Jerusalem in May of AD 57. He had no idea he would be unable to return because of his arrest in Jerusalem and long imprisonment in Caesarea (Walker 2012b, 122-23).

Paul wants Timothy to bring **my scrolls, especially the parchments.** It is unclear whether these materials were with Carpus in Troas or with Timothy in Ephesus. That Paul wants these whenever Timothy arrives shows that he expects a significant delay in his trial and potential death. The adverb *malista* could mean **especially** ("above all" [ESV]) or *namely*. It is possible that the parchments were part of Paul's book collection (Poythress 2002).

Following the Jewish practice of calling Torah scrolls "books" (1 Macc 1:56; 12:9), the word **scrolls** (*ta biblia*) in the NT usually refers to Scripture (→ 2 Tim 3:15). Scrolls were typically made of papyrus, a paper-like material made from reed plants that grow in the warm, wet parts of the region.

"Parchment" (*membranas*), a loan word from Latin, describes a material made of animal hides used for making **scrolls.** Sheets of prepared skins were sown together to form scrolls. Early Christians began to adopt a newer technology of using codices, books sown together at a common seam like modern books. Parchment was more expensive and durable than papyrus. Since Paul was a leather worker, he could have prepared his own parchments (Collins 2002, 283).

We can only speculate about the content of these documents. Their importance to Paul is evident in his specific request. He was a student of Scripture and a writer of letters. These would have been essential tools for his ongoing ministry and spiritual growth. They may have included copies of the

Jewish Scriptures, legal documents (such as proof of citizenship), copies of sent letters, or materials upon which to write new letters (Richards 2004, 156-69; Skeat 1979, 173-77).

■ **14-15** Paul continues to think about his challenges and reflects on one of the difficult people in Ephesus. He warns Timothy to watch out for **Alexander the metalworker. Alexander** was a common Greek name coming from the great conqueror Alexander the Great. There is no further identification of this person here, but Timothy would know about whom Paul wrote. In Acts 19:21-41, a Jewish Alexander was a spokesman involved in the riots of the silversmiths. In 1 Tim 1:19-20, Paul mentions a former Christian named Alexander.

Whoever this Alexander was, Paul claimed, He **did me a great deal of harm** (lit. *many bad things*). Paul was confident Christ would repay Alexander at the final judgment (see 4:1, 8). He takes seriously the conviction he expresses in Rom 12:17-21—God alone is qualified to avenge wrongdoing (appealing to the OT: Deut 32:35 [Rom 12:19]; 2 Sam 3:39; Pss 28:4; 62:12; Prov 24:12; 25:21-22 [Rom 12:20]).

Verse 15 of 2 Tim 4 explains why (*gar:* **because**) Timothy (emphatic **You** [*sy*]) **should be on** his **guard against** Alexander in the meantime. **He strongly opposed our message.** The mission in Ephesus could suffer from the opposition of people like Alexander (→ 3:8). As the final negative example in the letter, he serves as a warning that all who oppose Paul's message will face judgment.

B. Paul's Confidence in the Lord (4:16-18)

BEHIND THE TEXT

There are several noteworthy similarities between what Paul writes here and Ps 22. It is impossible to tell if he is intentionally echoing this passage or if Scripture has simply shaped the way he writes. This psalm begins with a cry of abandonment by God. Jesus quoted Ps 22:1 as he hung on the cross: "My God, my God, why have you forsaken me?" (Mark 15:34). John saw a fulfillment of 22:18 in one of the details of the crucifixion: "They divided my clothes among them and cast lots for my garments" (John 19:24). The psalm recognizes God's deliverance and concludes with a commitment to make this deliverance known to others. Parallels with Paul's thoughts:

Theme	Psalm 22	2 Timothy 4
A sense of having been forsaken	1-2, 6-7	16
Cry for help and deliverance	5, 9, 20	17
A mission to the nations	27-28	17
Delivery from death and the lion's mouth	21	17

IN THE TEXT

■ 16 Paul offers one final reflection on his current situation, ending with a testimony of confidence that the Lord will ultimately deliver him to "his heavenly kingdom" (v 18). The letter shifts to the third person as Paul details his circumstances (Quinn and Wacker 2000, 827). Paul uses this final opportunity to appeal to Timothy once more.

The problem is that **no one came to . . . support** Paul at his **first defense**. This creates numerous historical challenges to constructing a chronology of this apostle's life and the place of this and other Pastoral Epistles within the Pauline corpus.

Defense (*apologia*) was a technical legal term used in courtrooms for a defendant's answer to accusations. The mention of **first** assumes Paul expects a second chance to defend himself in the near future, possibly in the next year. The context assumes his first defense had occurred before people deserted him, which was recent enough that Paul still felt abandoned.

Historical Questions

There are several possibilities as to when Paul's first defense took place and what happened afterward. In Roman antiquity, the initial hearing (*prima actio*) was used to determine the status of the case and the evidence against the defendant (Ferguson 1993, 49-52; Towner 2006, 637). In such a hearing, Paul would have had to give an account of himself (*apologia*). The magistrates would have assessed his threat to society and determined the kind of imprisonment he required as he awaited trial.

There were two possible outcomes after this hearing: (*a*) *Non liquet*: release due to insufficient evidence. (*b*) *Amplius*: there was enough evidence to proceed to the trial proper, the *secunda actio*. Paul wrote in Greek and did not use any of these Latin words. So, it is impossible to determine how his description fits. His Roman citizenship guaranteed him a due trial. Three major solutions exist (→ Introduction).

First, this section, the letter, and all the Pastoral Epistles are pseudonymous letters written much later than Paul. The details of this passage were added to lend credibility to the fictive historical setting. But the actual author was only remotely in touch with anything related to the historical Paul.

Most, if not all, of the historical problems pointed out by this position can be resolved by comparing the Pastorals to Paul's other letters and the book of Acts. The major problem with this perspective is that it is based on much speculation and appeals more to stylistic than historical differences with other "undisputed" letters.

Second, a more conservative position holds that Paul had an earlier trial after his Roman imprisonment recorded in Acts 28 and was subsequently released (see 2 Tim 4:18). He continued his ministry, possibly traveling even to Spain (Rom 15:24, 28), for an unknown period of time before being rearrested. He wrote 2 Timothy during this second imprisonment.

This perspective, like the first, is based on conjecture. It overlooks a plain reading of the text. Paul clearly states that he was not released after his first trial. He wanted to go to Spain (Rom 15:23-29), but there is no evidence he did (but see *1 Clem.* 5.7).

Third, Paul faced a preliminary hearing once he arrived in Rome (Acts 28; see Walker 2012b). His hearing did not go as expected, because he hoped for acquittal based on the lack of evidence. Instead, he had to remain imprisoned until his full trial. Because he posed no risk, he received the more lenient house arrest (Acts 28:16). Things had settled down with his house arrest, which he interpreted as deliverance "from the lion's mouth" (→ 2 Tim 4:17).

Second Timothy shows Paul's initial response of discouragement and his desire to have Timothy with him. His isolation meant that the Christian community in Rome had been unable to contact him. Only those who traveled with him on his journey to Rome, such as Luke, knew his location at first. Timothy had not received word of the outcome until this letter. The abrupt ending of Acts with Paul under arrest awaiting his final trial fits well with Luke spending time with Paul, helping him reflect on the early Christian movement and with personal needs and necessary administration.

4:17   Paul has two basic problems: **No one came to my support.** And, **Everyone deserted me.** Support (*paregeneto*) is literally *came forward for me* and was used in the defense of a prisoner (Kelly 1963, 218). Paul may be referring to the actual hearing in the Roman court: no witnesses appeared to testify to his innocence. The statement may be more emotional that factual. **No one** could be hyperbolic; Paul had at least Luke with him when he wrote the letter and likely during the whole time (note the "we" in Acts 28:16). Paul's arrest apparently had a chilling effect upon the Christian community, if he was as isolated as he felt when he wrote this letter.

Rather than become bitter over his isolation, Paul offers a prayer of forgiveness using the rare optative mood: **May it not be held against them.** The verb **held** (*logisthein*) is an accounting term meaning to count or reckon something against (with the use of *mē*) someone (Heidland 1967, 284-92). He does not want any wrong against him counted against those who abandoned him (compare Luke 23:34; Acts 7:60; contrast 2 Tim 4:14).

■ **17 But the Lord stood at my side and gave me strength.** The conjunction **but** (*de*) shows that the **Lord** will have the final word in Paul's outcome. The **Lord** Jesus Christ was **present** (*parestē*; BDAG 2000, 778) with Paul through the Holy Spirit (→ 1:7). This assured him that whatever happened to him was ultimately for his good (Rom 8:28).

Christ **endued** him **with power** (*enedynamesen*). Paul had personally experienced God's strength at various points of difficulty in his ministry (Acts 23:11; 2 Cor 12:9; Phil 4:13). He had earlier urged Timothy to "be strong [*endynamou*] in the grace that is in Christ Jesus" (2:1). "What Paul commanded earlier in the letter for Timothy is substantiated here on the basis of personal experience" (Towner 2006, 642). The reason the Lord stood by Paul is given in a two-part purpose (*hina*) clause:

First, that **the message might be fully proclaimed** through Paul. **Through me** stands in the emphatic first position to show Paul's obedience to the divine commission. **The message** clearly refers to the gospel of Jesus Christ. **Fully proclaimed** refers to Paul's continued ministry even while he was imprisoned (see Acts 28:30-31; Phil 1:12-18). It is a two-part verb: *plēro*, to fulfill or complete, and *phoreō*, "to carry or bear habitually or for a considerable length of time" (BDAG 2000, 1064).

Second, that **all the Gentiles might hear** the gospel. This perhaps simply restates the first. The conjunction **and** could mean "namely" (Mounce 2000, 596). Preaching to non-Jews was the driving motive in Paul's mission (Acts 9:15; 22:21; 26:17; Rom 1:5, 13; 3:29; 4:18; 9:24; 11:11, 25; 15:9-12, 16, 18; 16:26). **Gentiles** here is (lit.) *nations* (→ 1 Tim 2:7). So it could include Jews who lived in Gentile lands (Rom 1:16; Rom 15:11; 16:26; Gal 3:28). Salvation for all people is a key theological theme throughout Paul's letters.

When Paul wrote this letter, he had finally reached the center of the empire (Acts 23:11); now even the emperor would hear the gospel. As a result of his trial, his testimony would reach more people than it might have otherwise.

Paul's first defense must have been somewhat successful, at least temporarily. The delay of his second trial and possible execution meant that for now he was **delivered from the lion's mouth**. The passive verb **delivered** implies that the Lord was his Savior.

The delay of his trial allowed Paul time to communicate with Timothy and for Timothy to join him in Rome. But he fears that the outcome of his second and final trial will not be so good (2 Tim 4:6-8). Success should be measured more by the opportunity to testify of the gospel before the great powers of the world.

The reference to **the lion's mouth** has challenged interpreters since the early church fathers. Lions were greatly feared in the ancient world. They were used as symbols of power. The use of the image of a lion for extreme danger stretches back to the OT period (1 Sam 17:37; Ps 7:2; Prov 22:13; 26:13; 1 Macc 2:60). The wording here resembles Ps 22:21. Daniel's experience in the lions' den (Dan 6:22) could have been in Paul's mind as well. The identity of the lion in this verse is unknown. Josephus called the reigning emperor Nero a lion (*Ant.* 18.228; Michaelis 1967, 253 n. 20). Chrysostom identified the lion as Nero (*Hom. 2 Tim.* 10). Paul's initial hearing was likely before one of Nero's representatives (Acts 25:10-12).

Paul faced other lion-like challenges, such as the snare of the devil (→ 2 Tim 2:26; 1 Tim 3:7; 6:9; 1 Pet 5:8). It is possible to interpret the reference literally. In 1 Cor 15:32, Paul claims to have "fought wild beasts in Ephesus." Most contemporary interpreters take this as a reference to sinful people. In this instance, as well, it is likely a figure of speech.

■ **18** This statement continues the contrast (untranslated *de*, "but") between Paul's dire situation and his confidence in **the Lord**. Paul's thought shifts to the future with the verb **will rescue**. The basic meaning of *rhyomai* is to come to the aid of, deliver, or save from danger (see Matt 6:13). Paul is confident that the Lord, who helped him in the past (2 Cor 1:10) and present (Phil 4:13), will do so again in the future.

The Lord did not rescue Paul from all danger, as the many troubles he faced in his ministry amply witness (2 Cor 11). But he views his life through spiritual lenses; his concern is with **every evil attack**, like Alexander's attempts (→ 4:14). **Attack**, (lit.) *work* contrasts with the "good work" he mentions in 2 Tim 2:21 and 3:17. These attacks were **evil** because they tried to distract Paul from his calling.

These attacks at best were only temporary. Paul's eyes are on a greater goal—entering the Lord's **heavenly kingdom**. There is an implicit comparison between **heavenly kingdom** and the earthly empire of Rome that sought to destroy Paul and the gospel (Mounce 2000, 598). The verb translated **will bring . . . safely** is simply the common NT word for save (*sōizō*). Paul's concern is his eternal salvation, not temporal rescue (Col 1:13). He would rather be with the Lord than sustain his bodily existence a bit longer (2 Cor 5:8; Phil 1:21). His confidence in the Lord, from the beginning of his ministry (→ 1 Tim 1:12) to the end, should encourage Timothy and the Ephesians (2 Tim 1:8; 2:3; 3:12; 4:5).

Thoughts of heaven evoke a doxology with four key components (→ 1 Tim 1:17). **To him** in the context refers to the Lord Jesus Christ, the subject of this chapter (→ 2 Tim 4:1, 8). The same doxology in Gal 1:5 is addressed to God. **Glory** (*doxa*) is God's overwhelming revelation of his splendor that elicits worship (Exod 33:18; 34:6-8). The (lit.) *unto the ages of ages* (and variations) is the NT idiom for *eternally* (Luke 1:33; Eph 3:21; Heb 1:8; 7:3; 1 Pet 4:11; 5:11; Jude 25). This is a fitting doxology to a completed mission.

C. Final Greetings and Benediction (4:19-22)

BEHIND THE TEXT

Paul's letters often close with second- and third-person greetings to personal friends (Rom 16; 1 Cor 16:19-21; 2 Cor 13:12-13; Phil 4:21-22; Col

4:10-15; Phlm 23). This gives evidence of the large Christian network that had already developed in the early decades of the church. The closing also gives final directions to Timothy that reiterate Paul's dire circumstances in Rome.

IN THE TEXT

■ **19-21** Greet (*aspasai*) means "to engage in hospitable recognition of another" (BDAG 2000, 144). In Christian circles, the greetings can be warm (1 Cor 16:19) and affectionate (2 Cor 13:12) but will vary from culture to culture. In 2 Tim 4:19 Paul directs Timothy to greet two individuals and an extended family. This is Paul's second reference to **the household of Onesiphorus** in the letter (→ 1:16-18).

Paul mentions specifically **Priscilla and Aquila**. The Greek and most modern translations use the nickname *Prisca*. Her full name appears in Acts; the shortened version, in Paul's letters. **Priscilla** is listed before **Aquila** four of the six times they appear in the NT. Unusual in the ancient world, this order points to her significant ministry role or social prominence (Fee 1988, 300).

Priscilla and Aquila were Jews from Pontus who fled Rome after Claudius issued his edict expelling Jews in AD 49 (Acts 18:2). They were tentmakers like Paul, which allowed them to be mobile. They met Paul in Corinth and became important coworkers with him. In Rom 16:3-4, Paul claims they "risked their lives" for him. They hosted him in their home during his eighteen-month stay there (Acts 18:3). They then accompanied him to Ephesus and hosted the church in their house there (vv 18-22; 1 Cor 16:19). In Ephesus they befriended Apollos and trained him in the gospel (Acts 18:26). When Paul wrote Romans, they had apparently returned to the capital of the empire and were hosts of one of the house churches there (Rom 16:5). But here, they are again in Ephesus.

The statement in 2 Tim 4:20 about **Erastus** and **Trophimus** is ambiguous. It may further reveal Paul's sense of loneliness. **Erastus** was a coworker with Timothy who went with him to Macedonia while Paul made plans to go to Jerusalem (Acts 19:22). At some point, Paul sent him to Corinth. Paul mentions Erastus in his final greetings in Rom 16:23 as the treasurer of the city of Corinth. From there Paul most likely wrote Romans. A limestone paving block archaeologists found in Corinth bears the inscription, "Erastus, director for city works, laid this pavement at his own expense" (Cadbury 1931). There is no way to know if this refers to the same person. Christians of high social standing are rarely mentioned in Paul's letters.

Paul **left Trophimus sick in Miletus**. According to Acts 21:29, Trophimus was a Gentile from Ephesus who accompanied Paul on his final visit to Jerusalem. His presence contributed to the riot that led to Paul's arrest and imprisonment. Miletus was about thirty miles from Ephesus at the mouth of the Meander River. Paul met the Ephesian elders there for a final exhortation (Acts 20:17).

Paul gives no indication as to when he left Trophimus in his home area. It could have been on his journey to Rome or during Paul's imprisonment in Caesarea. The verb **left** need not suggest that Paul was in Miletus, only that he *permitted* him to return home (see BDAG 2000, 115 s.v. 1) or *assigned* him there (Johnson 2001, 447-48).

Sick translates the adverbial participle *asthenounta*, which refers to some type of physical weakness. It can be interpreted concessively ("although he was ill") or causally ("because he was ill"). Paul was the instrument of divine healing for some people (Acts 14:9-10; 19:11-12; 20:10; 28:8-9), but he obviously did not heal everyone (Knight 1992, 477).

Trophimus was near Timothy in Ephesus. This information may have hinted that Timothy needed to adjust the administration within the vicinity of Ephesus or needed to stop in and check on Trophimus on his way to Rome.

Verse 21*a* of 2 Tim 4 briefly interrupts the greetings with a repeated (→ vv 9, 13) exhortation to Timothy: **Do your best to get here before winter.** This time reference suggests that Paul was writing sometime during the summer. Travel by land through Macedonia would have been difficult. It was likewise dangerous to travel by ship.

The usual route to Rome from Ephesus was by ship, passing overland through the Isthmus of Corinth. Major shipping on the Mediterranean was closed in the winter. If Timothy did not leave soon, he would not be able to get to Rome until the next spring.

Finally, Paul sends greetings from **Eubulus** and **Pudens, Linus, Claudia and all the brothers and sisters.** None of these last four names are mentioned elsewhere in the NT. Evidently, they were with Paul or were a part of the Roman church. This lends support for taking the statement in v 16 as hyperbolic. Not **everyone** had deserted Paul. Some Christians had found him and were with him during his house arrest. The last three names are all Latin, the common language of Rome. Irenaeus claims that Linus became Peter's successor as bishop of Rome (*Haer.* 3.3.3). Claudia is the only woman besides Priscilla (v 19) mentioned in the greetings.

■ **22** The letter ends with a final, double benediction in the form of an abbreviated prayer. Two different audiences are involved. The first uses the singular pronoun **your** and is intended for Timothy as the direct recipient of the letter. The second uses the plural **you,** which implies that the letter was also for the whole church through the agency of Timothy. The letter to Philemon ends in a similar way (Phlm 25).

The Lord consistently refers to Jesus in this letter. **Spirit** refers to Timothy's inner person. Paul asks the Lord to strengthen Timothy inwardly so he may be better able to deal with his outward challenges.

Praying for God's **grace** to be with the recipients is a typical part of the closing of Paul's letters (1 Cor 16:23; 2 Cor 13:14; Gal 6:18; Eph 6:24; Phil 4:23; Col 4:18; 1 Thess 5:28; 2 Thess 3:18; → 1 Tim 6:21; Titus 3:15; Phlm 25).

FROM THE TEXT

This is a very personal passage that rehearses some of the major themes of the letter. First, it is obvious that Paul was distressed about the opposition in Ephesus and its affect upon the church. This comes through in his reflections on his own imprisonment in Rome.

One principle we can gain from the closing of the letter is that *ministry often involves dealing with difficult people.* If ministers or church leaders are not spiritually and mentally prepared, these people can wreck a church, leave wounds, or cast burdens upon the leadership that force them to leave ministry. Sometimes it is those closest to us who cause pain. The pain may simply be from our own loneliness.

As he closed the letter, Paul longed for his colleagues who could help him in ministry. This offers a second principle: *companionship in ministry is important, especially during difficult times.* Jesus sent his disciples out in pairs (Mark 6:7; Luke 10:1). Having a friend in ministry helps in prayer support (Matt 18:19). The presence of Christ is with those who gather together (Matt 18:20). This group can become the nucleus of a church or an effective witnessing pair. In Scripture, two witnesses can verify an event (John 8:17; 2 Cor 13:1). The testimony of two people adds strength to the message.

A ministry team can have gifts that complement one another (Eph 4:11-12). Having a mentor in ministry can be an effective way to train future leaders, as Paul did Timothy (Acts 16:1-3). Having a friend in ministry can bring encouragement, as Timothy would do for Paul when he arrived in Rome (on Titus, see 2 Cor 7:6). Priscilla and Aquila are an example of a married couple who were effective in ministry (Acts 18:26). Paul's desire to see Timothy again was both personal and strategic. At this low point in his ministry, Paul believed God was with him, but he still longed for human companionship.

God gave Paul strength to preach the gospel even to the Roman officials who would later condemn him to death. A third principle is that *God's strength is sufficient in our sufferings and time of need.* Supreme power belongs to God who provides us hope and assurance that there is more to our existence than this life. God's promises of eternal life in heaven with him are true, and these promises sustain us through any difficulty we may face in this life.

We get a glimpse in this passage of the humanness of Paul as he dealt with a sense of abandonment. It is noteworthy that after reflecting on God's presence with him (2 Tim 4:17-18), he shifted his focus from those who left him to those who shared in his ministry, both in Rome and in Ephesus. Like many of the psalms of lament, our sorrows can turn to joy. Whether or not Paul intentionally reflected on Ps 22 when he wrote this closing, this psalm offers us a pattern that goes from distress, "My God, my God, why have you forsaken me?" (v 1), to confidence, "He has done it!" (v 31).

COMMENTARY

TITUS

I. OPENING GREETINGS: TITUS 1:1-4

BEHIND THE TEXT

The letter to Titus shares many of the same concerns as 1 and 2 Timothy: false teachers and doctrine, church health and structure. Paul urges Titus to develop godly leaders in the churches on Crete to protect them from false teaching and establish them in the truth of the gospel.

Significant historical problems lay behind this letter (→ Introduction), but the complex and unknown historical background does not change the letter's message. We lack sufficient information to make more than educated guesses about the historical occasion of the letter:

- There is no hint of where Paul was when he wrote. He must have been traveling, since he planned to spend the winter in Nicopolis (3:12).

- Titus may have been in Corinth when he received this letter, which ordered him to sail to Crete (→ Titus 3:12).
- The letter presumes there were churches in Crete when Paul sent Titus there.
- Paul's only known contacts with Crete were brief, on his way to Rome under arrest (Acts 27:7, 12, 13, 21). These were far too brief to allow him time to evangelize or start churches there.
  ○ These churches may have been started earlier by Paul's associates or other early Christian missionaries.
  ○ Perhaps Jewish pilgrims from Crete returned with the Christian message soon after the day of Pentecost (see Acts 2:11).
  ○ It seems odd for Paul to impose order on churches he had not started.
- Paul expected Titus to return to Rome after his tour of duty in Crete.
- Neither Paul's other letters nor the book of Acts refer to Titus' ministry in Crete.
- Paul may have written 2 Timothy early in his Roman imprisonment (→ Introduction). By this time, Titus had been with Paul in Rome.
- Paul sent Titus from Rome to minister in Dalmatia (→ 2 Tim 4:10).

The rhetoric of the opening of Titus creatively gives the theological basis for the exhortations that follow. This is a personal letter in the form of a *mandatum principiis*, "a letter from a ruler or high official to one of his agents, delegates, ambassadors, or governors helping him set up shop in his new post and get things in good order and under control" (Witherington 2006, 90).

The letter to Titus follows the style of ancient letters, which typically began with author, recipient, and a form of greeting (→ 1 Tim 1:1). These verses comprise one long, complex Greek sentence of forty-seven words (compare Romans at sixty-four words, 1 Timothy with thirty-two, and 2 Timothy with twenty-nine). The letter employs deliberative rhetoric, which attempts to change behavior by the use of positive and negative examples (Titus 2:7). In ch 1, there is a sharp contrast between elders and false teachers. Paul follows the rabbinic doctrine of "two ways," rejecting the path of the opponents and urging the church to choose his better way.

The letter opening distinctly shows the purpose of Paul's apostleship within salvation history. It establishes his ethos as an authoritative representative of God. "It helps locate the author within a presumed set of shared values; it anticipates several of the letter's key topics and themes; and it begins establishing itself as an 'official' document" (Richards 2002, 76-77). It also gives Titus credibility as Paul's emissary with apostolic authority to appoint leaders and correct problems.

IN THE TEXT

■ **1a** As typical in ancient letters, the author begins with his name, **Paul**. Saul of Tarsus used this name exclusively in his ministry among Gentiles (→ 1 Tim 1:1). His ministry role as **a servant of God and an apostle of Jesus Christ** sets the tone for the letter and Titus' mission in Crete.

The phrase **a servant** [or *slave*; → 1 Tim 6:1-2] **of God** occurs only here (but compare "servant of Christ" in Rom 1:1; Jas 1:1; 2 Pet 1:1; Jude 1). Paul became a slave, figuratively speaking, when he was captured by Christ on the road to Damascus (Acts 9; Phil 3:12). Paul's reference to *slave* here may anticipate his directions to slaves in Titus 2:9-10.

More importantly, this self-designation connects Paul with Israel's past (Collins 2002, 302-3). *Dolos theou* is a frequent synonym for "prophet" in the LXX (1 Kgs 18:36; 2 Kgs 17:23). It also describes Israel (Ezra 5:11; Isa 49:3), Abraham (Ps 105:42), Moses (1 Chr 6:49; 2 Chr 24:9; Neh 10:29; Dan 9:11), Daniel (Dan 6:20), and David (2 Sam 3:18; Ps 89:3).

God has exclusive claims on his servants and thus demands exclusive loyalty from them. Paul implies that he had carried out God's will, and so should Titus and the church leaders in Crete. **God** appears five times and is the focus and primary actor in this paragraph.

Paul was bound to the service to which God called him, specifically, to be **an apostle of Jesus Christ** (see Rom 1:1). "Apostle" is always used with "Christ" in the NT. God appoints apostles, but they represent Christ (Marshall 1999, 118). The Greek *apostolos* describes one sent as Christ's ambassador with the commission to preach the gospel (→ 1 Tim 1:1). Paul became an apostle by God's will (1 Cor 1:1; 2 Cor 1:1; Eph 1:1; Col 1:1). Paul's authority as apostle prepares readers for the commands he will give later (Titus 2:2, 15; 3:1, 8; Richards 2002, 73).

■ **1b-3** Paul assigns his apostleship three purposes in three prepositional phrases. They emphasize three core values of God's people: faith, knowledge, and hope. The more typical Pauline triad is faith, hope, and love (1 Cor 13:13; Col 1:5; 1 Thess 1:3; 5:8). Paul may have included knowledge here because Cretan Christians needed a clearer understanding of God to battle the false teachings infiltrating the church (Titus 1:9-13; Black and McClung 2004, 216). The hope of eternal life is the theological basis for godliness, the key characteristic of the people of God (2:11-13; 3:4-7; Knight 1992, 282).

The first purpose of Paul's calling is **to further the faith of God's elect**. The word **elect** in the OT identifies the people God chooses for special purposes (1 Chr 16:13; Pss 89:3; 105:6, 43; Hag 2:23; Isa 42:1; 45:4; 65:9, 15). Paul uses it for the church, which continues Israel's mission (Rom 8:33; 9:11; 11:5, 7, 28; 16:13; 1 Cor 1:26-27; Col 3:12; 1 Thess 1:4; → 2 Tim 2:10). The elect refers to those who have already come to faith in Christ (Towner 2006, 667). Using it here connects the believers in Crete with God's comprehensive plan of salvation by faith (Rom 2:2-29) and isolates the errant teaching of the opponents, who stressed works of the Law (Titus 2:14).

The preposition *kata* (**toward**) introduces "the sphere in which Paul exercises his apostleship and the ends he hopes to achieve by it" (Kelly 1963, 226). One primary goal of his apostleship was to lead people to **faith** (*pistin*), to **trust** in Christ alone for salvation (→ 2 Tim 2:10). Faith is an important theme in this letter (Titus 1:13; 2:2, 10; 3:15).

A second purpose of Paul's apostleship was to develop **knowledge of the truth that leads to godliness**. *Epignōsin* describes complete understanding. The phrase **knowledge of the truth** is parallel to salvation in Christ in 1 Tim 2:4. The opponents in Crete were attempting to redefine "truth" (Titus 1:12, 16). So Paul wants Titus to be clear about the **truth** (3:3-8). Faith and knowledge go together (1 Tim 2:4; 2 Tim 2:25; 3:7). "Those who know God's name . . . put their trust in him" (Stott 1996, 169).

Knowledge has the goal of developing godly character. **Godliness** (*eusebeian*) is one of the key words in the Pastoral Epistles (→ 1 Tim 2:2; 3:16). Godliness for Christians begins theologically with reverence for God and shows up ethically in a lifestyle of obedience to God's commands (→ Titus 2:12). Correct knowledge of God should lead to correct behavior (→ 1 Tim 6:3). Acceptance of the truth of the gospel should be evident in godly character.

A third aim of Paul's apostleship was **the hope of eternal life**. The preposition *epi* shows goal or purpose in parallel with *kata*. **Faith** and **knowledge** lead to **hope**. Hope (→ 3:7) is an important theme in Paul's letters to Timothy (1 Tim 1:1; 3:14; 4:10; 5:5; 6:17; 2 Tim 2:25). Hope is the sure expectation that something in the future will become a reality (→ 1 Tim 1:16).

Eternal life is the goal of Christian hope. The hope of receiving eternal life inspires believers to stand strong despite opposition. This reward comes as a result of God's justifying grace in Christ Jesus (→ Titus 3:7; 1 Tim 1:16; 2 Tim 1:1). Paul's shares this hope with all God's elect people. Paul lists three reasons why we can be assured of eternal life:

The first is based on the one who made the promise: **God, who does not lie**. Christian hope is not based on some innate human quality. It does not arise from wishful human speculation. It depends on God's grace in Christ. The rare attributive adjective *apseudēs* shows that God is completely trustworthy, unlike the opponents in Titus 1:12 (→ 2 Tim 2:13; Num 23:19; 1 Sam 15:29; Rom 3:3-4; Heb 6:18).

Because Paul is a servant of God sent by Christ, his message is reliable and should be heeded. This statement could be a subtle critique of the stereotypical Cretan identity. Lying had become an acceptable cultural practice on the island (Winter 2003, 150; → Titus 1:12).

The second basis for the hope of eternal life arises from God's plan **before the beginning of time** (see Eph 1:4; Col 1:16-17). God created the human race in order to experience his loving grace through the Son (→ 2 Tim 1:9; Eph 1:4-5). This message of hope was not something Paul made up (Gal 1:11). It was **promised** through the prophetic word (Rom 16:25-26; 1 Pet 1:10-12). God's covenantal promises (Rom 4:21; Gal 3:13-18) were fulfilled at a specific point in time through the incarnation of the Son. Believers can participate in this promise of eternal life now through the Holy Spirit (1 Cor 2:7-10; Col 1:25-26).

The Time Spectrum of Salvation

There is a noticeable shift in Titus 1:2-3 from the eternal past to the present (→ 2 Tim 1:9-10). The Greek conjunction *de* marks the contrast. Paul uses two different words for time in these verses:

Time (*chronōn*) in Titus 1:2 can refer to an indefinite period of time—an "age"—or to a specific "date" (Delling 1974, 581-93). The prefix *pro-* indicates that Paul refers to the eternal "period" before creation (→ 2 Tim 1:9). God had prepared the plan of salvation before he created the universe (1 Cor 2:7; Eph 1:4).

Time (*kairois*) in Titus 1:3 refers to a particular **season** of time. The plan of salvation was revealed at a specific point in history. The word *kairois* refers to a point (2 Tim 4:3) or event (2 Tim 4:6) in time. In Titus 1:3, Paul specifies it with the dative *idiois*, **his own**: This was the decisive moment in history when God's plan of salvation was revealed through the death and resurrection of Jesus Christ (→ 1 Tim 2:6). God determined the perfect timing for Christ to come (Rom 5:6; Gal 4:4).

A third time period is included in Titus 1:3: the proclamation of God's plan after the Christ event. This is the point in time when the church is called to witness to the plan that has its origins in eternity. Eternal life is made known through the message Paul preached and passed on to Titus. The church is the key instrument through which God makes his eternal plan known. "When the time was ripe, he went public with his truth" (v 3 [TM]).

The third assurance of eternal life is that God has revealed this truth *through the preached word* (2 Tim 3:16; 4:2, 4:17). The verb *ephanerōsen* indicates that God has **brought to light** what was once hidden and invisible (Rom 1:19; 16:26; 1 Cor 4:5; Col 1:26). Its aorist tense refers to an undesignated period of revelation that includes the present moment (2 Cor 6:1-2). The preposition *en* followed by the dative *kērygmati* shows the means by which God reveals this word of hope: through **the preaching**—the message or the activity of proclamation (Towner 2006, 673).

The passive verb *episteuthēn* shows Paul's part in God's plan. **God our Savior** was the one who **entrusted** the message to Paul. The emphatic *egō* (*I*) makes it clear Paul was not the originator of the message of salvation, only the herald sent by Christ (Gal 1:1, 11, 12; → 1 Tim 1:1). The prepositional phrase **by the command of God** refers to Paul's divine commission (→ 1 Tim 1:11; 2:7; Marshall 1999, 130). Paul was under orders as God's servant to preach the message he received through revelation. The phrase further augments Paul's trustworthy ethos (character) and gives authority to Titus to deal with a difficult situation.

Paul ends the paragraph attributing salvation to *our Savior, God.* This major clue to the theme of the letter is intended to shape the thinking of the Cretans (Knight 1992, 286). Salvation will be the end result of hope in Christ.

Salvation in Titus

Paul refers to salvation in numerous ways in this letter:

- "The faith of God's elect" (1:1).
- "The hope of eternal life" (1:2).
- God (1:3; 2:10; 3:4) and Christ (1:4; 2:13; 3:6) are both called Savior.
- "Our common faith" (1:4).
- Offered through "the grace of God" (2:11).
- Redemption "from all wickedness" (2:14).
- "The kindness and love of God" (3:4).
- God saved us from destructive attitudes and behaviors (3:3, 5).
- Salvation comes by "the washing of rebirth and renewal by the Holy Spirit" (3:5).
- Salvation does not come by works (3:5).
- "Justified by . . . grace" (3:7).
- Becoming "heirs having the hope of eternal life" (3:7).

■ **4** The greeting in this letter is similar to 1 Timothy. Both letters are addressed to individuals who were missionary colleagues of Paul. **Titus** is not mentioned in the book of Acts but was an important emissary in several of Paul's letters. He was part of the delegation of "certain other men" who went to Jerusalem to enquire about how to incorporate Gentiles into the church (Acts 15:2; Gal 2:3). It may be noteworthy that Paul sent Titus, this uncircumcised Gentile Christian, to deal with opponents in Crete who emphasized circumcision (→ Titus 1:10).

Titus had an important ministry in Corinth, with eight references to him in 2 Corinthians. He met Paul in Macedonia (2 Cor 2:13) with good news of a change of heart by the Corinthians (7:5-7). Paul sent him back to Corinth to help with collecting the offering for the believers in Jerusalem (8:18-23; 12:18). His success in Corinth showed how well he could deal with difficult situations.

Paul must have thought that Titus could again use his skills to deal with the problems in the Cretan churches. After his ministry in Crete, Titus was to join Paul in Nicopolis near the Adriatic coast (Titus 3:12). It is unknown if he made it there and what he did. At some later point, when Paul was imprisoned in Rome, he sent Titus on a third known mission to Dalmatia (2 Tim 4:10). The tradition according to Eusebius (*Hist. eccl.* 3.4.6) is that Titus returned to Crete and became its first bishop and died of old age there.

Titus was Greek by birth, although his name is Latin. He became a Christian under Paul's ministry (Gal 2:3). The designation ***[my] true child according to a common faith*** reveals a spiritual kinship that Paul as his mentor felt for Titus. **True** (*gnēsiō*, **legitimate**; → 1 Tim 1:2) or **authentic** connects the authority of Titus directly to Paul. **Child** (*teknōi*) is a term of fictive kinship that bonds Titus to Paul in faithfulness and obedience. The word **common** (*koinēn*) refers to something **shared**. Paul reminds Titus, the churches in Crete, and the false teachers that this uncircumcised Greek shared the same faith as Paul, the circumcised Hebrew (Knight 1992, 286).

Paul gives his typical greeting of **grace and peace** (→ 1 Tim 1:2; Rom 1:7; 1 Cor 1:3; 2 Cor 1:2). He transforms these typical Greek and Jewish greetings into a blessing **from God the Father and Christ Jesus our Savior**. Theologically, the greeting summarizes the source and outcome of his message. The reference to Christ as Savior prepares for the theological emphases of the letter in Titus 2:11-14 and 3:4-7. Conspicuously missing in the most reliable manuscripts is "mercy," found in the greetings of the other Pastoral letters, but in no other Pauline letter.

FROM THE TEXT

Paul had keen insight into God's purpose for him. Service to God does not need to be complicated; it begins simply with an attitude of submission. As new creations in Christ, believers are no longer slaves to sin, but slaves to God. There has been an essential change of ownership that transforms all we do (Rom 6:15-18, 20-23; 8:15; 1 Cor 7:22; Gal 4:4-5). For Paul, being a slave of God was a badge of honor to be lived out in humble service. In Christ we have the greatest model. He took the form of a slave, dying on a cross for our salvation (Phil 2:7-8).

Paul understood God's purpose for him as planting seeds of faith (1 Cor 3:6). Knowledge is a vital ingredient to help these seeds grow. Fundamental to Christianity is an informed faith. Both faith and knowledge are necessary foundations for establishing a firm hope in eternal life. Faith is built upon knowledge and knowledge adds support to faith. If either one is missing, the gospel loses its convicting power. Our minds must engage our faith. Paul understood this and wrote about the mind being renewed in Christlikeness (Rom 12:1-2; 1 Cor 2:16; Eph 4:23; Phil 2:5; Col 3:2). Our Christian faith cannot be grounded on emotions or religious experiences but in relational knowledge of God found through study of the Scripture and obedience to the Holy Spirit. Knowledge is the anchor that holds us firm against the highs and lows of emotions and experiences.

Paul saw the vital connection between his ministry of preaching the gospel and God's eternal plan for creation. This was not presumption on Paul's part. He was not boasting of the importance of his own ministry. Rather, it shows how crucial he saw the gospel message to be. His mission was not like the many other traveling teachers of his day. His message of the cross contained the very power and wisdom of the Almighty God (1 Cor 1:18-25). This ought to inspire all Christians to remember that we are part of something big; so big, in fact, it is the reason why the universe was created (Eph 1:3-10)!

II. THE ESSENTIAL NEED FOR QUALIFIED LEADERS: TITUS 1:5-16

BEHIND THE TEXT

Paul begins the body of the letter by addressing unfinished business Titus must complete in Crete. He entirely omits the typical thanksgiving section, which normally follows the greeting in contemporary letters. This is possibly because of the urgency of the situation. Titus must resolve three major issues (Black and McClung 2004, 222): (1) a lack of organization and leadership (v 5), (2) the influence of false teachers who needed to be corrected (vv 10-11; 3:10-11), and (3) believers who needed doctrinal and moral instruction (2:1-10; 3:1-2).

The basic problem was that false teachers from the "circumcision group" (1:10; see vv 10-16) were leading the church astray into false doctrine. Paul's solution was for Titus to appoint leaders with certain character qualities who could strengthen the church against these heretics. He emphasizes the character of elders, not their specific duties. He uses the rhetorical tool of *synkrisis* to contrast the traits of the appointed elders with those of the false teachers.

The genre of this comparison is a virtue and vice list (→ 1 Tim 1:9-10), which resembles the lists for overseers and deacons in 1 Tim 3:1-13. There are several possible explanations for these similarities: (1) They were written by the same author around the same time. (2) The offices of "bishop," "elder," and "deacon" overlapped and were still in the process of being defined. Or, (3) Both lists were dependent upon a common list (oral or written) of qualifications for church officials (Arichea and Hatton 1995, 269). The traits here are harsher and the virtues more rudimentary than in 1 Timothy, possibly because the church in Crete was still in its infancy (Johnson 1996, 223). Elders were already present in Ephesus (Acts 20:17), but Titus had to find and appoint them in Crete.

A. The Qualifications of Leaders (1:5-9)

IN THE TEXT

■ **5** Paul begins the body of the letter with a clear statement of Titus' two-part mission in Crete: (1) continuing evangelism and (2) finding local people to guide new converts. This was Paul's typical strategy in his own mission (Acts 14:21-23). This rather abrupt and forceful opening statement functions as the *propositio* of the letter and creates urgency for Titus' mission.

The island of **Crete** is located in the Mediterranean Sea south of the Aegean Sea. It is 156 miles (251 km) east to west and 35 miles (56 km) north to south. In ancient times, it was known for its many towns. It served as a major stopping place for commercial sea trade on the Mediterranean. Its location made it a strategic place to spread the gospel, but also a melting pot of diverse philosophies and religions. It had been the center of the Minoan civilization, which had faded by the time Rome came to power. By the second century BC there was a growing Jewish population on the island (Tacitus, *Hist.* 5.2).

Unresolved Historical Questions

Nothing is known of how the church in Crete started or when Paul or Titus may have spent time there. **I left you** implies that Paul and Titus were on the island together, Paul left, and Titus remained to continue the work. This coheres with nothing we know from Acts or Paul's other letters. There are several major approaches scholars have taken to solve this problem:

1. The traditional approach is that Paul spent some time in Crete evangelizing after his release from his first Roman imprisonment (Acts 28). Since there is no mention in Acts of Paul or Titus ever visiting Crete, their ministry must have been later (Mounce 2000, 385-86). The major problem with this approach is that there is no evidence that Paul was ever released from prison (→ Introduction).

2. During Paul's brief layover in Crete en route to Rome (Acts 27), he heard of problems in the church there and sent Titus to resolve them.

This possibility, however, neglects Paul's plan to meet Titus in Nicopolis (Titus 3:12). This assumes he was free to move about as needed, not under house arrest in Rome.

3. Paul could simply have commissioned Titus to help resolve issues in the young church because word had reached him that Judaizers were causing trouble there as they had in other churches. Paul need not be present in Crete for this to happen. **Leave behind** often translates the verb *apoleipō*, but it can also mean **dispatched, deployed,** or **assigned.** What is crucial is the transferring of authority from one person to another; the geographical location need not be part of the consideration (Marshall 1999, 150). Paul could have sent Titus to Crete at some point or left him there during one of their Mediterranean Sea journeys. We need not assume Paul evangelized in Crete to interpret this letter.

4. There is no reason to assume Acts exhaustively reports all of Paul's missionary travels. We know from his letters that he apparently evangelized in Arabia (Gal 1:17) and in Illyricum (Rom 15:19), neither of which are mentioned in Acts. Paul and Titus may have evangelized Crete during the long three-year stay in Ephesus or during one of their trips across the Mediterranean. Silence in Acts does not mean it did not happen. Paul may have written the letter to Titus after leaving Ephesus, while traveling through Macedonia to Corinth. Nicopolis would have been a convenient place for them to meet before winter once things had settled down in Crete (Walker 2012a, 10-11).

Paul's goal for Titus in Crete is given in a two-part purpose (*hina*) clause. He explains these purposes more fully, in reverse order, in the rest of the chapter:

First, so that Titus **might put in order what was left unfinished.** The verb *epidiorthōsē* (only here in the Bible) means **amend, set right,** or **further correct** (BDAG 2000, 371). This rare verb may have a background in the Cretan legal language for "reforming" treaties and law (Towner 2006, 678).

Ta leiponta simply means **the remaining things.** What required attention was the influence of the opponents, discussed in Titus 1:10-16. There was work to do, and since Paul could not be there to do it, Titus needed to do the job. Titus' effectiveness in Corinth gave Paul confidence in his ability to guide this difficult situation.

Second, Titus must **appoint elders in every town,** the topic of 1:6-9. **Appoint** (*katastēsēs*) means to designate someone to a particular office or duty (BDAG 2000, 492 s.v. 2.b.). The translation "ordain" (KJV) may be anachronistic, since formal ordination was still developing in the early church. By appointing leaders, Titus gave them authority to enact necessary reforms (Marshall 1999, 151). The first order of business was to appoint strong and worthy indigenous leaders (Acts 14:23).

Literally, **elders** (*presbyterous*) refers to "old men," who are still held in high esteem in traditional cultures. Philo wrote that what makes a person an elder is not age but wisdom and understanding of Scripture (*Contempl. Life* 67). In the early church, elders became important leaders alongside the apostles (→ 1 Tim 3:1; 4:14; 5:1; Acts 15:4, 22; 20:17, 28; 1 Thess 5:12; Jas 5:14; 1 Pet 5:1, 5; 2 John 1). Among their primary tasks was teaching and preaching the true gospel and making sure believers lived godly lives (1 Tim 5:17).

The plural form may refer to **elders** in the various house churches located **in every town** on the island (BDAG 2000, 512 s.v. B.1.d.). Paul's usual strategy was to go to the urban centers of the Roman Empire where people gathered for commerce, news, and various cultural or religious celebrations. The many small towns in Crete made this different strategy important.

The closing thought, **as I directed you**, strongly reminds Titus of an earlier oral command that sent him on his mission. The situation in Crete called for quick and decisive action. An emphatic **I** (*egō*) adds further stress. The verb *dietaxamēn* (only here in the NT) is a forceful word used by emperors to give orders (Acts 18:2; 23:31). There was no shirking this assignment.

■ **6** Paul lists twelve qualifications of elders, six positive and six negative. These emphasize personal integrity more than personality, and who elders are more than what they do. These qualities are not uniquely for leaders only, but leaders should set the example for the rest of the church (→ Titus 2:12).

(1) **An elder must be blameless** (*anenklētos*; → 1 Tim 3:2, 10). Leaders must have such good reputations that no one can say anything bad about them. Their personal integrity cannot be questioned. How this may be achieved in that culture is described in the next four qualities that focus on their lives at home.

(2) An elder should be **faithful to his wife** (lit. *a one woman man*; → 1 Tim 3:2, 12). Church leaders should be models of mutual love and respect in their marriages (Eph 5:22-33).

(3) An elder should be **a man whose children believe**. The father as the head of the family should live out his faith in such an attractive way that the rest of the family comes to believe (Acts 16:15, 31; 18:8). Elders do well by raising their children in the Lord (Eph 6:4). Instruction in Scripture is one aspect of Christian child-rearing (2 Tim 3:15-17). Leadership ability begins at home.

Parents' Responsibility for the Faith of Their Children

Parents cannot control the salvation of their children (see Liefeld 1999, 313). Not all children accept the faith of their parents. Responsibility ultimately rests with each child. Jerome wrote,

Parents should not be faulted if, having taught their children well, these turn out badly later. Indeed, if anyone had taught his sons well, it was Isaac, who must be viewed as setting even Esau on a firm foundation. But Esau turned out to be profligate and worldly, when he sold his birthright for a single meal. Samuel also, though he invoked God and God heard him, and he obtained rain at the time of the winter harvest, had sons who declined into greed. (*Comm. Tit.*, quoted by Gorday 2000, 287)

The multigenerational households of the first century made parental influence significant. The individualism of Western culture today makes spiritual nurturing more difficult, but not impossible. It takes great wisdom in knowing how to influence children through discipline and strong love, which are two important qualities in the church as well.

(4) An elder's children should **not** be **open to the charge of being wild and disobedient**. They were to be **blameless**, not even suspected of having a bad reputation, in two respects:

They were not to be **wild** (*asōtias*)—given to "reckless abandon, debauchery, dissipation, profligacy" (BDAG 2000, 148). The word describes the prodigal son in Luke 15:13. His life was marked by "senseless and reckless and excessively riotous behavior with no concern at all for the consequences of such action" (Arichea and Hatton 1995, 210).

They were not to be **disobedient** (*anypotakta*)—"refusing submission to authority, undisciplined, disobedient, rebellious" (BDAG 2000, 91). Eli's sons illustrate this "unruly" (KJV) lifestyle (in 1 Sam 10:27). The word in Titus 1:10 describes the opponents in Crete.

It could be asked, how does one measure these qualities in an objective manner? Every family has its faults, weaknesses, and quirks. The public nature of the word **blameless** assumes the community is involved in the assessment of elders and can testify to their character quality. The word should not be interpreted to mean "faultless." This word is important because it is repeated again in v 7.

■ **7** The positive qualities continue but with a noticeable shift in vocabulary describing the leader. Paul now refers to **an overseer** (*episkopon*). Is this the same official as the **elder** in vv 5-6 or a different one? Two issues influence this:

First, the connective *gar*, **Since**. This word usually introduces the reason for a previous statement. The reason an elder should be blameless is because he "oversees" God's household, the church.

Second, the Greek *dei* (**must**) describes something as ordained by God: (lit.) *it is necessary that an elder be blameless*. Paul makes reputation the highest criterion for church leadership.

Episkopos combines a preposition (*epi* meaning "over") and noun (*skopeō*, "watch") to describe the *function* of an elder: to provide church oversight and leadership (→ 1 Tim 3:1). A similar shift from the position of an elder to the job of oversight occurs in Acts 20:17 and 28. "Bishop" is a possible translation, but the ecclesial position by this title was a development well after the writing of the NT. The use here of the two terms together describing the same person suggests an early date for the letter (Mounce 2000, 390).

(5) An overseer should be blameless *as a manager of God's* household. **Blameless** is the same word that starts the list in Titus 1:6. Its repetition here combines the qualities of v 6 with vv 7-9. For this reason some interpreters take this as a position separate from the elder of v 6.

A *manager* (*oikonomon*) is responsible for administering the affairs or property of another person. A household manager was "the overseer of the house" (*Eum.* 740; Collins 2002, 324). Managers needed to be faithful and trustworthy with the owner's property (Luke 12:42; 16:1, 3, 8; 1 Cor 4:1-2). Their authority is delegated by the rightful owner. The church as God's household is an important theme in 1 Tim 3:15 and 2 Tim 2:20-21. As stewards, elders are to give oversight to the church, but must remember that it is God's family, not theirs.

Certain moral qualities are required for any would-be leader of God's family. In what respects an overseer must be blameless continues with a list of negative qualities to be avoided. Each begins with the Greek negative *mē*. These vices were strong temptations for all leaders in that era.

(6) First, an overseer should **not** be **overbearing**. The word *authadē* has at its root a selfishness that does not care about others. They are so intent on their personal agendas that they are "arrogant," "stubborn," "headstrong," "self-willed," "obstinate." They always want their own way, no matter what it takes (Arichea and Hatton 1995, 272). **Overbearing** leaders use the power of their position to take advantage of others in order to achieve personal goals. They have poor listening skills. It is difficult to work under such persons.

(7) Overseers should **not** be **quick-tempered** (*orgilon*). This adjective describes people who get angry easily. In ministry, it is easy to lose patience with difficult people. Overseers will have their share of stress from the false teachers. An even temperament and self-control will keep them on course.

(8) Overseers should **not** be **given to drunkenness**. The consumption of too much alcohol can lead to many relational problems (→ 1 Tim 3:3). Drunkenness can lead to a loss of self-control. This opens the door to the next vice:

(9) Leaders cannot use **violence** (*plēktern*) even to achieve worthy objectives. A violent person bullies others and may even abuse them physically or verbally. The end does *not* justify every means.

(10) Ministry leaders cannot be motivated by money, power, position, or prestige. Overseers should **not** be **pursuing dishonest gain** (*aischrokerdē*). Ministers should be supported for their work so they may devote their time to ministry. But they should not take advantage of their position for material gain (→ 1 Tim 3:3, 8; 5:17; 6:5; Gal 6:6). Greed motivates people to take more than they need. Some paraphrasing translations include: "involved in

any shady finance" (TNT), "money-grubber" (NEB), and "dishonest in business" (CEV) (Arichea and Hatton 1995, 273). Caution is especially important in relation to church finances. Greed was a well-known problem with many Cretans (Polybius, *Hist.* 6.46).

Each of the preceding negative qualities does terrible damage to community. Appointing leaders with these vices will only harm the church. Cretans had a bad reputation for many of these character flaws. Paul urged Titus to look for leaders who had been so transformed by Christ as to be Christians first, not stereotypical Cretans (→ Titus 3:3-7).

■ **8** The adversative **rather** (*alla*) marks a shift from the negative vices to the desirable positive virtues for overseers. The first two are compound words using *philos*, "love."

(11) Overseers **must be hospitable** (*philoxenon*, lit.), *a lover of strangers*. Hospitality was important in the early church because of the dangers faced by itinerate ministers. Travelers needed welcoming places to stay and safety from persecution (→ 1 Tim 3:2-3; 5:10). Leaders who welcome and care for people set a good example for the church. "The practice of hospitality among Christians was often urgent, sacrificial and risky: urgent because Christians might be forced from homes or jobs with no one to turn to but fellow Christians; sacrificial because material goods were often in short supply; risky because to associate oneself with those who had been forced out meant to identify with their cause" (Towner 1994, 227).

(12) The next quality desired for a church leader is a unique compound word: he **loves what is good** (*philagathon*). The overseer should embrace noble virtues that lead to godliness—"whatever is true, . . . noble, . . . right, . . . pure, . . . lovely, . . . admirable, . . . excellent or praiseworthy" (Phil 4:8).

(13) The leader should also be **self-controlled** (*sōphrona*). This is essentially the same virtue described later in this list (16) as **disciplined**. It is the basis for many other positive behaviors mentioned in the letter. Six of the sixteen occurrences of the word in the NT are in this letter, particularly in the section on home life (Titus 2:2, 5-6, 12). Self-discipline must have been a challenge in Cretan culture. This virtue involves being able to master one's passions. According to Philo, this virtue "takes its stand against pleasure, which thinks that it can direct the course of human weakness" (*Alleg. Interp.* 1.69, quoted by Collins 2002, 325). Modern translations resort to a variety of English equivalents: "prudent" (NRSV), "sober-minded" (NKJV), "live wisely" (NLT), "self-restrained" (TNT), and "sensible" (NASB). Controlling oneself is a by-product of the Holy Spirit's work (→ 1 Tim 3:2, 8; Gal 5:22).

(14) Overseers ought to be fair and honest by being **upright** (*dikaion*) or "righteous" (1 Tim 1:9; → 2 Tim 2:2). This virtue has both a theological and moral sense to it. Morally, righteousness is a human endeavor and responsibil-

405

ity in obedience to God's commands. Theologically, it is a gift of God's grace that leads to new relationship with him. Since this list stresses human qualities, the moral sense is the likely emphasis here. The word is used theologically in 3:5 and 7.

(15) Their inward change will be evidenced in **holy** (*hosion*) living. *Osios* is a more intentionally religious term than *dikaios*. That which is holy is pleasing and acceptable to God because it has been purified and dedicated to him. Our relationship with God impacts our relationship with others. Outward purity results from a pure heart. Paul uses the antonym *anosios* in 1 Tim 1:9 and 2 Tim 3:2 to characterize the impious behavior of the opponents in Ephesus.

(16) The way to accomplish all these virtues will come through being **disciplined** (*enkratē*). This entails controlling passions and desires by pursing godliness through the help of the Holy Spirit. This word is a synonym for "self-control" in Gal 5:23. The Holy Spirit empowers believers to control their passions and appetites.

■ **9** The last quality particularly stands out as crucial in the context of the problems in Crete:

(17) An overseer **must hold firmly to the trustworthy message as it has been taught**. The participle *holding firmly* graphically describes a clear understanding of and ability to articulate the truth. The word has the connotation of commitment. Jesus used it in Matt 6:24 (‖ Luke 16:13) for the devotion one has toward a master. A **trustworthy message** is (lit.) a *faithful word* (→ 1 Tim 1:15; 3:1; 4:9; 2 Tim 2:11) and specifically refers to the gospel (Mounce 2000, 391).

The gospel message is **trustworthy** because it was handed down from the apostles, who received it firsthand from Jesus. In this situation, Paul is the primary authority who has handed the message on to Titus, his representative. This chain of transmission guarantees the church stability and consistency. Devotion to orthodox doctrine will enable elders to do two things (indicated by *kai . . . kai* followed by two infinitives):

Positively, elders should **encourage others by sound doctrine**. The infinitive "to encourage" (*parakalein*) can have the rhetorical nuance of strongly urging, appealing, or exhorting (BDAG 2000, 765 s.v. 2). The source for encouraging the church is **sound doctrine**. The phrase speaks of teaching (*didaskalia*) that is "healthy" (*hygiainousēi*; → 1 Tim 1:10; 2 Tim 4:3; Titus 1:13; 2:1). Orthodox teaching will lead to spiritual health. Scripture is one primary tool for building up the church (→ 2 Tim 3:15-17). The goal of this encouragement should be unity, knowledge of Christ, maturity, and Christlikeness (Eph 4:12).

Negatively, knowing the truth of the gospel will enable qualified church leaders to **refute those who oppose it**. Refute or *rebuke* (*elenchein*) has several nuances. It shows people "where they are wrong" (NLT). The truth can "bring to light, expose, set forth" (see Eph 5:11, 13) what is false. Overseers are to preserve orthodox teaching. If they fail to do so, opponents may lead the church astray. Knowledge of the truth is necessary to correct false doctrine (→ Titus 1:13; 1 Tim 4:6; 6:2-3; 2 Tim 3:16). It can also be restorative, helping misguided people recognize their wrongdoing (→ Titus 1:13; BDAG 2000, 315). The goal of church discipline is to restore those who have departed from the truth. This will be apparent by their ungodly lifestyle (→ 1 Tim 1:9-11) or their false teaching (→ 2 Tim 2:25-26; 4:2).

Descriptions of the Gospel in the Pastoral Epistles

Various expressions for the gospel appear in the Pastoral Epistles:
- The *gospel* (1 Tim 1:11; 2 Tim 2:8)
- The *teaching* (1 Tim 1:10; 4:6; 6:1; 2 Tim 1:13; 2:2; 3:10; Titus 1:9; 2:1)
- The *faith* (1 Tim 1:19; 3:9; 4:1; 5:8; 6:21; 2 Tim 4:7; Titus 1:13)
- The *truth* (1 Tim 2:4; 3:15; 4:3; 2 Tim 2:25; 3:8; 4:4; Titus 1:14)
- The *deposit* (1 Tim 6:20; 2 Tim 1:12, 14)
- The *mystery* (1 Tim 3:16)
- The *promise* (2 Tim 1:1)
- The *testimony* (2 Tim 1:8)
- The *solid foundation* (2 Tim 2:19)
- The *word* (2 Tim 4:2)
- The *trustworthy message* (Titus 1:9)

FROM THE TEXT

Paul understood the important principle that everything rises and falls on leadership (Maxwell 1999, xi). Strong local leadership is essential for any new mission to be successful, especially if there is any potential for false doctrine. The surest way to deal with heresy in the church is to make sure strong leaders know the truth of the gospel. Jerome wrote,

> In fact, want of education in a clergyman prevents him from doing good to any one but himself. Even if the virtue of his life may build up Christ's church, he does it an injury as great by failing to resist those who are trying to pull it down. (*Epist.* 53.3, quoted by Gorday 2000, 288)

It takes management skills and character to be a good leader in the church. The situation in Crete called for leaders of the highest character. No two situations are the same. Context may influence the specific skills needed in leaders. But the core character qualities Paul lists are universal.

There are many voices crying for attention in today's world. With easy and instant communication, the average Christian is exposed to many different ideas on any given day. Some of these ideas may sound Christian, but they breed only misunderstanding or feed selfishness. Competent leaders must be lighthouses pointing the way clearly through this sea of confusion. A leader must model both compassion and strength when dealing with potential heresy or misunderstanding of the gospel.

The greatest model for this type of leader is Jesus Christ. He showed compassion to those who came to him in humble repentance (Matt 8:5-13; Luke 19:1-9). He corrected those who intentionally deceived people (Matt 23). The only way leaders will be effective today is by imitating the love of Christ.

B. The Crisis of Character in Crete (1:10-16)

BEHIND THE TEXT

This section of the letter gives insight into the situation that led Paul to write. Although the letter is addressed to Titus, its contents deal with the house churches in Crete. Paul here explains why Titus must appoint leaders in Crete: there were some "rebellious people" (v 10) who were leading the church astray with false doctrines influenced by Judaism. Paul uses strong language in this paragraph to help Titus identify the problem people and decide what to do about them. We get some description of these people but few details.

The relationship between Judaism and Christianity was one of the major challenges the early church faced. Acts devotes significant attention to this tension (chs 10, 15). The frequent mention of issues related to Jewish practices and interpretation of the Law in the letters of Paul shows that the issue was widespread (especially in Galatia, Ephesus, Philippi, and Colosse). There was no single, uniform, organized, or united movement of so-called Judaizers (Gal 2:14), those who wanted to combine elements of Judaism and the new faith in Jesus Christ. Rather, there were regional variations and emphases. General similarities among the groups include emphases on Jewish law, practices—especially circumcision, festivals, and genealogies. Many of these issues affected the churches in Ephesus and Crete, prompting Paul to write the Pastoral Epistles.

The issues in Crete were similar to those in Ephesus. This may explain why Titus and 1 and 2 Timothy share similar themes and vocabulary. Titus mentions nothing of the realized eschatology and asceticism found in Ephesus (1 Tim 4:1-5; 2 Tim 2:18; Marshall 1999, 192). There is no clear indication in the letter as to how Paul learned of the opponents in Crete. Titus 1:10-16 closely resembles 1 Tim 1:3-11 (Knight 1992, 296):

Titus 1	1 Timothy 1
Full of meaningless talk (*mataiologoi*) (v 10)	**Full of meaningless talk** (*mataiologian*) (v 6)

Paying no attention to Jewish myths (*mē prosechontes Joudaikois mythois*) (v 14)	*Not to devote to myths* (*mē de prosein mythois*) (v 4)
By teaching things not necessary (*didasktontes ha mē dei*) (v 11)	*To teach false doctrine* (*heterodidaskalein*) (v 4)
Pure to the pure (*kathara tois kathrois*) (v 15)	*A pure heart* (*katharas kardias*) (v 5)
Conscience (*syneidēsis*) (v 15)	*Conscience* (*syneidēseōs*) (v 5)

This section has two rhetorical purposes: It functions as a warning against false teachers and as a negative example (*synkrisis*) of what to avoid. Paul's polemic isolates the opponents. His position represents wisdom and truth; the opponents' represent false wisdom and sophistry (Karris 1973, 563). The description of the false teachers stands in stark contrast to Titus' elders (Witherington 2006, 127):

Elder	False Teacher
House manager	House wrecker
Blameless	Defiled conscience and works
Not pursuing dishonest gain	Unscrupulous teaching for gain
Not quick-tempered or intemperate	Acting like a wild beast
Holding fast to sound tradition	Embracing myths and human commands
Truthful and refuting error	Liar, deceiver, embracing and teaching error

Paul's argument is moved forward by the use of catchwords and maxims. It is a logical syllogism that forms a thematic chiasm:

A The evidence of the threat of Jewish opponents to the church (Titus 1:10-11).

    B An example in the form of a Cretan maxim (v 12).

        C Therefore Titus should rebuke them (vv 13-14).

    B' An example in the form of a proverb (v 15).

A' Second description of the opponents' behavior (v 16).

IN THE TEXT

■ **10** For (*gar*) identifies this section as the reason why Titus must appoint elders (in 1:5-9). Paul lays out Titus' challenge, describing opponents in three ways:

First, they are **rebellious people** (*anypotaktoi*) because they reject the truth of the gospel and apostolic authority. They are unwilling to submit to the authority of others (BDAG 2000, 91). Although they were part of the church, they refused to submit to the church. The same word describes the "disobedient" in 1:6 (→). Their behavior revealed their rebellion.

Second, they are **full of meaningless talk**, "babblers" (*mataiologoi*; → 1 Tim 1:6) with nothing of substance to say.

Third, they make empty promises with their **deception** (*phrenapatai*). They intentionally lead the church astray into false doctrine—"attractive nonsense" (Marshall 1999, 195). One of those doctrines apparently involved circumcision.

There was a substantial Jewish population in Crete (Acts 2:11; 1 Macc 15:23; Philo, *Legat.* 282; Josephus, *Ant.* 17.327; *Vita* 427; Tacitus, *Hist.* 5.2). Paul identifies the leading (*malista*: **especially**) opponents as **those from the circumcision**. They were Jewish (whether natural born or proselytes) Christians who taught that circumcision was essential for salvation (Acts 10:45; 11:2; Gal 2:12; 5:1-12; 6:15; Col 3:11). If they had heard of the apostolic decree of Acts 15 (that Gentiles need not become Jews to become Christians), they rejected it.

■ **11** Circumcision is not the main problem Paul addresses. The problem is what the opponents were doing to the house churches. Jewish missionaries were threatening these fragile churches by attempting to persuade new converts to accept their interpretation of the Law (Johnson 1996, 213).

Titus' response must be *to silence* them. This infinitive stands out grammatically with the strong opening, ***Therefore, it is necessary [dei] that***. There was no room for compromise or dialogue. Paul does not say how Titus should proceed at this point. The word *epistomizein* implies only that he "gag" (Collins 2002, 333) or "bridle" (BDAG 2000, 382) them with the truth of the gospel and exposure of their error. In 3:9-11 (→), he effectively directs Titus to bar them from the Christian community: "Warn a divisive person once, and then warn them a second time. After that, have nothing to do with them" (see Matt 18:15-18).

The implicit reason why they must be silenced follows: **because they are disrupting whole households by teaching things they ought not to teach**. The term *oikos* describes the extended family, which could include several generations and slaves. **Disrupting** (*anatrepousin*: **overturn**) has the figurative sense of "ruining" (LEB). The false teachers were "upsetting" (ESV, NASB, NRSV) entire households, corrupting the churches that met in them. The plural indicates this widespread problem threatened the early Christian movement in Crete. An instrumental participle **by teaching** indicates how they operated. Paul offers two descriptions of their teachings:

First, *it was not necessary* (*mē dei*). They **ought not to teach** such things. Their teaching did nothing to help believers grow in their faith, knowledge, and hope in Christ. They were directly opposing Paul's own mission stated in Titus 1:1-3.

Second, they taught for **dishonest gain** (*aischrou kerdous*). Their pecuniary motivation disqualified them from being elders (→ v 7). Compensation for ministry is not the issue (→ 1 Tim 5:17-18). Their gain was "shameful" (*aischros*; BDAG 2000, 29) because of the content and motive of their teaching (Knight 1992, 298). They were like the sophists, contemporary traveling teachers, often criticized for wanting money for their work (Winter 2003, 147-48). Christian teachers are not sophists. The gospel must be given out freely and accurately because it is an extension of the mercy of God in Christ Jesus (Titus 3:4-7).

■ **12** In support of his warning about the opponents, the apostle appeals to a well-known maxim that is a generalization about the stereotypical Cretan character. "Maxims persuade because they hit upon opinions or famous sayings that the audience already accepts or is familiar with" (Witherington 2006, 94; referring to Aristotle, *Rhet.* 1395b1-11). Paul cites a widely accepted ethnic prejudice as a rhetorical tool to shame the Cretan opponents and warn others in the church (see 1:13).

This saying comes from **one of Crete's own prophets**. This is the only place in the Bible a pagan is called a prophet. Interpreters since the church fathers have been bothered by the idea of Paul calling a pagan a "prophet." This narrow reading misses Paul's point. There are several plausible explanations: (1) Paul may accept the prophetic ability of the saying as an accurate assessment of a Cretan cultural weakness. (2) He strategically appeals to Cretan culture and memory as a rhetorical tool. (3) He could write from the perspective of Cretans who claim this saying as coming from their prophet (Arichea and Hatton 1995, 277). (4) The term could simply have its broad sense of "spokesperson" (Collins 2002, 334).

Scholars debate the source of this saying, but its application is clear. Most think it comes from Epimenides of Knossos (sixth-fifth centuries BC). Plato and Aristotle considered him a prophet (*Rhet.* 3.17). Clement of Alexandria (*Strom.* 1.14), Jerome (*Comm. Tit.* 1.12), Chrysostom, and Augustine also identify him as the source (Hanson 1982, 176). The **prophet** gives three characteristics matching the description of opponents in vv 10-11:

First, **Cretans are always liars**. The Cretans developed a reputation of being liars because they claimed that the grave of Zeus was located on their island. But since Zeus was immortal, he could not have died (Lucian of Samosata, *Philops.* 3; *Tim.* 6; *Anth. pal.* 7.275; Callimachus, *Hymn. Jov.* 1.8-9). This reputation entered the Greek language as *kreitzō*, "lie or cheat." The opponents were likewise deceitful in their teachings (v 10).

Second, Cretans are called **evil brutes**. The word *thēria* refers to animals. Used figuratively for people, it describes wild, uncontrolled behavior. The adjective **evil** only makes the imagery more vivid. Their behavior is abusive and malicious. The teaching of the opponents was similarly having detrimental effects on the churches in Crete (v 11).

Third, they are **lazy gluttons.** This figurative description also applied to the Cretan opponents. *Argai,* "idlers" in 1 Tim 5:13 (ESV, RSV), describes those who refuse to work. The Greek *gasteres* (lit.) refers to the entrails—the stomach or womb (BDAG 2000, 190). Figuratively, it describes an insatiable appetite for more—a life devoted to selfishness and pleasure. Cretans were known for being greedy mercenaries (Polybius, *Hist.* 6.46; Livy, *Hist. of Rome* 44.45.13; Collins 2002, 334). The selfishness of the opponents only feeds into this cultural pattern.

■ **13-14** The rhetorical value of the famous saying appears in the next two verses. Paul makes the connection between the saying and the false teachers clear. The NIV's **saying** is literally ***testimony***. The Cretans should already know their bad reputation. This assessment should ***cause*** (*aitian*) Titus to **rebuke them sharply.**

The antecedent of the pronoun **them** is unclear. Two groups are possible: (1) those who will listen and repent, and (2) those who have rejected the truth and refuse to amend their ways. The first group does not rule out the opponents, but the second group captures the opponents' present activity.

Paul charges Titus as mission director for Crete to **rebuke them sharply.** **Rebuke** (*elengche*) in 1:9 is translated "refute." The adverb *apotomōs* is a strong term that can mean "harshly" or "severely." This is an urgent, serious problem. Such a response is necessary because of the threat to the truth of the gospel. Titus knows the truth and should appoint leaders who do. His rebuke has a two-part purpose:

Positive: The goal is for the Cretans to **be sound in the faith. Sound** (*hygianinōsin*) has the connotation of healthy and orthodox (→ 1 Tim 1:10). Those who follow false teaching become sick spiritually. Replacing this with sound teaching leads to spiritual vitality. Paul hoped the heretics would return to orthodox faith (→ 1 Tim 1:20; 2 Tim 2:25-26).

Negative: The preventative goal was that the Cretans should abandon their error, ***by not being devoted*** [*prosechontes*] ***to Jewish myths or the commands of people.*** The instrumental participle expresses a focused attention or response to something that can lead to devotion or preoccupation (→ 1 Tim 1:4). **Jewish myths** would be extrabiblical legends that take the attention away from the truth of the gospel (→ 1 Tim 1:4). This hints that the heretical teachings resembled what Timothy faced in Ephesus.

Human commands could include interpretations and opinions about the Law (Jewish *halakah*) or even tangential opinions related to the gospel. The merely human commands contrast with God's commands in Scripture (Isa 29:13; Matt 15:9; Mark 7:7).

Paul is ambiguous about the content of these commands. His focus is on the source: **people who have turned away from the truth**. Truth refers to the orthodox Christian message received by the apostles from Jesus (→ 1 Tim 2:4; 2 Tim 4:4). The participle **turned away** (*apostrephomenōn*) vividly describes their intentional rejection of God's commands revealed in the gospel.

■ **15-16** Paul now offers his own proverb to counter the speculations of the opponents. The saying has a chiastic structure that uses antithetic parallelism (Quinn 1990, 102):

A *all things [are] pure*

   B *to the pure*

   B' *but to the corrupted and unbelieving*

A' *nothing [is] pure.*

Pure (*katharos*), three times in this saying, describes something clean and free from defilement (→ 1 Tim 1:5). The saying's broad and inclusive statement would trouble many Jews, who interpreted OT purity laws very narrowly. The logic is simple: because God created all things, all things are good (Acts 10:14-15, 28; 11:8-9; 1 Cor 8:4-6; 10:26; 1 Tim 4:3-5; see Luke 11:41; Rom 14:20).

The proverb hints that the "human commands" of Titus 1:14 may have focused on issues of clean and unclean, including matters of food (→ 1 Tim 4:3-4). The opponents confused moral and ritual purity. They may have thought that obeying human interpretations of purity laws made them morally pure. They tried to be holy by their own efforts rather than through the power of the gospel. The first **pure** refers to ritual purity; the last, to moral purity (Mounce 2000, 401). Paul insists that ritual purity does not influence moral purity (→ 1 Tim 4:1-5).

Paul illustrates how the opponents had misinterpreted purity by confusing knowledge of the Law with obedience to God. **In fact** is the strong adversative **but** (*alla*). It contrasts the opponents' interpretation of ceremonial purity with the moral purity that comes from trusting in the gospel. The sequence of defilement is noteworthy: from mind, to conscience, to words, and finally to deeds. Once the inner person is defiled, everything about a person is affected (Oden 1989, 64). Ritual purity is dependent on moral purity, not the other way around (Arichea and Hatton 1995, 279). A heart purified by the Holy Spirit through faith (Titus 3:5; Acts 15:9) is possible because of Christ's sacrificial death (Titus 2:14; see Eph 5:26).

Those who allow their **minds and consciences** to be **corrupted** (*memiantai*) by rejecting the Holy Spirit misunderstand salvation. The verb describes something that has been stained, making it ritually unclean or morally defiled (Hauck 1967, 644-47). Its perfect tense indicates that this defilement has been ongoing. Their descent to impurity started at some earlier point of rejection and has had continuing effects. The same verb appears again in the third line of the proverb.

Paul knows the issue is deeper than outward defilement, despite the opponents' preoccupation. So, he includes **minds** (*nous*; → 1 Tim 6:4-5), the center of thinking and understanding, and **consciences** (*syneidēsis*; 1 Tim 1:5), the center of moral judgment. If the mind becomes corrupted, it cannot understand the truth of the gospel (2 Tim 3:8). And this will become apparent in one's living (Mark 7:15). The Holy Spirit begins the cleansing process in the inner person (Rom 8:5-6). Those who harbor corrupted thoughts often compensate by external ritual. Those with purified minds see the good in God's world (Liefeld 1999, 320).

Paul charges that the opponents **claim to know God, but by their actions they deny him.** This **claim** (*homologousin*) is an open confession of faith, allegiance, and loyalty (Arichea and Hatton 1995, 280). It is the opposite of **deny** (*arnountai*). The actions of the opponents too much reflected Cretan culture for their profession to be taken seriously. Their hypocrisy showed that their knowledge had not produced genuine faith. The chapter ends with three terse descriptions summarizing the character of the opponents:

First, they are **detestable** (*bdelyktoi*, only here in the NT)—"repugnant," "abhorrent," "repulsive," even "disgusting" before God. But they have no shame for their condition (Foerster 1964a, 598). Leviticus 11:10-42 gives an example of things God detests.

Second, they are **disobedient** (*apeitheis*). It is ironic that they may be involved in "quarrels about the law" (Titus 3:9) but do not actually obey the Law. Disobedience is characteristic of the old life controlled by sin (3:3; Rom 1:30). This adds further proof that the opponents had rejected the truth of the gospel.

Third, all this makes them **unfit for doing anything good. Unfit** (*adokimoi*) summarizes the thought of the entire paragraph. These people are "unqualified" to do good works, the thing they attempt to do. They are "counterfeits," "rejected" because of their poor quality. They fail the test because they are unable to do good (→ Jannes and Jambres in 2 Tim 3:8). Their actions betray their true nature. No legitimate fruit; therefore, no authentic faith (Towner 2006, 711). They were just like the Pharisees Jesus criticized in Luke 16:14-15.

Titus 1:16 serves as the hinge connecting the letter's introduction to the rest of the letter. It anticipates the key thought that obedience should be the response to salvation and result from salvation (Mounce 2000, 402).

FROM THE TEXT

One clear message Paul sends to the modern church is *do not compromise with false doctrine*. The saying that there are no new heresies, just reworked old ones, should draw believers to what Paul says in this letter. The threat of false teaching and preachers with selfish motives has only intensified with the ease of communication through modern technology. Anyone can get his or her message out to the public. There is no place for pluralism in the church when it comes to the truth of the gospel.

The best way to expose heresy is by clearly preaching the truth. There are three essential steps when dealing with heresy: identify it, do not compromise with it, and rebuke it. Replace heretical teachers or those who get caught up in trivial or controversial matters with teachers who have a knowledge and passion for the gospel. Jerome wrote, "If ravening wolves are to be frightened away it must be by the barking of dogs and by the staff of the shepherd" (*Epist.* 69.8; quoted by Twomey 2009, 194).

Stott (1996, 183) offers a series of questions to test the truth of a doctrine: First, is its *origin* divine or human, revelation or tradition? Secondly, is its *essence* inward or outward, spiritual or ritual? Thirdly, is its *result* a transformed life or a merely formal creed? True religion is divine in its origin, spiritual in its essence and moral in its effect.

A second message, which will be emphasized in the next section of the letter, is that we should see *the vital connection between holiness of heart and holiness of lifestyle.* The opponents in Crete misunderstood true purity. Purity is not simply a matter of outward obedience to rules. It must begin with the inner transformation of the mind and conscience (v 15). Jesus said, "A good man brings good things out of the good stored up in his heart, and an evil man brings evil things out of the evil stored up in his heart. For the mouth speaks what the heart is full of" (Luke 6:45). Rules for ritual purity have their symbolic place only as an expression of inward purity and not the cause of it.

Third, *the character of leaders will influence the direction of the communities they lead.* The church must not be led by unqualified people. They are unfit for leadership if they do not live up to Paul's positive list in Titus 1:5-9 or if they share any characteristics of his negative list in vv 10-16. Unfit church leaders can do great harm to the reputation of the gospel. The selection of church leadership is crucial.

How clergy are trained and how lay leaders are discipled will set the direction of the church in the future. Paul knew this and was constantly putting out fires in the early churches caused by false teaching. The positive outcome of this is that we now possess his inspired wisdom in the letters of the NT.

III. LIVING AS REDEEMED PEOPLE IN COMMUNITY: TITUS 2:1-15

BEHIND THE TEXT

Chapter 2 is one complete rhetorical argument nestled in the heart of the letter. Paul gives practical instruction for living in community (vv 1-10) and the reason for this lifestyle (vv 11-14). Godly behavior must be based upon sound theology. Paul begins with the existing situation in Crete and attempts to move believers closer to the ideal of new life in Christ.

There is a noticeable shift from the polemic against the opponents in 1:10-16 to ideal character qualities within Christian house churches. The two sections are connected: in order to deal with false teaching, the church must grow in its understanding of "sound doctrine" (2:1). Paul advises Titus as to how to instruct five different groups: older men (v 2), older women (v 3), younger women (vv 4-5), young men (v 6—with Titus as an example in vv 7-8), and slaves (vv 9-10). These divisions have more to do with gender and age than with responsibilities within the church. Here Paul responds to the threats of those disrupting Christian households (1:11).

Paul's strategy calls for Titus to teach the various groups within the Cretan churches to adopt godly lifestyles that arise from sound doctrine. His guidelines resemble the conservative ethical norms for ancient households (*oikoi*) of Greco-Roman pagan philosophy. The household was the basic unit of society. There were widely shared cultural expectations and responsibilities for each person. If these were not observed, shame and internal problems could result. The Pastorals endorse existing household and family structures and reflect dominant social values (Verner 1983, 145; → 1 Tim 2:8-15). Many of the values Paul lists were espoused by moral philosophers of the time. The primary difference between them was Paul's emphasis on the Holy Spirit as the divine means through which these ideals might be realized (→ Titus 3:4-7).

This list is unlike other NT (Eph 5:21—6:9; Col 3:18—4:1; 1 Tim 2:8; 3:1-13; 5:1—6:2; 1 Pet 2:18—3:7) and early church (*1 Clem.* 1.3; 21.6-8; Ign. *Pol.* 4.1—6.1; *Did.* 4.9-11; *Barn.* 19.5-7) household codes, because it does not address the family unit. Instead, its focus is the larger, multigenerational house church in which outsiders could participate (Titus 2:5, 10). It differs from such lists in Colossians and Ephesians by (1) not giving direction to reciprocal pairs (wives-husbands, children-parents, slaves-masters), and (2) having no legitimating language such as "in the Lord," "because of the Lord," or "as pleasing the Lord" (Johnson 1996, 233). Most of the characteristics are not particularly unique to each age-group but universally applicable to all.

The first section is carefully structured with three strategic purpose clauses (Titus 2:5, 8, 10). These express Paul's goal of strengthening the Christian witness before unbelievers by reinforcing traditional structure and authority within the typical household (Witherington 2006, 132). The reputation of the church and its message were at stake. The Cretan believers should rise above the problems of their culture (→ 1:12) because grace through Jesus Christ had made a fundamental change in them and should influence how they lived.

A. Directions to Various Groups within the Church (2:1-10)

IN THE TEXT

1. Teach Sound Doctrine (2:1)

■ 1 The emphatic **but you** (*sy de*; → 1 Tim 6:11; 2 Tim 3:10, 14; 4:5) marks the shift from polemic to exhortation. Paul compares what Titus should teach with what the opponents were teaching. The verb (lit.) **speak** (*lalei*) clearly refers to instruction. Paul will repeat this idea in v 15, forming an inclusio (literary bookends) to this second major argument. Titus is the primary recipient of the letter, but Paul's directions are for the whole church (3:15).

The message Titus is to communicate to the Cretans is **what is appropriate to sound doctrine**. Appropriate (*prepei*) describes something suitable, fitting, or proper (1 Cor 11:13; Eph 5:3; 1 Tim 2:10). The antecedent to the pronoun **what** is unclear, but would include the directions that follow in Titus 2:2-10 and anything else that agrees with **sound doctrine**. This (lit.) *teaching* (*didaskaliai*) should be *healthy* (*hygiainousēi*, → 1:9; 1 Tim 1:10) as compared to the "sick" teaching of the opponents. Titus' approach and message stand out against their Jewish myths and deception (1:10-16). Correct teaching should have at its core the truth of the good news of Jesus' death and resurrection (1:1-3; 3:4-7). Paul will explain this **doctrine** in 2:11-14.

In this opening verse, Paul introduces the two key thoughts of the chapter: orthodox doctrine (vv 11-14) and the behavior that agrees with it (vv 2-10). The basis for the virtues that follow is sound doctrine. Ethics should be based on doctrine, and behavior should result from knowledge and faith (v 10; → 1:3). The opponents failed to connect behavior with belief and focused only on outward activity, not the inward change that inspires godly outward behavior.

2. Older Men (2:2)

■ **2** Paul begins his list with those who would have held the most esteemed position in that culture: **older men**. The Greek word *presbytas* is related to *presbyterous*, used in 1:5 for the "elders" who were to lead the church. The word in the singular (only here and in Luke 1:18 and Phlm 9) refers to the age-group, not church leaders (Quinn 1990, 117). Most of the "elders" likely came from this group because of their maturity and cultural esteem.

The age for an "old man" varies in ancient texts. With the short life expectancy in antiquity, anyone over forty was "old." Philo, following Hippocrates, divided ages into seven stages. The sixth stage he called *presbytēs* for ages fifty to fifty-six (*Spec. Laws* 2.33; *Creation* 105; Collins 2002, 339). "Old" may refer more generally to grandparents older than "young people." Since age does not guarantee maturity, older men also need instruction.

Paul points out four key qualities of these men that form a chiasm of positive-negative, negative-positive. The last positive quality is expanded into three more. Each of these is also part of the lists for overseers in 1 Tim 3:2 and 8.

First, older men should be **temperate** (*nēphalious*; 1 Tim 3:2, 11). Literally, this word means sober—not drunk. Excessive drinking was a problem in Cretan culture (Titus 1:12; Spicq 1969, 2:618-19), especially among older people (Quinn 1990, 130). Figuratively, it refers to being clear headed or self-controlled. Either possibility befits older men. Drunkenness is incompatible with Christian faith (see Rom 13:13; 1 Cor 5:11; 6:10; 11:21-22; Gal 5:21; Eph 5:18; 1 Thess 5:6-8; 1 Pet 4:3).

Second, these men should be **worthy of respect** (*semnous*; 1 Tim 3:8). Their reputations should be unsoiled, like that of the "elder" of Titus 1:7. They should have the respect of others and have a "noble" (Phil 4:8) and attractive character. A reputation takes time to develop and can be lost in a moment.

Third, they should be **self-controlled** (*sōphronas*; 1 Tim 3:2). Being **self-controlled** is one of the changes resulting from God's grace (Titus 2:12). It requires restraining one's passions, and self-awareness, thoughtfulness, and sensibility. It takes self-discipline, but God gives believers his grace to assist. The idea of controlling oneself is important in this passage with the *sōphr-* root occurring in vv 2, 4, 5, 6, and 12.

Fourth, "spiritual health" (*soundness*) has three dimensions: **sound in faith, in love and in endurance**. **Sound** (*hygiainontas*) is the participial form of the adjective used in v 1 to refer to healthy doctrine. Spiritual health will result when these three qualities are consistently lived out (present tense). This directly confronts the opponents' teaching (1:9, 13).

a. **Faith** is the active human response to God's grace. It involves intellectual ascent expressed through trusting in his promises. The Greek article used here stresses the content of Christian faith—what Christians believe, stated in 2:11-14 (Mounce 2000, 409). **Faith** occurs with **love** nine times in the Pastoral Epistles.

b. **Love** is a verbal noun. It must be demonstrated by actions in relationship with God, others, and oneself. It will show up in good deeds done in the behalf of others.

c. **Endurance** does not compromise under pressure (1 Tim 6:11; 2 Tim 3:10). It is "the element of constancy and perseverance which maintains faith and love in the face of opposition and every temptation to discouragement until the believer reaches the end of the long journey" (Marshall 1999, 241). Faith, love, and hope are a common Pauline triad (→ 1 Tim 6:11; 1 Thess 1:3). Here, **endurance** replaces "hope" with much the same force. The two words are closely related in Christian theology. Endurance is how hope is expressed in difficult situations and in the face of opposition.

3. Older Women (2:3)

■ **3** **Likewise** compares and connects what follows with what came before, referring to sound doctrine in v 1. *Presbytidas* is similar to *presbyteras* in 1 Tim 5:2. Philo uses the term for women over sixty (*Spec. Laws* 2.33)—grandmothers as in v 2. Older women were leaders in Greco-Roman culture by virtue of their age and respect in the home. The four characteristics in this verse follow a chiastic positive-negative, negative-positive pattern. The qualities are both personal and relational.

a. **Reverent** (*hieroprepeis*, only here in the Bible) is a spiritual quality essential for older women (like faith, love, and endurance for older men). It is a compound word describing a "temple" that is holy and dedicated to God. It is an inward, spiritual commitment evident in outward holiness (see in 1 Tim 2:15 and 2 Tim 2:21). Because the women had dedicated themselves to God, they should act like it (Schrenk 1965, 254). Their lives were a form of "living liturgy" (Collins 2002, 341; Rom 12:1). Older women had limited opportunities in that culture, but they could devote themselves to God in prayer (→ 1 Tim 5:5).

The next two qualities are related in experience. Too much wine can lead to a loose tongue that may be tempted to slander. Timothy faced these two issues in Ephesus as well (1 Tim 3:11; 5:13). Both problematic behaviors were stereotypical marks of liberated older women in that culture:

b. Gossiping (→ 1 Tim 5:13) was a vice of speech. The Greek root behind **slanderers** (*diabolous*) is the word for "devil," the great deceiver. Slandering is telling lies or half-truths, causing harm to another person.

c. Drunkenness was a vice arising from deficient self-control—drinking too much alcohol. Some in antiquity considered drinking wine a virtue (Spicq 1969, 2:618-19). But others condemned consuming it in excess (Quinn 1990, 135). **Addicted** is a perfect passive participle from the verb "enslave" (*dedoulōmenas*). Addiction to wine or any intoxicant is a form of slavery that has an overpowering influence both physically and mentally. Origen wrote, "Sobriety is the mother of virtues, drunkenness the mother of vices" (*Hom. Lev.* 7.4, quoted by Gorday 2000, 295).

d. The last quality prepares for v 4: **To teach what is good** is a compound adjective (found only here) meaning literally being *good* [*kalo-*] *teachers* (*didaskalous*). This is a clear and measurable activity directed toward younger women. Beyond the topics to be urged on them (v 4), there is no indication of what form this teaching should take. It assumes some degree of authority and acceptance of the leadership of older women within the home and house church. Generational teaching like this is still common in many cultures. Much more is caught through example than by precept. Often, the best way to learn is to watch another person.

4. Younger Women (2:4-5)

■ **4-5** The fourth characteristic for older women expands to a purpose clause not clear in the NIV. Older women should seek to be good teachers *so that* they can mentor the **younger women**. The verb **urge** (*sōphronizōsin*) shares the same root as "self-controlled" in v 2. As a verbal noun, here it means to bring others to their senses by encouragement or advice (BDAG 2000, 986). The young women in the church needed a wake-up call to their social responsibilities.

The seven qualities that follow were important in the ancient world for the ideal woman and for keeping peace in the home. The home was the one place in that culture where women had a major influence. Notions about the "new Roman woman" were sweeping the Greco-Roman world, leading some women to claim new rights for themselves and causing considerable social tension (Winter 2003, 152-59; → 1 Tim 2:8-15; 5:11-14).

The opponents in Crete may have exploited these cultural freedoms, causing problems within homes and the churches that met there. This would have given the church a bad reputation before others. The **younger women** were probably in their twenties to thirties, the typical ages for having children at home.

First, the young married women should show strong family commitment with *a.* **love *for* their husbands** and *b.* ***love for their* children**. These characteristics translate two compound words (only here in the NT). Both include the root "love" (*philo-*). The first place for women to minister was to those closest to them.

The next two qualities are also related. *c.* **To be self-controlled** (*sōphronas*) is one of the key words in this passage (→ Titus 2:2). In the context of marriage and family, it connotes *modesty*, an important feminine quality in the Hellenistic world (Collins 2002, 342).

d. To be **pure** (*hagnas*) adds emphasis to the need for young women to control their passions. To do so would cause them to stand out in a culture in which women's liberation and immorality were becoming vogue. Behind both of these words is the need to be faithful to their husbands (→ 1 Tim 5:2).

e. These women should also **be busy at home**, (lit.) ***work at home***. This highly contextual idea refers to carrying out typical household duties. Women should avoid laziness and being neglectful of their responsibilities to their families (→ 1 Tim 5:13-14). "If a woman accepts the vocation of marriage, and has a husband and children, she will love and not neglect them" (Stott 1996, 189; see Prov 31:27).

f. Women should have the universal quality of **kindness** or **benevolence** (*agathos*). They can do this by being considerate of others and being pleasant people to be around. This will witness to the inner grace that is transforming their lives.

g. Finally, the young women should **be subject to their husbands**. This directive echoes a common theme in the NT (Eph 4:21-23; Col 3:18; 1 Pet 3:1). The present tense verb here is in the middle voice: their submission is to be voluntary and ongoing. This is a specific submission of a wife to her ***own*** (an untranslated *idiois*, ***one's own***) husband. This is not calling for the submission of women to men in general (Mounce 2000, 412). Submission begins with an attitude of mutual respect that creates space for love to be given and received. There is no mention here of the husband's part, but Paul emphasizes this in Eph 5:21 and 25. Here, he offers a timely solution to a current problem in some Christian homes in Crete.

Paul's reason for pursuing these qualities appears in one of the significant purpose clauses in this chapter: *in order that* the word of God *may not be blasphemed*. The genitive construction **the word of God** could refer to God as the source of the speech (subjective) or about God (objective). The focus of this **word** is the gospel message (→ 2 Tim 2:9; Marshall 1999, 250).

The passive verb can mean **malign**, "discredited" (NRSV), "reviled" (ESV), or "dishonored" (NASB). Paul assumed that unbelievers have a basic sense of what is right and can recognize bad behavior when they see it (Rom 1:32; Knight 1992, 318). They will judge the truth and appeal of the message by the messengers (→ 1 Tim 6:1). There should be a qualitative difference between the characteristics of Christian women and the culture around them. If these women can be a good testimony of God's power and grace, others may come to know the truth of the gospel (→ 1 Tim 2:2-4).

5. Younger Men (2:6-8)

■ **6** Paul's instruction to **young men** resembles (*hōsautōs*, **Similarly**) that to the other groups. Their good deportment should result from Titus' teaching of sound doctrine (Titus 2:1). **Be self-controlled** (*sōphronein*) is the only direct exhortation to this group.

This is the fourth occurrence of a word from the *sōphr-* word group in this passage (vv 2, 4, 5). These words have the basic idea of self-mastery and clear thinking. The young men in Crete needed to think clearly in facing the threat of false teaching. The list is short because by following this one directive, they would master many other ethical challenges in their immoral culture. There is also the implicit elaboration in the call for **young men** to imitate Titus' "example [of] doing what is good" (v 7).

Paul changes from "teach" in v 3 to **encourage** in v 6. The type of instruction Titus should use ought not to be coercive but something that cooperates with the work that God's grace is already doing in the lives of these men (→ 2:12). This type of behavior cannot be forced but lived out in a positive, consistent, and exemplary way.

■ **7-8** Paul next instructs Titus to **set . . . an example** to the young men. **In everything** that begins v 7 could go with the directions in v 6 (CEB, NEB), that the young men should be self-controlled in every area of their lives, or with the specific directions for Titus in v 7. Since Paul appeals to Titus at this point, it is likely that Titus is a young man himself. At the least, he urged the young men to look to him as a role model.

a. Following the pattern of others was an important mission strategy for Paul (→ 1 Tim 4:12; 1 Cor 4:16; 11:1; Phil 3:17; 1 Thess 1:6-7; 2 Thess 3:9). Titus could set an example **by doing what is good**, an instrumental participle. Doing good is an important topic in this letter (1:16; 2:14; 3:1, 8).

b. A second way Titus could influence the young men was through his teaching. Here, Paul's emphasis is not on *what* Titus taught, but on *how*. The context clearly indicates that his teaching begins with the gospel message and its expression in practical living. Titus' example could be imitated by young men in other areas of their lives.

Titus should show (*i*) **integrity** (*aphthorian*, only here in the NT; but compare 1 Cor 3:17). It (lit.) means "without decay" (Collins 2002, 344). Such teaching is pure, sound, and uncorrupted (BDAG 2000, 156).

His teaching should be done with (*ii*) **seriousness**. He needed to be absolutely clear in his message because the eternal destiny of his listeners was at stake. He could do this with "a high moral tone and serious manner" (Kelly 1963, 242).

And finally, he should use (*iii*) **soundness of speech that cannot be condemned**. A cognate of the now familiar "healthy" is used here (*hygiē*; → Titus 1:9; 2:1). Titus should teach "sound doctrine" with "sound words." The measurement for this will be that these words **cannot be condemned** (*akatgnōston*). This rare word comes from the courtroom and "describes the innocence of a person who is acquitted of a crime of which he or she has been accused" (Collins 2002, 344). Paul does not promise that Titus will never experience rejection in his teaching. But if he accurately teaches the gospel, his message will be proven true in the end. Paul gave a similar directive to Timothy (1 Tim 4:12-16). Again, Titus stands out in sharp contrast to the opponents who were unqualified to be mentors (Titus 1:16).

A second (→ 2:5) important purpose clause comes at the end of v 8: **so that those who oppose you may be ashamed because they have nothing bad to say about us**. No one can say anything bad about an uncorrupted and respectable life devoted to doing good. One way to silence criticism is to have nothing about which to be criticized. There is no further description of those who opposed Titus, but it probably included the false teachers of 1:14.

The shame of being condemned was more than personal for Titus. It would influence the witness and relationship of the whole church. If Titus preached the gospel accurately, the only ones to experience shame would be the false teachers.

Titus vs. the Opponents

There are some noteworthy contrasts between the behavior of Titus and the false teachers in Crete:

Titus	The Opponents
Do "good" (2:7)	"Unfit for doing anything good" (1:16)
"Show integrity" (2:7)	"Deception" (1:10) and lying (1:12)
	"Dishonest gain" (1:11)

"Seriousness" (2:7)	"Lazy" (1:12)
	Caught up in trivial matters of "myths" and "human commands" (1:14)
"Soundness of speech that cannot be condemned" (2:8)	"Full of meaningless talk" (1:10)
Good reputation (2:8)	"Disrupting whole households" (1:11)

6. Slaves (2:9-10)

■ **9-10** Slaves receive the final exhortation of this unit. The NIV's **teach** is not in the Greek text. It is plausibly assumed from the context. Slaves were common in households of that time and had a key part in the economy. The majority population of cities was slaves. Some slaves were well educated or had significant responsibility within homes and local governments. Often slaves became believers with the rest of a household or as individuals, such as Onesimus who met Paul on his travels (1 Cor 7:21-24; 12:13; Gal 3:28; Phlm 10; → 1 Tim 6:1-2). Slaves were known for embracing new religions, which could have created social tensions within the home and resulted in suspicion of the new Christian faith (Johnson 1996, 235; Towner 2006, 737).

Titus is to direct slaves **to be subject to their masters in everything**. The passive verb *hypotassesthai* describes how any Christian should respond to someone in authority (Rom 13:1; 1 Cor 16:16; Eph 5:21; Col 3:18; Titus 3:1; 1 Pet 2:13). Paul lists four tangible ways slaves can do this. Each of these is related to submission and to one another.

a. Slaves should try **to please** (*euarestos*) their masters. The term in the NT usually refers to pleasing God (Rom 12:1; 14:18; 2 Cor 5:9; Eph 5:10; Phil 4:18; Col 3:20). Paul could imply a wider application here, since the direct object **them** is omitted in Greek. "If a slave does what is pleasing to God, the slave will usually be pleasing to the master" (Mounce 2000, 415). The next two can be temptations particularly for slaves and are given in the negative:

b. Slaves are **not to talk back**. Talking back is not only disrespectful but can lead to verbal and physical confrontation. It lowers the respect from both parties and can create lasting relationship problems.

c. Slaves are **not to steal**. Stealing takes advantage of another's property by fraud, hiding, or embezzlement. The only other occurrence of the word **stealing** (*nosphizomenous*) in the NT refers to Ananias and Sapphira in Acts 5:2-3. The sad part about both of these problems is that selfishness usually leads to pain.

d. The last quality is positive: slaves are **to show that they can be fully trusted**. Slaves often had significant responsibilities within their households. These included caring for market purchases, cleaning a house or grounds, taking care of children or animals, and even stewardship of businesses. Any of these required trust. Trust is something that must be earned and **demonstrated** (*endeiknymenous*) and comes as a result of honesty, integrity, and faithful service.

Life was not always easy for slaves. This could lead them to resent or rebel against their masters. The new spiritual freedom experienced by Christian slaves could have led them to seek liberation from their physical bondage, resulting in a negative response or even punishment from their masters. Paul directs them to rise above their situations by living respectably. This would result in a testimony to God's salvation within them. Christian slaves will be different from other slaves who were known for talking back and stealing.

The reason for this behavior is given in the third (vv 5, 8) purpose clause of this passage: **so that in every way they will make the teaching about God our Savior attractive.** The goal is that their masters will be so pleased with their performance that they will be attracted to this new teaching. "In the Greco-Roman world, insubordination or instability in the *oikos* was reason enough to condemn a religious movement" (Johnson 1996, 235, referring to Livy, *Hist. of Rome*, 39.8-19).

The focus of this effort is the **teaching about God**, a phrase that prepares for the theological discussion of the good news about Jesus Christ in vv 11-14. The genitive *of God* can be subjective, teaching *from God*, but more likely here as objective, **about God.**

The Greek word translated **attractive** (*kosmōsin*) is associated with the English "cosmetics," the skill and tools used to enhance the beauty of a person, and "cosmos," the ordered universe. The word literally means "to put in order," and figuratively "to have an attractive appearance through decoration" (BDAG 2000, 560; → 1 Tim 2:9-10). Slaves should share the same worthy goal of those in honorable positions in the culture; they are to be attractive witnesses to God's grace in Christ.

FROM THE TEXT

Paul's missionary motive shines through again in this passage. The principle is clear: *Christians ought to live in a way that authenticates the claims of the gospel.* This passage illustrates that Christian teaching ought always to lead to changed living. Purity begins within (→ 3:4-7) and serves as the wellspring for holy living. Christians are called to participate in the world as salt and light and not withdraw from it. The motive for this is so that unbelievers "may see your good deeds and glorify your Father in heaven" (Matt 5:16). Chrysostom wrote, "For the Greeks judge not of doctrines by the doctrine itself, but they make the life and conduct the test of the doctrines" (*Hom. Tit.* 4).

Paul deals with several groups in the church who have significant influence as mentors. Those who find themselves in positions of influence should heed Paul's directions and *develop self-control that shows up with integrity and godly influence*. "The misconduct of any Christian, and especially of a leader in the church, will have consequences for the entire Christian community" (Knight 1992, 313).

One does not need to be in a place of high honor or responsibility to have influence. Even "slaves" can live catalytic lives that draw people to Christ. Whatever spot in society we may have, we can live out our faith in full assurance. "The way that one conducts oneself, appropriate to one's state of life, bears prophetic witness to the gospel message" (Collins 2002, 347).

The behavior Paul calls for in this passage does not come naturally for most people. We have to work at it and be trained in it. Intentional discipleship, especially in the home or between the generations, will lead to internal strength and external witness.

The story of the incarceration, release, and rise to power of Joseph is a good illustration of what Paul means. As a slave in Potiphar's house, Joseph found favor with his master and rose to be responsible for the whole household (Gen 39:2-6). His integrity and self-control were put to the test when Potiphar's wife wanted to sleep with him. This cost him his freedom. While in prison, he continued to live with integrity. The prison warden saw this and made Joseph responsible for the whole prison (39:20-23). After his miraculous release from prison, Joseph was given even more responsibility as the chief steward of all of Egypt (41:41-43). There is a key element in this story that prepares for what Paul writes next. In each of these incidents, the writer of Genesis makes it clear that God was with Joseph (39:2, 21; 41:16, 28, 39). Joseph did not accomplish any of this on his own. Likewise, as believers, the only way we can live out a strong testimony is through the grace of God.

B. Grace as the Source for the Christian Ethic (2:11-15)

BEHIND THE TEXT

This section contains one of the most significant christological passages in the NT. It is a summary of the core of Christian theology. It lies at the heart of the letter and gives the theological foundation for the Christian ethics of 2:2-10. Verses 11-14 form one sentence in the Greek, although most modern translations break it into two or more parts. The main idea is that God's grace appeared in Jesus Christ (vv 11, 13), as the revelation of our saving God mentioned in v 10. This grace transforms how a person lives now (v 12). Thus, the lifestyle Paul urges Titus to teach comes as a result of God's grace.

This theological section was anticipated in v 10 with Paul's reference to "God our Savior." In vv 11-15, Paul will expand this thought and explain how this grace is the resource for saying no to ungodliness and yes to a new way of living. The focus is on what God has done in Jesus Christ. Both the Father and the Son are key actors in the plan of salvation. "God is the author or source of the grace through which salvation came, and Christ *is* the manifestation of that grace and the means of salvation (cf. 1 Tim 2:3-6; 2 Tim 1:9-10)" (Towner 1989, 109).

The time frame of salvation in these verses covers the past, present, and future, with stress on present behavior (Fee 1988, 192). The historical appearance of Christ stands at the center of God's saving grace (Towner 1989, 111). In the past, salvation was revealed through what Christ has done by giving himself for us (Titus 2:11, 14). The salvation in which we now stand produces a life of piety (v 12). This leads to hope in future salvation when Christ will come again (v 13).

Paul introduces the theological theme of God's grace in v 11. He follows this with its ethical implications in v 12. Verse 13 speaks of the ethical tension of living in the world as we await the second coming of Christ. Verse 14 gives the historical basis for the Christian ethic in Christ's redeeming sacrifice for us. Verse 15 returns to the theme of v 1—teaching sound doctrine. In it Paul calls for Titus to teach the Cretans with authority. This passage repeats the key themes introduced in 1:2-4: grace, salvation, appearance, and God's salvation in Jesus Christ.

IN THE TEXT

■ **11** The transition **For** (*gar*) links this section to the previous one. Paul reaches the height of his discussion by providing the theological basis for how the Cretan Christians ought to live and what will make their lives attractive to unbelievers (2:2-10). He begins to define in this section what he meant by "sound doctrine" in v 1.

The main subject and verb of the long sentence that makes up this section is given at the start: **the grace of God has appeared** (*epephanē*). The verb comes first in the sentence for emphasis. It designates a divine appearance— here the first coming of Jesus Christ (Luke 1:78-79; 2 Tim 1:10; Titus 2:11; 3:4). Paul mentions no specific point of Jesus' life. But his sacrificial death on the cross must be in view because of the phrase "who gave himself for us" in 2:14. The word will occur again in v 13, this time referring to his second coming (Acts 2:20; 2 Thess 2:8; 1 Tim 6:14; 2 Tim 4:1, 8; Titus 2:13).

The word "epiphany" was used in the Hellenistic world for the appearance of a god or divinized emperor. It describes their intervention in the affairs of the world to bring some form of salvation (Collins 2002, 349). In Cretan beliefs, the god Zeus was said to have appeared in the past bringing aid and gifts to the people who responded by worshipping him as savior. Paul may be intentionally countering this claim by showing that true salvation ("sound doctrine") has a different source.

This source is found in the main theme of **grace**, personified as an indirect reference to what Christ embodied. The rest of the paragraph will describe the effects of this grace. *Charis* (**grace**) is simply an expression of God's freely given love. We experience it as unconditional *favor* and *mercy* that overcome the penalty and power of sin and its affects in our lives. Paul experienced this grace in a powerful way in his own life (→ 1 Tim 1:14-16) and often wrote of it in his letters.

This grace **offers salvation to all people.** The word **offers** is not in Greek. The NIV paraphrase attempts to capture the relationship between the grace of God and the salvation that results from its appearance. **Salvation** here is an adjective (*soterios*, only here in the NT) describing **grace**: this grace is God's saving intervention in the human predicament.

The balance of the passage defines what effects this saving grace has for life on earth. The change grace brings now offers deeper assurance of the hope we have in the second coming of Christ (Titus 2:13).

God offers salvation to **all people.** This is a universal invitation, but not universalism (→ 1 Tim 2:4; 4:10). Faith is still required (→ 2 Tim 1:9). Liefeld writes, "Grace brings the *potential of* salvation to an unrestricted number of people, many of whom accept it" (1999, 338). The "we" of Titus 2:13 are some of those who have responded. This statement may directly challenge opponents who preached a narrow view of salvation for only certain people (1:10; Gal 3:2-5).

The Wesleyan Doctrine of Prevenient Grace

Verse 11 of Titus 2 is one of the key verses in the Bible in support of the Wesleyan doctrine of prevenient grace. John Wesley maintained that God alone is the source of salvation (1986, 10:230-31). Because of the power of sin, people are totally dependent on the grace of God. They cannot choose salvation without God's prior grace. Wesley used the term "preventing grace" to describe

the first dawn of light concerning his will, and the first transient emotion of having sinned against him. All these imply some tendency towards life, some degree of salvation; the beginning of deliverance from a blind, unfelling heart, quite insensible of God and the things of God. (1986, 6:509)

Contemporary Wesleyans use the word "prevenient" for the grace that "goes before"—awakening us to our sin and enabling us to accept God's offer of salvation. Prevenient grace gives us the choice; as Wesley wrote, one "has in himself the casting vote" (1986, 6:281).

The ultimate goal of prevenient grace is to lead everyone to justification in Christ. Prevenient grace leads to the point of decision, if we accept it. It helps us realize our need for salvation by an ultimate, creative power. Wesley wrote,

Before justification; in which state we may be said to be unable to do any thing acceptable to God; because then we can do nothing but come to Christ; which ought not to be considered as doing any thing, but as supplicating (or waiting) to receive a power of doing for the time to come. For the preventing grace of God, which is common to all, is sufficient to bring us to Christ, though it is not sufficient to carry us any further till we are justified. (1986, 8:373)

■ **12-13a** What this salvation involves is given in part here and more emphatically in 3:4-7. The idea is simple: God's grace brings moral transformation in this life and hope for eternal life. The change in this life is expressed in two parts: one negative; the other positive. This two-way approach was a common pattern in Paul's writing. But it was not unique to him. Other Jews and Christians of the time took a similar approach (compare Rom 6:5-15; Gal 5:16-26; Col 3:8-14; *Barn.* 18—21; *Did.* 1—6; 1QS 3.13—4.26).

The personification of grace becomes more explicit here. Grace saves (v 11) and goes on and **teaches us.** Paul uses a different word for "teach" here than earlier in 1:11; 2:1, 3, 7. *Paideuō* has the connotation of training or instructing a child, often in a negative way through discipline (→ 1 Tim 1:20; 2 Tim 2:25; 1 Cor 11:32; 2 Cor 6:9; Heb 12:6, 7, 10). Positively, its intention is to bring about change for responsible living—to help people make appropriate choices (Acts 7:22; 22:3; BDAG 2000, 749). Because God is the source of this grace, the result will be the development of love expressed in affirming relationships with others. The present participle used here refers back on the main verb "appeared" in v 11, showing how God's grace has the ongoing effect of "teaching."

Grace encourages repentance from and rejection of sin. Negatively, we must cooperate with grace by saying **"No" to ungodliness and worldly passions.** The aorist participle translated **to say** shows a decisive choice to break from the life of sin in response to grace. *Arneomai* means deny any association with (Louw and Nida 1996, 34.48) and to renounce especially something evil.

Ungodliness (*asebeia*) is the opposite of the important quality in the Pastoral Epistles of "godliness" (→ 1 Tim 2:2). An adverbial form of this term appears later in Titus 2:12. Ungodly behavior is marked by a rejection of God and God's laws. This shows up in a breakdown of relationships with other people. Those who live in **ungodliness** reject God's laws, preferring to live an irreligious life without reference to God.

The ungodly way of life is destructive because it worships something other than God and succumbs to **worldly passions** (*epithymia*). *Epithymia* always has a negative connotation in the Pastoral Epistles (→ 1 Tim 6:9; 2 Tim 2:22; 3:6; 4:3). These passions are a manifestation of sin (Rom 1:24; Gal 5:16, 24) and ultimately lead to self-destruction. When the invitation of God's grace is rejected, the sin-controlled self takes over, spiraling into further bondage, eventually leading to death (Rom 6:15-23). Many of the Cretan Christians had likely lived like this before their conversion. The radical change Christ brings should have become apparent to others, resulting in a positive testimony for the gospel.

Positively, a new life replaces the old one (Rom 6:6; Eph 4:22-23). Grammatically, the emphasis in this verse is on the positive result (*hina*) with the verb **to live**. Paul points out three important characteristics of how grace teaches us to live: **self-controlled**, **upright**, and **godly**—all adverbs modifying the verb **live**. These three were cardinal virtues for Stoicism. But read in the context of grace, they take on Christian meanings and applications (Mott 1978, 22-30).

Being **self-controlled** (*sōphronōs*), as Paul urges these Christians a number of times to be (Titus 1:8; 2:2, 5, 6, 12), can only truly happen when people cooperate with the Holy Spirit and allow God's grace to transform them (Gal 5:23). Cooperating with God's grace will help us develop a lifestyle characterized by prudence and moderation and lead to respect in the eyes of others. Grace enables a person to live **upright** (*dikiaōs*) in obedience to God's laws (→ 1 Tim 6:11).

The order is significant in Paul's thinking. Grace leads to righteousness. Righteousness does not make one deserving of grace (Eph 2:8-9). Grace inspires a deeper desire to commune with God, producing godliness. Godliness is the path to becoming Christlike. God draws people to himself through his loving grace and transforms those who will say "yes" to his will.

This promise is for **this present age**. Salvation is a present (*nyn*, **now**) experience (2 Cor 6:2; Phil 2:12). God's grace, when allowed to work, will ultimately lead to final salvation. Salvation begins in this life. We tangibly experience it through freedom from sin and the newness of a holy and morally transformed lifestyle (Rom 6; 12). This present age will end with the appearing of Christ Jesus, for which **we wait** (Titus 2:13). Only then will we experience salvation in its fullness.

Growth in Grace

John Wesley taught that believers should continue to grow in the grace of God after justification. Grace compels believers forward and deeper in their relationship with God. This will involve cooperating with and obeying the leading of the Holy Spirit. This results in a "gradual spiritual recovery of the likeness of God" through the process of sanctification (Maddox 1994, 177). The primary evidence of this will be growth in love. Wesley wrote,

> The conviction we feel of inbred sin is deeper and deeper every day. The more we grow in grace, the more do we see the desperate wickedness of our heart. The more we advance in the knowledge and love of God, through our Lord Jesus Christ . . . the more do we discern of our alienation

from God, of the enmity that is in our carnal mind, and the necessity of our being entirely renewed in righteousness and true holiness. (1986, 5:257-68)

Growth in grace is helped by the "means of grace." "By means of grace, I understand outward signs, words, or actions ordained of God, and appointed to this end, to be the ordinary channels whereby he might convey to men, preventing, justifying, or sanctifying grace" (ibid., 187).

Wesley divided these into three types. The *general* means of grace included keeping God's commands, denying ourselves, taking up our cross, and exercising the presence of God. The *instituted* or *particular* means of grace were taught by Jesus Christ to his disciples and include prayer, studying the Bible, the Lord's Supper, fasting, and Christian fellowship. Finally, the *prudential* means of grace include participating in small groups, various prayer meetings, visiting the sick, doing whatever good one can, and reading devotional classics. By developing these various disciplines, one will grow in holiness and experience the purpose of God's grace toward us.

■ **13b** Here Paul reaches the theological highpoint of the letter. Unfortunately, it is one of the most challenging to interpret. The syntax and punctuation are ambiguous. Many different interpretations are possible.

The meaning of the first half of the verse is clear: Christian life is lived between the times. Between the first and second comings of Christ. Between our old lives dominated by **ungodliness and worldly passions** and the **blessed hope.** For now we are *awaiting* the blessed hope *and appearance of* the glory. The NIV rightly translates the present participle as temporal: **while we wait.** The waiting takes place *while* grace does its transforming work in our lives (v 12).

The participle has two objects, **hope** and **appearing,** governed by the same article. Thus, they point to the same event—the object of hope is the revealing of glory. We are waiting for **the blessed hope,** which will be a fulfillment of what God has already promised in Christ (Eph 1:18). This hope is called **blessed** because it will complete the purpose of God's grace and bring an end to the struggle with a fallen world.

"Blessed" is used for God in 1 Tim 1:11 and 6:15. The hope of believers brings blessings because of its source and target. Hope is an important theme in the Pastoral Epistles. Jesus is called "our hope" in 1 Tim 1:1. Paul urges believers to put their hope in God rather than in things of this world because salvation is found only in him (1 Tim 4:10; 5:5; 6:17). Twice in Titus Paul specifically identifies eternal life as the object of our hope (1:2; 3:7).

The object of hope here is **the appearing of the glory of our great God and Savior, Jesus Christ**. This second occurrence of the Greek root *epiphan-* (→ 2:11) refers to Christ's second coming, when the hope of eternal life will be finally and fully realized (1 Thess 4:16-17). **Glory** (*doxēs*) is the overwhelming manifestation of the presence of the transcendent God (→ 1 Tim 1:11; 3:16; 2 Tim 2:10; 4:18). The KJV tradition and the NIV[84] translate this noun as an attributive genitive, "glorious appearing." This has been corrected in the 2011 NIV. The clear emphasis is on the revealing of God's glory.

This passage makes an important link between grace and glory. God reveals his grace fully only in the appearing of Christ's glory. The only response one can give to this glory is worship (Phil 2:9-11). God's glory was revealed in the first coming of Christ (John 1:14; 1 John 3:2) and is an expected part of his second coming (Matt 16:27; 24:30; 25:31; Mark 8:38; 13:26; Luke 9:26; 21:27; 24:26). Christ is "the hope of glory" for Christians (Col 1:27; see Rom 5:2).

The major interpretive issue of this verse is in its last phrase. Is Paul referring to two different persons, God the Father and Jesus Christ, or one? Is he calling Jesus Christ both God and Savior? The place to begin to approach this difficulty is with the *grammar*. The problem is that four nouns and two adjectives are in the genitive case. How they relate to one another is the question. Since the original Greek had no punctuation, there is no way to know if there was a comma of apposition, as the NIV has between "Savior" and "Jesus Christ." Interpreters have generally followed one of three major options:

First, simply follow the literal Greek word order: "the appearing of the glory of the great God and our Savior Jesus Christ." The KJV essentially takes this approach. With this translation, two persons will appear at the second coming: the great God and our Savior. "Jesus Christ" stands in apposition only to "Savior." The major objection to this view is that nowhere else in the NT does the verb "appear" (*epiphainō*) occur with the Father, but only with the Son (1 Tim 6:14; 2 Tim 1:10; 4:1, 8). Nowhere else is God the Father joined with the Son in the second coming (Fee 1988, 196).

Second, a majority of modern scholars and translations prefer a translation much like that in the current NIV: **the appearing of the glory of our great God and Savior, Jesus Christ**. Here, "our" and "great" modify both "God" and "Savior," "God" and "Savior" refer to one person, and "Jesus Christ" stands in apposition to both "God" and "Savior." A similar phrase occurs in 2 Pet 1:1. This position essentially identifies Jesus Christ as God. This would be a significant claim by Paul.

In major support of this position, Granville Sharp's rule for a Greek construction like this is that two nouns governed by the same article refer to the same person (Wallace 1996, 270-90). In this case, the article *tou* governs both "God" and "Savior," making these refer to the same person. Thus, "Jesus Christ" stands in apposition to the whole phrase, "our great God and Savior." Those who presume pseudonymity for the Letter to Titus take this statement as evidence for a later development in christological thinking (Dibelius and Conzelmann 1972, 142-44).

Third, Fee (2007, 445) and Towner (2006, 752-58), following the work of F. J. A. Hort (1980), take "Jesus" as an apposition to "glory." The resulting

2:13b

translation would be: "the appearing of our great God and Savior's glory, Jesus Christ." Fee points out that in 2 Cor 3:7—4:6, Christ is the revelation of God's glory as God's true image.

> Christ is the coming manifestation of God's glory precisely because he was first of all the manifestation of God's grace as the one who has stepped into the divine role of redeeming and cleansing "for himself a people for his name." (Fee 2007, 445)

In addition, this clause follows a common pattern in Greek of adjective-noun-and-noun-adjective; thus, "great" and "our" modify both "God" and "Savior." This position takes into consideration Sharp's rule and takes the identification of Jesus as God to remain somewhat ambiguous.

Contextual considerations must be taken seriously in this discussion. In the Letter to Titus, both Jesus and God are called Savior (1:3, 4; 3:4, 6). In the immediate context (2:10*b*), God is the first of the pair to be called Savior. We would then expect Jesus to be called Savior in the near context, which is indeed what we find here. As we will note in v 14, several characteristics of God in the OT are attributed to Jesus. The construction "great God" is not found elsewhere in the NT but is quite common in the LXX (Deut 10:17; Ezra 5:8; Neh 8:6; Isa 26:4; Jer 39:18 [LXX numbering]; Dan 2:45; 9:4; and others). In addition, "God" and "Savior" were often found together in Hellenistic Greek (Spicq 1969, 1:249-51). Harris points out that the expression "God and Savior" was a stereotyped formula in reference to one deity in the religious language of the time (1980). Paul's claim here may be an intentional confrontation against imperial and pagan cults that claimed divinity for their heroes. The universal early Christian belief was that salvation is found in no one else but Christ (John 14:6; Acts 4:12). Paul is making the connection between Jesus and salvation clear in this passage.

The *theological claims* implied by this phrase are significant. Our interpretation of the divinity of Christ is not in question in this passage. It is confirmed throughout the NT (John 1:1, 18; 20:28; Heb 1:1-3, 8-10; 2 Pet 1:1; 1 John 5:20; Harris 1980, 271). The question is whether Paul, as a monotheistic Jew, could equate Jesus with God. Paul's clearest statement on this is found in 1 Cor 8:6: "For us there is but one God, the Father, from whom all things came and for whom we live; and there is but one Lord, Jesus Christ, through whom all things came and through whom we live." In was in Christ that God was reconciling the world to himself (2 Cor 5:18; see also Rom 9:5).

The next question becomes whether these are the same person or only share divine identity. The grammar supports the possibility that Paul affirms that Jesus is God, but this is not indisputable. The interpretation here may be influenced to some degree by how one reads passages like Rom 9:5 and Col 1:19, which have their own challenges and questions. The early church fathers almost universally read this clause as referring to one person. There is a close link between God and Christ. Both are the source of salvation. So the two cannot be distinguished. This passage could be evidence of the development in the early church of a clearer understanding of the divine nature of Christ. This may be the clearest statement in the Pauline Epistles of Jesus as God.

Beyond this uncertainty, Paul's key point is clear: Christ Jesus brought salvation. When he comes a second time, the purpose of God's grace in our lives will have reached its purpose of bringing God's sons and daughters into glory (Phil 3:20; Heb 2:10). The insertion of the name "Jesus Christ" at the end of this verse prepares for the thoughts about salvation in Titus 2:14. This salvation is not a far-off potentiality but a present transformative power for those who allow God's grace to work in their lives. Jesus Christ is the divine source and agent for this.

The Arian Controversy

The struggle of the early church to understand the divinity of Christ came to a crisis with the Arian controversy of the fourth century. Arius (ca. AD 250—336) was a presbyter in the Church of Alexandria who emphasized absolute monotheism. He argued that the Son could not be of the same substance as the Father but had to have been created as "the firstborn over all creation" (Col 1:15). The controversy was resolved in part with the First Council of Nicea (AD 325), which rejected Arius' teaching. A majority of the council agreed that the Son is of one substance (*homoousios*) with the Father. Thus, the divinity of the Son was enshrined in one of the core creeds of the church.

The controversy continued, however, even after this historic meeting. Arianism gained support from various segments of the church and the newly converted Emperor Constantine. The greatest defender of the Nicene Creed became Athanasius, bishop of Alexandria (ca. AD 296—373).

Athanasius considered Arianism a threat to the doctrine of the incarnation. Athanasius was a great thinker and writer and one of the most influential theologians in the history of the church. He argued against Arianism by articulating a clear doctrine of the Trinity. One biblical passage Athanasius used as proof of Christ's divinity was Titus 2:13-14 (*Ep. Adelph.* 60.6). The First Council of Constantinople in 381 confirmed Nicea and effectively ended the influence of Arianism, although traces of it have reappeared throughout church history in various groups.

■ **14** As he often does in his letters, Paul bursts forth in praise of Christ and what he has done as our Savior (→ 1 Tim 1:15-17). This is summarized in the succinct phrase **who gave himself for us**, which describes the divine part in our salvation. The phrase sums up the fundamental gospel truth of the doctrine of atonement. That this statement begins with a relative pronoun (*hos*) has led some interpreters to see this as possibly part of a preexistent hymn (Collins 2002, 353). However, the grammar and flow of the sentence necessitate this structure. The idea is so basic to Christian theology that any such statement will be creedal to some degree.

Although the cross is not mentioned in this letter, the death of Jesus clearly stands behind this statement. **Gave** (*edōken*) is a historical aorist referring to the past event of Jesus' sacrificial death. The most significant display of God's grace, the central theme of this section, was seen on the cross where Jesus died to take away the sins of the world (John 1:29; 3:16).

Himself translates a reflexive pronoun (*heautō*). Jesus went to the cross and willingly sacrificed himself. The doctrine of atonement is dependent upon the doctrine of incarnation. The latter asserts that Jesus was fully human and suffered a real death. Athanasius wrote, "For the coming of the Savior in the flesh has been the ransom and salvation of all creation" (*Ep. Adelph.* 60.6, quoted by Gorday 2000, 300).

The object of this sacrifice is **us**, those who have come to believe and accept this message of hope. The simple prepositional phrase *hyper hēmōn* expresses the depths of divine grace and the reason Jesus died on the cross. The preposition *hyper* is used when one's action affects others and can be translated here as ***in our behalf.*** This phrase reflects the traditional understanding of Jesus' sacrifice preserved in Matt 20:28 and Mark 10:45. This idea was important to Paul's theology and is repeated in Gal 1:4; 2:20; Eph 5:2, 25; and 1 Tim 2:6.

Jesus became one with us by suffering death. But death could not win because Jesus rose from the dead. By conquering death, Jesus also conquered the power of sin (1 Cor 15:56-57). This is both on the cosmic level of defeating the evil powers that wage war against us, and the individual, by opening the way to God by the forgiveness of sins (Eph 2:2-6, 14-16). Jesus' death and resurrection removed the alienation and guilt caused by disobedience to God's law and shame before his holiness.

Various Theories of the Atonement

The short prepositional phrase ***in our behalf*** has led to much discussion throughout church history about how Jesus' death and resurrection bring salvation. Various theories have been offered throughout church history. The four major interpretations of the atonement are:

- Christus Victor or Ransom (Irenaeus ca. AD 130-202; Gregory of Nyssa ca. AD 330-395): Through his resurrection, Jesus gained victory over sin and paid the ransom to free us from Satan and the forces of evil.
- Satisfaction Theory (Anselm 1033-1109): This rejection of the ransom theory argued that Jesus' sacrificial death satisfied the debt owed to God because of sin.
- Moral Influence (Peter Abelard 1079-1142): Jesus' life and death demonstrated God's love. This incomparable demonstration should cause sinners to repent and return God's love.

- Penal Substitution (John Calvin and the Protestant Reformers of the sixteenth century): Jesus suffered the sin we deserve because of our disobedience. Jesus died the death we should have died.

The church as a whole has never reached consensus on which theory is the one orthodox view. In fact, none of these theories individually or together capture the depth of what Jesus did. Paul called the cross event the great mystery of God (I Cor 1:18-25; 2:6-7). We will spend eternity discovering the riches of this event that lies at the heart of God and his plan for creation.

Paul offers two reasons why Jesus died for us, given in two parallel purpose (*hina*) clauses. The first refers to liberation from sin, and the second, cleansing from sin.

First, Christ's death and resurrection had this purpose in relation to the past: **to redeem us from all wickedness. To redeem** (*lytrōsētai*) means to deliver from the control of others. It is an important biblical concept with basis in the OT story of Yahweh setting his people free from Egyptian slavery (Exod 6:6; 13:13-15). The slavery from which believers are set free is **all wickedness** (*anomias*, lit.), **lawlessness**—rebellion against the law of God (1 John 3:4). God intervenes in the human struggle against sin and opens the way to freedom through Jesus Christ's sacrifice (Rom 6:19; 1 Cor 6:19-20).

Second, Christ's death had for its purpose to open the possibility of sanctification: **to purify for himself a people that are his very own, eager to do what is good.** Freedom in Christ makes purity possible. Cleansing (*katharisē*) is a cultic term describing how defilement is washed away, making something or someone worthy to be in relationship with or proximity to the holy God (→ Titus 1:15; 2 Tim 2:21). What must be washed away is the stain of sin. This cultic terminology can be applied to everyday life in which the immorality of the world tempts believers to live to please the pull of the flesh (1 Cor 6:9-11). Cleansing is a gift of God that comes as a result of Jesus' death (Eph 5:25-26; 1 John 1:7) and our response of obedience and commitment (2 Cor 7:1). It is possible that Paul is reflecting on Ezek 36:25, 28-29, 33 and 37:23, which look forward to a time when the Holy Spirit would sanctify people through a new covenant relationship (Heb 9:14-15).

There are two results of this cleansing. The primary goal is the creation of a new people. The phrasing of this verse echoes covenantal formulas from the OT. By cleansing disobedient Israel, God was able to establish a relationship with them as his special people (Exod 19:5-6; Deut 7:6; 14:2; 26:18; see 1 Pet 2:9-10, applying this to the church). Even Gentiles who were not part of the OT covenant can be incorporated into this new people of God through faith in Christ (Rom 9:25; Eph 2:11-18).

The word *periousion* means chosen, special, a choice treasure, or a costly possession (Preisker 1968, 57-58). A secondary reason for redemption comes from the first and reflects the purpose clauses of Titus 2:5, 8, 10: the church as the new people of God is his **special instrument** in the world to bear witness to his transforming grace.

Paul uses an attributive adjectival clause to describe God's new people as **eager to do what is good**. *Zēlōtēn* means zealous, committed, or enthusiastic for a cause (BDAG 2000, 427). God's grace revealed through Jesus Christ's sacrifice leads to a zealous desire for **good works**. We live to please our master. The internal change through sanctification inspires outward acts of goodness (→ 1 Tim 5:10, 25; 6:18).

Paul's last point here echoes his last point in Titus 1: he contrasts the good works of sanctified believers with the opponents who were unfit for any good works (1:16). Paul's real concern is not abstract theology. His aim is to show how the church should practically live out its faith in Christ. The logical syllogism should not be missed:

1. God's grace through Jesus' sacrifice leads to holiness of heart manifested in good deeds that bear witness to this grace (2:11-14).
2. The opponents lacked this inner change because of their selfishness, misplaced priorities in trivial human myths, and outward religiosity (1:10-16).
3. Therefore, the Cretans should listen to Titus' instruction and not that of the false teachers (2:2-10).

■ **15** This unit ends with a restatement of Titus' mission in Crete (→ 1:5; 2:1) and a pause before Paul begins to conclude the letter. Three second-person imperatives are followed by a final third-person imperative.

The first repeats the command of v 1, **speak these things**, using the same verb *lalei*. Paul knew that the best way to strengthen the church was through communicating the gospel clearly (1 Tim 4:6, 11, 15; 5:7, 21; 6:2, 11). This verb has the nuance of teaching, as noted in the NIV. **These things** could refer to the directions in 2:2-14 or the entire letter up to this point. Titus must teach this doctrine without shame or compromise and with full authority because this was the message most needed in the Cretan church.

Titus could do this best by encouraging the Cretans by teaching sound doctrine (1:9). The imperative *parakalei* can mean urge or appeal. It has the positive nuance of coming alongside of someone to offer an inspiring word. Titus might also need to **rebuke** those who resisted his message (→ 1:9, 13).

Titus should do these three things **with all authority**. His authority would come from several places: (1) his message, based on the truth of the gospel, (2) his association with the Pauline mission, and (3) his ability in interpersonal communication.

The last command, **Let *no one* despise you**, is a quick note of personal encouragement from Paul. He uses a similar rhetorical strategy for Timothy

438

in 1 Tim 4:12 (1 Cor 16:11). *Periphroneitō* occurs only here in the NT but is similar to *kataphroneitō* in 1 Tim 4:12. One of Timothy's challenges was his youth. Paul does not say what potential criticism Titus might have faced. Both colleagues faced resistance to their authority.

FROM THE TEXT

God's grace is universally offered to all people. This grace was most clearly revealed in the life, death, and resurrection of Christ. God's grace is beyond defining, but Paul gives significant insights into it in this passage.

First, we see that *this grace goes before us*. It draws us closer to God with gentle nudges. We experience this grace as the Holy Spirit speaks to our hearts through Scripture, the testimony of others, our own conscience, the events of life, and even nature itself. The goal of grace is to lead us to a saving knowledge of and faith in Jesus Christ (Eph 2:8). Our experience of grace on an individual level connects us to the historical event of the life, death, and resurrection of Christ. There is no greater revelation of grace than Jesus' sacrifice *in our behalf* (Titus 2:14; Rom 5:8; 2 Cor 5:14; 1 Thess 5:10).

Second, *this grace, when allowed to work, will bring transformation*. God's grace goes with us all throughout our spiritual journey. His mercies are "new every morning" (Lam 3:23). We experience grace through the Holy Spirit (Titus 3:5) who transforms us into the likeness of Christ (2 Cor 3:18) by teaching us "the mind of Christ" (1 Cor 2:16). These are significant links in Paul's thought and NT theology because they connect theology to practical living. Paul understood well that grace is the key component that changes the old life to the new. The human response is simply to say yes to God and no to the world.

Although saving grace begins at a personal level, it will influence others by our change in lifestyle (Titus 2:5, 8, 10). Embracing God's grace will lead to transformation of culture. Without grace, this world would indeed be a bleak place.

Third, *this grace gives hope*. Grace sustains us as we await the second coming again of our Lord Jesus Christ. We live in anticipation of this moment, sustained by God's mercy through the trials and temptations of life. Spiritual victory comes only through dependence upon God. Hope is more than a subjective feeling but is based on the historical event of Christ's sacrificial death. By looking to the past and longing for the future, we find the strength to live in the present (Rom 5:2; 8:22-25; 1 Thess 4:13-18).

IV. THE MOTIVE AND RESOURCE FOR DOING GOOD: TITUS 3:1-11

BEHIND THE TEXT

The letter continues the unique "household code" from 2:2-10 but expands beyond the house church to how believers should relate to outsiders. The underlying theme is the Christian testimony before the world of God's grace in Christ. The central message is simple: how Christians live will affect how unbelievers receive the gospel.

Believers in Crete faced the challenge of false teachers who were preoccupied with trivial matters (1:10-16). This was a major detraction that would (1) harm their testimony of the gospel, (2) lead to division within the church, and (3) create a fundamental misunderstanding of the transformation that happens in Christ through the presence of the Holy Spirit. Paul urges Titus to call them back to the core tenets of the gospel.

This chapter follows a similar structure to ch 2. Paul first exhorts Titus to speak to the Cretans about certain behavioral matters (2:1-10; 3:1-2). He follows this up with the theological basis for Christian ethics (2:11-14; 3:3-7).

Paul's paraenesis in 3:1-11 is supported by one of the more concise statements about salvation in the NT (vv 4-7). He is not theoretical in this letter. His theology is always practical. In this case, the concise reminder of the gospel serves two purposes: (1) it gives the resource of God's grace as the basis for doing good (vv 1-2, 8), and (2) defines the right path against false teaching or wrong motives (vv 9-11).

Verse 12 begins the closing conventions of the letter, including final personal instructions. Within vv 1-11, three smaller, thematically related units depend upon one another. They form a logical and coherent argument:

1. What the Cretans should do: be living testimonies before outsiders (vv 1-2).
2. Why and how they should do this: because the indwelling Holy Spirit has fundamentally changed them from within through the grace of God in Christ Jesus (vv 3-7).
3. The challenge they faced: opponents misunderstand God's grace and focus on divisive opinions (vv 8-11).

A. Directions to the Whole Church (3:1-2)

IN THE TEXT

■ **1-2** The exhortation of 2:15 ("teach" [*lalei*]) continues here with the imperative **remind**. One of the primary tasks of a teacher is to remind students of what they should already know. The present tense of this verb has an iterative sense: *Keep reminding* (→ 2 Tim 2:14). **The people** (lit. *them*, *autous*) refers to the various groups mentioned in ch 2. But it includes all believers in Crete. The topics for reminder focus on how Christians should live their public lives. It is human nature to become self-focused and forget that how we live reflects what we believe.

(1) A list of seven virtues begins with a series of five infinitives that complete the action of the main verb. The first relates particularly to civil government. Christians ought voluntarily **to be subject to rulers and authorities**. **Rulers** ("beginning" or "first" [*archais*]) are those in charge, who make decisions for others. The word **authorities** particularly makes reference to their power to make those decisions. When these two words occur together elsewhere in Paul's letters, they usually refer to spiritual powers (Eph 6:12; Col 1:16; 2:15). Here, however, Paul likely has in mind governmental officials (Delling 1964b, 482-84).

The **and** (*kai*) is missing in better manuscripts but added in later ones (Metzger 1994, 586). The two adjoining words could form an asyndeton meaning ruling authorities, or "rulers who have legitimate authority" (Collins 2002, 357).

First Timothy 2:1-2 provides a motive for submission to the government: "that we may live peaceful and quiet lives." The status quo provided a stable environment in which the gospel could be freely and openly proclaimed. Early Christians generally espoused a positive view of government when the church was not widely persecuted. They believed God delegates authority to civil governments to promote good and punish evil (Rom 13:1, 4; 1 Pet 2:13-14). For this reason, Christians ought to be model citizens by respecting those in authority.

(2) Submission recognizes the authority by an attitude of ***obedience*** **to rulers** (*peitharchein*). Obedience is a more effective witness than rebellion (→ Titus 2:10). Jesus set the pattern by urging paying taxes—giving to "Caesar what is Caesar's" (Matt 22:21; see Rom 13:1-7). Jeremiah encouraged the exiles from Judah to seek the good of the place they lived (Jer 29:7). The Greek word for "empire" (*oikoumenē*) shares the same root as "house" (*oikos*). The empire was a large-scale model of the household and should provide a place of safety for its members (Bassler 1996, 205; Cicero, *Resp.* 1.43).

Obedience to rulers is not unconditional. Even they were to be subservient to the lordship of Jesus Christ. Wesley notes that Christians should show active obedience as far as conscience will allow (1813, 246). Christians cannot compromise their core convictions or commitment to the supremacy of Christ. Christians were severely tested in this regard from the late first through the early fourth centuries. If this letter is authentically Pauline, it was written before emperor worship was compulsory and before the persecution under the emperor Domitian (Barrett 1963, 139-40). Paul enjoyed the Pax Romana, which brought peace and prosperity to the Mediterranean world. But, according to tradition, he lost his life because he would not compromise his core conviction that Jesus alone is Lord.

(3) The Christian witness extends beyond obedience to those in authority. Believers should **be ready to do whatever is good**. **Whatever** (*pan*) is a broad term meaning ***any*** or "every" thing (ESV, NASB, NRSV). This calls for creative initiative that looks for opportunities to be a positive and proactive force for good in society. The call to do good appears eight times in the Pauline Letters, including the Pastorals (2 Cor 9:8; Col 1:10; 2 Thess 2:17; 1 Tim 5:10; 2 Tim 2:21; 3:17; Titus 1:16). The believers in Crete should stand out from the false teachers who were *up to no good* (→ 1:16).

(4) The next three virtues give examples of how to have good relationships with others. The first is formulated negatively: **slander no one**. This di-

TITUS

3:1-2

443

rective is based on the familiar verb *to blaspheme* (*blaspēmein*), which, when used of humans, means to speak ill of another by using coarse or demeaning words. Although the word often has a religious sense as applied to God, here it means to "malign" (NASB) or "speak evil of" others (NKJV), tarnishing their good name.

The indefinite adjective *mēdena* (**no one**) is broad and unconditional. We should not speak evil even of enemies. There are times to confront difficult people (3:10), but Christians should not ruin another's reputation deliberately. The false teachers again may stand in the background (→ 3:9).

(5) The next two qualities are governed by the same infinitive: **to be peaceable and considerate.** The adjective **peaceable** (*amachous*) describes a person who is easy to get along with—not argumentative or combative. One can do this by not responding to difficult situations with violence. This may require the personal sacrifice of turning the other cheek instead of fighting for one's rights (Matt 5:38-42). This should be a characteristic of overseers (1 Tim 3:3; → 2 Tim 2:23-24 and Titus 3:9).

(6) Being peaceable can be shown by being **considerate** (*epieikeis*) of others. This entails being courteous, respectful, gentle, and kind (Phil 4:5). To do this requires following the example of Jesus in not insisting on our own way (see Phil 2:1-11). This is how an overseer should use authority (1 Tim 3:3).

(7) The last quality of *gentleness* underlies all the others. The circumstantial present participle *always showing* (*endeiknymenous*) concludes the Greek sentence. *Prautēta* (**gentle**) is essentially a synonym of **considerate**. It is "the quality of not being overly impressed by a sense of one's self-importance" (BDAG 2000, 861). Different translations attempt to capture its range of nuances: "courtesy" (ESV, NRSV), "meekness" (KJV), "consideration" (NASB), and "humility" (NKJV).

This **gentle** demeanor is not passive or internally focused; it is active and visibly evident **toward everyone**. There should be no limit or condition for this virtue. This was one of the character traits of Jesus (Matt 11:29; 21:5; 2 Cor 10:1) and is part of his kingdom ethic (Matt 5:5). Being gentle may require people not to retaliate when they are wronged (Rom 12:14). It is an essential quality for church leaders (1 Tim 6:11).

FROM THE TEXT

Obedience to authority is not natural, but a supernatural possibility of grace. When interpreting these verses, we must keep in mind their original context. Paul's primary concern is for the Christians in Crete to be credible witnesses to those around them, to transform society by their positive influence. They were to be "in the world," but not be "of the world" (John 17:13-14). How is this lived out? The only effective way is by allowing God's grace to transform us from the inside out. In this way our witness flows from inner strength given by the Holy Spirit. Peace with God makes peace within communities possible (Jer 29:7; Ezra 6:9-10).

Paul knew the harsh realities of abusive authorities. He had been often beaten and imprisoned unjustly (2 Cor 11:21-33). Yet, he had a confidence that Christians could make a difference in the world. Christians ought to be model citizens who serve as channels of God's grace, becoming Christlike in whatever civil setting they find themselves. The only way this will be possible is through the renewal Christ brings (Titus 3:3-8).

B. The Change Christ Brings (3:3-8)

BEHIND THE TEXT

Here Paul provides the theological basis for his directions in 3:1-2. He explains the purpose of God's action of redemption: to create a people who would do good works. Christians are capable of doing good works only because God has saved them (Marshall 1999, 305).

There is a clear comparison in the passage between what Christians used to be and what they can become through God's grace. The evidence of a changed life demonstrates the power of the gospel.

Verse 3 sets up the contrast with a vice list—negative features of the old way of life. Verses 4-7, one sentence in Greek, describe the salvation God gives those who trust in Christ. This sentence has five parts signified with these strategic words:

- Time: "When" (v 4)
- Basis: "Not . . . but" (v 5)
- Main thought: *we were saved* (v 5)
- Means: "through . . ." (v 5)
- Purpose: *in order that . . .* (v 7)

Significant theologically in this passage is that all three persons of the Godhead are identified as involved in salvation. The before-after shift—from the "then" of the old life to the "now" of the new life—comes because of what Christ has done as Savior. The Holy Spirit brings the historical event of the cross and resurrection to each person through an internal, spiritual change. The evidence of this change consists in how Christians live before unbelievers. Titus is to remind the Cretans of this because it is so basic to the Christian faith.

IN THE TEXT

■ **3** Paul prepares for the contrast between how Christians lived *formerly* and live *now* because of Christ. The contrast appears with the time formula, **at one time** (*pote* [v 3]) vs. "But when" (*hote de* [v 4]). The transition between the two is the experience of salvation. Paul often contrasts past and present—what we once were and what we have become in Christ (Rom 6:20-22; Gal 1:23; Eph 2:11, 13; 5:8; Col 1:21-22; 3:7-8; 2 Tim 1:9-10; Phlm 11; see 1 Pet 2:10).

The emphatic *we ourselves were* (*hēmen ēmeis*) includes Paul and all believers (Rom 3:23; Gal 1:4; 2 Tim 1:9-10). This subtly contrasts believers with unbelievers in Titus 3:1-3: one motivation for being courteous to others (v 2) is that we once were like them (Stott 1996, 200).

Paul describes the old life with a list of nine vices marking the general condition of human depravity (Rom 1:29-31; 1 Cor 6:9-11; Gal 5:19-21; Fee 1988, 202). He portrays the opponents in Ephesus and Crete in similar ways (1 Tim 4:1-2; 2 Tim 3:1-13; 4:3-4; Titus 1:16; 2:12). These vices reflect on three types of shattered relationships—between (1) us vs. God, (2) us vs. ourselves, and (3) us vs. others.

(1) We first rejected God. The first two vices use an alpha privative (*a-*) to negate clear thinking (*noē*) and persuasion leading to a decision about a matter (*peitho*).

a. The old life was **foolish** (*anoētoi*). Without spiritual understanding we refuse to acknowledge the truth of God's revelation and become spiritually insensitive (Luke 24:25; Rom 1:14; Gal 3:1, 3; 1 Tim 6:9). Rejecting God (= rebellion [Rom 1:18-31]) leads to ignorance of God's ways (Eph 4:18-19). The Cretans used to be foolish (Titus 1:12). But so was Paul. His **we** includes himself. Once, he too was deceived and rejected God's revelation in Jesus Christ (Phil 3:5-6; 1 Tim 1:15).

b. Believers were also once **disobedient** (*apeitheis*). The parallel in Titus 1:16 suggests they once disobeyed God and rejected his laws (Luke 1:17; Acts 26:19; Rom 1:30; 2 Tim 3:2). They deliberately walked away from the right path and got lost in their own foolishness (→ Titus 3:1). Disobedience to God is evident in disobedience to those in authority (Rom 13:2).

(2) Paul moves deeper into the consequences of rejecting God. The second entity that suffers from these vices is ourselves. The next two problems translate passive participles, indicating that we are the victims of others' actions, especially the great deceiver, Satan (1 Tim 4:1-2; 2 Cor 4:4; 11:3; 2 Tim 2:26).

c. Being **deceived** (*planōmenoi*) results from another person twisting the truth so that the wrong way looks attractive. This was one of the problems of the false teachers in Ephesus (2 Tim 3:3) and a real danger for the Christians in Crete (Titus 1:10, 16). The first two vices (*a* and *b*) are the cause and result of this deception.

The NIV's punctuation and inclusion of **and** between **deceived** and **enslaved** assumes that **passions and pleasures** are what deceive. But grammatically these are clearly the objects of the second participle **enslaved** (*dou-*

leuontes). **Passions and pleasures** can be part of the deception as the weapons of temptation.

d. **Passions** (*epithymiais*) always have a negative connotation in the Pastoral Epistles (→ 1 Tim 6:9; 2 Tim 2:22; 4:3; Titus 2:12). Passions are God-given desires, distorted and controlled by sin. As such, they lead to destruction (→ Titus 2:12). Even good passions can disrupt full devotion to God.

e. **Pleasures** (*hēdonais*) are feelings or sensations that bring delight. Another strategy of Satan is to distort God's blessings to satisfy selfish desires. We deceive ourselves by using other people as tools or objects for our own self-gratification. Pleasures replace love of God for love of things in the world (Rom 1:24; 2 Tim 3:4). When sin is master, it controls our bodies, leading us further into disobedience and death (Rom 6:19-23; Gal 4:8-9; 1 Tim 6:9).

"Hedonism" is the pursuit of pleasure as the means of securing happiness. Exhortations against this were common in antiquity (Quinn 1990, 204; Fiore 2007, 218). The words **passions** and **pleasures** are closely related: when the passions are satisfied, the result is pleasure; when pleasure is sought, we have passions (Büchsel 1965, 171, n. 36). **All kinds** (*poikilais*), describing both terms, shows this trap as a lifestyle. People are remarkably creative in how they satisfy selfish desires.

(3) The last image depicts the breakdown of relationships with others that occurs when we reject the grace of God (2:11). Paul begins internally with attitudes that move outward and begin to affect other people.

f. **Malice** is *bad* (*kakia*) intentions toward others—wishing that evil or ill might befall them (Rom 1:29; Col 3:8). It is a broad term that can include many types of mean activity intended to cause others harm. It is the opposite of gentleness in Titus 3:2.

g. **Envy** (*phthonō*) is being jealous of what others have. This leads to resentment and coveting (Rom 1:29; Gal 5:21; 1 Tim 6:4). It is another manifestation of selfishness.

h. The next attitude begins inwardly and quickly moves outward, eliciting a response from others. Paul uses two different words for "hatred." The first, **being hated** (*stygētoi*, only here in the NT) is the response others give someone who is despicable, detestable, or loathsome. Christians ought to look at everyone as created in God's image, and although marred by sin, still having the potential for transformation.

i. The second word, **hating one another** (*misountes*) is the more common NT word for hatred. It describes a strong aversion toward others shown in disregard and rejection (BDAG 2000, 652-53).

These characteristics portray a life controlled by sin and lacking in love, where relationships and community break down because of selfishness. This is a clear and honest description of the human predicament. When God is ignored, hatred and brokenness result. These attributes are the opposite of what Paul urges in Titus 3:2. Cretan believers should show none of these characteristics because God's grace has changed them.

■ **4** Because of God's grace and salvation in Christ, there is hope for resolving the chaos described in v 3.

Verses 4-7 form one sentence in Greek. It is one of the more concise statements about salvation in the NT. It is one of the "faithful saying[s]" found in the Pastoral Epistles (→ 3:7). Scholars debate the possible background for this statement. One opinion is that Paul quotes a preexistent baptismal hymn (Kelly 1963, 254; Collins 2002, 359-60). But this sentence lacks the clear poetic elements common in hymns. Any parallelism is simply due to its grammatical structure. More likely this is a carefully crafted creedal confession (Mounce 2000, 440-41).

Verse 4 introduces the condition for salvation. **But when** is an important temporal indicator. It gives a time stamp for the revelation of God's grace in 2:11 and confirms the hope of 2:13. This revelation is made explicit in the verb **appeared** (*epephanē*; → 2:11, 13).

The historical aorist tense of the verb could point to the first coming of Christ (Mounce 2000, 438). Paul mentions no specific period of Jesus' life. But it is likely that the crucifixion was not far from Paul's thinking (2:14; 1 Tim 2:6).

But it is also possible that the verb refers to the personal epiphany people experience when they hear the gospel and respond to it (Knight 1992, 339). This is implied in the "we" statements in this section. Neither alternative changes the central idea of this sentence—that God has intervened with grace to create the possibility of new life in Christ.

This revelation was of **the kindness and love of God**. **Kindness** (*chrēstotēs*) is one of God's characteristics and is a manifestation of his generous grace toward us (Rom 2:4; 11:22; Eph 2:7).

The word for **love** is the basis for the English word "philanthropy" (*philanthrōpia*). This rare word is literally a "love for humanity" that is shown through acts of kindness (Acts 27:3; 28:2). These were two of the highest virtues in Hellenism and Hellenistic Judaism. They were used to describe the benevolence of both deities and human rulers, which led people to call them "saviors" (Fee 1988, 203; Collins 2002, 361-62; Plutarch, *Comp. Dem. Cic.* 3; Isocrates, *Evag.* 43; Pliny, *Pan.* 3.4; Luck 1974, 107-12; 2 Macc 14:9).

God as the sovereign and benevolent Ruler has intervened in human history with the message of salvation. Paul calls God **Savior** for the third time in this letter (→ Titus 1:3; 2:10). In terms of Hellenistic culture, God is the patron who gives benefits to his people. God alone, not any emperor or human benefactor, brings salvation. These characteristics of God as **Savior** are emphasized in v 5: "He saved us." Verses 6 and 7 point out that both the Holy Spirit and Jesus Christ also participate in effecting human salvation.

■ **5** Two prepositional phrases here emphatically contrast two possible means of salvation. For the sake of English syntax, the NIV puts the main clause, **he saved us**, first and then repeats it for clarity: **He saved us**. But it actually comes only after some introductory phrases and occurs just once. The word order in Greek emphasizes first the *means* of salvation—not by (*ex*) our own effort but **because of** (*kata*) God's **mercy**.

The negative is given first: **not because of righteous things we had done**. Righteousness (*dikaiosynē*) is an important requirement in Scripture. It is a key characteristic of God who expects those in relationship with him to evidence also. God defines what is right through his law. Paul knew firsthand the futility of trying to be righteous by his own effort (Rom 9:30-32; Eph 2:9; Phil 3:4-7).

Good works were important to Paul (→ Titus 2:14), but he reminds the Cretans here that these do not bring salvation. Rather, they are evidence of it (→ 3:8). No human can be righteous enough to earn salvation because of the pervasive problem of sin (Rom 3:20, 23). Works of righteousness result from God's grace in our lives; they are not the cause. This is an important theme in Paul's letters, especially when he dealt with misuse and misunderstanding of the Law, a problem in Crete (→ 1:10; see Rom 4:4-5; Gal 2:16-17; Eph 2:8-9; Phil 3:9; 2 Tim 1:9).

The only source of salvation that can deliver us from sin is God's **mercy** (*eleos*). **Mercy** is an aspect of God's love, not deserved but freely given (→ 1 Tim 1:2; Eph 2:4). The contrast between ***works of righteousness*** and **mercy** is clear with the strong adversative *alla* (**but**). The pronoun **his** also emphatically stands in contrast to the pronoun **we** in the previous clause. **Mercy** is a manifestation of God's grace—God's free gift that allows sinners to receive forgiveness and reconciliation. God has already acted to bring about our salvation.

Verses 4 and 5*a* of Titus 3 prepare for the main emphasis in the sentence (vv 4-7). Just two words in Greek summarize the gospel: *esōsen hēmas*, **he saved us**. Everything else in vv 3-7 clarifies what this means. Salvation is the solution to the predicament of v 3.

How God saved us is indicated by a prepositional phrase beginning with **through** (*dia*). A literal translation is ***through washing of rebirth and renewal of the Holy Spirit***. The syntax is difficult to interpret because its string of genitives leaves its theology unclear. Words in the genitive case in Greek are usually related to another word. Defining this relationship involves interpretive decisions, which here are much debated.

Three significant words in some way reflect the salvation experience. **Washing** (*loutrou*, lit.) refers to hygienic washing with water to remove dirt. This was a ritual/ceremonial act in many ancient religions. For Christians, literal baptism serves as a figurative washing away of the defilement of sin. The word occurs also in Eph 5:26 in which cleansing comes by means of "the *washing*" in "the word."

Rebirth is a compound word, consisting of "again" (*palin*) and "to be born" (*genaō*, elsewhere in the NT only in Matt 19:28—"the *renewal* of all things"— emphasis added). Jesus and Nicodemus discuss being (lit.) "born from above" or "born again" (*gennēthēnai anōthen*) by water and the Spirit (John 3:3, 5).

New life in Christ is a central theme in Paul's theology (Rom 6:4-14; 2 Cor 5:17). **Renewal** is similar in meaning to **rebirth.** **Renewal** is another compound, here "again" (*ana*) and "new" (*kainos*). Romans 12:2 describes the "renewing" of the mind into a new pattern of thinking that is pleasing to God. The Holy Spirit makes this possible (Rom 8:9-13; Behm 1965a, 453) as part of the *new* creation in Christ (Rom 6:4; 2 Cor 5:17; Gal 6:15; Eph 2:15; 4:23).

How do the three words—**washing, rebirth,** and **renewal**—relate to one another? And, what part does the Holy Spirit have in each? Grammar should guide our theological conclusions. The preposition **through** always takes genitive objects. Here that could be **washing, washing of rebirth,** or **washing of rebirth and renewal.** Is Paul referring to one, two, or three different aspects of salvation?

And, what is the relationship between **washing** and **rebirth**? The NIV puts the two together as one event. But in Greek, there is no conjunction. Literally, Paul refers to **washing of rebirth.** This, of course, leaves their genitive relationship vague. Most likely, **rebirth** and possibly **renewal** are the results of the **washing.** Thus, *the washing that leads to rebirth and renewal.*

What is the function of the conjunction **and** connecting **washing** and **renewal**? Are these two parallel statements, as the NIV translation assumes?

And what is the place of **the Holy Spirit** in all this? Is the Spirit agent of all three verbal nouns or only in the last, **renewal**?

The answers to the foregoing questions are significant, because they may provide a biblical foundation for the doctrine of salvation. Often interpreters adopt a final reading that is determined by theological agendas. Three major approaches to the phrase vie for acceptance (Fee 1988, 204-5).

First, Paul describes two different events: (*a*) conversion and confirmation (the traditional view), or (*b*) conversion and the baptism of the Holy Spirit (the Holiness-Pentecostal view). The KJV translation assumes this reading by the insertion of a comma after "regeneration" (**rebirth**).

The argument against this is the similarity in meaning of **rebirth** and **renewal.** These more naturally seem to refer to a single event. Otherwise, we would expect a repetition of the preposition **through** before **renewal.**

Second, the whole phrase describes one event. **Washing** refers to water baptism. The preposition **through** governs two events. Both are the work of the Holy Spirit. Early church fathers and many interpreters today prefer this reading. Baptism and the gift of the Holy Spirit were linked in early Christian practice and theology (Acts 10:47-48).

The major challenge to this view is that it goes beyond what Paul says elsewhere about baptism. Elsewhere, he never suggests that water baptism saves. It is merely the outward symbol of the inner work of the Holy Spirit (Acts 22:16; Rom 6:3; Gal 3:27; 1 Pet 3:21; Mounce 2000, 448).

Third, **washing** here is a metaphor for internal spiritual cleansing, not literal water baptism. The emphasis is on the cleansing and regenerative work of the Spirit. The Holy Spirit is the source of all three actions. The first metaphor (**rebirth**) deals with the past problem of sin; the second (**renewal**) looks forward to the new life in Christ.

The Spirit cleanses believers of the stain of sin and transforms them into the likeness of Jesus Christ (Ezek 36:26-27; John 3:5-8; Rom 6—8; 1 Cor 6:11; 2 Cor 3:18). "Paul is describing the one event of becoming a Christian in as rich and full a way as possible" (Dunn 2010, 167). A paraphrase that takes seriously the grammatical issues might be: *the washing done by the Holy Spirit that results in renewal and rebirth.*

■ **6** The relative clause here modifies "the Holy Spirit" in v 5. The implied subject of the verb **poured out** continues to be God (v 4; compare Peter's quotation of Joel 2:28 in Acts 2:17-18). The coming of the Spirit fulfilled the prophetic vision that God would change the human predicament through the new covenant (Jer 31:31-34; Ezek 36:25-27).

Poured out (*execheen*) literally refers to the streaming of a liquid. A cognate describes the cultic cleansing ritual in Exod 24:6, 8. The OT also uses the word in its figurative sense of "fully experiencing" God's wrath (Hos 5:10; BDAG 2000, 213). The aorist tense looks back on this as a completed action. God's promise in Scripture has been fully realized in time and is available for all who will put their trust in Christ.

The adverb **generously** (*plousiōs*; → 1 Tim 6:17) indicates that this is not a trickle, but a saturation! The metaphoric language of Titus 3:5 continues here. Both Ezekiel and Joel looked forward to a time when God would shower his people with his Spirit, purifying them from sin and empowering them for new life (Ezek 39:29; Joel 2:28).

Paul connects this outpoured fulfillment of prophecy with **Jesus Christ our Savior**. The Christology in Titus is quite high (→ 2:13-14). This is the third time Paul refers to Christ as Savior in this letter (→ 1:4; 2:13). Each of these is closely connected to a statement about God as Savior (1:3; 2:10; 3:4).

It is **through** Christ that the Spirit is given. Both the Father and Son send the Spirit (as in John 14:26; 16:7; Acts 1:4-5; 2:33). There are four references to the Spirit's coming from Christ in Paul's other letters (Rom 8:9; 2 Cor 3:17;

Gal 4:6; Phil 1:19). Through the work of the Holy Spirit, Jesus fulfills the promises the Father made in the OT.

Significantly, all three persons of the Trinity are involved in human salvation. Out of kindness and love, the saving God (3:4) sent Jesus the Savior, who "gave himself for us" (2:14) and sent the Holy Spirit to make this salvation personal by cleansing from sin and renewing us in his likeness. The focal point of God's plan of salvation (1:2) and the one who made it all possible is Jesus.

Paul reflects back on Easter and Pentecost and personalizes these historic moments. These events may transform the present moment for Titus and the believers in Crete. The promise of Pentecost was not just a onetime event. It exists as a present possibility for all who put their trust in Jesus Christ.

The Father took the initiative in love to save us.

The Son gave himself to make us right with God.

The Spirit renews us into God's image, to be like Christ.

■ **7** The Greek sentence continues with a clause dependent on the main statement in v 5: "He saved us." Here we find out why God saved us. Paul begins with the purpose indicator, **so that**. But the participial phrase **having been justified by his grace** interrupts the explanation.

Justification is a forensic (legal) metaphor. It entails release of the guilt and penalty for wrongdoing, forgiveness of the wrong, and the establishment of a right relationship with the wronged party.

Theologically, justification refers to God's forgiveness of our sins. This allows us to enter into a right standing before him. Forgiveness of our sins preserves God's righteousness as judge. Paul deals especially with justification by grace in Romans and Galatians.

Justification comes **by his grace**. Justification is not deserved nor can it be earned. It remains a gift (Eph 2:8-9). The closest antecedent for **his** is "Jesus Christ our Savior" (Titus 3:6). But Christ is the agent of *God's* grace (Rom 3:23-24; 1 Tim 1:14). The grace of God is foundational in this letter.

The aorist tense of the participle *dikaiōthentes* (**having been justified**) points to an event that occurred before the main verb *genēthōmen* (**we . . . become**). We are justified so that we may inherit eternal life. Justification refers back to the regeneration and renewal (Titus 3:5). "The work of Christ in justification and the work of the Spirit in regeneration are simultaneous" in Christian experience (Stott 1996, 205).

After this brief but important thought, Paul finishes the sentence with the reason why God saved us: **so that . . . we might become heirs having the hope of eternal life**. An heir is someone who receives an inheritance or the fulfillment of a promise. In this case, the promise is **the hope of eternal life** (Matt 19:29; Luke 18:18; 1 Pet 1:3-4).

Paul returns here to his opening thought in Titus 1:2. Adoption as God's sons and daughters qualifies us to be **heirs**. In Rom 8:15 and Gal 4:5 Paul used adoption as a metaphor for the new relationship justified believers have with God. Eternal life begins now through the presence of the Holy Spirit. His presence in the lives of believers guarantees that this new life is real and everlasting (→ 2 Tim 1:14; 2 Cor 1:22; 5:5; Eph 1:14). Being justified gives believers reason to hope that God will fulfill all his promises (Rom 5:1-5; 1 Tim 4:10).

■ **8** This is the final **trustworthy saying** of the Pastoral Epistles (→ 1 Tim 1:15; 3:1; 4:9; 2 Tim 2:11). It emphasizes that the creedal statement in Titus 3:4-7 is important and worthy of careful consideration and acceptance. Each of these sayings in some way stresses core doctrines of the Christian faith and urges readers to embrace them in practical ways.

Titus was to focus his mission in Crete on teaching this "sound doctrine" (2:1). The saying is **trustworthy** because of its source: Paul taught what he had received from God. The church and Scripture confirmed this revelation (see Rom 16:25-26; 1 Cor 15:3-4; Gal 1:11-12).

Paul explains the main reasons why he wrote Titus this letter, stressing his apostolic authority (→ 1 Tim 2:8; 5:14; Knight 1992, 351; Towner 2006, 780): **I want you to stress these things**.

The word translated **stress** (*diabebaiousthai*) means to insist confidently and with certainty (BDAG 2000, 226). This is how Titus should approach the task of teaching believers in Crete (Titus 2:1, 15) and correcting the false teachers (3:9-10). He can do this is by knowing deeply the truth of the gospel Paul just articulated.

These things signals that the letter is coming to a close. Paul begins to summarize the reasons why he is writing by calling Titus to reflect back on the creed and all that comes before it (→ 1 Tim 6:2).

The result (*hina*) of Titus' teaching should be that **those who have trusted in God may be careful to devote themselves to doing what is good**. The phrase **those who have trusted** translates a substantive perfect participle (*pepisteukotes*). The verb *pisteuō* is usually translated "believe," accepting something as true. The object of the trust often takes the dative case as here. Paul describes Christians as those who have decided to follow God and accept his message of salvation through Christ. They have personally experienced what Paul describes in Titus 3:4-7.

The practical outcome of salvation should be **doing . . . good**. Paul will use the exact phrase *to be devoted to good works* again in v 14. This statement repeats one of the central themes of the letter (→ 2:7, 14; 3:1). The repetition emphasizes the vital connection between faith and behavior. Evidently, the opponents had missed this (→ 3:9-10).

The infinitive *to be devoted* has an implicit imperatival force: this is what the Cretans should give their attention. *Good works* summarizes and generalizes the specific commands of 2:2-10 and 3:1-2. It goes beyond them by including anything that will lead to a positive outcome for others. This is all filtered through and determined by the gospel as described in 3:4-7.

The motive for doing good things is that they **are excellent and profitable for everyone. Excellent** translates the same word rendered **good** (*kalos*) in the preceding clause. **Profitable** (*ōphelima*) can also mean useful or beneficial (BDAG 2000, 1108). When one cooperates with the transforming leadership of the Holy Spirit, one will produce fruit that will be obvious to others and influence situations in a positive direction (Gal 5:22-23). Notably, the object of Christian good deeds is **everyone**, not just those in the church. Paul's emphasis on mission to the lost once again drives his instructions to the church (Titus 2:5, 8, 10). Sanctification by the Holy Spirit leads to mission to the world.

FROM THE TEXT

The message of this part of the letter is clear: salvation is available to all people because of the mercy of God. Only because of what Christ has done may the power of sin in all of its manifestations be broken. The abiding presence of the Holy Spirit enables believers to experience real transformation. Believers are not the only ones who live good lives. But they know that this goodness is not good enough to save them (Rom 3:23). The theme of this passage is similar to Eph 2:1-10: God's grace saves us so we can do the good works he created us to do.

The application is more difficult because it calls for a choice on the reader's part. The theological declaration is sandwiched between two statements about doing good. How should we respond to the good news? Since believers have the benefit of God's kindness and mercy, they ought to cooperate fully with the Holy Spirit and produce fruit that bears witness to what they profess. God saves, *but* we must respond in obedience.

C. Dealing with the Opposition (3:9-11)

IN THE TEXT

■ **9** Paul's exhortation here turns again (1:10-16) to the opponents in Crete. It stands in direct contrast (*de*, **but**) to 3:8. There is a time to silence opposition (1:11) and a time to reject it altogether.

Titus needed to be careful not to get personally caught up in what he was to clean up. The verb **avoid** (*periistaso*) vividly describes turning around and looking the other way. He was to "steer clear" of the opponents (Quinn 1990,

235). Paul does not mean Titus should simply ignore them, but he should not allow them to influence him. To do so meant shunning four things:

Foolish controversies (*zēteseis*) only produce more problems (→ 1 Tim 4:7). Not all controversy is bad. The Greek word simply means an investigation seeking information (BDAG 2000, 428 s.v. 1). Problems arise when the topic is based on mere opinion or speculation (→ 1 Tim 1:4; 6:4; 2 Tim 2:23). Those who teach and preach ought rather to focus on the truth of the gospel. At times, it is necessary to confront false teaching (1 Tim 1:18-19; 6:12; Titus 1:11, 13), but church leaders must carefully avoid curiously exploring false doctrines.

Genealogies are an example of useless speculation based on one's family heritage. Genealogies were important to Jews (→ 1 Tim 1:4). Locating one's place could be a basis for an individual's religious authority (Wall 2012, 372) and result in people thinking highly of themselves.

The next two problems are nearly synonymous. **Arguments** are quarrels that result from useless debates (→ 1 Tim 6:4; 2 Tim 2:14, 23). Paul is particularly concerned here with **quarrels about the law** (→ 1 Tim 1:7). Law is not so much the problem as its misinterpretation and misapplication. The false teachers apparently used it to gain power and position through coercion (→ Titus 1:10).

Teaching not based on solid gospel truth often arises from selfish motives and leads only to division (Rom 1:29; 13:13; 1 Cor 3:3; 2 Cor 12:20; Gal 5:20). Titus should shun "stupid controversies" (NRSV), etc., **because these are unprofitable [*anōpheleis*] and useless** (*mataioi*).

The first word describes something that is neither advantageous nor beneficial, perhaps even damaging or harmful (BDAG 2000, 93). It is the exact opposite of "profitable" good works (Titus 3:8).

These activities are also ***futile***. They do nothing to develop spiritual maturity or positively influence outward behavior. The opponents were engaged in the very activities Paul says characterize the old life of sin (→ v 3).

■ **10-11** Paul tells Titus how to respond to the opposition, whom he calls **divisive** (*hairetikos*). This word is used in situations in which some form of correction is needed (Acts 20:31; Rom 15:14; 1 Cor 4:14; Col 1:28; 3:16). In later church history it describes "heretics," those who depart from the truth of the gospel and divide the Christian community.

Paul is not simply referring to personal disagreements here. Division is the result of false teaching because it reflects selfish motives or feeds selfish ambitions (1 Cor 3:3). Heresy divides because it distracts people from the unifying truth (Eph 4:2-6).

Titus must **warn** the offenders up to three times. The syntax of this verse is terse and to the point. The word translated **warn** (*nouthesia*) is actually a noun meaning "counsel about avoidance or cessation of an improper course of conduct, admonition, instruction" (BDAG 2000, 679). Such warnings attempt to turn misguided people from the wrong way to the right (Behm 1967a, 1021-22; 1 Cor 4:14; 10:11; Eph 6:4; Col 1:28).

It is noteworthy that Titus should begin optimistically and positively, expecting the divisive people to change (→ 2 Tim 2:25-26). The three warnings Paul advises should give them time to realize their error and repent.

After the third warning, if they remain unrepentant, Titus was to **have nothing to do with them**. There comes a point when correction is a waste of time; eventually, the time comes to *reject* them. This long English phrase translates one Greek word: *paraitou*. In the Pastoral Epistles it means reject, repudiate, decline, dismiss, drive out, or even expel (→ 1 Tim 4:7; 5:11; 2 Tim 2:23; Stählin 1964, 195). There are two implied reasons for this rejection:

First, rejection might do what warnings could not. By shaming the unrepentant, Paul hoped they would see their error and return to orthodoxy. Shame was a powerful social force in antiquity. To avoid it, people often adjusted their behavior (→ 1 Tim 1:19; 5:11).

Second, this rejection might spare the church further shame in the eyes of unbelievers. Expelling intransigent and divisive heretics would preserve the integrity and witness of the church (1 Cor 5:1-5; 2 Cor 2:5-8).

Verse 11 of Titus 3 gives the reason why this type of response was called for, using a causal participle: *because you have come to know* (*eidōs*). Titus should be able to recognize the error of these people. Paul uses three vivid descriptions of the resulting state of these people:

First, they are **warped** (*exestraptai*: "perverted" [NASB, NRSV]). This verb in the perfect tense shows that their deviation from the truth began in the past and continues to malform them. Their stubborn persistence in error is evidence of their corrupt minds (Guthrie 1990, 231).

Second, they are **sinful** (*hamartanei*). This verb in the present tense describes their current condition and lifestyle. Preoccupation with trivial doctrines and speculative opinions can lead to sin.

Third, their perversion and sin is *because* [causal participle *ōn*] **they are self-condemned** (*autokatakritos*). These people have sealed their own doom by their actions. They have only themselves to blame.

FROM THE TEXT

Paul's directions to Titus in v 10 resemble those recommended by Jesus for dealing with unrepentant one-time believers (Matt 18:15-17):

Jesus	Paul
Step One: Personal discussion between you and the sinner (18:15)	Step One: Warn once

Step Two: Take one or two others to establish a witness (18:16)	Step Two: Warn a second time
Step Three: Take the matter before the whole church (18:17a)	Step Three: Have nothing to do with the person
Step Four: Treat as an unbeliever (18:17b)	

Jesus contrasts "if they listen" (Matt 18:15) with "if they will not listen" (18:16), "if they still refuse to listen," and "if they refuse to listen" (v 17). The goal in both Jesus' and Paul's direction is restoration of the sinner (2 Cor 2:5-11; 2 Thess 3:14-15; → 1 Tim 1:3-5; 2 Tim 2:25-26).

It is significant that this comes after Paul has written of the transformation that God's grace, mercy, and kindness bring in the life of sinners (Titus 3:3-7). All church discipline should be done out of godlike love (see Heb 12:4-13, quoting Prov 3:11-12). There is the ever-present danger that those correcting another person may only make matters worse (see Gal 6:1-5). Discipline should be done gently and out of love. Leaders must realize that God's grace is already at work in the lives of sinners and be ready to offer restoration and reconciliation. By rejecting loving gestures intended to help, unrepentant sinners refuse God's grace and bring harm to the fellowship in the church.

Confrontation within the church is never easy. Emotions are often a significant part of this. Anger and defensiveness are typical reactions. Too many churches divide over the power struggles involved in these confrontations. But avoiding confrontation can be even more divisive.

Paul explained to the Corinthians that there was one legitimate reason why a church should be divided: "No doubt there have to be differences among you to show which of you have God's approval" (1 Cor 11:19).

Professing Christians must abandon their stubborn attachment to false doctrine and the reprehensible lifestyle it fosters. If they refuse to change their ways, the church must reject them to preserve the integrity of the gospel message.

Crete was not the only place where this type of activity was going on in the early church (Rom 16:17-20). Early Christians needed to be constantly vigilant against growing heresy. The best preparation was a firm grounding in the gospel (→ 1 Tim 1:3-7).

Those who lead churches today must balance these two poles: preserving orthodoxy at all costs and lovingly restoring those who have wandered away from it. The only effective way to do this is seeking the grace of God and recognizing its presence and its goal of saving all people.

TITUS

3:9-11

V. LETTER CLOSING: TITUS 3:12-15

BEHIND THE TEXT

The letter closing provides important background information about Paul's ministry. But it still leaves unanswered a lot of historical questions for modern readers. Paul mentions several names, giving a personal quality to the letter.

Wherever Paul was when he wrote, he was not alone. He mentions no co-sender or secretary (Rom 16:22). Neither does he note that he was writing the closing greetings in his own hand (1 Cor 16:21; Gal 6:11; Col 4:18; 2 Thess 3:17). The closing of the letter to Titus is brief and abrupt. By saying farewell immediately following his directions about dealing with opponents, we get the impression that Paul has said all he needed to say and stopped.

459

The letter closing contains four parts: personal instructions (Titus 3:12-13), a restatement of the main concern of the letter about "doing . . . good" (v 14), a final greeting (v 15a), and a simple benediction (v 15b). Paul reincorporates two key themes of the letter in the closing: doing good and God's grace. The tone of the closing is warmly marked by greetings offered to and from various segments of the early church. There is the strong sense that this is a team endeavor and many people have a part to play in the mission of spreading the gospel.

IN THE TEXT

■ **12-13** Paul gives personal instructions at the close of the letter that would lead to more effective ministry. He writes that he intends to send either **Artemas** or **Tychicus** to Crete. When he wrote, he had not decided which. **Artemas** appears only here in the NT, so we know nothing more about him. That Paul would entrust him with a crucial assignment indicates his confidence in Artemas as a valuable ministry colleague.

The better-known Tychicus may have been Paul's eventual choice. **Tychicus** was Paul's companion on his third missionary journey and accompanied him to Jerusalem with the collection for the poor believers in Jerusalem as a representative of Paul's Gentile churches (Acts 20:4). He delivered the letter to the Ephesians (Eph 6:21) and, along with Onesimus, the letter to the Colossians (Col 4:7-9). All this suggests that he could have done well in bringing relief to Titus in Crete and later to Timothy in Ephesus (→ 2 Tim 4:9, 12, 21).

The indefinite ***whenever*** (*hotan*) followed by the subjunctive verb **send** suggests that Paul refers to future plans that are still unsettled as he writes. Whenever Artemas or Tychicus arrive to relieve Titus of his responsibilities in Crete, Titus is to leave to meet Paul in **Nicopolis**.

There were seven known cities in the ancient world named Nicopolis. The one to which Paul refers here was likely located on the western coast of Greece across from Italy and 200 miles (322 km) northwest of Athens. Augustus founded it in 31 BC after his victory at Actium against the forces of Antony and Cleopatra. So he named it "Victory City." By Paul's day, it had become a major city and the capital of the province of Epirus.

Paul planned to winter in Nicopolis because travel on the Mediterranean was virtually impossible during the winter. This note may be a subtle encouragement for Titus to make haste, lest his journey be blocked because of the weather. Paul probably wrote this letter in the late summer or early fall. At a later point, Titus appears in Dalmatia, just north of this Nicopolis (2 Tim 4:10). So it seems likely that Paul's plans worked out.

Titus was to help two others on their journeys. **Zenas**, a Greek name, is called a **lawyer**. It is unknown whether he knew Jewish or Roman law or if he used his profession to assist Paul in his imprisonment. As a lawyer, he was well educated.

Apollos is possibly the well-known teacher who followed Paul in Corinth (1 Cor 16:12). He was a highly educated Jew from Alexandria who knew the Scriptures. He became a believer while in Ephesus through the ministry of Priscilla and Aquila (Acts 18:27—19:1). Evidently, both men were with Paul as he wrote. Their travel plans were to take them to Crete, a frequent intermediate stop in travel across the Mediterranean. They could have delivered the letter from Paul to Titus. There was no postal service for private citizens in that era.

Paul asked Titus to show both men Christian hospitality by helping them on their journey by providing financial or other tangible means of support to assist them. The last phrase of Titus 3:13 is (lit.): *in order that they might lack nothing.* Paul gives no more details. But Titus needed no more direction. He knew the apostle well enough to know what he was to do.

Hospitality like this was crucial for the early Christian mission and is a significant theme behind much of the NT ($\rightarrow$ 1 Tim 5:17). The events of this verse have no clear correspondence to anything mentioned in Acts. This makes it highly unlikely that Luke was with Paul at this point. Nothing more is known about the journey of these two brothers.

■ **14** The theme of hospitality continues but broadens to encompass the whole church. What Titus is to do for Zenas and Apollos (v 13) should be imitated by the entire Christian community. This verse recapitulates a major theme of the letter: **doing what is good** ($\rightarrow$ 1:16; 2:7, 14; 3:1, 8).

Christians can **learn** (*manthanetōsan;* $\rightarrow$ 1 Tim 2:11; 2 Tim 3:7) to *care* for the needs of others. The goal of these *good works* should be *the pressing needs* of others. Paul does not say specifically what these **needs** (*chreias*) were, only that they were urgent and necessary (*anankaias*). The purpose (*hina*) for this is so that the people *would not be unfruitful* (*akarpoi*).

Again, Paul's concern for active faith is evident. Bearing fruit should begin by providing for the basic needs of others. This will (1) show that the Holy Spirit is at work (Gal 5:22-23; Titus 3:4-7), and (2) lead to a stronger witness to unbelievers (2:5, 8, 10). Believers should "never tire of doing what is good" (2 Thess 3:13).

■ **15** Paul was not alone when he wrote this letter. It is unknown who *all those with* him may have been or where he was when he wrote. Although the letter is personal, from Paul to Titus, others joined them in Christian fellowship and greetings.

Love (*philountas*) is a term of affection and friendship. It is qualified here by **in the faith.** Faith in Christ is the common bond among Christians. When faith is genuine, it breaks down social, economic, and gender barriers (Gal

3:28). Faith in Christ allows complete strangers to call one another "brothers" or "sisters." Letters such as this communicated the affection that existed within the fictive Christian family—even those separated by great distances or who had never met one another.

The closing blessing, **Grace be with you all**, is fraught with meaning in this letter. **Grace** has been a key theme throughout (→ Titus 1:4; 2:11; 3:7). The plural **you** (*hymōn*) shows that the letter was intended to be read eventually to all the believers in Crete. Paul hopes that the grace of which he has written will continue to empower them to give visible expression to their Christian faith.

FROM THE TEXT

This brief letter reminds modern readers that the Christian life must be practical. The source for effective Christian living must be first and foremost God's grace revealed in Jesus Christ's sacrifice of himself for us. The Holy Spirit takes this message of hope and spiritually forms Christlike character and conduct within believers.

We must teach this "sound doctrine" effectively within the church. Everyone must learn how to appropriate this in their lives in ways that bear a winsome witness to others. Leaders must be carefully chosen whose own character shows that God's grace is active in their own lives.

The collection of letters known as the Pastoral Epistles calls us to engage our world with active faith. There are countless and repeated challenges to orthodox Christian doctrine. Some come from intentional heretics; most, from people who started off well but wandered off the right path following interesting but irrelevant and controversial ideas. Satan and his minions help this deception along.

Paul's answer for the problems in both Ephesus and Crete is *strength in relationship* with God in Christ through the indwelling Holy Spirit and *knowledge of the truth* of the gospel. Faith, piety, and discipleship will hold the church on course: to bear witness to the good news of his offer of mercy and kindness to all who will put their faith in Christ.

The many practical issues addressed in these letters all boil down to how we should be faithful stewards of the message God and the church have entrusted to us. These letters are a call to transformed lives. Christ in us will influence every area of our lives and bear witness to a world in desperate need of God's grace.